THEORY AND PRACTICE OF EXPERIENTIAL DYNAMIC PSYCHOTHERAPY

THEORY AND PRACTICE OF EXPERIENTIAL DYNAMIC PSYCHOTHERAPY

Edited by

Ferruccio Osimo

Mark J. Stein

KARNAC

First published in 2012 by
Karnac Books Ltd
118 Finchley Road
London NW3 5HT

British Library Cataloguing in Publication Data

A C.I.P. for this book is available from the British Library

ISBN-13: 978-1-78049-063-2

Typeset by V Publishing Solutions Pvt Ltd., Chennai, India

Printed in Great Britain

www.karnacbooks.com

This book was conceived within the first Experiential Dynamic Therapy training group in the UK. Together we have built on the inspirational work of colleagues who dedicated so much to helping ease the suffering of others. We hope our writing stimulates and nurtures creative new beginnings.

—gratefully, the authors

CONTENTS

ABOUT THE EDITORS AND CONTRIBUTORS

Dr Richard Aubrey is a Health Professions Council (HPC) registered clinical psychologist. He specialises in the psychological treatment of complex physical health problems. He has completed core trainings in Intensive Experiential-Dynamic Psychotherapy with Dr Ferruccio Osimo and Dr Diana Wais, and Intensive Short-Term Dynamic Psychotherapy with Dr Josette ten Have-De Labije and Kees Cornelissen.

Amanda Baker is a UKCP registered psychodynamic counsellor and BACP accredited counsellor and psychotherapist who specialises in short-term counselling in higher education. She has worked at the universities of Nottingham, Oxford, and Portsmouth where she is currently based, as well as practising privately. She has degrees from Melbourne and Oxford universities in music and psychodynamic studies. She studied EDT with Ferruccio Osimo and Diana Wais in London, completing core training in 2010.

Dr Jessica Bolton, BA Hons (Oxon), DClinPsy, works as a clinical psychologist with adults with common and severe mental health problems. She works in a variety of ways to attempt to ensure that the broadest spectrum of clients can access psychological formulation, treatment, and psychoeducation. She uses courses, groups, and individual therapy as well as a variety of therapeutic models. Dr Bolton has worked as a senior manager in primary care psychological services. Currently, she is working in NHS adult mental health services in the West Midlands and runs a small private practice from Sutton Coldfield, drjessicabolton@hotmail.com. She started developing her skills in experiential dynamic therapies in 2002 and completed core training with Ferruccio Osimo in 2009. Dr Bolton is the current chair of EDT-UK, an association affiliated to the International Experiential Dynamic Therapy Association, which organises core trainings and educational seminars in EDT.

Ronete Cohen has a BA and MA in psychology from Leiden University in the Netherlands. She has completed the English core training in IE-DP with Dr Ferruccio Osimo and has trained in Short-Term Dynamic Psychotherapy/Affect Phobia Therapy with Kristin Osborn. In her private practice, she works with children, adolescents, and adults. She diagnoses and treats educational, behavioural, and emotional problems in children and adolescents, specialising in comprehensive treatment—parent and school consultancy, and individual and family therapy. Her expertise includes giftedness, eating disorders, abuse, and sexuality (lesbian, gay, bisexual and transgender affirmative therapy, specialising in bisexuality). She writes advice columns and articles for magazines and online. She is a member of the British Association for Counselling and Psychotherapy.

Arno L. Goudsmit, PhD, has degrees in psychology and philosophy. He is a psychotherapist, and trained with Dr Osimo in Milan between 2003 and 2007. He founded and directs EDT Maastricht, a psychotherapy institution (funded by insurance companies) where a variety of EDT styles are practised. He also teaches at the School of General Practice at Maastricht University. He has published on psychotherapy and on living systems. See: http://www.edtmaastricht.nl/goudsmit and http://www.personeel.unimaas.nl/arno.goudsmit.

Silvia Landra, MD, is a psychiatrist and psychotherapist. She was a member of the first Italian core training group in Intensive Experiential-Dynamic Psychotherapy with Ferruccio Osimo. She is open to innovative experimentation, and her main focus has been the interface of EDT with social rehabilitation. For ten years, she ran the mental health section of Caritas Ambrosiana and was the medical director of a rehabilitation centre of the Lombardy region. Currently, she works as a clinical psychiatrist at Bollate prison, is the director of Casa della Carità, and of Souq, centre for studies on urban suffering. Dr Landra maintains a psychotherapy practice in the area of Milan, Italy.

Dr Margarita Lobeck is a clinical psychologist and has been providing treatment to children and adults with experience of physical trauma in the South and West Yorkshire region since 2003. She has completed a core training in Intensive Experiential-Dynamic Psychotherapy with Dr Ferruccio Osimo and Dr Diana Wais, and is currently training in Intensive Short-Term Dynamic Psychotherapy with Dr Josette ten Have-De Labije and Kees Cornelissen. More recently she has become interested in a more integrated and interdisciplinary approach to health and hopes to explore this further when she moves to work and live in Dresden, Germany.

Dr James Macdonald, PhD, DClinPsy, is a clinical psychologist working in an NHS psychological therapies service in Buckinghamshire and as an academic tutor on the Oxford doctoral course in clinical psychology. He has trained in Gestalt Therapy as well as EDT and was a member of the first UK EDT core training group with Ferruccio Osimo and Diana Wais. He was the first chair of EDT-UK.

Dr Joop Meijers is a clinical psychologist and senior lecturer at the Department of Clinical Child Psychology, School of Education, Hebrew University, Jerusalem. He is a former chair of the Israeli Association of Cognitive-Behaviour Therapy.

Ferruccio Osimo, MD, psychiatrist, is one of the founders of the International Experiential Dynamic Therapy Association and was its first president. He trained in dynamic psychotherapy at the Tavistock Clinic in London, where he carried out in-depth clinical studies on the quality of outcome, co-authoring with David H. Malan the book, *Psychodynamics, Training, and Outcome in Brief Psychotherapy* (1992). He attended Habib Davanloo's core training in Intensive Short-Term Dynamic Psychotherapy, and took part in the Short-Term Dynamic Psychotherapy Research Programme directed by Leigh McCullough at Harvard Medical School. His model of Intensive Experiential-Dynamic Psychotherapy is described in the *Comprehensive Handbook of Psychotherapy* (2002), in his book, *Experiential Short-Term Dynamic Psychotherapy: A Manual* (2003), and in several scientific articles. Dr Osimo founded the Italian, UK, and Israeli core trainings in IE-DP. He maintains a psychotherapy practice in Milan, where he teaches at Università Statale, School of Psychiatry. He is the president of the Italian EDT Association, www.apde.info. His clinical work has been presented internationally.

Mark J. Stein, PhD., DClinPsy, is a Health Professions Council (HPC) registered chartered clinical psychologist at the Adult Psychological Therapies Service in Kirklees. He has completed core trainings in Intensive Experiential-Dynamic Psychotherapy with Ferruccio Osimo, and Intensive Short-Term Dynamic Psychotherapy with Josette ten Have-de Labije and Kees Cornelissen. His background has included research in clinical health psychology at the universities of Kent at Canterbury, Warwick, and Sheffield. In addition to treating patients in the National Health Service, he is a clinical supervisor for clinical psychologists in training at the universities of Leeds, Sheffield, and Staffordshire, and provides teaching on the experiential dynamic psychotherapies to clinical psychology doctoral students at the universities of Leeds, Sheffield, and Nottingham.

Dr Naomi Wilson, BSc (Hons), DClinPsy, is a Health Professions Council (HPC) registered clinical psychologist and completed a core training in Intensive Experiential-Dynamic Psychotherapy with Dr Ferruccio Osimo and Dr Diana Wais in 2009. She works as a senior clinician within the Institute of Psychotrauma, East London NHS Foundation Trust, a specialist psychology service for adult survivors of trauma. Her clinical interests are in the integration of experiential dynamic therapies and trauma focused therapies within cross-cultural work. Naomi is also a senior academic tutor on the Clinical Psychology Programme, University of Surrey. Her research interests are the psychological impact of trauma, narrative methodologies, psychotherapy process, and critical perspectives on the political, professional, and ethical frameworks to which NHS clinicians are accountable.

FOREWORD

Jeremy Holmes

On the whole, Brits don't do *Festschrifts*. Maybe we are too suspicious of hierarchies, too allergic to idealisation, too democratic, healthily sceptical, too polyphonic—or perhaps just too envious! And, so often, "a prophet is not without honour, except in his own country, and among his own kin, and in his own house". But if any UK psychoanalytic psychotherapy researcher deserves to be celebrated for a lifetime contribution, it is David Malan. This book is perhaps best thought of as a species of *Festschrift*, with Italian overtones.

It is more than sixty years since Malan first started his MD thesis on brief psychotherapy at the Tavistock—and he is still going strong. One of his many attributes is that he has always been open to influence and change. There have been significant mutations since Malan first enunciated his seminal brief dynamic psychotherapy credo in *Individual Psychotherapy and the Science of Psychodynamics* in the 1970s, especially those attributable to Davanloo and McCullough. Nevertheless, EDT still retains the fundamental features first enunciated by Malan, and this book should be seen as the coming of age and culmination of his work, together with a celebration of the fact that EDT is beginning to find a place for itself within the UK National Health Service.

What are the essential qualities which Malan has brought to the field? They can be summarised as: openness and honesty, clarity of thought, the scientific spirit of enquiry, simplicity that does not sacrifice subtlety, and an active stance that does not preclude receptiveness.[1]

One of the key features of his work from the start, and permeating the spirit of this volume, is the recognition that if psychotherapy is to be properly studied, both for purposes of research or supervision, it must be in the public domain. The use of audio or videotape recording—with appropriate confidentiality safeguards—is integral to EDT in a way that is notably absent from all other established therapies.

Nevertheless this spirit of openness is beginning to be accepted within the psychodynamic research community. It is not that therapists' own written process recordings are deliberately dishonest, but rather that unconscious forces are ubiquitous. Therapists, no less than their clients, are shaped by narcissism, the Oedipal need to please, obsessional fears of failure, the desire to bend reality to conform to a preconceived story or theory.

Malan's second great contribution, his clarity of expression and thought, sets him apart from many psychoanalytic writers. "Malan's triangles" may not be entirely of his own making, but in his hands they become a rubric in which the therapist can reflect upon what he or she is doing and where he or she "is" in relational space at any given moment.[2]

This capacity to demystify and penetrate the aura of mystique which surrounds psychoanalytic work, yet not devaluing or vulgarising it, is one of Malan's extraordinary gifts. As this volume attests, therapists from a variety of backgrounds can understand the EDT approach, without feeling that they need to undergo a prolonged period of priestly initiation before they can embark on psychoanalytic therapy. Malan's triangles are an invaluable *vade mecum* in introducing the principles and practice of dynamic therapy to trainee therapists. These are often experienced professionals from medicine or clinical psychology who need to "unlearn" the tendency to "help", advise, prescribe, and begin to acquire a new set of skills, including receptiveness and "active passivity". Like many great ideas, the triangles are deceptively simple, yet however convoluted the clinical situation or sophisticated the analyst, it is always worth thinking about what is going on in Malan's-triangles terms.

Malan started off his professional life as a scientist and remains one to this day. From the outset he promoted the need for accurate, reproducible clinical descriptions, and the prediction of desirable outcomes prior to embarking on therapy (i.e., "intention-to-treat"), followed by unbiased evaluation post-treatment. This approach was viewed in the 1950s with intense suspicion by the analytic community, to its detriment and shame, not least among Malan's colleagues at the Tavistock Clinic. Malan managed, far ahead of his time, to do justice to the subtlety of psychoanalytic assessment of character and dynamics, while at the same time to subject it to scientific scrutiny. Brief dynamic therapies are finally beginning to accumulate a respectable evidence base (Abbass, 2006), an impetus which can be traced directly back to Malan's influence.

Another of Malan's crucial contributions, manifesting his analytic heritage through Balint and Ferenczi, is that of the "active therapist". This is the "masculine" psychoanalytic vector whose counterpart is the "feminine" capacity for the receptive encouragement of free association. The "active therapist" reaches its apotheosis with Davanloo's quasi-surgical (i.e., using violent means for curative ends) assault on the patient's defences. This is based on the conviction that once the walls come tumbling down, the patient will finally get in touch with warded-off affects in need of expression. This book is replete with examples of the therapist's active engagement with the patient—challenging, guiding, questioning, suggesting—all skills that are sharpened by the context of time-limited therapy. As Dr Johnson famously said, nothing concentrates the mind more than the prospect of a hanging (the built-in termination for brief therapies) in the morning.

Malan's heirs, Osimo and Stein and their collaborators in this book, illustrate a set of EDT-based concepts that have wide applicability to dynamic therapies generally. One of the most useful EDT formulations, deriving directly from Davanloo, is the distinction between strategic and tactical defences.

The wider psychoanalytic community is familiar and comfortable with the range of strategic defence mechanisms, originally systematised by Anna Freud, and explored empirically by Vaillant. The innovative aspect of the idea of tactical defences arises out of EDT's focus on the "minute particulars" (a Keatsian phrase picked up by another brief therapy theorist, Robert Hobson, 1985) of patient-therapist interaction. The ways in which people avoid painful affect in the here-and-now—by gaze aversion, vague generalisations, changing the subject, adopting a physically defensive posture and so on—are all grist to the psychodynamic mill. They provide the entry point for therapists' compassionate probes into the psychic pain they are designed to protect.

There is an obvious link between video recording and tactical defence analysis in that in supervision the therapist can observe defences in action and how he or she responds: by collusively going along with the avoidance; by over-enthusiastically trying to break them down in a species of "friendly fire" (another useful EDT concept introduced in the book), which may merely serve to reinforce defensive manoeuvres; or by a sensitive sticking to the point so that the patient feels both sufficiently held and challenged to be able finally to express and to let go long-suppressed painful emotions.

Relevant to tactical defence is the idea of the "character hologram", a metaphor based on the idea that, like a hologram, every part of the client's existential being is contained in each fragment of interaction and behaviour. Thus the first session contains in embryo all of the subsequent treatment; focusing on a fragment of clinical interaction can illuminate not just the whole of a session, but may typify the patient's problems more generally. Malan-influenced therapists strive always to make a Strachean (1934) "complete interpretation"—one that brings together into a single focus the patient's current relationship outside therapy, the transferential constellation in the consulting room, and the childhood and family structures which underlie both—T, C, and P.

An interesting facet of EDT is the way in which it strives to breathe fresh life into classical psychoanalytic formulations. The idea of the character hologram for instance loops back to Freud's observation that:

He that has eyes to see and ears to hear may convince himself that no mortal can keep a secret. If his lips are silent, he chatters with his finger-tips; betrayal oozes out of him at every pore. And thus the task of making conscious the hidden recesses of the mind is one which is quite possible to accomplish. (Freud, 1905e, p. 94)

One difference that distinguishes EDT, and perhaps contemporary psychodynamic therapy generally, from Freud's 1905 formulation is that in the latter, the therapist's task is primarily cognitive: to "make conscious the hidden recesses of the mind". EDT, with its Ferenczian antecedents, sees emotional avoidance—affect phobia—as the crucial target for interpretation and intervention. Many of the case examples in this book illustrate the movement from avoidance of painful affect to release of pent-up feelings, as the therapist both warmly holds and vigorously challenges old-established patterns of defensiveness. Thus EDT would always be pushing towards a present moment, an in vivo experience, as opposed to an intellectual detached discussion, which would be construed as a tactical defence.

Another standard psychoanalytic concept that animates much of the EDT therapist's activity is working with, or rather against, the "sadistic superego". This too can be traced back to

Strachey (1934), and his idea that people's problems flow from the prohibitions located in an internalised parent-figure—thou shalt not love, hate, cry, assert yourself, protest, etc. In the Strachey model, the patient assumes transferentially that the therapist will similarly be cruelly critical; but there is a discrepancy between that expectation and the therapist's benign and validating, albeit challenging, presence; that then leads to psychic reorganisation and the internalisation of a portion of a more loving superego.

The idea of the superego's "sadism" derives in part from the Kleinian tradition, where the child's own death-instinct-derived hostile impulses are postulated as projected into the parents, and then re-introjected in the form of the superego. In my view the sadistic superego concept is questionable (Holmes, 2011), and to some extent incompatible with the idea of affect phobia. From this perspective, the reason why people try to stop unwanted feelings surfacing into consciousness is primarily because a) they are by definition painful, and b) because to feel them threatens security. Expressing protest and manifestations of fear in situations of insecure attachment reduce further the sub-optimal security offered by the caregiver: their suppression is not a manifestation of sadism, but the need to achieve a modicum of safety. Indeed, conceptualising emotional inhibition as deriving from a harsh anti-hedonic internal parent may in itself be a defence against a sense of helplessness and vulnerability (Fairbairn's "better a bad self in a good world rather than a good self in a bad world").

The therapeutic consequence of that perspective is that the key provision of the therapist is not so much that of a benign superego-figure ousting a sadistic one, but someone who provides conditions of real security, which in turn releases the capacity for exploration of affect. In the latter situation it becomes safe to ventilate feelings, whether these be angry protest at poor caregiving, grief at loss and absence, or cries of unrecognised distress.

Implicit acknowledgement of the limitations of the "sadistic superego" concept may lie behind Osimo's development of the idea of maieutics in contrast to Davanloo-esque challenge. The midwifery metaphor—deriving originally from Socrates—is not original to EDT (see Feldman, 1966; Padel, 1991; Rycroft, 1985), but tends to be downplayed as psychoanalysts like to emphasise the mutative impact of interpretation as opposed to the holding, soothing, function they provide as the patient pushes to give birth to a new self—or rather a new version of the old self—which might be seen as the aim of analytic work.[3]

As this book magnificently attests, the next generation of EDT leaders is now well established. The anecdotal evidence is persuasive, but a new set of tasks present themselves. There is a need for full manualisation of EDT so that it can stand alongside CBT, and the newly emerged Dynamic Interpersonal Therapy (Lemma et al., 2012) as an established evidence-based effective therapy. That in turn will allow for outcome studies and for incorporation into the Increasing Access to Psychological Therapies programme as a treatment for complex depressive and anxiety disorders. In his much-quoted article defending psychodynamic therapy Shedler (2010) cites the Castonguay et al. (1996) study showing that many of the features integral to psychodynamic work are, despite its declared anti-analytic stance, associated with good outcomes in cognitive therapy. These include three factors central to EDT: the working alliance (or "real relationship" as Osimo dubs it); emotional experiencing; and developing conscious awareness of previously implicit affects. EDT is a powerful technique for fostering lived affective experience, and then moving on from that to verbal and cognitive awareness of avoided feelings.

In my view the next decade will see a progression from "brand name" therapies to integrated and dimensional approaches which highlight the structural ingredients of intimate relationships that lead to change and those that inhibit it. The task for EDT is to continue to develop its identity as a distinct psychodynamic school, while beginning, in collaboration with other therapies, to identify key mutative elements and theoretical constructs. The intelligence and commitment of this volume suggest that that is not just a pious hope, but an achievable aspiration.

References

Abbass, A. (2006). Intensive short-term dynamic psychotherapy for treatment-resistant depression: a pilot study. *Depression and Anxiety, 23*: 449–452.

Castonguay, L., Goldfired, M., Wiser, S., Raue, P. & Hayes, A. (1996). Predicting the effect of cognitive therapy for depression: a study of unique and common factors. *Journal of Consulting and Clinical Psychology, 64*: 497–502.

Feldman, A. (1966). Psychoanalysis and Shakespeare by Norman Holland: Review. *Psychoanalytic Review, 53*: 148–153.

Freud, S. (1905e). Fragment of an analysis of a case of hysteria. *S. E., 7*. London: Hogarth.

Hobson, R. (1985). *The Heart of Psychotherapy*. London: Routledge.

Holmes, J. (2009). *Exploring in Security: Towards an Attachment-informed Psychodynamic Psychotherapy*. London: Routledge.

Holmes, J. (2011). Superego: an attachment perspective. *International Journal of Psychoanalysis, 92*: 1221–1240.

Lemma, A., Target, M. & Fonagy, P. (2012). *Brief Dynamic Interpersonal Therapy: a Clinician's Guide*. Oxford: Oxford University Press.

Padel, J. (1991). Fairbairn's thought on the relationship of inner and outer worlds. *Free Associations, 2*: 589–615.

Rycroft, C. (1985). *Psychoanalysis and Beyond*. London: Chatto & Windus.

Shedler, J. (2010). The efficacy of psychodynamic psychotherapy. *American Psychologist, 65*: 98–109.

Strachey, J. (1934). The nature of the therapeutic action of psychoanalysis. *International Journal of Psychoanalysis, 18*: 139–145.

Notes

1. If we accept Jung's aphorism that all psychological theories are a disguised form of autobiography, one might say that these typify not just Malan's theoretical approach, but also his mode of being-in-the-world.
2. He borrowed the idea from Menninger, and of course Freud in that nothing could be more triangular than the "Oedipal situation". Also, the moment a sibling is added, the geometry becomes a four-way matrix rather than a triangle (cf. Holmes, 2009).
3. My anxiety as an obstetrically naïve medical student doing his "midder" was alleviated by a very experienced midwife who reassured me, "Don't worry – you don't have to do anything – it's the woman who is having the baby, not you. Just be there and accept her gratitude when the baby is born!" I sometimes tell this story to reassure beginner psychotherapists who are often in a similar state of panic.

INTRODUCTION

Ferruccio Osimo & Mark J. Stein

This book has many co-authors, all of us experienced clinicians, mostly working within the National Health Service in England, who met regularly, for up to eight years, to train in Experiential Dynamic Therapy (EDT). As is the custom in an advanced EDT training setting, learning was facilitated by supervision of audio-visual recordings of direct clinical work. One of us (FO), due to his longer experience with EDT, served as teacher and supervisor. Over time, the process of learning from each other's experience familiarised us with the techniques and the atmosphere of EDT. The idea of co-writing a book arose from the wish to share some of our ways of applying theory to clinical practice with fellow practitioners, by bringing together the essence of the experience gathered from different contexts and perspectives. The result is this fairly exhaustive account of how EDT is really applied by people experienced in the approach as well as those at different stages of learning, and the effective tools it can offer in day-to-day clinical work.

EDT developed during the last two decades of the twentieth century and therefore is a relatively recent methodology, but its historical roots are longer. Its scientific reliability stems from clinical research as well as from a process of Darwinian selection of the most effective techniques that, starting with Sandor Ferenczi and Otto Rank, was powerfully boosted in the last thirty years by David H. Malan, Habib Davanloo, and their students. As we set out to present EDT to colleagues, our aim is to offer therapists and counsellors a rich and articulate body of theory-grounded, technical interventions whose effectiveness is supported by process and outcome research. We are immensely grateful to the authors and patients who have allowed the inclusion of a great deal of annotated transcript from real psychotherapy sessions to illustrate how EDT is and can be applied to a wide range of presenting problems in our work with patients, achieving remarkable therapeutic results, even in a limited time.[1] To this end, we decided to focus on the interventions that characterise EDT, and, one of us (FO), began to articulate the essential ingredients of the therapeutic approach. In addition, we wanted to provide illustrative examples, from several service settings, of treatments for different presenting problems, and with patients at different levels of global functioning. Contributions were invited from interested colleagues and the result is the book you are now reading.

The essence of Experiential Dynamic Psychotherapy

Experiential dynamic therapy is intended to be a comprehensive system of psychotherapy that involves much briefer treatment than traditional psychodynamic or psychoanalytic psychotherapy. It is considered one of the short-term dynamic psychotherapies (STDP). EDT is based on creating a relational setting and atmosphere favourable to experience of all human emotions, whether they are primitive, as rage impulse, sexual arousal, disgust, and total despair can be, or more differentiated, like anger, concern, sadness, grief, and desire. EDT relies on a set of techniques administered in the context of a genuine, personal, and respectful human interchange, in this way guiding the individual to experience all of their emotion as fully as possible. The process leading to such emotional experience, and helping the individual to attain an understanding of the roots of their suffering and its pathological perpetuation, is regarded as the main way to activate the potential for healing and integration at its best. The ultimate objective of EDT is to remove or repair the causes of pathological suffering in a reasonably short time, and to help patients achieve a good-enough integration of the Self, personal happiness, and adaptation to their interpersonal and socio-cultural milieu.

EDT is experiential and psychodynamic or "dynamic". It is experiential in that it promotes the actual physical (through the body), and mental (related mental representations, thoughts, and fantasies) experience of feelings, impulses, and desires. Indeed, EDT practitioners regard emotional experiencing as a deep and meaningful expression of the Self. Moreover, EDT is psychodynamic in that it relies mainly on the basic dynamic theory of conflict and on transference phenomena to make sense of the mental mechanisms whose interplay is responsible for much of human suffering: in particular, the interplay of defences (D), anxiety (A), and deep emotion (X). EDT is, however, open to integration with concepts and techniques drawn from other paradigms/models, whenever this is felt to be appropriate in order to help the patient or to make sense of the complexity of the human mind.

Overview of the book

Part I, "Experiential dynamic therapy: from history to theory and clinics", opens with Ferruccio Osimo's introduction to and history of the experiential dynamic therapies, including the groundbreaking Intensive Short-Term Dynamic Psychotherapy (ISTDP) of Habib Davanloo and its subsequent development. The centrality of relationship in therapy is emphasised, and the current state of the art and science is described. Amanda Baker then presents material from interviews with David Malan, sharing some of his experiences, thoughts, and insights over decades of clinical practice, research into and promotion of short-term dynamic therapies. Ferruccio describes the nine essential ingredients of experiential dynamic therapies, and the reader is escorted step-by-step towards the discovery and understanding of the main treatment guidelines and technical interventions. Key characteristics of taking care of the real relationship, mirroring, history taking, and putting into perspective are described. In addition, high technical content, experiential-dynamic interventions, including defence restructuring, emotional maieutics, anxiety regulation, dealing with the pathological Superego, connecting corners of the Triangle of Others, and Self- and Other-restructuring are explained and discussed. The reader is introduced to a coding system, used throughout the clinical chapters, to clarify the nature, and application, of therapist interventions in the therapies presented. Ferruccio then describes Intensive Experiential-Dynamic Psychotherapy (IE-DP), a form of EDT, illustrating how, in IE-DP, the personal relationship between therapist and patient, and the physical experience of conflicting emotions are regarded as the basis of therapeutic change. Various aspects of IE-DP are touched upon and Ferruccio explains in detail, and illustrates with clinical material, his conceptualisation of the "character hologram". The associated transcript provides an example of IE-DP from assessment to six-month follow-up, with an Axis I and Axis II disordered patient taken on for IE-DP within the Servizio Sanitario Nazionale (Italian national health service).

Part II, "Clinical applications of experiential dynamic therapy", describes the application of experiential dynamic individual approaches within the UK National Health Service and counselling services, primarily, but also in other countries (Holland, Israel, and Italy) which have similar public health services.

Jessica Bolton outlines the provision of primary care mental health services (PCMHS) in the UK, and the characteristics of a typical primary care mental health service. Jess then discusses the relevance of experiential dynamic approaches in treating the more complex presentations of common mental health problems in primary care. The case Jess presents demonstrates taking care of the real relationship, and the subsequent acceleration of therapeutic gains that were maintained at two-year follow-up. In particular, the case focuses on the early therapeutic work with a patient for whom the more common therapies (i.e., CBT and counselling) offered in PCMHS teams were thought to be less suitable. Notable aspects of the therapy include prioritising the real relationship, emotional maieutics, and helping the client free herself from a pathological Superego and embrace her creative, humorous, and healing parts. Jess asserts that the therapeutic relationship needs only to be *good enough* and *long enough* to encourage the healing Self to emerge, and how emotional maieutics need only cover a *good enough* range of feelings to enable the patient to be free from fear of emotional experience and expression. Furthermore, Jess nicely illustrates how encouraging/helping the patient to stay with feeling leads to an uncovering of important dynamic links, a clear understanding of character pathology, and provides an opportunity for a corrective emotional and relational experience.

Mark J. Stein presents a therapy with a patient suffering from intrusive thoughts in the aftermath of cancer. The reader is introduced to psychological aspects of cancer and the presenting problems of patients attending treatment for cancer-related difficulties. Through linking the psychological aspects of cancer with specific therapeutic activities of EDT, Mark provides a coherent rationale for a circumscribed, but important, role for EDT in augmenting the range of interventions available in psychological therapies services working in oncology. In particular, he argues that developments in EDT, and in particular, aspects of ISTDP and IE-DP (mirroring, anxiety assessment and regulation, emotional maieutics, defence work, attention to the "real" relationship, interventions that focus on Superego pathology), and AEDP (acknowledging mastery, mourning-the-self, receiving affirmation), make EDT approaches particularly helpful to patients with cancer, for whom psychological adaptation is associated with regaining a sense of control, restoration of self-esteem, and finding meaning in their experiences.

Margarita Lobeck then discusses interconnectedness of physical trauma and psychological symptoms. Specifically, Margarita describes the psychological issues that can arise from physical trauma such as a burn injury, hand injury, or road traffic accident, highlighting their complex interplay, and shows how a modified and creative use of aspects of EDT can facilitate healing, helping a person with psycho-physical trauma to shift from a position of being split off from their injured part to integration. Psychological treatment of patients who have suffered physical trauma has only recently begun to receive increased attention from mental health professionals and, as a result, therapeutic approaches are still at a very early stage in their development. Margarita draws on the literature and her clinical experience to suggest that experiential dynamic therapies, with their explicit focus on the patient-therapist relationship, and moment-to-moment tracking and regulation of emerging emotion, are well suited to treatment of patients who have suffered physical trauma. Two case vignettes illustrate how an experiential approach can be both a starting point for trauma work as well as a means of helpfully guiding the patient experientially through trauma.

Also within clinical health psychology, Richard Aubrey suggests that experiential dynamic therapies, with their consideration of affective factors, are an appropriate treatment option for patients with treatment-resistant poly-symptomatic somatic problems. Richard presents a clear and concise account of helping a patient to build ego-adaptive capacity. In particular, Richard demonstrates a comprehensive assessment of anxiety manifestations, interventions to help a patient turn against automatic, habitual, and self-defeating defences (including ignoring and self-neglect), unmasking of Superego pathology, and exploration of deep feelings towards current and past attachment figures.

Ferruccio highlights the unique way in which EDT can undo the triggering and maintenance of depressive mechanisms and describes a therapy of a patient with long-standing depression. In particular, Ferruccio suggests that, by promoting emotional experience in mind and body, EDT sets in motion a benign circle of being oneself, feeling in touch with emotion, and having a sense of being oneself and capable of feeling. The case presented highlights some of the salient dynamics that tend to characterise depressive patients, and their treatment with Intensive Experiential-Dynamic Psychotherapy, in particular, focusing on some aspects of the patient-therapist relationship, handling of the pathological Superego and character defences with the help of the Character Hologram, and restructuring the relationship with Self and Other.

Ronete Cohen then introduces the reader to the problem of underachievement in gifted adolescents, and illustrates how aspects of EDT, in particular, anxiety work and separating healthy Ego from pathological Superego, can be helpful in addressing the problems faced by underachieving gifted adolescents. Parts of the therapeutic process are illustrated with transcript from a psychological therapy with a young gifted adolescent. Ronete describes significant and measurable improvements in aspects of the presenting problem reported by the patient, staff at the patient's school, and the therapist at (premature) termination of therapy.

Amanda Baker describes the context of university counselling, and presents a rationale for the inclusion of experiential dynamic therapy-informed work among the range of therapeutic responses offered by a university counselling service. Amanda makes links between the issues facing university students, developmental issues relevant to therapy with university students, and specific therapeutic activities of EDT. Transcript of therapy with a student presenting to a university counselling service illustrates how some experiential and dynamic interventions were applied within the counselling, with an emphasis on taking care of the "real relationship", restructuring the client's sense of Self and Others, and facilitating use of fantasy, to explore hidden impulses, and desensitise the client to experience and expression of anxiety-provoking and painful feelings, especially anger.

Thereafter, Derek, a client who had recently completed a brief course of EDT in an NHS psychological therapies service, writes about his journey through therapy. Derek shares his views on the difficulties and achievements in his therapy and describes how, through facing his emotions with his therapist, he ultimately was able to resolve the legacy of trauma in his early attachment relationships. James Macdonald adds an afterword.

Part II of the book concludes with a chapter by Arno Goudsmit who discusses and illustrates the development of an interpersonal transitional space in which corrective emotional experiences can take place. In particular, Arno suggests that therapy can offer a new interpersonal space, from which the patient can develop a new or an enhanced Ego position. The case presented illustrates how a patient begins therapy failing to distinguish between pathological Superego and healthy Ego parts and how, once the distinction between the two parts becomes clear, the inner conflict in which the patient had been trapped becomes visible and can be worked through. Arno argues that a full acknowledgement of this crucial distinction is made possible in the course of the formation of an interpersonal experiential therapeutic space.

Part III, "Training and Research", opens with Silvia Landra's chapter on an EDT group psychotherapy. In a public health service—like the Italian one—in which capacity to provide psychotherapy is exceeded by growing demand, any treatment options that allow therapy providers to respond to the greatest number of requests for treatment, in the shortest possible time, are welcome. Group treatments have the potential to achieve this. Although EDT is mostly administered in a two-person setting, Silvia Landra, together with Ferruccio, recently offered an EDT group psychotherapy. In her chapter, Silvia shows how two consolidated approaches—group analysis and EDT—can merge into something new and effective. Eight patients, four male and four female, with Axis I and Axis II disturbances, and different degrees of resistance and levels of ego-adaptive capacity, were treated with group IE-DP. Based on review of the video recorded material and reflection on the experience of providing an EDT group psychotherapy, nine learning points stand out as being crucial in bringing about meaningful therapeutic effects. Silvia discusses the lessons learned from this pioneering clinical experience, and presents transcript to illustrate important aspects of the therapy process.

Naomi Wilson then describes how experiential dynamic principles can improve the workplace, through privileging relationships within National Health Service teams. In particular, Naomi argues for accumulating evidence of the centrality of relationships, attunement, and a highly affective focus as prerequisites to psychological healing, that these aspects of clinical work can be motivating for caregivers, and that emotional connection is personally and professionally sustaining. In contrast, current "quality" indicators are objective and exclusively derived from scientific, economic, or political rationalities. Naomi argues that such quantitative scrutiny can sabotage discourses around human connectedness, thus rendering the vital relational dimension of care invisible. Using EDT frameworks Naomi then formulates how services might operate to validate the experiential aspects of professionals' roles.

An erudite chapter by Joop Meijers, a respected cognitive behavioural psychotherapist, who has recently begun to explore the use of experiential-dynamic activities in his practice, follows. Joop carefully compares and builds a bridge between two streams of therapy that, on the surface, appear very far apart, if not contradictory to each other: cognitive-behaviour therapy (CBT) and EDT. Joop explains how mainstream CBT focuses on the role of cognitions as a determinant of emotions and, therefore, in its interventions, stresses the importance of changing beliefs, interpretations, perceptions, and, in this way, brings about change in emotion and emotion-driven behaviour. EDT, instead, assumes that, at the root of the problem there is an inability to connect with, experience, and express authentic feelings and impulses, due to the anxiety they provoke. In particular, it is thought that, because of the individual's guilt, grief, and fear—lest their authentic feelings and impulse should threaten attachment bonds—they become anxious about their authentic feelings and longings. To bring about change it is then necessary to help patients regulate their anxiety, so as to be able fully to experience and express their true feelings. For EDT therapists, "cognitive" pathology is regarded as impaired ideation linked to insufficient opportunities to take in health-promoting stimuli or "experience of nonexperience [for example, severe sensory or educational deprivation]" (Vaillant, 1993, p. 44), defensive processes (e.g., rumination, selective attention, ignoring), and self-attacking and self-diminishing thoughts and ideas linked to Superego pathology. In EDT, it is the reawakening of dormant feelings and impulse that is believed to be pivotal in bringing about change. The EDT therapist—similarly to the CBT therapist—helps the patient to distinguish between cognitions that reflect their real Self, and those originating from deprivation and their pathological Superego (dysfunctional core beliefs, in CBT terminology). In EDT, however, the focus will be, in particular, the patient's emotional response to this new awareness, for example, enabling them to take a stand against the pathological cognitions, and to experience, acknowledge, and express their authentic feelings, impulse, and longings. Only at this stage can the patient revise their impaired ideation, and relinquish cognitive defensive processes, inasmuch as they have had an experience of the Self (and Other) that is very different to previous Self (and Other) experiences, and defences have ceased to serve a "useful" function. In other terms, when the individual has dealt with the painful and anxiety-provoking feelings, the defensive avoidance of authentic feelings is no longer required. Joop shows how understandings of CBT and EDT, and techniques deriving from those understandings, can complete each other and be integrated. The case of a patient with severe obsessive-compulsive disorder (OCD) is presented. Joop describes how, in this particular case, the patient was first treated with traditional CBT (exposure therapy), and how, after the patient decided that the CBT was not helpful enough, he approached Joop, who, being trained in both CBT and EDT, decided to change the approach and apply principles of EDT. Joop presents transcript to illustrate how, in the EDT part of therapy, the patient overcame some of the fear of his authentic feeling of anger, which resulted in a significant decrease in OCD symptoms and improvement in well-being and functioning. Although Joop asserts that this was accomplished without using the typical CBT techniques of exposure and response prevention, he acknowledges that Leigh McCullough's conceptualisation of affect phobia (McCullough Vaillant, 1997; McCullough et al., 2003) provides a framework for understanding the therapy in precisely those terms. Similarly, Joop's chapter makes a meaningful contribution to the dialogue between two schools of therapy that can only gain by learning each other's language and—eventually—creating a new, richer, language that merges and integrates the existing ones.

Part III concludes with James Macdonald's chapter on EDT in the context of psychotherapy research. James spells out the key elements of EDT, linking them with evidence-based "principles of change" derived from process-outcome research, and examines the evidence base for EDT relative to other therapies and to psychodynamic therapy. In particular, James introduces the reader to the relevant research indicating the equivalent effectiveness of different therapy models and notes that these findings apply also when EDT has been compared to other approaches in formal research studies. James argues that, while EDT may not have been demonstrated as more effective than other models of therapy, it provides a coherent theoretical approach that is congruent with a variety of evidence-based therapeutic processes, drawn from diverse models of therapy. This lends itself to an integrative perspective on EDT and its relationship to other models of therapeutic practice. James also reviews the randomised controlled trials of EDT and summarises EDT's place in recent efforts to promote evidence-based practice in the field of psychological therapies in the UK. James concludes that EDT holds promise as a contemporary model of psychodynamic psychotherapy that harnesses a variety of evidence-based processes of therapeutic change with evidence of its efficacy in a growing number of formal research studies.

References

McCullough, L., Kuhn, N., Andrews, S., Kaplan, A., Wolf, J. & Lanza Hurley, C. (2003). *Treating Affect Phobia: A Manual for Short-Term Dynamic Psychotherapy*. New York: Guilford Press.

McCullough Vaillant, L. M. (1997). *Changing Character: Short-Term Anxiety-Regulating Psychotherapy for Restructuring of Defenses, Affects and Attachment*. New York: Basic.

Vaillant, G. E. (1993). *The Wisdom of the Ego*. London: Harvard University Press.

Note

1. It is certainly the case that, within the UK, demand for psychological therapy from commissioners and referrers has tended to exceed resources, and many services have found it necessary to operate a waiting list. Therapists working in the public (and even the private) sector are under an increasing time constraint and pressure to obtain good results while remaining cost-effective and competitive.

PART I

EXPERIENTIAL DYNAMIC THERAPY FROM HISTORY TO THEORY AND CLINICS

CHAPTER ONE

A historical overview of experiential dynamic psychotherapies

Ferruccio Osimo

Experiential dynamic therapies descend from the line of thinking and research historically initiated by Alexander and French (1946), who were the first to declare their aim of making psychoanalytic therapy "briefer and more effective". Before Alexander and French, some of the theoretical contributions by Sandor Ferenczi, Otto Rank, and Wilhelm Reich have been particularly relevant to the development of EDT and, more recently and specifically, David Malan and Habib Davanloo are the most prominent proponents of experiential dynamic therapy. For an account of these contributions the reader is also referred to Amanda Baker's chapter (Chapter Two), that includes an interview with David H. Malan.

A precursor

Charles Darwin, in a pre-psychoanalytic era, had already understood the links between emotion, defence ("force of habit"), body muscles, and conscious and unconscious mental mechanisms.

> Certain complex actions are of direct or indirect service under certain states of the mind, in order to relieve or gratify certain sensations, desires, etc.; and whenever the same state of mind is induced, however feebly, there is a tendency through the force of habit and association for the same movements to be performed, though they may not then be of the least use. Some actions ordinarily associated through habit with certain states of the mind may be partially repressed through the will, and in such cases the muscles which are least under the separate control of the will are the most liable still to act, causing movements which we recognize as expressive. (Darwin, 1872, p. 34)

Thirteen years after publishing his great work on the origin of species by means of natural selection, the great scientist published *The Expression of the Emotions in Man and Animals*. Ekman (1996) commented on the importance to Darwin of universality and emotional expression:

> Universality mattered to Darwin because it provided support for his theory of evolution. Universality would make more plausible his claim that emotional expressions are not unique to humans but are shared with other primates. (p. 366)

As elaborated by Ekman in his book, currently such universality is substantially demonstrated for the facial expressions of happiness, disgust, surprise, sadness, anger, and fear.

Origins of experiential dynamic therapy

Experiential dynamic therapy (EDT) historically originates from short-term psychotherapies, especially Malan's brief psychotherapy (1963, 1976a, b, 1979). EDT is a comprehensive approach, aiming to take care of all the significant aspects of an individual at a deep level, but more quickly than in previous dynamic therapy models. This is achieved by means of an *acceleration* of the therapeutic process. The idea of accelerating the therapeutic process is not new in the field of psychodynamic therapy and, perhaps surprisingly, even in psychoanalysis. Ferenczi (1920), in the first lines of his essay, *The Further Development of an Active Therapy in Psychoanalysis*, wrote: "Psycho-analysis, as we employ it today, is a procedure whose most prominent characteristic is passivity" (p. 199).

Ferenczi deeply sensed the need to introduce more active techniques and this played a major role in the more conflictual aspects of his relationship with the founder of psychoanalysis. A few pages further he goes on:

> In seeming contradiction with the fundamental rule of psycho-analysis I had in a few cases to decide to encourage or discourage patients directly towards or against the production of thoughts and fantasies. I have in this way induced patients to carry out this plan who threatened to deceive me, for instance, to feign dreams. But when I became aware of the "misuse of freedom of association" by means of misleading, futile, and sidetracking ideas or fantasies, I did not hesitate to show the patient that by this he was only trying to escape the more difficult task, and to bid him resume the interrupted train of thought. These were just cases in which patients wished to *avoid* what touched them closely … (1920, p. 207)

When the new science he founded was dawning, even Freud carried out a number of treatments we would define as short-term. Osimo (2003a, chapter 11) describes a case of short-term psychoanalysis reported by Breuer and Freud (1895), seen through the theoretical lens of contemporary short-term psychotherapy. However, it is important to say that an abbreviation of psychoanalysis was never the intention of its founder who, moreover, regarded with suspicion all attempts in this direction. Rather, he took utmost care to let the fundamental discovery of the unconscious world unfold its potential in all possible directions and always opposed alternative approaches aiming at accelerating the process, like those by Ferenczi (1908–1933), Rank (1924), Ferenczi & Rank (1925), Adler (1928–1937), and Reich (1933). His recommendation for a *passive* attitude, where the analyst behaves as a sounding board to the analysand's free associations, and keeps attention "free-floating", promoted a progressive lengthening of psychoanalytic treatments.

It was certainly no coincidence that Freud put an end to the relationship with his brilliant disciple Otto Rank, when the latter published *The Trauma of Birth* in 1924. Rank's theory of the birth trauma as prototypical of all subsequent traumas led him to propose that the re-experiencing of it and of the related fears in the analytic transference would prevent the "unconscious reproduction of the same in the severance from the analyst" (p. 214). A somewhat cruel irony is that the painful "severance" between Freud and Rank occurred precisely because of the publication of this theoretical viewpoint. Rank's enormous insistence regarding the birth trauma and his idea of setting a time limit to treatment certainly triggered Freud's fierce opposition but, nevertheless, Rank's theoretical position is relevant to the development of short-term psychotherapies. Indeed, Rank was deeply concerned with the healing side of psychoanalysis, thus with emotional experience, rather than simply theoretical aspects: "… therapeutic possibilities do not conform, in any expected degree, to the increase of our knowledge, and […] even simple therapeutic action can be arrested by too much knowledge and too much [cognitive] insight" (1924, p. 202).

Adler's theoretical focus on the complexes of inferiority and superiority, thus also on the power aspects inherent in the analyst/analysand relationship, and his consequent modifications of technique and setting are certainly relevant to the shortening of therapy. Indeed, Adler was the first analyst who gave up the couch and, choosing to sit face to face with his patients, emphasised that: "… the psychological development of a person can reach a normal condition only when he can achieve the necessary degree of ability to co-operate" (1928–1937, p. 199).

Adler also addressed the problem of "over-gratification" as a by-product of therapy, leading to a patient's dependence on the therapist, and consequent difficulty in terminating treatment. He called this the "psychopathology of the pampered child", or "a view of life in which the individual assumes that the other person is there for him" (p. 195). In calling for a countering of the patient's strivings to get the therapist to take on the pampering role at a very early stage, Adler's approach can be regarded as a contribution to the acceleration of the therapeutic process.

The analytical psychology of Carl G. Jung included the concept of *archetypes* (1912, 1934–1954) as primordial images deriving from the *collective unconscious*. Archetypes are elements of a matrix that is common to all peoples, a virtual image that is genetically transmitted. As such, archetypes would not seem to help shorten treatment, rather to make things more complicated by populating the unconscious with an endless crowd of mythological characters. In clarifying what he meant by "archetypal images" Jung (1964) stated:

> … some contents of modern man's unconscious resemble products of the mind of ancient man … the archetype is a tendency to form such representations of a motif—representations that can vary a great deal in detail without losing their basic pattern … [rather than an] "inherited representation" … [they are] an instinctive trend … Instincts are physiological urges, and are perceived by the senses. But at the same time, they also manifest themselves in fantasies and often reveal their presence only by symbolic images. These manifestations are what I call the archetypes. (pp. 66–69)

In *Psychological Types*, Jung (1921) paid tribute to a clinical application of archetypes when he focused on the way the effect of archetypes is manifest in each individual, and articulates the concept of co-existence of two opposites: (i) the *persona* or the social mask, and (ii) the *shadow*, representing its repressed negative. Seen through the lens of EDT, this concept becomes clinically incisive inasmuch as, by focusing on the overall mode of presentation of an individual, it can be used to address the character defence. As such, Jung's (1964) conceptualisation of dream and archetypal images has particular relevance to the conceptualisation of the character hologram articulated by Osimo (2009) (see also pp. 107–132):

> They form a bridge between the ways in which we consciously express our thoughts and a more primitive, more colourful and pictorial form of expression. It is this form, as well, that appeals directly to feeling and emotion. These "historical" associations are the link between the rational world of consciousness and the world of instinct. (Jung, 1964, pp. 47–49)

Furthermore, Jung was interested in the therapeutic power of images as messages from the unconscious because he believed that modern life had led to a stripping away of the emotional energy from ideas, but that symbolic images retained their potency, thereby having the potential to make an impact on the perceiver: "… its symbolism has so much psychic energy that we are forced to pay attention to it" (1964, p. 49).

Again, referring to the energy attached to these images:

> We can perceive the specific energy of archetypes when we experience the peculiar fascination that accompanies them. They seem to hold a special spell … They [archetypes] are, at the same time, *both images and emotions*. One can speak of an archetype only when these two aspects are simultaneous. When there is merely the image, then there is simply a word-picture of little consequence. But by being charged with emotion, the image gains numinosity (or psychic energy); it becomes dynamic, and consequences of some kind must flow from it … they are pieces of life itself—images that are integrally connected to the living individual by the bridge of the emotions … it must be explained in the manner indicated by the whole life-situation of the particular individual to whom it relates … archetypes come to life only when one patiently tries to discover why and in what fashion they are meaningful to a living individual … they gain life and meaning only when you try to take into account their numinosity—i.e., their relationship to the living individual. (1964, pp. 79, 96–97, italics added)

In 1933, Reich published *Character Analysis*, in which he outlined a totally new dynamic approach to personality disorders. Reich was a radical critic of Freud's "basic rule" of free association and held a different position as regards the approach to analytic patients. Instead of privileging verbal communication, that is, speech and language, Reich started to look to the body as a major source of interpersonal communication, and information about the individual's unconscious mechanisms and conflicts. Davanloo's confrontation of character pathology would seem related to Reich's view of character, which is also relevant to the concept of character hologram (Osimo, 2009) (see also pp. 107–132). It is therefore worth quoting from Reich's (1933) book that the character of an individual

> is usually expressed in a specific *attitude* or *mode of existence* … [that] represents an expression of the person's entire past … The way the patient speaks, looks and greets the analyst, lies on the couch, the inflection of the voice, the degree of conventional politeness which is

> maintained, etc., are valuable cues in assessing the secret resistances with which the patient counters the basic rule. (pp. 48–49, italics in original)

In other words, when we are faced with a character problem, we are faced with defences that have been incorporated into the patient's behaviour, or "character armour" (p. 48) which the patient perceives as the way they *naturally* are, that is as a part of their ego. Consequently, Reich's technical recommendation is to focus consistently on the patient's "ego defence" (p. 70), because "unless the ego defence has been systematically and thoroughly worked through beforehand, no interpretation would evoke an *affective* response" (p. 68, italics added). Another fundamental recommendation by Reich is,

> … we merely single out from the orbit of the personality the character trait from which the cardinal resistance proceeds, and, if possible, we show the patient the surface relation between the character and the symptoms. But for the rest, we leave it up to him whether or not he wants to make use of his knowledge to change his character. (p. 59)

Reich's theoretical position, technical recommendations, emphasis on emotional experiencing, and his view of the body as a source of information about human conflict, are highly relevant to most EDT models.

The first clinical trial explicitly aiming to make psychoanalysis "briefer and more effective" is the one reported in the book by Alexander, French, and colleagues published in 1946, a true milestone of psychotherapeutic reading. These authors regarded emotional experience as the major therapeutic factor, and this led them to elaborate an *ante-litteram* form of EDT. Historically, moving the focus of attention from giving interpretations at a cognitive level to actively promoting the experience of buried feeling within the therapeutic relationship represented a paradigm shift in psychoanalysis, and a shift in emphasis from theory to clinical practice. For example, I would like to summarise an interesting clinical case described in Alexander and French (1946, pp. 293–299).

> The patient was a highly intelligent man of nineteen. Symptomatically he was remarkably depressed and this interfered with his university studies. He was also anxious and worried to have to face his father's disappointment. Dr Adelaide McFayden Johnson offered him thirty-five sessions. "In giving his history the patient had difficulty in reporting that his mother had been accidentally burned to death when he was three."

For a full account of the case the reader is referred to Alexander and French's (1946) book. Here, I wish to highlight the therapist's attitude of focusing on the emotionally charged incidents, paving the way to the in-session experience of deep emotion and sharing it with the patient.

> The treatment lasted for three months and in the third month, the patient's resistance about recalling his mother's death led the therapist to focus on this. At some point, the patient asked out of the blue: "But did I tell you I went to the hospital and got my birth certificate three weeks ago?" This was done to learn his mother's last name, but, surprisingly, the patient now could not remember it. The therapist commented that the patient possibly harboured angry feelings at his mother for dying and abandoning him. The patient said: "I must have been a

> stinker, for no relative would take me." The therapist related this to anger and asked again for his mother's name. In response to the therapist's putting pressure, the patient answered angrily: "I have it on me. I don't want to look, because before when I looked at it, I was uneasy for hours afterwards." After some further resistance and further pressure the patient took out the certificate bearing his own mother's name, but did not hand it over. He commented, "The name is G-," and replaced the paper in his wallet. After a few lines the therapist said empathically: "... I feel you have been repressing not only your angry feelings for her, but also, perhaps, the fact that you and she loved each other." To this the patient said the thought came to him of writing to his aunt asking her to send him a picture of his mother. Suddenly tears welled up and the patient threw himself sobbing on the couch. After ten minutes he grew calm and said, with great feeling, "Silly, but I feel as if my own mother were all around me here. It's something so familiar." He then embarked on a kind of accelerated imaginary recapitulation of some crucial questions he would have wanted to put to his mother, to which the therapist gave some answers. What he was most probably seeking were not the answers, but the corrective relational experience, which could give him the emotions he wished he could have experienced with his mother. In fact, before the end of the session, he exclaimed: "I know who I've been talking to: my mother! And I feel wonderful! "I feel my mother is all around me." After the session the patient's depression lifted, he was able to successfully complete his courses, and his view of his parents became more realistic. In the two-year follow-up period he remained symptom-free and many changes occurred in his life. In his last letter to the therapist the patient wrote that he had "never been so satisfied with his relationships with people as now".

This case provides the unbiased observer a clear suggestion of the following:

- The intense re-experiencing of buried emotions in the actual relationship with an emotionally responsive therapist brings about therapeutic change. This is what Alexander and French (1946) called *corrective emotional experience* and is pivotal to dynamic change.
- If such re-experiencing can be brought about rapidly, dynamic change will also be rapid, that is, the phase of consolidation of change or "working through" is not quite a matter of time, but of good-enough emotional experience.
- When an effective approach is employed, even relatively early traumas can be re-activated and solved independent of the length, frequency, and total number of sessions.

Alexander and French's innovative and somewhat revolutionary therapeutic approach triggered an adverse reaction from the traditional psychoanalytic establishment, some of whose most prominent representatives attacked these authors savagely and quite irrationally (e.g., Eissler,1950; Jones, 1946). In contrast, other independent thinkers were more open to the idea of accelerating the therapeutic process. For example, Fromm, though more recently, wrote:

> ... by having the courage of using analytic insight to approach the patient very directly [a therapist can] possibly do in twenty hours what one feels obliged to do, as an analyst, in 200 hours. There is no reason for false shame to use direct methods when they can be used. (1964, p. 41)

In an article about Fromm's technical views we can read: "This is reminiscent of certain modern techniques of brief psychotherapy … and confirms that Fromm had a very active approach to resistance" (Bacciagaluppi, 1989, p. 237).

When Balint started to experiment with brief forms of therapy at the Tavistock Clinic in 1955, notwithstanding his acquaintance with Alexander, he developed a similar but independent research and study setting. Balint founded the Brief Psychotherapy Workshop (BPW), consisting of a group of selected and gifted clinicians, one of whom was David Malan. Their initial idea was to circumscribe the area of conflict, designated by Balint with the term *focus*, on which to concentrate dynamic work. According to Malan (1999), the therapies supervised within the BPW were never *really* focal, since interpretations actually involved all the meaningful material, and not only the focal conflict. However, the popularity of the term *focal* applied to brief therapy became enormous, to the point of being regarded as a necessary attribute of all brief therapies. This term also appears in the title of Balint's posthumous book on the subject, published by his wife, Enid, and his disciple, Peter Ornstein (Balint, Balint & Ornstein, 1972). Its value seems to have been mostly diplomatic, in that circumscribing the area of intervention by selecting a therapeutic focus made it easier for long-term analysts to accept brief therapy as something different—therefore less confusing or threatening—from what they did. In this way, it was seemingly focality—and not more effective techniques—that made brevity possible. This is, however, untrue, as even a dynamically simple case with a single and highly meaningful focus offers no guarantee for brief and effective therapy. In other cases, using an effective approach, resolution of dynamically complex, or "multi-focal", conditions, may be achieved within a relatively short time. Given the contribution of different factors, the term "focal" as a label for short-term psychotherapy is as misleading as it would be to use "couch" or "free-association" to label long-term psychoanalysis. Malan (1999, personal communication) told me that Balint once told him: "I used to think that the essence of analysis was five times a week on the couch, free association, etc., but now I realize that the essence of analysis lies in the attitude of the therapist" (Balint, personal communication to Malan).

Sifneos's (1972) Short-Term Anxiety-Provoking Psychotherapy (STAPP) is probably the purest example of really focal and really brief psychotherapy. His emphasis on the crucial role of anxiety in closing or indeed opening the gates of deep, unconscious communication is certainly relevant to contemporary EDT. However, Sifneos failed to develop effective tools to *regulate* the level of anxiety, with the consequence that selection criteria for STAPP were very narrow, and made it applicable to a very low proportion of patients, probably three to five per cent of all psychotherapy referrals.

Malan and Davanloo

In the mid 1960s Malan took over the Tavistock BPW from Balint. The members of his workshop were all trainees, making the group quite different from Balint's, which consisted entirely of experienced therapists. Malan postulated the crucial interplay of selection criteria, therapeutic technique, and the *quality* of results obtained. His elucidation of the dynamic process and of factors of change in brief psychotherapy and, subsequently, in EDT, is invaluable. His (1963, 1979) books, translated in various languages, contain a rich harvest of clinical material, illustrating the backbone on which the "science of psychodynamics" is based. In this respect they represent an ideal continuation of the book by Alexander and French. Thanks to his extensive clinical research, Malan was able to reject the "hypothesis of superficiality", according to which brief psychotherapy is a *superficial treatment*, applicable to *superficially ill* patients, and bringing about *superficial results*. His pivotal contribution to psychotherapy in general, and EDT in particular, should never be ignored and can be encompassed under four sub-headings: (i) theoretical position, (ii) scientific approach to change mechanisms, (iii) follow-up studies, and (iv) respect for the Other.

Malan's (1979) theoretical position was eminently experiential and dynamic: "The aim of every moment of every session is to put the patient in touch with as much of his true feelings as he can bear" (p. 74).

Malan was a chemist before becoming a doctor and specialising in psychiatry and psychotherapy. His scientific approach to change mechanisms is consistent with his interest in transformative phenomena and may partly explain his unique skill in measuring change by keeping a clear distinction between real deep change and simple migration of pathology from one to another symptom. Most of Malan's published studies include long-term follow-up. These studies are actually process *and* outcome studies, since they mostly include both a narration of the unfolding therapeutic process and a detailed analysis of change. By means of these studies over a period of five decades, Malan set in motion a two-way process. On the one hand he was able to measure the effectiveness of selection criteria and technical method and, as a parallel process and further bonus, he distilled the essence of what really matters in terms of quality of results; what makes the difference in someone's quality of life (Malan & Coughlin Della Selva, 2006; Malan & Osimo, 1992). Malan trained many therapists at the Tavistock—me being one of the lucky ones—and one of the things he taught us was deep respect for the patient-as-a-person. His attitude to trainees was respectful but could be harsh too. The following anecdotes will help to highlight his attitude to patients, trainees, and the unfolding of truth.

In my training years it happened to me—and I believe it to be a common experience—to take for granted that a patient, in a given circumstance, must surely feel a certain feeling. In my first supervisions with David I found it surprising—and indeed frustrating—when he asked, "What is the evidence that that was what he felt?", or plainly, "How do you know this?". I would hastily try to articulate a plausible explanation, calling upon my psychoanalytic concepts of Oedipal jealousy, rivalry, and the like, without realising that, in so doing, I was just trying to make up for my actual ignorance of what feeling was being experienced. David found this infuriating. Once, I had to report to David about my first follow-up interview with a former patient from his workshop, and I got a lot of criticism for not having gathered clear-enough evidence that things were exactly the way they seemed to be. The interview had lasted for two-and-a-half hours and, at the end, the patient and I were both exhausted; he had shared a lot of his life history with me, and I had had to keep focused and attentive in my effort to find what I was looking for and prove myself a good trainee. At supervision I initially felt fairly proud, but it did not last very long: "You let him talk too much without interrupting"; "How do we know if the quality of the relationship with the wife is really improved? You should have got him to give you a detailed description; what do they do when they are together, go to the movies? Do they talk or not? What is their social life like? How do they deal with differences?" I answered what I could, that is, what I *thought* it was, or that *surely* it was and … that was the last time I did that, since the more I used my imagination to fill the gaps of my interview the angrier David got. The cherry on the cake came when I reported that, towards the end of the interview, the patient had told me he remembered almost nothing of his therapeutic sessions, including his decision to terminate before the term of fifteen sessions. At that point, feeling moved by this man who, after telling me all the details of his life, told me he had forgotten all of his therapy, I thought it would be reassuring to hear me saying that many think this means that therapy is still working inside him and this is a good indicator. The patient did actually feel reassured, and left the place feeling as happy with his ignorance as I felt with mine. When I reported this, however, David asked why on earth I said that—I again tried to justify—then he stared at me in the eye and said, "This is rubbish: you must never lie to patients." That time I gave up trying to answer, and never again tried to make things up with David, and indeed with patients.

On another occasion, while I was reporting to him about the follow-up interview with one of his own former patients, Malan suddenly recalled an incident that had occurred in a session with that patient, many years earlier. This patient was very rigid, his emotional life thwarted, and Malan felt disappointed with their interchange. At some point, exasperated by the patient's coldness, Malan put to him the following question, "Why you think I do this job?", to which the patient promptly answered, "Because they pay you good money." Malan responded, "Did it ever occur to you that I might enjoy helping people?" This time the patient kept silent, but his nose started to bleed. I found this incident extremely touching and, also, dynamically interesting. Malan's humble comment was, "That was the first time I realised that nose-bleeding may have a psychological basis."

Malan (1963, 1976a, 1979) first conceived the importance of placing, side by side, the two triangles known as the "Triangle of Conflict" (Ezriel, 1952) and the "Triangle of Others" (Menninger, 1958) (Figure 1). Taken together, they serve to shed light on the psychodynamic content of every verbal and non-verbal communication of the patient.

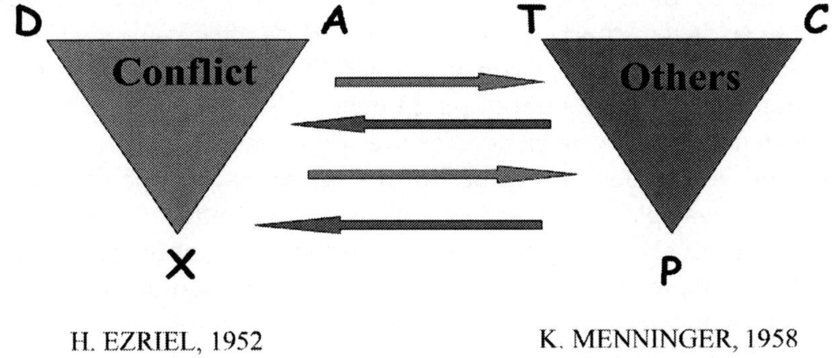

Figure 1.

The Triangle of Others allows a therapist to distinguish three categories of patients' interpersonal relationships: (i) those that are current or belong to the recent past (**C**), (ii) the relationship with the therapist (**T**), and (iii) relationships of the more distant past (**P**), that is, with the primary attachment figures (Bowlby, 1982). This last corner of the Triangle of Others is placed at the bottom, signifying that it is "deeper" and typically reached at a later moment with respect to the other two. The Triangle of Conflict represents the three elements on which psychodynamic theory is based, that is, defence (**D**), unconscious feelings, desires, representations, and impulses (**X**), and anxiety (**A**), which is often accompanied by other inhibitory emotions such as pain, guilt, and shame. Again, the **X** corner of the triangle is placed at the bottom since feelings and impulses that are excluded from consciousness are regarded as "deeper" because they tend to be reached only after the anxieties and defences that are mobilised for the purpose of excluding them. The Triangle of Others actually represents the other people in the patient's life, and the Triangle of Conflict represents the patient's psychodynamic Self. Drawing a few arrows joining the two Triangles highlights also the relationship between the individual and the other significant people in their life. The two Triangles are well known and their use by dynamic therapists is widespread.

In the 1970s Malan first saw Davanloo's video recordings of his clinical work. Witnessing his innovative approach of directly confronting, identifying, clarifying, and challenging patients' defences raised Malan's enthusiasm to the point that he stated, "Freud discovered the unconscious and Davanloo discovered how to use it therapeutically." Thus Malan envisaged a totally new therapeutic power in Davanloo's work, something that he deemed missing in psychoanalysis and dynamic therapy hitherto: the power to address and undo patients' defences from the first therapeutic session, by means of highly specific techniques. Malan's excitement was understandable given that he was a clinician and researcher who was already internationally known and respected for his clinical studies. Moreover, Malan immediately decided to devote himself to study and articulate Davanloo's techniques and associated theory, something he has never stopped doing for the last twenty-five years (e.g., Malan 1986a, b). He was always eager to lend his unique understanding of psychodynamics to all those he believed to be valid contributors to the development of EDT—and this is indeed rare—like McCullough Vaillant (1997), Osimo (2003a), and Coughlin Della Selva (Malan & Coughlin Della Selva, 2007).

In the early 1980s, by means of video recorded clinical cases, Davanloo was the first to demonstrate that even severe character problems could be effectively dealt with in less than forty sessions. As a medical doctor and psychiatrist, Davanloo was experienced in psychoanalysis and dynamic therapy before developing Intensive Short-Term Dynamic Psychotherapy (ISTDP). Notwithstanding his appreciation for the way in which psychoanalysis made sense of the conscious and unconscious dynamics in the human psyche, he found that the way in which psychoanalysis was *practised* was too lengthy and not effective enough, that is to say, inadequate to deal effectively with the complexity and intensity of human emotion, and bring about the desired change. He therefore deemed it necessary to elaborate new technical interventions, catalysing the change process more efficiently and giving therapists more healing power. His idea—and indeed his accomplishment—was to give psychoanalysis new tools to counteract pathology and promote healthy functioning. Davanloo's view of the human unconscious is centred on the conceptualisation of two conflicting parts: (i) the Self-sabotaging, pathological

Superego part, and (ii) the Ego part, healthy but for having become a hostage and victim to the Superego. Davanloo spent some twenty years studying his own video recorded therapy sessions and, as a result of this endeavour, was able to identify, select, and maximise the really useful interventions and drop the rest. His prevailing therapeutic attitude—with which his patients are immediately confronted—is one of calling upon the patient's potential to ally with the therapist and fight against the self-sabotaging Superego, in order to defend and finally rescue the prisoner Ego. This does not fail to make his clinical presentations on video extremely involving and fascinating. Some of his strategies for breaking through the defensive barrier of even the most resistant patients are remarkably effective. Seeing his patients change in real time, in response to his surgically accurate interventions, administered by a therapist who is only apparently uninvolved—and sometimes even irritating—but can be empathic at a deeper level, makes him a highly charismatic therapist.

Davanloo's discoveries

Davanloo's model has two main distinctive technical features that make his Intensive Short-Term Dynamic Psychotherapy the prototype of all subsequent EDT models: (i) his new conceptualisation of defence mechanisms, the way they are met in the here-and-now of the session, and his new ways of dealing with defences, and (ii) the techniques leading to rapid uncovering and experiencing of even the most primitive layers of human feeling and impulse, shedding light on aspects of human conflict—indeed of human nature—that do not usually surface, nor do they tend to be welcome, in the soft tone atmosphere of more traditional consulting rooms.

Davanloo called the overall process, "unlocking of the unconscious" (1986, 1990). His way of handling defences is extremely dynamic in that it follows the unfolding of the moment-to-moment interaction with the patient. Defences are not interpreted—as in psychoanalysis and dynamic psychotherapy—since this type of intellectual explanation makes the process over-cognitive. The more a therapist keeps on interpreting defences one by one at the cognitive level, the more the patient will mobilise new sets of defences, for example, tactical defences, such as vagueness, tentativeness, evasiveness:

> In ISTDP the process set in motion by the therapist differs profoundly from traditional psychoanalytic psychotherapy in that the therapist does not concentrate on a single defence in a static way, but is trained to recognize every defence the moment it arises, rapidly shifting from one defence to the next and addressing each one in highly specific ways. (Osimo, 1991, p. 44)

Davanloo's model is especially suitable for highly resistant personality disorders presenting with ingrained character pathology. To break through these character defences, Davanloo recommends a standard set of interventions, the "central dynamic sequence" (Davanloo, 1989, pp. 35–36), which incorporates the major technical interventions in the process of unlocking the unconscious. At the core of this sequence is pressure for feeling. Resistance is thus mobilised in the form of tactical and character defences. As defences come to the forefront they can be clarified and challenged by the therapist. This promotes deeper and deeper emotional experiencing, until new defences are mobilised and come to the forefront. These new defences are clarified and challenged in their turn, and the process continues, in this way, until a breakthrough of feeling occurs, followed by an unlocking of the unconscious, that is, when the therapist and patient have a clear view of the pathological components within the psyche. After this has happened repeatedly, the unconscious becomes open and fluid. According to Davanloo, this means that there is no resistance in operation and the deep dynamic content can now flow freely. More on the central dynamic sequence can be found in my later chapter (pp. ??–??). For a thorough and exhaustive description of Davanloo's model of ISTDP, the reader is referred to his own writings (e.g., Davanloo, 1990, 2000) as well as to Coughlin Della Selva (1996), Malan (1986a, b), and ten Have-de Labije (1999, 2001a).

Current state of the art

All the EDT approaches are indebted to Davanloo's discoveries, his innovations, and his demonstration of how it is possible to have an understanding of all defences much more quickly than it was previously believed. Because of the reverberation of Davanloo's own personality on his theoretical conceptualisation, this is historically linked to the idea of a challenging attitude of the therapist. However, subsequent clinical studies revealed that, if defences are correctly identified, understood, and clarified to the patient, their renunciation can be achieved also with a different personal attitude, for instance a validating attitude (McCullough et al., 2003; McCullough et al., 1991; McCullough Vaillant, 1997). In time, this has made it easier to keep the personal aspect distinct from the crucial technical requirement of timely identification of and effective dealing with the patient's defences. Osimo (2003b) elaborated on the complementary functions of challenge/wind and empathy/sun in the therapist's attitude and techniques. The "sun and wind" theory was taken up and further elaborated by Tunnell (2006) who emphasised that the patient's as well as the therapist's position on the sun vs. wind spectrum is relevant to the success of both the patient-therapist and the therapist-supervisor interchange.

Over the last three decades, various EDT approaches originating from the Malan and Davanloo pioneering work have been empirically tested and scientifically investigated. Each of them has some characteristic features of its own, whereas other features are common to all. Some of Davanloo's former students went on elaborating Davanloo's theoretical-technical framework, keeping the founder's acronym (e.g., Abbass, 2002; Coughlin Della Selva, 1996; ten Have-de Labije, 2001a, b, 2010), or modifying it slightly, as in Attachment Based (AB) ISTDP (Neborsky, 2003). Others modified some of Davanloo's theoretical-technical principles and the new acronyms are indicative of differences rather than similarities. Examples include Accelerated Empathic Therapy (AET) (Alpert, 1992; Fosha, 1992; Sklar, 1992), Accelerated Experiential-Dynamic Psychotherapy (AEDP) (Fosha, 2000, 2003; Russell & Fosha, 2008), Intensive Experiential-Dynamic Psychotherapy (IE-DP) (Osimo, 2002, 2003a, 2009), Mindfulness Informed Experiential Dynamic Therapy (MI-) EDT (Kalpin, 2003, 2008), Personality-Guided Relational Psychotherapy (Magnavita, 2005), and Short-Term Anxiety-Regulating Therapy (START), also known as Affect Phobia Therapy (APT) (McCullough Vaillant 1997; McCullough et al., 2003a). McCullough, though, never abandoned the STDP acronym.

The process of learning from each other was greatly catalysed by the scientific events promoted by the International Experiential Dynamic Therapy Association (IEDTA), founded in 2001. This process has been bringing about a sort of Darwinian selection of the most effective techniques and productive concepts. Based on experience, our recommendation is not to miss any opportunity of a prolonged and repeated exposure to clinical videos. Viewing sessions carried out by highly experienced EDT therapists, shown at symposia and immersion courses, with a teaching purpose, may be especially intensive, moving, and spectacular. Also, clinical videos presented by colleagues who are less experienced and still in training, do not fail to mobilise our deep emotion and have an activating effect on our unconscious. Such involved and attentive observation of the therapist-patient interaction does in time increase therapists' capacity to tolerate the intensity of emotional experiencing in their patients as well as in themselves. As a result of this, and of advanced training, therapists will stop inadvertently avoiding, and instead facilitate and sustain, the surfacing of very intense emotional experiencing, on which EDT relies as its main change factor.

Indications and contraindications of EDT

There is more than one way of approaching the theme of indications and contraindications for any therapeutic model. For example, we can focus on the range of disturbances treatable with a given model in ideal conditions, that is, with a fully trained and sensitive therapist, and without any time constraint or other external limitation. If we do so, we run the risk of overestimating the potential of our model, since these ideal conditions rarely occur. We will likely include some candidates who can theoretically be helped in a substantial way, but in actual fact will not benefit substantially from the therapy. Alternatively, by taking into account the specific conditions in which treatment is going to take place, we will be in a better position to predict therapeutic outcome more reliably. If we do so and decide to use our therapeutic model in a flexible way, we are also more likely to make the most of the time and expertise that are available. Another relevant factor is the goal we set out to achieve with our treatment. For example, do we always aim for a full resolution of all symptoms, disturbances, and maladaptive behavioural patterns? Getting *as close as possible* to excellence is an excellent resolution! There are times, however, in which the severity of disturbance, time constraint, or some other external limitation makes it unrealistic to aim for a complete cure. In this case a therapist may be left with two less ambitious options: (i) trying to give at least some help, or (ii) giving up altogether.

Our philosophy is to aim for the best possible result given the circumstances of the patient, and the setting in which therapy is offered. A pragmatic approach is to assess all the disturbances accurately, before committing to treatment, and to evaluate the actual conditions in which therapy will take place as well as our own motivation to treat that patient in those conditions. Psychotherapy in general, and EDT in particular, requires a true personal involvement of the therapist. As human beings, we should assess our limits carefully. As will be shown in subsequent chapters, EDT is a comprehensive psychotherapeutic model, capable of bringing help to people suffering from a wide range of disturbances. A fundamental indication for EDT, however, is the patient's response to EDT. How is it possible to know this before committing to treatment? The answer, of course, lies in the nature of the initial interviews used in EDT, called trial therapy or trial relationship (see also my later chapter, pp. ??–??). This involves one or two extended sessions lasting two and a half to three hours each, prior to making any commitment to treat the patient. These extended sessions are designed to assess how a patient responds to exposure to EDT therapeutic techniques and therapeutic ingredients (see pp. ??–??) as well as the relationship with the therapist. In this way the selection of candidates rests, ultimately, on the outcome of the extended trial sessions. No scale, questionnaire, or diagnosis, by themselves, would sufficiently answer two crucial questions: (i) did *this* person respond to *this* therapist using *this* approach, and, in the affirmative case, (ii) was the response good enough to make a full therapeutic result a realistic objective given the circumstances of the patient, the setting in which the therapy will be offered, and the motivation of the therapist?

This careful, fine-tuned assessment makes it possible to optimise the use of therapist time and energy, reducing therapist burnout from unsatisfactory, frustrating interaction with patients. Moreover, it helps make the best use of highly specialised professionals, especially in the public sector. The use of descriptive diagnosis, like those provided by the Diagnostic and Statistical Manual (DSM-IV, American Psychiatric Association, 1994) is widespread and useful to orientate the treatment provider to the nature of the patient's problems. Projective testing and the administration of scales and questionnaires may further refine diagnosis. Their level of accuracy is, however, insufficient for a really accurate and specific selection process. To use a metaphor, if a physician suspects an infectious disease, the prescription of a broad-spectrum antibiotic may be at times correct even before the origin of symptoms is proven. Yet, if the specific bacterium is isolated and its sensitivity to different antibiotics tested, this will enable the doctor to make a more accurate prediction, making the healing process more effective. The same applies to EDT, where the descriptive identification and classification of a syndrome or "disturbance", per se, do not give enough information as to the extent that the profound forces underlying the symptoms can be satisfactorily modified, and sensitivity to therapeutic ingredients needs to be tested. Having clarified this point, I will outline the main indications and contraindications for EDT at the clinical and, subsequently, at the descriptive level.

The clinical microscope

The main clinical indicators are the quality of interpersonal rapport developing between therapist and patient during the first trial extended sessions, their ability to come to a clear understanding of the patient's core conflicts, and achievement of an adequate level of emotional activation. The therapist will offer their best personal and professional resources, making use of themselves as well as of their techniques. As a result the patient will generally make dynamically meaningful communications, showing some degree of emotional activation. If this process gives rise to a good-enough emotional experience (Osimo, 2001), and the patient can tolerate the anxiety that is provoked, they can be accepted for EDT. Carrying out this initial assessment and extended trial interviews is a complex undertaking, requiring specific training involving use of videotaped sessions. This is made worthwhile by the level of accuracy—thus of cost-effectiveness—it allows. Depending on the quality of emotional response, on the clarity of the relevant dynamics, and on the actual diagnosis (see next section), a patient may be eligible for a rapid, or a more gradual activation of their unconscious conflicting emotions. If a rapid activation is possible the total number of sessions will tend to be relatively lower than when a gradual activation is needed. Therapy usually lasts between three and approximately thirty-five sessions in the case of rapid activation, and between thirty and seventy sessions if the activation has had to be more gradual. It goes without saying that the faster the healing process, the better for all those involved and, especially, for the patient. EDT's main goal is not, however, brevity per se, rather a quality of outcome satisfying to both patient and therapist. EDT is not feasible if the trial extended sessions did not result in a clear view of the patient's dynamics, access to emotional experiencing, and indicated an inability to tolerate anxiety. Rather, if the anxiety mobilised during the interaction with the therapist who is trying to activate the patient's conflicting forces, exceeds the patient's tolerance, this is a contraindication to EDT. It does not imply that the patient is unsuitable for dynamic psychotherapy tout court. A more supportive dynamic approach or a different form of treatment can be considered.

The descriptive categories

There are indeed so many scales and classification systems that one can be suspicious that their huge number might inversely correlate with the relevance of the parameters they measure. Although these scales provide some accurate measures of single or groups of items, they only represent an aspect of a far more complex reality. Contemporary descriptive diagnostic manuals such as DSM-IV (American Psychiatric Association, 1994) and ICD-10 (World Health Organization, 1994) do indeed strive to make up for this complexity by resorting to multi-level diagnosis. Nevertheless, the descriptive diagnosis needs to be integrated and confirmed case by case on the basis of clinical indicators. The same diagnostic tag may indeed serve as an umbrella for a number of conditions that differ remarkably, in terms of their objective and subjective severity, and of the strategies used by the patient in their attempt at adaptation. Finally, a diagnostic label will not provide any information regarding the origins and causation of the disturbance. Three descriptive indicators will be considered here: (i) diagnosis, (ii) defensive style, and (iii) Global Assessment of Functioning.

Diagnosis

Patients with personality disorders and most neurotic disturbances are the main targets of EDT. Therapy and its duration are always patient-tailored. However, patients presenting with personality disorders, such as the avoidant, dependent, passive-aggressive, depressive, antisocial and some obsessive-compulsive, borderline, and histrionic tend to require between three and thirty-five to forty sessions. The same applies to a number of Axis I syndromes like the dysthymic, anxiety, and somatoform disorders, sexual dysfunctions due to psychological factors, bulimia nervosa, binge eating, and others. Patients with narcissistic or paranoid personality disorders and patients "with traits of" (McCullough Vaillant, 1997, p. 408) schizoid and schizotypal disorders tend to require a higher number of sessions, usually ranging between forty and seventy to eighty.

Defensive style

As regards the prevailing defensive style, Vaillant's (1977) hierarchy of defences is an extremely useful frame of reference. In particular, his distinction between neurotic and immature defensive styles provides a helpful indicator for the EDT selection process. The more projection, schizoid fantasy, hypochondriasis, and other immature defences are woven into the structure of the patient's defensive system, the greater the therapeutic task ahead of therapist and patient.

Global functioning

Even after a DSM-IV diagnostic category and the main defensive mechanisms have been identified, our sense of the patient's level of "functioning" may still be quite vague. Although the term "functioning" is far from being satisfactory, as it relies on a similarity between man and machine (and what's worse a defective one), the concept of "functioning" may help the clinician to understand the extent to which the patient's problems do actually interfere with their daily life. This aspect of assessment should guide the therapist's management of therapy, since when the level of adaptation is good enough, life experience is itself therapeutic—thus a therapist's ally. The same cannot be said when the patient's ways of interacting with "reality" are vastly limited or plainly self-destructive. A practical way of measuring this aspect with ease is represented by the Global Assessment of Functioning (GAF) scale (American Psychiatric Association, 1994). When the other requirements are fulfilled, a GAF score higher than sixty is likely to allow for a short-term course of EDT. A lower GAF score (with the other requirements fulfilled) will generally require a more gradual approach, thus a progressively longer EDT course.

Concluding remark

As the reader will notice, the EDT selection process lays much emphasis on the empirical, clinical assessment of the patient's in-session emotional and anxiety response. As a matter of fact, the accumulated knowledge and techniques deriving from many years' use of video technology applied to psychotherapy and pioneered by Davanloo enables EDT trained professionals to attain a degree of accuracy and specificity much higher than previously possible, by means of the trial extended sessions. Training, trying out techniques, and getting supervision on the video recorded sessions makes a huge difference to the degree of accuracy with which the well-trained interviewer can assess a patient's responsiveness to the specific therapeutic model.

References

Abbass, A. (2002). Intensive short-term dynamic psychotherapy in a private psychiatric office. *American Journal of Psychotherapy*, *56*: 225–232.

Adler, A. (1928–1937). *Superiority and Social Interest*. H. Ansbacher and R. R. Ansbacher (Eds.). New York: Norton, 1964.

Alexander, F. & French, T. M. (1946). *Psychoanalytic Therapy, Principles and Application*. New York: Ronald Press [reprinted New York: John Wiley & Sons, 1974].

Alpert, M. (1992). Accelerated empathic therapy (AET): A new short-term dynamic psychotherapy. *International Journal of Short-Term Psychotherapy*, *7*: 133–156.

American Psychiatric Association (1994). *Diagnostic and Statistical Manual of Mental Health Disorders* (4th edition). Washington, DC: American Psychiatric Association.

Bacciagaluppi, M. (1989). Erich Fromm's views on psychoanalytic "technique". *Contemporary Psychoanalysis*, *25*: 226–243.

Balint, E., Balint, M. & Ornstein, P. (1972). *Focal Psychotherapy: an Example of Applied Psychoanalysis*. London: Tavistock.

Bowlby, J. (1982). *Attachment and Loss: Volume 1. Attachment* (2nd edition). New York: Basic.

Breuer, J. & Freud, S. (1895). *Studies on Hysteria. S. E., 2*. London: Hogarth.

Coughlin Della Selva, P. (1996). *Intensive Short-Term Dynamic Psychotherapy: Theory and Technique*. Chichester, UK: John Wiley & Sons.

Darwin, C. (1872). *The Expression of the Emotions in Man and Animals*. London: Murray [reprinted London: Harper Collins, 1998].

Davanloo, H. (1986). Intensive short-term dynamic psychotherapy with highly resistant patients. II. The course of an interview after the initial breakthrough. *International Journal of Short-Term Psychotherapy, 1*: 239–255.

Davanloo, H. (1989). The central dynamic sequence in the major unlocking of the unconscious and comprehensive trial therapy. Part II. *International Journal of Short-Term Psychotherapy, 4*: 35–66.

Davanloo, H. (1990). *Unlocking the Unconscious*. Toronto: John Wiley & Sons.

Davanloo, H. (2000). *Intensive Short-Term Dynamic Psychotherapy*. Chichester, UK: John Wiley & Sons.

Dupont, E. (Ed.) (1988). *The Clinical Diary of Sandor Ferenczi*. M. Balint & N. Zarday Jackson (Trans.). Boston: Harvard University Press.

Eissler, K. R. (1950). The Chicago Institute of Psychoanalysis and the sixth period of the development of psychoanalytic technique. *Journal of General Psychology, 42*: 103–157.

Ekman, P. (1996). Universality of emotional expression? A personal history of the dispute. In: Darwin, C. (1872), *The Expression of the Emotions in Man and Animals* (pp. 363–393), republished 1996.

Ezriel, H. (1952). Notes on psychoanalytic group therapy: Interpretation and research. *Psychiatry, 15*: 119–126.

Ferenczi, S. (1920). The further development of an active therapy in psychoanalysis. In: J. Rickman (Ed.), *Further Contributions to the Theory and Technique of Psychoanalysis* (pp. 198–217). London: Karnac, 1994.

Ferenczi, S. (1955). *Final Contributions to the Problems and Methods of Psychoanalysis*. M. Balint (Ed.), E. Mosbacher (Trans.) [Reprinted by Maresfield Library]. London: Karnac, 1994.

Ferenczi, S. & Rank, O. (1925). The development of psychoanalysis. In: G. H. Pollack (Ed), C. Newton (Trans.), *Classics in Psychoanalysis Monograph Series*, Monograph 4. Madison, CT: International Universities Press, 1987.

Fosha, D. (Ed.) (1992). Accelerated empathic therapy (AET): history, development and theory. *International Journal of Short-Term Psychotherapy*, special issue, *7*: 3.

Fosha, D. (2000). *The Transforming Power of Affect*. New York: Basic.

Fosha, D. (2003). Dyadic regulation and experiential work with emotion and relatedness in trauma and disordered attachment. In: M. F. Solomon & D. J. Siegel (Eds.), *Healing Trauma: Attachment, Trauma, the Brain and the Mind* (pp. 221–281). New York: W. W. Norton.

Fromm, E. (1964). *The Art of Listening*. New York: Continuum.

ten Have-de Labije, J. (1999). Maintaining Davanloo's discovery for uncovering the unconscious: an attempt at formulating operational definitions of the dependent variables. Part I and II. *Ad Hoc Bulletin of Short-Term Dynamic Psychotherapy, 3*: 4–21.

ten Have-de Labije, J. (Ed.) (2001a). Red and green traffic lights on Davanloo's road to the unconscious. Part I. In: J. ten Have-de Labije (Ed.), *The Working Alliance in ISTDP: whose Intrapsychic Crisis?* Amsterdam: VKPD.

ten Have-de Labije, J. (2001b). Davanloo's road to the unconscious: Working with a wartraumatized patient and working with a phobic patient. Proceedings of the 1st IEDTA Conference, Milan. *Quaderni di Psichiatria Pratica, special issue, 54–76.*

ten Have-de Labije, J. (2010). *The Collected Writings of Josette ten Have-de Labije*. Del Mar, CA: Unlocking Press.

Jones, E. (1946). Review of Alexander, F., French, T. M. et al., *Psychoanalytic Therapy: Principles and Applications. International Journal of Psychoanalysis, 27*: 162.

Jung, C. G. (1912). Psychology of the unconscious: a study of the transformations and symbolisms of the libido, a contribution to the history of the evolution of thought. B. M. Kinkle (Trans.). London: Kegan Paul Trench Trubner, 1916.

Jung, C. G. (1921). *Psychological Types, or, The Psychology of Individuation*. H. G. Baynes (Trans.). London: Kegan Paul Trench Trubner.

Jung, C. G. (1934–1954). The archetypes and the collective unconscious (2nd edition). *Collected Works, Vol. 9, Part 1*. Princeton, NJ: Bollingen, 1981.

Jung, C. G. (1964). *Man and His Symbols*. Garden City, NY: Doubleday.

Kalpin, A. (2003). The use of "being present" in facilitating emotional closeness and emotional experience. *Ad Hoc Bulletin of Short-Term Dynamic Psychotherapy, 7*: 46–63.

Kalpin, A. (2008). Implementing mindfulness in experiential dynamic therapy with a depressed patient. *Ad Hoc Bulletin of Short-Term Dynamic Psychotherapy, 12*: 22–38.

Magnavita, J. J. (2005). *Personality Guided Relational Psychotherapy: A Unified Approach*. Washington, DC: American Psychological Association.

Malan, D. H. (1963). *A Study of Brief Psychotherapy*. London: Routledge, 2001.

Malan, D. H. (1976a). *The Frontier of Brief Psychotherapy*. New York: Plenum.

Malan, D. H. (1976b). *Toward the Validation of Dynamic Psychotherapy*. NewYork: Plenum.

Malan D. H. (1979). *Individual Psychotherapy and the Science of Psychodynamics* (2nd edition). London: Hodder Arnold, 1995.

Malan, D. H. (1986a). Beyond interpretation: Initial evaluation and technique in short-term dynamic psychotherapy. Part I. *International Journal of Short-Term Psychotherapy, 1*: 59–82.

Malan D. H. (1986b). Beyond interpretation: Initial evaluation and technique in short-term dynamic psychotherapy. Part II. *International Journal of Short-Term Psychotherapy, 1*: 83–106.

Malan, D. H. (1983–2012). Personal communications.

Malan, D. H. & Coughlin Della Selva, P. (2007). *Lives Transformed: A Revolutionary Method of Dynamic Psychotherapy*. London: Karnac.

Malan, D. H. & Osimo, F. (1992). *Psychodynamics, Training, and Outcome in Brief Psychotherapy*. Oxford: Butterworth-Heinemann.

McCullough, L., Kuhn, N., Andrews, S., Kaplan, A., Wolf, J. & Lanza-Hurley, C. (2003). *Treating Affect Phobia: A Manual for Short-Term Dynamic Psychotherapy*. New York: Guilford.

McCullough, L., Winston, A., Farber, B., Porter, F., Pollack, J., Laikin, M., Vingiano, W. & Trujillo, M. (1991). The relationship of patient-therapist interaction to outcome in brief psychotherapy. *Psychotherapy, 28*: 525–533.

McCullough Vaillant, L. (1997). *Changing Character: Short-Term Anxiety-Regulating Psychotherapy for Restructuring Defenses, Affects and Attachment*. New York: Basic.

Menninger, K. (1958). *Theory of Psychoanalytic Technique*. New York: Basic.

Neborsky, R. (2003). A clinical model for the comprehensive treatment of trauma using an affect experiencing-attachment theory approach. In: M. F. Solomon & D. J. Siegel (Eds.), *Healing Trauma: Attachment, Mind, Body and Brain* (pp. 282–321). New York: W. W. Norton.

Osimo, F. (1991). Time limit, focality and intensive short-term dynamic psychotherapy. *International Journal of Short-Term Psychotherapy*, *6*: 35–51.

Osimo, F. (1994). Method, personality and training in short-term psychotherapy. *International Journal of Short-Term Psychotherapy*, *9*: 173–187.

Osimo, F. (2001). The good-enough emotional experience (Italian original: L'esperienza emozionale sufficientemente buona). Proceedings of the 1st IEDTA Conference, Milan. *Quaderni di Psichiatria Pratica, VII, special issue, 138–141*.

Osimo, F. (2002). Brief psychodynamic therapy. In: J. J. Magnavita (Ed.), *Comprehensive Handbook of Psychotherapy: Psychodynamic and Object Relations Psychotherapies*. New York: John Wiley & Sons.

Osimo, F. (2003a). *Experiential Short-Term Dynamic Psychotherapy: A Manual*. Bloomington, IN: AuthorHouse.

Osimo, F. (2003b). Annotations for the Sun and the Wind. *Ad Hoc Bulletin of Short-Term Dynamic Psychotherapy*, *7*: 23–46.

Osimo, F. (2009). The character hologram. *Ad Hoc Bulletin of Short-term Dynamic Psychotherapy*, *13*: 25–50.

Rank, O. (1924). *The Trauma of Birth*. Mineola, NY: Dover, 1993.

Reich, W. (1933). *Charakteranalyse: Technik und Grundlagen*. Vienna: Zelbstverlag. [First English translation by Mary Boyd (1945), *Character Analysis*. New York: Noonday Press, 1998.]

Russell, E. & Fosha, D. (2008). Transformational affects and core state in AEDP: The emergence and consolidation of joy, hope, gratitude and confidence in the (solid goodness of the) self. *Journal of Psychotherapy Integration*, *18*: 167–190.

Sifneos, P. (1972). *Short-Term Psychotherapy and Emotional Crisis*. Cambridge, MA: Harvard University Press.

Sklar, I. (1992). Issues of loss and AET. *Proceedings of the Conference: The Sequelae of Trauma*. Denville, NJ.

Tunnell, G. (2006). Postscript 10 years after: "The Oedipal Son" revisited. In: S. Minuchin, W. Y. Lee & G. Simon, G. (Eds.), *Mastering Family Therapy: Journeys of Growth and Transformation*. New York: John Wiley & Sons.

Vaillant, G. E. (1977). *Adaptation to Life*. Boston: Little, Brown.

World Health Organization (1992). *ICD-10 Classification of Mental and Behavioural Disorder: Clinical Descriptions and Diagnostic Guidelines*. Geneva: World Health Organization.

CHAPTER TWO

David Malan and the genesis of experiential dynamic psychotherapy in the UK[1,2]

Amanda Baker

Introduction

This chapter has been formed around David Malan's own recent reflections, and presents verbatim comments (shown in extracted text) from two interviews with David and his wife Jennie, which took place in June 2009 and February 2010. Malan's pioneering career as a psychiatrist, psychotherapist, teacher, researcher, and writer provides us with a remarkable case study of the journey from psychoanalysis to evidence-based brief psychotherapy. Throughout his professional life he has focused on the psychodynamic underpinnings of therapeutic change, but this psychodynamic conviction was accompanied from the start by deep reservations about 1950s psychoanalysis as the mainstay of the UK's National Health Service psychotherapy at the time he was setting out on his career. This conflict drove his search for the radical developments that eventually catalysed his contribution to Experiential Dynamic Therapy (EDT). Malan was ahead of his time in worrying about things like evidence base, brevity, and accurate follow-up. Motivations such as these, which have permeated his life's work, are becoming crucially pertinent to the experience of therapists today who want to work psychodynamically within the public sector. It is hoped that, by presenting here some of what David Malan said as he looked back over the development of EDT, this chapter will be interesting to readers who are practitioners in the current UK climate, where there is a growing appetite among public sector psychotherapists for therapies which are relational, experiential, and dynamic while also matching the requirements of public sector commissioning. A new generation of psychotherapists, counsellors, and psychologists is welcoming EDT as a psychodynamic framework which prioritises brevity and demonstrable effectiveness, and is applicable to work with a wide range of people in a wide range of settings.

The development of brief dynamic therapy in the UK

David Malan has long had a wide influence on dynamic psychotherapy in the UK and his seminal (1979) textbook, *Individual Psychotherapy and the Science of Psychodynamics*, is essential reading on psychodynamic trainings. From well before the advent of EDT, David Malan was a driving force behind the development of brief dynamic therapy in the UK:

> I had read the literature and particularly I had read Stekel. He was really the original person who was concerned with brief psychotherapy. And I even went to Stekel's widow—he had died by that time—for therapy. I needed help with my own problems—but I also wanted to see how this worked. And it wasn't a success … I wasn't ready for her approach.

This did not diminish his interest in brief therapy and he decided in the late 1940s to train as a psychiatrist and psychotherapist, partly because he wanted to research the effects of brief psychotherapy. This made Malan's relationship with mainstream psychoanalysis radical right from the start.

> I entered psychoanalytic training from the very beginning with the aim of becoming a researcher and practitioner in this form of psychotherapy. I'd been brought up on an exact science [*chemistry*] and the experimental method … So I employed that in my approach to this work.

Malan was convinced of the importance of opening up the practice and effects of analytic psychotherapy to scrutiny. He believed that psychodynamic processes should be scientifically studied and that the most important tool for this "objective study of subjective material" would be long-term follow-up interviews, to obtain reliable psychodynamic outcome data.

> I gave a talk to the Psychoanalytic Society and, at the end of it, appealed for patients that I could follow up as I wanted to know what the true results of analysis were. You can imagine the reaction amongst them. "Very interesting" yes, but volunteering patients, goodness me, no! One analyst [*Eva Rosenfeld*] offered her patients. Winnicott spoke to me out of the corner of his mouth—"You can have my seventy!"
>
> So [*Rosenfeld*] phoned up the first patient she wanted to offer me and the patient had an anxiety attack over the phone. And she didn't offer any more. And you know that tells a story … What I made of that was that the patient was very far from cured, and this was her prize patient whom she had read a paper about to the British Society. So Winnicott said I could have his seventy. And he started getting in touch with his patients and I saw two of them for follow-up. The therapeutic results were only partial and he didn't offer any more.

Malan concluded:

> … that these patients were still in a state of high transference to their therapists … The trouble with these analyses is that the patient lies on the couch and you go on

> and on and on. Every analyst is told "You must resolve the transference before you terminate" and they did their best to do so, but it didn't work. Whereas in Stekel's brief therapies this dependence on the therapist did not develop.

These discoveries reinforced the urgency of the need for research which could more formally differentiate myth from fact regarding the effects of both psychoanalysis and brief dynamic psychotherapy. Malan was already a research chemist, and his interest in researching psychotherapy always balanced his personal stance as a therapist.

> I wanted to see objectively what the results were and whether or not dynamic therapy was effective.

Compared with psychoanalysis, EDT more overtly incorporates experimental investigation of therapeutic effects. For example, EDT practitioners video record and review video recordings of their clinical work in supervision and as part of their reflective practice. When asked to speculate as to how Freud—"the original brief therapist" (Coren, 2001)—might have viewed the possibility of video recording sessions which Davanloo used to such potent effect, Malan commented that he thought Freud would have seen this as interfering with transference and would have been "highly against it". When asked what Winnicott, with whom David Malan was in analysis at the time he became interested in the work of Habib Davanloo, would have thought of Davanloo's work, Malan said:

> He was thoroughly sympathetic to what we were doing. He was a very nice and very broad-minded person.

But Winnicott seems to have been exceptional and, as when he was appealing for follow-up patients, Malan met with what he describes as a polite but unenthusiastic response from the psychoanalytically dominated adult psychotherapy community at the Tavistock. A similar response came from the British Psychoanalytical Society when he tried to introduce Davanloo's approach. The resistance led him to realise what he describes as:

> … an awful truth about analytical psychotherapy or psychoanalysis, which is that it was a religious belief, and anybody who challenged this religious belief, they didn't want to know. It was as simple as that. … And I used to use the parallel of medical problems. Supposing I had said that I've discovered a new drug that was applicable to a large number of patients with neurotic illness and it appeared to cure some of them permanently and they didn't relapse even after two or three years. One would think that everyone would say "Yes, please tell us about this", "Can we have some?", "Can we try it out?" But you know, not a bit of it. They said "How very interesting" and then completely ignored it.

And yet it was out of psychoanalysis that both Malan's and Davanloo's work emerged. Asked if he thought the Balint Workshop developments in brief dynamic work were evolutionary or revolutionary, Malan said:

> I think it was a revolution. It was most certainly not accepted by the majority of psychoanalysts. And the fundamental hypothesis which analysts believed,

> without any actual experience, was what I call the hypothesis of superficiality. That is that brief psychotherapy has to have superficially ill patients; the technique needs to be superficial, and it's very questionable whether the transference should be used; and the results are only superficial. And that was the standard view of dyed-in-the-wool analysts, without any evidence whatsoever. So there was potentially a lot of hostility towards what we were doing. But I like to feel that Balint and I handled it in such a way that the analysts were not made resentful.

It seems that, perhaps following in the footsteps of other eminent Tavistock dissenters from the classical analytical canon—such as Bowlby with his then revolutionary development of attachment theory—divergence from classical psychoanalysis was an obstacle to the acceptance of brief dynamic therapy by analysts and, subsequently, the wider psychotherapy community in the UK. Over the span of his career, Malan painstakingly gathered, collated, researched, and presented evidence for the validity of brief dynamic psychotherapy in several detailed studies (Malan, 1963, 1976a, b; Malan & Coughlin Della Selva, 2006; Malan & Osimo, 1992). This gave Balint, Malan, and their colleagues encouragement to persevere.

Brief psychotherapy in the forties and fifties

In the United States, Alexander and French (1946) were developing a model of brief dynamic therapy which was a close antecedent of EDT, positing the therapeutic importance of "corrective emotional experience" in present relationships with the therapist and others, in which old established conflicts are re-enacted with adaptive rather than maladaptive consequences. That therapy can work in a short time is predicated on the view that recovery can result from repair, not re-parenting. Psychopathology is often thought to arise when someone's response to attachment trauma kindles affect-regulatory conflict. Unravelling dynamic conflict is seen as a discrete rather than cumulative event once restorative experiences become possible.

> In all forms of etiological psychotherapy, the basic therapeutic principle is the same: to re-expose the patient, under more favourable circumstances, to emotional situations which he could not handle in the past. The patient, in order to be helped, must undergo a corrective emotional experience suitable to repair the traumatic influence of previous experiences. (Alexander & French, 1946, p. 66)

Along similar lines, the active, focal approach being pioneered in Balint's Brief Psychotherapy Workshop, from its 1955 inception at the Tavistock Clinic in London, contrasted with mainstream psychoanalysis and seemed to offer promising solutions.

Another influence on brief psychotherapy at this time was the "anxiety-provoking therapy" being developed by Sifneos in America, following discoveries about change arising via reaction to present experience. Lindemann's work with survivors of the Coconut Grove fire in Boston in 1942 generated new ideas on crisis intervention and emergency treatment (Lindemann, 1944; Malan, 1976a). Brief psychotherapy for patients in crisis, aimed at "restoring them to their previous level of functioning", led Sifneos to realise that "[T]here was a type of patient who could be helped in a more radical way by brief psychotherapy" (Malan, 1976a, p. 21). Sifneos developed brief anxiety-provoking dynamic psychotherapy and pioneered wider use of brief psychotherapy in outpatient treatment.

Malan found striking resonances with Sifneos:

> I remember a most beautiful moment in my interaction with Sifneos when I was talking to analysts and said that the factor that came out from our statistical study of these twenty patients was motivation, and Sifneos was in the audience and he came up to me afterwards and he said "You've blown my mind, because we have always regarded motivation as the most important factor."

Malan describes the approach developed in the Balint Workshop as identical to Sifneos's anxiety-provoking therapy in most of its characteristics:

> He [Sifneos] emphasizes the importance of early and repeated interpretation of resistance, ambivalence, and negative transference in order to maintain the therapeutic alliance; deliberately raising the patient's anxiety by concentrating on interpreting defences, repeatedly using examples from the transference; and making the patient aware of repetitions of past patterns in the transference relationship. (Malan, 1976a, p. 23)

The therapists in Balint's workshop were all experienced psychoanalysts. However, they were sitting face-to-face with their patients, being active and aiming to be focal, using interpretation intensively, and working within a brief framework which patients knew about and expected. They initially set out assuming that "Prognosis is best in *mild illnesses* of *recent onset*" (Malan, 1976a, p. 49), but Malan found that "Neither *severity of pathology* nor *chronicity* seemed to have any bearing on outcome" (p. 49). While they initially tried to keep their work focused, and avoid what they believed would be dependent transference-inducing deep interpretations, they found that:

> The technique used could be thoroughly radical and involve all the main types of interpretation occurring in full-scale analysis, including interpretation of dreams and fantasies, analysis of resistance, interpretation of the transference, and the link between the transference and childhood (Malan, 1976a, p. 47).

> [*Balint's*] idea was that therapy had to be "focal", that is that you had to have a focus. If you wanted to be brief you had to pick a certain aspect of a patient's problems, or rather, a certain aspect of a patient's pathology, and to concentrate on that, and ignore everything else. This actually didn't work. And it didn't work because the analysts who came to try to employ this technique under Balint's leadership were quite unable to follow any limited aim in fact, and they waded in with making interpretations which were supposed to be superficial but they forgot about that, and they made as deep interpretations as the patient required. It became obvious that the deeper you worked, even in brief therapy, the better your results were.
>
> It was a most excellent result, because in fact, it soon transpired that you could go as deep as you liked without doing any harm. Our terror was that if you started

> making interpretations to a patient, you'd get deeply involved in the transference neurosis, and then termination would become impossible. This was the opposite of the truth. If you were active and dealt with the problems as they came up, then it made the work brief.
>
> Balint's fantasy was that the less ill the patient appeared to be initially, the better the results would be. And this was quite useless as a prognostic factor. It soon transpired that the only effective prognostic factors were dynamic ones, that is, concerned with the interaction between the patient and the therapist in the initial interview. What emerged from this was that when I scored Balint's criteria of the patient being less ill initially, this was a useless criterion. But when I scored motivation, suddenly this came out as correlating strongly with outcome. I remember Balint saying "motivation?!" in a tone of contempt. Nowadays one shouldn't be surprised by the importance of motivation because it's concerned with the interaction between therapist and patient. Particularly those patients who started with low motivation but became highly motivated in response to a dynamic interview had the best outcome. They were given a taste of what they were going to experience in therapy and those who reacted well to it were the ones that you expected to do well. Nowadays there's nothing surprising about that but it was surprising to us then. I called these "dynamic" criteria, as opposed "static" criteria which is how ill the patient was and recent onset and things like that. Recent onset had no correlation at all. It was everybody's fantasy that if you caught the patient as soon as they developed symptoms, this would be a good prognosis, and it wasn't. It's how the patient reacts to the therapist.

The American crisis work of Lindemann and Sifneos had created an accepted niche for brief dynamic therapy, but now the evidence for the more "radical" position on brief psychotherapy was convincing Malan and others that the presence of an acute current conflict is not a necessary requirement for brief therapy. In parallel with his counterparts in America, Malan voiced frustration with the situation at the Tavistock, with long waiting lists causing high dropout before many of those who could most benefit from brief therapy, including those in crisis and those with milder difficulties, even began. This left "those with severe chronic problems who are either downright unsuitable for interpretative psychotherapy, or only suitable for exactly what we provide: therapy of a long-term reconstructive kind." (Malan, 1976a, pp. 15–16)

Looking back on his career, Malan emphasised in our interview that this recognition, i.e., the "debunking" of the hypothesis of superficiality, was one of his most important achievements.

> If one had to put in one sentence what Davanloo and I and other therapists have shown, it is to explode the hypothesis of superficiality. That's the crucial thing. And what training therapists need to know is that you don't need to pull your punches, you don't need to hold back. You can go as deep as you like, within reason and watching for danger signals. But if one can get that across, then that is the really important thing.

> What I did was to debunk the fantasy that it was dangerous to go too deep and if you get involved in the transference you'll never be able to get out, and so you must keep your interpretations superficial and you can't expect any deep-going results. The hypothesis of superficiality was that you must use a superficial technique and the results will only be superficial, which was everybody's fantasy about brief psychotherapy before I came along. Alexander and French employed these deeper interpretations but they didn't try and study the correlation between that and outcome. They just used them, and they used them to good effect.

In fact a major finding of Malan's initial doctoral research (1963) and replication study (1976b) on the outcomes of the Balint Workshop therapies was that good outcome correlated to therapies in which therapists had reported a high frequency of interpretations making a link between the transference and childhood (Malan, 1976b; Malan & Osimo, 1992).

> Eventually a factor emerged which correlated very strongly with outcome, namely the therapist making interpretations which linked the transference with the past. I got the impression that this was a very important factor. I then undertook as objective a study as was possible with this highly subjective material. I did a count of the number of times that the therapist recorded this kind of interpretation in which they linked the transference with the past. Eventually I saw that I had to make a complete content analysis of each of these therapies in order to get as much information as possible and to use other kinds of interpretation as controls. And this took six months!
>
> The link with transference and distant past was a clinical impression. And what I did was to use an objective method to count the number of times that a therapist recorded this kind of interpretation. This was not necessarily the number of times he made the interpretation, but it is meaningful that an account of a therapy in which these interpretations appear most frequently is an account of a successful therapy.

This type of evidence and the refuting of the "hypothesis of superficiality" provide a scientific basis supporting deep and incisive intervention even in the short term, which is strongly encouraging to contemporary therapists who are more and more pressed by time constraints demanded by third-party employers and commissioners—like the NHS and health insurance companies—as well as patients wanting to feel the benefits of therapy as early as possible.

"Malan's Triangles"

Malan's clear understatement of the unique contribution he made to theory, as well as to clinical practice, by connecting the Two Triangles (see Osimo, 2012a) was:

> Both of them had been seen before, but I put them together.

In fact, the linked triangles have become a fulcrum which continues to connect all EDT approaches. The conceptualisation of the triangles works as a prism making dynamic unconscious processes clearly perceptible, which is helping EDT to flourish, in therapy, in supervision, teaching, research, and writing. This gives a clear language for understanding dynamic conflict at source—in its interpersonal beginnings—and as it maps onto present situations including transference phenomena. This means that the linked triangles also very neatly fit with contemporary attachment theory.

Malan's workshop

Malan took over the Tavistock brief psychotherapy workshop in the mid-1960s. He established attendance for at least a year by all trainees on the Tavistock's four year psychoanalytic psychotherapy programme. To deliver brief dynamic therapy via trainees was another radical step, and the way to evaluate this was to set up an outcome study evaluating all the patients seen and supervised in the workshop within a given time-span. This sample consisted of a series of twenty-four consecutive therapies from the 1970s (Malan & Osimo, 1992). While noting that this brief work required more sophisticated skill than its long-term counterpart (Malan & Osimo, 1992, p. 323), the study confirmed that brief dynamic therapy delivered by talented and intensively supervised trainees, adopting "fearless use of a radical purely interpretative technique, in certain patients with long-standing and relatively severe disturbances, can lead to therapeutic effects that are wide-ranging, deep-seated, and permanent" (Malan & Osimo, 1992, p. 325).

Malan's work became influential internationally and, among the visitors Malan attracted from abroad, in 1974, was Habib Davanloo.

> Davanloo was invited to give a series of seminars in Norway and he decided to go back to the States via London, visiting the Tavistock Clinic. He came to one of my seminars and that is how we met.

Malan and Davanloo

> I was extremely put off by his challenging style. The patient would say, "I think I feel ..." He responded, "You think?! You're not sure?" And I didn't like this at all, but the patients lapped it up, because it got to their deep feelings and they got better.

What Malan saw when Davanloo showed his video recordings was a revolutionary way of inducing breakthrough into a patient's unconscious core affective experience, by means of very active engagement with aspects of the patient's here-and-now behaviour, especially resistance. "Once the patient has been acquainted with his defences, he will begin ... to see the sense of the therapist's challenges and turn against the defences himself" (Davanloo, 1990, p. 107). By this means potential "external conflict between patient and therapist is transferred to ... internal conflict between the patient's therapeutic alliance and his resistance" (Davanloo, 1990, p. 107). Davanloo is at pains to emphasise that his method of direct challenge is only effective if the patient can understand that it is aimed towards their *defences*, and in the presence of a conscious and unconscious therapeutic alliance. If this is not clear the patient will feel personally under attack and a misalliance and therapeutic impasse will ensue (Davanloo, 1990). The fine-tuned sensitivity in making this distinction was something Davanloo developed over years of meticulously studying his own videotapes.

> He did it more or less in secret—it was most extraordinary. He would watch his tapes of the day in the evening and try and work out what worked and what didn't, and if something worked he tried it out on the next half dozen patients. An incredible piece of work.

The skill this gave him is evident in Davanloo's published transcripts (see Davanloo, 1990), but the subtlety and the pace at which these interactions unfolded may account for the initial discomfiture of therapists witnessing this sort of work.

> [*Jennie Malan*] That abrasive challenging approach was a total anathema, especially at the Tavistock Clinic, and people said "We don't want any more of this."

But in spite of Malan's own initial aversion, he felt that the evidence in patients' responses could not be ignored.

> You just couldn't brush them off ... As a scientist you need evidence. And if you get evidence, you've got to pay attention to it.

Davanloo's work appeared to Malan to be more consistently and effectively producing the results Malan and his trainees were aiming for, and applicable to a far wider range of patients.

> [*Jennie Malan*] Davanloo was struck by David's writing and lecturing, and so the two of them did many international conferences together. David then undertook to study very carefully what Davanloo was doing and to work out the central dynamic sequence and all the rest of the techniques to see what was happening in these interviews. And the two of them worked closely together.

Malan's encounter with Habib Davanloo led to an extensive collaboration, as he worked with Davanloo to re-conceptualise and formalise the mechanisms of Davanloo's Intensive Short-Term Dynamic Psychotherapy (Davanloo, 1990), including the "Central Dynamic Sequence" (Davanloo, 1990, pp. 101–123; 1996, pp. 301–302).

While Davanloo's therapy had much in common with the work being undertaken at the Tavistock Clinic, it led Malan to striking realisations, such as the central importance of the intensity of affective experiencing:

> We didn't know about intensity in experience being a crucial factor. It happened. But we didn't observe that that was what mattered.

Echoing a phenomenon they had seen in some of the Tavistock therapies, Malan was struck to see in Davanloo's work how this access to unconscious affect "seems to occur especially when the patient expresses *anger* about the therapist's *correct* interventions, which threaten major defences" (Malan & Osimo, 1992, p. 319). This is complementary to Malan's earlier finding that interpretations linking transference with distant past were especially important, since the present interpersonal upheaval of major defences brings patients in touch with reverberations from their distant past attachment experience. The clinical use of the central dynamic sequence capitalises on these processes, and a key to its effectiveness seems to be that, in contrast to classic psychodynamic method, it uses interpretation to consolidate emotional breakthrough only after transference feeling is aroused, rather than to precipitate it (Malan, 2006).

Davanloo's therapy may have been applicable to a wider group of patients (for example, "those treated in Malan's Workshop represented just over 4 per cent of patients who applied for treatment at the Tavistock Clinic during the period studied"—Malan & Osimo, 1992, p. 323), but it was much more difficult to teach than the Tavistock brief dynamic therapy which was feasible to deliver via trainees. This has been partly because, for most therapist personalities, it is very difficult to master, and partly because aspects of Davanloo's style remained unpalatable to many therapists.

> [*Jennie Malan*] What some of the clinicians in America have said is that they also didn't like the abrasive approach, and were put off by it, but David's conceptualisations of it made it tolerable and they would go back and see more, and became convinced that this actually was a very effective tool. But they couldn't themselves do it, and that was why they then developed their own alternative means of getting the same results. Challenging the defences but in a much less abrasive way.
>
> [*David Malan*] Yes, the abrasiveness is quite unnecessary. That is what they demonstrated ... Challenge is not the essential ingredient. It's concentrating on dealing with the defences over and over again. And you don't have to do it by challenge. But you do have to do it by getting the patient to see that his defences are counterproductive.

Underpinning this diversification in therapeutic style is the ever increasing recognition of the importance for therapeutic success of the dynamics of the therapeutic relationship itself, both from within EDT and outside. Second generation EDT practitioners now seem to be converging over the value of the "genuine and compassionate relationship between therapist and patient, within which deep feelings and impulses can be freely experienced, intimate thoughts are shared, and new revealing insights are achieved" (Osimo, 2009, p. 25).

Relationship and techniques

In Malan's early research, the most intransigent of difficulties that therapy might address proved to be in the area of intimate relationships and commitment to intimacy (Malan, 1976a).

> The quality of intimate relations is perhaps the most searching test of an individual's mental health and adjustment, and it is this area that has always received the greatest weight in our judgements of outcome. (p. 239)

Perhaps it is no surprise then that a form of therapy that can overcome this difficulty is one that makes intensive use of relationship. Alexander and French (1946) highlighted the effects of rapport between patient and therapist, and Malan (1979) too used the concept of rapport as a way of monitoring how emotional depth in the real relationship between therapist and patient, i.e., the dynamic of the therapy itself, affects its success. In his research he found that "intense involvement on both sides" (Malan, 1976b, p. 272) underpinned the factors which correlated with good outcome.

EDT therapists try to establish real contact with their patients, which can enable "corrective emotional experience" in conjunction with cognitive insight.

> It seems to be true that, for therapeutic effects to be permanent, both a cognitive and an affective element must usually be present. In other words the patient must both *experience* X [feelings] and *understand* the nature of the defences, in relation to C [current] and P [past]; must also understand the similarities between the two areas; and ... this can usually only be done via the same kind of experience and understanding in the transference. (Malan & Osimo, 1992, p. 36)

Among second generation EDT therapists, Diana Fosha, in particular, moved away from the confrontational stance in her Accelerated Experiential Dynamic Psychotherapy (Fosha, 2000, 2001), suggesting that unlocking does not have to arise from challenging maladaptive defensive resistance, but that adaptive affective functioning can be catalysed by means of affirming, empathic, attachment-oriented therapy using dyadic regulation of affect, in which the therapist's own affect is used to scaffold the client's under-developed and avoided areas of affective experiencing. McCullough, Fosha, and others (e.g., Fosha, 2000; McCullough Vaillant, 1997) argue that therapy is about helping patients to activate their own adaptive and healing attachment systems, in relationships. The therapeutic stance capitalises on the fact of patients' attachment drive, which will seek comfort and healing for the pain of their original trauma, by means of intimacy with another person, if conditions become safe enough. Along with more recent developments of ISTDP, other meaningful second generation models include Kalpin's (2003, 2008, 2009) Mindfulness-Informed EDT, Magnavita's (2005) Integrative Psychotherapy, and Osimo's (2003, 2012b, c) Intensive Experiential-Dynamic Psychotherapy (IE-DP). Each of these models has a view of—and approach to—the therapeutic relationship. As Osimo (2003, 2009) points out, amongst all these different approaches, the personality of the therapist is as important as the personality of the patient in determining an approach that is workable.

All EDT therapists aim to find ways of showing a patient their self-defeating resistance and defences in a way that can be taken in by the patient. In our interview, Malan emphasised that, with the majority of patients, he believes that the only effective therapy involves reaching buried painful feelings through persistently pointing out and blocking defences, resulting in what is known as the "central dynamic sequence" (for a clear description see Malan & Coughlin Della Selva, 2006, pp. 21–29). Intensive Short-Term Dynamic Psychotherapy (ISTDP), which remains the most faithful to the approach pioneered by Davanloo, aims to utilise this procedure. Malan described the way that the central dynamic sequence commonly unfolds, especially in ISTDP, as follows:

> There is some pressure from the therapist for the patient to acknowledge and express their painful or anxiety-laden feelings.

> This results in the patient going into resistance. The resistance takes the form of defences against expressing or experiencing the underlying feelings.
>
> The therapist refuses to accept the patient's avoidance and points out the nature of the defences against expressing the underlying feelings. The therapist persists in this blocking of the defences, and sooner or later the patient gets angry about not being able to use their customary defences.
>
> This leads to further resistance which now involves the transference.
>
> The therapist now points out the defences being used against expressing feelings in the transference.
>
> Eventually the patient is able to acknowledge, express, and experience the feelings in the transference.
>
> This results in a breakthrough and a freeing of the patient's unconscious.

In our second interview, however, he also emphasised that the central dynamic sequence is a dynamic phenomenon rather than a sequence of technical steps that appears differently in different forms of EDT, more or less overtly.

Other forms of EDT such as Fosha's (2000, 2001) Accelerated Experiential Dynamic Psychotherapy (AEDP) or Osimo's (2012b, c, d) IE-DP do not necessarily aim to catalyse rising transference resistance and mobilise complex transference feelings in the therapeutic relationship.

All in all, the current "second generation" EDT therapists show that EDT techniques can be adapted to different therapeutic models and therapist personalities. It goes without saying that the therapist needs to be at least aware of their own character traits and problem areas, but David Malan believes that, although it requires a complex set of skills, modern-day EDT is accessible to a wide range of therapists. He does not believe that experience as a psychoanalyst or an analysand is an essential prerequisite to successful acquisition of modern-day EDT skills:

> [*It's not essential*] to have been analysed, no. Certainly it's an advantage. One thing you can be sure of if you've undergone analysis or therapy is that you won't take your problems out on your patients which is the risk.

The EDT therapist's position in relation to their patient is openly collaborative and experimental. For example, patients are made aware that studying the videos helps the therapist to think about how the therapy is working. Besides this research-active attitude being integrated into the process of the therapy, Malan has always been interested in framing the practice of therapy within a research-active context, and the Tavistock workshop was a forum for developing psychotherapy research. As described in the introduction to this chapter, Malan spoke emphatically about the importance to him of research from the very beginning of his career.

The discovery of something rich and powerful can exert a fundamentalist tug away from the exploratory attitude that led to its discovery; and the substitution of believing for seeing can obscure the value of ever-refreshing evidence. If Malan has had an axe to grind, it is with sectarian positions that obscure the simple value of looking for truth about subjective individual human experience. Testament to this is his openness to the possibility that other approaches can succeed where dynamic ones fail, or that they can be complementary, since, for example, behavioural approaches "may sometimes *activate a patient's unconscious* and thus have a major facilitating effect on dynamic psychotherapy" (Malan, 2001, p. 193; also see Meijers, 2012). Experiential dynamic therapies have embraced instruments for self-scrutiny, for example, video recording, and the very open exchange of working and thinking practice which it enables. The following section highlights Malan's reflections on research, especially in terms of psychodynamic follow-up interviews.

Research

Malan and Davanloo share a preoccupation with the importance of examining and refining therapeutic effect, and experiential dynamic therapies put a premium on monitoring the moment-to-moment, session-to-session effect as part of the work of the process. An increasing number of EDT practitioners in the UK are adopting the use of session-by-session measures to track the progress of patients in therapy (see Harmon, Lambert, Smart & Hawkins 2007; Hawkins, Lambert, Vermeersch, Slade & Tuttle, 2004; Lambert, 2005, 2010; Lambert, Harmon, Slade, Whipple & Hawkins, 2005; Lambert, Whipple, Smart, Vermeersch & Nielsen, 2001; Lambert et al., 2002; Lutz et al., 2006). In addition, as has already been stated, video recording has been a powerful and natural tool for therapists' personal monitoring and review of their work (Abbass, 2004; Alpert, 1996; McCullough, 2003). Coming too late for Malan's Tavistock research, routine video recording of therapy has also provided a valuable store of data for larger-scale psychotherapy research such as that being carried out by Leigh McCullough (see Macdonald, 2012). Conventional medical-style trials comparatively evaluating outcome have provided mounting evidence for the effectiveness of EDT (Abbass, Sheldon, Gyra & Kalpin, 2008; Macdonald, 2012). However, Malan has argued that the evidence from controlled studies using averages does not distinguish the particular quality of psychodynamic change. There are "certain qualities of a therapeutic result that indicate that a patient's neurosis has been truly resolved" (Malan, 2001, p. 197), and which reveal the validity of psychodynamic therapy more sharply than can be done with quantitative measures. Discussing the problem of comparative studies that rely on quantifying via averages, he wrote: "… although many of the results of [dynamic] psychotherapy are no more than *moderately* favourable, and are indistinguishable from those given by non-dynamic methods, the best results possess qualities that are specific to dynamic psychotherapy" (2001, p. 194).

In his lifelong quest to gather evidence that does justice to the specific effects of dynamic therapy, Malan has consistently advocated follow-up interviews as the essential instrument. He believes that the richness of therapeutic results can best be picked up only in an interview in which deep and real relational contact is made. Hence:

> It has to be a personal interview … I advocate the follow-up being done by the therapist because the therapist has already made proper contact with the patient, and it's essential to have deep contact in the follow-up interview. Just ticking answers to questions is absolutely no use … And you need to record what the patient actually

> said, because one of the factors is the real depth of feeling that the patient can show in a good follow-up. And you can only do that by knowing the actual words.

While patients have great insight into *how* they feel different, Malan believes that only a few patients have accurate insight into what led to the change.

> Only really insightful patients can answer that question meaningfully.

For example, talking of the therapeutic power of deep emotional experiencing,

> I don't think they report it. I think one observes it and makes a judgement about it. The really good patients who have got really good results will tell you and it's meaningful, but the intermediate ones are quite likely to be giving an answer that just isn't relevant. But still, it's evidence, whatever they say.

So Malan has always pushed for psychodynamic measures and, in most of his clinical studies (e.g., Malan, 1963, 1976a, b; Malan & Osimo, 1992), applied them to all the patients seen during a given time span, and adopted outcome criteria tailored to individual patients on the basis of their presenting situation. These individualised criteria were then independently tested against outcome data obtained in long-term follow-up interviews, thus creating a form of single-case experimental design. The power of this experimental design stems from the fact that it provides a binocular view, integrating the information specifically gathered from every single case with that drawn from the sample as a whole. The details of Malan's process and outcome studies are reported in his publications, but in our interview he emphasised some fundamental principles.

> The essential thing is a follow-up of at least six months, preferably more, since termination. Otherwise you can't tell a thing because, if the patient is just finishing then they're still involved in the therapeutic process. ... What I always used to do was make a list of the patient's original disturbances in every area of their life that you knew about, and then you write down how you would like this to change and what you would like to find at follow-up. ... I think the essential thing is to lay down before you see the patient for follow-up what you want to see, and then match what they actually say against that. This is the objective approach to subjective material and it is absolutely essential that one should strike that balance.

He points out that patients at the start of therapy cannot necessarily define what their own criteria for success would be:

> They don't know—you know that better than they do.

And in terms of how to identify the efficacy of the particular interventions a therapist is employing—

> This is a lot of work. Before seeing the patient for follow-up, you have to make judgements about variables that you think would be relevant. You have to think up a series of hypotheses about what ought to be important in prognosis, and give some account of those before you see the patient ... And how you do the follow-up is also extremely important. You must go into the follow-up with a series of questions you want to know the answers to ... So you've got a series of criteria for a successful outcome and you tailor your interview to elicit relevant information. Then you need to make judgements about whether the criteria have been fulfilled. You don't have to score them, but it helps to score them.

Malan developed, applied, and refined this approach in the major studies he conducted which span his career, generating a large body of evidence about the validity of psychodynamic therapy.

Malan has always argued that, at the same time as being the instrument of radical personal transformation that is unique in every case, psychodynamic work can bear and benefit from scientific scrutiny, and that these are not incompatible. He is passionate about the "objective study of subjective material" as something which dynamic therapists and researchers should engage in. He has always argued that there are psychodynamic ways of being scientific, and scientific ways of being psychodynamic.

> Before I was a psychiatrist I was a chemist, and one of the things that chemists have to do is called qualitative analysis. That is, you're given an unknown substance and asked to find out what it is. Well, I used to love doing this, and I used to approach it intuitively. And I remember a particular occasion on which I looked at a substance and I said "That looks like so and so." I did three tests on it which would be positive if it was that substance and it was. I loved to work intuitively on chemical analysis, and I love to work intuitively with patients.

This research-consciousness is among several facets that equip EDT well for developing within the current evidence-based climate of public sector psychotherapy, but it is only very recently that interest in EDT has begun to grow within the UK. The brief dynamic psychotherapy which Malan and others were pioneering at the Tavistock several decades ago became subsumed into EDT as, in collaborating with Davanloo, his own efforts became increasingly focused on developing and disseminating ISTDP which was initially far more influential abroad than in the UK. The psychoanalytic community in the UK, as described earlier, was sceptical about Davanloo's approach, and until recently Malan has been something of a lone voice in his home country.

Current situation in the UK

In the UK as elsewhere, the more traditional psychoanalytic tradition maintained a strong place, and has continued to flourish in different forms which are sometimes differentiated as psychoanalysis, psychoanalytic therapy, and psychodynamic counselling. In one form or another, psychoanalytic practice has remained influential in the public as well as the private sector, evolving and adapting itself, often in response to the institutional settings in which therapists work, including secondary care psychotherapy services, primary care counselling services (Bolton, 2012), and university counselling services (Baker, 2012). As funding and accountability structures have changed the horizon of public sector psychiatry and psychotherapy, the briefer more active approach developed in the Tavistock workshops has gained strength in the public sector. The rise of evidence-based practice and the cognitive therapies has also influenced psychodynamic therapy which has moved in a more integrative direction, for example, in Coren's (2001) short-term psychodynamic psychotherapy. Additionally, modern attachment theory and developmental psychology have interacted with psychoanalysis to spawn a new generation of research-informed approaches to, and conceptualisations of, psychotherapy. These include Brief Attachment-Based Intervention (BABI) (Holmes, 2001), Mentalisation-Based Treatment (MBT) (Allen & Fonagy, 2006), Psychodynamic Interpersonal Therapy (PIT) (Guthrie, 1999; Hobson, 1985), and Interpersonal Psychotherapy (IPT) (Weissman, Markowitz, & Klerman, 2007). They diverge from psychoanalysis in being structured, goal-directed, focused, more diagnostically determined, and brief- or time-delineated.

While EDT continues to identify itself as a psychodynamic therapy and, perhaps, in essence, remains closer to psychoanalysis, it differs from psychoanalytic therapy in giving less weight to analytic processing, and more to emotional experiencing. The psychoanalytic discourse in the UK has continued to adopt a therapeutic stance which, in keeping with its psychoanalytic roots, prioritises dyadic processing of unconscious relational phenomena (especially transference, countertransference, and projective identification). As do other new generation therapies, EDT more clearly establishes "treatment" goals. EDT aims to facilitate direct emotional experiencing in the patient, to which end the therapist takes a less transference-laden "real relationship" stance alongside the patient. In these ways EDT seems to be well-aligned with the outcome-focused language and agenda of clinical psychology and other public sector contexts, and more closely aligned with CBT (EDT pioneers such as Leigh McCullough and Josette ten Have-de Labije both started their careers as behavioural therapists). Thus, post-Davanloo EDT, having been developed and researched largely abroad, seems to be converging with the changing needs of UK contexts.

> [*Jennie Malan*] I got totally frustrated, because I went to conferences with David and saw how these American and European therapists were using ISTDP effectively, and became very distressed that it wasn't available in Great Britain.

Ferruccio Osimo was among Malan's brief dynamic therapy trainees at the Tavistock and also went to learn ISTDP from Davanloo. He invited Malan as a co-teacher in the first EDT training to be set up in the UK in 2006 with Diana Wais, a London-based practitioner of Diana Fosha's AEDP and member of the AEDP training faculty. Jennie and David Malan organised conferences in Oxford in 2006 and 2008, and invited some of Davanloo's former trainees from abroad to present their own brands of EDT work, in the hope of gaining wider acceptance for these in the UK.

Ferruccio Osimo and colleagues founded the International Experiential Dynamic Therapy Association (IEDTA—www.iedta.net), with an inaugural conference in Milan, Italy in May of 2001. IEDTA has supported pluralism and promoted robust cohesion amid the proliferation of approaches emerging in second-generation EDT through clinical, teaching, and research exchange. Two EDT organisations have recently been established in the UK: (i) EDT-UK (www.edt-uk.com), and (ii) ISTDP-UK (www.istdp.org.uk).

Conclusions

This chapter has presented David Malan's reflections as he recently described his career from the 1950s to the present time, tracing his view of the process by which EDT emerged from its psychoanalytic roots. The motivations which drove Malan have informed the way EDT has developed under his influence, and, at the same time, the broader climate of the last five or so years in the UK seems to be reaching a point which is converging with the ethos which Malan's career epitomises. In particular, the link between motivation and therapy outcome has been highlighted. Published EDT transcripts (e.g., ten Have de-Labije, 2010) clearly reveal interventions that aim to improve patients' capacity to attend to themselves, and understanding of the ways in which they perpetuate their suffering, as well as the consequences of their self-defeating patterns of behaviour, in the hope that they will be motivated to relinquish their defences, and take a more self-compassionate and self-valuing position. In addition to cognitive insight, intensity of in-session emotional experiencing was also identified as a significant factor associated with positive outcome in psychotherapy, and several authors (e.g., Coughlin Della Selva, 1996; Fosha, 2000; McCullough Vaillant, 1997; Osimo, 2003; ten Have de-Labije, 2010) have described approaches to deepen the affective experience of patients. Similarly, Malan emphasised the importance of dealing with defences—a topic that has received much attention in the EDT literature (see for example, Coughlin Della Selva, 1996; Fosha, 2000; Frederick, 2009; Malan & Coughlin Della Selva, 2006; McCullough Vaillant, 1997; McCullough et al., 2003; Osimo, 2003, 2012b; ten Have-de Labije, 2009). Attention to, and the quality of, the relationship between therapist and patient, a focus on what is happening in their interaction in the here-and-now of the session, and making links between what is emerging and what has played out in the patient's relationships with significant others is of crucial importance to Malan and many psychotherapy practitioners, in particular those working within an EDT approach, and several authors expand upon this aspect of their work (e.g., Fosha, 2000; Osimo, 2003, 2012b; ten Have-de Labije, 2010). The scientific method, so important to Malan, is reflected in the willingness of EDT practitioners to embrace video technology, and open their practice up to scrutiny and empirical study. Indeed, an increasing number of clinical psychology trainees are carrying out psychotherapy process and outcome research based on tapes provided by patients and therapists working in an EDT approach, and EDT practitioners are participating in session-by-session data collection and/or providing data for researchers interested in improving the outcome of psychotherapy through provision of feedback on the progress of therapy. One of Malan's major hallmarks has been having the boldness to know that "science"—as a check to the currents of competing and ultimately self-defeating messianic tides—need not take the wonder out of dynamic psychotherapeutic engagement. It is perhaps this attitude that appeals to a new generation of psychologists and psychotherapists who, like Malan, think that emotional and intuitive complexity in psychotherapy does not need to be opaque, unsystematic, or unscientific. EDT provides a rationale and guiding framework capable of dealing with this complexity, as the chapters of this book illustrate.

References

Abbass, A. (2004). Small-group videotape training for psychotherapy skills development. *Academic Psychiatry, 28*: 151–155.

Abbass, A. & D'Arcy, B. (2007). Bringing character changes with Davanloo's intensive short-term dynamic psychotherapy. *Ad Hoc Bulletin of Short-Term Dynamic Psychotherapy: Practice and Theory, 11*: 26–40.

Abbass, A., Sheldon, A., Gyra, J. & Kalpin, A. (2008). Intensive short-term dynamic psychotherapy for DSM-IV personality disorders: A randomized controlled trial. *The Journal of Nervous and Mental Disease, 196*: 211–216.

Alexander, F. & French, T. M. (1946). *Psychoanalytic Therapy, Principles and Application*. New York: Ronald Press.

Allen, J. G. & Fonagy, P. (2006). *Handbook of Mentalization-Based Treatment*. Chichester, UK: John Wiley & Sons.

Alpert, M. (1996). Videotaping psychotherapy. *Journal of Psychotherapy Practice and Research, 5*: 93–105.

Baker, A. (2012). Intensive experiential-dynamic psychotherapy in a university counselling service. In: F. Osimo & M. J. Stein (Eds.), *Theory and Practice of Experiential Dynamic Psychotherapy*. London: Karnac.

Beck, A. T. & Greenberg, R. L. (1996). Brief cognitive therapies. In: J. E. Groves (Ed.), *Essential Papers on Short-Term Dynamic Therapy*. New York: New York University Press.

Bolton, J. (2012). Experiential dynamic therapies in primary care mental health services. In: F. Osimo & M. J. Stein (Eds.), *Theory and Practice of Experiential Dynamic Psychotherapy*. London: Karnac.

Coren, A. (2001). *Short-Term Psychotherapy: a Psychodynamic Approach*. Basingstoke, UK: Palgrave.

Coughlin Della Selva, P. (1996). *Intensive Short-Term Dynamic Psychotherapy: Theory and Technique*. Chichester, UK: John Wiley & Sons.

Davanloo, H. D. (1990). *Unlocking the Unconscious: Selected Papers of Habib Davanloo, MD*. Chichester, UK: John Wiley & Sons.

Davanloo, H. D. (1996). Unlocking the unconscious. In: J. E. Groves (Ed.), *Essential Papers on Short-Term Dynamic Therapy*. New York: New York University Press.

Ezriel, H. (1952). Notes on psychoanalytic group therapy; interpretation and research. *Psychiatry, 15*: 119–126.

Fosha, D. (2000). *The Transforming Power of Affect: A Model for Accelerated Change*. New York: Basic.

Fosha, D. (2001). The dyadic regulation of affect. *Journal of Clinical Psychology/In Session, 57*: 227–242.

Frederick, R. J. (2009). *Living Like You Mean It: Use the Wisdom and Power of Your Emotions to Get the Life You Really Want*. San Francisco, CA: Jossey-Bass.

Guthrie, E. (1999). Psychodynamic interpersonal therapy. *Advances in Psychiatric Treatment, 5*: 135–145.

Harmon, S., Lambert, M., Smart, D. & Hawkins, E. (2007). Enhancing outcome for potential treatment failures: Therapist–client feedback and clinical support tools. *Psychotherapy Research, 17*: 379–392.

ten Have-de Labije, J. (2009). Helping our patients to experience feelings: Understanding the role of defences in emotion regulation and the implications for ISTDP practitioners. *Ad Hoc Bulletin of Short-Term Dynamic Psychotherapy: Practice and Theory, 13*: 15–23.

ten Have-de Labije, J. (2010). *The Collected Writings of Josette ten Have-de Labije*. Del Mar, CA: Unlocking Press.

Hawkins, E., Lambert, M., Vermeersch, D., Slade, K. & Tuttle, K. (2004). The therapeutic effects of providing client progress information to patients and therapists. *Psychotherapy Research, 10*: 308–327.

Hobson, R. F. (1985). *Forms of Feeling*. London: Tavistock.

Holmes, J. (2001). *The Search for the Secure Base: Attachment Theory and Psychotherapy*. London: Routledge.

Kalpin, A. (2003). The use of "being present" in facilitating emotional closeness and emotional experience. *Ad Hoc Bulletin of Short-Term Dynamic Psychotherapy, 7*: 46–63.

Kalpin, A. (2008). Implementing mindfulness in experiential dynamic therapy with a depressed patient. *Ad Hoc Bulletin of Short-Term Dynamic Psychotherapy, 12*: 22–38.

Kalpin, A. (2009). Mindfulness, experiential dynamic therapy, and a case of somatization disorder. *Ad Hoc Bulletin of Short-Term Dynamic Psychotherapy, 13*: 16–51.

Lambert, M. (2005). Emerging methods for providing clinicians with timely feedback on treatment effectiveness: An introduction. *Journal of Clinical Psychology, 61*: 141–144.

Lambert, M. (2010). "Yes, it is time for clinicians to routinely monitor treatment outcome". In: B. L. Duncan, S. D. Miller, B. E. Wampold & M. A. Hubble (Eds.), *The Heart and Soul of Change: Delivering What Works in Therapy* (2nd edition). Washington, DC: American Psychological Association.

Lambert, M., Harmon, C., Slade, K., Whipple, J. & Hawkins, E. (2005). Providing feedback to psychotherapists on their patients' progress: Clinical results and practice suggestions. *Journal of Clinical Psychology, 61*: 165–174.

Lambert, M., Whipple, J., Smart, D., Vermeersch, D. & Nielsen, S. (2001). The effects of providing therapists with feedback on patient progress during psychotherapy: Are outcomes enhanced? *Psychotherapy Research, 11*: 49–68.

Lambert, M., Whipple, J., Vermeersch, D., Smart, D., Hawkins, E., Nielsen, S. & Goates, M. (2002). Enhancing psychotherapy outcomes via providing feedback on client progress: A replication. *Clinical Psychology & Psychotherapy, 9*: 91–103.

Lindemann, E. (1944). Symptomatology and management of acute grief. *American Journal of Psychiatry, 101*: 141–148.

Lutz, W., Lambert, M., Harmon, S., Tschitsaz, A., Schürch, E. & Stulz, N. (2006). The probability of treatment success, failure and duration—what can be learned from empirical data to support decision making in clinical practice? *Clinical Psychology & Psychotherapy, 13*: 223–232.

Macdonald, J. (2012). EDT in the context of psychotherapy research and mental health policy in the UK. In: F. Osimo & M. J. Stein (Eds.), *Theory and Practice of Experiential Dynamic Psychotherapy*. London: Karnac.

Magnavita, J. J. (2005). *Personality-guided Relational Psychotherapy: A Unified Approach*. Washington, DC: American Psychological Association.

Malan, D. H. (1963). *A Study of Brief Psychotherapy*. New York: Plenum Press.

Malan, D. H. (1976a). *The Frontier of Brief Psychotherapy*. New York: Plenum Press.

Malan, D. H. (1976b). *Toward the Validation of Dynamic Psychotherapy*. New York: Plenum Press.

Malan, D. H. (1979). *Individual Psychotherapy and the Science of Psychodynamics*. Oxford: Butterworth-Heinemann.

Malan, D. H. (2001). The way ahead. In: M. Solomon, R. Neborsky, L. McCullough, M. Alpert, F. Shapiro & D. H. Malan, *Short-Term Therapy for Long-Term Change*. New York: W. W. Norton.

Malan, D. (2006, May). *The Essence of Experiential Dynamic Therapy*. Paper presented at the Oxford Conference on Experiential Dynamic Therapy, Oxford.

Malan, D. H. & Coughlin Della Selva, P. (2006). *Lives Transformed: A Revolutionary Method of Dynamic Psychotherapy*. London: Karnac.

Malan, D. H. & Osimo, F. (1992). *Psychodynamics, Training and Outcome in Brief Psychotherapy*. Oxford: Butterworth-Heinemann.

McCullough, L. M. (2003). Videotaping and rating your own sessions: Two valuable ways to improve the quality of therapy. *Addendum to Treating Affect Phobia*. Retrieved April 18, 2011 from http://www.affectphobia.org/docs/VideoATOS/VideoATOSArticle.pdf.

McCullough, L., Kuhn, N., Andrews, S., Kaplan, A., Wolf, J. & Lanza Hurley, C. (2003). *Treating Affect Phobia: A Manual for Short-Term Dynamic Psychotherapy*. New York: Guilford Press.

McCullough Vaillant, L. M. (1997). *Changing Character: Short-Term Anxiety-Regulating Psychotherapy for Restructuring of Defenses, Affects and Attachment*. New York: Basic.

Meijers, J. (2012). Experiential short-term psychodynamic therapy from the perspective of a cognitive-behaviour therapist: a personal account. In: F. Osimo & M. J. Stein (Eds.), *Theory and Practice of Experiential Dynamic Psychotherapy*. London: Karnac.

Menninger, K. (1958). *Theory of Psychoanalytic Technique*. New York: Basic.

Osimo, F. (2003). *Experiential Short-Term Dynamic Psychotherapy: A Manual*. Bloomington, IN: AuthorHouse.

Osimo, F. (2009). The character hologram. *Ad Hoc Bulletin of Short-Term Dynamic Psychotherapy: Practice and Theory, 13*: 24–49.

Osimo, F. (2012a). A historical overview of experiential dynamic therapies. In: F. Osimo & M. J. Stein (Eds.), *Theory and Practice of Experiential Dynamic Psychotherapy*. London: Karnac.

Osimo, F. (2012b). The essence of experiential dynamic therapies. In: F. Osimo & M. J. Stein (Eds.), *Theory and Practice of Experiential Dynamic Psychotherapy*. London: Karnac.

Osimo, F. (2012c). Intensive experiential-dynamic psychotherapy and application of the character hologram. In: F. Osimo & M. J. Stein (Eds.), *Theory and Practice of Experiential Dynamic Psychotherapy*. London: Karnac.

Osimo, F. (2012d). Intensive experiential-dynamic psychotherapy with long-standing depression. In: F. Osimo & M. J. Stein (Eds.), *Theory and Practice of Experiential Dynamic Psychotherapy*. London: Karnac.

Weissman, M., Markowitz, J. & Klerman, G. L. (2007). *Clinician's Quick Guide to Interpersonal Psychotherapy*. New York: Oxford University Press.

Notes

1. I am deeply indebted to David and Jennie Malan for their very generous involvement in the process—two interviews, much reading and thinking, and many email exchanges—which produced the material upon which this chapter is based.
2. It should be stated at the beginning that David Malan views EDT as an overarching term that covers all experiential dynamic therapies. Personally, he has always been an advocate of ISTDP, but he recognises that IE-DP and other approaches have an important contribution to make.

CHAPTER THREE

The essence of experiential dynamic psychotherapies

Ferruccio Osimo

The present chapter outlines the essential ingredients of experiential dynamic psychotherapies, orientating the reader to the practice of Intensive Experiential-Dynamic Psychotherapy (IE-DP). Key characteristics of taking care of the real relationship, mirroring, history taking, and putting into perspective are described. In addition, high technical content, experiential-dynamic interventions, including defence restructuring, emotional maieutics, anxiety regulation, dealing with the Superego, connecting corners of the Triangle of Others, and Self- and Other-restructuring are introduced and discussed theoretically. Annotated extracts from real therapy sessions are presented to illustrate characteristics of experiential dynamic psychotherapies in clinical practice. The reader is also introduced to a coding system used throughout the clinical chapters to clarify the nature, and application, of therapist interventions.

Introduction

As was illustrated in the first two chapters, over the last three decades we have witnessed the birth and development of experiential dynamic therapies. A customary feature of EDT is that clinical work is video recorded enabling us to view real therapy sessions and provide accurate annotated transcripts. Witnessing audiovisual recordings of real therapies can have a strong impact, especially when it includes intense emotional experiencing as well as the opportunity to directly observe character change. Video technology also gives us an opportunity to play back the process of change and its outcome in a vivid and real way. Habib Davanloo was the first to apply video technology to psychotherapy on a large scale for his research studies and scientific presentations, which proved stimulating to many. His former trainees identify with his psychotherapeutic method to a greater or lesser extent, each emphasising certain aspects and introducing new ones, or even budding new approaches, attuned to and enriched by their own personalities. Generally, these EDT approaches are more powerful than previous forms of short-term intervention, since they can be effective in a relatively short time with people presenting with complex problems, severe symptoms, and a strong resistance to change. Some illustrative clinical examples are presented herein, but interested readers are strongly advised to take advantage of any opportunity to attend seminars where they can see and hear the therapeutic process in operation with their own eyes and ears.

In physics, Heisenberg's *uncertainty principle* relates to the problem inherent in accurately measuring both position and velocity of subatomic particles. According to Heisenberg, it is impossible to determine simultaneously, with accuracy or certainty, both the position and velocity of a subatomic particle as the more accurate the approximation of one, the worse the approximation to the other becomes. That is to say that the action of (or process involved in) observing affects what is observed. Now, applying the same concept to EDT, while it is possible to give an accurate description of techniques, we cannot disregard the personal variables of the clinician proposing and using them. The present chapter presents an overview of the ingredients of EDT from the perspective of the author who leans towards Intensive Experiential-Dynamic Psychotherapy (IE-DP) (Osimo, 2001, 2002, 2003, 2009). The following section will therefore outline the main features characterising IE-DP, to assist the reader in identifying where the account of EDT in the remainder of the chapter may lean towards IE-DP.

Intensive Experiential-Dynamic Psychotherapy (IE-DP)

In IE-DP, the patient's whole person—rather than his or her pathology—is the focus. As a therapeutic approach, IE-DP highlights three key characteristics: (i) the real relationship between patient and therapist, (ii) deep experience of feelings, and (iii) experiential-dynamic technical interventions. The IE-DP therapist therefore takes a comprehensive view of the patient-therapist relationship that is seen as both a real, personal interchange between human beings, and a matrix enhancing the healing power of all technical interventions. This is achieved by total openness on the therapist's part and facilitated by the mirroring interventions (see pp. 49–54). Physical (through the body) and mental (related mental representations, thoughts, and fantasies) experience of feelings, impulses, and desires are welcomed and valued as deep and meaningful expressions of the Self. Experiential-dynamic technical interventions include identifying unhealthy defences and motivating their renunciation, regulating anxiety to ease distress and facilitate emotional experiencing of deep feeling and impulse. In addition, the therapist aims to identify the overall character hologram (Osimo, 2009, and chapter 4) and the self-sabotaging aspects of character and Superego, and calls upon all the individual's resources to establish the supremacy of the Self. Interventions also clarify links between the patient's experience and behaviour in session with the therapist and those with significant Others in their current life and past, to make dynamic sense of conflicting emotion and recurrent maladaptive patterns. Individuals are helped to make relationships with Others and with the Self more adaptive, with regard to both the actual handling of the relationships in life and their inner representation. Application of therapeutic interventions is guided by close monitoring of the moment-by-moment shifts of the patient around the corners of the Triangle of Conflict, rather than a predetermined sequence of therapist activities. In other words, a therapist's choice of intervention is guided by the way the therapeutic relationship unfolds, as well as their careful assessment of what is at the forefront, i.e., impulse/feeling, anxiety, or defence, using the Triangle of Experiential-Dynamic Activities (Osimo, 2001) as a compass. These endeavours pave the way to the powerfully healing in-session experience of deep, painful feeling and impulse in an atmosphere of safety and interpersonal connection, enabling the individual to promote the desirable changes in a reasonably short time.

Experiential Dynamic Therapy (EDT) and its general setting

Therapist and patient sit in front of each other preferably without anything, like a table or such, between them. It is customary to audio and video record therapeutic sessions so as to enable both therapist and patient to review sessions whenever they find it appropriate or useful. Patient or therapistgenerally review sessions independently and, in most cases, this does not take place after each session. Recorded sessions can be used also for study and teaching purposes if a patient has agreed to this in writing. More generally, no recording can take place before a patient has been fully informed and has signed a consent form. If the patient does not give their consent, the therapy can still take place without recording if the therapist agrees to this. Sessions are generally scheduled once a week and have fifty to sixty minutes' duration. Some therapists find it useful to have longer sessions, such as ninety minutes each fortnight. The initial one or two interviews are always longer, lasting two and a half to three hours each. EDT especially aims to bring about activation and experiencing of emotion, and the activation and experiencing of feelings needs time. This is the reason that therapists, especially at the start of therapy, may allow more time. This initial part of EDT is called the "trial therapy" (Davanloo, 1986), or "trial relationship" (Osimo, 2001), because its main purpose is to assess how a patient responds to exposure to EDT therapeutic techniques, as well as to the relationship with the therapist. The trial therapy is the most difficult phase of EDT and requires advanced training and supervision before a therapist can carry it out correctly. Its difficulty mainly stems from the twofold requirement of a therapist who is emotionally present, responsive and, at the same time, capable of mastering all EDT techniques and combining them together. Not an easy task indeed! To start making it a bit easier, the present chapter will include theoretical explanations and give clinical examples of each and every EDT technique, whether they are implemented in the trial therapy or in subsequent sessions.

A virtual therapy?

In the pages that follow, excerpts from real IE-DP clinical sessions are presented to illustrate the characteristics outlined above, and as an introduction and orientation to the other clinical chapters. The transcripts are derived from recordings of real clinical work with different patients. A system of coding was developed to assist the reader in making sense of the clinical dialogue and the therapeutic activities of the therapist. These include taking care of the real relationship (RE), mirroring (MI), history taking, perspective, and portrayal (HP), as well as high technical content interventions,that is, defence restructuring (DA), emotional maieutics (XA), anxiety regulation (AA), dealing with Superego (SE), making dynamic links (TCP), and restructuring representations of Self and Others (SO). The codes are summarised in Table 1.

Table 1. Essence of EDT: Therapist Activities, Definitions and Codes for Annotation of Transcripts.

Therapist activity/focus (code)	*Definition*
Real Relationship (RE)	Taking care of the real human relationship with the patient—including the personal aspects of therapist and patient—putting a premium on connection and closeness
Mirroring (MI)	Drawing the patient's attention to aspects of the patient's Self, especially those of which s/he is less aware
History taking, Perspective and Portrayal (HP)	Collecting and sharing the patient's personal history, helping him/her to put into perspective and offering alternative perspectives, portraying and re-actualising specific incidents in the patient's life by carefully focusing on them
Anxiety Regulation (AA)	Identifying patterns of anxiety discharge and regulation of anxiety
Defence Restructuring (DA)	Dealing with tactical and character defences (clarification and relinquishing)
Emotional Maieutics (XA)	Creating a safe connection and facilitating emotional experiencing and expression
Superego Restructuring (SE)	Unmasking the Superego and changing attitude/turning against
Transference-Current-Past links (TCP):	
(TC)	Dynamic link of here-and-now/transference/therapist and current/recent life
(CP)	Dynamic link of current/recent and past/primary attachment figures
(TP)	Dynamic link of here-and-now/transference/therapist and past/primary attachment figures
Self- and Other-Restructuring (SO)	Restructuring of perception/representation/behaviour of Self and Other and of relational patterns

Taking care of the real relationship (RE)

How *real* is a therapeutic relationship? The obvious answer would be, of course it is real, or there would be no relationship at all. As therapists, however, we tend to focus on what we deem to be therapeutically effective and this may lead us to overlook or underestimate other aspects. A typical example of this would be a psychiatrist prescribing an antidepressant, and assuming that, if the patient gets better, then they responded to the medication. If not, the patient is a "non-responder". This is a way of overlooking the potential therapeutic effect of the personal interchange with the doctor, as well as the role played by life events outside the therapeutic setting. Even with the different types of intervention we administer in psychotherapy, we may assume that, since our patient got better, our technical intervention has been effective, thus overlooking a number of other elements of our interchange.

If, instead, we attend to the overall complex interchange we have with the other person, we will immediately realise that there is much more to it than the technical aspects, and that all is equally real. In IE-DP, the therapist puts a premium on closeness in the therapeutic relationship, and what we mean here by "real relationship" is the most personal part of the interchange, occurring along with the more specifically technical interventions. In other words, all that is common to human relationships, therapeutic or other. The encounter of two people creates a unique interpersonal current, flowing in largely unconscious and mysterious ways. This represents a fundamental part of the actual relationship as well as of the transformational process, and training to tune into and give attention to these very personal aspects of the therapist-patient relationship will significantly empower a therapist's technical work. Through putting a premium on the human connection and closeness, there is the potential for patients to benefit from feeling the therapist's genuine interest in them and perceiving the therapist as a *true person*, which makes the therapeutic action more powerful.[1] As the reader knows, therapists—the same as their patients—are not perfect and may also have some unresolved problems. The point here is not to aim for an ideal—or idealised—therapeutic relationship, but to renounce hiding oneself behind the therapist role. This can be achieved by means of personal therapy and advanced EDT training with IEDTA teachers, which involves many hours of supervision of the trainee's clinical videos. Last but not least, aside from techniques, research has demonstrated the potential therapeutic effects of the real relationship. McCullough Vaillant (1997) expresses a similar view:

> Although transference distortions are important to resolve, the real affectively shared human relationship between the patient and the therapist may be more fundamental to character change than transference phenomena [...] This collaborative [...] and emotionally present therapist is essential to the creation of the "holding environment", in which a rapid growth and change can take place [...] The relationship with the therapist is a vehicle for the transmission of affect and carries in it the power to harm or to heal. (pp. 433–434)

By broadening this concept, we may extend it to all levels of real interchange, from the first telephone or email contact, to the mutual responses to each other's demeanour, voice, look, expression, the handling of finances, the way of greeting each other, the physical distance, the degree of mutual liking, and so forth. What here is called "real relationship" is thus all that belongs to the matching and the interaction between two specific people and, therefore, to the way their personalities, culture, and conflicts complement and resemble each other or otherwise. This gives rise to an "interpersonal current" (Osimo, 2001), rendering each therapist-patient dyad unique.

Clinical example to illustrate "Taking care of the real relationship" (RE)

The Dirty Man—session 6

This example of "taking care of the real relationship" (RE) is taken from a partly successful therapy with a man presenting with very severe obsessive compulsive disorder (OCD) with pervasive cleaning rituals, leading to loss of employment and getting in the way of a normal family life. As a result of IE-DP, he retrieved his family, and social and work life. Although his rituals were not totally renounced they did improve significantly. The real relationship interventions, and relevant remarks made by the patient, will be identified by the code "**RE**". What the reader will notice is that, through the therapist facilitating the patient's experience of associated feelings, there is a surfacing of sadness, immediately followed by a spontaneous TCP link (see pp. 96–103) with the wife, and, subsequently, the mother. The latter is omitted as, in the present section, the focus is on RE.

In response to the therapist giving attention to the here and now of their relationship, the patient comments:

Pt: ... in actual fact, as I go out from here, I feel better. It may not last for long but, at least, I get back to an acceptable level ... (**RE**)

Th: ... and how come? What gives you this sense of feeling well?

Pt: ... someone who speaks with me and listens to me. Let's be direct, someone I trust and value. Actually, if it wasn't so, I, the patient, would myself reject the doctor, no ... someone listening to me! (**RE**)

Th: ... OK, well!

Pt: ... because for me ... for me it's important, let me say ... (**RE**)

Th: ... hmm.

Pt: ... because what destroys me is indifference, void ... because if you listen to me ... two weeks ago, yes! I went to dinner with some friends of mine who run for the city council, you know. We had a tough confrontation about certain issues and, because I know I'm right about these issues, re: the war, USA, Iraq, and the mayor's position, re: all that ... We are all against the mayor, but in different ways. At any rate, this confrontation didn't exhaust me. It actually made me feel stronger. Some time ago, the day after having a struggle like this, I would have got that mechanism whereby I would start thinking—well maybe they were right and I'm wrong. This didn't happen and hasn't happened for some time now.

Th: ... so, you feel that I listen to you! (**RE**)

Pt: ... yes. (**RE**)

Th: ... are you sure? (**RE**)

Pt: ... that you listen to me? (**RE**)

Th: ... yes. (**RE**)

Pt: ... physically yes, you're here ... you're even taping me! Apart from jokes, physically yes.

Th: ... physically? (**RE**)

Pt: ... no, no, I mean to say: I believe that you listen to me, understand me and wish to help me, beyond my resistance to your help which maybe ... beyond my stubbornness ... there is a willingness to help me that may go beyond your role here, that's what I feel, and that's what pleases me, because clearly, in a way, in inverted commas, you "have to" heal me. (**RE**)

Th: ... so, all in all, you feel I'm here. (**RE**)

Pt: ... yes. (**RE**)

Th: ... that I'm not indifferent. (**RE**)

Pt: ... yes.

Th: ... so, what do we do with this? (**RE**)

Pt: ... this is very important for me. (**RE**)

Th: ... very important. (**RE**)

Pt: Well, you perfectly understand that this is what I lacked, no, and what I'm still lacking. I may have been too demanding for the people around me [an indirect reference to the patient's mother].

Th: Saying that you've been too demanding is a way of justifying them.

Pt: Well, but it may well be, no? Objectively ...

Th: What we can objectively state is that you got less of that than you needed.

Pt: I don't know if there is a standard measure for human beings ...

Th: What surely exists is your measure.

Pt: Yeah, I know my measure exists.

Th: Now the issue here is not to find fault with others but, honestly, if we look at what your need was, you got too little involvement and too much indifference. This mostly applies to your intimate being, the way you are inside ... not especially regarding other things. So, since you now feel that I'm here with you, this is good! (**RE**)

As shown in the next lines, the patient's response to the therapist valuing closeness between the two of them is twofold: (i) he makes a spontaneous link with "other people", that is, at the C and P corners of the Triangle of Others and, (ii) in so doing, the patient becomes visibly sad:

Pt: Well, you see, if also other people would join you in this (snorts) ...

Th: What's the matter, because you seem to be feeling something ...

Pt: Well, no, some embarrassment about addressing the relationship with my wife.

Th: Do you wish to talk about it?

Pt: (Becomes sad) Well, the point is that it's a strange relationship this one with my wife, doctor ... true, real rapport between us is extremely rare ...

Th: You mean sexual intercourse?

Pt: Yes, sexual intercourse, but this goes beyond my obsessions, which led me to avoid ...

At this point we leave the interview. The point is that focusing on the patient's perception of the *real relationship between two human beings* triggered a significant emotional experience, bypassing the patient's symptoms ("this goes beyond my obsessions") and resistance ("which led me to avoid ...").

Mirroring Interventions (MI)

Human beings—and, to a lesser degree, animals too—are endowed with complex systems capable of perceiving and reproducing the behaviour of other living beings. This phenomenon, occurring naturally and mostly out of the individual's consciousness, is often referred to as "mirroring". EDT mirroring interventions (MI), that are described here, rely on these natural systems in order to actively detect signals from the patient and convey them back. Since mirroring interventions are grounded in our psycho-neurological make-up, it is not surprising that they bear a connection with various human features and skills. This prompts the following digression on the respective roles of normal human functioning, specialised functioning involving specific skills, and the emerging knowledge from neuroscientific research.

Yawning, laughing, and therapeutic alliance

The commonest observation of an automatic form of mirroring is probably yawning. When two or more people have been in physical proximity for some time, and one of them starts yawning, the same reflex is often activated in the others in a matter of seconds, sometimes triggering a series of yawns that start bouncing from one person to their neighbour. In this example, there is hardly any conscious and deliberate attempt to imitate, nor desire to convey a specific message to others. No doubt, however, it is a signal that gets exchanged and has the power to catch people's attention. Another example, involving more active participation, is when laughter contagiously migrates from person to person in a group. A third example of a more differentiated and specialised quality is that of acting; the art and technique of an actor reproducing in themselves the facial and body expression and, partly, the inner atmosphere of the character they are interpreting. In general, all these phenomena imply a form of physical closeness, and one of their effects is to enhance a sense of familiarity and emotional closeness. The observation that children take on the facial expression and demeanour of adults, especially their parents, is widespread.

There can be no doubt that this ability to activate in oneself and mimic a behaviour we perceive in another person and make it our own must have a correlate in our brain. A first exciting step in the direction of identifying the neural circuits responsible for our mirroring ability is the discovery of mirror neurons. Indeed, mirror neurons are thought to lie at the core of our ability to resonate with others' internal states (Iacoboni, 2008; Rizzolatti & Craighero, 2004). Siegel (2010) wrote at length, and competently, on the inter-related phenomena of presence, resonance, and attunement, but was not exceedingly seduced by neuroscience mermaids when he pointed out, "We literally soak in what we sense inside another to shape our internal world. However this sponge-circuit works, mirror neurons or not, it seems apparent that we move rapidly from cortical perception to subcortical response … These subcortical shifts are what changes in us when we attune to someone else" (p. 38).

Neuroscience is providing some precious input to our understanding of human interchange but, like Daniel Siegel, we do not wish to lose sight of a more comprehensive view of things, whether or not neuroscience has already claimed to have illuminated them. Empirical observation—and indeed EDT practice—maintains a crucial role in our understanding of such things as familiarity, closeness, trust, and positive feeling. When a guitar or violin string vibrates, another string, close to the first one, may start vibrating too without being touched. In physics this is referred to as vibrating by sympathy, but we can reformulate and say that when two human beings are close enough to each other, emotional vibrations in one of them are likely to mobilise emotion in the other. This we usually refer to as closeness, resonance, and attunement, and their role in human relationships, as well as in psychotherapy, is crucial. Most importantly, the experience of being present and resonating with each other, tuning in to this interpersonal current (Osimo, 2001, 2002, 2003) can be enhanced by active mirroring by the therapist of all that they observe in the patient. By so doing we put the brain systems we are naturally endowed with to the service of conscious and unconscious therapeutic alliance, an equivalent of "making friends" in non-therapeutic relationships.

Mirroring interventions in clinical practice

Mirroring (MI) interventions involve the therapist drawing the patient's attention to aspects of the patient's Self, especially those of which they are less aware. These are perceivable aspects, revealing emotions, fears, and defensive attitudes. In particular, mirroring involves giving the patient constant and accurate feedback of what they are conveying verbally, physically, or on any other level. In EDT mirroring is highly active and lively, in that the therapist reflects what he or she is actively and independently observing: for example, regarding the patient's position or manner of speech and expression, and use of voice. In this way, the therapist may at times reflect a distorted or not entirely accurate image, but patients readily learn to accept, reject, or correct what is being mirrored.

Mirroring in practice

One of the features of EDT is that it aims to maximise the effects of therapeutic interaction, and this applies from the very beginning of the relationship with each patient. For example, if we think of a first encounter, quite some time may go into getting acquainted. The patient arrives in a state of suffering and is understandably anxious about their feelings and experiencing them with the therapist. The therapist knows almost nothing of this new person, and will not be able to predict what their own emotional response to the new patient is going to be. In EDT we wish to accelerate the therapeutic process. We believe that a powerful healing factor is to get to the emotional experience of painful feelings safely and as soon as possible. Mirroring (MI) interventions are of great help in catalysing the therapist-patient interaction. Theoretically, it is enough to say that a mirroring intervention serves to catalyse the personal interchange and relationship. Therefore, it does not require that the therapist has already understood the patient's problems and dynamics; mirroring interventions can be administered independently of the level of understanding. What usually happens is that a therapist starts with mirroring before knowing much of the patient's problems and, as the mirroring goes on, further aspects come into focus, enabling the therapist to make their interventions more accurate. As previously stated, patients also quickly learn to fine-tune the therapist's mirroring if they perceive a discrepancy between what feels right to them and what has been mirrored. Through this process, previously hidden aspects of the patient come more clearly into focus. The more often mirroring interventions bring to the patient's attention what the therapist sees, or otherwise perceives, the more this will lead to a *rapid* interaction between therapist and patient. This will also maximise the use of time. As well as drawing the patient's attention to their physical presentation, or hidden aspects of the Self, by pointing out to the patient what the therapist sees, mirroring can also serve to focus patients on, for example, their physical experience, posture, or manner, by asking specific questions that encourage them to attend to their moment-to-moment experience.

Clinical example to illustrate mirroring (MI)

The Mad Child—trial relationship

In this extract the therapist starts the initial extended interview, "trial relationship", with a new patient by mostly playing the role of a living mirror, actively observing and reflecting what the patient conveys in verbal and non-verbal ways. The patient's first complaint is frigidity and pain during intercourse. She and her husband have been seeing a sex therapist for the last year. The patient opens with a general request for help that is acknowledged by the therapist, who then immediately focuses on the here-and-now of the relationship. This leads to a series of mirroring interventions concerning the patient's sensations, catalysing the new relationship and paving the way to emotional experiencing. The surfacing of emotion, in turn, leads to the recollection of a highly meaningful memory from the patient's childhood. In passing, we may notice that what is mirrored includes each of the three corners of the Triangle of Conflict i.e., Defence, Anxiety and Impulse/Feeling (see chapter 1, p. ?). The mirroring interventions will be identified by the code "MI". We take up the interview from the moment the camera was switched on, a few seconds after the patient started talking:

Pt: … perhaps I need to face things in a clearer and more direct way … one of the last things that were left somehow pending was … hmm, that I have an intense feeling of desertion … and this conditioned the relationship with my husband … and she [sex therapist] said this is likely to stem from my life experiences … in my childhood, or …

Th: … sure …

Pt: … OK, but … I don't know where it all comes from …

Th: … but how is it for you to be talking of that with me now?

Pt: … I don't know.

Th: … you seem very compressed … where do you feel this compression

Pt: (Points to her throat)

Th: … in your throat? (**MI**)

Pt: … hmm, yes, hmm, hmm …

Th: … how is your throat? (**MI**)

Pt: … closed … these subjects can even trigger responses like crying … I mean …

Th: … there is something very intense inside you … also … my sense is that you feel compressed also in your head … like something that is … bigger than you and you can hardly contain, no? … it's enough to just mention your sensitivity to abandonment … and what other sensation do you have in your body? (**MI**)

Pt: … well I feel a kind of … hmm, oppression here.

Th: … oppression …? (**MI**)

Pt: … hmm, at the level of my breast.

Th: … something more inside … **(MI)**
Pt: … yes, it is like tears coming to my eyes …
Th: … not like a pressure from outside … rather a sense of inner Oppression …? **(MI)**
Pt: … hmm, hmm!
Th: … hmm, hmm …
Pt: … it is as though I had a sort of bronchial constriction … how to put it … physically, I mean …
Th: … yes, yes, as one can figure out a kind of … constraint … **(MI)**
Pt: … hmm, hmm …
Th: … hmm, hmm, hmm, hmm … and you are also tense in your shoulders … as it seems … **(MI)**
Pt: … very much so …
Th: … perhaps on the right side, more than on the left … **(MI)**
Pt: … hmm … yes, it's true.
Th: … and the rest of your body, legs, tummy, hips …? **(MI)**
Pt: I often have a back pain … in the lumbar region …
Th: … also now? **(MI)**
Pt: … no, not now in this moment … now I have this oppression … from here upwards …
Th: … from there upwards … and how is your neck? **(MI)**
Pt: … the neck is a bit stiff here on the back …
Th: … hmm, and this thing from here to here … is it still there? **(MI)**
Pt: … I also have some … tightness in my stomach …
Th: … I see … at the same time you seem to have an intense wish to … eventually manage to open a few doors … **(MI)**
Pt: … yes, being at the same time a bit scared … about having to start again from square one …
Th: … well, maybe that will come on its own … instead of making an effort to explain things, how about staying with what you feel? … and all these different sensations you have in your body … and also some anxiety, as it seems … in your stomach, as we say … beside this sense of constraint here … and of pressure … higher up … is your heart beating normally? **(MI)**
Pt: … so it seems …
Th: … and what do you feel in this very moment? … as my impression is that, from time to time, there is like a feeling surfacing … a wave of feeling …
Pt: … yes, tears come to my eyes …
Th: … tears come to your eyes … **(MI)** and how do you manage not to cry, hmm?
Pt: … when I realise I am about to cry, it stops coming …
Th: … ah! So there is something holding back this crying …
Pt: … hmm …
Th: … and what is it, a sort of blocking?
Pt: … some embarrassment …
Th: … some embarrassment? **(MI)**
Pt: … hmm, hmm

Th: ... at the thought of crying here with me? (**MI**)

Pt: ... yes, or anyway the sensation that this cry is somehow coming, but it is a feeling that ... it's as though it cannot get released ... it's partly embarrassment, and partly as though the stimulus was not sufficient to really make me sob ... I have a lump in my throat ...

Th: ... is it getting your goat this thought of having to come here and cry?

Pt: ... no, no, not that ...

Th: ... and what can it be the thought linking with this cry or the tears coming up to your eyes?

Pt: ... that's what I was wondering ... well, what we touched upon re: desertion, brought back a bit of ... yes, I think that's what it was ...

The patient is now fully in touch with her deep emotion of sadness. In this trial relationship, mirroring interventions played a primary role in helping the patient to focus emotionally on a highly traumatic memory from her childhood—soon after her parents separated (mother left), her father completely forgot to collect her from kindergarten. The impact on the patient of being forgotten by her father so soon after her mother left was predictably devastating.

History taking and putting into perspective (HP)

Focusing on the real relationship obviously concerns the here-and-now of the relationship and, as for mirroring, cannot but take place in the moment-to-moment interchange between therapist and patient. So, neither type of intervention, per se, addresses patients' history or the problems bringing them to therapy. It is preferable, however, not to split a session into two parts, as would happen if we *first* listen to problems and take the history, and *then* "start" offering our therapeutic action. If we were to do so, in a way, we would be postponing the moment in which our therapeutic relationship "officially" begins, forgetting that the relationship begins at the very first moment of our interaction with the patient. At any rate, if we start interacting more naturally—and hopefully without wearing a professional mask—we will still listen to, explore, and share the patient's suffering and put questions on their personal history. This we actually need to do also in order to assess the level of global functioning (American Psychiatric Association, 1994), an important indicator of whether an exploratory or supportive approach would be beneficial (McCullough Vaillant, 1997). Also, eventually, to make a diagnosis and/or arrive at a formulation, that is to say, to get an accurate clinical picture.

Using our receptivity, psychodynamic eye, and prospective view, as we elaborate all this information we will start mapping the origins of the patient's suffering and the nature of their conflicts. Moreover, we will get an account of an individual's habitual ways of staying in relationships. Furthermore, the patient is now in a relationship with us. This gives us a chance of directly observing some of their relational patterns and comparing them with their ways of interacting with others. To cut a long story short, we are in a privileged position to get a picture of the patient's character. Now, one of the main characteristics of EDT is its emphasis on character, through which we get a view of someone's defensive system as well as their adaptive traits. Also, the ultimate objective of EDT almost always includes character change indicating that the individual's approach to life has become different and more constructive. No doubt this also involves a change in the way of looking at life, that is, a change of perspective. This aspect will be further addressed below, especially in the section about Self- and Other-Restructuring, and in my later chapter (chapter 4, pp. 107–132), in which the concept and operational use of the character hologram (Osimo, 2009) is described.

Another aspect of putting things into perspective is when we aim to get closer to the experiencing of feeling and impulse. To achieve this, we focus on a specific incident in the patient's life. Let us imagine having started our session taking care of the real relationship, in particular the degree of closeness with the patient. We have mirrored a number of aspects of the patient's presentation, and collected information on their reasons for seeking help. If we now wish to enable the patient to experience deep emotion (X), we need to focus on a specific incident of his or her life that we deem relevant to the patient's problem or conflict. Since the incident is related to this, by focusing on it, we can certainly get to its emotional content, assisting the patient's emotional experiencing. Emotional experience of conflicting feelings is painful and, most of the times, the patient will try to stay vague—perhaps the commonest tactical defence (see pp. 64–65). By keeping our attention focused on the incident, however, we *are* with the patient in that situation and frame of mind, and can *stay* there until deep emotion surfaces and is experienced. Whenever appropriate, we will further enhance emotional experiencing by helping the patient to focus on every detail of the incident in question. To this purpose we will reconstruct the exact sequence of frames within the incident like in a slow-motion film, for example, who was present, who said what, what the patient answered/thought/felt, how was the room, what was the patient's position, were they looking at the Others involved, were there any sensorial stimuli like smells, sounds, colours, and so on. In this way a patient's perception of the relevant incident is re-actualised and put into perspective, thus fully portrayed. By being emotionally present, we sustain and share the patient's emotional experiencing and even have an opportunity to carry on the portrayal until the patient is enabled to focus on what they could have said or done differently, in order to effectively express their deep feeling or impulse, thus offering the patient an alternative perspective.

Clinical example to illustrate "history taking, and putting into perspective" (HP)

A Stressed Wife—trial relationship

Working with a psychotherapy model capable of bringing about deep change in the short term almost invariably reverberates on the individual's significant Others. Positive and constructive as it is, change may not be easy to accept for some patients' partners, especially if adapting to the new situation requires a deep change also in the partner. The patient presented below was married to a man who, as a result of his IE-DP, changed his character, renouncing certain maladaptive behaviours that, though defensive, well matched the patient's anxieties and defences. Since the new situation was clearly triggering huge anxiety and distress in the wife, the therapist proposed that the three of them, that is, therapist, wife (current patient), and husband (former patient) should meet for a joint session. Two couple sessions took place and, during the second, the wife's state of crisis and character problem became apparent. The therapist offered to see her individually. The following vignette is taken from the beginning of the extended individual trial relationship interview. The main interventions were centred on helping the patient to keep things in perspective regarding both current situation (C) and past (P). It is worth noticing that, in her family of origin, the patient had gone through multiple traumas from an early age. She lived in an atmosphere of constant threat, including that of her parents separating and rejecting her. It is not surprising, therefore, that her husband's change imbalanced her deeply, throwing her into deep distress, confusion in time and space, and hallucinations, although there was no previous indication of a psychotic disorder. By focusing on the complex events in the here-and-now (T), and current (C) situations, it was possible to resolve the confusion and put things in perspective again. This reduced the patient's huge anxiety, enabling her to connect to the therapist, and spontaneously share meaningful incidents from the past (P), linking them to what she was currently experiencing in her relationship with her husband. This type of C-P link is one of the main *dynamic* interventions with this patient (see pp. 96–103). The numerous "history taking and putting into perspective" interventions are identified by the code "HP". The patient was vividly ambivalent about coming for an individual session, which had made it difficult to find a mutually convenient time to meet. The therapist begins by acknowledging agreement on a mutually convenient time:

Th: … so we were able to find a time …
Pt: … yeah, sorry, at work I can't always look at my email, so …
Th: … well, we managed, good! … so, you decided to have a session for yourself … (**HP**)
Pt: (Nods)
Th: … it's quite a decision …
Pt: … (laughing) … yes, I know at the moment I'm feeling quite vulnerable … it is not as if I did not want to come, it's just that this will bring things up and I am scared of dealing with that … I think lately I've been kind of … on autopilot, and it's been necessary for me, because I feel kind of on the edge.
Th: … you say you feel vulnerable?
Pt: … yeah, yeah … I've been better lately, but … I've been very tearful and … usually I am much aware of how I'm feeling, but when things get really hectic it's … as if somebody steps in and … I don't know who I am and … I'll wake up in a panic attack … and that's not like me …
Th: … you mean you wake up in the night? (**HP**)
Pt: … yeah, screaming and I can't breathe, so … but it isn't recently, that was just before I saw you … I was having this awful …
Th: … do you mean in between the two times we met? (**HP**)
Pt: … no, no, when I saw you last, just before then … The patient clearly has huge anxiety, and does not appear to recollect having attended the couple sessions on two occasions. In between the two sessions, her husband—we'll call him Bob—had been away for a week, which exacerbated her inner threat of abandonment. Her distress becomes evident. The therapist keeps a holding attitude with several HP interventions:
Th: … (puzzled) … because you came twice! (**HP**)
Pt: … did I come twice? Oh, you are right! … did I? Yes, I did, sorry, yeah, in between those two …
Th: … OK, so it was just before the second time? (**HP**)
Pt: … just before the second time, over the weekend and … I've had these dreams forever that the devil's coming for my soul …

Th: … Oh!

Pt: … yeah and I have to fight off the devil and the devil was really coming close and I was managing to fight it, but I was screaming, 'cause I was really scared …

Th: … hmm, and how was the devil like? (**HP**)

Pt: … it depends … the devil is sometimes in a friend, a person, or the devil can be somebody that I haven't expected … my dreams are very odd … and the weird thing is that sometimes I'll be walking and the dream will come back to me like a déjà-vu experience … or I'll have a dream and it is the continuation of another dream I had before and in the dream I remember that I had a dream before … it's pretty weird, and the other thing that's been bothering me is that when Bob went away I was feeling very stressed and … I would hear music and the music would play … when it wasn't on … I would hear music!

Th: … where? (**HP**)

Pt: … in my head … it wasn't in my head …

The patient is clearly confused and trying to identify the source of the music. Her communications convey her distress. The therapist once more tries to help her maintain perspective. He also wants to bring in more reality aspects by focusing on the time and space in which the acoustic hallucination happened:

Th: … I mean … where were you? (**HP**)

Pt: … in different places, I would be in bed or in the sitting room and I'd hear this music playing, and it sounded like music was playing outside … and I knew that it wasn't so because it was always the same song … or it would be a speeded-up version, or different versions of a song, and I knew it wasn't playing somewhere else, but it sounded so realistic I wanted to go through and ask …

Th: … and you said this happened when Bob was away to see his family … (**HP**)

Pt: … and I was feeling very stressed about what was happening between the two of us …

Th: … you were left on your own and had this … (**HP**)

Pt: … (laughs nervously) got crazy! … hearing the music! … it was like it was real music!

Th: … do you like music? (**HP**)

Pt: … I love music, yeah … it was beautiful music …

Th: … and you remember where you were exactly when this started? (**HP**)

Pt: … that one time I was in the sitting room, and I thought it was upstairs and when the music speeded up I realised it couldn't be … but it was worrying … it was odd …

Th: … you didn't even need a CD … hmm, hmm … so you felt something really strange was happening … (**HP**)

The therapist offered mostly HP interventions, helping the patient to decrease her anxiety and get out of her confusion. This enabled the patient to bring her mother into the scene and start disclosing some meaningful material:

Pt: … yes, to my head … it's the same also … my mum called … and Bob and I are finding equilibrium again and it's getting better …

Th: … you mean now? (**HP**)

Pt: … yeah, and my mum called and we were talking about that and we talk lots and she's the only one who knows about what's going on … and partly the big reason that I am so scared of what is happening with Bob is because I don't want to be like my mother, live the life she made us live and … I love my mother and understand the choices that she made: I just don't want to make the same choices.

Th: … can you be more specific? (**HP**)

Pt: … sorry, my dad was an alcoholic and my mother would constantly threaten to get divorced but she wouldn't … like we pack our bags and we go and then she just drives back home and … my parents got very nasty, they were breaking each other down all the time …

Th: … verbally? (**HP**)

Pt: … verbally, but my dad got very violent … for instance, he didn't hit my sister but … she was standing near the wall and he hit the wall or … he pointed a gun to me once and said he was going to shoot me …

Th: … hmm! … well, it's …

Pt: … yeah, not good!

Th: … well, "not good" is a nice way of putting it, and how come that he pointed the gun? (**HP**)

Pt: … it was on various occasions … he always used to carry his guns around with him, and I remember once I said, "Why don't you just put it away?" and he turned at me and pointed it at me and said, "Why? Are you scared I would shoot you?" … and I remember going … (patient shows by raising her hands and showing speechless and filled with fear) and thinking, "My goodness, he's going to shoot me!"… and he just kept it there until he put it away …

After making a spontaneous and highly meaningful link between the trouble and risk of separation she is experiencing with her husband (C), and the atmosphere in her upbringing (P), the patient has now introduced the traumatic relationship with her father. As we will see, father hallucinated too, revealing that the patient's recent hallucinatory symptom was something familiar, and might result from identification with father rather than psychosis, which reassured the therapist regarding the possibly non-psychotic quality of this symptom in the patient, who grew up in such a pathological family. She in fact went on:

Pt: … he got so drunk that one night he hallucinated and saw someone standing at my mum's side in the car … and he shot the "person", and the bullet passed my mother's nose, and we were in the back of the car (nervous laughter).

Th: … you laugh!

Pt: … it's not funny, I mean …

Th: … you have a lot of pain about it …

Pt: … I used to, I don't so much any more … it's not the way I want to live … I don't drink a lot, but I understand why … The patient tells a very sad story concerning her father, which is here omitted. Let's see how she goes on, trying to push back her sadness using tactical defences:

Pt: ... the sadness of this is that my dad always ... funny, I'm getting sad ...
Th: ... is this funny?
Pt: ... I get sad! (smiles).
Th: ... yes, but you smile ...
Pt: ... because I don't want to cry ...
Th: ... yes ... you cry!
Pt: (Smiles and raises her right hand, like trying to keep the therapist distant from her feeling)
Th: ... there is no reason that you push it back ...
Pt: ... (crying) I never cried about that, though ... it's just ... something that happened, so ...
Th: ... (interrupting) so ... you are sad ...
Pt: ... yeah, I think I'm just sad ...
Th: ... don't think. You are sad!
Pt: (Nods)
Th: ... and your sadness is important ...
Pt: ... and I've dealt with it ...
Th: ... you want to push it back ...
Pt: ... no! ... my past isn't part of my present as such!
Th: ... it is! ... you are crying now!
Pt: ... yes, but I just felt sad for my dad. It's weird ...
Th: ... you are feeling sad for your dad ...
Pt: (Nods and cries)
Th: ... what is the sad thought?
Pt: (Sobbing) he would always tell mum that she wasn't good-enough ... and his mother never made any mistakes ... he was the perfect father ...
Th: ... take a breath!

The patient is experiencing deep sadness and the therapist helps her stay in touch with her sad feeling to completion. She then says that she is aware of her anger, but she nevertheless understands and loves her father. She then moves to her unresolved rage at her mother, whom she rightly makes responsible for having perpetuated the violence, exposing the patient to it, and denying her the love and closeness she needed. She is very frightened by her rage at mother, but will manage to get in touch with it and work it through:

Th: (Interrupting) ... if you let your rage come ...
Pt: ... I've told her before, she knows ...
Th: ... but what do you want to tell her?
Pt: ... nothing, I don't!
Th: ... you are very well behaved!
Pt: (Laughs) no!
Th: ... yes!
Pt: ... my mother knows, trust me, I've told her ...
Th: ... but I don't know!

Pt: ... fine! Your choice was to stay with my dad ... and if you want to get divorced, get divorced! Don't push us along while deciding what you want to do and expect us to take the rollercoaster! I am angry with her for the choice that she made ...

Th: ... so your anger is about her being the martyr?

Pt: ... yeah! She was playing a game after she reconciled with my father ... she was a complete witch to me: she wanted me out of the house. How dare you!

The patient is now in touch with her rage at mother and the trial relationship interview can proceed in a satisfactory way. We leave the dialogue at this point. It is worth noticing, in this case, that the highly meaningful dynamic data and emotional experience were attained mainly by means of HP interventions.

High technical content interventions

The interventions described above have the following purposes and combined effects:

- Take care of the dawning relationship with the patient by giving them concerned attention;
- Catalyse the personal interchange, training the therapist-patient dyad to work together, and fostering mutual trust and motivation to advance in their shared journey;
- Shed light on mannerisms, thoughts, and other physical and emotional aspects of the patient;
- Collect information on problems, conflicts, and life history and put them into perspective.

If we use a sailing metaphor, carrying out these operations is helping the two sailors to gradually become more familiar with their boat. The boat has been made ready, sails and lines are in place, and there is a supply of water and food. There is an underpinning of confidence, an orientation, and they can set sail into the deep sea. However, if our two sailors wish to sail safely, they will also have to know how to deal with the changing conditions of, for example, sea, wind, and weather.

Moreover, they had better be prepared to face unexpected occurrences, like sudden windblasts or, at worst, an iceberg, a monster giant octopus, or even a pirate attack. There are dangerous seas, like the Bermuda Triangle (Figure 1), where people become lost. The deep sea of the human unconscious we set out to navigate can also be perilous, when its hidden feelings, impulses, thoughts, and memories, with their emotional charge, emerge out of the blue. So, we will now leave the Bermuda Triangle and return to the Triangle of Conflict (Figure 2), that helps people navigate the experiential and dynamic waters of the human unconscious.

In EDT, the achievement of deep dynamic change is mostly based on creating a relational setting and atmosphere enabling the patient to *experience* their anxiety-provoking and/or painful emotions safely. We will therefore need to regulate our trim and speed according to the three corners of the Triangle of Conflict, Defences, Anxiety, and Deep Feeling/Impulse. In particular, we need to reduce or neutralise the forces blocking experience. Since we need to activate the conflicting and anxiety-laden emotions, represented by **X** in the Triangle of Conflict, and since these are kept unconscious by defences (**D**) and anxiety (**A**), we need to alter the complex balance of

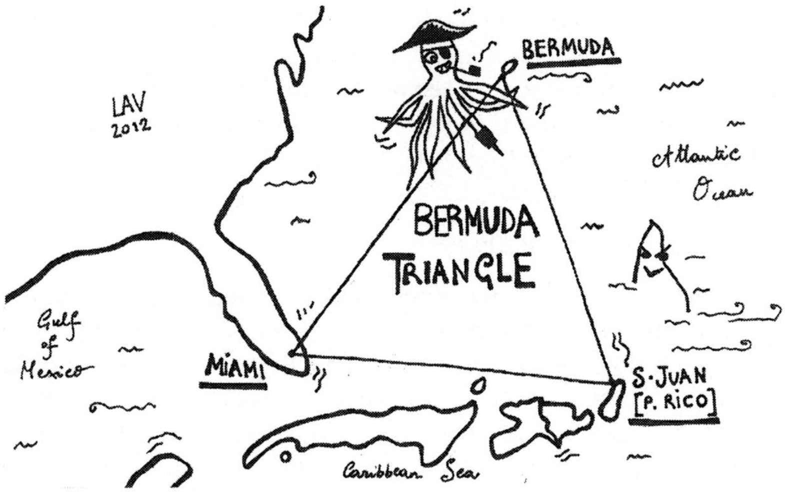

Figure 1. Triangle of Bermuda.

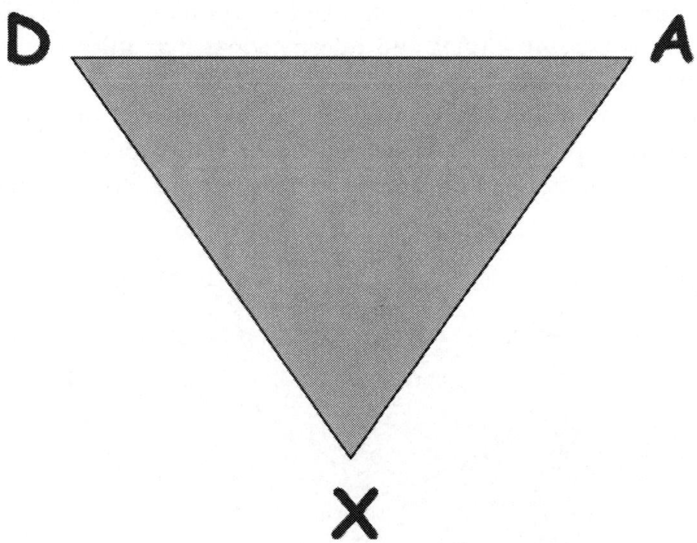

Figure 2. Triangle of Conflict.

the three forces. We therefore have to act on the D corner to weaken defences. Depowering D, and approaching X, will mobilise anxiety, which we need to regulate and keep within a range of intensity that allows for the experiencing of X (Abbass & Bechard, 2007). If we can also act on the X corner by means of a *direct facilitation* of emotional experiencing and expression, we will be acting on *all* the three forces involved in the maintenance of the conflict. We also need to be prepared to face whatever opposing force or unpredicted attack should emerge against us. Freud (1923b) described a component of the human psyche, mostly carrying a guiding function, that, at times, operates against the individual's best interests, hindering and threatening the smooth and balanced unfolding of their inner resources. Freud called it Superego and, whenever it materialises as a destructive force in the way of the healing process, we will need to counter its destructive power. The following sections describe some techniques specifically addressing the Superego and each of the corners of the Triangle of Conflict.

Introduction to experiential-dynamic activities

"Experiential-dynamic activities" refers to the three clusters of techniques a therapist implements in order to influence and modify the dynamic and emotional forces represented at the three corners of the Triangle of Conflict: (i) defence restructuring, (ii) anxiety regulation, and (iii) emotional maieutics (Osimo, 2001, 2003). Since each activity addresses one of the corners of the Triangle of Conflict (D, A, and X, respectively), in short, they can be referred to by adding a capital "A", standing for "activity", to the letters D, A, and X, as illustrated in the Triangle of Experiential-Dynamic Activities (Osimo, 2001, 2003) (see Figure 3).

In Figure 3, the Triangle of Experiential-Dynamic Activities, also representing the therapist, is placed in relation to the Triangle of Conflict, representing the patient. The arrows represent the interplay of patient and therapist, sitting in front of each other, and link the therapist's technical interventions to the patient's inner and interpersonal dynamics. According to this scheme, application of therapeutic interventions is guided by close monitoring of the moment-by-moment shifts of the patient around the corners of the Triangle of Conflict, rather than a predetermined sequence of therapist activities. In other words, a therapist's choice of intervention is guided by their careful assessment of what is at the forefront, that is, impulse/feeling,

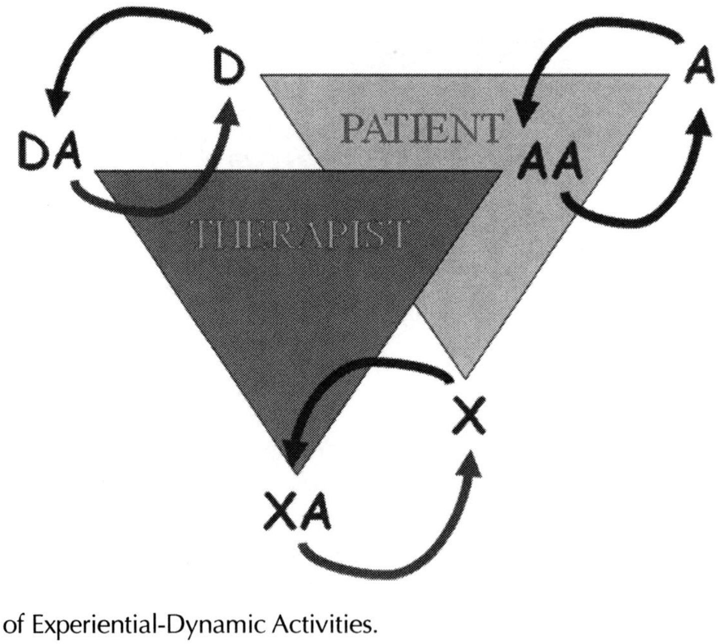

Figure 3. Triangle of Experiential-Dynamic Activities.

anxiety, or defence, using the Triangle of Experiential-Dynamic Activities as a compass, and harmonising technical interventions with the real personal relationship.

The therapist, from the first moments of the session, carefully observes all the verbal and bodily signals coming from the patient, detecting which aspect of the Triangle of Conflict is at the forefront. As will be further elaborated, if anxiety and other inhibitory feelings are at the forefront and inhibit experience of deep emotion X, this is an indication for the therapist to focus on and regulate anxiety, AA, so as to lift its inhibitory effect, and uncover deep impulse and feeling. If the therapist is faced with tactical and/or a character defence, what is called for is DA, defence work. If emotions are surfacing, the therapist will instantly resort to XA, using their maieutic skills to facilitate the rise, experiencing, and expression of that emotion.

The interactive system thus created between therapist and patient is made complex by its continuous evolution through the session, but the therapist can refer each of its discrete instants to the present scheme to determine where they are standing in experiential and dynamic terms. The rapid shift from one dynamic and experiential activity to another, according to the prevailing signals from the patient, is dependent on the active involvement of the therapist, who attends to the moment-by-moment shifts in the patient's presentation, their own inner state, and the dyadic interaction. What actually happens is that therapist interventions constantly influence the balance of forces among D, A, and X. For example, when the therapist offers XA, the patient may switch to D, requiring the therapist to move to DA, at which point the patient may become anxious, indicating the need for AA. In this way, it can be seen that intervention disrupts the homeostatic balance among the three aspects of the Triangle of Conflict, and that change in one aspect leads to change in another.

Defence restructuring (DA)

Following Freud's early work on describing unconscious processes, human defence mechanisms have been conceptualised by many authors (e.g., Freud, A., 1937; ten Have-de Labije, 2009; Vaillant, 1977). Some have carried out studies on the evolution of defences through the life cycle (e.g., Soldz & Vaillant, 1999). Given the operational scope of the present book, interested readers are referred to the scientific literature concerning the classification of structural defences (e.g., American Psychiatric Association, 1994, pp. 751–757). Here we focus on defences in clinical work and, specifically, on the two categories of *character* and *tactical* defences (see Davanloo, 1995).

Character defences

As Reich (1933) observed, there is a layer of defences sculpted in character and body, working as a fence shielding the Self from deep emotion (see also Osimo, 2012, in chapter 1 pp. 6–7). Terms such as *manner of presentation* or *position* refer to the overall attitude a person may have to somebody else, or in a particular situation. This applies to patient and therapist sitting in front of each other. Such presentation styles reflect specific character traits and crystallise moment by moment in the different positions taken by the patient. The term "position" applies to both the mental attitude and the body posture, thus embracing different levels of a person's character. *Facial expressions* and *glances* can indicate distance or proximity. *Posture* might indicate openness or lack thereof and, at times, conveys the conflicting presence of both. Striated, voluntary muscle tension is an indicator of anxiety (Coughlin Della Selva, 1996; Davanloo, 1990). The *tone of voice* will reveal anxiety and, indeed, the overall attitude. Voice can be circumspect or arrogant, joyous or angered, open or shy, leaning towards embellishing or sweetening or pessimistic, plaintive, or sarcastic, seductive, childish, etc. Finally, the content of the dialogue may clarify and reveal, but it may be used to hide and distort meaningful aspects of the Self. These factors combine to form the manner of presentation, giving voice to the individual's character. When faced with personality disorders, working with character defences is of prime importance (see also my later chapter, chapter 4, pp. 107–132).

Tactical defences

If character defences are well-established patterns that have become crystallised into the personality, the *tactical* level of defences is more fluid. It becomes activated at the moment of interaction between people, and has the prevailing aim of lessening emotion and repelling intimacy. The credit for the discovery of the crucial role of tactical defences goes to Davanloo (1986b, 1990). In the therapeutic relationship, they arise automatically, either out of anxiety about experiencing and sharing intense feeling, or in obedience to a pathological Superego that would have the patient ignore or dismiss their feelings (ten Have-de Labije, 2008). Much as the patient deeply desires to supply the therapist with all that they need to make therapy effective (what could be called the healthy part of the patient), they also tend to keep the therapist *at a distance*, not letting either of them get too close to the most painful and frightening emotions. The patient maintains the emotional distance by putting defences into action. The patient's disposition to *work together* with the therapist represents the *therapeutic alliance*. The tactical moves used to maintain distance are referred to as tactical defences, mobilised in the here-and-now. Tactical defences include being vague, diluting the emotional content, evasiveness, diversion, retraction, as well as non-verbal defences, for example, avoiding eye contact, frequent smiles, laughs, whining, or taking a detached attitude (Coughlin Della Selva, 1996).

Tactical defences are highly relevant clinically, since they sometimes play a crucial role in keeping the therapist "at bay", and/or supplying them with apparently important material, but without really committing to what is being said. Phrases such as, "*I believe* I am angry", or "I have interpersonal problems", "*I think* I am sad", or "The relationship with my wife *seems* good" are so deprived of the emotional content to which they refer, as to represent pure dialectic exercises. If the therapist does not realise this, they will take for granted material that the patient has indeed expressed, but in the absence of any emotional connection. Simple but targeted interventions from the therapist such as, "Are you, or aren't you angry?", "Are you sad or not?", "Are you really happy or is it only a phrase for me?" convey the therapist's determination to face things in all their depth and calibre, motivating the patient to get closer to deep emotion. Initially, this may increase the patient's need to increase distance, and result in putting forward even more defences. At the same time, however, by spotting the tactical defences, the therapist conveys to the patient they are strong enough to take care of emotions that, for the patient alone, may be extremely frightening (see Fosha, 2000). In summary, the effective management of tactical defences plays a significant part in "reducing the distance", thereby increasing the emotional involvement of patient and therapist in their relationship.

During defence restructuring a crucial variable is the patient's awareness of their defences and their self-defeating aspects. Often, a patient habitually makes use of character and tactical defences without being aware of their defensive function and self-defeating effect. Rather, they are satisfied with their defensive manoeuvres. In these cases, the defences are said to be "ego-syntonic", meaning that the patient identifies with their own defences to the point of neither "seeing" nor comprehending their defensive function. This term was first introduced by Reich (1933), meaning that the person then experiences their defences simply as natural parts of the Self, as could be the case of an arm or a leg. In response to the efforts of the therapist to mirror a highly ego-syntonic defensive attitude, for example, "Do you notice that you address important topics speaking quite vaguely, generally, and in a monotone?", the patient might say, "Yes, yes, this is the way I am", or "It is part of my character", with an attitude of one who affirms a truth taken for granted, that can rightly be presented as an unchangeable fact. The same attitude as one who would say, "Yes, I have blue eyes, did you notice?"

The level of "ego-syntonicity" of a defence influences the way of carrying out defence restructuring, in that the more ego-syntonic the defence, the more actively and repeatedly the therapist will mirror the defence, until the patient "can see" the defensive moves as well as their defensive and self-defeating function.

Summing up, the aim of defence restructuring is the identification, mirroring, and clarification of the self-defeating aspect of tactical and character defences. This may involve repeated mirroring and clarification of the most ego-syntonic (satisfied with and not seen for what they are) defences and their functions until they become clear and accessible to the patient. ten Have-de Labije (2001) refers to the therapist interventions of confrontation, identification, clarification, and challenge. Patients can be helped to relinquish the defences either through *validation*, that is, acknowledging the validity of their use *in the past but not at present*, or through *challenge*, that is, questioning directly *their validity at present*.

Clinical example to illustrate defence restructuring (DA)

The Phantom Strangler—trial relationship

The patient, a thirty-four-year-old man, was referred by an outpatient clinic for treatment of a major depressive episode of one and a half years' duration. He was on antidepressant medication—Paroxetine. An episode of orchitis had precipitated the depression. He feared even the slightest responsibility, perceived himself as being abnormal, and was clearly depressed, with a cluster of symptoms such as insomnia, daily headaches, and anxiety. He also had a compulsion to repeatedly check a few actions, such as locking the house door. His attitude of passivity in the face of injustice, and his total inability to get in touch with feelings and impulses showed a markedly Self-punishing and Self-devaluing character. From a diagnostic point of view, the patient also fulfilled the criteria for avoidant personality disorder. His level of general functioning (based on the Global Assessment of Functioning scale) was rated fifty-five. A full description of this therapy, from trial relationship to follow-up, can be found in Osimo (2003).

The impressive variety of tactical and character defences put into operation by the patient, and frequent defence restructuring interventions of the therapist, provides a good clinical example. The reader is encouraged to note, in the passage that follows, the main character defences of *passive-aggression* and *projection*, with *intellectualisation*, *displacement*, and *reaction formation*. The patient also presented an impressive array of tactical defences including *evasiveness, generalisation, rationalisation, intellectualisation, avoidance, diluting emotional content, retraction, avoidance of eye contact, postural bending, and small and distorted voice*. From the beginning of the session, the patient showed noticeable anxiety, and used a lot of generalisation and rationalisation. The defence restructuring interventions are identified with the code "DA".

Th: Please sit down here. Well, please tell me what you wish to deal with in here.

Pt: Well simply, I would like to try and solve my problems, because I am aware of the fact that I have been dragging them behind me for a long time (trembling voice).

Th: Are you always that anxious?

Pt: Well, today especially. Today in a particular way.

Th: When did you get this anxiety?

Pt: Well, we can say in particular circumstances. Always. Every time in which I feel or in which I am subjected to judgement. Evaluation.

Th: Hmm.

Pt: So from the exams at school, any circumstance. A sport competition. At work when I have to collaborate with someone new. It is enough that someone watches me while I am working, I find it disturbing.

Th: Therefore you tend to avoid direct exchange? (**DA**)

Pt: Let's say that I prefer working on my own, not collaborating and ... yes, well, handling the thing on my own. I think that in any case I fear a confrontation with someone and so ... I don't know ... maybe ... I know I am slower, maybe I may need more time to get organised, therefore I systematically avoid ... facing the other person ... with anybody ...

Th: So, what is it that you would like to deal with, here?

Pt: I would like ... exactly ... I would like ... to try and solve these problems of mine, I would like to succeed in having a full life.

Th: This is a bit vague, isn't it? (**DA**)

Pt: Solving my problems? I think the other doctor showed you my clinical file ... I think that you are already familiar at least with a first diagnosis. That is, I would like to solve those behavioural problems.

Th: Yes, could you please give me an example?

Pt: Well, exactly, for example the fact that, in any case, I feel inadequate, I feel profoundly different from others ... and therefore I am never on the same wavelength ... I don't know how, but people see something wrong in me ... They may appreciate me at a later stage, but the first impact is always negative.

At this point the therapist repeatedly mirrors the patient's evasiveness and presses for a specific example of "once when this happened". The patient gives a vague response:

Pt: Well, in the working environment I tend to duck out.

Th: But do you notice that you tend to duck out here also? I mean, I ask you for a specific example and you tell me that "in the working environment …" you tend to duck out. This isn't very specific: the working environment is vast … (**DA**)

Pt: Yes, for example … yes, of course … a …

The patient responds with a contorted monologue, supplying a series of irrelevant data regarding the organisational aspects of his work. To highlight the patient's avoidance once more, the therapist enquires about the specificity of his response:

Th: Is this a specific example? (**DA**)

Pt: (Irritated by the insistence of the therapist) Yes! … well, what happened … is that a colleague who had been hired after me …

The patient describes how a rather overbearing female colleague got ahead of the patient, despite having been employed two years after him.

Th: How did it happen?

Pt: How did it happen? This person has more charisma, has more courage to come forward, let's say that this happens because I never step forward and …

Th: (Interrupting, in order to mirror a character defence) You are taking the attitude of someone who is incapable. (**DA**)

Pt: Yes, that is, of an incapable … I am afraid to undertake this type of work because I am afraid I may be inadequate […] I duck out, sure! Then, obviously, this creates … I don't know … it gives me problems …

Th: So, you'd like to stop ducking out? (**DA**)

Pt: Yes.

Th: Then is this the reason why you are here?

Pt: … Yes … but … also being depressed, well! In September, in the morning, while I was going to work I used to burst out crying on the tram, like this, on my own!

Th: Do you notice, however, that even here you tend to remain on your own? I mean, you avoid looking at me, go over a number of issues you have already touched upon, giving an explanation to keep yourself calm! That is, you work on your own. (**DA**)

Pt: Hmm, anyway let's say that … a big problem of mine is, let's say … a certain lack of self-confidence, the fact of being afraid to step forward.

Th: Hmm, but this is another thing you are telling me about … so what you are telling me is that your life is poor, miserable, because you put yourself in the position of being incapable. (**DA**)

Pt: Yes, because … because, more than anything at work I always avoid responsibility, and let's say that … this reflects upon …

Th: You are ruminating on your own! (**DA**) It seems to me that you are a bit … that you are almost paralysed to tell me, to speak about yourself …

Pt: But … Maybe …

Th: And you keep on looking down, you keep on interrupting yourself. (**DA**)

Pt: I find it difficult to look you in the eye.
Th: Do you ever stammer? Usually… (**DA**)
Pt: Only during exams.
Th: Because now also … I am not saying that you are stammering, but that you are speaking with some effort … Do you have any feelings about being here with me?
Pt: Well, yes, at this moment I am quite agitated.

The active mirroring of the patient's defensive strategies mobilises anxiety, so the therapist switches to anxiety regulating interventions (see p. ?). After helping the patient to regulate their anxiety, the therapist returns to the patient's feelings:

Th: Are you uneasy because of what I say?
Pt: The interviews that I had so far, maybe, had a different form, that is on the other side there was a person that welcomed these things; you, on the other hand, are … I would not say inquisitorial, you are inexpressive … and you are a man …
Th: How am I then?
Pt: A machine.
Th: And what else?
Pt: You are analysing me, while in the previous interviews I never had this feeling.
Th: What do you feel towards me because I am a machine?
Pt: Nothing … I don't feel anything. That is, nothing, I know that you are analysing me.
Th: Hmm, you are ruminating quite vaguely (**DA**), but obviously there is something you do not like in the way in which I look at you, the way I "analyse" you, the way I talk to you …
Pt: I don't know … I think … You tell me that I look elsewhere … that is true, yes, that is true … on the contrary, I am working on myself. Maybe I am not interacting with you.
Th: You are avoiding me. (**DA**)
Pt: Yes.
Th: Ah, and I make you notice it. (**DA**)
Pt: Yes, exactly.
Th: Hmm, and what do you feel towards me because I make you notice it?
Pt: Uneasiness […] I am not managing to make contact with you, or maybe it is you who is not managing to make contact with me (smiling)!
Th: (Ironic) Hmm, but this is fine reasoning! But you are not telling me what you feel about me being a machine, not welcoming, when you say I am "not" inquisitorial, although this word came to your mind … (**DA**)
Pt: Mistrust.
Th: Ah, mistrust! But, again, mistrust is just a description. (**DA**)
Pt: I am always tense, but no … special effect.
Th: You are paralysed, you duck out, is that what you do? (**DA**)
Pt: Yes.
Th: But you said that you wanted to stop ducking out. (**DA**)
Pt: Sure.

Th: And there is something you feel towards me because I am not welcoming … but you are paralysed at the idea of telling me what you feel about it. (**DA**)

Pt: Yes … it makes me feel like a liar, like a child who is being naughty, who is telling you … that is telling you … that is being naughty, that is telling you lies.

Clearly, here, the therapist might be tempted to give an interpretation but instead he chose to go on enquiring about the patient's feelings towards the therapist and challenging the patient's defences:

Th: Hmm, so now I treat you as a liar as well! What do you feel about the way I treat you?

Pt: What do I feel? How can I describe my uneasiness? I defend myself (the patient clenches his fists).

Th: (Ironically, looking at the fists) So I see! (**DA**)

Pt: Yes, I defend myself.

Th: But these fists here, what do they mean, that you are defending yourself? (**DA**)

Pt: Or maybe that I attack, you mean? (smiles).

This gesticulation, the increased mobility, the unexpected smile appearing on the patient's face, all reveal that deep emotion is surfacing from the patient's unconscious.

Th: So, you described many ways in which I annoy you … Yet, when I ask you what do you feel towards me, since I am inquisitorial, not welcoming and actually a machine …

Pt: Hostility, but not an aggressive hostility, that is, I just stay on the defensive, first I need to understand.

Th: Yes, but do you see that you are paralysed, that you shut off? (**DA**)

Pt: First I need to understand …

Th: Then who knows how long we need to wait! (**DA**)

Pt: Yes, exactly (smiles).

Th: But, on the contrary, you already have a feeling. Do you want to go on like this? (**DA**)

Pt: No, I don't want to continue like this […]

Th: Then I ask you again, what do you feel towards me, not being welcoming, being a man, being a machine, inquisitorial, practically inexpressive …

Pt: Mistrust!

Th: Hmm. This is a description of how you keep me distant. (**DA**)

Pt: Yes.

Th: (In a resolute tone) And while you shut off and need to understand, you are incapable of saying what you feel, although you already feel something. (**DA**)

Pt: What do I feel? I am not preparing to attack you, nor to be attacked.

Although the patient denies it, we can note the progressive surfacing of actively aggressive material in relation to the therapist.

Th: So, do you want to make it, or don't you want to make it? (**DA**)

Pt: Of course I want to make it!

Th: Then let's see what do you feel towards me! Once and for all!
Pt: (Snorts).
Th: When you snort for example! (**DA**)
Pt: (Smiles).

Half an hour into the session, the patient's attitude has completely changed. Emotional activation is clearly visible from his posture, body movements, and facial expression. Defensive responses are progressively giving way to expressive ones, which also need to be mirrored to the patient. For clarity, only DA interventions are coded.

Th: But what do you feel?
Pt: (Smiles) The wish to punch you? I don't know, but it isn't true!
Th: And since you laugh while you say it, this isn't clear … even if before you showed these fists! So, if you decide to remain in this impotent position … (**DA**)
Pt: (Continuing the sentence, a signal of unconscious therapeutic alliance)… then it is useless for us to see each other again …!
Th: … there you stay! I cannot drag you out of that position. But, if you decide to give up that position, you should manage to tell me what is the effect in you of all these things you said about me, which are not small! Because you said inquisitorial, not welcoming, a machine, inexpressive, and a man! (**DA**)
Pt: (Snorts) I cannot tell you that I am getting as angry as a beast, because it is not true! I want to collaborate with you!
Th: You tell me you want to co-operate … but you don't tell me how you feel, which would be your way of actual collaboration. (**DA**)
Pt: But doctor I can't do it!
Th: You see, it is automatic for you to say "I don't know", "I can't do it", "I can't", "This is not true", these are almost automatisms. But you came here to deal with these things, to solve them … (**DA**) Let's see how you feel towards me.
Pt: I feel as if I am facing a person who is capable of looking inside me (emphasising each word considerably).
Th: And what do you feel?
Pt: What do I feel? (looks away).
Th: Do you notice that you are avoiding looking me in the eyes? (**DA**)

The therapist now notes that the patient's feelings are increasingly visible on his face, and that *now* the patient is more aware of them and, with a part of himself, is *really* looking for the words to express them.

Pt: I feel a great desire to tell you what I am feeling …
Th: And how is this desire? What kind of desire is it?
Pt: A desire to tell you that I feel … I feel rejected by you …
Th: So, I am rejecting you.
Pt: This is what I feel.

Th: Hmm (forcefully) and what do you feel if ... if you want to leave your impotent position, of not succeeding in saying what you feel because I am rejecting you, and what would you like to say or do? If you are sincere, if you do not want to remain paralysed, because it is a lifetime you are paralysed regarding this thing here. (**DA**)
Pt: Yes (voice broken by sobbing).
Th: Would you like to continue? (**DA**)
Pt: No.
Th: Hmm, so what would you like to tell me?
Pt: To go stuff yourself! (crying) ...
Th: There is rage in you. Do you have an impulse to do something to me?

The patient is clearly under the effect of extremely powerful emotions.

Pt: There is so much anger, to kill the entire world, doctor!
Th: But in your thought what would you do to me, in your fantasy? If you let it out, this anger?
Pt: (Feeble voice) Nothing.
Th: It is whiney this voice here, hmm? It is a thread of your voice! The rest doesn't come out, the same way as only part of your anger is coming out ... (**DA**) and you actually said it ... that if you let it all out ... how is this anger that you have inside ... endless ... destructive.

The patient is visibly shaken by the surfacing of extremely intense emotion and impulses that, for the moment, he is unable to put into words.

Th: Do you feel it now?
Pt: No, it went away ... Yes, but I am always extremely rational ... I know that you are here to provoke me and have a row with me (slip of the tongue).
Th: I am here to have a row with you?
Pt: No ... I said: "I know that you are not here to provoke me."
Th: So the idea has come to you! And how, in your thought, would you have that row? How do you imagine it in your fantasy?
Pt: But ... but right now it doesn't come to me to think how I would strangle you ... in reality I dream it.

The murderous rage of the patient emerges in a way that is so surprising to him that, though being wide awake, he experiences himself like in a dream. In the case presented, persistent challenge to the patient's defences enabled him to connect with his deep feeling and impulse. The vignette concludes with the following dialogue, showing that the patient is no longer putting defences into operation:

Pt: I would kick you in the face!
Th: Hmm, as the first thing.
Pt: I would smash up your head with knee blows and then I would strangle you.

As the reader will predict, this powerful arousal of murderous rage will be followed by very intense feelings of guilt, Self-attacking, sadness, and grief. The patient will then start making spontaneous links with meaningful episodes of his past and current life. The sequence of defence restructuring leading to emotional experiencing and expression, and to spontaneous dynamic links (TCP links, see pp. 96–103), is paradigmatic of the EDTs, differentiating them from previous psychodynamic therapies and psychoanalyses.

Emotional maieutics (XA)

After practising EDT for some years, I realised that there is a varying degree of resistance in each patient, *directly deriving from the fear of experiencing and expressing feelings* in and of itself. In other words, when the patient perceives a deep emotion rising inside, they have a natural desire to experience it fully and put it out but, simultaneously, they are afraid and, in some cases, paralysed by the fear of experiencing and expressing their feelings. This fear is specifically related to the experiencing and expressing of feelings and is different from other types of anxiety or defence, because of its intense, primordial quality. It is not accessed by consciousness for the very reason that it precedes conscious awareness of emotional experiencing and may actually interfere with conscious processing. If this specific level of resistance is identified, it becomes possible to deal with it by directly sustaining the emotional experiencing. If, instead, the therapist does not see this specific level of resistance, they will see the patient as being obstructive and may exert a stronger pressure, trying to "push" the patient to experience their deep feelings and impulses. This, however, involves a type of interchange based on an active therapist versus a passive patient and introduces a battle atmosphere, which detracts from the patient's capacity to be a fully active participant in the therapeutic relationship. Whenever possible, it seems preferable to melt this specific fear of emotional experiencing and expression by acting directly on it. This is the aim of emotional maieutics (Osimo, 2001, 2003).

The *New Oxford Dictionary of English* (1998) defines "maieutic" as pertaining to intellectual midwifery, in other words to the Socratic process of helping a person to bring into full consciousness conceptions previously latent in his mind. When applied to EDT, we can define maieutics as pertaining to *emotional* midwifery, the process of *helping a person to experience deep emotion and the impulse present in themselves*. A midwife (*maia*, in ancient Greek) helps the mother to give birth, and withstand the pain of delivery, and the parallel with a therapist's actions is not just metaphorical. Emotions are felt through the body, and giving birth to them by moving them out (in Latin, *emovere* means "move out" or "move from") can indeed be painful.

Contemporary cultures are often forgetful of these aspects of human emotion, namely their close relation with the body and their being contagiously interpersonal. The maieutic therapist makes their Self as emotionally available to the patient as possible, giving them a sense of being connected. All of their faculties are concentrating on the emotion that is being experienced, mirroring what they perceive and helping its bodily and verbal expression. For the therapist, the emphasis here is on lending their physical and emotional perceptive capacity, and on *being close to* the patient. Being at ease with one's body and emotions, and having access to one's instinctive, animal nature, are important qualities for a therapist wishing to act maieutically.

As a metaphor, the act of giving birth represents the quality of a specific event that, by its very nature, requires co-operation between two people—both being active participants—and one of them *facilitating* the coming out of something vital from the other. If this metaphor serves to illustrate the relational and interactive elements connecting these two people, it is also true that it does not comment on *what* is being brought to life, transported from the interior to the exterior or *expressed*. Now, leaving the metaphor and reverting to psychotherapy, it is crucial to discuss in detail the nature of what is let out, that is, of *expression*. An infant within the mother's womb is an independent being and is, at least partially, "other" from the mother, who carries it inside her. In contrast, what a person may be helped to express, that is, an emotion, possibly connected to a wish, need, memory, representation, thought, or experience, derives solely from whoever expresses it. It is a part of them. Nevertheless, although unintentionally, until the moment immediately preceding expression, the individual guards it. This explains the sense of wonder often accompanying the expression—indeed the *birth*—of a buried feeling.

The aim of emotional maieutics is to facilitate the rise and experiencing of feelings, and to welcome their expression. Through gaze, verbal expression, tone of voice, facial expression, and posture, the therapist contributes an overall attitude of presence, facilitation, holding, and contact—a state of readiness to welcome the Other's emotions. The emotional, sensorial, and cognitive faculties of the therapist are actively concentrated on the Other's whole being. It is not a matter of pressing, rather caressing, giving strength to the patient who is trying to comply with the interior pressure to "let out", but, at the same time, is afraid of doing so. The therapist's emotions, communicated through body attitude, words, and sounds, conveying a sense of connection and participation, can accompany those of the patient and resonate with them, offering closeness to their emotional experience.

Verbal intervention is not always necessary and may be moderate, for example, using phrases such as, "There is a feeling in you", "What is the feeling you have in this moment?", "A feeling is coming", "I perceive that you are afraid of what you feel", "You seem afraid/paralysed/terrified of something you are feeling inside". In my experience, words more often distract and hinder than help the patient to focus on body sensations and feeling. Although the best way to illustrate emotional maieutics is showing videos of patients, through transcript from a therapy session, I will attempt to convey something of these endeavours. The emotional maieutic interventions are identified with the code "XA".

Clinical example to illustrate emotional maieutics (XA)

The Night Creature—sixteenth session

The following dialogue is taken from a session that took place after this severely traumatised patient returned from a visit to her family, whom she had not seen for eight months. During that time, the patient's attitude towards her relatives had been modified by psychotherapy. In particular, the patient had previously shown a thoroughly compliant attitude relative to her family's needs, but in this visit there was no such attitude. However, she resorted to a different defence, namely an emotional detachment that persisted throughout her stay. This detachment, notwithstanding its defensive function, was different from dissociation, since it enabled the patient to perceive her family dynamics clearly, becoming aware of the ways she had always interacted with her family, and the historical and current nature of her family life. In particular, her childhood experiences within an abusive and violent family, the ongoing terror of expressing anything genuinely personal, and the consequent complete blocking of affective expression had massively conditioned her behaviour. The vignette starts with a mirroring intervention by the therapist, reflecting the sense of defensive detachment the patient was conveying while describing the psychological state she was in during the time spent recently at her parents:

Th: You are saying that something froze you.
Pt: It wasn't even numbness; it was a total absence of feelings. All through the time I spent with them I was totally dead. I have no other word for it, because it wasn't even not-being-in-touch-with-feelings. It was being totally devoid of any kind of feeling. I was there and there was nothing. It wasn't even a sense of distance. It was a sense of there-is-nothing-inside-me.

A few minutes later:

Pt: Somewhere I am very angry and somewhere I also feel that my mother has deprived me of so much: she has actively denied me a lot of things, starting with the protection and the ease and the closeness and the intimacy that I could rightly expect. She withheld these things almost knowingly.
Th: She actually used the withholding of it to have power over you?
Pt: Yes, but I am angrier about being denied those things than about the playing with it. It's like I feel this right to demand these things.

In the following intervention, the therapist calls the patient's attention to her identification with her mother, whereby she went on denying herself all that her mother had denied her:

Th: But, at the same time you ended up taking up her role and started to deny these things to yourself. The same applies to when you deny your feeling, when you are detached and you feel guilty about your feelings.
Pt: No, I guess I felt too afraid.
Th: Hmm, of what?
Pt: Of having any feelings in their presence.

This is a perceptive comment; the patient was afraid of feeling. It is worth noticing here that the fear was not about expressing, but rather the very fact of feeling was associated with a sense of vulnerability to abuse. The preceding as well as the following therapist intervention aim at easing up the patient's emotional experiencing and expression:

Th: Uh huh (expressing interest). (**XA**)
Pt: Because having feelings means being exposed.

So, because of the constantly abusive atmosphere the patient lived in, she developed a terror of even feeling—the thought of other family members seeing or sensing what she felt represented a threat to the patient's ability to protect and defend herself.

Th: So your real fear was to have any feelings in their presence. (**XA**)
Pt: Maybe. I guess so. I was really quite paranoid all through the visit and I reverted back immediately to my ...

Here comes a crucial insight:

Pt: I didn't remember this way of being as being so pronounced, but it came back to me that I used to live at night and, during the time I spent there, I reverted back to this habit immediately. It is like when you have jet lag; I didn't sleep, not even for one night. And I remember doing that in the past. This is a pattern that I developed when I was living with them, I just didn't remember it so ... so distinctly, but it was like that, I was a creature of the night, really and I just ... the moment I stepped back into the house is where I ... I immediately got back to this pattern, immediately, immediately ... like not doing anything, not thinking anything, not feeling anything during the day ...

The patient is surprised and excited by her own discovery.

Th: During the day means when they were around?
Pt: Well, they were always around, yes, but ... and then coming to life when she [mother] went to sleep ...
Th: When she went to sleep?
Pt: Yeah. Yeah, that's what I meant, yeah. So I had this feeling constantly that I was hiding and that I came out in the night, when she was away. Like, it was strange, I wouldn't even eat during the day and I would eat during the night, alone. When I say: "I have to go home", it's the same feeling about hiding and it's hiding every feeling and every need ....

After realising this defensive strategy, which she had implemented with an unconscious aim to preserve her real Self, at least during the night, the patient goes on to describe her perception of her relatives' complete failure to understand her, and the consequent ignoring of her feelings and emotional needs. We return to the session:

Pt: There was no hint in their behaviour that something was wrong. I feel like I have been dreaming these days. There is not even ... you see, when people hide things, you kind of perceive it ... they don't, they're just totally oblivious of me. So I feel like I am the only one who tells this story, like I am inventing it. I guess that I find it quite irritating ...

This and the following "I guess" are obviously tactical defences, but the patient is undoubtedly making a quantum leap in terms of her understanding of crucial intrapsychic and interpersonal dynamics.

Pt: I see no guilt, no hidden … I don't know, any kind of disturbance or imbalance or trying to avoid something. They are so peaceful (spelt out with anger) with this reality. It is a sense of me being the crazy one.
Th: Because you are out of their reality.
Pt: Yeah, their reality is so solid, and I guess that I am envious, because their reality is the reality. Like the family is there, around them, I am the outcast!

The patient looks visibly emotionally aroused and is trying not to be overwhelmed by her emotion.

Th: What do you feel about this? (**XA**)
Pt: I guess I feel angry …

As this patient so clearly explains, as a result of highly pathological family dynamics, some people develop a *fear of* emotional experiencing and *expression*, which is so great as to paralyse any spontaneous expression of the Self, conditioning their behaviour in the most conspicuous way. In the case of the "Night Creature", I would say that this conditioning was manifest to the extreme. With these patients, a holding or a generally accepting attitude is not sufficient, and neither is acting on their defences. They need the therapist's *active support of their emotional experience and expression* because they are not able to sustain it themselves. Of course, there are other individuals for whom this particular fear is less relevant. They have easier access to their emotional life and know what feelings are all about. With such individuals, the role played by emotional maieutics is not as crucial. With more fragile and traumatised patients, who carry a crushing anxiety connected to their emotional life, maieutic interventions and overall attitude can make a tremendous difference and are uniquely effective in facilitating access to innermost emotions.

The ways of carrying out maieutic, or midwife, activity are simple and, I would say, almost as primordial as the fear of expression. As has been considered, the purpose of maieutic activity is to lift the fear of emotional experiencing and expression and, in this way, provide a very specific support to get in touch with deep feelings and share them with the therapist. Here, the therapist's presence, openness, and overall attitude are of the essence, and verbal intervention is not always necessary. The fact that the verbal component is the least important accounts for the difficulty in describing maieutic activity solely through words, as I am trying to convey something of a complex interaction between therapist and patient. Indeed, the fundamental aspect, be it accompanied by words or not, is the therapist's global disposition towards the patient. This involves the therapist's *presence*, which includes the spirit of willingness to accept the patient's emotions, an openness, which is expressed through looks, modes of expression, tone of voice, facial expression, and body posture. The Latin root *obstare* (to be present) gives rise to *obstetrics*—another term for midwifery—and emotional maieutics is indeed *all about* being present, facilitating, and holding. For this purpose the therapist also will express their being present with looks and tone of voice. They will convey togetherness, echoing emotion, underlining, offering a sense of closeness, and participation in such emotional experience, most often without the interruption brought on by excessive verbal intervention.

According to Malan (personal communication, p. [chapter 1]), Balint identified the approach of the therapist as the main core of the analytical process, and Malan too underlines the importance of the therapist's attitude, constantly monitoring the depth of rapport with the patient (D. Malan, personal communication, (1984). Emotional maieutics is, in essence, exactly this, an *attitude*. If that is the case then why should it be so crucial to insist on what the "maieutic" therapist *does*? The answer is that this attitude is also a "doing" and requires calling upon all the sensorial, affective, and cognitive faculties of the therapist and focusing them on the being, in a broader sense, of the Other. This results in a sort of connection with the Other which, however, does not hamper the ability to observe. In order to assist the rise of emotional experiencing and attend to expression, it is crucial to participate and connect at all possible levels with the other person. This involves actively getting close to them, not limiting communication to a verbal level, since this notably reduces the chance of experiencing and expressing, and favours defences, such as intellectualisation, detachment, and emotional coldness in both the patient and the therapist. The less the therapist confines the dyad to verbal communication, the more they will develop the capacity to activate themselves at all possible levels of the relationship, facilitating and supporting the rise, experiencing, and expression of the emotions that are kept distant from consciousness. As a result of this, the patient-therapist relationship is strengthened and the therapeutic process can proceed in the best way, avoiding the slow-downs and impediments deriving from an inadvertent fear of emotional arousal in either partner of the therapeutic dyad. The maieutic attitude and activity is natural to some extent, but it mostly needs to be awakened and trained in the therapist. The extensive use of videotapes of sessions to observe, review and re-experience the patient-therapist interactions helps to progressively increase the therapist's ability to tolerate the intensity of deep emotion, enabling them to facilitate this process, allowing emotion to exist and welcoming it. In this way the therapist gets progressively desensitised to his or her own emotional experiencing and expression that can give rise to anxiety.

Maieutic activity gives emotion an additional strength, arising from the emotional connection formed with the therapist. In such instances, the therapist functions as a *symbolic extension* of the other person, and as a container filled with his or her expression. One cannot give birth into emptiness. Furthermore, someone must greet an infant into the world. Hence, maieutic activity also has an accepting, welcoming function.

In summary, maieutic activity facilitates the patient's experience of emotions and is therefore life-giving. It provides both the patient and the therapist with first-hand data on feelings that previously were repressed or otherwise excluded from consciousness. It almost invariably provides the patient with a corrective emotional and relational experience (Alexander & French, 1946), and strengthens the relationship with the therapist, who is perceived as a living human being, truly involved in the relationship. It catalyses the therapeutic process, helping to avoid excessive use of the intellectual defences. It creates the foundations for compassion (McCullough Vaillant, 1997), engenders a sense of gratitude in the patient, and can be gratifying and life-giving for the therapist as well.

Anxiety regulation (AA)

Patients may present with anxiety at the forefront, prior to any specific interventions. In other cases, especially following defence restructuring and emotional maieutics, anxiety can become so intense as to act as a cloud, covering up the patient's emotions. Consequently, the main purpose of anxiety regulation in EDT is to optimise emotional experiencing. In addition, careful assessment of a patient's anxiety manifestations provides invaluable psychodiagnostic information (see ten Have-de Labije, 2006).

The psychodynamic significance of anxiety as a basically inhibitory force was clarified by Freud (1926d) who defined it as "a reaction of the Ego to danger" (p. 129), whereas "symptoms are created so as to avoid a *danger-situation* whose presence has been signalled by the generation of anxiety" (p. 132). Freud affirms that "as a feeling, anxiety has a very marked character of unpleasure" (p. 132), and that it "arose originally as a reaction to a state of *danger*, and it is reproduced whenever a state of that kind recurs" (p. 134). In other words, following a past trauma, whenever one of the feelings or impulses linked to the trauma might be again stimulated, anxiety sets in, inhibiting their expression in order to avoid the re-experiencing of trauma.

Anxiety regulation (AA) is here proposed as the experiential-dynamic activity addressing *those inhibitory forces hindering a good-enough experience of conflicting* (painful and anxiety-provoking) *emotions*. Its aim is to facilitate their experience and expression. McCullough Vaillant (1997) makes a fundamental operational distinction between the *physiological* and the *pathological* functions of anxiety and other inhibitory forces:

> The original evolutionary function of the inhibitory affects was for self-guidance or self-control, but when pathology occurs, these reactions represent feelings and associated beliefs that have been intensified beyond the bounds of adaptive control into some degree of self-inhibition, self-thwarting, or in extreme cases, punitive self-attack. This sometimes results from inadequate caretaking and sometimes from unknown causes. *Whatever the reasons, the unnaturally exaggerated inhibitory or self-attacking affects are a major cause of defensive behavior and thus a major cause of environmentally based psychopathology*. (p. 139)

The rationale for anxiety regulation

In the Triangle of Conflict, only one pole (X) represents authentic Self-experience. The other two poles (D and A), in different ways, get in the way of such emotional experience. Do you remember Heisenberg's *uncertainty principle* applied to EDT (see p. 44)? Also concerning anxiety, the specific EDT orientation of the therapist may affect the way in which they perform anxiety regulation. Some manifestations can indeed be addressed as anxiety or, instead, as defences, and the therapist will have to choose which way to go. For example, talking in a torrential way simultaneously allows defensive avoidance of emotional content, and motor discharge of anxiety. It is up to the therapist whether to point out and challenge the defensive aspect, or to regulate the patient's anxiety in order to contain their relentless speech. Another example is when the patient experiences a feeling that is real, but, at the same time, inhibits the experience of another feeling that is also authentic and adaptive. Anger, for example, can represent an adaptive expression, aiming to set clear limits. However, there are cases in which anger can inhibit more authentic Self-experience. Let us take the case of a man who responds with anger towards women to whom he is attracted. Since anger is brought about by sexual desire (adaptive = X), this anger would actually have an inhibitory function = A—this example applies also to women who react with anger towards men they find attractive, and within same sex relationships.

Another frequent occurrence is anger inhibiting grief, for example, in complicated mourning. In these examples, anger can be regarded as either an inhibitory force or a defence, depending on the therapist's theoretical orientation, which will also influence the technical interventions in relation to the patient's anger. The IE-DP approach, in particular, adopts a radically dynamic perspective, whereby *any* emotion may have an inhibitory function, the same as anxiety, whenever its experience covers another emotion. As a consequence, in the above example, IE-DP views anger that inhibits sexual excitement or grief as akin to anxiety in that—the same as guilt, shame, and fear more often do—the anger has an inhibitory function. The IE-DP therapist will thus be more likely to use anxiety regulation in these cases.

The more defences are effective in keeping authentic emotion and impulse distant from consciousness, the less anxiety's inhibitory effect is needed. Since EDT brings the anxiety-provoking and/or painful emotions back to consciousness, this will inevitably increase the intensity of anxiety. An overly intense anxiety has paralysing effects on psychological functioning, so in order for the dynamic process to proceed smoothly and rapidly, anxiety must be kept within a useful range, that is neither so low as to favour regression, nor so high as to block the therapeutic process. To this purpose, the therapist monitors the patient's level of anxiety and identifies the ways in which anxiety is experienced; its localisation in the body (physical perceptions and manifestations), or corresponding mental experience of it (for example, confusion, drowsiness, disturbed ideation). Questions are posed to patients regarding their perception and intensity of anxiety. Their inner experiences, thoughts, and mental representations connected with anxiety are explored and shared with the therapist. In these ways, anxiety inhibiting the *experiencing* of deep feeling and impulse is kept at a level that is bearable rather than overwhelming. This process also makes the experience of anxiety more *familiar*, thereby increasing the patient's sense of being able to *master* their anxiety. The awareness of the *connection* between anxiety and hidden conflicting emotions is encouraged. Patients are helped to regard anxiety as a *normal* phenomenon when unconscious emotion is coming to the surface.

Manifestations of anxiety

The term "anxiety" is associated by each of us with a complex set of internal events. These images, feelings, and physical experiences are similar to those of fear. Actually, anxiety is nothing more than the fear of *experiencing* our own feelings and impulses, and the associated expected *consequences*. For the purpose of anxiety regulation in psychotherapy, it is essential that the therapist is able to deal with their own anxiety. When intense grief, rage, and sexual excitement are aroused in the patient, this may indeed affect us therapists deeply as persons. Repeated exposure to clinical videos of EDT sessions and advanced EDT training will increase the therapist's ability to sustain and share emotions and the related anxiety while remaining calm but not detached. This will, in turn, have an anxiety-regulating effect on the patient. In his study on the evolutionary importance of emotional expression in man and animal, Charles Darwin (1872) described the typical manifestations of anxiety. These include widely opening one's eyes while raising the eyebrows and the central fascia of the forehead, in order to increase the visual field, and to be able to look in all directions. The mouth is often open or semi-open, to facilitate breathing, and the muscles contract, producing movements in the arms and shoulders and causing changes in posture. Generally, the torso slants backwards, with a deep inspiration followed by a series of frequent and superficial respiratory cycles. Voice may be altered, emitted with effort, restrained, or absent. Mouth may become dry, because of diminished salivation. Other neurovegetative reactions include accelerated and energetic heartbeat, dilation of the pupils, pallor, "cold" sweats, and erect body and scalp hair. In clinical practice, not all of these reactions occur simultaneously each time anxiety is intensified. What is constant is the appearance of some of them, sometimes in a mild form. It is thus crucial to be trained to recognise any slight manifestations of anxiety, signalling a feeling, a desire, or an impulse that the patient needs to bring into consciousness. Some physiological aspects of anxiety, like sweating and accelerated heartbeat, though frequent, are not directly evident. Therefore, in order to get a clearer view of how anxiety is being experienced, we have to put questions such as, "How is your heartbeat?", "Are you sweating?", or "How are your shoulders?". In addition to providing useful information, these simple questions will help the patient see the therapist as a person who is interested in everything they are feeling, both physically and emotionally.

Conscious and unconscious anxiety

Davanloo (1990) identified three main channels for the expression of conscious and unconscious anxiety. This is also described by Coughlin Della Selva (1996) and ten Have-de Labije (2006). The first channel passes through the striated voluntary musculature that governs movement, the second takes the route of the smooth, involuntary musculature, and the third produces an alteration of perceptual and cognitive processes. According to Davanloo, anxiety channelled through the striated musculature is closer to consciousness and patients "tend to associate their physical tension with anxiety and to have a fairly accurate idea what they are anxious about" (Coughlin Della Selva, 1996, p. 10). On the other hand, when a larger portion of anxiety and its causes are unconscious, the elements mainly involved are the smooth muscle function and the perceptual-cognitive sphere. Smooth muscles are present in most organs and viscera, and are controlled by the neuroendocrine system. People who channel most of their anxiety in this direction tend to somatise. Patients are often unaware of the connection between their physical ailments, such as headaches, meteorism, diarrhoea, irritable bowel, gastritis, etc., and their state of anxiety and nervousness. In these cases, a rapid mobilisation of anxiety is dangerous, because of potential for its direct release on the organs involved, with potentially damaging consequences in the presence of important pathologies such as asthma, ulcerative colitis, or duodenal ulcer. These conditions require a slower pace, so as to help the patient to become gradually aware of the way they experience their own anxiety physically. This graded process (Abbass & Bechard, 2007; Davanloo, 1990) increases tolerance to anxiety. Finally, when anxiety is altering the perceptual-cognitive processes, it is the functioning of the Ego rather than the body that is the victim. In these cases the mobilisation of anxiety can result in losing one's train of thought, or experiencing disorientation. The barrier between mental and physical is rather thin and slips in perception and cognition may be accompanied by sudden sensations of weakness, dizziness, or drowsiness or, instead, an urgent need for motor discharge. In other cases the thought processes may become disrupted or disorganised to the point of activating delusional ideation. The appearance of these symptoms would signal that the Self is unable to tolerate the level of anxiety reached, and that we are in the presence of a relative fragility of the Ego. The consequence is that the process of anxiety-regulation needs to last longer and the unconscious anxiety-provoking and/or painful emotions should be approached at a slower pace.

Anxiety in the psychotherapeutic clinical practice

The different configurations of anxiety that need anxiety regulation in clinical practice can be traced back to three possible types (Osimo, 2003): (i) the patient spontaneously reports that they are anxious, and the manifestations of anxiety are, at least partly, clear to both the therapist and the patient, (ii) the patient does not spontaneously acknowledge anxiety that is evident to the therapist, and (iii) the patient does not spontaneously acknowledge anxiety and there is an absence of overt manifestations of anxiety.

In the first case, when the patient *states* they feel anxious, a guided identification process should be conducted with the active participation of the patient, by asking them *how* and *where* anxiety is perceived. This process will make it possible to measure the intensity of anxiety and evaluate the somatic pathways channelling it. It is particularly important to make sure if anxiety is at least partly channelled through the striated muscles, thus being closer to consciousness. If this portion of anxiety is little or negligible, it is necessary to look carefully for any symptoms or ailments in the body.

In the second instance, when the patient makes no direct reference to anxiety, but their *body* is signalling its presence (e.g., fearful facial expression, muscular rigidity with tension in the shoulders, neck or other regions, superficial breathing or voice alteration, increased sweating, a need to shift position frequently to discharge part of the tension), it would be wrong to assume that the patient is fully aware of these manifestations and of their significance. It is therefore necessary to mirror these signals to the patient and help them to see the connection between these physical manifestations and the underlying subjective experience of anxiety.

In the third scenario, when the patient makes no direct reference to anxiety and their body is sending no signals, but the *content* of speech, and the circumstance it relates to, suggest the presence of anxiety, it will be necessary to first establish a purely cognitive connection, asking the patient whether they have any sensation, or any reaction to what the therapist is saying. Individuals are not always aware of their *being* also a body; therefore it may become necessary to make specific reference to this aspect, by asking them whether they have any sensations *in their body* and *where* are these located.

Clinical example to illustrate anxiety regulation (AA)

The Lonely Boy—trial relationship I

The following clinical example, from the first extended session with a man in his late thirties with over fifteen years of previous psychotherapies, shows how anxiety can go undetected and remain unconscious if not systematically addressed with anxiety-regulation. This bright but severely Self-sabotaging man complained of fits of violent rage with his girlfriend (mother of their two-year-old child), compulsive sex with transvestite men and other women, chronic irritable bowel, recurrent severe back pain keeping him in bed for months, and underachievement in his profession. A former eating disorder (binge eating) had been cured before starting IE-DP. Anxiety-regulating interventions are coded as AA.

Th: ... hmm, what would you like to face today?
Pt: ... well, don't really know ... I don't have a clue ... no real priority ... er ... perhaps yes, I'd like to get back to a good relationship with Joanne ... thinking that we may have to split due to my behaviour, or to hers ... this feels to be total bullshit to me ... so, I'd like to see how to improve things with Joanne ...
Th: ... so, is this what you want to face?
Pt: ... yes, if we go by subjects, yes ...
Th: ... we want to do something useful, since you are talking of everything, but, in a way, you are neglecting yourself!
Pt: ... in what way ...?
Th: ... because you came here to get done with things, didn't you?
Pt: ... yes, but I am used with Dr S. [former analyst] ... maybe I don't know how this relation is ... I used to talk and talk ... well, I have an illumination; now I know why I stopped seeing Dr S. ... One day after a session with her I thought to myself, "Shit! I've been talking about exactly the same thing a hundred times!"... sort of what I am doing now ... I said this a thousand times ... what you are asking me is interesting ...!

As we see, the patient is used to talking a lot, but had lost hope of ever managing to face and solve his complex problems. This led him to remain superficial, touching on many subjects without dealing effectively with any of them. It is crucial to realise that when patients are talking in general, in spite of touching on crucial aspects of their lives, they are not emotionally active and their efforts come to nothing. This is probably one of the major shortcomings of couch-based, passive forms of psychoanalysis. The therapist has to bring the patient back on track:

Th: ... so: you are destroying your relation with Joanne ... are you interested to talk about this?
Pt: ... well, it is surely very important! ... in terms of priorities, I see the relation with Joanne plus, next time, me among other people, in my job etc., why I always feel so jinxed ... and why I keep on frustr-... whipping my life ... my back, and ...
Th: ... you said "whipping my life and my back?"
Pt: ... yes ... I don't know if it is a slip of the tongue ...
Th: ... it is what you said! ... now, since you also have a back pain ...
Pt: ... actually, I've just made the link! ... and there is also another thing ...
Th: ... I wouldn't like to spend three hours talking uselessly ... (**AA**) Talking a lot is at the same time part of this patient's character defence and a way of discharging anxiety. For this reason the above intervention is coded here as **AA**.
Pt: ... no, I don't want this either ... no, no, shit, no ... and I need to understand the way you work ...
Th: ... I am showing you ... so, do we start from your relationship with Joanne?

Pt: … yes, sure, yes, because it conditions a lot of other things … my rage conditions me a lot …
Th: … you mean you are enraged with Joanne now?
Pt: … yes, I am a bit angry, because …
Th: (Interrupting) … you say you are angry …
Pt: … yes I am, she says I've never forgiven her since the first day we've been together and I am always angry at her …
Th: … this is what Joanne says. What do you say?
Pt: … it is true by half … she is right … not totally …

The following two therapist interventions should be coded as both DA (talking instead of feeling), and AA (torrential talking to discharge anxiety). For the purpose of illustrating anxiety regulation, here they are coded as AA only:

Th: (Interrupting) You talk a lot! (**AA**)
Pt: … I …?
Th: … you talk! (**AA**)
Pt: … yes, earlier on she actually said, "You pissed me off with your monologues; you talk a lot, but never listen to others", so, yes I talk a lot …

The patient stated he is angry, but this is not visible, nor is it indeed credible that he is in touch with the actual physical experience of his rage. There are clearly defences as well as inhibitory forces in operation. In order to explore this, the therapist goes along with the word "anger" since the patient used this term, but is looking for the physical experience of anxiety. For this reason the next three therapist interventions are coded as AA:

Th: … when you say you are angry is it because you experience anger somewhere? (**AA**)
Pt: … yes!
Th: … where do you feel it? (**AA**)
Pt: … my anger I feel it here … and also in my arms …
Th: … what do you feel there? (**AA**)
Pt: … it might come to me to grab something and throw it somewhere … or …
Th: … that is anxiety … what you have there … (**AA**)
Pt: ah yes?
Th: … what do you feel?
Pt: … well, now (coughs) to tell the truth … in this moment I do not feel anxiety … I mean I am always short of breath …

The patient denied anxiety, but is giving evidence of it in various ways; motoric discharge, talking a lot and quickly, shortness of breath. The therapist focuses on the physical experience of anxiety:

Th: … what do you feel there? (**AA**)
Pt: … here I always feel bad. I've had an ongoing colitis (irritable bowel) since I was thirteen, so …

Th: ... tension in your bowel? (**AA**)
Pt: ... yes ...
Th: ... air? (**AA**)
Pt: ... yes, some air and a lot of colitis ...
Th: ... do you often go to the bathroom? (**AA**)
Pt: ... yes, very often, and generally badly ...
Th: ... is it hard or soft? (**AA**)

The therapist's enquiry about the patient's stools might be regarded as excessive, but it actually conveys his unconditional interest in all aspects and levels of the patient's life. Moreover it can provide information on the functions of the autonomous nervous system as well as on the patient's character.

Pt: ... generally hard ... well, normal ... in real difficult moments I have diarrhoea ... I have a pain here, I feel bad, go to the bathroom ...
Th: ... you are short of breath, with superficial breathing ... (**AA**)
Pt: ... yes a lot ...
Th: ... you keep on talking, moving and gesticulating ... it's all ways of discharging your anxiety ... (**AA**)
Pt: ... yes ...
Th: ... do you realise that? (**AA**)
Pt: ... well, re movement, no ... but now that you say, I can understand ...
Th: ... it is a way of dispersing your tension ... talk and talk and talk ... move and move ... (**AA**)
Pt: ... ah! ... so also with Joanne I talk a lot ...
Th: ... and very fast too ... (**AA**)
Pt: ... yes, a bit fast ... yes, to say as much as I can, because I want to convince her ... so I talk as much as I can ...
Th: ... you keep moving your foot ... (**AA**)
Pt: ... what?
Th: ... your foot is moving! (**AA**)
Pt: ... I actually always wear comfortable shoes ... and with Joanne ...
Th: ... so, there is anxiety now ... (**AA**)
Pt: ... yes, yes, there is anxiety ...
Th: ... you are tense ... all tensed, even in your muscle ... (**AA**)

The patient is gradually getting to know his own anxiety manifestations and, with the therapist's help, he starts seeing them for what they are:

Pt: ... well ... this I don't know ... are you asking if I feel tense?
Th: ... yes, can you see your shoulders were tensed and now relaxed? (**AA**)
Pt: ... yes, a bit perhaps ... what I don't feel so much lately is tension at the physical level ... I felt it for many years ... now I feel it mostly in my belly, stomach ... breathlessness ...

Th: ... and you have a back pain ... (**AA**)

Pt: ... yes, bloody hell, I always have a back pain ...even if not too terrible lately ... I don't know if all this tension is what brings about my problems ...

Acknowledging his anxiety with the therapist's help has also a relational side to it; for the first time in his life, the patient is allowing another human being to share some very intimate aspects of his life, closely connected with his feelings and inner world. It is not surprising if he now tries to avoid fully acknowledging that what is going on in the session is also the dawning emotional closeness with the therapist.

Th: ... do you notice you try to heal on your own? ... you put hypotheses, give answers ... all by yourself ...

Pt: ... ah yes! ... no, I had not noticed it ... to be honest ...

Th: ... you are finding it difficult to connect with me ...

Pt: ... oh my! ... and I thought I was so relaxed and saying all that comes to mind! I understand what you mean, but I don't see what I should do ...

Th: ... let's go on. We saw there is much anxiety that you have in many different ways. ... You started by saying you are angry at Joanne ... I then asked you where you feel your anger, and you mentioned some anxiety signals ... (**AA**)

Pt: (Coughs)

Th: ... including the cough, which is nervous cough ... (**AA**)

Pt: ... that makes me smile ... no, I don't smile ... you are right, because I've had this bloody cough for one year! ... and my voice goes down and then comes back ... without any physical cause ...

Th: ... can we look at what happens? ... because—you see—you keep on trying to take care of yourself on your own ... instead of letting me take care of you .... Can you give me a specific example with Joanne?

Pt: (Coughs)

Th: ... and—you see—anxiety comes when I ask you to be more in a relation with me ... or to get closer to a specific example, hmm? (**AA**)

Pt: ... yes ... in spite of the fact that I couldn't wait to come here ... it may be a defence, but ...

Th: ... let's see one example ...

Pt: ... OK, our last discussion ...!

The patient's anxiety is now better regulated and he has become more aware of his anxiety; in particular, he is familiar with the ways his anxiety is channelled and discharged. He was shown that part of his anxiety is connected to emotional closeness with the therapist. He intuitively understood that by accepting to be guided by the therapist, he will see parts of himself and his painful feelings and conflicts that he has hitherto played around with and avoided taking seriously. The patient is eventually ready to go deeper into his painful emotions as he now gives a specific example by portraying that morning's discussion with Joanne in a detailed way; it was about preparing dinner for a guest. He starts, "... at some point Joanne looked at me and her look was belittling and spiteful ..."

We leave the clinical example at this point, knowing that therapist and patient are now set to start working closely together on this specific incident (HP, see pp. 54–60). Rage and other feelings will become activated and be experienced. Meaningful links with the patient's symptoms and life history will become possible.

Dealing with the Superego (SE)

Every patient in our day-to-day therapeutic work demonstrates how human beings have a part of their psyche carrying a set of guidelines and rules influencing the individual's moves, choices, mental processes, and life strategy. The individual is endowed with this set of psychological functions and starts developing them from the very early phases of life. The same as the rest of human development, this *guiding part* results from the interplay and interaction of the individual with their physical, relational, and cultural environment, and it is largely unconscious. Since it carries precepts and directions to some degree influenced and moulded by external stimuli from early phases of individual development, this set of rules may clash with the line of thought and action consonant with the individual's Self at a later developmental stage, that is to say, based on what the individual currently feels, thinks, and wills. Freud (1923b, 1924c) called this part of the psyche "Super-Ego", the term itself referring to something standing above the individual's Ego, thus, and more broadly, above one's personal identity, that is to say, the sense of "being oneself".

The existence of the Superego and its possible clash, or conflict, with the interests of the Self, gives rise, to a greater or lesser extent, to behaviours and ways of being that are not in tune with what the individual feels and wants. In the worst case, the Superego can be overriding and rule the individual's life in a highly destructive way, undermining pleasure, satisfaction, and self-realisation, even fostering the pursuit of afflictive, painful, and penalising behaviours and life choices. This is a true psychological conundrum on which Freud's genius started to shed light. As therapists, we are certainly concerned with the role played by these phenomena in psychotherapeutic practice, especially when the punishing, sabotaging, and self-stifling component significantly underlines the patient's defensive style. Even though, as shown by Vaillant (1977, 1993), each and every defence is born first of all as a means to confront life and represents a striving for adaptation; when clogged by the Superego, the whole defensive system can stop serving its adaptive function and—similar to a Trojan Horse—carry within it the mechanism for destruction.

As Vaillant (Soldz & Vaillant, 1999) also demonstrated, in the absence of stimulation deriving from significant changes in the socio-cultural and relational context—like, for instance, an energetic psychotherapy—the individual's defensive system maintains itself over time. In other words, human beings are endowed with a marvellous adaptive potential but, once defences are established, there is some major or minor degree of inertial resistance towards replacing them with more adaptive ones. So, even if defences serve an adaptive function, some defensive patterns involve bigger sacrifices than others, in terms of personal and social realisation, satisfaction, and pleasure. This "sacrificial" component, when carried to the extreme, takes the characteristics of an endless perpetration of self-destructive behaviour. Collecting failures, self-inflicted or letting others inflict humiliation, physical pain, even wounds and mutilation, are forms of self-sabotage and self-punishment. Some theoreticians (e.g., Klein, 1984) describe the

Superego as more of the individual's *response* to the reality of their early experience, therefore mostly as their own *production*. Others (e.g., Bowlby, 1982) reject this view and the very term, Superego, instead resorting to the concept of an inner representation or "working model", faithfully reflecting how caregivers *really* were and behaved, thus as an inner realistic *reproduction* of external reality. Davanloo (1990) regards the Superego as the major source of pathology and human suffering, therefore as an enemy to fight, stressing the part of it that clashes with the individual's healthy interests. This motivated him to focus on techniques to bring about and exacerbate an intrapsychic crisis, that is, an induced splitting between the part of the individual identified with their healthy needs and the pathological Superego part that demands self-sabotage and undermines constructive life strategies. Indeed, Davanloo made the process of "turning the Ego against the Superego" a core part of treatment, and postulated that the way of turning the Ego against the Superego is by activating the primitive murderous sadistic rage against punitive, critical, and neglectful attachment figures.

Whatever the theoretical position, terms used, and way of conceptualising this human aspect, the therapist's task is to identify the parts of an individual that are acting as a sabotaging, destructive force, and make it visible to the patient. The patient may be more or less rationally aware of behaving in destructive and ruinous ways, but is *never* in touch with the related *emotional experience*. As usefully pointed out by ten Have-De Labije (2009) patients suffering from Superego pathology will *diminish*, *neglect*, *ignore*, and *deny* their real feelings, needs, and desires, instead of observing and taking good care of them. In part, because acknowledging one's feelings, needs, and desires involves the painful experience of all the love that has been missed, there follows the related unconscious desire to take revenge against one's caregivers, with the consequent guilt and grief over the loss of love and emergence of tender feelings. Kalpin (2001) wrote:

> It is the remorse that is defended against, and it is the defence against the experience of this remorse which cripples the whole emotional system and inhibits the person's potential … In order to successfully avoid the experience of this remorse, one must make sure to never experience anger toward someone who is also loved … Therefore anger must be avoided and love and closeness must also be avoided … [When, instead, sadistic impulses towards someone who is also loved *are* experienced] with sufficient intensity, then remorse and sadness ("guilt and grief") are also experienced … Once the feared affects have been experienced, the defences against these feelings are no longer necessary. (p. 51)

Independent of the theoretical position one takes, it is useful to maintain a distinction between the parts of the patient that are well integrated, and congruent with self-compassionate and self-actualising values, wishes, and needs, and the neglecting, punishing, diminishing parts that obstruct integration, self-compassion, and self-actualisation. In the experience of the author, this distinction has tremendous clinical value and we may hope that, in the future, developments in neuroscience will shed further light on the delicate interplay of these parts of the Self. My comprehensive operational definition of Superego is as follows:

> An inner reflection *and* a response to the power and the love we experienced in our early environment with our primary attachment figures. In the course of life, this set of mental functions

> does constantly guide and inspire us. In so doing, however, at times it happens to exceed its adaptive function and may even become our omnipotent god or torturing jailer.

When the individual is plagued by a pathological Superego, the therapist will need to enable them to gain control of and not be dominated by it. This cannot be achieved without an emotional activation. A clinical example follows to show how to illuminate the obscure faces of Superego that can appear in therapy, make the patient familiar with it, and show how its power can be harnessed to achieve a higher level of integration. The interventions aimed to restructure the Superego are identified with the code "SE".

Clinical example to illustrate dealing with the Superego (SE)

The Daughter of five parents

The patient, a woman in her thirties, came for therapy because of a severe—and apparently mysterious—inability to assert herself, and a dependent relationship with her mother and family of origin. She was married with a child, and steadily employed. At first, she denied having any relational problem and talked about her very special family. Before the patient was conceived, her mother had had five miscarriages, and the patient grew up within an extended family comprising her parents and two aunts, one of them single, and the other married. In other words, she was raised by five caregivers, all of them eager to "spoil" their only child. From the first extended interview, it was clear that, as a child, the patient had suffered from remarkable inhibition of social skills, had almost no peer relationships, and felt filled with guilt and shame. She had had no material restriction and was apparently privileged, which accounts for some of the difficulty in identifying the Superego parts in this patient, as well as her own shame at the prospect of needing therapeutic help. Two excerpts from the fourth and fifth sessions provide an example of Superego work. In particular, identifying the self-sabotaging and self-stifling parts, showing them to the patient, using the experiential-dynamic activities to activate deep emotion, calling upon the patient's strength and therapeutic alliance and, finally, the patient turning against her Superego and establishing the supremacy of the Self.

Pt: Today a colleague told me that the boss was around, so I thought to go and ask him to be sent to that course, but …

The therapist knows that the Superego is often projected onto people in authority. Moreover he notices anxiety and decides to enquire about her physical experience in the moment:

Pt: Difficulty breathing, this weight on my stomach and, the moment I think to go and ask, this anxiety comes over that blocks me completely …

Th: So this anxiety is very strong. To the point of preventing you from feeling what you wish … (**SE**)

Pt: (Nods)

Th: … in your head you do know … but then this painful anxiety comes, and all that you feel is this anxiety … (**SE**)

Pt: (Nods)

Th: … so it's powerful and instant this thing disconnecting you from what you wish … so it disconnects two parts of you, one that keeps on working efficiently, and another that … should feel but cannot feel because it gets disconnected … (**SE**)

Pt: (Face expressing painful feeling)

Th: … what do you feel as I say so?

Pt: … I keep on having this weight blocking me (squeezing her chest) … as though I had a big stone here …

Th: … so this is really terrible … even in this very moment, this big stone, this weight, this tension, this squeezing thing that gives you pain … (**SE**)

Pt: (Is filled with tension and has a suffering face)

Th: … is paralysing your being and preventing you from feeling what you feel beyond this squeeze … you can't feel what is being squeezed … so, the way of freeing yourself from this big stone is to feel whatever you feel, wish and want … so, shall we see if you can throw away the big stone and tell me what you feel? Or maybe there is an image that comes to you? (**SE**)

This intervention is coded as SE because the Superego, self-sabotaging part is still much more powerful than the patient's ability to free her Self. For the time being, all that she can do is become more familiar with her superego part:

Pt: (Deep sigh, suffering face, moving on the chair, like she is trying to push away something very annoying) … the image is … of myself trying to free myself from this thing …

The therapist notices the patient's effort and knows that, because of her anxiety and tension, she needs to regulate her anxiety and find her pace before she can turn against her Superego part. He therefore acknowledges the patient's commitment and tries to use her mental image of herself to focus on a specific incident and portray that moment in the patient's life:

Th: … very well then … what is the way you see yourself in this image, is it the way you are now?

Pt: (Very anxious and suffering) … yes like now …

Th: … where do you see yourself, here, at your job …?

Pt: … in an empty space …

Th: … are you alone or with other people?

Pt: … alone … it's like I am locked inside a box …

Th: … oh! (interested) … and you've been locked up there for much too long … so let's see how you manage to get out of it …! (**SE**)

The therapist is pleased that the patient can now see the "box", an image of something imprisoning the patient/her feeling part, thus a metaphor of the Superego.

Pt: (Suffering, anxious, paralysed, head bent forward, a hand before her eyes) I don't manage to get out, can't …

Th: (Interrupting to call upon the patient's inner strength) … do you want to stay inside the box? (**SE**)

For the first time here the therapist tests where the patient stands; now that she *sees* the box, what is her attitude to it?

Pt: (Laughing nervously, and shamefully) … no, but I am not managing to see myself out of it …
Th: … you do not see it is possible to get out …? (**SE**)
Pt: … (denies with her head)

The therapist sees that the balance of the two parts, Self and Superego, is still weighted towards the Superego, so he needs to further motivate the patient. He does this by indirectly highlighting the misery in which the patient condemns herself to live:

Th: … so it's a real prison, like a castle without a drawbridge, you are very efficiently boxed up, it's horrible! … don't you feel like getting out? (**SE**)
Pt: (Nods, though she is totally stiff)
Th: … you may need to call upon all of your strengths to manage getting out … I can only call you from outside … don't get stiff … I can only tell you: "Get out … you are not well inside there" … is there anything you feel or think? (**SE**)

In this last intervention, not only does the therapist once again ask the patient where she decides to stand—stay inside or come out of the box—he is also probing for the patient's feelings at the thought of being imprisoned. The response is some mobilisation of anxiety and, later, shame:

Pt: … it's like it comes to me to stomp my feet …
Th: … do stomp your feet for God's sake, don't refrain all the time …! (**SE**)
Pt: (Hiding behind two hands) I feel ridiculous!
Th: … oh no, you are not! Don't hide and don't feel ashamed …! (**SE**)
Pt: (Is filled with shame, and hiding behind her hands)

In this case shame is clearly having an inhibitory function and the therapist wants to regulate it:

Th: … do you feel so ashamed? Well, you don't need to, and anyway I can see even behind your hands … there is nothing to be ashamed of … what an effort you are making! … but it comes to you to stomp your feet … so you feel like kicking somebody with these feet … whom do you want to kick? (**SE**)
Pt: … I want to kick the box!
Th: … OK, let's start with kicking the box [Superego], then we'll see whomever else you want to kick … (**SE**)
Pt: (Keeps on having jolts in her legs)

Th: ... you really feel like kicking ...! So, if you wish to stop being the well-behaved girl ... **(SE)**
Pt: (Kicking movement)
Th: ... to whom is that kick directed? To me (therapist)? **(SE)**
Pt: ... no, I want to break this thing ...
Th: ... then you need all of your strength ... do you feel your strength or are you still tense? ... let's see what comes out of the box if you open it ... what is it like, Felicia coming out, and what does she feel ...
Pt: ... yes, in my arms and shoulders ... and I have two images: one of me kicking the box, and the other of me kicking the wall ...
Th: ... all this tension is also part of the cage ... like a cage of tension imprisoning you ... so, if the beast comes out of the cage, what does she do? Shall we free her? **(SE)**

At last, the therapist's effort to keep the patient focused on her box/prison/wall/Superego enables the patient to see something beyond this Great Wall:

Pt: ... I have an image of myself as a child of four or five being totally enraged at my aunt and shaking the sink, spilling the water, and flooding the bathroom and then my father scolding me ... my aunt tried to cool me down but was totally powerless ...
Th: ... was this the aunt that taught you to read and write?
Pt: ... yes, but at some point she stopped because I had a sort of rejection ...
Th: ... do you see that child as happy or not?
Pt: ... actually my memory is of a diligent child, rather sad and resigned ...
Th: ... well, I don't mean to play the philosopher, but a child of five needs to play, it's a bit early to be "diligent" ... so ... whom do you want to kick? **(SE)**
Pt: ... I have this image of my family [extended family of five people] ... maybe it was them who were my box, even if out of excess love ...

Here the patient starts associating the "box" with her attachment figures, though still in a general way. Moreover she absolves them, by confusedly supposing their love was in excess. The therapist clarifies, and guides the patient back on track:

Th: ... love can never be too much ... is this the reason that you cannot kick anybody? The first thing that came to you was about kicking ... **(SE)**
Pt: ... I am thinking of these three women. I see myself surrounded by these three, that one was my mother and the others my two aunts ... and it's like I had to compensate something to each one of them ...
Th: ... by being the doll they never gave you ...

During the weekend following this session the patient went to her mother's, having a chance of spending some time in her former bedroom. In the following session (5) she is describing her visit and says:

Pt: ... for the first time, after I got out of my room I felt sad ... but as I left I also felt guilty for having felt sad ... (looks very sad) ... later at night I saw myself as a child and felt very intense compassion and distress and … I recalled … my mother had a shop and they sold many toys. Once my mother said I could choose a toy for me … so we were in the store and I really chose one.

Th: … what toy?

Pt: … a doll with a comb … in a matter of a few hours, after we got home, she grabbed it from my hands …

Th: … what do you feel?

Pt: … a deep pity for this child.

No doubt one of the patient's feelings, beside her deep sadness, may have been compassion for herself. We already know, however, that she tends to put a positive spin on everything and would consciously find it unbelievable that her mother's action was inspired by anything else but love.

Th: … what do you feel towards your mother?

Pt: … well …

Th: … is it difficult?

Pt: … yes …

Th: … but important!

Pt: … when I think of her in that incident she is cruel!

Th: … what do you feel?

Pt: … I don't manage to feel any anger.

Here the patient is mentioning—and at the same time denying—her anger. In the next intervention the therapist will have to show the patient that if she rejects the emotional experience of her anger by getting tense, then it will keep her a prisoner of the Superego "box":

Th: … if you don't get stiff … or do you want to go on staying in the box? (**SE**)

Pt: … in this moment I only have feelings at the child and it comes to me to hug her and be close, but I am unable to …

Another step forward has been made; the patient now sees that she is powerless, even to experience and express her loving feelings. In the next intervention, the therapist will show her that, unless she takes a different position towards her Superego, she will stay paralysed regarding both types of feeling:

Th: … hugging is not enough if you cannot protect her, and that you can only do by expressing what you feel at your mother treating you that way … or you are like an accomplice to your mother! (**SE**)

Pt: … I never rebelled …

Th: … do you wish to go on this way? (**SE**)

This is a direct challenge to the patient's will to stay compliant or, instead, to disobey her Superego and take her own position. In the next line, the patient starts doing so, but her voice gets smaller (tactical defence):

Pt: (Small voice) I don't want this to happen again …
Th: … with that small voice? (**SE**)
Pt: … I go to my mum and take back my doll!
Th: … do you feel the anger?
Pt: … no …
Th: … if you can't do that you stay paralysed, you are bent over on yourself instead of putting out what you feel …

The patient is gradually changing her position, but the therapist notices that her body language is now carrying the Superego part. She is actually bent over herself, is weepy, and has a lot of tension in her shoulders and whole body. In EDT, there is a belief that the process of deep change requires emotional experiencing and expression of hitherto defended-against feeling and impulse. This is why the therapist needs to help the patient call upon her whole being if she wants to experience the whole of her emotion.

Pt: … I want to tell her to let me be …
Th: … look at your shoulders, they are all tense! (**SE**)
Pt: … what did I do! Let me do what I want!
Th: … weeping that way? You are all tense and cannot let out your rage this way … and you've had it for forty years and it doesn't fade away, even if you ignore it! Do you feel ashamed? (**SE**)
Pt: (Cries in anguish) Yes, if I think of me being angry I feel shame and I am afraid of changing the relationship with my mother!

It is worth noticing that the patient is absolutely aware of what is happening in herself, as well as with the therapist, namely, that experiencing her deep feeling and impulse will make them conscious, and change her perception of the relationship with her mother. The therapist gets a fix on the therapeutic boat:

Th: … so there are these feelings … so what do you want to tell your mother if you don't paralyse yourself? Because the moment I ask you this, your right arm and shoulder get stiff, you bend your head and get all tense. Do you wish to go on this way or to say what you feel? (**SE**)
Pt: … rather than feeling, I have images … at any rate, my mother …

Visualisation of relevant images can indeed help focus on a specific moment and get closer to the related feelings, but that phrase "… at any rate, my mother …" will most probably displace the attention onto the mother, introducing some rational thought and distancing the patient from her feeling part. Hence the therapist's interruptions:

Th: (Interrupting) No, YOU, what do YOU imagine? (**SE**)
Pt: … I see my mother very nervous, tough, stiff …
Th: … cold?

Pt: … yes, which is contradictory, because …

Th: (Interrupting the rationalisation) You reason instead of feeling: what do you feel at your mother being cold to you? Unless you wish to spend all your life feeling ashamed. What do you want to say or do, if you wish to get out of this "good-girl cage"? (**SE**)

Pt: … it comes to me to very childishly say that she is wicked (starts sobbing)

Th: … and what is the feeling?

Pt: … I feel guilt for having said so (hides behind handkerchief and fist)

Th: … the moment you say "wicked" you hide behind your hanky; if you stop punching your nose, what do you feel? (**SE**)

Pt: … you don't!

Th: … so, what is the image of you telling her this? Now or when you were small?

Pt: … small …

Th: … how small?

Pt: … five or six …

Th: … where?

Pt: … in the sitting room …

Th: … so it is you and your mother?

Pt: … no, my mother is not there. I am in the sitting room, standing …

Th: … what do you feel or do?

Pt: … just thinking she is wicked and doesn't give me any attention (patient is sobbing) … she is always in haste …

Th: … doesn't give you time, attention, and presence … (**SE**) and what do you feel about this, if you give yourself a chance of feeling your feeling?

Pt: … I am just disappointed …

Th: … this way you become passive and put yourself in a resigned position and you neglect yourself … if you now want to give yourself the attention your mother did not give you and give yourself the chance of feeling what's there, you can make it … unless you wish to stay passive and resigned … (**SE**)

Pt: … the image faded away …

The Superego has not yet given up, and now the patient has a sense of "losing touch" with her images and feeling. The therapist has to get her back on track by reminding her of her habitual character defence:

Th: … so you decide to go on being the "good girl" even if this makes you unhappy … (**SE**)

Pt: (Sighs) I am trying to …

Th: … you are trying to hide behind your hand … if you think of your mother who is cold, what do you feel, if you don't wish to go on with your useless suffering? Is this what you want to be? Forever paralysed by this feeling! Do you see you are hiding from me? (**SE**)

Pt: … I can't!

The patient needs some additional strength from the therapist:

Th: … do you feel that you hate her? Do you want to let it come? It's your feeling! What is the way you feel it physically? If you want to get out of the box … like when you get stiff … it's all box ... where do you feel it in your body? If you don't paralyse and hide ... where is it? If you don't put this fist here ... (**SE**)

Pt: ... it comes and goes ...

Th: ... do you still feel squeezed there? (**SE**)

Pt: ... no, I have two images ... of her now as a sweet old lady, and her young and strong and that is worse ...

Th: ... Felicia, do you want this tooth pulled out? (**SE**)

Pt: ... I'd like to ...

Th: ... there is no censure here, shall we get here? You don't like her because she is cold, never has time for you, doesn't give you any attention and neglects you. What do you want to do to her if you are honest and don't hide, and want to put it off your chest and not be a larva, if you don't stifle yourself ... (**SE**)

Pt: ... once she cursed me ...

Th: ... she said what exactly?

Pt: ... "Go to hell", and I told her: "You go! She slapped me ... there I imagine myself ...

Th: ... ok, you are strong ... you think of yourself doing what? (**SE**)

Now the therapist is sustaining the patient, who is trying to complete her change of position and turn against her paralysing Superego.

Pt: (Laughing) ... me giving back, beating her up!

Th: ... if you don't laugh, let's see how you beat her. You are strong if you don't paralyse. You have a fist there ... (**SE**)

Pt: ... no, I want to slap her!

Th: ... right or left [hand]? (**SE**)

Pt: ... right!

Th: ... where? (**SE**)

Pt: ... on her head!

Th: ... only once? (**SE**)

Pt: ... no ...

Th: ... how many?

Pt: ... I give another (laughs).

Th: (Referring to the laughter) See how painful it is for you? The second time, again with your right hand? (**SE**)

Pt: ... yes ...

Th: ... both strong, then what happens? (**SE**)

Pt: ... then one with the left ...

Th: ... your mother keeps standing up? (**SE**)

Pt: ... yes she does and tries to shelter from me ...

Th: ... and you? (**SE**)

Pt: ... I keep on slapping her!

Th: ... you give many, with both hands? (**SE**)

Pt: ... yes ...

Th: ... so you go on with both hands until ...? (**SE**)

Pt: (Sobbing) She starts sobbing!
Th: ... and what do you do? (**SE**)
Pt: ... I start sobbing too ... she was always capable of giving me guilt ...
Th: ... so you feel like saying something to her ...? (**SE**)
Pt: ... but tell her "Enough, I won't let you do it ever again!"
Th: ... you won't? (**SE**)
Pt: ... you don't tell me how I have to behave, don't get into my life, don't tell me what I am supposed to like or not like!
Th: (Lending words) "You stop trying to make me be the way you want." And what do you feel when you say so? (**SE**)
Pt: ... bitterness ...
Th: ... where?

The therapist wants to make sure that the patient is fully in touch with her feeling, but she is not. Her bodily experience shows that there is still some inhibitory force in operation:

Pt: ... chest ...
Th: ... you let yourself be squeezed still ... then there is more you need to express ... (**SE**)
Pt: ... I told her what I felt!
Th: ... did you really manage? (**SE**)
Pt: ... something is missing, I feel partly relieved ...
Th: ... so we will have to go on facing this ... (**SE**)

The session is coming to a close and it is important to acknowledge exactly how far the therapist and patient have come in the process of dealing with the Superego and establishing the supremacy of the Self. This is part of the overall change process and will continue in the subsequent sessions and throughout the therapy.

Two additional EDT constituents, yet to be illustrated, also relate closely to the change process and accompany it throughout the therapy: (i) connecting the corners of the Triangle of Others, and (ii) restructuring of inner representations of Self and Others.

The actual process of therapeutic change: connecting the corners of the Triangle of Others (TCP) and restructuring the inner representations of Self and Others (SO)

As the reader is by now well aware, therapeutic change may only come as the result of a number of complex and interrelated factors. Each of those already described above—personal relationship and a real connection, history and perspective, mirroring, Superego work, and the experiential-dynamic activities—can play a crucial role in facilitating change. The ways in which a therapist can attend to the patient's actual change and help it happen will now be described.

A change that is felt to be good-enough, by both therapist and patient, is what the patient—knowingly or partly unconsciously—came for in the first place and, consequently, it is a necessary condition for the therapeutic relationship to come to a happy conclusion. Even though the ultimate evaluation of a constructive and lasting therapeutic change can only be determined through after-termination follow-up, even before therapy ends we wish that patients not only *understand* the origins of their suffering, but are also in a position to make a good-enough use of themselves in facing life. According to EDT theory and in-depth process and outcome studies on the *quality* of therapeutic change (Malan & Coughlin Della Selva, 2007; Malan & Osimo, 1992), in addition to cognitive understanding, successful outcome is actualised in relation to experience and expression of emotion, self-awareness, character change, and improvements in interpersonal relationships and functioning. In particular, the individual can now experience intense emotion and impulse (X) without giving rise to symptoms (D) and/or unbearable anxiety (A), that is, they can now *feel and express what they feel*. In addition, they have become aware of their maladaptive character patterns, maintained by self-sabotaging Superego forces, and achieved the motivation and power of changing their character in order to improve their interpersonal relationship and adaptation to life. The three indicators of successful outcome are therefore: (i) a good-enough dynamic understanding, (ii) a different and more favourable balance of the three corners of the Triangle of Conflict, and (iii) a change in the representation of Self and Others, positively affecting the actual interpersonal relationships. In technical terms, this amounts to offering patients T-C-P interventions (TCP), that is, making dynamic links between feelings and behaviour patterns experienced and performed with the therapist (T), in current relationships (C), and in past relationships (P). The therapist will further assist the patient to bring their new cognitive and emotional mastery to fruition in their real relationships with their significant Others. This is referred to as Self- and Other-restructuring (McCullough Vaillant, 1997; McCullough et al., 2003). Realising the impact of their inner mechanisms on the quality of their lives, and the power they have to change things, will complete and stabilise the process of change. Before moving to a clinical example of TCP and SO, a short digression on the specific role of TCP in EDT will clarify an important difference between EDT and all previous forms of psychodynamic therapy.

An annotation on change process in EDT

As described in my earlier (Chapter 1, pp. 4; 9–14), EDT historically originates from brief psychotherapy, also called STDP in North America. STDP, in turn, stems from psychoanalysis and, more specifically, from the work of those analysts who, like Adler, Ferenczi, Rank, Reich, Alexander, and others, were more interested in the healing side, the patient's needs, than in the edification of a perfect theoretical castle. In all these pre-EDT dynamic models, including psychoanalysis, interpretations linking transference (T) with other situations in the patient's life, past or current (P and C respectively), represented the main type of intervention, aiming to access the patient's unconscious. In other words, offering a T-P, T-C, or C-P interpretation—a mostly rational, cognitive type of intervention—was meant as a lever, hopefully impacting the patient's instinctual and emotional level. We all owe respect to the founders of psychoanalysis and dynamic psychotherapy, but relying on interpretation as the main technical tool proved technically weak, especially with highly resistant and fragile patients, resulting in lengthening of treatment and unsatisfactory results. In EDT, we *first* access the level of emotional experiencing by using all the technical ingredients described above and only *then* start using TCP interventions. This basically amounts to reversing the sequence of events by moving from emotional to cognitive rather than the other way around.

Another distinctive feature of EDT is represented by the introduction of Self- and Other-restructuring interventions, coded as SO, assisting the patient in their endeavours to improve their approach to life, and relationships with their significant Others. In pre-EDT therapeutic models, the therapist's focus was mostly intrapsychic, and change in real life was regarded as more of a natural consequence of deep inner change. In EDT we are equally interested in the two sides of the coin, intrapsychic and interpersonal, moving swiftly between the two. As soon as the in-depth change process has begun, we can start right away to help the patient make good use of the new parts of the Self they can now access. As our reading colleagues will have by now come to see, the aspects of EDT just described are part of the overall attitude of an EDT therapist, who is trained to be deeply connected, emotionally attuned, and a real and significant Other in the patient's life.

Clinical example to illustrate connecting the corners of the Triangle of Others (TCP) and Self- and Other-restructuring (SO)

The Reassurance-seeking Young Woman

The patient presented with a depressive breakdown, seemingly precipitated by the threat of her relationship with her boyfriend coming to an end. During the first extended interview, trial relationship, it was possible to create a good-enough real relationship with the patient, assess symptoms accurately, explore and regulate anxiety (which turned out to follow healthy pathways, and be discharged via the striated musculature without any somatisation or other interference), start dealing with the Superego, get to the emotional experience of rage at mother, and bring into focus the character hologram (Chapter 4, pp. 107–132) of the "little ill one". The following account of session 4 aims to illustrate several aspects of the therapy. First, even though the character hologram of the needy and dependent "little ill one" had been already addressed in previous sessions, at the start of session 4, the patient again takes the dependent position. Second, the therapist refuses to take the complementary position of being reassuring and comforting and, instead, helps the patient to give up this character defence and state clearly what she wishes to work on in this session. The focus then shifts to the relational pattern with her boyfriend, which arouses the patient's feelings of rage, at which point, the therapist is able to make a meaningful CP link, connecting her rage at her boyfriend to her rage at her mother. The patient and therapist are able to address the patient's self-perception and relation with Self as the "little ill one" or, instead, as the independent woman free to follow her deep feeling. Finally, the patient and therapist address the patient's perception of, and relation with, Other (therapist, boyfriend, mother = TCP) as a projection of the patient's Superego, that is, as protecting, reassuring, but deeply angering Others or, alternatively, as individuals with whom the patient can deal in a specific, personal, and meaningful way.

The patient opens the session talking about her current cold and linking it with the asthma that she suffered from as a child. The therapist listens for a minute or two and then, meaningfully, says:

Th: So, with your cold we are done … I mean …
Pt: (Laughs, showing she understood the indirect reference to her character defence)
Th: Let's see what you'd like to look at, unless you still need to play the little ill girl in order to find reassurance …
Pt: no, no, not this time … I am here present (patient sits up, conveying her wish to be an active participant in the session)
Th: You wish to be here … and now you even sat up, very well … so you did want to come …
Pt: It is something I want to do … so, even if it's not the same as when I want to go to the movies …
Th: … if it was the same, that would be really serious! So you actually wanted to come here today, or just out of duty?
Pt: There is that too, but I really want …
Th: Then let's see what you want to face, take in your hands and solve today, or anyway improve …
Pt: (After a short silence while trying to get focused) I would like to become a bit more independent … I mean, thinking it all through, I realised that my emotional life depends a lot on what happens around me … and if I were to find myself alone without Steve … and this dependence on external factors …

The therapist, by pointing out the tactical defence of superficiality, helps the patient to focus on the actual relationship, thus making a SO intervention:

Th: Is Steve an "external factor"? (**SO**)
Pt: Well, in a way, yes, since I cannot base my feeling well on being with someone … I'm telling you this because, even with Steve, at times I do not understand how genuine is my love for him or, instead, I am scared to end up alone without him … but not out of my being in love, rather as a sort of dependence … so, this thing I don't like and I'd like to decrease it …

The therapist again points out the tactical defence of *not fully committing* by saying:

Th: Excellent, so you'd like to decrease it …?
Pt: This dependence …?
Th: Yes … or you wish to take it away?
Pt: At times I say "take it away" (gets instantly sad and starts crying, an example of the powerful effect of neutralising the tactical defence) … with this person I have a very weird relationship: he is the one with whom I get most enraged … at times I feel as though my face goes maroon and I feel like hitting him (shows how, accompanying with sound of slapping Steve's face repeatedly)
Th: So, there is a clear connection between being the needy-and-dependent and this rage underneath …

After establishing the link between character hologram and the feeling of rage, the therapist helps the patient to focus on the actual triggers of this rage. The patient describes herself as emotionally transparent, honestly admitting her faults. Steve, on the contrary, would always take the position of he who is *in the right*, having been brought up in the *right* way within the *right* family ... the patient perceives him as being cold, detached, bossy, judgemental, and blaming, putting all the fault on her and accusing her of "spoiling everything". The patient's description of Steve's attitude fits in with some aspects of the patient's mother and, also, of her self-blaming and bossy Superego. The patient had discovered that Steve, having some informatics expertise, had been spying on her computer and personal mail for six months, without letting her know. This, based on previous material, is giving the therapist a silver-plated opportunity to make a major CP link between Steve and the patient's mother:

Th: ... the other time we saw he is a bit detached, a bit cold ... which is reminiscent of your mother ... and now this thing of spying on your computer reminds us of your mother's similar habit of reading your teenager diary without ever saying anything ... (TCP)

The patient promptly acknowledges and accepts this CP link. There is an obvious advantage in offering this type of link while the patient is emotionally aroused, which makes the connection self-evident to her. So, we know *what* the patient defends herself against (**X** = rage at mother, Steve), *how* she does that (**D** = taking the needy, dependent position), and *why* she does so (**A** = fear of her own rage + losing Other's affection). How can we now actually help the patient to use her new knowledge in order to facilitate change? By identifying and marking out the exact trigger of her Self-sabotaging moves. In so doing, we help the patient see that she has the power to decide to respond to the same trigger in a different and more adaptive way. To this purpose the therapist recapitulates as follows:

Th: So, what takes place is that some aspects of Steve, like being cold, detached, controlled, manipulating, and blaming it all on you, do actually infuriate you ... but, in spite of this, you depend on them ... (**SO**)

Pt: Yes.

Th: So, instead of drawing the correct conclusion and taking away the dependent attitude, what happens is that you stay in a relationship with someone like Steve and, moreover, you play the dependent-and-needy-one. (**SO**)

Pt: Yes and, as a matter of fact, this is something I myself don't understand ...

The patient is now understandably puzzled at her own behaviour, as this behaviour is based on a distorted image of the Other (Steve). Is Steve a nice, understanding, loving man, or the opposite of all this?

Pt: At some point I told him I needed him to be closer to me ... he used to send me tons of text messages ... the moment I had an evident breakdown, he really withdrew. Now that I am better, he got back to be close ... the moment he sees me a bit more fragile, shit he's gone ...

The "Other" described by the patient is thus unreliable, self-centred, rejecting. hence clearly unsatisfactory. What is the complementary "Self" the patient puts into this type of interaction? This is what the next therapist intervention aims to discover:

Th: It's often easier to see what the Other does than what we ourselves do ... you described how unbearable it is for you when Steve puts all the blame and the negative on you and manages to be judgemental, nonchalantly keeping a stiff upper lip, which gets on your nerves ... It seems to me, though, that when you play the needy-and-dependent you also become indirect and, instead of expressing your rage, you put up with coldness, distance, manipulation, and all the rest that you described ... so, talking of you ... (**SO**)

The words "talking of you" stress the patient's distorted perception of her own Self in this pathological interaction; at the end of the day she is as indirect and hiding her deep feeling as is Steve. The therapist continues:

Th: ... there are some aspects, probably those triggering your rage, that also trigger your compliance, dependence and weepy-neediness, that is what you most need to change! This is your problem. (**SO**)

Pt: When he lets me down I freak out and start wrapping it up and telling myself that I want to stay with him ...

Th: So, why have you been staying with him until now? (**SO**)

Pt: Because I paradoxically feel safe with him. The truth is that as long as we keep superficial I feel well with him, not if we go deeper.

This is a crucial realisation by the patient. The therapist can now accurately keep the focus on the actual trigger of the patient's maladaptive behaviour:

Th: Then Steve's behaviour, in spite of being cold and uncaring, is felt by you as a balm, a warm and reassuring presence ... (**SO**)

Pt: Yes, I absurdly feel safe with him, and keep telling myself that a perfect man doesn't exist ...

Now the patient is seeing the paradox. Moreover, she is seeing her defence of rationalisation. The therapist keeps the focus on the defensive attitude in the relationship with Steve and recapitulates:

Th: He really pushes the right button and the L.E.D. "good and affectionate" lights up in you but, at a deeper level, you don't feel good resonance and attunement. Giving up this belief, however, feels like a catastrophe, so you become dependent and weepy, instead of talking your mind and heart ... (**SO**)

Pt: Yes, this is exactly the way it happens ... when I realise he gets distant, I really freak out ... but this is not what I want ... I believe I am trying to persuade myself I want to be with him to keep myself quiet ...

While saying so, the patient is emotionally activated, present, in touch with the therapist and with herself. This is what gives her realisation the power to facilitate change. The therapist just empathically says:

Th: I'm starting to believe the same myself … (**SO**)

Pt: With my former boyfriends I always managed to separate … with Steve, I believe I really idealised him … I "decided" he is good and just and I am sort of aspiring to be as good and just as him … because when I had my breakdown I wanted to do all the things that he did … for example I never was a religious fundamentalist and I made an effort to accept all what he believed … also because he blamed my jumpiness on not having been given rigid enough rules and good enough values in my upbringing …

Th: So the only good rules and values are his … (**SO**)

Pt: Yes, I always sensed this aspect of his, but the actual realisation came only as a result of my breakdown. It came as a surprise, something I didn't expect …

These last communications by the patient are an excellent description of various defence mechanisms she is now seeing clearly while being in the middle of her change process. In particular, she can now correct her formerly distorted vision of Steve; she has acknowledged that she *projects* idealised parts of herself onto Steve; she further acknowledged her own desperate attempt to "be like him", thus using *projective identification* in order to deny conflict, and describes her *sense of surprise*—her realisation came as something new, like a newborn part of herself. Finally, she also realised that giving birth, that is to say, emotionally experiencing this—formerly repressed—part of herself involved suffering ("only as a result of my breakdown"), that is now being healed by therapeutic work. The patient goes on:

Pt: … so I still don't know if I am disbelieving when I realise Steve is deeply different from how I thought he was, or if I just wish a safe and easy life and what Steve brings is simple and effective … since I actually never was dependent on someone as I am with Steve … really never … perhaps except with my parents when I was a little girl … when I was ten and I had to be two weeks away from my parents and it felt like … the end of the world … it is the same feeling of the most devastating thing … and he always takes the martyr position with me, sort of "Poor Steve, how can he bear with someone like me, so angry and demanding …" (**TCP**)

Wow! Here the patient made a spontaneous CP connection by linking Steve with her parents—based on previous material, mainly her mother—when she was ten years old. This is an example of the close connection between the perception of Self and Other, interpersonal patterns, and dynamic links. Moreover, it shows that correcting the perception of Self and Other (SO) can bring new dynamic insight (TCP). Finally, the combination of the two, the experiential and dynamic levels, fuels the patient's motivation to change. As it appears from the following dialogue, at the close of the session, the patient is growing more and more eager to accelerate her change process. The image of Steve as a martyr is making her indignant and she now wants no further delay when she asks the therapist:

Pt: So, what is your advice for me now?
Th: I encourage you to focus on when it comes to you to play the needy, dependent, weepy and ill with Steve … (**SO**)
Pt: (Patient nods)
Th: … and see if this is, by any chance, happening because you are really angry about something that is really important for you … (**SO**)
Pt: (Patient is totally attentive to what the therapist is conveying to her)
Th: … and if, by any chance, you can manage to sit up as you did with me (now the link is also with T) and say whatever you have to say! (**SO, TCP**)
Pt: (Patient smiles)
Th: … fearlessly … (**SO, TCP**)
Pt: So when I'd start getting weepy I'd better say what I feel …?
Th: Yes! Well, you may or may not say … but you certainly need to focus on what you really wish and how come this is so frightening and if you really need all that fear or can do without! (**SO**)

The session is over and the patient gets up from her chair uttering:

Pt: What the hell!

TCP and SO interventions like the ones described in this session with the "Reassurance-seeking Young Woman" specifically aim to facilitate and sustain new dynamic insight and character change, by helping patients to apply their new potential in real life. TCP and SO interventions are used throughout therapy but tend to be more frequent in the change phases.

Concluding remarks

The EDT codes exemplified in this chapter are also included in the clinical chapters that follow, within the associated transcript and/or annotation. However, within the complexity of clinical dialogue—verbal and non-verbal—different types of intervention do at times mix and overlap. The coding and annotation is therefore not meant to be exhaustive but rather to help identify the main specific components of therapeutic dialogue, the prevailing sense of each intervention, its immediate impact, and subsequent therapeutic effect. Just as for any other therapeutic approach, the saying, "the proof is in the pudding" applies to IE-DP. So, for those who wish to learn *how* to make EDT successful from the beginning, the list of ingredients, together with guidance as to when and how to combine and mix them together, is an important guideline as to how to conduct the whole therapeutic process, from the first extended interview to the last session.

References

Abbass, A. & Bechard, D. A. (2007). Bringing character changes with Davanloo's intensive short-term dynamic psychotherapy. *Ad Hoc Bulletin of Short-Term Dynamic Psychotherapy: Practice and Theory, 11*: 26–40.

Alexander, F. & French, T. M. (1946). *Psychoanalytic Therapy, Principles and Application*. New York: Ronald Press [reprinted New York: John Wiley & Sons, 1974].

American Psychiatric Association (1994). *Diagnostic and Statistical Manual of Mental Health Disorders (4th ed.)*. Washington, DC: American Psychiatric Association.

Bowlby, J. (1982). *Attachment and Loss: Vol 1. Attachment* (2nd *ed.)*. New York: Basic.

Coughlin Della Selva, P. (1996). *Intensive Short-Term Dynamic Psychotherapy. Theory and Technique*. Chichester, UK: John Wiley & Sons.

Darwin, C. (1872). *The Expression of the Emotions in Man and Animals*. London: HarperCollins, 1998.

Davanloo, H. (1986a). Intensive short-term dynamic psychotherapy with highly resistant patients. Part I. Handling resistance. *International Journal of Short-Term Psychotherapy, 1*: 107–133.

Davanloo, H. (1986b). Intensive short-term dynamic psychotherapy with highly resistant patients. II. The course of an interview after the initial breakthrough. *International Journal of Short-Term Psychotherapy, 1*: 239–255.

Davanloo, H. (1990). *Unlocking the Unconscious*. Toronto: John Wiley & Sons.

Davanloo, H. (1995). *Intensive Short-Term Dynamic Psychotherapy: Selected Papers of Habib Davanloo, MD*. Chichester, UK: John Wiley & Sons.

Fosha, D. (2000). *The Transforming Power of Affect*. New York: Basic.

Freud, A. (1936). *Ego and the Mechanisms of Defense* (The Writings of Anna Freud, Vol 2). New York: International Universities Press.

Freud, S. (1923b). *The Ego and the Id. S. E., 9*. London: Hogarth, pp. 12–59.

Freud, S. (1924c). The economic problem of masochism. *S. E., 19*. London: Hogarth, pp. 157–170.

Freud, S. (1926d). Inhibition, symptoms and anxiety. *S. E., 20*. London: Hogarth, pp. 77–174.

ten Have-de Labije, J. (2006). When patients enter with anxiety on the forefront. *Ad Hoc Bulletin of Short-Term Dynamic Psychotherapy: Practice and Theory, 10*: 35–69.

ten Have-de Labije, J. (2008). She only wanted some understanding: Separating ego and superego parts with an extremely anxious woman. *Ad Hoc Bulletin of Short-Term Dynamic Psychotherapy: Practice and Theory, 12*: 40–80.

ten Have-de Labije, J. (2009). Helping our patients to experience feelings: Understanding the role of defences in emotion regulation and the implications for ISTDP practitioners. *Ad Hoc Bulletin of Short-Term Dynamic Psychotherapy: Practice and Theory, 13*: 15–23.

Iacoboni, M. (2008). *Mirroring People: the Science of Empathy and How We Connect with Others*. New York: Farrar, Straus and Giroux.

Kalpin, A. (2001). Murder, guilt, and the rapid alleviation of superego imprisonment. Proceedings of the 1st IEDTA Conference, Milan. *Quaderni di Psichiatria Pratica, VII, special issue*: 48–53.

Klein, M. (1984). *Love, Guilt and Reparation: and Other Works 1921–1945*. London: Hogarth.

Malan, D. H. (1981–2012). Personal communications.

Malan, D. H. & Coughlin Della Selva, P. (2007). *Lives Transformed: a Revolutionary Method of Dynamic Psychotherapy*. London: Karnac.

Malan, D. H. & Osimo, F. (1992). *Psychodynamics, Training, and Outcome in Brief Psychotherapy*. Oxford: Butterworth-Heinemann.

McCullough, L., Kuhn, N., Andrews, S., Kaplan, A., Wolf, J. & Lanza-Hurley, C. (2003). *Treating Affect Phobia: A Manual for Short-Term Dynamic Psychotherapy*. New York: Guilford.

McCullough Vaillant, L. (1997). *Changing character, Short Term Anxiety-Regulating Psychotherapy for Restructuring Defenses, Affects and Attachment*. New York: Basic.

Osimo, F. (2001). *Parole, Emozioni e Videotape: Manuale di Psicoterapia Breve Dinamico-Esperienziale (PBDE)*. Milan: Franco Angeli.

Osimo, F. (2002). Brief psychodynamic therapy. In: J. J. Magnavita (Ed.), *Psychodynamic and Object Relations Psychotherapies*, Vol 1 in *Comprehensive Handbook of Psychotherapy*. New York: John Wiley & Sons.

Osimo, F. (2003a). *Experiential Short-Term Dynamic Psychotherapy, a Manual*. Bloomington, IN: AuthorHouse.

Osimo, F. (2009). The character hologram. *Ad Hoc Bulletin of Short-Term Dynamic Psychotherapy, 13*: 25–50.

Reich, W. (1933). Charakteranalyse: Technik und Grundlagen. Vienna: Zelbstverlag. [First English translation by Mary Boyd (1945) *Character Analysis*, reprinted New York: Noonday Press, 1998.]

Rizzolatti, G. & Craighero, L. (2004). The mirror-neuron system. *Annual Review of Neuroscience, 27*: 169–192.

Siegel, D. (2010). *The Mindful Therapist: a Clinician's Guide to Mindsight and Neural Integration*. New York: W. W. Norton.

Soldz, S. & Vaillant, G. E. (1999). The big five personality traits and the life course: a 45-year longitudinal study. *Journal of Research in Personality, 33*: 208–232.

Vaillant, G. E. (1977). *Adaptation to life*. Boston: Little, Brown.

Vaillant, G. E. (1993). *The Wisdom of the Ego*. Cambridge, MA: Harvard University Press.

Note

1. Some patients suffer from disturbance or deficits in their receptive capacity towards others (McCullough, Kuhn, Andrews, Kaplan, Wolf & Lanza Hurley, 2003) and intervention may be required to help the patient adapt to "successive degrees of relatedness" (p. 275) and to build a real relationship.

CHAPTER FOUR

Intensive Experiential-Dynamic Psychotherapy and application of the character hologram

Ferruccio Osimo

Intensive Experiential-Dynamic Psychotherapy (IE-DP) is one of the experiential dynamic therapies (EDTs) stemming from Davanloo's Intensive Short-Term Dynamic Psychotherapy (ISTDP). All the EDT approaches emphasise accessing the patient's unconscious in order to bring about the conscious experiencing and working through of their painful feelings. These models involve the creation of a genuine and compassionate relationship between therapist and patient, within which deep feelings and impulses can be freely experienced, intimate thoughts are shared, and new revealing insights are achieved. IE-DP holds the personal relationship between therapist and patient and the physical experience of conflicting emotions as the basis of therapeutic change. A few crucial aspects of IE-DP are described in an earlier chapter (see pp. 44–45), and herein, one of them, the character hologram, is introduced and specifically addressed in greater detail.[1] For a more thorough theoretical and clinical description of IE-DP, the reader is referred to Osimo (2002, 2003).

The essence and ingredients of IE-DP

IE-DP aims to bring about a good-enough emotional experience and holding relationship within which all emotions can be experienced safely. This is achieved by staying focused on the body and the emotional experience in ways that are tailored to every single patient because they arise from that specific therapeutic relationship. In this way, even the most primitive impulses and feelings can be thoroughly activated and effectively worked through, without forcing the therapeutic relationship through a fixed sequence of steps, like, for example, always helping the patient to make a mental image of their murderous sadistic rage and the burial of their victims. A preordained sequence of therapeutic moves is not regarded by IE-DP as healing—and therefore desirable—insofar as its repetition may become ritualistic and weaken the value of the real personal relationship. The real personal relationship needs to develop freely and will thus be different with different patients. This is based on the assumption that the more the interchange is naturally inspired by spontaneity, the more a relational and emotional experience is likely to carry a really transforming potential (Alexander& French, 1946; Osimo, 2003; Palvarini, 2010).

IE-DP therefore places the more personal aspects of the interchange between patient and therapist at the centre of the scene, and makes this the foundation of the clinical work, whatever the technical intervention or therapeutic activity. Paying so much attention to the personal relationship and taking good care of it makes the working alliance stronger and technical interventions more powerful. From this perspective, technical interventions of whatever kind, that aim to deal with defences, regulate anxiety, and accompany the experiencing of deep feelings, are valued by IE-DP, provided that they have roots in a good-enough relational ground. Over the years, this aspect of IE-DP has been found to be productive by a number of IE-DP trainees and therapists, who gradually came to discover that their own personality and character, when harmoniously matched to the techniques they use, are the most powerful therapeutic tools. The techniques to address defences (D), anxiety (A), and deep feeling and impulse (X) are then used according to the signals coming from the patient at any given moment, that is, according to specific patient variables. This is schematised by the Triangle of Experiential-Dynamic Activities (Figure 1) -defence restructuring (DA), anxiety regulation (AA), and emotional maieutics (XA) (Osimo, 2002, 2003).

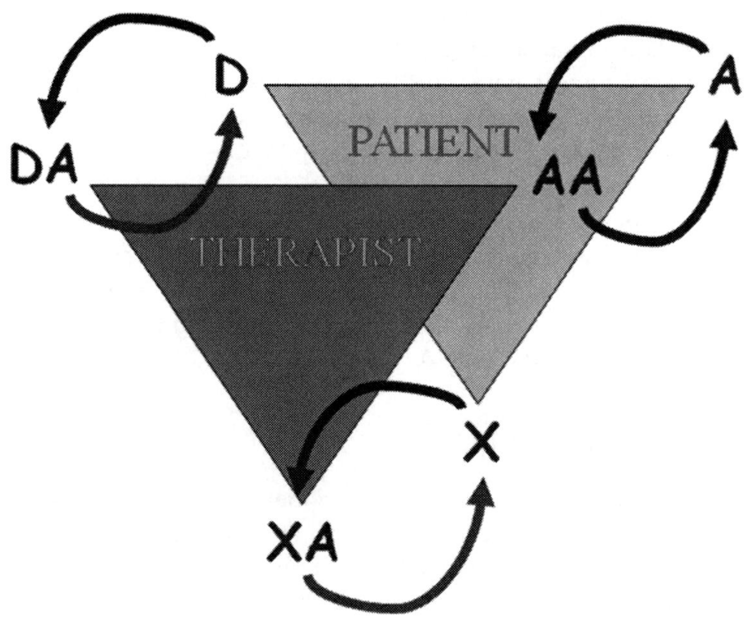

Figure 1. Triangle of Experiential-Dynamic Activites.

Another characteristic feature of IE-DP is the concept and technique of emotional maieutics. This activity addresses all that a therapist can do to pave the way to the experiencing of deep feeling, from the moment it arises, along the arch of its bodily and mental experience, through to its verbal and behavioural expression in the relationship with the therapist and in real life. This is achieved by a deep and thorough emotional connection to the Other, in a way that is somehow similar to a midwife helping a woman to give birth to a baby. It is true that deep emotion, though belonging to the individual and being part of them, is often experienced as something completely new—the same as a newborn baby—the moment it emerges from the unconscious. IE-DP therapists often present to the patient the character hologram as a way of addressing the most ingrained, self-destructive personality traits, and mobilising feeling.

The character hologram

The term hologram comes from the ancient Greek words *hòlos* = whole, and *gramma* = graphic sign, picture. It is generally used for a laser-based technology producing three-dimensional images. The idea of a *character* hologram is to produce a three-dimensional image of the character that is perceived by the patient in a bright and vivid way. Patients are more often aware of one aspect of their character but not another. For this reason, the character image needs to be whole as, otherwise, patients might go on seeing only those character aspects of which they are already aware but not, to put it this way, the other side of the moon. So, both the ego-dystonic (known to the patient) and the ego-syntonic (unseen) character traits must be encompassed in the hologram in order to be effectively conveyed to the patient. However, there is more to it than simply bringing previously unseen aspects of character to the patient's awareness. The hologram holds a unique power in that, simultaneously, it is a reflection of an individual's whole being and the way they interface with Others. It is no coincidence that the hologram is generated by the close interaction of therapist and patient. The same way a nerve ganglion connects sensory and motor information, human character connects, in mostly unconscious ways, inner life and social life. This gives it a crucial role in facilitating or hindering harmonious adaptation.

The idea of wholeness is that of a comprehensive picture and/or of a sign rendering the essence of the prevailing mental, emotional, and physical position someone takes. Patients are helped to visualise the character hologram, and actively collecting and processing all the available information accomplishes this. Technically, the therapist resorts to a frequent and indiscriminate mirroring of whatever he notices of the patient's presentation and ways of interacting in the moment. This amounts to assessing and feeding back to the patient whatever signal is coming from the patient, whether or not the therapist immediately realises its meaning and relevance in the moment he mirrors it. Mirroring will address posture, movement, facial expression, way of looking, tactical defences, pathways of anxiety, manner of speech, use of language, tone of voice, mood, degree of connection and empathy, body posture, way of dressing, social demeanour, overall attitude (diffidence, seductiveness, niceness, rudeness), slowness vs. quickness, passivity vs. activity, idiosyncrasies like tics, stereotyped movements, and involuntary jolts, even smell and, indeed, any other perceivable clue or piece of information. Proceeding in this way, the hologram's constituent elements are being put together until its whole image is clearly outlined and it wholly crystallises before the therapist's eyes.

Elements of the character hologram may come from many sources. Above all, the patient's personal history will help to throw light on repetitive behavioural patterns. The manner of speech will partly help to describe and clarify, partly tend to conceal and disguise. The degree of closeness vs. distancing with the therapist will convey the patient's general type of contact and pattern of attachment. The patient's subjective perception and representation of themselves, their Others, and of the relational patterns between the two provide first-hand data of the patient's inner images of relationships and the related fantasies, projections, and projective identifications. Moreover, they indicate to the therapist communication preferences and sensitivities of the patient. For example, the use of metaphors can be instantly illuminating to someone yet puzzle someone else. The core idea of the character hologram is to come to formulate, intuitively, the essence of the patient's position in a way that is, at the same time, highly symbolic, as a signature or an icon, and three-dimensional, thus perceivable through one's senses.

As to the way of sharing the hologram with the patient, this will depend on what form of communication feels more viable and promising with each patient. Basically the hologram can be shared using a metaphor, an image provided by the patient or delivered by the therapist, by means of a verbal description, by making reference to some famous character like an actor, a politician, a mythological, literary, or fairy tale figure, a character from a TV serial, a cultural commonplace like Santa Claus, a social figure like the beggar, the boss, the nurse. In contrast to Jung's (1964) archetypal images (see Chapter 1, pp. 5–6), the character hologram is constructed by the therapist through observation and interaction with the individual patient, rather than drawing on the parallel world of symbols. It is clearly best if the manner of sharing the character hologram arises from the interaction between therapist and patient, thus becoming a further element strengthening their dawning relationship. The technique of visualising a character hologram will be illustrated in the clinical transcript.

Case study: A Treacherous Woman

The transcript illustrates the use of the character hologram in the initial phase of IE-DP, providing an example of psychotherapy with an Axis I and II disordered patient, taken on for IE-DP in a public setting, specifically Servizio Sanitario Nazionale (Italian national health service). The therapy from session 2 through to session 26, and the clinical picture of the patient at six-month follow-up will be summarised. This young woman had narcissistic, obsessive, and avoidant personality traits. She was very successful in her job and rather perfectionist in all areas of her life. However, she showed a repetitive pattern of getting involved in treacherous relationships, in particular, being betrayed or ill-treated and, at times, in her turn, perpetrated the betrayal. The patient was totally unaware of the ways in which she brought about these outcomes, and of their defensive nature. Her impulse control was poor. This ego-syntonic character defence and behavioural pattern had been the cause of multiple losses, insofar as her relationships either lacked stability, closeness, and mutual support or were terminated bitterly and prematurely. Moreover, the patient had three consecutive miscarriages after having become pregnant with the same man. Even if her reproductive system had been widely investigated and found to be functioning perfectly, an organic aetiology of these miscarriages cannot be totally excluded. However, it is only right to suppose that, to some extent, they may have been influenced by emotional factors. What we can say is that this personal tragedy added to the sense of loss and unresolved mourning. Finally, for the last two years the patient suffered from panic attacks.

Five months before starting therapy, the patient participated in three assessment interviews, one with the therapist (FO) and two with a psychiatric resident. She was then put on a waiting list and eventually invited for a first extended interview, trial relationship (Osimo, 2002, 2003). The patient began by describing a devastating panic attack she had had two months earlier, which clearly was precipitated by finding her boyfriend with another woman. We join the interview from the beginning.

The first trial relationship interview

Th: So, some time has passed, and your situation may have changed or still be the same … (**HP**)

Pt: It's slightly improved in some respects … however in January I had a panic attack, which was the worst I ever had, and I ended up in hospital …

Th: To the casualty ward? (**HP**)

Pt: Yes, I had to call for an ambulance, because I was driving on the highway and I felt really bad, I thought it was a heart infarct, actually … because this event followed an emotional trauma … hmm, and I started feeling pretty bad, going short of breath, having accelerated heartbeat, I was unable to calm down …

Th: Were you alone? (**HP**)

Pt: I was alone in my car … I'd impulsively left the place and drove away—because I'd driven 300 kilometres to go and see my boyfriend and caught him with another woman. So, I would either kill him, which was my instinct, or …

Th: Another woman at his place, what do you mean? (**HP**)

Pt: Well, I already suspected that he was seeing someone else, but I wasn't sure …

Th: Your boyfriend wasn't expecting you? (**HP**)

Pt: No, I wished to give him a surprise … so as to see with my eyes if what I thought was true or not, and clarify things. So, I went there, pressed the buzzer, he opened the door, nothing was going on … they'd just got back home, but it was enough to understand the dynamics … nor did he deny. He actually confirmed all what I said, that is that the relationship with this woman was more than friendly. And … I took the car and drove away, because I was furious and … along the way I started feeling dizzy, and wobbly … at some point my whole body was trembling, really shaking like this, my hands became like hooks, like this … then I had pins and needles in this arm, pain at my breastbone, I realised also my other hand was becoming hooked and I couldn't open it, and I ended up calling for an ambulance because I was on the highway and feared something would happen and I would die. So they took me to the hospital, put me on a drip and gave me a lorazepam tablet to put under my tongue …

The patient gave an excellent clinical description of her symptom, a panic attack, and its medical treatment. She even correctly reported that it followed an emotional trauma that, as I have written, has a connection with the patient's self-sabotaging pattern of endlessly getting involved in treacherous situations. In a way, the patient is offering the therapist some meaningful dynamics on a silver plate. However, it is also true that her self-destructive behaviour involves keeping the other person distant and/or setting up a vicious circle of mutual ill-treatment. The therapist then, though acknowledging that what the patient is bringing is important, wishes to privilege what is happening in the here-and-now. For example, what kind of interchange is taking place between therapist and patient? What interpersonal pattern is the patient starting to enact even with the therapist? How willing (motivated) is she to become aware of her self-sabotaging behaviour, take responsibility for what she is doing, and acknowledge its disastrous consequences? Let's see how the therapist tries to put the more personal aspects of the interchange between patient and therapist at the centre of the scene:

Th: Well, we'll get back to this very shocking incident, however … I'd like to first understand with you … where we are … in what mood you are coming here, and what you would like to face … clearly we'll also talk about incidents like this but, more in general, what do you regard as something useful, important to face here with me … regarding your life? **(RE, HP)**

Pt: I would like to find a way to handle some emotions and some life situations that I can't handle, and give me tremendous pain. So, then there is my behaving impulsively, at times also in my job.

A promising beginning indeed! However, the next sentence shows that the patient uses rationalisation and projection mechanisms, as though she was not herself bringing about this type of interchange:

Pt: I cannot stand false, hypocritical people and when I come across them, I become kind of ruthless, get angry and impulsive … of course when I am involved. I would like to be false too, the same as many others with whom I work, but I don't manage … that is, I'm so transparent. Unfortunately my conscience tells me to do what is right, correct, according to certain principles that I was taught …

The patient mentioned "tremendous pain" and a therapist showing no interest in this would be uncaring. In her rationalisation, the patient said, "I am so transparent." Now, this might be a distorted self-perception, but the therapist noticed that the patient did indeed exhibit a kind of totally sincere and somewhat childlike attitude. Moreover, he also noticed a somehow childish tone in the patient's voice, and this element will be used later in the formulation of the character hologram. So, now, the therapist enquires about the tremendous pain, to which the patient responds, "It is a pain arising in the deepest part of me, in this area here," while pointing to her breastbone. Some further room is given to anxiety symptoms, which included severe lack of sleep and agitation for two months after the "incident" with her, now former, boyfriend. Having done this, the therapist wishes to call attention to the patient's main defensive pattern, by focusing on the relationship which is dawning between the two of them. In response, the patient tries to keep the therapist distant by rationalising and using tactical defences, for example, generalisation and diversion.

Pt: Bromazepam gave me some relief, but I felt a bit stunned, also in the following days … so I decided not to take it, because I generally don't want any addictions, I can't bear them … (generalisation, diversion)

Th: Nor can you bear husbands … (**DA**)

Pt: Well, I thought of this actually, but … I don't know … (leaving things vague)

Th: We'll have to see what way you will handle this with me, in terms of dependence … (**RE, DA**)

Pt: Hmm, I see that … however, since this is my first experience I'm having … with you and this psychological or psychotherapeutic approach, whatever … don't know … (leaving things vague)

Th: Let's see if we manage to learn something from the position you take with me from the beginning, since you had a number of boyfriends … (**DA, RE**)

Pt: A number … three! Three meaningful ones in thirty years! (diversion)

Th: I'd like to understand what is the position you take at the beginning, you know … even though I am not a potential boyfriend, I am still a man, another person with whom you are beginning a relationship, so I wonder what is your first approach, to put it this way … (**DA**)

Pt: You know, I also work with male doctors at the hospital, and I currently put males in two categories, those with whom I work, and I see the doctor figure, which is the way I see you, with whom I have to speak, to interact and that's it … there is no interchange of emotion, liking, affection … I see the figure, I have to interact with my colleagues in my job, and you now represent someone who in a moment of doubt can help me find a way, or understand a problem or an aspect that I am finding difficult to face.(generalisation, rationalisation, distancing)

Th: So, in a way you are stating that I am like one of the doctor colleagues with whom you have to deal with in your work, whom you plan to use for a moment, or for an aspect. (**DA**)

Pt: In this moment I see you as though I were "using" you, like my goal to feel well and find a way … some answers to doubts … I hope you will help me find a solution.(a fair description of her attempt to get what she wants while keeping the therapist distant)

Th: Yes, well, this is very general, it doesn't say what kind of use … well, this we will see. It seems to me, however, that you are keeping me very distant, when you put me in the bunch of your colleagues … (**DA**)

Pt: Well, I have to distinguish between two categories of men; those with whom I have a professional relationship, or anyway one not involving affection, friendship, love or sex. The others belong to the other group, men with whom there may be just friendship, or also sex, or a love story. And you don't belong to this category. You belong to the other; men with whom I have to interact … (further rationalisation and distancing)

Th: Here it is different then, because you do tell me about all that … (**DA**)

Pt: I know, but today we are meeting for the second time and I cannot put you in the category of people for whom I feel affection, not like being in love, but like valuing ... I don't feel I know you and I want to keep you in that category of people with whom I interact, but ... (further rationalisation and distancing)

To this moment, symptoms of panic, acting impulsively, and sleep disturbances have been explored, together with the patient's mostly ego-syntonic character defences, which have led to an inability to form a satisfactory and lasting relationship with a man. Her motivation to face her defensive behaviour was put to the test and an attempt was made to set shared objectives. The dialogue, though, became one between two people seemingly turning a deaf ear. Unless one of the two could introduce some new element, it could unproductively go on for some time. One way to get out of this type of stalemate is to formulate the character hologram and share it with the patient.

A character hologram for the Treacherous Woman

Now we will see how, after the therapist shared the character hologram with the patient, her attention, which was hitherto totally caught by her symptoms and defensive moves, became focused on the way in which her two parts, or poles of her conflict, were reflected in her overall attitude. Also we will see that this mobilised the patient's unconscious anxiety.

Th: Sure ... to sum up, looking at the position you took with me from the beginning, I notice two things: one is that you took the position of a little innocent, a kind of tiny bird who is lost, and with a voice that is rather small and timorous ... and this is one aspect. The other aspect is that, in spite of this, you have already firmly and inflexibly put me in the category of people with whom you keep distant ... category A, or B, I don't remember ... I notice these two aspects so, as it seems, on the one hand you wish or need to show parts of you that are highly ... woundable, that give you a lot of suffering. On the other hand, at the same time, you try to keep a distance of many kilometres ...

In passing, we may notice that the therapist's unconscious brought to his lips the words "of many kilometres", creating an involuntary link with the real distance the patient had driven to go and see her boyfriend on the occasion of the recent traumatic incident.

Th: ... now, if we look at it for a moment, all this is rather logical ... but clearly not resolved! It's like you are sending two opposite messages: then you'll tell me if I am totally out of track or if you agree with what I say—one of the messages is, "I am little and fragile, I am suffering badly, please help me, because I can't take more of this." The other message is, "I have a fear of you which is ... smashing! So I cannot afford to really be in a relationship with you." The resulting message then is, "I find myself in an impossible situation ... because I am totally puzzled regarding coming close or keeping distant and I can't find any way that is viable and satisfactory." What do you think of what I said? **(MI, DA, RE)**

Up to this moment the therapist's way of conveying the hologram has relied on a mainly verbal description. However, he also used a few images and metaphors, and mentioned the "position with me" the patient took from the beginning, thus including the patient-therapist relationship. He also mentioned conflicting stances and defences, including the quality of the patient's voice and her overall posture. In so doing, he referred to a few things the patient herself had said, adding other elements from his own elaboration. The conflicting nature of all these messages was highlighted in an empathic way. Finally the therapist showed his interest in the patient's opinion -also in her deep response, of course. Let's see what the patient said.

Pt: That it happens also in life with other people. Not only with you. That is, I try to trust people … in general … both in the relationships with men, boyfriends or whatever …, but manage up to a point … then I never let myself go completely. In your specific case … this aspect of the little girl … is something I'd never thought of. I see more of myself in the other aspect …

As is immediately clear in the video, but here we can only describe in words, at this point the patient has changed her attitude completely; now, there is no trace of resistance in her remarks. She acknowledged what the therapist said as true and eventually agreed to look at the relationship with the therapist ("In your specific case …"). Her therapeutic alliance has suddenly strengthened and she is ready to accept also the parts of the hologram of which she was not aware ("this aspect … is something I'd never thought of"). The therapist then makes a further effort to find ways to convey this hidden aspect even more convincingly, partly even mimicking the patient's intonation and tone of voice, as he says:

Th: I noticed this voice of yours …, which seems like very hesitant, a bit like a little girl. I am just describing, I don't mean to say that you are a little girl, but it's like a small voice … like a small voice of someone saying, "May I …?", or "I wish I could …". This type of attitude, you see, of the kind, "Don't do me harm". I don't know, something like that. (**MI, DA**)

Now, the patient is making an effort to take in—rather than to keep out—what the therapist is saying. Her changed attitude is evident from the way she speaks and, even more meaningfully, from an involuntary contraction in her whole trunk, an indirect confirmation that something deep was hit and intense unconscious anxiety was mobilised. From now until the end of the trial relationship, there will be full co-operation of patient and therapist, and their joint efforts will bring about an activation of deep feeling and highlight the main dynamics. The following dialogue ends this vignette from the trial relationship:

Pt: Yes, yes … no, I got it …
Th: You jolted? (**MI**)
Pt: When?
Th: Now. (**HP, MI**)
Pt: No, I mean …

Th: Your shoulders ... (**MI**)
Pt: Jolted in what way?
Th: A contraction. (**MI**)
Pt: Ah, I didn't realise ... no, this made me think of something ...

Implications of the character hologram

The patient is now more open and receptive. She spontaneously starts talking of her pattern of relationship with boyfriends. By now, the therapist knows that the patient is superficially self-assured but, deep down, very doubtful of being loved. He can now spell out to the patient the deep sense of being neglected that she conveyed to him, and which is clearly connected to the issue of betrayal—actually neglect is a form of betrayal. The following excerpt is taken from later in the first trial relationship interview.

Th: This realising to be neglected ... (**MI**)
Pt: Neglected?
Th: I believe you are afraid that others couldn't care less about you, umm ... deep down ... (**SO**)
Pt: That I'm afraid to go unnoticed?
Th: No, no, what I mean is that it seems to me that there is a type of betrayal that you feel constantly threatened by and exposed to ... and it is the betrayal of not-being-loved, it is about discovering that it is not true that someone loves you, that it was false ... This thing feels VERY present in you ... like a pain that you've ... almost always had. (**SO**)
Pt: Yes.

There are moments in which nothing is more convincing than a simple "yes" and this is one of them. The patient, on the wave of preconscious feelings and sensations mobilised by the character hologram, goes on quietly to elaborate along the lines of neglect and betrayal, with the therapist assisting her. Later in the interview, this leads to, and links with, having lived with her grandparents until the age of six. At that time, she felt loved and enjoyed life.

Th: So with your grandparents you felt good? (**HP, XA**)
Pt: Yes, yes ...
Th: Are they still alive? (**HP**)
Pt: Yes, yes ...
Th: How are these grandparents? (**HP**)

The patient describes her grandparents as being loving and affectionate with her. To this the therapist enquires:

Th: With your parents instead, you did not feel equally well? (**HP**)
Pt: I don't know, the memories I have of my parents as a child are of sadness and suffering.
Th: You are actually becoming sad ... when this sadness comes over you, what are you thinking? What is the thought or the image that comes? (**MI, XA**)

Pt: I don't know, that I hate them.
Th: That you hate them … (**MI**)

The patient now becomes more and more sad, with tears and sobbing. At first, the impact of these deep complex feelings makes her a bit confused. However, interacting quietly with the therapist, who is maieutically helping her to stay focused on her feeling, things fall into place. In this way, hatred becomes hatred and anger anger; love is referred to as love, and betrayal as betrayal. Meanwhile, meaningful personal history is collected. She got no affection whatsoever from her father and this made her suffer. Mother was a narcissistic, self-centred woman who triggered father's physical violence by playing the victim. From the age of eight until seventeen, when the beatings took place, the patient sided with her mother, and tried to defend her by putting herself in the way between mother and father. As a result of this, father hit her as well. In the patient's words:

Pt: Yes, and I only saw the wicked ogre harming my mother … because she cried … I identified the good and the bad, OK? So I comforted her and felt very sorry, and I started hating my father, and thinking you are a real shit, I hate you! And I wished my father died … I prayed God in order for my father to die …

So, based on the patient's account, it seems that neglect and betrayal were very present in her upbringing, and some aspects of her character and personality can now be matched to some aspects of her history. During the whole process the patient is totally attentive and fully co-operating. She even spontaneously acknowledges her character armour—a signal of strong unconscious and conscious alliance with the therapist. Let's have a look at the final part of this first trial relationship extended session:

Pt: I don't talk about them often, but when I think of my childhood, if I think of them … sadness actually comes. If, instead, I talk about them as an adult woman, like from when I was seventeen, I talk the way I'm talking now, as though I took on an armour whereby they couldn't harm me, I don't know. I am not sorry I cried here, I am sorry I still suffer for all this, and I do not understand why … I'd like to spot … an event for which …
Th: Well, there have been a number of events, however, something that seems to have come into focus, in this last part of our session, is this figure of your mother as a treacherous, deceiving person … (**TCP**)
Pt: It is true, that is, I'd never thought in those terms, but now that you say this word, what comes to me is, yes it is true … my mother taught me, taught us … to lie.
Th: Listen, as I said, in a few moments we have to stop. It seems to me that this initial phase of getting an overall picture and of planning the work ahead of us is not over. We've seen some aspects but we need to look at others too, this is my feeling. How was your experience here? (**HP, RE**)
Pt: Better … talking with you, you mean?
Th: Better than what? (**HP**)
Pt: I feel more relaxed now.

Th: Ah, better than before … (**HP**)

Pt: Yes, better than the first time [initial assessment] and better than at the beginning of this conversation.

Th: Do you think this way of working together as we did today makes sense to you? (**HP**)

Pt: Today you made me think of a few things that I never ever thought of in my life. This idea of my mother and the betrayal … I mean, honestly I unconsciously felt it must be connected to my mother, because I am still very resentful and angry, as though I wanted to rub her away from my life, but I didn't manage to make the link with betrayal, which is something very ingrained as a thought, in my job, in my affects. And unfortunately in my life I betrayed too, I was betrayed, but betrayed too …

The second trial relationship interview

The therapist opens the second extended interview, with a general question aiming to re-establish contact and explore the patient's response to the first trial relationship session. In response, the patient brings a mixture of anxiety, defences, and feeling. The dialogue that follows is an example of the way IE-DP works; taking care of the relationship and using the Triangle of Experiential-Dynamic Activities as a guide. In short, the exploration and regulation of anxiety, working around defences, and staying connected with the patient to facilitate the experiencing and expression of emotions and impulses. Based on the Triangle of Experiential-Dynamic Activities, the therapist constantly monitors which corner of the Triangle of Conflict (Ezriel, 1952; Malan, 1963) is at the forefront and resorts to the corresponding intervention.

Th: Did you think of anything? (**HP**)

Pt: Yes, yes, I thought a lot of that thing about my mother … what you raised regarding betrayal, because it was something I'd never ever thought. I could not understand why my mother, since I was fifteen … was so annoying for me. This made me think a lot, and as I walked out of here I had a strange image of myself … because I went to a beauty spa with a friend of mine, and she told me that I was really … a bit weird, very reflective, thoughtful, also sad in my look …

Th: And what was the way you felt? (**XA**)

Pt: I felt tired, emptied, but not of content … as though I had surfaced something that … I didn't know …

Th: And this made you feel slightly weird? (**AA**)

Pt: No … like having grown more frustrated at my mother …

Th: So, it's better to look at this anger isn't it? … (therapist's tone of voice is determined, the word "anger" is spelt out) (**DA**)

Pt: How do we look at it? (helplessness)

Th: You say you have it even now … (**XA**)

Pt: Yes, but when I am so angry, I don't manage to let it out … anger at times gives me agitation, I speak or scream … at times … (helplessness and description of anxiety discharge)

Th: When you scream and get agitated you are very tense and burst out, but that is not really anger … maybe there is anger underneath, but the fact of screaming and getting agitated is different … (distinguishing between anger, anxiety and helplessness) … shall we look at how it is in yourself what you call "anger"? When you say you are angry, even now when you think of certain things with respect to your mother … (**AA, XA**)

Pt: I'd actually like to put her sitting there and tell her … something nasty.

Th: This thing that you are feeling, to start with, where are you feeling it? When you say you are angry … (dismissing generalisation + attention called to physical experience of her anxiety and feeling, by asking where) (**DA, AA**)

Pt: It originates from my stomach, something like a punch … propagates till the neck, and there it gets stuck (anxiety)

Th: What do you feel exactly in your stomach, physically? (**AA**)

Pt: I imagine something like moving, a tangle of … like something twisting …

Th: Twisting in your stomach and … (**AA**)

Pt: 'til my throat, and gives me a knot in my throat, the same as when I get an anxiety attack.

Th: This twisting in your stomach … besides the twisting is there any sensation, like is it annoying, painful or what? (**AA, XA**)

Pt: Not painful, but annoying yes …

Th: And at the same time this sense of something twisting inside, however … there is a lot in-between stomach and throat … how is the physical sensation throughout this pathway, I mean … what else do you feel in the other parts? (keeping the patient focused on her overall physical sensation) (**AA, XA**)

Pt: Now I have a knot in my throat, and at times I have difficulty swallowing …

Th: Where in your throat? (**AA**)

Pt: Here.

Th: Ah, high up here … hang on, because I am very interested in the actual physical sensation … when you say "knot" it is a figure of speech, you know … (**AA**)

Pt: At times it is a sense of suffocating.

Th: Where from? (**AA**)

Pt: From where there are … my tonsils, it's like something obstructing, which stays on …, but I don't see it as a mechanical obstruction, well, actually I do feel the obstruction … like when I read a book, I bend forward to read it and after some time I have this sense of suffocating, but it's not exactly suffocating, it's like a need to take deep breaths so as to relax and attenuate this sense of suffocation in my throat.

Th: Like something weighing on what you might feel, on your living, breathing deeply. (**AA**)

Pt: Yes, even now it is annoying, but I can tolerate it.

Th: Have you got it now? (the therapist is interested in knowing exactly how her A is now) (**AA**)

Pt: Yes … instead, the times when I've needed to take bromazepam, I also had this knot in my throat, but the constriction in my breastbone was so intense that I couldn't even lie down (this indicates that, differently from previous occasions, the patient now can tolerate her A).

Th: Then it was actually painful? (**AA**)

Pt: It was very annoying, it wasn't panic, because panic I had three times in all my life, the last was in January …

Th: Because in a sense it seems that there is, at the stomach level, tension above all, like stiffness, blocking, restraint, whereas higher up in your throat or at times even in your breastbone, it feels more like a weight weighing or … (**AA**)

Pt: Impending …

Th: Impending, very well, over what is your most genuine feeling, that you have and would need feel, together with your deep breathing … and you'd need to express them, but there is this weight, even physically, which is impending and keeps them down there, instead of letting them be … (**AA, XA**)

Pt: And I noticed something, which may be unrelated, but it came to me now …

Th: Yes.

Pt: As a teenager I was untidy, creative, impulsive, but not in the violent way, I mean joyful and open to life; now I've become sort of perfectionist … now it's like … I tidy up at home, I fold my dresses and put them away in perfect order … as trying to tidy up also my life. (revealing something of her deep being and the self-damaging way of stifling it)

Th: It is a police-like type of order … (**DA, SE**)

Pt: Yes. (the patient gave up her D and is now becoming sad)

Th: What do you feel as you say so? (**XA**)

Pt: Sorrow.

Th: It is very intense this sorrow you are feeling, as though there was the actual need of suffocating a highly vital part of you for the sake of this external order, to put it this way … did anything come to mind about when you were around sixteen … before this change took place? (**XA, HP**)

Pt: My life was more carefree … in the end life experiences I had to go through changed me in order to survive.

Patient and therapist go on staying in touch with each other and the patient stays connected to her more vital part that had got lost far from consciousness. Staying with the feelings leads to a spontaneous link with the theme of the lost babies. The patient actually had three consecutive miscarriages with the man with whom she stayed for seven years. The patient now is not using any defence and co-operates fully with the therapist. The therapist is resonating with the patient's grief and asks for more information, aiming to evaluate how much of the causation of the miscarriages might be psychological:

Th: You had miscarriages; you lost the children or stopped the pregnancy? (**HP**)

Pt: No, no, I lost all three in the third month of pregnancy.

Th: And do you know why? (**HP**)

Pt: I underwent all sorts of investigation, including the genetic, and I am healthy and, theoretically, I can have all the kids I wish. I took all the fertility tests … so I put myself in the hands of God, of destiny and if they don't want … I remember, however, that whenever I got pregnant, at first I wept all the time feeling desperate, unhappy for the first weeks, because my life would have to change … I would lose what I had, in order to take on a new role, sort of more mature … I feared losing my freedom of travelling, studying, taking courses. So I was in despair for the first weeks, then everything felt marvellous as I felt my tummy grow … then by the third month everything disappeared … here as well … I believe we should dig into it.

The patient's account is crystal clear; her reproductive system is healthy and she can have all the babies she wishes. As we know, in some cases, there happens to be a biological incompatibility between two specific partners. However, in the present case, the patient clearly describes her conflicting feeling when she first realised that she was pregnant, then through to the loss of the baby; a progression from despair to happiness and again to despair and grief. This supports the hypothesis of a non-negligible psycho-emotional factor in the causation of the miscarriages. The patient's last comment, " … here as well … I believe we should dig into it" is another signal of the strong therapeutic alliance. The therapist empathically echoes:

Th: Sure …
Pt: I never wanted to face these things … around the miscarriages … all the three times I had to go to hospital because my womb wasn't clean, and all the times I had to undergo general anaesthesia for the surgical operation, and the last time I asked the doctor to please give me a double dosage so I don't wake up anymore … well, he partly listened to me since I didn't manage to wake up and I had to stay in hospital two or three days more …

This last communication conveys the intensity of the patient's unbearable—and unresolved—grief over the loss of her babies and, by extension, of her "baby-part". It also signals suicidal ideation and feelings of guilt at the thought of having prevented her children from being born. These aspects will be thoroughly worked through, two sessions on but, for now, the second trial relationship session is approaching its end. Ten minutes later, the patient wonders if this therapy can really help her. As we know, she has had a tendency to sabotage her goals, making her question even more to the point! A nice chance for the therapist to express his optimism and to stress once more that the outcome will depend on the joint work of both therapist and patient:

Pt: This therapy, what we are doing, will it help me to develop a new attitude toward life and people? Will it help me to feel better, to face those days in which I have anxiety attacks … can it help me?
Th: Surely, but we also need you to answer the question, is it helping you? **(HP)**
Pt: I believe it is. I am not 100% sure, because it is quite a new experience … I'll be able to say so when the things I am talking about won't make me cry any longer … I see that for the last two weeks I kept on thinking of my mother and the thing of betrayal … this really gave me a lot to think …
Th: So we are doing something here … **(HP)**
Pt: It kept coming back, and even when I was doing other things … click! My thought would fly on its own … but it did so in a smooth way, like meaning, OK let's face this too …
Th: OK, so you agree to go on with this experience … **(HP)**

Pt: Yes, well now that we opened the little drawers, we can't leave stuff out there ... I either close or empty them!

Th: True, it's been the goal of this starting part ... (**HP**)

The second extended interview ends in this way with therapist and patient agreeing on their therapeutic contract.

Session 1: Superego and the ego-syntonic defence of acting-out

All in all, the twotrial relationship extended interviews made a good start to this therapy. In spite of this, the patient postponed her firstfifty-minute session (session 1) twice, thus delaying the beginning of the weekly sessions by twenty-five days and taking a break from the therapeutic work as well as from the relationship with the therapist. The patient later explained that, on one occasion, she'd had to take extra duties and, on the other, she had to assist her mother who needed to undergo some clinical tests. The therapist will have to deal with this type of self-sabotaging acting-out within the therapeutic relationship. He starts by clarifying to the patient that, whatever the reason that she skipped her sessions, this is interfering with their therapeutic work. We take up the interview from the patient's response to this:

Pt: Work, my mother ... I wonder what it is all about?! There must be something I'm not realising, so I am not aware of myself!

Th: Well, there may be some distortion ... however, it is true that, as you said, out of your own will you've been able to accomplish a few things that gratify you, and really are in your interest ... regarding your job, travelling, professional and scientific interests, these are all highly positive things (defence validation) ... and you also mentioned "love for yourself" ... (**DA**)

Pt: Well, I am probably unable to give love to myself as well as to a hypothetical man or to a friend. I actually find it difficult to have friends; I mean real friendship, whether with women or men.

After dealing with the defence of distancing in the relationship with the therapist (skipping two sessions), the patient can now acknowledge that emotional distancing makes her personal relationships unsatisfactory. The therapist once more chooses to focus on the relationship with him to have a chance of looking at how the self-sabotaging behaviour actually takes place:

Th: Let's look at this, because there seems to be something you do ... if we look at you and me ... it seems to me that, without doing any injustice, you neglect both me and yourself in an even and identical way; you don't neglect me more than you or the other way round ... I mean; the job here, we have to carry it out together for you ... and this stand-by of twenty-five days ... seems negligible to you ... that is, if I hadn't called your attention to it ... (**SE**)

Pt: (Now half-defending herself and showing some irritation) Got it, but if I've been busy, what could I do?! That is, where are you getting at, I'm not with you! What should I think? That I've been on standby for these twenty-five days and neglected our job, and it is unhealthy of me to have let twenty-five days go by in this way, in connection with the working relationship we are in the process of building? I don't understand!

Th: Actually, I don't think it's particularly healthy, but my goal now is not to give you a score—which would be rather poor in this case—what I wish is to highlight this pattern you have … (**DA, SE**)

Pt: A way in which I behave?

Th: A way of behaving which, I believe, amounts to n-e-g-l-e-c-t-i-n-g, whereby during these famous twenty-five days, you surely did a number of things, so there are some things you did NOT neglect … you may have not neglected your job … (**SE**)

Pt: I didn't neglect my job, period.

Th: You haven't neglected your mother … well, according to her you surely did … (an indirect reference to the projected Superego) (**SE**)

Pt: Surely!

Th: But, as a matter of fact, you spent a lot of time going around with her, making phone calls for her … (**DA, SE**)

Pt: What the hell should I be doing different from this?

Th: I may well hope you busied yourself also with other things, like plans for your future or so … if you did, very well! (**SE**)

Pt: Not really … I unfortunately didn't. I am actually neglecting something … this word "neglecting" … is probably right … I paid the annual fee of a gym club and for the past four months I didn't go for a single time. This gets really on my nerves … and I don't find the strength to go, why? I don't know. When I get home I am tired and when I have time to rest, I say, if I go I get tired.

Now the patient has acknowledged her self-neglect and the ways in which she perpetrates it. Moreover, she then illustrates the secondary gain—an indirect sign of therapeutic alliance. She actually explains with pride that "something special" happened in her job; her female boss chose to entrust the patient, rather than any other nurse, with the transportation of a very ill newborn baby by helicopter. Now, the therapist has a chance of dealing thoroughly with this defence, including its secondary gain:

Th: I mean … on the one hand there is your interest and pleasure in doing your job well, plus doing something unusual. Besides, the boss is conveying that you are good, capable and reliable, which is gratifying, OK … but, in order to get some affection, or whatever it is—for you it feels like a form of affection, anyway—do you always need to work hard for someone? I mean, can't there be someone, or indeed yourself, who cares for you even without you having to take all this trouble? Then, flying by helicopter is a nice experience, and you are rightly proud of your professional skill (defence validation)provided that it does not become the only way to get some appreciation and feel valued … and perhaps even a bit cared for … because this way life becomes like being sentenced to hard labour to get some appreciation. (**DA, SE**)

Pt: I hadn't thought of this aspect, obviously …

Th: Well, it would seem worthwhile to reflect on these ways of behaviour we tried to describe today and see to what extent your life is good enough even in this way and, if not, you may want to try and change a few things … and I'd say, to start with, you might try to come to the sessions regularly, so as for us to keep the ball running and not uselessly still … since this is a place for you only … actually few other places are only for … **(DA, SE)**

Pt: … me …

Th: Right, you know …?

Session 2: murderous and suicidal feelings, mourning of unborn babies

The second session opens with another signal of good therapeutic alliance, by way of a spontaneous motivation to face her hidden mechanisms and go through all the suffering this entails. "All that the therapist does" is to listen carefully to the patient's appalling account of a baby's autopsy, helping her to stay tuned in to her feelings and accompanying her:

Pt: Well, today I came to talk to you of something.

Th: Ah, something in particular … **(HP)**

Pt: Yes, we'll see if it's related to other things, it's something that happened, and left me a bit surprised … for various years I've wished to see a baby's autopsy. So I went, and as the pathologist began dissecting, opened the body and things … I remained absolutely impassable, unaffected, nothing … at some point it felt like we were dealing with a doll …

Th: Was it a newborn baby? **(HP)**

Pt: Yes, so it was … a doll like those we all played with as kids, and I couldn't get the feel of the human being … the pathologist took all the little bits from the various organs, giving explanations, trying to understand the cause of this inexplicable death … he'd just been born, and after ten minutes suddenly died … they tried to resuscitate him for fifty minutes. Nothing! So the pathologist took from all the organs …

Th: Were you present at the resuscitation? **(HP)**

Pt: No, because it was not during my duty. I just wanted to see the post-mortem … when he was ripping up the baby, I mean … at the end only an empty body was left over … with nothing inside … I had an association to my parents or grandparents … because they lived in the countryside, and when they killed animals to cook and eat them it was the same identical scenario … and it's a time of my life I've been working through during these last weeks … I thought about all this in various moments, like during breaks … then I went to the supermarket, I saw the liver and I saw the kidneys … I went near to being sick … meat has become almost disgusting for me as a reaction …

Th: So you had a delayed reaction … **(HP, XA)**

Pt: When I saw the liver at the supermarket I immediately associated the two … the pathologist cut the liver with the same knife I have at home! I saw the kidney there and I got a flashback, now, I don't manage to understand if this reaction is normal or of someone mentally disturbed.

Th: Well, I don't know exactly, I am interested in the reason that this incident affected you deeply inside … **(RE, XA)**

Pt: What upset me was also the mother's history; she'd tried to kill herself while pregnant ... and while giving birth, she said to her baby, "I hate you and wish you could die, I hate you, hate you, hate you", and the baby actually died in ten minutes, this upset me!

Th: This actually upsets me too; to be honest ... she'd attempted suicide during her pregnancy? **(RE, HP)**

Pt: Yes, and the gynaecologist after some time went to the mother asking, "How do you feel, madam?" And the mother went, "Well, if I was at the Maldives I'd feel better", that was totally out of place, I mean her son had died that very moment! This brought about a ... a hole inside, hearing about this ...

Th: It is something indeed horrible. **(RE, XA)**

Pt: I actually said, "Holy Mary, what a cruel destiny!" ... or maybe this is right, since she didn't want the baby, but, hell, me, I wanted a baby ... that is, I don't have it, this shocked me ... you must know that, selfish as I am, I'd like to have a baby even without a husband! Why am I so selfish?

It was obvious from the beginning that the patient's interest and involvement in a baby's autopsy could not but bear a connection with personal aspects of her own. Moreover, she has now made the link with having a baby and, more than this, she actually mentioned "without a husband"—a transparent reference to her unresolved conflict about closeness and relationships with men. This patient is quick and intelligent, but it would be wrong to forget about her character armour, self-sabotaging ego-syntonic defences and, more generally, to suppose that she is not resistant. Rather, her resistance is overridden by her therapeutic alliance, fostered by the closeness in the relationship with the therapist. The explicit link with more personal issues then comes naturally:

Th: This incident is really sad and made you think of what happened to you? **(TCP)**

Pt: Yes ... yes, yes it's true ...

Th: Of what? **(DA)**

Pt: Of the children I didn't have.

Th: Can we talk about this? It is something meaningful for you ... where is your thought going? **(HP)**

Pt: It goes to the "why", why I didn't manage to have a baby.

The patient's hint at a rationalisation needs just a simple intervention by the therapist, who wishes to stay closely focused on the emotional parts. Because of the strong therapeutic alliance, this is sufficient to help the patient go deeper and deeper into her painful feelings of grief and missed happiness. She is fully in touch with her feeling:

Th: Yes, but to "when" does it go? What comes to mind, what moment are you thinking of? **(HP)**

Pt: When I was pregnant, the thing of being pregnant with a baby growing inside me ... that sense of feeling well, the feeling of happiness I felt.

Th: 'til what month had you got? **(HP)**

Pt: Third, third ... my boyfriend kept saying, let's try again and again ... it hasn't gone through this time, let's do it again ... hell! But this "again" was three times and it was me going to the operation room to go through that pain, like taking away, tearing away something from you … shit! He didn't understand, really not a bit of sensitivity, nothing … in the end I did not want this baby, because I was still afraid of having that pain, not so much the physical pain, more of a … really like tearing something away from inside.

Th: This feels very painful, but very important too … what thought comes to you? **(XA)**

Pt: The image that comes in all this thing is as though they had torn away bits of my heart … every time a child dies at the hospital, the moment of passing away, between life and death … or just dead, it always comes to mind that they fly towards Heaven, and then I think of my children.

Th: It comes to you that they fly to Heaven. **(XA)**

Pt: Yes … then I think of my children that I did not have and it's hallucinating to think of "my children", at three months they were this big, nine millimetres … but it is the idea one has that is difficult to eradicate.

Th: All this love … ending so badly … it feels like a great love always ending badly, always being betrayed … and dying, getting killed. **(XA)**

Pt: Perhaps, yes, it is something forever repeating.

Th: Something that can only live in Heaven … a few aspects of your life not involving a relationship with somebody who might betray, because they only depend on you … these have wings and go to Heaven … when instead there is a relationship with someone … real … there is a lot of fear of a deadly violence … occurring within the relationship … something you clearly experienced in your life … and there is this fear of your homicidal impulses towards a child, no? **(XA, SO)**

Pt: Yes, it's true this terrifies me.

The depth of this dynamic material and the intensity of the related feelings do not preclude the use of humour. Another reason for introducing a lighter tone is that the session time is over and the therapist would like to lighten up the atmosphere before saying goodbye. As we see from the patient's response, she would instead like to go on … and she is perfectly right in this! But the therapist really cannot prolong the session. He will actually make a comment that refers to her tendency to distance herself while simultaneously suggesting the potential benefits of relinquishing this defence:

Th: … the killing of those you love … so we'd better have a few other sessions before you have a baby, wouldn't we? **(XA, RE)**

Pt: The problem is that this homicidal instinct, this slightly macabre thing of mine, is something I've always had since I was a child … when my parents went to bed, I went to watch TV to see all the horror movies with deaths and things …

Th: So next time you tell me about that … **(RE)**

Pt: (Anxiously) … I'll discover I'm a serial killer.

Th: (Giving hasty reassurance) Don't worry. **(RE)**

Pt: I do worry instead! I behave like that nurse who killed her patients … that really upset me! … At times I think I must have a double personality since I have such hallucinating thoughts …

Th: We'll talk about this … when are you coming next time? (**RE**)
Pt: Will I be able to understand who I am?
Th: Yes, if you come to the sessions regularly you will! (**HP**)
Pt: Well I skipped two in all, uh!

Summary of the subsequent sessions

After the second session, the patient attended regularly. She had become aware that her tendency to distance herself in relationships with others, including the therapist, doomed her relationships to failure. She therefore tried to stop avoiding closeness and actually did better and better in this respect. In the fourth session, while navigating through feelings of compassion, physical closeness and love, the patient was mourning all the love wasted by her distancing and avoidance. Staying with all these feelings and talking quietly brought back a meaningful memory:

Pt: I remember only one incident from when I was a child, I must be five to six years old, and this I never forgave them … [parents] … there was … umm, some relative had been admitted to hospital, and they had to pay him a visit … these idiots, and this is the only way I can call them, left me in the car alone, and locked the car doors "because I was asleep"—and could not get into the hospital … when I woke up, and it was all locked up, it was hallucinating … I remember still now, I was crying like a crazy, obsessed person, I thought I would die, wanted to fly, get out, open, with my feet and hands I broke everything! Like a mad person. People who passed by stared at me and went away! … When they [parents] came back … they did nothing, don't remember if they picked me up and comforted me, but this incident really remained inside me, it's like it happened yesterday … what I really mean is, their two heads, even added together, don't make one whole head! … How can one leave a child alone in the car that way! … yes, I was a caged animal, if I look at myself now, the image of myself in the car, is that of an animal who tries to escape in whatever way it can … that experience was really devastating. I was left for I don't know how long locked up in the car … crying in despair, while people were passing outside, looked at me who was alone in the car …
Th: And what is the most terrifying part you experienced there? (**XA**)
Pt: Obviously feeling abandoned, and, hell, staying locked up in a box, I had a sense of stifling and lacking everything. … all this brought about a pretty strong sense of claustrophobia … can you imagine the extent that I worked within myself to try and master this fear of closed places?! It once happened I was in the car and got a panic attack because something reminded me of that experience.

The patient's account is given while she is experiencing fear, rage, and despair, and sharing them with the therapist. This incident and the related feelings clearly link with the panic attack, as well as with other aspects of her character, including being impulsive and avoidance of closeness.

In the fifth through to the eleventh sessions there was further emotional experiencing of her primitive part (impulsive, enraged), which led to a better integration and improved communication with her adult part. As a result she became capable of separating smoothly from her former long-term boyfriend, an attractive but rather crazy man, with whom she had been in love, on and off, for many years. With him, the patient was capable of facing the issue of commitment cards-on-the-table. He said he loved her and liked her but had no intention whatsoever of committing himself to a couple relationship. The patient ended the relationship in a quiet but extremely determined way.

The twelfth and thirteenth sessions give evidence of a change in her attitude towards therapy and in the way she was handling the relationship with Max, the man she recently started dating. Regarding coming to therapy:

Pt: Let's say, now for some time I'm happy to come and I always come willingly ... and as compared to a few months ago when you called my attention to me putting my job in the foreground or other things ... now, for instance the fact of having this appointment this morning ... I am committed and it's a pleasure even to wake up to come over and things, so ... I'm very happy to be doing this ... so I'm really willing to come ...

And regarding Max:

Pt: More in general, my spirits are good, I caught a cold, but that's another matter ... and with Max, after what we discussed here last session, I got the message and I am applying it, I believe ... I am assessing, gradually and slowly ... in my previous relationships with men ... I'd never spoken so clearly and explicitly ... as I did with Max a few days ago ... that is, what was not satisfactory ... I used to make do, I adapted and modelled myself ... this is probably what brought me to go through awful suffering ... I realise this.

Th: Oh, how good! And are you glad about this? (**XA, SO**)

Pt: I am serene, glad ... well sort of happy ... I am happy about the step I made ...

Th: Right, happy with yourself ... (**XA**)

Pt: Yes, I am proud of myself, in that ... I could have met someone crazy or not reach any objective ... instead, in front of me there was someone (Max) who didn't agree on everything, but listened, answered ... we said we wish to try to get to know each other better, our dynamics ... more calmly ... also I told Max that ... he seems not to have time, and I told him I believe the relationship needs time, I am a person who needs time ...

The fourteenth session might be called the "mother session", both because it was centred on the mother and because it seemed to work as a milestone of therapy, after which it would be impossible to resume the old self-sabotaging strategies. Mother, a markedly narcissistic woman, came over from the South and spent ten days at the patient's place. Mother needed to undergo a number of clinical investigations and the patient organised the whole thing to the best of her competence and care. She even slept on the sofa, to let mother sleep in her bedroom. But mother behaved in an appallingly irritating way, victimised the patient, and kept repeating that she will die soon. The patient then suggested to her mother that she might benefit from seeing a psychotherapist. To this, mother had a very aggressive reaction, becoming provocative and vexing the patient. The patient got extremely anxious and, for the first time in her life, had symptoms of acute gastritis. This incident provided a chance of regulating anxiety, uncovering murderous and sadistic feelings, and experiencing the related guilt for her rage and grief over the wasted love. All in all, this session represented a crucial moment in which meaningful dynamics could be worked through. In the second half of the session there was a deep sense of satisfaction about feeling more worthy, also thanks to therapy. The patient asks that the camera be switched off and reports a meaningful, though partly faded, memory from her childhood, in particular, of an abusive situation apparently involving mother and a priest. She is unclear regarding how accurate her memory may be, but wanted to share it and felt relieved afterwards.

During the period of the sixteenth through to the twenty-third sessions, the patient went on exercising her ability to be constructive in relationships. A further inner renunciation of mother, her ex-partner, self-centred people—and the patient's own narcissism—took place. Sessions started to be scheduled every other week, making it possible for the patient to go on developing and practising her new life skills with the therapist's support. The last session (session 26) took place three months after the previous one. The patient was well, and the therapist tried to get a clear picture of how things were, so as to be able to decide if more sessions were needed or not. The patient reported having gone on to face, experience, and work through her fear of closed places, with the awareness of a connection to her inner experience of oppressive and abusive relationships. She had trained her breathing, trying to learn to breathe more and more deeply. In connection with this, she also took a course in skin-diving; when underwater she had fear of dying, but went on and faced it successfully. She acknowledged the progress she made concerning fear of closeness. She was aware that she needed to progress further concerning making a good love relationship. Patient and therapist acknowledged that their work had been useful and that the patient now faced her anxiety instead of avoiding it. They agreed to conclude therapy.

Follow-up

When discussing the various therapeutic approaches and techniques, one should never be overly seduced by a theoretical model's elegance and coherence, forgetting that the only way to measure its effectiveness is by offering patients a thorough follow-up to find out how they are at some time after therapy—see, for example, Malan and Osimo's (1992) follow-up study of twenty-four consecutive cases, seen at the Tavistock Clinic, and supervised by Malan. We do not always offer follow-up and, at times, we may be unable to see a patient for this purpose, but with the Treacherous Woman this was fortunately possible. Six months after the end of therapy, the therapist invited the patient to a follow-up session. She was willing to come and grateful for being invited. After reporting about her latest professional success, she was asked by the therapist:

Th: Listen, in your opinion, what's been different after therapy?

Pt: What I gained out of our sessions is an ability to read myself, look at me and accept myself ... something that, previously, I was not capable of or I didn't have the tools or ...

those little words …

Th: Those little words?

Pt: Yes, those little key words, that now are difficult to describe … but by means of our talking together, by surfacing certain situations that made me suffer—and surely won't vanish and will make me suffer again—but becoming aware of certain things is a way to start solving, accepting or living with them … think of my mum or my family …

This was the patient's overall description of her change. The expression used by the patient, "those little words", conveys the idea of having accessed her inner "little" Self and, using words, having been able to share it with another human being. The following quotations from later on in the follow-up session give a more detailed account of what changed.

Relationship with others

Pt: … I brought home respect for myself, that I previously hadn't … nor—above all—was I even aware it was missing … how do I see this …? From the fact that previously I took some actions, did things in order to get others to tell me "Good for you", "You've done great". From my boyfriend, parents, my job, and so on … Now, instead I only do—well, not only—anyway, I do what is good for me: what does me good, and regarding the other person … I care about him or her, but only up to a point … I do my best to respect my neighbour … but I don't comply with what the other person expects of me, am I being clear?

Relationship with herself

Pt: … and this … before psychotherapy -it's called psychotherapy isn't it? (laughs) … Before these encounters we've had, I wasn't capable of this, out of fear of being judged, of making others suffer … so I often did the things I didn't feel right … including little things, like "Let's go out" … Now, instead I don't do so … when I did things for others I wasn't happy and I had anxiety, because I didn't feel like, but was unable to listen to myself … I did feel those sensations, but was not connected, and didn't take them into account, so our encounters brought about an effect here, that I subsequently built on it at home … in time … now I feel very well with myself … when I'm at home on my own reading, watching TV or eating I feel well, I am serene … when I am away I look forward to coming back home … and, for example, when I'm at home I cook for myself. I cook well, in a dignified way, not like shit, as single people often do, just because they have to …

Relationship with a man and future children

The patient is still seeing Max and they get on well with each other in a constructive way, but they did not move in together.

Pt: For how my life is now, I believe he is the right person for me, because he is not oppressive, lets me breathe and I let him breathe, we call each other regularly, just to know how are you, what are you doing … it's alright … also, he's totally different from me, therefore it is interesting to have an interchange re: cultural, intellectual things … either our relationship will become like a friendship—and I am very clear about what a friendship is—or it will become a love relationship, what I mean by a constructive couple relationship. So I feel well with myself, but in this moment I may not be capable of living with a man … however, if I fall in love or find the right person … I believe in the first phase of the relationship, I will manage … it is when we'll decide to have a child, this will be tragic for me because of my past experience. I try not to think of that, but I see that it is still painful …

Th: Good, congratulations!

Pt: I haven't built anything. These are just facts …

Th: Why you say you built nothing?

Pt: I didn't build a real relationship, we are going out together …

Th: Well, you haven't yet labelled it in a specific way, but you see each other, and this means your overall interchange is a good one.

Pt: For me it is something new, because this way of staying in a relationship had never happened to me, I actually think it is really the only way, because I feel adequate, serene …

Th: Good, all is clear, and, as it seems, the keys are now in your hands. So, if you need me you'll let me know, but it actually seems you already have all the keys that you need … this doesn't mean that you shouldn't come to see me from time to time if you so wish and … it'll be a pleasure for me as well, so, no problem!

Pt: Thank you, thank you.

Comments

The patient's symptoms are almost completely resolved, and no new symptom took their place. Her character has undergone deep change and her approach to all areas of life is remarkably different from before. She acknowledges her change also in relationship to men ("This way … had never happened to me") but slightly underestimates her improvement in this area. She is aware of her residual anxiety concerning living with a man and giving birth to a child, but there are signals that she is facing these anxieties and managing to make further progress. She is grateful to the therapist and knows that she can count on his future help, if required, especially if she gets pregnant. It is in the spirit of IE-DP, and of short-term dynamic psychotherapies, not to keep a therapy going if patients can go on improving on their own.

References

Alexander, F. & French, T. M. (1946). *Psychoanalytic Therapy, Principles and Application*. New York: Ronald Press [reprinted New York: John Wiley & Sons, 1974].

Ezriel, H. (1952). Notes on psychoanalytic group therapy: interpretation and research. *Psychiatry, 15*: 119–126.

Jung, C. G. (1964). *Man and His Symbols*. Garden City, NY: Doubleday.

Malan, D. H. (1963). *A Study of Brief Psychotherapy*. London: Tavistock [reprinted London: Routledge, 2001].

Malan, D. H. & Osimo, F. (1992). *Psychodynamics, Training, and Outcome in Brief Psychotherapy*. Oxford: Butterworth-Heinemann.

Osimo, F. (2002). Brief psychodynamic therapy. In: J. J. Magnavita (Ed.), *Comprehensive Handbook of Psychotherapy: Psychodynamic and Object Relations Psychotherapies*. New York: John Wiley & Sons.

Osimo, F. (2003). *Experiential Short-Term Dynamic Psychotherapy: A Manual*. Bloomington, IN: AuthorHouse.

Osimo, F. (2009). The character hologram. *Ad Hoc Bulletin for Short-Term Dynamic Psychotherapy: Practice and Theory, 13:* 25–50.

Osimo, F. (2012). A historical overview of experiential dynamic therapies. In: F. Osimo & M. J. Stein (Eds.), *Theory and Practice of Experiential Dynamic Therapy*. London: Karnac.

Palvarini, P. (2010). Is the concept of corrective emotional experience still topical? *American Journal of Psychotherapy, 64*: 171–194.

Reich, W. (1933). Charakteranalyse: Technik und Grundlagen. Vienna: Zelbstverlag [first English translation by Mary Boyd (1945), *Character Analysis*, reprinted New York: Noonday Press, 1998].

Note

1. This chapter is based on a previous article (Osimo, 2009).

PART II

CLINICAL APPLICATIONS OF EXPERIENTIAL DYNAMIC THERAPY

CHAPTER FIVE

Experiential dynamic psychotherapies in primary care mental health services

Jessica Bolton

In the present chapter, the provision of primary care mental health services (PCMHS) in the UK, and the characteristics of a typical primary care mental health service will be described. The nature of the presenting problems of patients referred to PCMHS, recommended treatments, and the relevance of experiential dynamic therapies (EDT) will be outlined. In particular, the relevance of experiential dynamic approaches in treating the more complex presentations of common mental health problems will be discussed. The process involved in developing EDT formulations and the contribution of supervision will be emphasised. The chapter will include a case which was less suitable for the other therapies provided within PCMHS, for example, Cognitive Behaviour Therapy (CBT) and Person-Centred Counselling (PCC), but was amenable to EDT formulation. Pre- and post-therapy data will be presented, indicating clinical improvement as well as significant improvement in quality of life. The patient described herein completed therapy within six sessions (including Trial Therapy and one-month follow-up) after which they felt ready for the therapy to end.

Primary care mental health services in the UK

During the 1990s, mental health care within primary care services tended to be delivered in general practice settings by community psychiatric nurses, counsellors, psychological therapists, and psychologists. Patients included those with mild to moderate severity of, for example depression, anxiety disorders, and eating disorders. Service provision varied considerably, with some areas having no specialist primary care mental health input or relying on a lone worker. In other areas, although a multi-professional team offered mental health care to patients with common mental health problems and effective team working was possible, having different managers (i.e., secondary mental health care managers and psychological service managers) sometimes complicated service provision. Irrespective of these difficulties, there was widespread concern that provision of mental healthcare resources in primary and secondary care did not meet the needs identified by general practitioners and researchers (Strain, Hutnik, Gregory & Bowers, 2006). In 2001, the National Health Service Plan made provision for one thousand new primary care mental health workers (PCMHWs), often psychology graduates who had completed a one-year postgraduate training course. These practitioners were tasked with providing brief, evidence-based therapeutic interventions and disseminating appropriate self-help material, strengthening the information base of mental healthcare services available to patients, promoting knowledge among patients and within the community, and assisting in the development of practice-based information systems, audit, and outcome measurement (Strain, Hutnik, Gregory & Bowers, 2006).

Improving Access to Psychological Therapies (IAPT)

In 2007, the government pledged £173 million over three years to the development of the IAPT programme. Its remit was to deliver psychological therapies in accordance with the UK's National Institute of Clinical Excellence (NICE) guidelines, to those experiencing mild to moderate depression and anxiety. By 2011, the IAPT programme will have trained 3,700 new therapists to help extend access to psychological therapies and by late 2010 the services set up had already helped 72,000 people recover from depression and anxiety disorders (Department of Health, 2011).

IAPT services tend to be delivered in community settings (e.g., general practitioner surgeries, job centres, libraries, community centres, voluntary organisation premises), by a large stand-alone team of therapists (up to forty trained therapists—"high intensity" therapists and "psychological well-being practitioners"—for a population of 250, 000) (Department of Health, 2008). The IAPT team typically receives referrals from general practitioners, other health professionals, and patients directly, that is, self-referral. "Low intensity" therapy provided by the psychological well-being practitioners (PWPs) would include psycho-education courses, provision of self-help resources, guided self-help, computer-based therapy, and a limited number of sessions of one-to-one therapy using a cognitive behavioural approach. Some of the support offered by PWPs is given over the telephone. High intensity therapy offered by IAPT services includes up to twenty sessions of individual or group psychotherapy, or psychological courses provided by therapists who are trained psychotherapists. The starting point for IAPT services was to provide Cognitive Behaviour Therapy (CBT), often alongside pre-existing counselling services, with subsequent commissioning of competencies and training for psychodynamic therapy (Lemma, Roth & Pilling, 2008).[1]

Introducing a range of therapies, including brief dynamic therapies, into IAPT services constitutes an important development as the significance of choice within health care has long been recognised. A recent survey revealed that, in comparison to those who wanted but were deprived of a choice, people given a choice of therapies were three times more likely to be happy with their treatment (We Need To Talk Coalition, 2010). Furthermore, in comparison with those who were deprived of a choice, people offered a choice of therapy were five times more likely to report that therapy helped them back to work (ibid.). In addition, brief dynamic therapies have the potential to help patients with medically unexplained symptoms (MUS); 20—30 per cent of consultations in primary care relate to MUS and it has been suggested that 70 per cent of patients with MUS have depression or anxiety, with mental distress as a potential underlying cause of MUS in a significant number of cases (IAPT, 2008). Although CBT may be helpful for a proportion of patients with MUS, dynamic theory can offer explanations for the occurrence of MUS, and experiential dynamic therapies (EDTs), in particular, offer clarity regarding how best to understand and manage different manifestations of anxiety (Aubrey, 2012; ten Have-de Labije, 2006; McCullough Vaillant, 1997; McCullough et al., 2003).

The service delivery system widely adopted within IAPT services is the stepped-care approach, that is, identifying the least restrictive and least costly intervention likely to be effective for the presenting problem (Davison, 2000; Department of Health, 2007). Within a stepped care service, complexity or severity will lead to a more intense level of response,-cognitive behavioural therapy, counselling, or short-term dynamic therapy. Stepped care can be effective and efficient in the treatment of patients with mild to moderate problems because it offers easy and timely access to low intensity interventions that are less dependent on the availability of professional staff, and incorporates patient-initiated approaches to treatment, for example, use of self-help books (Cuijpers, 1997), and computer programmes (Proudfoot et al., 2004). Patients requiringlow intensity intervention but with input from a professional or paraprofessional may have access to courses (White, 2000), or guided self-help (Gellatly et al., 2007).[2]

The particular value of EDTs in primary care

Primary care mental health services are structured to work with patients who are likely to experience treatment gains within between six and twenty sessions (see NICE, 2009, 2011) and, in the experience of the author, much can be achieved within a short-term dynamic therapy when the therapist adopts a focused, structured approach as in EDT. Relevant aspects of EDT include time-sensitivity (McCulloughVaillant, 1997), working with anxiety (ten Have-de Labije, 2006), and frameworks for understanding resistance on the part of the patient and therapist (McCullough Vaillant, 1997). That an EDT practitioner aims to accelerate the therapy and to work "through therapeutic objectives in the shortest possible time" (McCullough Vaillant, 1997, p. 3) means that treatment fits the requirements of a PCMHS, while also offering a holistic approach, and the potential for enduring change. Understanding, carefully assessing, and attending to the different manifestations of anxiety is part of a responsible and effective formulation (ten Have-de Labije, 2006), and enables appropriate transfer (step-up) to longer-term treatment when patterns of anxiety indicate the need to proceed more slowly (see Coughlin Della Selva, 1996; Malan & Coughlin Della Selva, 2006). In particular, the graded format (longer) treatment is indicated by serious parasympathetic reactions such as gastro-intestinal disturbances in patients with ulcerative colitis or duodenal ulcers, or a predominance of cognitive perceptual disruption (e.g., tunnel vision, mind going blank, dissociation). Patients most likely to benefit from EDT in primary care settings have a predominance of somato-motoric anxiety manifestations, or striated muscle tension, and sympathetic reactions, experiencing anxiety in more universally recognised ways, for instance, heart thumping, sweating, shivering, tight chest.

Regarding understanding a patient's resistance, this can only be determined in the context of the therapeutic relationship. In EDTs, the initial session, an extended interview, referred to as a trial therapy, provides information about the quality of relationship that is possible and, for this reason, is also referred to as a "trial relationship" (Osimo, 2003). Its main goal is to establish if this patient responds to this therapist working in this approach (Osimo, 2001, 2003). The force of the opposition, in the face of the therapist's attempts to enable them to change, gives an indication of the patient's resistance. Distinguishing between *character* defences (their automatic and habitual way of interacting with the world) and *tactical* defences (a more fluid response to the here and now) helpfully informs expectations about a patient's ability to relinquish their defences. Identifying the defence with the client, collaboratively clarifying its self-defeating aspect, and inviting the patient to behave differently (particularly in the here and now with the therapist) will provide a wealth of clinical information regarding their level of resistance, motivation to change, psychological-mindedness, and ego strength.

When a patient is able to give up some of their tactical defences within the first session, it indicates their desire to change and their ability to work with the therapist. Although it is reasonable to expect that character defences will not be relinquished so quickly, from accumulated clinical experience with EDT, it is known that the resistance, as an opposing force, per se, is invariably overcome if the patient has a sufficient amount of *inner strength* (Malan, 1979). However, in providing psychological therapies within PCMHS, a patient's resistance to recognising and relinquishing their tactical and character defences would be an indication for referral to a service that offers longer-term treatment. That said, it is important to keep in mind that therapist resistance has the potential to influence their therapeutic activities, including the extent of anxiety regulation, defence work, and encouragement of emotional expression, as well as the timing of these interventions that, in turn, may have an impact on patient resistance.

Malan (1979) describes rapport as being the extent of emotional connection between patient and therapist. The match between what the patient is bringing and how the therapist responds (i.e., the extent to which the therapist offers what is needed by the patient at any particular moment) hugely influences rapport (ibid.). Review of video recordings of therapy reveals that, when the clinical work is not proceeding as effectively as one might wish, the therapist can be struggling to match their intervention to patient need, in the moment of the patient's need. Although the lack of progress may be linked to resistance or fragility within the patient, it is important to consider whether it is associated with the therapist's state of mind, level of experience, prejudice about the patient or their presenting problems, etc. The routine use of video recording in EDT, and of group supervision/intervision with an experienced trainer/colleague, helps to identify barriers to therapeutic gains, and contributes significantly to an understanding of what might need to change or be dealt with to enable therapy to proceed. In particular, with avoidable barriers within the therapist being identified by supervisor/peer group, the barriers (we could read here "defences") can be recognised and relinquished by the therapist, and the therapeutic work and relationship between patient and therapist can blossom.

It seems important to clearly state that the development of the real relationship between patient and therapist is not about having more lenient boundaries but rather using the Self of the therapist for the benefit of the patient. An example will help to demonstrate this, with the clinical case described later also focusing somewhat on this issue. When I trained with a highly skilled and inspiring psychoanalytic supervisor in the final year of my doctorate, I felt unsure whether to reveal to her that a patient had requested a hug at the end of therapy and, more importantly, that I had responded by *giving* her a hug! My reflections on the psychoanalytic model I had been taught told me that I should interpret this and see it as something important happening in the transference. My gut instincts as a therapist and human being, which I had thankfully also been taught to listen to by my supervisor, told me otherwise! Within my next supervision session, with a sense of shame, I revealed to my supervisor that I had given the patient a hug, and was thankfully validated by my supervisor for responding in this real way—the patient wanted to show their gratitude to *me, their therapist, for helping them*. We could have interpreted the patient's request as their longing for more expressions of love from their mother when they were a child, but the healing and most appropriate response in the moment was to take seriously their wish for a real and human relationship with me. As a patient of psychoanalysis myself, I also experienced the real relationship during my analysis, feeling it most significantly at the end of therapy, and experiencing it as one of the most healing parts of the process. Within EDT, and Intensive Experiential-Dynamic Psychotherapy (IE-DP) especially, the real relationship is central to formulation and intervention. Ideally, from the first moments of the trial therapy, the focus on and acknowledgement of the real relationship is consistent throughout the therapy, rather than being left until the end of a session or the therapy. An important aspect of EDT, and IE-DP in particular, is the emphasis placed on use of the real relationship to effectively and quickly communicate with the healing part of the patient in a way that ensures recovery and, moreover, the opportunity to thrive.

EDT in primary care mental health services

The case presented herein was undertaken within a pre-IAPT, stepped-care PCMHS in which counsellors and PCMHWs carried out the majority of the clinical work including assessments, psycho-educational courses, computerised CBT, guided self-help, and up to six sessions of therapy using a cognitive behavioural approach or counselling. I was the manager of the service and offered EDT to appropriate patients. At the time of the therapy, I was in the second year of a three-year Core Training in Intensive Experiential-Dynamic Psychotherapy (IE-DP).

Case study

The case presented will illustrate taking care of the real relationship and the subsequent acceleration of therapeutic gains that were maintained at two-year follow-up. It will be demonstrated that the therapeutic relationship needs only to be good enough and long enough to encourage the healing self to emerge.[3] I will also try to illustrate how emotional maieutics need only cover a good enough range of feelings to enable the patient to be free from fear of emotional expression. Furthermore, the case illustrates how encouraging and helping the patient to stay with feeling leads to an uncovering of important links, a clear understanding of character pathology, and provides an opportunity for a corrective emotional and relational experience.

The cheerful sad woman and her sumo devil

The patient, Bernadette (all names and some identifying features have been changed to protect her anonymity), of mixed Spanish and British ancestry, was in her mid-forties, married for ten years, with two sons aged six and two. She wanted help to deal with grief due to losing a child, a stillbirth, four years earlier. She was referred by her general practitioner who requested two therapies—grief counselling followed by cognitive behavioural therapy to help her reclaim her life. She presented with a mixture of complicated grief and severe depression, and the assessor, in common with the patient's general practitioner, was concerned that cognitive behavioural work and counselling may offer only partial interventions for her, and instead suggested EDT.

Psychometric data

The patient completed the Beck Depression Inventory (BDI-II; Beck, Steer & Brown, 1996), the Clinical Outcomes in Routine Evaluation Measure (CORE-34, Evans et al., 2002), and the Warwick and Edinburgh Mental Well-being Scale (WEMWBS; Stewart-Brown & Janmohamed, 2008) at the beginning of therapy, at the end of treatment (BDI-II only), and at follow-up. Prior to therapy the patient scores were within the severe range on the BDI-II, above the clinical cut-off score on all dimensions of the CORE, and 2.3 standard deviations below the population mean for the WEMWBS.

Session 1: trial therapy

The therapist used the initial part of the extended interview, trial relationship, to educate the patient about the experiential dynamic approach. In particular, teaching about the importance of feelings (so the patient could feel her emotions as they surfaced—XA), about how deep feelings can be inhibited by guilt and anxiety (AA), and how they can be pushed away by coping strategies (tactical defences, character defences, superego pathology—DA, SE).

The therapist starts by paying close attention to emotional maieutics, specifically trying to help the patient more fully experience the surfaced feelings because they were so present and confused. The therapist actively mirrors what the patient shows in both verbal and non-verbal ways. The initial question of what she needs help with reveals the patient's confusion about her feelings and her problem. The following transcript shows how the patient is inhibited by guilt, primarily, but also anxiety and shame, and reveals the Superego pathology. The patient had experienced a great deal of emotional and physical trauma in her life, having had many miscarriages as well as the stillbirth at a very late stage in the pregnancy, and, like many patients seen in psychotherapy rooms, does not truly understand the impact of her traumatic experiences on her, and does not take her feelings seriously. We join the session at the beginning:

Th: So what have you come today wanting help with? (**HP**)

Pt: Erm, OK. Forgive me if I get tearful (gets tearful), because that is part of the thing that I just can't seem to control at the moment. And half the time, I don't really even know what sparks that off.

The client has experienced significant anniversary reactions to the stillbirth every autumn and winter since she lost her son. The referral had been made to the service as a result of an anniversary reaction that she had hoped would be more manageable but that she had found very difficult to manage. The therapist is concerned that the patient is taking an attitude of neglect towards herself, paying very little attention to her feelings. The intervention at this point was an attempt to emphasise the need *to* pay attention (SO *by* paying attention—RE):

Th: So let's just, let's just notice shall we?

Pt: (Laughs, and shifts uncomfortably in her chair) It was like today, I have been absolutely, for me I've been doing pretty well recently, and thinking to myself, I'm feeling OK again, for me and I've gone longer without crying for a while, a couple of weeks without crying. But today at work, [there was] no one to cover and, immediately, I'm straight to tears. Up until this morning I was doing OK. Part of it is the fact that, as I parked the car, I thought there is someone there who is going to listen.

Th: And it sounds as if you have been holding it all together. (**XA**)

Pt: (Begins to cry, then tidies herself up with tissues)

Th: All sorts of feelings coming up. Come out as crying, sadness, but a lot of guilt in there as well. Guilt about having feelings? Why you and why now? Like you are not allowed to have feelings. (**XA, MI, AA, SE**)

Pt: I'm sure other people have issues from their past. I can't seem to leave them where they should be and not have them affect things on a day to day basis.

Th: Maybe here we can put the feelings of guilt to one side and let you have some feelings. So we can see what it is that you are feeling, find out what is going on underneath. (**XA, RE**)

Pt: I feel so stupid. Normally, I'm fairly rational, I do my job, I do other things, etc., etc. I feel. Part of me says focusing on it and dealing with it is a good thing, that's why I'm here, I need to go through this process. Another part of me says you just get on with it, don't you, that's what other people seem to do, you should just get on with it and focusing on it will only make it worse. Even when I feel fine though, it is only a temporary thing. Certain times of the year are worse than others.

Th: Such as? (**HP**)

Pt: It's coming into autumn. It just seems to be a time for me (tears come and then get pushed away).

The patient revealed her yearning for help and attention, but immediately experienced guilt about her needs, and expressed the ideas that others have greater needs, and that she should be able to cope with her experiences and move on. The therapist used this opportunity to encourage putting inhibitory feelings like guilt to one side to reveal deeper emotions. Through the therapist's encouragement, the patient begins to discuss the traumas that she has experienced and, gradually, connects more deeply with the emotional significance of the events and the ways that others have responded.

Th: We're here for these feelings (**RE**), so let's give them some space and let them be aired and not be squashed (**XA**)

Pt: Some things have happened to me about that time of year …

The patient spends a few moments describing a close, long-term relationship that ended during the autumn when she was in her early twenties. We rejoin the session five minutes later:

Pt: But then of course, four years ago, I lost Samuel, I had a stillbirth. I don't even know what to call it, well it wasn't a stillbirth … I'm sorry, there is no heartbeat. And my other little boy was with me at the time. I'd had miscarriages before, I'd had three miscarriages, then I had David. Then we moved away. We'd had problems conceiving, I'd had all the tests. We had a miscarriage about six weeks before moving up there. I then fell pregnant and I had David and while we were still up there when David was two, I fell pregnant again. I fell pregnant with Samuel and carried Samuel for thirty-eight weeks and then lost him. And because I'd had the other miscarriages … part of me feels, you know, because I've given this quite a lot of thought, as to why … I thought that I must have made a huge mistake, that I must have done something very wrong and that is why I have had these miscarriages … because I have these feelings inside. And I knew after I lost Samuel I needed … I tried to get some counselling. We spoke about it for about twenty minutes and she said, well, make another appointment at the desk on your way out and we'll meet in two weeks and see if your mood has picked up. And I thought, I've just given birth to a dead baby, my mood's not going to pick up, it's not just depression. I didn't go back.

The patient is weeping almost constantly, with bouts of laughing, while telling the therapist about the death of her son. The therapist focuses on helping the patient to connect with and express the emotion that begins to bubble up but is then immediately pushed down.

Pt: I tried to work and look after the family and deal with the friends' group, it backfired just a little bit.

Th: Take a moment and notice the feeling. You have just told me all about the things that you have going on, this huge mountain of responsibility on your shoulders and there is some feeling coming out. Can you notice where that feeling is? In your body? On your chest? In your hands? **(XA)**

Pt: Here.

Th: Top of your shoulders. **(MI)**

Pt: I feel like the whole of my body is closing in.

Th: So a tense feeling, a tight feeling? **(MI)**

Pt: Yeah, everything contracting I think, probably just the stress of it all …

The patient is not labelling her tension as anxiety but instead refers to it as stress. The therapist could have helped the patient to understand that the muscle tension she was experiencing was anxiety (AA), and that talking about the death of her son gives rise of feelings that provoke anxiety. This would have helped the patient to recognise and regulate her anxiety, and to gain an understanding of causality—important aspects of ego adaptive capacity (see ten Have-de Labije, 1999, 2001, 2006). The therapist offers a mirroring intervention to make the links for the patient but says "as you talk about things" rather than "as you talk about the death of your son" (vagueness on the part of the therapist) and repeats the patient's term "stress" rather than labelling the patient's experience of contraction as anxiety:

Th: So, as you talk about these things your stress builds up, and there's also tears that are coming at the moment so … (**MI**)
Pt: A complete mess.
Th: So. I'm not thinking you are a complete mess, I'm … (**RE, SO**)
Pt: I do (laughs).
Th: I'm interested in these feelings, you know that come out, and somehow get a bit bulldozed over. You want them to go away and you want them to disappear (**DA**). And one of the things that is important here is to have space for feelings (**SO**). That if we get into a habit of trying to keep ourselves busy and not have any feelings and not have any space for them (**DA**), then they find a way of just bursting through and becoming a bit volcanic.
Pt: Yeah (smiles).
Th: So if as we go, we have a bit of space for feelings, then it allows that to not happen and it means that they can be what they need to be, not what they have to be in order to get noticed. (**SO, RE**)
Pt: Yeah.
Th: So as this feeling is coming you notice this tension here … (points to shoulders), it's still there. (**AA**)
Pt: Yeah, across the base of my neck. But you see, you say it out loud and it all seems like, there is no reason why you shouldn't be able to deal with that. Other people do. And I just don't feel like I'm doing a very good job at any of it.

Interventions that helped the patient to recognise and relinquish her defences, and increased rapport between patient and therapist, initially increased her tension (anxiety) and then her guilt. The therapist tries to use the empathy in the real relationship and emotional maieutics to help the hidden feelings of grief break through the guilt and defence of neglecting her emotions.

Th: I don't think you are giving yourself credit. Here you are, a woman who has huge amount of strength, who has had the terrible trauma of having to give birth to a dead baby … (therapist is emotionally moved). (**SO, XA, RE**)
Pt: He's buried in [name of city some distance away] as well so it isn't as though I can go and see him every week … (patient goes into detail of the cemetery and explains that she didn't want her son surrounded by death).
Th: He's far away from you. (**XA**)
Pt: Yeah, yeah. I can't just go (cries).

The picture is building up of a deeply traumatised woman, whose superego is preventing her from grieving her losses and facing her anger. She has a strong sense of how she should behave and does not give her feelings in the here and now the importance they deserve. We rejoin the session forty minutes into the two-and-a-half-hour session. The therapist draws Bernadette's attention to her defence of covering up her sadness with laughter:

Th: One of the things I'm noticing is, you picked up on your laughing when you are crying. (**MI, DA**)
Pt: Yes (smiles then starts crying).

The patient acknowledges her defence and continues to cry. The therapist moves to helping the patient identify and turn against a neglectful Superego (SE):

Th: And that in the context of you pushing your emotions away, it seems very important that you take yourself and your feelings seriously (**SO**). And I wonder if there is part of you that feels, "I don't deserve to take my feelings seriously because others have it worse, and because this isn't legitimate, and what am I doing here". (**SE**)
Pt: (Looking desperately guilty and shameful) I don't trust my own judgement anymore, I just don't. That's why I mentioned the earlier experiences—I made a bad decision.
Th: You let yourself down? (**HP, XA**)
Pt: I let myself down badly (crying).

The patient seems to be connecting in this moment to her feelings about the consequences of not listening to herself fully: her tendency to neglect and cover up her feelings. The therapist could have checked this out by asking the patient to say what she was crying about before proceeding to encourage her to take a different position towards herself (SE, SO), to stay with her feelings (XA), and, as appropriate, drawing her attention to her self-defeating and neglectful defences (SE, DA):

Th: Let's just stay with that feeling for a moment because that is really important (**XA, SO**)
Pt: (Looking down) It is. (Looks up, shrugs)
Th: It is, but you are shrugging. This is another part of you that doesn't want to take you seriously. To try to get rid of it. This isn't a shrugging matter. (**SE, DA**)
Pt: I don't know how to deal with it, where do you go (whining). There's nothing anyone can do about it. I don't know how to handle it and it annoys me. There's no reason for me to be unhappy. Yes, bad things have happened but I have two gorgeous children, a husband who loves me, end of. That should be … (tails off)
Th: Do you notice how you are not listening to yourself. You are not taking yourself seriously. You are saying I should be happy, full stop, even though I have feelings, I should be happy. I should ignore my feelings of grief, I should ignore my feelings of letting myself down and I should just be happy. (**SE**)
Pt: Yeah.
Th: This is not a reasonable way to treat yourself. (**SE, SO, XA**)

Following the therapist drawing the patient's attention to her self-neglect, self-dismissal, and rigid expectations, the patient reveals some experiences in which she was desperate, and others did not take her emotional needs seriously. Firstly, she reveals her terror when a midwife left her alone during labour, giving birth to Samuel. We pick up the session a few moments later when the patient reveals having had an abortion at twenty-one years old, and going to church to speak to someone:

Pt: I can see the priest, he's at the front of the church, and I remember wanting him to come and talk to me. And I'm bawling my eyes out at the back of the church. He walked straight past me and straight out of the church. Right, I know I'm on my own.

Th: But you are not on your own here. I am here, and I want to be with you, and I want to see this through together (**RE**). We can do that successfully if you take yourself seriously (**SO, SE**). The priest didn't take your pain and anguish seriously, and the midwife didn't take it seriously. I am here to be with you taking you and your feelings seriously (**RE**). But I can't do that on my own ...

Pt: (Laughs)

Th: Does that make sense? But what that means is you putting some of this to one side. This way you have had to cope for a long time, of putting your feelings to one side and looking after other people, looking after your sons and husband, and looking after Samuel. (**DA**)

The above transcript reveals the patient's habitual and automatic position towards herself, as well as past relationship experiences that have contributed to this position. Through the therapist drawing the patient's attention to her self-neglect, self-dismissal, and rigid expectations, the way was paved for Bernadette to recognise the powerful effect this was having on her. Towards the end of the trial therapy, she was able to see this part as a devil on her shoulder, watching and reacting to her every move, crippling her spontaneity and liveliness. She and I played with this concept and, in recognising the power of this part, labelled the Superego as "the Sumo Devil" (as sumo wrestlers are rather large characters!). This playful, creative act in itself enabled her to begin turning against this punitive part of herself.

Summary of the trial therapy

During the trial therapy, the therapist began to develop an understanding of Bernadette's way of managing herself, and the importance of her listening to and taking her emotions seriously, rather than neglecting or laughing at them. Bernadette had experienced a range of, firstly, inhibitory (guilt, shame, anxiety), then, hidden feelings (grief, anger). Although she appeared to have experienced a breakthrough of sadness about the way she had been behaving towards herself, there was neither a partial nor a complete breakthrough of deep hidden feeling towards others. We had discovered, however, that her punitive Superego worked her guilt to crippling effect, and blocking her defences was followed by guilt that needed to be regulated prior to hidden feelings emerging. The hidden feelings were also quickly followed by the punitive Superego response, crippling the full expression of her emotions with guilt. Bernadette had a strong sense of how she should behave, and what she should say, and linked these ideas to her beliefs about her mother's expectations and hopes of her. Meeting her mother's expectations became a heavy burden for Bernadette, and failing to live up to an unrealistic ideal led to intense guilt.

The additional process in the trial therapy, that paved the way for success in the subsequent sessions, was the development of the real relationship. The interventions to help Bernadette recognise and relinquish her defences were most effective when contained within the relationship with the therapist. For example, when I said, "I am here to be with you, taking you and your feelings seriously but I can't do that *on my own*", I was helping Bernadette to restructure her defence of neglecting her emotions, her sense of self-worth, and to take a different position in relation to herself, but in the context of our collaborative relationship. Soon after this intervention, Bernadette began to turn against her punitive Superego, and find a creative way of accepting, objectifying, and relinquishing that part. Bernadette had given clear examples of being neglected by caring professionals (counsellor, priest) and alluded to her mother's expectations of her neglecting the reality of her situation—a likely transference reaction would be her perceiving me as neglectful. Instead of interpreting this dynamic, the IE-DP approach makes explicit what is possible in the relationship (I can help you by not neglecting your feelings), and gives the patient the opportunity to use it in a healing way (get close to the therapist) or to react against it (feel angry towards the therapist for trying to get close to them), offering the opportunity for therapeutic and adaptive experience and expression.

This working on the real relationship can also be more subtle. For example, when I say, "Take a moment and notice the feeling. You have just told *me* all about the things that you have going on, this huge mountain of responsibility on your shoulders and there is some feeling coming out. Can you notice where that feeling is? In your body? On your chest? In your hands?"—the patient responds clearly and directly to the question, without immediately going to guilt. I am rooting the intervention in the context of the relationship by using the word *me*, rather than saying for instance—"You have just been talking about"—which is much more vague and individually focused. I also convey empathy in this way and give some psychoeducational information regarding where the patient might be feeling the emotion. This also gives the patient some time to notice her feelings rather than give an automatic response of self-neglect.

Supervision

So, helpful work so far, but I was feeling blocked by my sense that just helping Bernadette to relinquish her sumo devil and take her feelings seriously would not be enough given the complexity of the emotions she was experiencing, and was concerned that she would continue to feel overwhelmed. Perhaps my inexperience in using EDT had left me somewhat overwhelmed by the intensity of her emotions too? When reviewing the videotape of the trial therapy, I was intrigued by the patient's anger signals that I had not mirrored or focused upon as closely as her grief, guilt, and defences.

Her character hologram (see Osimo, 2008, 2012) was given more depth by taking a video of our work to the group supervision attached to core training.[4] The character hologram is a three-dimensional view of the character of the patient and drew on my own style of using metaphor in therapy. The patient had already become aware of a previously ego-syntonic part of her character—the sumo devil—the pathological Superego that was punishing her for failing to live up to an unreasonably idealised self image, and the mere labelling of this part was helping to make it more ego-dystonic (in conflict with her healthy sense of Self). However, we needed a broader understanding of the interactions between her Superego and other parts, and between Bernadette and others. Supervision generated the idea that Bernadette's pathological Superego (her sumo devil), and resulting tactical defences, got in the way of her focusing on specific moments and experiences, thereby preventing her from processing and effectively working through. In particular, Bernadette generalised her experiences, preventing the specifics being given time and attention. She also covered up her feelings, for example with wit (laughing), and guilt that inhibited grief, anger, and terror. These defences created conflict between the part that was feeling appropriate emotions in response to her experiences, and the part that "should be" coping, happy, etc. The developing character hologram was of a controlling sumo devil sitting on the shoulder of a feisty, creative, humorous woman, resulting in a battle of wills that allowed little creativity or healing to flow. My understanding of Bernadette's character hologram helped me to be more precise about her "not taking herself seriously"—she takes different positions towards herself and takes them all simultaneously. This prevents her being in touch with any of her feelings, thereby letting herself down badly. This developing understanding enabled me to fully realise the importance of not only helping Bernadette to separate her adaptive feelings from inhibitory emotions, but also to focus on each, carefully and seriously.

Session 2

At the beginning of the second session, a fortnight after the trial therapy, Bernadette demonstrated a more generous spirit towards herself, and reported having taken a similar, self-compassionate attitude between sessions. She also reported being more connected with her children and their feelings. In session, it was easier to help Bernadette to connect with her emotional experience. We join the session twenty-five minutes in, as Bernadette is beginning to talk about her sense of vulnerability to harm:

Pt: Something bad is really gonna happen and I'm anticipating that. It's kind of a safety thing. I expect to receive shocking news, that's what I expect (tearful). If the children are out of the house and the phone rings, instantly in my head it is someone phoning to say that your son has been involved in an accident, or your son is dead.

Th: Take a moment. Take stock to notice what is going on in you at the moment. Notice your body, where are the feelings? **(XA, SO)**

Pt: Erm. I don't know, I kind of feel a bit pins and needly. Just all *down my legs. And again here* (points to chest).

In response to the therapist's invitation to attend to her feelings, Bernadette refers to her anxiety. To the therapist, this highlighted the importance of helping Bernadette to distinguish between her experience of anxiety and her experience of adaptive feelings. The therapist identifies a part of the patient that made a link between vigilance and saving her child's life—an assumption that presumably has the potential to lead to self-criticism given her previous experiences of miscarriage and stillbirth:

Th: Part of you has made a link between being always alert because if you'd been quicker you could have saved … [Samuel] **(SE)**

Pt: Yeah (crying). I remember being on the sofa. Time frames get mixed up but in my head it's very close to the time I lost him, a day or so. And I could feel him and he was moving side to side and I remember saying to Fred, "Oh, he'll be a footballer or a swimmer, he's really, really active." In hindsight I think, "No, it's because he was really distressed" (crying). He wasn't just an active baby he was in distress and you were just sitting there. You didn't do anything, you really didn't do anything. And I know in my head I couldn't have known, I know I couldn't have done anything but …

The therapist hears Bernadette express a rational and compassionate attitude towards herself as well as self-criticism. The therapist chooses to draw the patient's attention to the harshly critical part of herself—to continue helping her to recognise the persecutory position she automatically takes towards herself:

Th: But yet you still persecute yourself. (**SE**)
Pt: Because maybe that was, I don't know. I know that none of it changes anything, but …

The patient maintains a self-critical position and, in response, the therapist clarifies the role and impact of the defence (DA), validating its prior use while challenging its continued use. The preceding and subsequent extract provide examples of both anxiety-provoking ("You are persecuting yourself") and anxiety-regulating ("What it helps *us* to do is to see *what it does to you …*") defence- and Superego-focused interventions. The former may provoke anxiety as underlying feelings begin to rise, and can be very helpful in providing the patient with a clear understanding of their behaviour. The latter is anxiety-regulating because it is in the context of the relationship, and focuses on the impact on the Ego. In the following extract, the therapist tries to convey something of the character hologram described above, as well as to help the patient understand the consequences of the pathological Superego being given so much power, and the importance of giving up the persecutory position and becoming more self-compassionate and caring. Anxiety regulating components of defence restructuring interventions that hold the patient in the real relationship are underlined.

Th: But the thing that it does help *us* do is to see what you do to yourself, and what it does to your family, being in this state of arousal constantly. (**SE, RE**)
Pt: Yeah.
Th: And of course it's a very natural part of the process of grief to think, "Could I have done something?", but it seems like, it's gone on for too long now. (**AA, SE, SO, XA**)
Pt: Yes. Yes (crying). Never expect that things are going to go OK because you are a statistic. Like with the miscarriages, "It happens to lots of people"—really, well not that I know.
Th: What I want to notice with you is that there are ordinary things that have happened that get very mixed up (**DA**). Ordinary things like wondering whether the baby is going to be a footballer [joy] that get mixed up with this awful, awful experience of him dying [sadness, grief] (**XA**). Which on one level is quite common but it lets you down (**SE**). Because instead of saying, "Gosh, wasn't that hard for me, to think one day, wow, I'm gonna have a baby,"

and then the next day to face that no, it's not going to happen (**SO**). Instead, it's all mixed up with, "I should have done that differently, I should have done that instead" (**SE**). So you cannot grieve what really happened. It's all so mixed up in your head, the good bits, the bad bits. (**HP**)

Pt: Yeah.

Th: To continue to let yourself down in this way, to make it all mixed up together and then impossible for you to then do anything with. It feels so important to start separating it out, and the only way we are going to be able to do that is if this cruel heartless part of you that just keeps telling you it's all your fault is told to shut up for a bit (**SE**). And actually then feel the proper feelings, the anticipation, the terror, the anger, the grief (**XA**). It all gets mixed up with this self-blame and that ends up being the main feeling. It messes it all up, does that make sense? (**SE**)

Pt: (Rubbing legs—the grief is coming through) I remember when I had Samuel, when he actually came out, the midwife, she held him and she looked at him, and looked at me and said, "He's beautiful, he's perfect." And I thought,"What a fucking stupid thing to say, 'cause he's not perfect, he's dead" (crying). I was so angry with her (waving fists).

The therapist notes that the patient is failing to distinguish between anger and grief, and focuses on helping her to differentiate her mixed feelings:

Th: Here we have anger at the midwife, and grief. Let's give them separate space, to either focus on the grief or the anger. It gets so mixed up, I don't think you do either justice and then it all feels overwhelming and horrible. (**DA, SE, XA**)

Pt: Yeah it does (blows nose).

In separating and working on the feelings of anger, guilt, and grief (XA) the therapist may take their lead from the patient. However, according to Davanloo's (1990) theoretical position, during a "breakthrough", deep unconscious emotions would be experienced in a sequence proceeding from sadistic, murderous rage to guilt, grief, love, and joy. This view of human emotional experience would suggest always dealing first with the watchdog of sadism and rage, before moving to the guilt over one's sadism and rage, grief linked to the consequences and, finally, the reparation of love. Indeed, in the author's practice, this sequence tends to be followed, and experience of anger would tend to be explored when a combination of feelings is being half-expressed. In contrast, other EDT clinicians (e.g., Osimo, 2002, 2003) recommend following the patient's lead rather than adhering to a preordained sequence of intervention. In the present case, as I was unsure where to start, I chose to follow the patient's lead. You will notice anxiety regulation occurring with maieutic activities—where I use "we" rather than "you"—an implicit reference to the holding of emotions in the relationship.

Th: So which direction shall we go in? Shall we look at the anger or shall we look at the grief? (**RE, XA**)

Pt: (Pause) The anger. Yeah, let's do the anger because there's more of an (clenches fists and pushes them forward sharply) aggressive feeling going on here.

The patient clearly indicates that she wants to follow the feeling of anger. She demonstrated clear verbal (labelling her feeling as anger) and physical (clenching her fists) signs that anger was an underlying feeling rather than a defensive cover-up. The therapist invites the patient to attend to her feeling and explore it with the therapist (MI, XA):

Th: There's some feeling there, that's where they are, in your hands when you're angry. Can you feel it there? Are you holding it back? Can you tell me? (**MI, XA, DA, RE**)
Pt: Yeah (tearful). My arms feel really, really tense.
Th: And your jaw, mouth? It's there as well? (**AA**)
Pt: Yeah (blows air through mouth).

The patient is experiencing anxiety as well as anger—shown by the discharge of tension in blowing air through her mouth—but does not distinguish between them. The therapist now knows that there is more work to do on restructuring the Triangle of Conflict, in particular helping the patient to distinguish her anxiety from her anger, thereby building the patient's ego adaptive capacity (see ten Have-de Labije, 1999). From the transcript, we might also reasonably conclude that the patient was ignoring her anxiety until the therapist drew her attention to its manifestations, indicating the need for further work, directing the patient's observing Ego towards her inner experience/anxiety, her defence of ignoring, and clarifying the self-defeating function of ignoring her inner experience/anxiety. Rather than regulating the anxiety directly or educating the patient about anxiety, the therapist chose to simply focus on the anger.[5]

Th: Who is the anger directed towards, if you allow it, (**XA**) not if you push it away and blame yourself? (**SE**) If you just allow yourself to have this anger? (**XA**)
Pt: Maybe at the midwife. The one who delivered him and also the one who I saw two days before.
Th: Let's focus on one or the other and focus on doing things separately and not doing it all at once. (**DA**) So which, the choice is yours. (**RE**)
Pt: The most immediate anger is the midwife who delivered him. I don't know if it's because she was the only other person around.
Th: I think you know there are things that she did that made you angry so let's say that. (**XA**)
Pt: There are things she did that made me angry. She left me on my own (voice is raised) and she seemed flustered and then she told me he was perfect. And all three … (crying, sobbing interrupts speech).

With the emergence of grief the therapist was faced with a choice between exploring either anger or grief. The therapist invited the patient to focus on the feeling of anger (XA) to avoid colluding with the part that does not take her feelings seriously enough to allow them to be fully expressed, experienced, and "delivered". At times, asking the patient to stay focused on the anger was difficult, as her grief for her son also needed attention. In addition, I was asking myself if the anger towards the midwife was a defence against the experience of grief.

Th: If we focus on the feelings, the sadness is coming and getting in the way, (**DA**) and of course it is legitimate to be sad but we're trying to focus on the anger. (**XA**)

Pt: It's like it builds up inside me (hand moves up torso like a rising water level) and then it gets to there (chest level) and I have to hold it so tight and then it will go back down again. It's not like a sickness feeling or anything, it's like a pressure and I have to hold on tight and then it goes back down.

Th: So this sense of emotion coming, which you don't fully let out, it comes half way? (**HP**)

Pt: Yeah, absolutely (nodding vigorously). Because it does just make me feel like screaming and shouting.

Th: Expressing your emotions is hard, scary; often that's why we get all these anxious feelings when we are also feeling angry or sad. (**AA**) But they are allowed here, you can express them as fully as you are able to. (**RE, XA**) So there is anger at the midwife for saying your baby was perfect. Where can you feel it? (**XA**)

Pt: In my hands, like I want to grip onto something really hard.

Th: What do you want to grip onto? (**XA, HP**)

Pt: It's like I'm back there, on the bed, so angry, enraged, also primal—I growl rather than scream. To be told he was perfect.

The patient is looking furious but shifts to talking about something "bizarre". We rejoin the session a few moments later when the therapist invites her to focus on her anger (XA):

Th: Can we focus on the anger now and create space later for the bizarreness? (**DA**)

Pt: Yeah (laughs). Yeah.

Th: The memory of the primal anger. What are you feeling right now? (**XA**)

Pt: The same thing, when I think about it, that's what it makes me want to do, to scream, to growl.

The patient talks for some minutes about not being able to scream and growl in the session due to shame and guilt regarding the potential impact on others. The therapist has a keen sense of the link between the patient giving birth to her baby who had died and her killing off her feelings before they are fully alive and experienced. The importance of the therapist, the patient's emotional midwife enabling a successful birth, to bring the emotion to life was a responsibility of which, at this moment, I was fully aware, and somewhat scared. Knowing that fear is a recommended state for therapists at times also—"In every consulting room there ought to be two rather frightened people: the patient and the psychoanalyst. If they are not one wonders why they are bothering to find out what everyone knows" (Bion, 1990, p. 5)—I find courage and continue.

Th: So you'll keep half in here (points to torso) just so that people don't have to hear you?

Pt: Yep (laughs).

The patient describes another situation in which she blocked her expression of anger, and the therapist begins to point out the cost of keeping her anger hidden (DA) before inviting the patient to think about what it might be like to experience her anger (XA) with her (RE). We rejoin the session at fifty-two minutes:

Th: The long-term impact of not expressing anger at the time is that years later … (**DA**)
Pt: I'm still sat here.
Th: With your anger half expressed (speaking gently but firmly). What would it be like now to connect with this anger with me? (**RE**) So when you feel this anger, what is it that you feel? (**XA**)
Pt: Not a tight anxiety feeling, it's a really strong hard feeling. If it came out it would be a really hard punch or something aggressive and violent (moving hands in fist).
Th: And that's what happens with anger, isn't it. So there's a feeling in here (points to own chest) which is a powerful feeling, which would come out as a punch. (**MI**)
Pt: Yes.
Th: Have you got an image of you doing that? (**XA**)
Pt: Don't know who I'd hit. I guess if I imagine the image of me hitting a punch bag.
Th: You can see that?

The patient is using displacement—instead of connecting the anger with the relevant person she connects it with an inanimate object. The therapist first focuses on helping the patient connect with her feeling of anger (which is one step forward in having the feeling despite the displacement) and then moves on to connect it with a human being. There are three parts to experiencing an emotion: (i) the cognitive part—"I am angry", (ii) the bodily experience of anger in the body, and (iii) the action impulse of the emotion—protecting oneself (see ten Have-de Labije, 2009; Malan & Coughlin Della Selva, 2006). Given the patient's tendency to experience intense guilt, the therapist decided to take a gradual approach in helping her to connect fully to her anger *towards the Other and her impulse to protect the Self/harm the Other.*

Pt: Yeah, I can see that (laughs). I can see that it would be quite frenzied.
Th: So it would be very frenzied. All your body being used. (**XA**) And how does your body feel now? There are those tears coming again (weepiness). (**DA**)
Pt: Actually it feels lighter.
Th: Connecting with the anger makes you feel lighter? (**MI**)
Pt: Imagining it in my head makes me feel like I've done it, I'm doing it and it lightens it.
Th: Great. And if we connect to the who? (**XA**)
Pt: (Laughs) The punch bag, I can't do that …
Th: You are not doing it in real life; you are just in here with me. (**RE, AA**)

As the patient gets closer to connecting fully with her anger towards the midwife, another defensive reaction occurs, specifically, replacing anger with the joy connected to the birth of her first son.

Pt: It's bizarre because I can't see a face. I can see the face of the midwife who delivered David (smiles broadly).
Th: So that's a nice face? (**HP**)

Pt: Yeah.

Th: A face you want to punch? **(HP)**

Pt: No.

Th: So let's put her to one side. **(DA)** It's nice that you remembered her. So you don't have to see the face but can you see a body? Can you see that shape? **(HP)**

Pt: Oh yes, she's slim, late thirties. But actually, God it's amazing actually, I'm just making a connection between her and the way things were then and what makes me frustrated in other people now. I can't bear inefficiency, I can't bear people faffing, I can't bear people not knowing how to deal with something ...

The patient is making important links for her understanding of her current difficulties as they begin to make sense for the first time. However, going with this distraction and avoidance would deny the patient having the fullest experience in expressing their emotion in a focused and healing way. Hence, the therapist invites the patient to continue exploring her anger towards the midwife (XA):

Th: So what does that make you want to say to this midwife? **(XA)**

Pt: Don't be scared, you have no right to be scared, to feel anything; I know it might be difficult, but it's your job. Do not presume you have any idea, any idea of what to say to me, to make this better.

Th: There's all these words, let's connect also with that feeling, the frenzied punching part, how would you express this in that way? **(XA)**

Pt: There's a punch bag on the floor in front of me.

The patient talks about being unable to hurt the midwife's feelings. She is responding to her guilt about expressing her feeling of anger. The therapist intervenes by acting on this defence (DA) in the real relationship (RE), valuing the patient (SO) and encouraging her to continue to explore her anger towards the midwife (XA).

Th: The midwife thinks about her feelings and not yours, you can worry about her too but let's not make that mistake, let's think about you. If we're thinking about you what do you want to say, what do you want to do? **(DA, XA)**

Pt: It's almost like (leans forward) if I was watching a training video for midwives and she behaved like that and I would want to pick her up by the scruff of the neck and give her a massive slap and say, "Look what you are doing to this woman. You are the only other person in the room that she can focus on and you look unsure of what you're doing. You look really flustered because you don't have another pair of gloves! You don't do it like that, you just don't." You really don't.

Th: You've picked her up, slapped her, told her that. Is that it? Is there any more or is the anger all gone? **(MI, XA)**

Pt: There's still anger there. It wasn't what I want to hear and she assumed at a time like that. She should not have said anything to me. It was not for her to say what she said. She interrupted what was going on. It was not for her to tell me about my baby.

Th: You wanted to have that for yourself. **(MI)**
Pt: Only a mother could say that he was perfect even though he was dead (deep sobbing).

We return to the session ten minutes later, after some work on allowing the grief to come through, and Bernadette sharing some intimate information about the aftermath of Samuel's birth.

Pt: The sadness comes and goes during the year. I can help prevent it, I can accept it, and it can come and go. But I realise now that the anger is a constant. It affects my relationships with people, the way I approach my job, the way I look at my boss. That's quite a huge thing to recognise actually, quite incredible. A good thing.

The patient's comment demonstrated that the link between her deep feeling (X) and her character is now fully conscious. The therapist tries to help the patient stay with her feeling of relief, and make conscious the restructured representation of herself and others, making connections between her past and present difficulties and ways of managing.

Pt: Do you know that's a huge relief, like wow, you know I'm not. I couldn't understand why.
Th: You were struggling so much. **(RE, MI)**
Pt: Yeah. Why I was finding it. You know I didn't used to be like that. I had patience, and was good at just going—"That's their way of doing it", but I can't now, I find it difficult and find myself saying it as well, I guess that's the anger coming out but I can't physically hit something at work so I have to say it and whinge, all I ever am is cross.
Th: So the relief is … **(XA)**
Pt: Now I know why I do it. It's not really about that, it's not that I'm overreacting, I'm reacting to the past—I hadn't understood where that was coming from.

Bernadette experiences some freedom from the crippling effect of the Superego, and the struggle between Ego and Superego, during the session. As a result, she can see more clearly both her character pathology—what she does to herself, and the underlying feelings that she has been carrying since the traumatic events of her past. Moreover, during the session she begins to turn against the punitive nature of the Superego, and experiences her underlying feelings, separately and attentively, in the context of a contained relationship and feels better for it.

Sessions 3–5 and termination

Bernadette's depression lifted following the second session; she reported alleviation of her low mood, concentration difficulties, and crying, and an increase in connectedness with her family, colleagues, and friends. During the subsequent weekly sessions we explored her relationship with herself and her children, her self-destructive avoidance reactions, and Bernadette was helped to process her grief more fully. Her focus shifted from the past to the here and now. Her first five sessions were weekly or fortnightly (due to illness and adverse weather) and her final session was planned to allow a month to elapse. During the last session, she described appropriate and proportionate feelings of anger towards a friend that were processed quickly, easily, and effectively. At termination, her BDI-II score was at the lower end of the mild range.

Follow-up

An unusual experience when working in the NHS, I telephoned the patient after almost two years to request a follow-up appointment to find out how she was (in order to provide follow-up material for this chapter). Bernadette was pleased to hear from me and was especially pleased to schedule an appointment to discuss her progress. Prior to the follow-up interview, I reviewed the trial therapy and identified resolution criteria to indicate the patient had completely resolved the conflicts and difficulties that had brought her to therapy (see Malan & Coughlin Della Selva, 2006):

1. Loss of symptoms—low mood, generalised anger, weepiness
2. Good enough relationship with her children and closeness with them
3. Less emotionally intense and overwhelming reactions to bereavement anniversaries
4. Good enough relationship with husband, sharing responsibilities and closeness with him
5. Free and guilt-free expression of herself and her creativity.

The patient led the session, initially describing her current life and offering reflections on the therapeutic work. The first vignettes reveal a touching account of a woman who felt connected with her therapist, and who felt she had been attended to and held by the therapeutic process. She was grateful for the impact of therapy on her, thanking me joyfully, in a way that recognised us both as participants in the work that was done.

Pt: [My husband] asked me "Did she give you any specific coping strategies?" and I said no she didn't, it wasn't like that. All I have to do, when I struggle, is remember being in the room with you. It calms me down, makes me take stock, and then I can go on. I just have to remember being there, physically being in the room and it helps, it genuinely helps. Which is, fabulous, it's just great.

A few seconds later she says:

Pt: The thing that I realised, I remember feeling that someone was finally taking me personally seriously and really focusing on me as an individual, rather than somebody else who has been through that scenario and this is the way you should deal with it. I didn't feel processed. I felt this really is my bubble, this is my time, this is just me. That helped enormously, just enormously … I remembered the physicality of it. When I was talking, at whatever stage I was in, you would take me back to ask "Where do you feel it?". The realisation that a lot of the time with general stress I get it in my jaw. One of the things that made me think, this really is me, this is really getting inside me, was the fact that I would feel it at the backs of my legs, which was that sense of spring-boarding into running away, I've got to get out of here, I need to leave, I need to go. That's what my body is saying to me and that's what made it so hard mentally to stay and face things. But I think that combination of being made to face it mentally, while your body is going "Move, move, just walk away", no, I'm going to stay and I'm going to deal with it. The other thing was about making eye contact, making eye contact when I'm dealing with things that are tough to deal with, and most other people would be quite comfortable for you not to make eye contact, for you to go off into your own little world but you made me focus and come back to you.

Th: Come here!

Pt: Exactly, come back to me, talk to me, let me know. And again they are things that really stick in my mind. And it's all that bit about, you really wanted. It certainly gave me every feeling that you wanted to talk to me (big smile). Just amazing stuff.

Here Bernadette is describing the impact of the focus on tactical defences (avoidance of eye contact), anxiety regulation (becoming aware of anxiety manifestations), defence restructuring (becoming aware of her impulse to avoid), and the emotional maieutics (focusing the patient on their bodily experience of feelings) in the context of a real relationship. Her comment about others being happy with emotional distance at times of distress, and the difference in the therapy that she had me to connect with, reveals her relief about the neglected and unknown parts being taken care of, giving her and me a three-dimensional view of her character. The emphasis she put on "You wanted to talk to *me*", irrespective of what was being said or done consciously, seems also to reflect the taking care of the unconscious therapeutic alliance, taking care of the Ego. Regarding the emotional upheaval around bereavement anniversaries, her current symptomatology, and the way she manages her emotions, she says:

Pt: It's recognised, it's OK, it's alright now. Just do what you need to do, it's absolutely fine, it's not something you have to cope with, it's something you deal with and you deal with it every day. In different ways, in tiny bits, in massive bits, or whatever. You learn to carry it with you and I have learnt to carry it better, much much better, than I ever did … Before when I got referred to see you I'd just had to take two weeks off work with depression. This year I took a day and a half.

Th: And what you did with it?

Pt: Completely different. [This time] I need to be in a place where I feel safe so if I want to cry, I can just cry and I know why I'm crying and I want to have that release, that's fine.

Th: And you're acceptable.

Pt: Yeah. And I realised when I was crying that there were only moments that I was really crying about Samuel, about losing Samuel, the rest of the time it was the tiredness and the emotion about not being able to handle things because I was so tired. And being able to recognise that was great.

Regarding the free expression of herself:

Th: And the part that seems absent. I'm sure you'll remember the part. Sumo devil?

Pt: Oh yes (laughs), sumo devil on my shoulder (laughs again).

Th: I've been waiting and watching out for him but he doesn't seem to be around.
Pt: I don't know where he's gone but he's not about any more.
Th: You're being kind and generous and patient with yourself.
Pt: It is just accepting. It's like somebody turned the key. Not that somebody opened a door and it's all beautiful. Someone unlocked it, my choice to walk through.

And later in the session …

Pt: I can genuinely say to myself, you'll be OK and know that I will be, there is no "Who are you kidding, you're always going to be like this". No, I am going to be OK and I am going to feel much better than I feel right now. And that might be tomorrow or it might be the next day, it's not going to be weeks and months, which was the way it was before.
Th: I love this metaphor you have about treacle. Because the treacle is I can't pull myself out of it, I'm bogged down in it. It feels like emotions aren't like treacle any more, they are things that come and go more easily, they get separated out more.
Pt: In my head I had this river of treacle, going through, and I think it probably comes from Winnie the Pooh, I watch too much kids' TV! So there's a river of treacle and on the banks it's all lovely, green beautiful trees and stuff. And it feels like I've gone from being the swamp monster that has no idea there are trees and beautiful stuff and blue birds singing. And now I feel like I'm sitting on the side of the river and it's almost like all your emotions are like different bits of light flashing past, oh look that's the anger and that's joy, that's that. It sounds a weird picture. Not having them all heading into the mire where they look all brown and nasty. Degrees of separation of emotion that wasn't there before.

Bernadette's comments conjured up a beautiful sense of self-compassion, self-understanding, and at the same time a realistic view of her emotional world, with the full range of emotions that moved the therapist almost to tears of joy. She appeared to have freedom for creativity and self-expression and, in session, was assertive, expressive, and warm towards me.

The patient also described her relationship with both her husband and children in a warm, close way. She described a sharing relationship with her husband, sharing responsibility for emotional and practical issues. She also described her experience of going to Samuel's grave with her sons and finding that they brought life to the experience, and that she liked that. This experience seemed to unite the whole family, with all the varied feelings and truths having space and legitimacy in her mind, and in the reality of this shared experience.

Psychometric data

At follow-up, Bernadette completed the Beck Depression Inventory (BDI), the CORE, and the Warwick and Edinburgh Mental Well-being Scale (WEMWBS). Her scores were in the "minimal" range (BDI-II), substantially lower than the clinical cut-off and non-clinical population mean scores (CORE), and half a standard deviation above the population mean score (WEMWBS).

Conclusions

I have tried to demonstrate the valuable work that can be done, and the acceleration that can take place, in therapy through experiential and dynamic interventions while prioritising and taking care of the real relationship. I have given examples of where encouragement to experience emotions and relinquish defences has been more effective and potent as a result of making the relational context clear and visible. Being transparent with Bernadette about my wish to help, my readiness and availability, and our togetherness in tackling the difficulties, was as important as actually being those things. Not only was the impact apparent in moment-by-moment changes in Bernadette, but also in her conscious understanding of the value of the therapy for her. She felt my interest in her to be genuine and transformative. Hence, by prioritising the human connection and closeness, the patient, as suggested by Osimo (2012) was able to perceive the therapist as a *true person*, and experience a more powerful therapeutic action, and accelerated healing experience.

I have also tried to show that the emotional expression needs to be of a good enough nature. In this case, the character hologram revealed that the patient needed help in separating her emotions and freeing her healthy Ego from a neglectful pathological Superego. Prioritising these issues helped the work to be focused and effective. A potential concern that she had not fully expressed rage towards the midwife or any of the other people who had neglected her in her time of need was unwarranted. She expressed her anger in a good enough way, in a focused and separated way, and in the context of a connected, close relationship. These clearly were the important factors for this patient.

Her presentation at follow-up indicated that we had managed, in a good enough way, to connect as fully as we could, and as we needed to, to ignite, tend to, and bring fully to life the healing process. The healing process had continued beyond the end of therapy, with her self-acceptance, creativity, and connections with others improving over the two-year follow-up period.

While I believe in the specifics of EDT, I have always believed that healing in therapy has as much to do with being cared for effectively and consistently by another human being as any technique or theory that we have in our minds. For me, EDT has provided an understanding of how I can use the caring relationship I offer effectively and quickly, doing something which is so clearly an art, while being driven by science, that also complements and gives plenty of space for my own personality.

References

Aubrey, R. (2012). Intensive short-term dynamic psychotherapy and the treatment of poly-symptomatic somatic patients. In: F. Osimo & M. J. Stein (Eds.), *Theory and Practice of Experiential Dynamic Psychotherapy*. London: Karnac.

Beck, A. T., Steer, R. A. & Brown, G. K. (1996). *Manual for the Beck Depression Inventory—II (BDI-II)*. SanAntonio, TX: The Psychological Corporation.

Bion, W. R. (1990). *Brazilian Lectures: 1973 São Paulo; 1974 Rio de Janeiro / São Paulo*. London: Karnac.

Cuijpers, P. (1997). Bibliotherapy in unipolar depression: A meta-analysis. *Journal of Behavioural Therapy and Experimental Psychiatry, 28*: 139–147.

Davison, G. C. (2000). Stepped care: Doing more with less? *Journal of Consulting and Clinical Psychology, 68*: 580–585.

Department of Health (2001). *Primary Care, General Practice and the NHS Plan. Information for GPs, Nurses, Other Health Professionals and Staff Working in Primary Care in England.* London: Department of Health.

Department of Health (2007). *Improving Access to Psychological Therapies: Specification for the Commissioner-led Pathfinder Programme.* London: Department of Health.

Department of Health (2008). *Improving Access to Psychological Therapy (IAPT) Implementation Plan: National Guidelines for Regional Delivery.* London: Department of Health.

Department of Health (2011). *Talking Therapies: a Four-Year Plan of Action.* London: Department of Health.

Evans, C., Connell, J., Barkham, M., Mellor-Clark, J., McGrath, G. & Audin, K. (2002). Towards a standardised brief outcome measure: psychometric properties and utility of the CORE-OM. *British Journal of Psychiatry, 180*: 51–60.

Gellatly, J. L., Bower, P. J., Hennessy, S., Richards, D. A., Gilbody, S. & Lovell, K. (2007). What makes self-help interventions effective in the management of depressive symptoms? Meta-analysis and meta-regression. *Psychological Medicine, 37*: 1217–1228.

ten Have-de Labije, J. (1999). Maintaining Davanloo's discovery for uncovering the unconscious: An attempt at formulating operational definitions of the dependent variables, Part I. *Ad Hoc Bulletin of Short-Term Dynamic Psychotherapy: Practice and Theory, 3*: 4–16.

ten Have-de Labije, J. (2001). Red and green traffic lights on Davanloo's road to the unconscious. In: J. ten Have-de Labije (Ed.), *The Working Alliance in ISTDP: Whose Intrapsychic Crisis?* Amsterdam, Netherlands: VKDP—Dutch Association for Short-Term Dynamic Psychotherapy.

ten Have-de Labije, J. (2006). When patients enter with anxiety on the forefront. *Ad Hoc Bulletin of Short-Term Dynamic Psychotherapy: Practice and Theory, 10*: 35–69.

ten Have-de Labije, J. (2009). Helping our patients to experience feelings: Understanding the role of defences in emotion regulation and the implications for ISTDP practitioners. *Ad Hoc Bulletin of Short-Term Dynamic Psychotherapy: Practice and Theory, 13*: 15–23.

IAPT (2008). *Commissioning IAPT for the Whole Community.* London: Department of Health.

Lemma, A., Roth, A. D. & Pilling, S. (2008). *The Competences Required to Deliver Effective Psychoanalytic/ Psychodynamic Therapy.* London: University College London.

Malan, D. (1979). *Individual Psychotherapy and the Science of Psychodynamics.* Oxford: Butterworth-Heinemann.

Malan, D. & Coughlin Della Selva, P. (2006). *Lives Transformed: a Revolutionary Method of Dynamic Psychotherapy.* London: Karnac.

McCullough, L., Kuhn, N., Andrews, S., Kaplan, A., Wolf, J. & Lanza Hurley, C. L. (2003). *Treating Affect Phobia: a Manual for Short-Term Dynamic Psychotherapy.* London: Guilford Press.

McCullough Vaillant, L. (1997). *Changing Character: Short-Term Anxiety-Regulating Psychotherapy for Restructuring Defenses, Affects, and Attachment.* New York: Basic.

NICE (2009). *Depression in Adults with a Chronic Physical Health Problem: Full Guideline.* London: Department of Health.

NICE (2011). *Generalised Anxiety Disorder and Panic Disorder (with or without Agoraphobia) in Adults: Full Guideline.* London: Department of Health.

Osimo, F. (2003). *Experiential Short-Term Dynamic Psychotherapy.* Bloomington, IN: AuthorHouse.

Proudfoot, J., Ryden, C., Everitt, B., Shapiro, D. A., Goldberg, D., Mann, A., Tylee, A., Marks, I. & Gray, J. A. (2004). Clinical efficacy of computerised cognitive-behavioural therapy for anxiety and depression in primary care: randomised controlled trial. *British Journal of Psychiatry, 185*: 46–54.

Stewart-Brown, S. & Janmohamed, K. (2008). *Warwick-Edinburgh Mental Well-being Scale (WEMWBS), User Guide, Version 1.* Warwick and Edinburgh: University of Warwick and NHS Health Scotland.

Strain, J., Hutnik, N., Gregory, J. & Bowers, G. (2006). *Graduate Primary Care Mental Health Workers: the Process of Introducing the Role into Primary Care Trusts.* Unpublished manuscript, University of Surrey.

We Need to Talk Coalition (2010). *We Need to Talk: Getting the Right Therapy at the Right Time.* Retrieved April 30, 2011 fromhttp://www.mind.org.uk/assets/0000/1929/weneedtotalkreport.pdf

Notes

1. The competencies for psychodynamic psychotherapy were based on approaches with the strongest claims for evidence of efficacy (Lemma, Roth & Pilling, 2008), their published manuals (including *Experiential Short-Term Dynamic Psychotherapy*—Osimo, 2003), and other widely cited experiential dynamic therapy texts (including McCullough, Kuhn, Andrews, Kaplan & Hurley, 2003, and Malan & Coughlin Della Selva, 2006) that explained psychodynamic terminology and provided clear descriptions of how relevant concepts translated into clinical practice.
2. Depending on the model of service delivery, judgement of need can be made during assessment or may be self-assessed by the patient.
3. For a perspective on intrinsic motivation towards growth and healing, the interested reader is referred to Fosha (2008).
4. The three-year core training in IE-DP involved theoretical and clinical components, teaching the *relational* and *experiential* techniques of Experiential-Dynamic Therapy, applied to patients with varying degrees of resistance and fragility. The training programme also offered individual supervision and personal guidance within a small learning group of eight to ten participants.
5. Some might consider the affect focus to be premature given the indications for further work to build the patient's ego adaptive capacity, and address her automatic and syntonic defence of ignoring (see ten Have-de Labije, 2001).

CHAPTER SIX

Experiential dynamic psychotherapies in the psychological treatment of a patient attending oncology services

Mark J. Stein

In the present chapter, psychological aspects of cancer will be outlined and the presenting problems of patients attending treatment for cancer-related difficulties will be described. Reference will be made to a range of psychological interventions for the psychological treatment of patients with cancer, and links will be made between presenting problems of cancer patients and specific therapeutic activities of experiential dynamic psychotherapies. The transcript of an initial interview with a woman presenting to psychology services following therapeutic mastectomy will be presented to illustrate how an Intensive Short-Term Dynamic Psychotherapy (ISTDP) perspective informed the clinical work undertaken. Patient-reported changes at short-term follow-up will be described.

Psychological aspects of cancer

The UK estimated prevalence of cancer in 1992 was 2 per cent, hence 1.2 million people in the UK were living with a diagnosis of cancer (Forman et al., 2003) and, each year, more than a quarter of a million people are newly diagnosed with cancer (Office for National Statistics, 2007). Specific challenges associated with the disease include diagnostic and treatment procedures, and reactions such as fear, uncertainty, pain, treatment-induced nausea, and vomiting. Additional challenges include adjustment reactions to diagnosis, surgery (e.g., mastectomy), and disease recurrence following remission, impact of disease and its treatment on quality of life, complications, and disease progression. Patients may also be required to undergo extensive psychological assessment prior to risk-reducing surgical procedures. Survival may be problematic for some patients with cancer, for example, if, previously, a loved one was lost to the disease. Understandably, psychological distress is a significant issue for patients with a diagnosis of cancer, and their relatives (Brennan, Cull, Harvey & Parkinson, 1997; Derogatis, 1986; Rodin, 2003; Zabora, BrintzenhofeSzoc, Curbow, Hooker & Piantadosi, 2001).

In the 1980s, research in North America revealed that 47 per cent of people with cancer had a psychological problem (Derogatis et al., 1983). Research in the United Kingdom found that 25–33 per cent of women with breast cancer developed clinically significant depression, anxiety, and/or sexual problems in the year following (Maguire et al., 1980). More recently, clinical research has also demonstrated high levels of psychological morbidity among patients attending cancer centres (Fallowfield, Ratcliffe, Jenkins & Saul, 2001), patients with newly diagnosed lung cancer (Hopwood & Stephens, 2000), and patients with early breast cancer (Hall, A'Hern & Fallowfield, 1999). In particular, Hall et al.'s study revealed that 49.6 per cent of study participants with early breast cancer were clinically anxious, and 37.2 per cent were clinically depressed in the first three months after diagnosis.

In addition to anxiety and depression, patients with cancer may present to psychology services for help with anxious preoccupation (e.g., checking for lumps), treatment-related fears (e.g., of radiation, needles), marital, sexual, and relationship problems, perceived losses and perceived threats to physical integrity, body image, and autonomy, and fears concerning the future—Damocles' syndrome.

A recent audit of an integrated psychosocial oncology service for people with cancer and their families, based on review of case notes, patient reports, and psychometric assessment data from consecutive patients attending during a five-day period, revealed that anxiety (51 per cent), depression (28 per cent), existential concerns (28 per cent), and impact on quality of life (26 per cent) were the main reasons for referral (Walker, 2006). When data concerning patients who "dropped in" to the service, that is, self-referrals, were included (in addition to those referred by a health professional), staff reported that the main reasons for attendance were anxiety (27 per cent), adjustment reaction (23 per cent), quality of life concerns (19 per cent), depression (13 per cent), concerns about the family (13 per cent), social and welfare rights concerns (12 per cent), existential concerns (10 per cent), procedure-related distress (2 per cent), and suicide risk (2 per cent) (ibid.).

Psychological interventions for people with cancer

Evidence-based approaches appropriate to the treatment of psychological difficulties associated with experience of cancer include person-centred, psychodynamic, cognitive behavioural, and existential therapies (Burton & Watson, 1988; Holland, 1998). In addition to generic therapy texts, resources are available to psychological therapies practitioners that focus on a specific therapeutic approach in working with patients who have cancer. For example, Moorey and Greer (2002) present a cognitive behavioural approach to emotional difficulties encountered by people with cancer. Goldie (2005) describes how a psychoanalytic psychotherapeutic approach may help patients to cope with cancer.

Some authors (e.g., Allen, 2006; Straker, 1998) have suggested that psychodynamic psychotherapy is particularly useful for understanding the emotional reactions of patients with cancer as well as offering a perspective on the health professional-patient relationship. Based on his experience of working with patients with cancer at the Royal Marsden Hospital since the early 1970s, Goldie (2005) concluded that psychoanalytic psychotherapy, together with general medical care, could significantly help patients (who are not "psychiatric" cases) to cope with cancer through its potential for a new sense of integration for the patient and the resolution of long-standing conflicts that can make it difficult to adjust to a diagnosis of cancer, its treatment or recurrence.

Experiential dynamic psychotherapies are talking treatments that help a patient to solve problems associated with unconscious emotions or conflicts (Abbass, 2003; Abbass, Hancock, Henderson & Kisely, 2006). When current stress, for example, a diagnosis or recurrence of cancer, activates these emotions, anxiety and defences may emerge, leading to anxiety disorders, somatisation, depression, avoidance, self-defeating patterns, and interpersonal problems. Experiential dynamic psychotherapies help a patient to "overcome anxiety, defensiveness and emotional avoidance" (Abbass, 2003, p. 535) thereby preventing more serious problems, reducing distress, and promoting improvements in quality of life. The "experiential component, that is *the experience of previously unbearable affect in the here and now of the patient-therapist relationship* [is considered] the key agent of therapeutic change" (Fosha, 2000, p. 314, italics in original).

In the last forty years, there have been significant developments in the experiential dynamic psychotherapies (Abbass et al., 2006). These include therapeutic focus (Triangle of Conflict and the Triangle of Others—also known as the Triangle of Person), active therapist involvement, use of the transference/therapeutic relationship, time sensitivity, and several developments in relational, restructuring, and experiential/affective techniques (Abbass et al., 2006; Coughlin Della Selva, 1996; Davanloo, 1990; Fosha, 2000a, b; Frederick, 2009; Frederickson, 1999; ten Have-de Labije, 2001, 2006, 2008, 2009, 2010; Malan & Coughlin Della Selva, 2006; Osimo, 2003). To some extent this has led to an integration of psychodynamic psychotherapy with modern principles of learning and behavioural change (McCullough Vaillant, 1997; McCullough et al., 2003) as well as an integration of developmental theory, self psychology, emotion theory, and affective neuroscience (Fosha, 2001).

The experiential dynamic psychotherapeutic approach is unique in its integration of "affective neuroscience, psychotherapy, philosophy, and mindful Eastern practices" (Fosha, 2008, p. 31), and marks a shift in focus from models of psychopathology to a model of healing. Such an approach is relevant to the treatment of maladaptive self-perceptions that may be hampering adjustment of patients following diagnosis of cancer and/or medical and surgical treatments that have an impact on appearance and sense of self. The clinical methodology is firmly rooted in and occurs in the context of the interpersonal relationship between patient and therapist, which is seen as a genuine, personal, and respectful human interchange (Fosha, 2000a; Osimo, 2003).

Patients with cancer potentially experience several losses including loss of health, loss of a sense of control, loss of security in a relationship, loss of confidence, and loss of positive self-perceptions. Research evidence suggests that cognitive adaptation to serious health threat, including cancer, is facilitated by finding meaning, regaining a sense of control (i.e., mastery), and restoring self-esteem (i.e., self-enhancement) (Helgeson, 1999, 2003; Helgeson & Fritz, 1999; Taylor, 1983). For these reasons, acknowledging mastery, mourning the Self, and receiving affirmation, key meta-therapeutic processes (Fosha, 2000b) within the developmentally-based model of change associated with experiential dynamic therapies, are highly relevant to work with patients with cancer. Types of therapist activity that are specifically experiential and dynamic, and which are likely to help a patient to find meaning, regain a sense of mastery, and restore positive self-perceptions, include attending to the relationship, mirroring, anxiety assessment, and regulation, emotional maieutics, defence work, and interventions that focus on Superego pathology (see Osimo, 2003, 2012). In summary, experiential dynamic psychotherapy practitioners have developed ways of working with defences, anxiety, and adaptive affect, as well as Self- and Other-representations, and patterns of interaction that may hinder adaptation to diagnosis, successful and unsuccessful treatment, disease progression, recurrence of cancer, and survival. Through helping a patient with cancer to overcome anxiety, defensiveness, and emotional avoidance, more serious problems are prevented, distress is reduced, and quality of life is optimised. As such, the experiential dynamic psychotherapies have a circumscribed, but important, role to play in augmenting the range of interventions available in psychological therapies services working in oncology.

Experiential dynamic psychotherapies and working with cancer patients

Case study

The initial psychological therapy session reported herein was undertaken within a National Health Service hospital psychological therapies service that provides psychological interventions and support to patients with cancer and their relatives and carers. The therapist was a member of an Intensive Experiential-Dynamic Psychotherapy (IE-DP) core training group in his first year of post-qualification advanced training. The patient's breast care specialist nurse referred the patient to the service for treatment of anxiety, adjustment reaction, and quality of life issues. The patient, a woman in her mid-forties, had been diagnosed with carcinoma right breast fourteen months previously, and underwent mastectomy and sentinel lymph node biopsy thirteen months prior to psychological therapy. She had also completed a course of adjuvant chemotherapy and external radiotherapy, and had been prescribed medication included Tamoxifen and Fluoxetine. Discussion of reconstructive surgery was scheduled to take place four months after initial contact with the psychology service.

The Woman with the Lump

The therapist begins the session by inviting the patient to say what the problem is for which she is seeking help (HP):

Th: … it would be helpful to get a sense from you of what the problem is that brings you here.
(Patient is sitting forward in the chair, holding her hands together and fidgeting with her fingers)

Pt: (Patient sighs and looks away) Just so stressed out. I think (pause) having the cancer (gesturing with her left hand) then having the treatment, I was fine. But then once it all stopped, I don't know, I just felt, I feel so alone. (Patient looks away. Tear comes to patient's eye and she wipes tear away) Sorry.

The moment the therapist invites the patient to share her understanding of the problem for which she is seeking help there is an increase in the patient's anxiety and the patient looks away. The therapist could have taken this opportunity to bring the patient's awareness to her anxiety, which she is ignoring, and conduct a thorough assessment of the patient's manifestations of anxiety (AA). He could also refer to the patient's defence of looking away as an automatic withdrawal from the therapist, the moment the patient is asked to describe her problem (DA). The patient spontaneously referred to her sense of aloneness that invites intervention by the therapist who could refer to the therapeutic relationship (RE). There is an emergence of tears, for which the patient apologises, suggesting habitual self-neglect that is put into operation by the Ego, in agreement with a cruel and neglectful Superego that demands giving priority to others, and the suppression of the patient's own feelings. This will also require intervention by the therapist (SE). The therapist decides to continue with emotional maieutics (XA) and the real relationship with the patient (RE) by implicitly acknowledging the patient's tears:

Th: It's OK (therapist moves tissue box nearer to the patient).

Pt: I don't know. It's as if I blame myself for getting it. And I feel as though I've let everybody down (sharp intake of breath, patient rubs index finger and thumb together).

The patient again expresses a self-critical and self-blaming perspective and there is another rise in anxiety that has spread to the intercostal muscles. The therapist does not deal with the Superego pathology (SE), nor enquires about who the patient has let down (HP), but instead continues to work on emotional maieutics (XA), while also making reference to the therapeutic relationship (RE) to begin to counter the patient's sense of aloneness:

Th: There's a lot of strong feeling coming up for you now (patient's lower lip is trembling) as you're talking to me about this, isn't there?

Pt: Yes (slowly stepping with her feet and legs).

The moment the therapist directs the patient's attention to her feelings there is an increase in anxiety within the patient that she discharges by stepping with her feet. This is an opportunity for the therapist to assess the ways in which the patient experiences anxiety (AA) as well as to assess her ego adaptive capacity, an important step in therapy (ten Have-de Labije, 2006). Instead, he continues to focus on the emerging feelings (XA) and invites the patient to attend to what is happening within:

Th: What's coming up for you?

Pt: Erm.

Th: What do you notice happening if you sort of tune in to how you're feeling within yourself?

Pt: I've never really spoken to anybody about it. I've told people bits but it's here (touches chest over clavicle) all the time and it's here (points to right side of head) in my head, 24/7 (clenches right fist) I'm (pause) on the one hand I'm frightened of getting it back, on the other hand (gesturing with her hands and arms, palms upwards) it's just totally stressing me out (flexing fingers and gently clenching fists).

The moment the therapist invites the patient to attend to her inner processes the patient responds defensively saying that she never talks about these matters and refers in vague terms to something located in her chest and head. She also refers to having shared some of her feelings but not all. This could be explored by asking who she has spoken to, how did they respond, and what it was like for her to share her feelings (SO). The therapist could make a link between not talking about her feelings with others and what is happening in the session (TC). The patient begins to express her fear of recurrence of cancer and her experience of what sounds like anxiety. Before clarifying their understanding of what the patient has said, the therapist continues to regulate anxiety (AA), by focusing on the experiential level and the patient's struggle to cope:

Th: So it feels overwhelming.
Pt: Yes (fists clenched).
Th: But it felt OK while you were having the treatment …
Pt: Yes.
Th: … but now that's all finished …
Pt: It seems to have hit me like a ton of bricks. It really has.

At this point the therapist begins to work more specifically on the patient's harshly self-critical and self-blaming pathological Superego (defence restructuring—DA, HP, SE) and continues to regulate her anxiety (AA). In this way he is normalising the patient's reaction and implicitly validating her *past* use of the defence of self-neglect:

Th: I think that's quite normal. A lot of people find that the main thing is getting through the treatments. The way they cope with that is to really put all the worries and anxieties to one side …
Pt: Yes.
Th: … and just focus on getting through it …
Pt: Yes.
Th: … and so when it does come to an end, that's when people do feel they've got some time and space to actually think about what's happened to them.
Pt: Yes.
Th: So that's quite a normal reaction that you've been experiencing.
(Patient is holding her hands together and turning a ring on her finger)
Pt: I just feel so gutted with it all (hands together, palms up). Like I said, I feel as though I've let somebody (wringing hands) I've let all my family down. I really do. And it hurts (tears coming to her eyes, clenching teeth, lips pressed together).

The patient responds by revealing more of her harshly self-critical and self-blaming pathological Superego and its emotional impact. There is a rise of tears and anxiety. The therapist switches back to emotional maieutics (XA) by asking the patient to identify what she is feeling:

Th: What are you feeling now?
Pt: STRESS (said angrily, jaw clenched) (wipes tears from eyes). I'm so stressed out (wringing hands). I can't just seem to get it out of my head. I really can't. And then like I've got (wipes eyes) the other operation to go through.

The patient again refers to stress that could be her way of describing her experience of anxiety but it also appears that anger is rising to the surface. The patient continues to use the defence of vagueness so it is not clear what she is unable to "get out of her head". She begins to talk about her anxiety concerning future surgical procedures. The therapist seeks clarification:

Th: Right.
Pt: (Sigh) Erm. That's on my mind all the time.
Th: Is that the reconstruction?
Pt: Yes.

The therapist takes this opportunity to focus on anxiety regulation (AA) although in an imprecise way—he could have asked "What's the scariest thing about reconstruction" to counter the patient's automatic and habitual defence of vagueness, and/or pointed out to the patient her use of the defence of vagueness (and its self-defeating function) (DA) in conversation with the therapist (RE).

Th: What are you, what's the scariest thing about that? Or what's the most stressful thing about that?
Pt: How I'm going to look. I mean, because (pause) I look at myself so, sometimes, I stress myself out more because I look, to me, I feel like and look like a freak. I really do (wipes tear from face). I just can't get it out of my head.

The patient describes her concern about how she will look following reconstructive surgery and her sense that she looks like a freak, again suggesting an emotionally abusive self-perspective. The therapist could have focused on emotional experiencing (XA) and asked what it is like for the patient to feel such a "freak" or to ask the patient how she feels when she looks at herself, but instead enquires about the patient's relationships (HP), in preparation for investigating alternative perspectives and determining the extent to which the self-defeating perspective originates from within the patient or current significant others:

Th: Are you married? Are you in a relationship?
Pt: No. I'm in a relationship. I've been giving him so much grief as well. I've been taking it out on him. And it's not fair. I shouldn't. But I can't help it. I'm just so stressed out (lips pressed together).

The patient refers to her tendency to take out her anger on her partner and this defence is somewhat dystonic. She attributes the behaviour to the fact that she is stressed out. The therapist seeks clarification of the phrase "stressed out":

Th: What do you mean by stressed out?
Pt: Like everything seems to get on top of me (wipes tear from face). Everything seems to be a hassle (fingers interlaced tight together over stomach).

It remains unclear what the patient means by stressed out but it appears to be a combination of a sense of being overwhelmed, and a lack of motivation. The patient continues to ignore her tears. The therapist could have drawn the patient's attention to her tears (MI), her anxiety (AA), and the defences of ignoring the tears and giving the therapist priority (DA). Instead, the therapist invites the patient to provide a specific example of what she means by stressed out (HP), albeit in a less than precise way, in an attempt to get a better sense of what the patient is talking about:

Th: Can you give me a specific example?

Pt: Sometimes I just don't want to get up in the morning, I just want to stay in bed and not see nobody.

The moment the therapist invites the patient to provide a specific example that relates to her experience of "stressed out" the patient responds by saying what she does rather than describing a specific event—a defensive response. The therapist does not draw the patient's attention to the defence of not answering the question (DA) and keeping her feelings hidden from others and the therapist (TC), and instead returns to emotional maieutics (XA) and the patient's struggle to cope:

Th: It just feels too much.

Pt: Yes. It really does. And I'm not sleeping properly either so I don't think that's helping. But, I'm so stressed out (clenching teeth, lips pressed together).

The patient reports sleep disturbance and simply repeats that she is stressed out. The therapist now takes a different approach and decides to address the relationship with the patient directly (RE). He invites the patient to say how she was feeling about coming to the session, while implicitly continuing to address the patient's sense of aloneness by referring to his presence in the relationship (RE):

Th: How did you feel about coming here this morning and seeing me?

Pt: A bit hit and miss. But on the other hand, I was glad that I've finally asked for the help, to see somebody because I've tried to do it on my own, I've tried to [get] past it all on my own, if you understand what I mean …

The patient does not say how she felt but does acknowledge mixed feelings in a vague way. Her use of the word "somebody" is both a defensive generalisation and distancing from the therapist, signalling anxiety about emotional closeness as well as emotional experience. However, a more compassionate and accepting self-perspective begins to emerge that is positive about the patient seeking help rather than relying on what has become an automatic, habitual, self-defeating, and emotionally distancing, defensive coping strategy, one of trying to deal with everything herself. The therapist notes the adaptive response and boosts the patient's healthy Ego by acknowledging the patient's efforts to cope (SO), while also implicitly encouraging the patient to attend in a precise way to different aspects of her experience—emotional maieutics (XA):

Th: Sure. And you've done a phenomenal job it sounds like …
Pt: (Sigh)
Th: I mean you've got through, you've got through the surgery …
Pt: Yes.
Th: … you've got through the chemo [therapy] …
Pt: I intended to, but …
Th: … so you've obviously got a great deal of strength …
Pt: Yes.
Th: … that you can draw on …
Pt: It's just now.
Th: … when you need to.
Pt: It's just, all of a sudden, all of a sudden, it just hit me like a ton of bricks. And I thought (sighs) but I've tried to cope with it myself and I can't. You see I'm not one of these that'll talk to people much (slight smile) about what's going on inside. I just, everybody just knows me as [name of patient]. And I still try to put on a brave face but it hurts.

The patient responds by again referring to the sudden tremendous impact of her experiences. She reports her tendency to keep things to herself rather than open up to others as well as her tendency to cover up her feelings through the defence of putting on a brave face, thereby making the outside (what others see) different from the inside (what she feels) (J. ten Have-de Labije, personal communication, 2009). The therapist could make a link between the patient's tendency to keep others at an emotional distance and her use of defences in the session (TC). Instead, the therapist responds by drawing the patient's attention to the relationship with him in the room (RE) and how the patient feels doing something different that has the potential to be helpful to her (SO, XA), in beginning to look at her inner processes with the therapist. The therapist also acknowledges the anxiety (AA) the patient might feel in relation to increased emotional closeness (RE).

Th: So how do you feel about talking to me about what's going on inside …
Pt: (Deep breath)
Th: … because if I'm to help you to cope with this …
Pt: Good actually. Good actually (lips pressed together). Mm. Yes.
Th: … that's something that we are going to need to get into, together …
Pt: (Nodding head, wiping tears from face)
Th: … is how you're feeling inside …
Pt: Yes.
Th: … and what's going to be helpful to you to get through this.
Pt: Yes.
Th: And that might feel quite scary, particularly if it's not something that you usually do …
Pt: No, it's not.
Th: … but it's part of my job to make you feel as safe as possible …
Pt: Yes.

Th: ... to help you to do that.
Pt: Yes.

The therapist returns to emotional maieutics (XA):

Th: So if I could ask you again just to tune in to how you're feeling now, just inside your body, how are you feeling if you tune in?
Pt: (Looks upwards) Actually, I'm feeling a little bit better, because I'm here, talking to you. It's, the biggest part of the problem (scratches at the side of her eye) is I think, when I'm on my own as well. It just goes through my mind. I just can't seem to get the cancer out my head. I really can't (lips pressed together, fingers interlaced tightly).

The patient responds by saying that she is feeling better. The therapist could have pointed out her defensive, self-defeating, and automatic use of a vague term, "feeling better", sought the agreement of the patient that she wanted to explore her feelings with love, care, and precision, and asked the patient to be more specific (DA)—in what way does she feel better (XA), what does she notice that's different when she tunes into how she is feeling in the room with the therapist (XA, RE, SO). However, the patient also provided more information about her problem and it appears to be linked to rumination about cancer when she is on her own. This suggests that the patient may have been trying to distract herself from rumination (and avoiding her feelings) by keeping busy or by being with others, while also putting on a brave face. The therapist seeks further information, albeit in a less than precise manner, about the patient's rumination (HP—defence clarification):

Th: Has it always been like that since it's been diagnosed or is it only since you've finished the first lot of treatment?
Pt: It's more or less always since I've finished my treatment. Since about, it started about [month], because my treatment didn't finish while [ten months later—six months before psychological therapy session] ...
Th: OK.
Pt: ... so I was still getting over that, then all of a sudden (blows out air) it just hit me.

The patient clarifies that the rumination became a problem shortly after finishing medical treatment (although she still has reconstructive surgery ahead). She again refers to the sudden impact of "it". This is another opportunity for the therapist to draw the patient's attention to her defensive, self-defeating, and automatic use of a vague term, "it", seek the agreement of the patient that she wants to explore her feelings with love, care, and precision (attending to the working alliance), and ask the patient to be more specific (DA), for example, to say what exactly hit her, what does she mean when she says "it hit her". The emotional experience could then have been explored further (XA). Instead the therapist draws the patient's attention to the fact that there was a period of time after previous medical treatment when the problem was not present (HP):

Th: So there were a couple of months after you finished treatment where things were OK?
Pt: Yes. And then all of a sudden …
Th: … and then in January things changed.
Pt: Uh-huh.

The patient confirms that there was a period when there was no problem with rumination and the therapist seeks information about what was happening in the patient's life when she became aware that she was ruminating about cancer (HP):

Th: What was happening around that time? What do you think might be something to do with why it suddenly seemed to hit you, like a ton of bricks?
Pt: (Deep inspiration, holding breath, fists clenched) I don't, maybe, I've had a lot of worry, like my daughter, she was pregnant. I've had a lot of worry over her. Er. You see I seem to worry about everybody else but myself.
Th: Mm.
Pt: I seem to try and, how can I put it, (pause) get through things on my own.
Th: You're an independent woman.
Pt: But (sigh) I'm finding it so hard and it's frustrating. It really is frustrating because I can't do it anymore. So.
Th: So you're feeling quite angry with yourself.
Pt: Yes, I am (emphatic nodding). And more for getting the cancer (lips pressed together, fingers interlocked). I know people say it can happen to anybody but when it happens to you it's, it's not nice.

The patient informs the therapist about her daughter becoming pregnant and confirms that she has a habit of giving others priority, neglecting herself, and keeping her feelings and concerns hidden from others. These automatic and habitual patterns of coping are no longer effective and the patient has been blaming herself. At this point, there is another opportunity for the therapist to address the Superego pathology by pointing out to the patient different aspects of her character—the healthy part that attends to herself by asking for help (SO), and the self-defeating, self-neglecting, fiercely self-sufficient part that puts barriers up between the patient and her feelings, and between the patient and others, including the therapist (TC), that tells her that she should be coping better without bothering others, that it is her fault that she had cancer, leaving her feeling alone, frustrated, and overwhelmed (SE). The therapist does not draw the patient's attention to this conflict but rather tries to understand the self-blaming perspective (SE):

Th: Why do you think you are blaming yourself?
Pt: I don't know (pause) (lips pressed together). I blame myself, because, like I said, I let, I'm letting everybody down, by being like this, if you know what I mean. Screwed. Putting it mildly, mildly. Screwed. Totally screwed at the minute.

The patient again states her sense of letting others down, evidence that the pathological Superego continues to dominate. It is not clear what the patient means by the word "screwed".

The therapist could focus on the Superego pathology (SE) or explore what the patient means by "screwed". The therapist gives voice to the pathological Superego (SE):

Th: You think you should be taking it in your stride …
Pt: (Sharp inspiration)
Th: … coping, and that to do anything else is putting a burden onto other people?
Pt: Yes. YES. Yes, I don't. I look at it this way, people have their own problems. They don't need mine. But I know in myself, deep down, I've been stupid for not talking, for not asking for the help at first.

The patient responds positively to the articulation of the Superego voice and confirms her fear of being a burden to others. Although she refers to the healthier part of her that wants to approach others for help, there is further self-criticism. The therapist has another opportunity to make links between what the patient is doing with him and her tendency to protect others from her feelings (TC). Instead he continues to explore the harsh self-criticism (SE) but does not yet draw the patient's attention to the healthy part of the Ego (SO).

Th: It sounds like you're criticising yourself quite a lot.
Pt: Yes. It hurts because, I really do feel as though I've let everybody down (voice becoming quiet and whispery). I really do (lips pressed together, jaw clenched, hands together over stomach).

The patient restates her self-defeating and self-blaming belief that she has let others down, and does so in a way that suggests that she is trying hard to keep strong feelings at bay. The therapist seeks to understand if the patient is doing this to herself under the influence of a pathological Superego or if there are, in fact, others in the patient's environment who have expressed such a blaming view to the patient (HP, SO):

Th: Has anyone said anything or done anything to give you that impression?
Pt: No (shaking head emphatically). No, so why? I feel like it, I don't know. Nobody has. Everybody's been so good. But it's just how I feel. I really do.

The patient denies that others have expressed blame, signalling the presence of Superego pathology (and a past aggressor). The therapist could have started to address this by drawing the patient's attention to the self-defeating function of the self-blame, harsh self-criticism, and fierce self-sufficiency, and contrasted the critical position she automatically takes with that of the healthy Ego that has a more compassionate view towards self and others (SE, SO). Instead, the therapist switches back to emotional maieutics (XA) but again asks general questions—in talking with the patient it is important to be precise so, first, they could have asked, who in particular does the patient sense that she has let down:

Th: So how do you, what's the feeling that goes with that sense that you've let people down?
Pt: Gutted. Erm.
Th: Tell me more about that.

Pt: Really gutted inside, because I've always been a person to get on with life, no matter what was thrown at me, and then all of a sudden this happens, and I can't, I can't seem to get out of the rut …
Th: Right.
Pt: I really can't. I've tried.

The patient again uses a word that does not convey a clear sense of a feeling and restates that she is struggling with not being able to move forward, despite having done so in the past through the defences of ignoring, neglecting, and "getting on with life". The therapist acknowledges that it has been a difficult period for the patient and gently repeats the question about feeling (XA) but again without helping the patient to be more specific about who she senses that she has let down. This vagueness and generality helps the patient to avoid the full extent of her feelings and deprives the therapist and patient of a better understanding of the patient's feelings.

Th: That tells me how difficult it has been for you over the last few months to move forward from this, and to some extent that's understandable, you've still got a reconstruction to get through …
Pt: Yes.
Th: … what I'm wondering about is this sense that you have of letting people down, and what that actually, what's the feeling that goes with that?
Pt: Erm (fidgeting with fingers).

The therapist continues to invite the patient to attend to her inner processes (XA):

Th: If you notice how you're feeling when you think about having let people down.
Pt: I feel hurt inside. Really hurt. That I've (wipes tear from eye) …

The patient responds by saying that she feels hurt, and tears come to the surface. The therapist seeks confirmation that the hurt is an emotional pain before continuing with emotional maieutics (XA):

Th: It's an emotional pain that you have?
Pt: Uh-huh (nodding head).
Th: Where do you feel that hurt?
Pt: (Clenches fists)
Th: Where, where in (passing hand in front of face and down chest) …
Pt: All over. Just all over (raising and lowering her hands and arms, flexed at the elbow). It's weird. I've never been like this before.
Th: How would you describe it? What's your experience of it physically?
Pt: It's like a hurting pain.
Th: Like an ache or a stab or …
Pt: Yes.
Th: … how would you describe it?
Pt: Like, like an ache, but it hurts. It really hurts. So bad.

Th: Where does it hurt the most?
Pt: All over.
Th: Where does it hurt the most?
Pt: (Sighs) Here (pointing to her right temple). It really does.

The therapist then observes that the patient is anxious and draws her attention to the tension in her body (AA).

Th: I notice that you seem to be quite tense at the moment. Is that something that you're aware of?
Pt: No (fidgeting with fingers).
Th: (Mirrors fidgeting with fingers)
Pt: I know. I know.

The patient confirms that her Ego is not attending to her anxiety although it does appear to be observing because when the muscle tension is pointed out to her, the patient is aware of her fidgeting. This is how she is discharging the anxiety. Although intervention directs the patient to relax (AA), the therapist could have pointed out to the patient that she automatically and habitually ignores her anxiety and that it is self-defeating and neglectful to do so as the anxiety then does not get dealt with (DA). A thorough assessment of how the patient experiences anxiety (AA), linked to the wish of the healthy part to treat herself more kindly (SE), would have been appropriate at this point:

Th: Can you try and relax?
Pt: I'm frightened to, to be honest with you.

The patient expresses her fear of relaxing so the therapist continues with anxiety regulation (AA):

Th: What are you afraid will happen if you relax?
Pt: Because (pause) erm (scratches head)

The patient does not respond and the therapist enquires if she is afraid of feelings (AA)—if ignoring and maintaining the tension in her body is a way of keeping the feelings at bay:

Th: Some of the feeling will come through?
Pt: (Nods, tears welling in eyes, biting lower lip) Yeah.

The patient has tears welling in her eyes and the therapist continues with emotional maieutics (XA):

Th: What do you notice happening in your body now?
Pt: It's just so stressed out. I can feel the stress inside.

Th: Tension?
Pt: Mmm. Yeah. It really is bad.
Th: What's the feeling? If you put that tension to one side …
Pt: Right.
Th: … what's the feeling that comes up as you're relaxing?
Pt: Erm. Stress. More stress. Nothing else.
Th: Sounds like tension again.
Pt: Yeah.

The patient is only aware of feeling anxiety that the therapist does not name for her but simply refers to as tension. The therapist could explore the reason for the anxiety (AA) and link it to the patient being invited to attend to her inner processes (XA), with the therapist (RE), something that she has tended to avoid in the past (DA), and with others (TC).

The patient goes on to describe her usual way of coping and again points out that she is aware that it is no longer helping her. The therapist validates the *past* behaviour while emphasising the importance to the patient of finding new ways of dealing with her feelings (DA), before proceeding with emotional maieutics (XA) and directing the patient's attention to some of the costs associated with the defensive pattern (DA):

Pt: (Coughs). Just got on with it. Dealt with it. Got on with it. Like I did when I first got the cancer. I just thought, right, I've been dealt with it, I'll deal with it. I dealt with it in my own way. And, I got through it. I sailed through it all …
Th: Good. That's wonderful.
Pt: … yeah, until now.
Th: So what it sounds like is that this coping strategy you have of getting on with things has really been quite effective and very helpful to you …
Pt: Yeah.
Th: … erm, however, it doesn't seem to be working at the moment …
Pt: No.
Th: … so we need to find an alternative way of helping you to cope …
Pt: Right.
Th: … and it may be that part of getting on and doing things meant blocking …
Pt: Yeah.
Th: … and shutting down some of the feelings …
Pt: Yeah.
Th: … or pushing them away and actually looking into some of those feelings and reconnecting with them, while it might be painful, is probably going to be a way of opening up for you another range of ways of coping.
Pt: Yeah. Mmm.
Th: Because my sense is that you're keeping so much in.
Pt: (Nodding, lower lip trembling)
Th: That you're really …
Pt: Yeah.

Th: … holding onto it …
Pt: Yeah.
Th: … to get through it.
Pt: Yeah.
Th: Just to get through it.
Pt: Yeah.
Th: And that, that must be so tiring.
Pt: It is.
Th: It must take so much energy to …
Pt: It does.
Th: … just to keep it all in …
Pt: Yeah.
Th: … and to keep going.
Pt: It does.
Th: … and if you're not, if you've not been sleeping, then it's understandable why …
Pt: Yeah.
Th: … it might be getting, it might have become hard …
Pt: Yeah.
Th: … for you to keep going with that strategy because it is quite an energy consuming strategy.
Pt: Yeah. It's just, it's just so weird. The feeling, it's weird. It really is. It's frustrating because I'm trying to, I try and shake it off myself but it's just not working. I think I've tried maybe a bit too hard.
Th: You've really soldiered on when it's felt …
Pt: Yeah.
Th: … like you've really needed some support.
Pt: Mmm (nodding, lips pressed tight together), yeah.
Th: That's how you've coped.
Pt: Yeah. It's mad though.

There appears to have been a glimmer of self-compassion in the patient, and the therapist proceeds to taking history, enquiring about experiences around the time of diagnosis of breast cancer (HP). The patient reports a successful treatment, but refers to her fear that there may be residual cancer cells. She describes some of her hypervigilant behaviour:

Pt: … but, I can't accept that. Because, with it breaking away, like where it's at the back of my [chest] wall, I don't know if maybe … I don't know if there is a piece floating around somewhere. And I'm frightened. If I get a little mark on my hand or a little bump, or anywhere on my body, I'm thinking, "Oh, no". I just can't get it out of my head.
Th: So you're quite, you're noticing any little thing and thinking I wonder if that's anything …
Pt: Yeah, yeah, yeah.

The therapist proceeds to place the patient's fear of residual cancer cells in the context of facts and explore with the patient what would help her to accept the facts (HP, AA)—although it may be helpful to explore the fear (AA) and associated thoughts and feelings in greater depth (XA). In oncology, with some patients, it can be helpful to encourage a focus on what is known rather than what is feared might happen (L.G. Walker, personal communication, 2008):

Th: … but they've said they got it all.
Pt: They said they've got it all, yeah.
Th: What would help you to accept that? To accept what they say, that they have got it all?
Pt: I don't know, to be honest with you.
Th: Because presumably they've done a biopsy have they?
Pt: Yes. Yes.
Th: They've taken some tissue from around the margins?
Pt: Yeah.
Th: And they're happy that they got it all?
Pt: Yeah.
Th: Have you had any scans done?
Pt: I've had a mammogram on this [contralateral] side. They said this side's fine. They gave me a scan on this side and they said that they had got it all so, which I suppose in one sense is good but it's, it's, it's just on my mind.
Th: Can you allow yourself to feel any relief that they got it all?
Pt: No. I can't, honestly. I really can't. Not at the minute, I can't.

The patient reports blocking a sense of relief, not allowing herself to accept a successful outcome to surgery. The therapist explores this further with the patient (XA, DA):

Th: Would you say you were feeling anything at the moment or are you feeling quite numb?
Pt: Numb (nodding).
Th: So maybe the strategy of just getting on with things and blocking everything away, it's not only blocking some of the negative feelings but it's also blocking …
Pt: Some of the positive.
Th: … some of the positive feelings as well.
Pt: Yeah (shrugs shoulders).

The therapist returns to enquiries about experiences around the time of diagnosis (HP) after which the patient refers to her sense that she has awakened from a dream:

Pt: Yeah. Yeah. I just thought, no it's not happening to me, I'm dreaming. But obviously not. And I think the reality's starting to kick in now. I really do.
Th: What is the reality? How would you describe the reality?
Pt: Erm, that I have actually had cancer because I try to block it out, ah no I haven't. Even when, like this, erm.

Th: I'm encouraged by what you've just said.
Pt: (Looks quizzical)
Th: Do you know why?
Pt: Why?
Th: You said, because I've had cancer.
Pt: Mm.
Th: You didn't say I have cancer …
Pt: No, right.
Th: …you said I've had …
Pt: Yeah.
Th: … cancer. And that's encouraging …
Pt: Mm.
Th: … because there's a part of you, although there is a part of you that is anxious …
Pt: Mm.
Th: … and worried about them not having got it all …
Pt: Mm.
Th: … and about what might happen, there's also another part of you that has accepted, it was, it's in the past.
Pt: Yeah.
Th: You had cancer.
Pt: Yeah (nodding).
Th: And that it is now gone. They got it all. So there is a part of you that has accepted that.
Pt: Mm.
Th: It's just there's another …
Pt: Part that …
Th: … part of you that is still worried about it.
Pt: Yeah. Yeah.
Th: So we need to know about both parts.
Pt: Right.
Th: The part of you that's accepted that it's in the past, and the part of you that's anxious about it still being there.
Pt: Mm.
Th: So can we look at that together?
Pt: Yeah.
Th: So, the part of you that is still worried about it being there …
Pt: Mm.
Th: … tell me some more about that.
Pt: Erm, I don't know, it's just, I'm frightened to death it's going to come back.
Th: What would that mean?
(Pause)
Pt: The cancer. I know, the cancer's gone. I know at the back of my mind it has, but I can't help feeling it's just going to come back. I don't know if that's normal or what. I just, I don't know, I feel, I really feel as though it's going to come back.
Th: What would that mean to you, were it to come back?

Pt: Devastating. Devastating. It really would. I've been through it once, I don't want to go through it again.

Th: It was a real ordeal.

Pt: More or less, yeah. So like to have, how can I put this, to have like a piece of you missing, that really hurts. I know it had to be done. I know it had, that it had to come off, but I feel such, so much like a freak.

Th: As though you've been mutilated?

Pt: Yeah (nodding). Yeah. Yeah. I know it had to be done, but it hurts so much.

Th: That's another sign of your strength. Something that you so didn't want to do, and to let them do to you, you put yourself through because you knew …

Pt: (Nodding) Yeah. Had to be done.

Th: … it had to be done. For your health.

Pt: Yeah.

Th: For your family. For the people you care about.

Pt: Yeah.

Th: And for you.

Pt: Uh-huh.

Th: I mean, you didn't have a choice.

Pt: No. No, I didn't. And I don't want it happening again. I really don't.

Th: We don't know what's going to happen in the future. What we do know is that, right here, right now, they've got it all.

Pt: Yeah.

Th: And there's no sign of any cancer.

Pt: (Shaking head)

Th: That's what we do know.

Pt: Uh-huh.

Th: I would encourage you to focus on that. Just to take each step, one step at a time …

Pt: At a time.

Th: … and to ask yourself, how helpful is it to worry about what could happen?

Pt: Uh-huh.

Th: It might happen. It might not.

Pt: Not. Yeah.

Th: We don't know.

Pt: (Nodding)

Th: But at the moment, you're through it.

Pt: (Nodding) Uh-huh.

Th: You know. You've had surgery, you've had chemo …

Pt: Yeah.

Th: … and things are going well. Things have gone well.

Pt: Mm. Yeah.

Th: And hold on to that.

Pt: Mm. I never thought about that actually. Mm. (Pause) It's just clicked, putting it all in perspective.

Th: You've been through a lot. You've been through a tremendous amount.

The therapist begins to explore the impact of surgery, the patient's change in appearance, and the patient's avoidance of looking at her physical self (HP). The patient again refers to her sense of being a freak, and emotional maieutic enquiry reveals that the patient has been feeling "hurt, stress, and gutted". She denies any compassion for herself and expands further on her harsh self-criticism, her avoidance of telling people how she is feeling and her defence of minimisation. The therapist explores the defences (DA) including the possibility of their use by the patient in session with the therapist (RE):

Pt: I usually talk to [name of sister], but normally it's myself. I don't talk to many people about how I am feeling. I'll tell [name of sister] sometimes but it's not how I really feel inside that I tell them. And I should do.
Th: So you put a brave face on?
Pt: Yeah (nodding). More or less, yeah.
Th: So you'll tell them something but it won't be …
Pt: It's not …
Th: Maybe it's less than you really feel about something?
Pt: Yeah. Yeah.
Th: Do you think you're doing that here with me a little bit?
Pt: No. I can, I'm feeling more at ease now, to be honest with you, that I'm talking to you. And I think, in a sense, I'm one of these that, with the problems I've got, I feel stupid for talking to people, family and friends. I feel so stupid. Because, I can't express my feelings real well to them whereas I must admit I feel at ease now with you. I really do.
Th: Good. I'm pleased to hear that.
Pt: Like an outsider, somebody that knows what is, not actually going on with a person, but they can see another side to it whereas you get family and friends, they don't.

The patient appears to be saying that although she does not feel understood she does appreciate an alternative perspective, which may be linked to the therapist's intention to provide an alternative perspective rather than exploring some of her anxieties in greater depth. The therapist validates the defences of self-sufficiency and minimisation before drawing the patient's attention to some associated costs (DA):

Th: And you don't want to put on them.
Pt: No. Exactly.
Th: You want to protect them …
Pt: Yeah (nodding).
Th: … from how hurt you're feeling.
Pt: Yeah. I don't like to let them know that I'm down, half the time.
Th: I can see why you would do that because you care about them very much …
Pt: Yeah.
Th: … and you don't want to see them upset. Also, you're a very independent woman.
Pt: Yeah.
Th: The cost of that is it deprives you of support.

Pt: Yeah.
Th: Emotional support. Potentially it also deprives you of feeling close to them emotionally because you're having to protect them …
Pt: Yeah.
Th: … from how you're feeling.

The therapist could have referred to the patient's sense of aloneness and drawn her attention to the healthy part of her that longs to be close with particular people in her life, to share her feelings and concerns with them, and to receive support from them (XA, SO). He could then draw the patient's attention to the conflict within her between this healthy part that longs for closeness and care from others, to be equal to others, and the part that is telling her she should not burden others, that others are more important than her, and that she should neglect and minimise her anxiety and pain (SE, XA).

Pt: And I've been doing stupid things like drinking too much. I only drink on a weekend but it's not helping me … It kills the pain. It kills the pain. Because the pain's so bad sometimes. And it helps to kill it, but it isn't doing me any good. It's not working.
Th: So is that something that you'd like to change.
Pt: YEAH (forcefully), I am going to change it. Yeah.
Th: There's a real strength and determination in your voice then.
Pt: Yes. I am.
Th: Good for you.
Pt: I need to because I can't go on like I have been. So, it doesn't help. The pain's still there the next day. So.

The therapist asks permission to explore the patient's pain (RE) and returns to emotional maieutics (XA):

Th: Can we look into the pain a bit more together?
Pt: (Nodding)
Th: How would you describe it?
Pt: Really hurting. That's the only way I can describe it. It really hurts.
Th: Can you just tune into it. Tune into that hurt. Really notice it.
Pt: It's there all the time.
Th: Where are you feeling it?
Pt: All over. But mainly here (points to side of her head).
Th: In your head?
Pt: Mm. Mainly.
Th: And how are you feeling it in your head?
Pt: Just. It's as if, it's as if my head is just going to explode, half the time.
Th: So like a pressure?
Pt: Yeah. Yeah. Because it (pause), I'm constantly putting myself down actually.
Th: Right. That's interesting.
Pt: I am. Constantly putting myself down.

The harshly self-critical part emerges again and the patient begins to recognise this is something she is doing to herself. She reports that she tells herself she is no good to anybody but when asked does not identify the voice as that of a previous aggressor. The patient returns to describing her pain for letting family down. The therapist does not explore the conflict between the healthy and self-destructive and self-defeating parts (SO, SE) but instead returns to emotional maieutics (XA). The patient continues to report generalised feelings and the therapist encourages more precision by inviting the patient to attend to feelings in different parts of her body:

Th: OK. So, there's this pressure feeling, like your head's going to explode, and your sense that you're putting yourself down.
Pt: Yeah.
Th: Where else do you feel the pain? What about in your chest?
Pt: Yeah. All over. Yeah.
Th: What's the feeling there?
Pt: It's just like a constant ache because like I can feel the stress inside me.
Th: Tension.
Pt: Yes, the tension, yeah.
Th: What about in your arms? Do you feel it in your arms?
Pt: Yes, I do, a lot. Because I had the chemo in that one and they took the lymph nodes out of this one, so my arms are constantly aching, all the time. My legs, I can't. I'm finding it a bit hard walking distances and that's frustrating me because I was always one to be chasing about here, there and everywhere.
Th: Is that like tiredness or …
Pt: Yeah, yeah, tiredness. And I've had to like slow right down and that's frustrating because I like to chase about everywhere and I can't do it now. So that's a problem as well.

The therapist begins to explore changes in energy and performance and enquires about timeline of treatment and recovery, before returning to emotional maieutics using imagery (XA). The patient is aware of anxiety and feelings of hurt but takes a passive position. The therapist helps the patient to take an active stance and to connect with and to express her feeling of anger towards a visualised representation of the cancer:

Th: So when you tune into this hurt feeling …
Pt: Mm.
Th: Can you just tune into it again?
Pt: Yeah. It's just there all the time.
Th: Is there a picture or image in your mind that goes with that feeling?
Pt: Yeah, there is actually.
Th: Can you describe it to me?
Pt: Yeah. Lump. That's all I can see. It's as if I've got blinkers on. And all I can see is this lump.
Th: Describe the lump to me.

Pt: Just a round lump. I think like since I had this one in here I'm, I wake up in the morning and I'm checking myself because all I can see is this lump.
Th: What's the feeling towards the lump?
Pt: Hurt.
Th: If you picture in your mind, the lump, and connect with that feeling that you have, what's the feeling towards the lump?
Pt: Stress. I see that lump and I get stressed out.
Th: Is that tension or is that …
Pt: Yeah.
Th: What do you mean by stressed out? I want to be clear that I understand what you mean by it.
Pt: Erm.
Th: Because that sounds more like tension and anxiety rather than a feeling.
Pt: Right. When I see that lump I think, I ca[n't], I think to myself, "Oh, no, not again". Even though I know it's in here (points to head), to me it's like reality.
Th: So this lump that's led to you having mutilating surgery …
Pt: Yeah.
Th: … you've had to go through chemo, radiotherapy, you've been feeling like this …
Pt: Yeah.
Th: How do you feel towards that lump?
Pt: Erm, gutted (sighs). How can I put it? (Pause)
Th: It feels like it's taken so much away from you …
Pt: Yeah.
Th: … but how do you feel towards it?
Pt: But it's, it feels as though it's taking over me as well.
Th: So how do you feel towards it? Towards that lump?
Pt: Erm (sits forward). Hurt. Yeah. I feel hurt. It's there and I can't seem to get rid of it.
Th: It's clearly hurt you. How do you feel towards it? What's the feeling towards it?
Pt: Hurt back. I feel as though I want to (pause) get it and wring it. Or just grab it and chuck it.
Th: So what's the feeling?
Pt: (Sighs; increase in respiration; rocks forwards) Erm.
Th: You want to wring it. Grab it.
Pt: Yeah. Yeah. Kill it.
Th: So what's the feeling?
Pt: Mass murder (laughs).

The therapist could have commented on the patient's defence of laughing to discharge anxiety associated with the expression of murderous rage (DA), and helped her to label her feeling as anger. Instead, he continues to explore her experience of the feeling and focus on emotional maieutics (XA):

Th: Where do you feel that? Where do you feel it?
Pt: Here (places hand over centre of chest).

Th: In your chest?
Pt: Uh-huh.
Th: And what's that feeling? How would you describe it? What does it feel like physically when you have that feeling, wanting to rip it, grab it?
Pt: It feels as though it aches and I just want to rip it out. I just want to get it out and cut it up (gestures with her hand). Then I'll know. Does that sound daft?
Th: No. It sounds wonderful. Sounds like fighting spirit.
Pt: Yeah. Yeah. I just want to grab it and …
Th: Can you picture that in your mind's eye? Can you picture this lump …
Pt: Oh, yeah.
Th: … and you grabbing it?
Pt: Yeah. And cutting it up and …squashing it or doing whatever with it.
Th: What would you do with it if you let that feeling come out …
Pt: Cut it up. Cut it up.
Th: OK. What are you using to cut it up?
Pt: Anything that I can get my hands on.
Th: OK. What are you going to use?
Pt: Knife. Sharp knife.
Th: OK. Tell me what you're doing to this lump that's hurt you so deeply.
Pt: Dissecting it. Cutting it up into little bits. And then burning it. Yeah.
Th: And what's happening to it now?
Pt: It's going. It's going.
Th: Disappearing?
Pt: Yeah.
Th: In smoke, up in smoke?
Pt: Yeah. Yeah.
Th: And what's left?
Pt: Nothing.
Th: What can you see? What's the picture in your mind's eye?
Pt: Well, there's no lump. Just (relaxing of shoulders) actually it sounds daft but clear sky.
Th: That's wonderful. Clear skies.
Pt: Yeah.
Th: What's the feeling that goes with that image?
Pt: Ease. A lot of ease.
Th: Where are you feeling that?
Pt: All over. It's weird.
Th: Just describe that feeling of ease to me.
Pt: Relaxed. More. I don't feel as though I've got any tension inside. I really don't. How weird, because I've been seeing that lump for a long time.
Th: You've been seeing it for a long time?
Pt: (Nodding). It's just gone. Totally gone.
Th: That's good. How does that feel now?
Pt: Ease. Easy.

Th: ... tuning in to how you're feeling.
Pt: Yeah. I feel, a lot better actually. I feel more at ease with myself.
Th: I can feel that.
Pt: I really do.
Th: I can feel that you're almost quite moved by how you're feeling ...
Pt: Yeah.
Th: Well you are moved by how you're feeling.
Pt: Yeah. I feel more at ease now. Oh, I really do. It's weird.
Th: Can you say some more about it? What are you feeling in your head? There was that pressure, as if your head was going to explode. What are you feeling in your head now?
Pt: Ease. There's no pressure. It just, erm, more relaxed. My brain seems to be breathing more.
Th: Wonderful. Breathing more.
Pt: (Laughs) If you can understand what I mean.
Th: You feel freer?
Pt: Yeah.
Th: Less constricted.
Pt: Yeah.
Th: You feel you're breathing easier.
Pt: Yeah. I never thought, just thinking about that lump, seeing that lump, grabbing it and doing that to it.
Th: You did wonderfully well.
Pt: Weird. It's gone. So unreal. I feel more at ease now.

During the following eight months, the patient attended five further sessions, focusing on anxiety regulation and preparation for reconstructive surgery, but, after the initial session, was no longer troubled by thoughts of residual cancer, and was able to put aside occasional worries about recurrence. She reported that she was feeling happier and more at ease with herself, and felt very positive about opening up to her family about how she was really feeling. Family members confirmed that the patient had been talking with them about how she was feeling and her concerns. These changes had resulted in the patient and significant people in her life feeling emotionally closer, and improvements in the patient's relationship with her partner. She no longer felt she was on her own. In addition, the patient reported a more compassionate position towards herself and felt as though a great weight had been lifted. She underwent reconstruction and, following surgery, reported being in good spirits and having no concerns, saying that she had maintained the gains described above.

Conclusions

Experiential dynamic psychotherapies have a circumscribed, but important role to play in augmenting the range of interventions available in psychological therapies services working in oncology. Anxiety is a common problem for patients attending oncology services and ISTDP interventions focusing on assessment of and regulation of anxiety can help patients to recognise and attend to all their anxiety manifestations rather than neglect themselves and accept high levels of anxiety. Superego pathology and self-defeating defences can be as much a problem for patients in medical settings as for patients in contact with mental health services. Interventions in ISTDP draw patients' attention to their self-defeating, automatic, and habitual defences and can help them to relinquish patterns of behaviour that perpetuate their suffering, and replace these with life-affirming and self-valuing coping strategies. Emotional reactions to diagnosis of cancer and its treatment may be enquired about rarely by medical staff, perhaps because health professionals in medical settings are afraid that dealing with a patient's feelings may take up too much time when only limited time is available for consultation. Alternatively, perhaps staying focused on the facts rather than the feelings enables health practitioners to protect themselves from the emotional impact of working with patients with cancer, some of whom will be terminally ill, and many of whom are likely to undergo painful, disfiguring, or distressing treatment experiences. Experiential dynamic psychotherapies offer patients an opportunity to experience and express feelings that may not be welcomed in a medical service, or that the patient is afraid would be too much of a burden or too distressing for their friends or relatives to bear. Metaprocessing questions have the potential to further the therapeutic process.

A question that arises from the case material presented is the extent to which emotional insight into unconscious conflicts is necessary for therapeutic gains or whether simply experiencing deep feeling can be transformative. In the case material presented, the patient connected with and expressed her anger towards cancer in a way that is similar to the experiencing and expression of murderous rage towards significant others reported in some ISTDP cases, and is consistent with visualisation procedures used by patients with cancer.

Strategies that patients use to cope with cancer and distressing treatment include visualisation and imagery (Rossman, 2003; Zaza et al., 2005). Visualisation as a coping strategy in adaptation to cancer has included both peaceful imagery and visualisation of host defences destroying cancer cells (Moorey & Greer, 2002; Rossman, 2003; Schaefer-Schiumo & Atwood, 2009; Walker et al., 1999). For some patients, use of visualisation is associated with a sense of control (Moorey & Greer, 2002). Walker et al.'s (1999) prospective randomised controlled trial involving ninety-six women with newly diagnosed large or locally advanced breast cancer revealed that, in comparison with standard care, patients using relaxation and guided imagery had fewer psychological symptoms. Low emotional suppression was linked to practice of relaxation and guided imagery (at least daily), and a modest correlation was found between vividness of imagery and clinical response.

In the case material presented, "the lump" is clearly seen as an aggressor. That the patient experienced relief following connection with and expression of rage towards the lump, and that she was not bothered thereafter by thoughts of residual cancer, suggest that experience of deep feeling can be therapeutic. Patient experience and expression of affect in many treatments including short-term psychodynamic psychotherapy is associated with improvement in psychological well-being (Diener, Hilsenroth & Weinberger, 2007; Iwakabe, Rogan & Stalikas, 2000; Lamagna, submitted for publication). However, according to Fitzpatrick and Stalikas (2008), "catharsis is not enough" (p. 145). Rather, verbalisation and visualisation of feelings and impulses is encouraged to facilitate the fullest experience of emotion, thereby validating feelings and transforming meanings to provide patients with a new perspective and understanding of self (Malan & Coughlin Della Selva, 2006). We might suggest that the lump as aggressor could be linked to a pathological, harshly critical, blaming and neglecting Superego (past aggressor), and that destroying the lump in fantasy had an impact at deeper levels of the patient's psyche. We can even speculate about who the lump as aggressor is associated with in the unconscious of the patient, while the material presented suggests the healing effect of having experienced deep, anxiety-provoking emotion within a secure interpersonal interchange.

Summary

The present chapter outlined psychological aspects of cancer and referred to treatment approaches including cognitive behavioural therapy and experiential dynamic therapies. Recent developments in the experiential dynamic psychotherapies, and in particular, aspects of ISTDP and IE-DP (mirroring, anxiety assessment and regulation, emotional maieutics, defence work, and interventions that focus on Superego pathology), and AEDP (acknowledging mastery, mourning the self, and receiving affirmation), were suggested to make these approaches especially helpful to patients with cancer. In particular, these developments facilitate a therapeutic process through which patients are able to regain a sense of control, restore self-esteem, and find meaning in experiences. Within each of the experiential and dynamic approaches, attending to the relationship is emphasised. Segments of a transcript from an initial session with a woman referred for therapy for help with anxiety, difficulties in adjustment to diagnosis of breast cancer and associated treatment, and quality of life issues were presented. Therapist interventions were identified and discussed to demonstrate how the approach can be applied in clinical practice in an integrated psychosocial oncology service. Short-term follow-up was presented and revealed clinically significant improvements in emotional, psychological, and social functioning.

Acknowledgements

I would like to acknowledge with deep gratitude the generosity of the patient in allowing me to include excerpts from the transcript of our session. I am also indebted to Professor Leslie G. Walker for helpful comments on an early draft of the chapter. My heartfelt thanks also go to Dr Ferruccio Osimo, who helped me to appreciate the importance of the real relationship, and to Dr Josette ten Have-de Labije, who encouraged me to be observant, attentive, and precise.

References

Abbass, A. A. (2003). The cost-effectiveness of short-term dynamic psychotherapy. *Expert Review of Pharmacoeconomics & Outcomes Research*, *3*: 535–539.

Abbass, A. A., Hancock, J. T., Henderson, J. & Kisely, S. (2006). Short-term psychodynamic psychotherapies for common mental disorders. *Cochrane Database of Systematic Reviews*, Issue 4. Art. No.: CD004687. DOI: 10.1002/14651858.CD004687.pub3.

Allen, L. (2006). The impact of the health professional on the individual's experience of cancer: A psychodynamic perspective. *Psychodynamic Practice*, *12*: 369–383.

Brennan, J., Cull, A., Harvey, P. & Parkinson, L. (1997). *Clinical Psychology Services in Oncology: a Guide for Purchasers of Clinical Psychology Services*. Briefing Paper No. 13. Leicester, UK: British Psychological Society.

Burton, M. & Watson, M. (1988). *Counselling People with Cancer*. Chichester, UK: John Wiley & Sons.

Coughlin Della Selva, P. (1996). *Intensive Short-Term Dynamic Psychotherapy: Theory and Technique*. Chichester, UK: John Wiley & Sons.

Davanloo, H. (1990). *Unlocking the Unconscious*. Chichester, UK: John Wiley & Sons.

Derogatis, L. R. (1986). Psychology in cancer medicine: A perspective and overview. *Journal of Consulting and Clinical Psychology, 54*: 632–638.

Derogatis, L. R., Morrow, G. R., Fetting, J., Penman, D., Piasetsky, S. & Schmale, A. M. (1983). The prevalence of psychiatric disorders among cancer patients. *Journal of the American Medical Association, 249*: 751–757.

Diener, M. J., Hilsenroth, M. J. & Weinberger, J. (2007). Therapist affect focus and patient outcomes in psychodynamic psychotherapy: A meta-analysis. *American Journal of Psychiatry, 164*: 936–941.

Fallowfield, L., Ratcliffe, D., Jenkins, V. & Saul, J. (2001). Psychiatric morbidity and its recognition by doctors in patients with cancer. *British Journal of Cancer, 84*: 1011–1015.

Fitzpatrick, M. R. & Stalikas, A. (2008). Positive emotions as generators of therapeutic change. *Journal of Psychotherapy Integration, 18*: 137–154.

Forman, D., Stockton, D., Møller, H., Quinn, M., Babb, P., De Angelis, R. & Micheli, A. (2003). Cancer prevalence in the UK: Results from the EUROPREVAL study. *Annals of Oncology, 14*: 648–654.

Fosha, D. (2000a). *The Transforming Power of Affect: A Model for Accelerated Change*. New York: Basic.

Fosha, D. (2000b). Meta-therapeutic processes and the affects of transformation: Affirmation and the healing affects. *Journal of Psychotherapy Integration, 10*: 71–97.

Fosha, D. (2001). The dyadic regulation of affect. *Journal of Clinical Psychology/In Session, 57*: 227–242.

Fosha, D. (2008). Transformance, recognition of self by self, and effective action. In: K. J. Schneider (Ed.), *Existential-Integrative Psychotherapy: Guideposts to the Core of Practice*. London: Routledge.

Fosha, D. & Slowiaczek, M. L. (1997). Techniques to accelerate dynamic psychotherapy. *American Journal of Psychotherapy, 51*: 229–251.

Frederick, R. J. (2009). *Living Like You Mean It: Use the Wisdom and Power of Your Emotions to Get the Life You Really Want*. San Francisco, CA: Jossey-Bass.

Frederickson, J. (1999). *Psychodynamic Psychotherapy: Learning to Listen from Multiple Perspectives*. London: Brunner/Mazel.

Goldie, L. & Desmarais, J. (2005). *Psychotherapy and the Treatment of Cancer Patients: Bearing Cancer in Mind*. London: Routledge.

Hall, A., A'Hern, R. & Fallowfield, L. (1999). Are we using appropriate self-report questionnaires for detecting anxiety and depression in women with early breast cancer? *European Journal of Cancer, 35*: 79–85.

ten Have-de Labije, J. (2001). Red and green traffic lights on Davanloo's road to the unconscious. In: J. ten Have-de Labije (Ed.), *The Working Alliance in ISTDP: Whose Intrapsychic Crisis?* Amsterdam, Netherlands: VKDP—Dutch Association for Short-Term Dynamic Psychotherapy.

ten Have-de Labije, J. (2006). When patients enter with anxiety on the forefront. *Ad Hoc Bulletin of Short-Term Dynamic Psychotherapy: Practice and Theory, 10*: 35–69.

ten Have-de Labije, J. (2008). She only wanted some understanding: Separating ego and superego parts with an extremely anxious woman. *Ad Hoc Bulletin of Short-Term Dynamic Psychotherapy: Practice and Theory, 12*: 40–80.

ten Have-de Labije, J. (2009). Helping our patients to experience feelings: Understanding the role of defences in emotion regulation and the implications for ISTDP practitioners. *Ad Hoc Bulletin of Short-Term Dynamic Psychotherapy: Practice and Theory, 13*: 15–23.

ten Have-de Labije, J. (2010). *The Collected Writings of Josette ten Have-de Labije*. Del Mar, CA: Unlocking Press.

Helgeson, V. S. (1999). Applicability of cognitive adaptation theory to predicting adjustment to heart disease after coronary angioplasty. *Health Psychology, 18*: 561–569.

Helgeson, V. S. (2003). Cognitive adaptation, psychological adjustment, and disease progression among angioplasty patients: 4 years later. *Health Psychology, 22*: 30–38.

Helgeson, V. S. & Fritz, H. L. (1999). Cognitive adaptation as a predictor of new coronary events after percutaneous transluminal coronary angioplasty. *Psychosomatic Medicine, 61*: 488–495.

Holland, J. C. (Ed.) (1998). *Psycho-oncology*. New York: Oxford University Press.

Hopwood, P. & Stephens, R. J. (2000). Depression in patients with lung cancer: Prevalence and risk factors derived from quality-of-life data. *Journal of Clinical Oncology, 18*: 893–903.

Iwakabe, S., Rogan, K. & Stalikas, A. (2000). The relationship between client emotional expressions, therapist interventions, and the working alliance: An exploration of eight emotional expression events. *Journal of Psychotherapy Integration, 10*: 375–401.

Lamagna, J. (submitted for publication). *Of the Self, By the Self and For the Self: Internal Attachment, Attunement, and Psychological Change*. Retrieved October 20, 2009 from http://www.aedpinstitute.com/images/pdf/Of%20the%20Self%20%20by%20the%20Self%20and%20for%20the%20Self.pdf.

Maguire, G. P., Tait, A., Brooke, M., Thomas, C., Howat, J. M. T., Sellwood, R. A. & Bush, H. (1980). Psychiatric morbidity and physical toxicity associated with adjuvant chemotherapy after mastectomy. *British Medical Journal, 281*: 1179–1180.

Malan, D. & Coughlin Della Selva, P. (2006). *Lives Transformed: a Revolutionary Method of Dynamic Psychotherapy*. London: Karnac.

McCullough, L., Kuhn, N., Andrews, S., Kaplan, A., Wolf, J. & Lanza Hurley, C. (2003). *Treating Affect Phobia: a Manual for Short-Term Dynamic Psychotherapy*. London: Guilford Press.

McCullough Vaillant, L. (1997). *Changing Character: Short-Term Anxiety-Regulating Psychotherapy for Restructuring Defenses, Affects, and Attachment*. New York: Basic.

Moorey, S. & Greer, S. (2002). *Cognitive Behaviour Therapy for People with Cancer*. Oxford: Oxford University Press.

Office for National Statistics (2007). *News Release*. Retrieved March 19, 2011 from http://www.statistics.gov.uk/pdfdir/ukcan0707.pdf.

Osimo, F. (2003). *Experiential Short-Term Dynamic Psychotherapy: A Manual*. Bloomington, IN: Author House.

Osimo, F. (2012). The essence of experiential dynamic therapies. In: F. Osimo & M. J. Stein (Eds.), *Theory and Practice of Experiential Dynamic Psychotherapy*. London: Karnac.

Rodin, G. M. (2003). Suffering and adaptation to cancer: What to measure and when to intervene. *Journal of Psychosomatic Research, 55*: 399–401.

Rossman, M. L. (2003). *Fighting Cancer from Within*. New York: Henry Holt.

Schaefer-Schiumo, K. & Atwood, J. D. (2009). Kristin's journey through breast cancer: A social constructionist perspective. *The American Journal of Family Therapy, 37*: 318–335.

Straker, N. (1998). Psychodynamic psychotherapy for cancer patients. *Journal of Psychotherapy Practice and Research, 7*: 1–9.

Taylor, S. E. (1983). Adjustment to threatening events: A theory of cognitive adaptation. *American Psychologist, 38*: 1161–1173.

Walker, L. G. (2006). *Oncology Health Service Audit June 2006: Executive Summary of Main Findings.* Retrieved January 29, 2008 from http://www.lgwalker.com/

Walker, L. G., Walker, M. B., Ogston, K., Heys, S. D., Ah-See, A. K., Miller, I. D., Hutcheon, A. W., Sarkar, T. K. & Eremin, O. (1999). Psychological, clinical and pathological effects of relaxation training and guided imagery during primary chemotherapy. *British Journal of Cancer, 80*: 262–268.

Zabora, J., Brintzenhofe Szoc, K., Curbow, B., Hooker, C. & Piantadosi, S. (2001). The prevalence of psychological distress by cancer site. *Psycho-Oncology, 10*: 19–28.

Zaza, C., Sellick, S. M. & Hillier, L. M. (2005). Coping with cancer: What do patients do? *Journal of Psychosocial Oncology, 23*: 55–73.

CHAPTER SEVEN

Experiential dynamic psychotherapies in the treatment of psycho-physical trauma

Margarita Lobeck

This chapter will highlight the importance of an integrated approach when treating patients who have experienced a physical injury, incorporating physical, psychological, and social aspects of the trauma. It will show how Experiential Dynamic Therapy (EDT) can facilitate healing, helping to move a person from a position of being split off from their injured part towards a position of integration. "EDT" is here used as an umbrella term being influenced by concepts, theories, and techniques from various teachers in the field including Davanloo (Intensive Short-Term Dynamic Psychotherapy), Osimo (Intensive Experiential-Dynamic Psychotherapy), Fosha (Accelerated Experiential Dynamic Psychotherapy), and McCullough (Affect Focused Dynamic Psychotherapy). However, the main principles of working in an experiential and dynamic way, using Malan's Two Triangles and the central dynamic sequence of working through defences and regulating anxiety to reach deep affect, are at the centre of all the work described herein.

Defining trauma for people who have suffered a physical injury

Trauma is a psycho-physiological experience of extreme stress. It is frequently described by trauma sufferers as an overwhelming fear of coming to harm, or even dying, connected with a sense of powerlessness and of not being in control. Every year a significant number of people suffer a physical trauma such as a fall, burn injury, hand injury, or a road traffic accident. It is very common to experience a number of psychological disturbances following the trauma as the brain attempts to process the event. The symptoms can be divided into three areas (see van der Kolk, 2003, p. 171):

1. The repeated reliving of memories of the traumatic experience (flashbacks, nightmares, intrusive thoughts).
2. Avoidance of reminders of the trauma, numbness, and emotional detachment that often coexist with intrusive recollections.
3. Experience of increased arousal such as hyper-vigilance, irritability, memory and concentration problems, sleep disturbance. and an exaggerated "startle" response.

Continued experience of trauma symptoms can lead to post-traumatic stress disorder (PTSD) as described in the *Diagnostic and Statistical Manual of Mental Disorders* (American Psychiatric Association, 2000). Some patients might not fulfil all criteria for a full diagnosis of PTSD but still suffer from post-traumatic stress. While the need for physical care is readily accepted by patients who have experienced physical trauma, and by doctors and society as a whole, the psychological aspect of the trauma is still often minimised or ignored. As a result therapies and support for this patient group in the NHS have been patchy.

Having worked with physical trauma for a number of years, I believe that, when trying to understand this patient group, the definition of trauma outlined above is not sufficient in describing what is a complex and multi-layered experience. Physical trauma might be better presented in terms of three distinct aspects that need to be addressed: (i) psychological, (ii) physical, and (iii) social. The psychological layer encompasses the trauma symptoms, as described by van der Kolk (2003). It might also include previous mental health and relational difficulties. I see the physical layer as the psychological response to the specific physical injury and its subsequent recovery. For example, some people will have reduced functioning of an affected limb or might be suffering from chronic pain, reduced muscle tension, or reduced flexibility and strength. The social layer encompasses the psychological reaction to the social impact associated with the injury such as loss of job, loss of finances, anxiety about return to work, or being faced with retirement. Frequently, it also involves a loss of identity.

Thus, when working with physical trauma, the therapist needs to address each of these three aspects, sometimes together, sometimes peeling them away one by one, and sometimes switching back and forth. Such complexity repeatedly calls for an approach that uses more than just one therapeutic method (see Rothschild, 2000), and can include necessary diversions to address acute issues such as facing yet another operation, or to support the patient through ongoing social stressors such as financial difficulties due to lack of income. Furthermore, from the wider group of trauma sufferers, we know that, for some patients, the current trauma reactivates earlier unresolved traumas. Indeed, most patients present with not just a single distinct psychological trauma, but frequently also with longer-standing dynamic interpersonal and/or intrapsychic conflicts that have been brought to the fore by the current crisis. Some authors (e.g., Ford, 1999) have defined this as complex PTSD, and Louise Reddemann (2007), a leading figure in trauma therapy in Germany, highlighted the often delicate balancing act trauma therapists have to perform in order to address complexity.

EDT and psycho-physical trauma[1]

Psychotherapy has developed considerably since Freud, and has incorporated research findings from fields such as neurology, physiology, and behavioural and cognitive sciences. There is also a growing interest in developmental psychology and especially attachment theory. At the same time, our understanding of trauma and post-traumatic stress has increased immensely over the last forty or so years and has helped forge therapeutic approaches more attuned to the needs of this patient group. Cognitive and behavioural trauma therapies (e.g., Ehlers & Clark, 2000) and Eye Movement Desensitisation and Reprocessing (EMDR) therapy (e.g., Shapiro, 2001) are now widely used but, more recently, emotion-focused experiential therapies, such as those discussed in this book, have also been shown to be effective with this patient group (see Gleiser, Ford & Fosha, 2008).[2] In particular, the experiential approach precisely focuses on defences and on the anxieties that have led the patient to avoid their emotional experience. Both anxiety and defence prevent the person from accessing and processing the emotions involved in trauma. Experiential dynamic therapies are thus well suited for patients who suffer from psycho-physical trauma (Gleiser et al., 2008). In addition, the active stance of the therapist in EDT is crucially important for this patient group. Reddemann (2007) stresses that, in trauma therapy, the adoption of a neutral and removed stance, as demanded by classic psychotherapy (to increase a passive displacement of transference dynamics from significant others onto the therapist), can be too dangerous for trauma patients with increased risk of dissociation, flashbacks, and shame. Instead the therapist must take a more active and involved stance supporting the patient when working through trauma material (as opposed to conflict material). In this respect EDT has the specific advantage over more traditional dynamic approaches of enabling the therapist to gradually guide the patient through the experience of the trauma, regulating the often fast and dramatic rise of anxiety, whilst also working with increased defence. This can allow a deeper and fuller experience of emotions before therapy moves on to process the experience cognitively. The therapist follows the changes in the patient moment-by-moment by monitoring physical signals indicating a rise in anxiety whilst ensuring that anxiety does not increase to a point where it becomes re-traumatising. Defence activity is constantly monitored by the therapist and made explicit to the patient

Another concept that has been elaborated upon by EDT practitioners is the patient-therapist relationship. For example, Osimo (2003) has written eloquently that the therapeutic relationship is not only the relationship of the patient and the therapist, but also the meeting of two people—the "real relationship" of two people sharing an experience. In trauma these aspects of two people interacting are in a very delicate balance; the therapist gives the patient enough support (feeling contained and cared for) to allow intense trauma work to be done, ensuring that the central focus on challenging defences and reducing affect inhibitors such as anxiety, guilt, and shame remains (McCullough Vaillant, 1997).

Case examples

The case examples chosen here have been selected to illustrate how EDT can be used in a modified and creative way when working with patients who have suffered a psycho-physical trauma. That is not to say that all patients require this integrated approach but, for the purpose of this chapter, the focus will be on the interplay between the physical, social, and psychological aspects of the trauma.

Although a potential barrier to the deeper, more unconscious "old traumas", the physical layer can be a starting point and vehicle for exploration. In particular, focusing initially on the physical injury can be helpful when developing the relationship and trust between the patient and the therapist. It also facilitates an increase in the patient's capacity to cope with powerful emotions that have been locked inside and sometimes have been suppressed for a long time prior to the physical trauma. In both cases this was the starting point of the deeper exploration of difficulties.

Apart from the classic PTSD symptoms, two themes present repeatedly when working with patients who have experienced psycho-physical trauma: (i) the patient struggling with a sense of guilt and self-loathing, especially in relation to the injured part, and (ii) finding it difficult to express anger, sadness, and fear appropriately. In the first case to be presented, therapy involved transforming the feelings of self-loathing into self acceptance. In the second case, access to deep emotions was made possible through a peeling away of layers from present to past, and from physical to psychological.

The therapist was in her third year of Core Training in IE-DP at the time of the case studies being taped.

Turning self-loathing into accepting the new Self

The first transcript illustrates the process of supporting a patient through the journey of accepting loss and change to her physical self, while encouraging her to take a more compassionate and less self-blaming (pathological Superego) position. The physical layer, a hand injury sustained when trying to catch a falling glass, was associated with considerable disability due to developing chronic regional pain syndrome. The psychological and social layer included symptoms of depression, heightened arousal, cognitive impairment, anger, loss, and grief, all associated with her injury and subsequent inability to return to work and to the life she had been leading. The patient described herself as having previously been a confident and very able person who would go out of her way to look after others. Since the accident she found she was often very angry with herself and described a tremendous loss in confidence.

The session's initial focus is on the physical layer but the therapist gently makes enquiries about the impact of the trauma (HP) and invites the patient to connect with her feelings towards her injured hand (Self) using emotional maieutics (XA):

Pt: I don't know, my life's changed. I don't go anywhere. I really don't go out you know. I might go to the supermarket. I never have a laugh, no enjoyment … and I used to love it. So, why? It all started with this (points at her hand)

Th: And that took all your confidence away. Took all your … (**HP, XA**)

Pt: … life (becomes sad and thoughtful)

Th: I guess there is a reality with your hand that you are not as stable and confident with this hand because you can't use it in the same way. So there is a reality that perhaps you feel a little awkward in public places and day to day … (**HP, XA**)

Pt: I don't, I don't, it's very rare I've probably been out once or twice since. But I don't like it.

Th: What happens? (**HP**)

Pt: I'd rather not go.

Th: No, what I mean, what happens that are you worried about? (**AA**)

Pt: I can't sort of cut my vegetables. I had to take my knife with me anyway, but [husband] had to cut it for me, I hated it. I hate my hand. Just looks like (looking at her hand) it's got all the veins sticking out, horrible. I just, I just hate it. But I'm stuck with it, so I've got to try and do something about it.
Th: That is a starting point. The way you feel towards this hand has an impact on how you feel. (**XA**)
Pt: I mean, if I do go out, well you've seen me I hide it (puts hand between her legs).
Th: When you go for a walk where do you have your hand? (**HP**)
Pt: I have it in my pocket ... I make sure I have something with a pocket on.

The therapist suspects that there may be a link between the patient's negative self-perceptions or pathological Superego position, her impulse to hide her hand, and her defensive tendency to avoid going out. The therapist enquires further (HP):

Th: So is, part of you not going out, is because of that?
Pt: Yeah and then I think probably ... it's wrong. I think it's because I stopped going out when it first happened and then you get to a stage where you don't want to go out, because my confidence went then.

The therapist encourages the patient to focus on her hand and to notice what emotions are stirred up within her (XA):

Th: So, if you want to just take a look at this hand right now, see whatever comes up for you, just take a look, what comes up? In terms of feelings towards this hand.
Pt: (Brings hand forward on knee and looks at her hand; touches her hand slightly) The fingers are turning up, there's a horrible vein here, not being able to close it, the soreness [of her palm] and it's smaller.

The patient's comment on the physical appearance of her hand and its soreness is a defensive response. The therapist does not explicitly address the patient's defence but continues to focus on the patient's feelings (XA) as she noticed emotions starting to be stirred up:

Th: Hmm, and how does that make you feel, looking at that and knowing that all those things are there?
Pt: I know there isn't anything anybody can do, well I ...
Th: How does that feel inside you?
Pt: I just want to hide it.

Recognising the defensive responses, the therapist now attempts to block the patient's defence before returning to enquiry about feelings (XA):

Th: So you just want to hide it. If you wouldn't hide, and keep the focus on it?
Pt: I hate it.

Th: So there is a hate.
Pt: I really do.
Th: How does that feel inside you?
Pt: It's like it disgusts me.
Th: What else comes up?
Pt: Things I can't do. I mean yesterday we were doing little, we were tidying the little cupboard out and I said to [husband] let me do that. I said no let me do it and everything I pick up I, I can't hold it and I drop it.
Th: So what does that make you feel?
Pt: When I drop something and it got something in it. I feel disgusted with myself and I just think "stupid hand" (says it very angrily) (Pause, patient is silent).
Th: So if you look at it right now again what is happening?
Pt: Stupid little hand.
Th: How does that feel?
Pt: (Big sigh) I don't know, I've got to learn to live with it and that's ...

The patient, having taken a position of self-rejection and self-disgust returns to a defensive position although the big sigh suggests to the therapist that feelings are rising and anxiety is being discharged. The therapist decides on a maieutic intervention, guiding the patient back to the anger, implicit in her expression of hate towards her hand, in order to increase the experience of the feeling (XA):

Th: But I want you to be aware that you have got this very strong feeling towards your hand, strong anger towards your hand, which ...
Pt: I think the anger is because it's spoilt my life, no doubt about it, it has spoilt my life and that sounds petty because a lot of people have lost a lot more than that. It's spoilt my life, stopped me going out because ...

The patient blames her hand for spoiling her life and does not see the possibility that she perpetuates her suffering through avoidance of going out. Instead of focusing on the patient's defensive use of blaming her hand, which would have been another option at this point, the therapist acknowledges the patient's blaming of her hand and continues with exploration of the patient's feelings (XA):

Th: So the meaning you give to the hand is "You spoilt my life". (**HP, XA**)
Pt: Yeah, me doing that silly thing yeah, me and my hand spoilt my life.

The patient now takes some responsibility for her hand injury, although the extent to which she is connecting to self-compassion rather than self-blame remains unclear. The therapist continues to explore her emotional response (XA):

Th: Now listening to what you've just said, what does that sound like, hearing yourself saying that towards your hand?
Pt: That's how I feel about it.

Th: What's that feel like, saying that?

Pt: What does this feel like? It's the end of my hand isn't it (stroking her hand). I'm never going to be able to do what I used to do, you know, when I …

The therapist notices that the patient has started to stroke her hand, suggesting that she has taken a more self-compassionate and self-caring position. The therapist mirrors the patient's action (MI):

Th: You're just stroking your hand as you are saying this.

Pt: Yes I know (continues stroking and now also looking at her hand) I'm trying to …

Th: Is there a part of you that also feels other things? (**XA, SO**)

Pt: No, when I rub it I think I probably, when I rub here (top of hand) it might get better, but, but I like gardening and I love cooking. But I'm doing very little cooking now, because I can't, I can rub the pastry which I do, you know, because it's therapy. But to make a cake or anything like that I can't do that … But I mean I suppose I should persevere with that.

The patient responds to the therapist's enquiry by describing what she cannot do, rather than saying what else she feels. The therapist could have pointed out that such a defensive focus on physical limitations and how the patient's avoidance of looking at her feelings prevents the therapist from helping her to the extent she would wish. The therapist continues to enquire about the patient's feelings (XA):

Th: Now I think it's very interesting what you said, you said that you felt very angry towards this hand, that you feel responsible for what happened, and how does it feel to feel that?

Pt: I think probably that I'm being honest.

Th: Hmm.

Pt: It's sad. I loved …

Th: Is there also some sadness about losing …

Pt: … losing what I used to have?

Th: Hmm, yeah.

Pt: Yeah, really, hmm.

Th: And what's that like, feeling that loss? (**XA**)

Pt: Sad, because not only has it ruined my life it also really stopped [husband's] life.

The therapist explores the sadness and anger further, especially the patient's anger towards the Self and encourages the patient to practise looking at the hand at home and allowing feelings to emerge. In the following session the patient reports how, having been on a walk with her hand outside her pocket, she began to feel less angry towards her hand and herself. Her shift away from self-blame towards a more self-compassionate position signalled the beginning of a clinically significant change. Over the next few weeks she started baking again, asking her husband for help rather than trying to do it all by herself and admitted she enjoyed it. She started to go out and invited friends round for a game of dominoes. Her husband told her that she seemed happier, laughing and joking with her friends, and singing in the kitchen when doing some cooking.

Pt: I was just in the kitchen doing some little things and he [husband] came in and he said, "I've just been sitting in [the lounge] and you're doing something I've not heard you do for a long time." And I said, "What?", and he said, "You've been singing." And I [thought], "I had?" It makes me really emotional, because this is another thing I used to love to do, singing ... You know, when he was saying it I felt really emotional because I felt there was a bit of me that's coming back ... I felt really, really good.

Th: There is a part of you, the seeds are growing. (**SO, XA**)

Pt: The seeds are coming up, yeah.

Th: And it's nice that it happened when you were in the kitchen. To me it sounds like you were doing something you enjoyed doing. (**SO, XA**)

Pt: I am very, very proud, I am proud to think, you know, like I was with the cooking, I was sort of throwing it away, you know I couldn't, but now I will think, well we'll try again. Whereas before I wasn't able to do that.

Th: Hmm, well, and accepting more the help will in some ways make you more independent.

Pt: Hmm.

Th: So you don't give up, you actually try some bits. (**HP, SO**)

Pt: Yeah, I can see, I suppose it's just getting to a point where you are happy with what's going on ...

Th: Hmm.

Pt: ... before I was sort of clawing at things and trying and sort of ... I was so frightened, so frightened, of not being able to do it, it was so big. I still get a little bit frightened but not like I was before.

And a little later:

Pt: Yes, I think, I don't know, I think it's because you've helped me to break it down. When I [first] came here it was just a big, it was like a sea of nothing. There was plenty going on, but I couldn't make sense of any of it. I hated lots of things about myself and that's beginning to ... I'm even going to the hairdresser's tomorrow: that's something I was going to tell you (smiles).

In subsequent sessions the patient linked her emotions to memories connected with those feelings. She remembered that, when she was growing up, her mother never praised her, leaving her believing that she was never good enough. The accident reaffirmed her sense of herself as "stupid". More work was done on working through her relationship with her mother (who died a long time ago) and freeing herself from the pathological Superego voice that she recognised as her mother's voice. This brought about more deep change and the patient was able to move forward, beginning to accept her (new) Self. In reviewing her therapy, the patient very fittingly said that she found it helpful for therapy to have focused on one thing at a time but, as work progressed, it all came together like pieces of a jigsaw, and eventually the whole person/picture emerged.

Peeling away the layers: learning to express anger following an accident

The patient in the second case to be presented had lost a finger as a result of a crush injury (physical layer). The accident happened on a boat which was battling high winds. A table that was not secured to the floor moved and crushed the patient's hand. She said that, at the time, she desperately tried to stay in control, but now, months later, felt utterly overwhelmed by her memories of the accident. The patient described ongoing trauma symptoms including flashbacks, depression, and mood swings (psychological layer).

The excerpts presented will illustrate how exposure work can be facilitated by using EDT. After some preparation around the accident recall (such as creating a safe place), the patient was ready to work on exposure to the trauma memory and to explore her feelings in connection with it. The excerpt begins with the patient responding to a question as to how she experiences her anger inside her towards the crew who failed to protect her (XA):

Pt: I think I'll be terrifying (voice louder and firmer, body tone increased).

The therapist noted a distinct increase in affect and took that as a signal to move forward to explore the anger (XA):

Th: OK, well go, go with that. What would you want to do, what would you want to tell them?
Pt: Well, I would shout, and I would tell them, ahm, and I'd point things out, make sure they could see things like, ahm … (Pause, patient is silent)

The patient is vague in her expression of her anger and the therapist draws her attention to her behaviour (DA). The therapist could have also clarified the self-defeating aspect of the patient's vagueness that keeps her away from experiencing her emotion more fully.

Th: That's still a bit vague.
Pt: I'd be seventeen foot tall and I would, ahm.
Th: That's pretty powerful.
Pt: Yeah and I would be sort of inconsolable really.
Th: Inconsolable in terms of? **(DA)**
Pt: In terms of the anger, you know, it would be kind of limitless (becomes very animated and moves her arm as if pushing someone/something away).
Th: Gosh this is a lot of power that you have.
Pt: (Nods)
Th: Stay with that, try not to push it away because this is really important to see what it feels like to have this anger. **(XA)**
Pt: Wow, I want to shake things and stomp about, shout and be critical and vile and yeah, be terrifying as much as I possibly can.
Th: Is there a particular person that comes to mind? **(XA, CP)**
Pt: Oh yeah, the person who, well, there would be two people. The person who didn't screw the table down and the other one who decided to have that granite table, that design on the boat. So it would be, definitely be the two of them.
Th: Well, what do you want to do?
Pt: Ahm …
Th: If you were seventeen foot tall.

Pt: I would just terrify them.
Th: Hmm.
Pt: I would be stomping and shaking them and really showing them the repercussions or the, the outcome of what they did or didn't do, and ahm …
Th: Is that enough, is that making you feel better?
Pt: Yeah, probably.

The patient's uncertain response suggests that she was not fully in touch with her feelings. To help this process the therapist moves to enquiry about the patient's here-and-now emotional experience (XA):

Th: How do you feel right now? Relaxed? Or is there some more anger?
Pt: I think I probably would have a few more, I would be like a wave and I would be coming back and would be ten foot tall and point out a couple of things.
Th: That sounds pretty nice to me, pointing something out, if you would actually go with the energy of being ten foot tall and the energy and the fury that goes with that.
Pt: Yeah OK, rather than caring about how terrified they are, ahm …
Th: So you're thinking about other people again.

The therapist identifies a defence that the patient had been using since her childhood, but that had been increasingly recognised by her as a problem. In addition, as the patient begins to connect to her anger, her anxiety increases, and she becomes vague. She moves away from the feeling into her head, intellectualising. The therapist both acknowledges and blocks her defence (but without clarifying how it is self-defeating), and tries to keep her in the experiential place by encouraging her to stay with feeling (XA):

Pt: Hmm.
Th: If you just go with the feeling you feel at this particular time, you feel just now, if you go with the energy that you are feeling rather than thinking about …
Pt: Well, I carry on for a good old while and I'd be unpredictable and they would have to stand there and shake, wondering what the hell is happening next, and know they haven't been dismissed yet, and they would have to put up with whatever happened.
Th: And what would happen?
Pt: Well, I would wander about and rant a bit like, ahm, sort of, ahm, King Lear I suppose … and I want to frighten them actually because I'm so annoyed with them that I want them to think where the hell is this gonna go and for them to not feel particularly safe either and, ahm (looks away and fidgets).

The therapist, noting an increase in the patient's anxiety and that she is distracted, offers encouragement (SO, AA):

Th: You are doing really well, you've managed to go a bit with your feeling.
Pt: And kind of enjoyed it a bit actually, and sort of feel better for it actually.

Th: Yeah.

Pt: But, ahm (goes quiet).

Th: What's happening?

Pt: Well, I suppose I don't like people getting cross with me, like I sort of avoiding it, so for me getting angry is not something I do very often because …

Th: What kind of feeling comes up just now?

Pt: Well, ahm, sort of a funny one, feeling like I should stop being angry because of looking after them, in a way they probably had enough …

The therapist and patient explore the rise in anxiety that stopped the patient experiencing her anger fully. The patient recognises that she felt good experiencing her anger but very quickly became frightened of her healthy anger in the face of her pathological Superego. She was surprised that anger could be positive as she always experienced anger as something that should not happen or as something to be feared. This led into a memory of her father, who could be very explosive and would shout at her, which, as a child, frightened her. It also triggered memories of other times when she was faced with conflict and anger.

Pt: Oh, he'd go red and, ahm, sort of shout. … One thing he would do, he would hit the dog and we would all go, oh don't hit the dog … I suppose I'm very frightened of anger and I don't like to witness it either. If I see anger in a film or in a book I would definitely absent myself. I would walk out the cinema, stop reading the book … Because I married somebody who definitely had big anger management problems … this guy would get angry about very odd things, it wasn't definitely normal triggers it was …

Th: Would you say that you changed since you had the experience with your partner or had you always … (**HP**)

Pt: I'd say I'd probably always had it.

Th: That issue with anger …

Pt: Because I didn't confront it in this partner I didn't say like, you frighten me or something, I would go like, uh-huh and sort of try and avoid it … I had this terror about how angry somebody could get …

The focus of therapy could now shift from the patient's current trauma (top layer) to her longer-standing interpersonal issues around expressing more difficult feelings including anger and tolerating conflict (deeper layer). Having felt safe in expressing some anger towards more distant people, such as the boat crew, gradually she became able to tolerate and express her feelings towards people closer to her.

Conclusions

The examples presented herein highlight how experiential therapies can complement trauma work and help patients connect to deep and painful feelings. Linking the physical and the emotional aspects of the trauma validates both and can make it easier for the patient to accept that they have been suffering not just from the physical impact but also from the emotional one. Likewise, understanding how past events can affect a current trauma, allows patients to move forward in their healing.

In the first case, it was shown that, through focusing on "the damaged hand" (the physical manifestation of the trauma), the patient became aware of and experienced emotions inside herself. She began to notice a harshly self-critical Superego and slowly was able to feel more compassionate towards her hand/Self. Moving away from self-loathing and self-blame signalled a clinically significant change for her and subsequently guided the path to recovery. The example showed how EDT had been a valuable approach in creating this opening by using a model that is both focused and active as well as containing.

In the second case, the visceral experiencing of anger (within the current trauma) unlocked deep and unconscious feelings from the patient's childhood. Noticing her energy and physical presence when challenging the sailing crew in her fantasy, gave the patient confidence and helped her to move on to challenge historical as well as ongoing relational issues. She became physically and emotionally more self-assured and returned to pursue her love of outdoor activity holidays. Socially the patient became more assertive with people.

Both vignettes have shown that EDT, and specifically the Triangles of Conflict and Others, provide a helpful framework for the therapist and the patient to stay focused whilst acknowledging the deep emotional experience of the trauma in a very safe (moment to moment monitoring of affect) set up. Understanding psycho-physical trauma as a complex and multilayered problem allows therapy to begin where the patient is at. However, it also requires the therapist to be able to recognise when movements between the layers are necessary and when they are avoidance. As discussed earlier in this chapter, acknowledging the physical, social, and psychological aspects is crucial for a full understanding and healing. I hope that the examples presented in this chapter have helped to illustrate how EDT, or at least parts of the model, can be used to great effect and with good results in patients who suffered a psycho-physical trauma.

References

American Psychiatric Association (2000). *Diagnostic and Statistical Manual of Mental Disorders (4th ed., text rev.)*. Washington, DC: American Psychiatric Association.

Ehlers, A. & Clark, D. M. (2000). A cognitive model of post-traumatic stress disorder. *Behaviour Research and Therapy, 38*: 319–345.

Ford, J. D. (1999). PTSD and disorders of extreme stress following warzone military trauma: Co-morbid but distinct syndromes? *Journal of Consulting and Clinical Psychology, 67*: 3–12.

Gleiser, K., Ford J. D. & Fosha, D. (2008). Contrasting exposure and experiential therapies for complex post-traumatic stress disorder. *Psychotherapy: Training, Research, Theory, Practice, 45*: 340–360.

McCullough Vaillant, L. (1997). *Changing Character: Short Term Anxiety Regulating Psychotherapy for Restructuring Defenses, Affects and Attachment*. New York: Basic.

Osimo, F. (2003). *Experiential Short-Term Dynamic Psychotherapy: A Manual.* Bloomington, IN: AuthorHouse.

Reddemann, L. (2007). *Psychodynamisch Imaginative Traumatherapie—PITT Das Manual.* Stuttgart, Germany: Klett-Cotta.

Rothschild, B. (2000). *The Body Remembers—The Psychophysiology of Trauma and Trauma Treatment.* New York: W. W. Norton.

Shapiro, F. (2001). *Eye Movement Desensitization and Reprocessing (EMDR): Basic Principles, Protocols, and Procedures (*2nd *ed.).* New York: Guilford Press.

Van der Kolk, B. (2003). Post traumatic stress disorder and the nature of trauma. In: M. F. Solomon & D. J. Siegel (Eds.), *Healing Trauma: Attachment, Mind, Body and Brain.* New York: W. W. Norton.

Notes

1. Rather then psycho-physical-social, I will refer to trauma as "psycho-physical" to represent the holistic and multi-layered nature of it, but it should be understood that this includes the social aspect.
2. Gleiser et al. (2008) suggest that an experiential dynamic therapy approach "addresses more factors associated with complex PTSD, such as severe and complicated forms of emotional dysregulation, entrenched defenses, dissociative symptoms, as well as attachment disturbances that perpetuate mistrust, difficulty in forming a therapeutic alliance, and withdrawal" (p. 3).

CHAPTER EIGHT

Intensive Short-Term Dynamic Psychotherapy and the treatment of poly-symptomatic somatic patients

Richard Aubrey

In the present chapter poly-symptomatic conditions for which psychological therapy is recommended will be identified and criticisms of Cognitive Behaviour Therapy (CBT) will be discussed. Experiential dynamic psychotherapies with their consideration of affective factors are suggested as a possible treatment alternative. In particular, Intensive Short-Term Dynamic Psychotherapy (ISTDP) treatment of a patient with treatment-resistant poly-symptomatic somatic problems is presented to illustrate the responsive and flexible stance of the therapist and how he helps the patient to build ego adaptive capacity. The transcript will illustrate comprehensive assessment of the patient's anxiety manifestations, interventions to help the patient turn against automatic, habitual, and self-defeating defences, including ignoring and self-neglect, unmasking of Superego pathology, and exploration of deep feelings towards current and past attachment figures. There will be an exposition of the process of somatisation as it pertains to the patient. The author will also highlight important differences between assessment from EDT and CBT perspectives. Last, there will be discussion of the possible mutative factors in the therapy and the limitations of the ISTDP approach.

Introduction

During the past decade there has been an increased interest in the role of psychological therapy in the treatment of poly-symptomatic somatic conditions such as irritable bowel syndrome (Kennedy et al., 2006), chronic pain (Grant & Threlfo, 2002), chronic daily headaches (Altieri et al., 2009), fibromyalgia (Dijkstra, Vlaeyen, Rijnen & Nielson, 2001), and chronic fatigue (Kinsella, 2007). In regard to chronic pain and chronic fatigue syndrome (CFS), the evidence is such that, in the United Kingdom, the National Institute of Health and Clinical Excellence (NICE) has recommended that psychological therapy be part of the National

Health Service (NHS) package of care for those patients suffering from these conditions (NICE, 2007, 2009).

Cognitive Behavioural Therapy (CBT) is the current psychological treatment of choice for chronic pain and CFS. Notwithstanding the evidence for its effectiveness (Morley, Ecclestone & Williams, 1999), there are criticisms of this approach in the treatment of poly-symptomatic somatic patients. First, there remains a significant number of patients who do not benefit from cognitive treatment or who fail to maintain gains at long-term follow-up (Bradley et al., 1987; Crook, Weir & Tunks, 1989). Second, there have been high rates of attrition associated with this modality (Turk & Rudy, 1991). Third, it has been stated that CBT fails to address the role of affective factors in the development and maintenance of such conditions (Grant & Threlfo, 2002). Indeed, it has been argued that interventions that focus more upon affect may increase treatment effectiveness (Barber, 1997). Given the emphasis that experiential dynamic psychotherapies place on the role of affective factors in the aetiology and maintenance of psychological problems, it seemed apposite to apply this approach to the psychological treatment of patients presenting with poly-symptomatic somatic conditions which had proven refractory to more orthodox interventions.

Case study

The therapy reported herein was undertaken within a clinical health psychology service that provides psychological treatment to patients with acute and chronic physical health problems. The therapist was a member of an ISTDP Core Training group and had also completed a three-year Core Training in Intensive Experiential-Dynamic Psychotherapy (IE-DP). The patient, who shall be referred to as Mrs D, was a thirty-four-year-old woman, with complex poly-symptomatic somatic difficulties that had failed to respond to medical, pharmacological, and psychological treatment. Her consultant rheumatologist referred her for assistance with adaptation to both chronic pain and chronic fatigue symptoms. The treatment is ongoing at the time of writing, although the patient is approaching the point of discharge.

Mrs D is married with a son. She was in part-time employment, but had not worked for twelve weeks due to an exacerbation of chronic fatigue. Her developmental history was one of abuse and neglect by her parents. She is the eldest child and has two sisters. She experienced her father as sadistic. In contrast, her mother was described as both submissive and compliant. Mrs D did not feel loved by either parent. She was self-reliant from an early age and took the role of caregiver to her siblings. Mrs D was bullied throughout school and endured this without seeking assistance. She married at the age of twenty-eight and gave birth to her son, Jack, two years later. Her husband was described as controlling. He would demand that she take care of the chores and was aggressive if his standards were not met.

Mrs D had experienced physical ill-health throughout much of her life. Her low back pain and chronic fatigue had become debilitating following the birth of her son and had not abated thereafter. At assessment, she complained of lower back pain, fibromyalgia, chronic fatigue, irritable bowel syndrome, and chronic daily headaches. She also reported a history of respiratory, neurological, and gynaecological problems. She met the DSM-IV-TR (*Diagnostic and Statistical Manual of Mental Disorders—Fourth Edition—Text Revision*, American Psychiatric Association, 2000) diagnostic criteria for Somatisation Disorder.

Initial session

The vignette below is a verbatim transcript from the opening of the initial assessment session. Due to restrictions within the service where the patient was treated it was not possible to offer an extended initial interview (trial therapy). This is recommended as the extended session allows more time for defence work (DA) and anxiety regulation (AA), thus building the ego adaptive capacity of the patient so that deep feeling can be facilitated and mobilised (XA). In the present case, the initial assessment session lasted sixty minutes.

Mrs D entered the session with anxiety at the forefront (see ten Have-de Labije, 2006). She sat on the edge of the chair and there was psychomotor agitation and upper body tension. The therapist noticed that Mrs D's legs were crossed and seemed rigid. Her breathing was shallow. In the author's experience, it is not uncommon for patients to present in this manner, especially those with chronic pain and chronic fatigue disorders. In such cases it can be helpful to focus immediately on the physical experience of anxiety (AA). The intention is to give the patient both a cognitive and affective experience of the value of psychological therapy. This reduces ambivalence, increases alliance, and raises awareness of the mind-body link.

Initial session (0.00–2.05 minutes)

The therapist and patient were sitting opposite each other.

Th: (Smiles) Hello.
Pt: (Smiles) Hello.
Th: So … let's begin by looking at the issues that you'd like help with? (**HP**)
Pt: (Pause) I'm not sure what they are (defence of ignoring).
Th: Not sure?
Pt: No … not really … I was thinking about that in the car coming over and I'm not sure if I'm … I'm right coming here. (There is a marked increase in psychomotor agitation.) I think that perhaps it's a mistake. I don't actually feel that bad today (defence of minimisation).
Th: OK … so there is some uncertainty about attending today. But do you notice that you're anxious? (**MI, AA**)
Pt: No … not really … it could be the medication … I'm on quite a lot of medication that's not … (defence of ignoring; rumination).
Th: (Interrupting) Hold on … hold on a moment … so you're not aware that you're anxious? (**MI, AA**)
Pt: No … well … a bit (defence of minimisation).
Th: So a bit?

Mrs D enters the session in a state of high anxiety but seems largely unaware of this—she automatically takes a position of ignoring her anxiety. Her speech is pressured and she is tense throughout her body. The fact that this is outside her conscious awareness indicates a poor observing Ego (ten Have-de Labije, 2006) and neglectful Superego (ten Have-de Labije, 2008). It is crucial therefore that this is mirrored back to her at the earliest opportunity (Osimo, 2003).

This will increase the observing Ego. However, in addition to a lack of observing Ego (and the consequent difficulty in regulation of anxiety), there are also defences of ignoring, minimisation, and rumination in operation. These defences need to be confronted, identified, and clarified so that they do not impede the process of the assessment and treatment.

Initial session (2.05–3.02 minutes)

Th: How do you experience your anxiety physically? (**AA**)
Pt: I don't know (defence of ignoring).
Th: But can we look at it? Can we look at how it sits in your body? (**RE, AA**)
Pt: If you want (defence of compliance and passivity).
Th: If I want? (challenge to defence). (**DA**)
Pt: If you want (defence of compliance and passivity).
Th: But what do you want? Is it important for you to look at how you experience the anxiety? (challenge to defence). (**DA, AA**)
Pt: I guess (defence of remaining indefinite).
Th: Is it guess or is it certain? (challenge to the defence of remaining indefinite). (**DA**)
Pt: Certain.
Th: (Smiles) Certain? (**DA**)
Pt: (Patient smiles). Certain!

The anxiety assessment becomes blocked from the outset. Thus rather than facilitating development of an observing Ego, the act of frequent mirroring increases anxiety which has to be defended against. The defences are consequently challenged and the therapist calls on the will of the patient to attend to her physical state. This leads to an increased conscious working alliance.

Initial session (3.02–3.45 minutes)

Th: So how do you experience your anxiety? (**AA**)
Pt: Tension. (Pause) But I don't like to think about it … I'd rather carry on and try ignoring it … (defence of ignoring).
Th: (Interrupting) Tension? (**AA**)
Pt: Yes … it's … it's mainly in my legs and back.

The patient begins to focus on her physical state. She is able to detail some tension but neglects large areas of her body. It is crucial that the therapist does not collude with the defence of ignoring and conducts a precise assessment of the physical manifestations of her anxiety. In so doing, the therapist acts as an observing Ego for the patient until she can develop her own.

Initial session (3.45–6.15 minutes)

The therapist continues with the anxiety assessment.

Th: Do you notice tension in the arms and shoulders? (**AA**)

Pt: Mmm … it feels tense here also (points to the back of the neck) and here (points to the chest).

Th: So, tension in the arms, shoulders, neck and chest. How's your jaw and throat? Tense? (**AA**)

Pt: Tense.

Th: Dry mouth? (**AA**)

Pt: Yes.

Th: Racing heart? (**AA**)

Pt: Yes.

Th: Body temperature? (**AA**)

Pt: I'm quite warm actually.

Th: Stomach? (**AA**)

Pt: I have IBS, but I've had that for a long time.

Th: Bloating? (**AA**)

Pt: Yes.

Th: These are symptoms of anxiety. These are all physical manifestations of anxiety. Do you see? (**AA**)

Pt: Yes.

Th: Tension in the arms, shoulders, neck. Dry mouth. Tension in the chest. Stomach bloating … increased body temperature … racing heart … these are all symptoms of anxiety. (**AA**)

Pt: Yes.

Th: Diarrhoea or constipation? (**AA**)

Pt: Constipation.

Th: Bladder problems? (**AA**)

Pt: No.

Th: Cystitis? (**AA**)

Pt: Sometimes.

Th: Right … so once again, anxiety. Legs? (**AA**)

Pt: Tense.

Th: Toes? (**AA**)

Pt: Curled.

Th: Headaches? (**AA**)

Pt: Yes.

Th: Tinnitus? (**AA**)

Pt: Yes.

Th: Tunnel vision? (**AA**)

Pt: No.

Th: Blurred vision? (**AA**)

Pt: Yes.

Th: Difficulties in concentrating? (**AA**)

Pt: Yes.

Th: Racing thoughts? (**AA**)

Pt: Yes.

Th: So ... tense from head to toe ... and to the extent it interferes with the ability to think and function. Goodness me. (**AA**)

There is far less resistance in operation now. However, the extent of the anxiety becomes clearly apparent. The rise in anxiety is immediate on entering the session and the spread is throughout the entire musculoskeletal, autonomic, and cognitive-perceptual systems. This indicates a fragile patient with poor ego adaptive capacity (Davanloo, 1990), and is therefore suggestive of someone with a high degree of Superego pathology (ten Have-de Labije, 2006).

The therapist proceeds to help the patient build an observing and attentive Ego. He aims to mirror to the patient not just the widespread anxiety that afflicts her life (and accounts for much of the pain and fatigue she experiences), but also to highlight the maladaptive defences in operation (MI, AA, DA).

Initial session (6.15–8.40 minutes)

Th: So this is the first problem we need to look at ... that you ignore your tension ... that you ignore the anxiety in your body. I can see the tension in your body and yet you don't. You ignore the anxiety and take it for granted. You ignore it and carry on regardless. It's become habitual. (The therapist confronts the defences of ignoring and neglect.) (**MI, AA**)

Pt: I guess (defence of remaining indefinite).

The therapist confronts, identifies, and clarifies the defence (DA) and proceeds to identify the neglectful Superego (SE).

Th: Guess or see? Because this is another thing that I've noticed that you tend to be vague (challenge to defence of remaining indefinite). You tend to leave things in the air and that stops me from getting to a good understanding of you and your issues. Do you see? (**RE, DA**)

Pt: Mmm ... I see.

Th: Because it seems to me that you treat yourself in a rather careless manner. The more that you ignore the pain ... the more that you ignore the tension and the tiredness ... the more it will continue. The more you leave things vague and indefinite ... the more the problems will continue and the less likely I'll be able to help. Do you understand? (The therapist again confronts the defences of ignoring and neglect.) (**DA**)

Pt: Yes ... no, yes ... I do.

Th: Because it's important. (Pause) So you ignore the anxiety. Now, that seems cruel to me, that you think so little of yourself that you ignore your pain and tension and fatigue. That seems cruel to me. (Therapist begins to highlight the Superego pathology of the patient.) (**SE**)

Pt: Yes.

Th: OK. So we know that you ignore your anxiety and it's become a habit. You become anxious and you tense. But you don't attend to it ... you don't look after yourself. (**AA, SE**)

Pt: No.

Th: But what happens if you ignore something?

Pt: It continues.

Th: It continues ... right. But is that what you want to do ... to continue to carry this tension? (The therapist calls on the will of the patient to relinquish her defences and take a stance against her neglectful Superego.) (**DA, SE, SO**)

Pt: Not at all ... that's why I came here ... to try to get rid of it. I don't enjoy having pain ...

Th: (Interrupting) I should imagine not. No ... but if you carry all this tension ... if your body is tense all the time ... there's little wonder that you complain of pain and fatigue. (The therapist connects the physical manifestations of anxiety to the somatic complaints.) (**MI, AA**)

Pt: Mmm.

Th: So that's the first job ... to start to attend to your tension ... because if you ignore it, then it continues. (The therapist notices a marked reduction in psychomotor agitation and muscle tension.) OK ... so if you look at it now ... how is the tension? (**AA**)

Pt: Less.

Th: Good. So what do you learn from this? (**AA**)

Pt: That it reduces.

Th: That it reduces when you start to observe and to attend to it. That you have some control over it.

Pt: I see.

Th: Good. So the tension is less? (**AA**)

Pt: Yes.

Th: Honest, or, do you say that because that's what I'd like to hear? (The therapist explores defence of compliance.) (**DA**)

Pt: (Smiles) Honest.

Th: (Smiles) Good.

In the extract above the therapist focused on the patient's presenting manifestations of anxiety. The patient's cognitive-perceptual system was directed at her anxiety and her ego-syntonic defences (ignoring, neglecting, denial, passivity, vagueness). The outcome of these interventions was an improvement in observing and an attentive Ego (the patient began to attend to her body), a reduction in the prevalence of the defences (enabling a clarity of discussion), and, most importantly, a lessening of the physical pain and tension. Mrs D was also introduced to the idea of there being a cruel and neglectful part of herself.

The above interventions also highlight a key difference between experiential dynamic psychotherapies and more orthodox CBT approaches to the assessment of poly-symptomatic somatic patients. In the latter, much time is dedicated to educating the patient about the potential benefits of psychological treatment (Kinsella, 2007). This is far less present in an experiential dynamic psychotherapies approach, as the patient rapidly gains a cognitive and affective understanding of the value of this method in the here-and-now of the session. Hence, there is little need to educate the patient in the mind-body link when they can experience this in session.

Returning to the case, following the anxiety assessment, Mrs D provided a historyand the therapist began to have a sense of the patient as someone who placed her needs second to those of others. She tended to comply with the wishes of others and to neglect herself. She had chosen a career (nursing) where her own emotional needs could be met vicariously—"helping profession syndrome" (Malan, 1979).

In this next section, taken from the mid-point of the assessment interview, the therapist begins to highlight her caregiving (but also self-neglecting) tendencies (SE). He opens by requesting a specific example. However, we see that the exploration of impulse/feeling towards her husband (XA) generates an overwhelming level of anxiety (A). This rise in anxiety is rapid and spreads throughout the musculo-skeletal, autonomic, and cognitive-perceptual systems.

Initial session (30.07–32.50 minutes)

Th: So there's a tendency to put others first. (**DA**)

Pt: Yes.

Th: Give me an example.

Pt: I'm not sure (defence of ignoring).

Th: Give me an example of when you put your needs second to those of somebody else (challenge to defence of ignoring). (**DA**)

Pt: (Pause) OK … last week. I was cooking in the kitchen and … no … it was Monday. Monday. Nick [husband] comes home … through the back door and I'm standing at the sink. I said "Hello" and he ignores me, throws down his bag and starts … "Not that again … I told you I didn't want sausages … I told you I didn't want sausages." So I explained that he was having … well … whatever he was having … I can't remember … and that the sausages were for me and Jack. So he goes off to the living room. Next thing he's back in … "So when is it going to be ready?" So I say …

Th: (Interrupting) Hold on … I want to slow the tempo here a moment. This seems important. Can we look at this in more detail? (**RE**)

Pt: OK.

Th: Good … so if we take it frame by frame … slowly … tell me how you felt when he starts to complain about the meal that you were preparing? (exploration of impulse/feeling). (**XA**)

Pt: I expect it … I know he'll behave in this way … particularly if he's had a tough day. I can't recall what had happened on … Monday … but he'd obviously had a bad day … (defence of rationalisation).

The therapist stays with the feelings.

Th: (Interrupting) I'm sure that you do expect it, but how'd you feel towards him? (**XA**)

Pt: I thought … "Here we go again" … (defence of rationalisation).

Th: (Interrupting) I'm not asking what you thought. I'm asking how you felt. How did you feel when Nick came in and started complaining? (**DA, XA**)

Pt: (Patient moves back in chair. She holds her hand to her mouth and there is clear gastrointestinal disturbance. This signals a rise in anxiety that is channelled into the smooth muscle of the gut.) Oh …

Th: (Interrupting) Tell me what's happening right now? (**AA**)

Pt: I feel … acid in my throat … acid … oh … horrible … (clears mouth).

Here we see an important technical error. Despite being aware of the patient's fragility, the therapist prematurely moved to an exploration of feeling towards the husband (XA). This led to a rise in the levels of anxiety (A) that was channelled automatically into the smooth muscle of the gut. Recognisinghis error, the therapist opts for an analysis of the somatic response (AA). This reduces the pressure towards feeling (i.e., the exploration of the impulse towards her husband—XA) and helps the patient to regulate her anxiety (AA). Further, it provides some important insight into the sequence of events for the patient. Thus, she is able to recognise that the exploration of feeling towards her husband (X) generates anxiety (A) that leads to somatisation (D).

Initial session (32.50–35.55 minutes)

Th: (Interrupting) Let's slow down a moment because this is important. There's acid in your throat ... what else? (**AA**)

Pt: Oh (clears mouth) ... my stomach is tightening now. It's really tight ... and turning ... oh ...

Th: (Interrupting) So acid reflux and stomach turning. If you look carefully ... what else? (**AA**)

Pt: I'm hot ... and pain ... in my back. (Pause) Oh ... and tiredness ... like I could just go to sleep.

Th: So acid, stomach churning, increased body temperature, pain in the lower back, nausea. Tiredness. Is there anything else? (**AA**)

Pt: No.

Th: How's your head? (**AA**)

Pt: Racing.

Th: OK. (Pause) So tell me about your vision. How's your vision? Do you see me clearly? (**AA**)

Pt: No ... not really ... you look blurred.

Th: So you have acid, stomach problems and you're hot. There's pain in your lower back and you feel nauseous. There's some fatigue ... your thoughts are racing and your vision is disturbed. (**AA**)

Pt: Oh ...

Th: Is there anything else? (**AA**)

Pt: No.

Th: OK ... OK. (Pause) Now I want to take this slowly so we can understand it. OK? (**AA**)

Pt: OK.

Th: OK. (Pause) So what I notice is that as we begin to look at the relationship between you and ... and ... Nick ... there is an immediate rise in your anxiety which manifests itself in a whole range of physical symptoms. OK? Do you understand that? (**AA**, building awareness of causality—an aspect of ego adaptive capacity)[1]

Pt: Yes.

Th: OK ... OK. So when we start to look at your feelings towards Nick in this example all these symptoms occur. These are all symptoms of anxiety. Do you understand? These symptoms are all physical manifestations of anxiety. Is that clear to you? (**AA**, building awareness of causality)

Pt: Yes.
Th: Symptoms of anxiety. (**AA**)
Pt: Yes.
Th: OK. So what we know is that exploring feelings in relation to Nick stirs up anxiety and … on the back of that … you experience all these physical symptoms. Yes? (**AA**, building awareness of causality)
Pt: Yes.
Th: OK. But we don't know why as yet.
Pt: No.
Th: Plus we still don't know what the feelings were towards him because the anxiety blocked them out. (**HP**)
Pt: Right … so the anxiety acts as a block?
Th: Exactly. The anxiety acts as a block to feelings and leads to a whole host of nasty physical symptoms. (**HP**)
Pt: Right.
Th: OK?
Pt: OK.
Th: So … so … there's something about feelings towards Nick that leads to anxiety that generates physical problems. Got it? (**HP**, building awareness of causality)
Pt: Got it.
Th: Good. (Pause) So … if you look carefully at your body … OK … how is the anxiety? (**AA**)
Pt: Less.
Th: The anxiety has lessened?
Pt: Yes.

Having regulated the anxiety through the process of recapitulation (AA), that also serves to build an awareness of causality (see ten Have-de Labije, 1999, 2001), the therapist returns to explore the feelings that the patient has towards her husband, Nick (XA). The therapist also encourages the patient to closely monitor her levels of anxiety during this process. In retrospect it could be argued that this is again a premature intervention and that the focus should have been on building an observing and attentive Ego. However, based on response to the recapitulation, the therapist decided to see if the patient could tolerate further exploration of affect (XA).

Initial session (36.40–40.04 minutes)

Th: So if we take it slowly, let's go back and have another look at that time in the kitchen. However, this time I want you to monitor your body as we do it. I want you to monitor your body and tell me as soon as the anxiety begins to come up. Does that seem OK? (**RE, AA**)
Pt: Yes.
Th: Good … good. So he comes in from work and you're preparing dinner. He starts to complain. Now, I want you to tell me how you felt towards him at that time? (**XA**)
Pt: (Patient swallows) I was feeling …(patient swallows again). I was feeling like I … like I don't have to put up with this … it's not on … that it's not on (defence of intellectualisation).

Th: So the feeling? (**XA**)

Pt: Frustration (defence of minimisation).

Th: But the feeling? (**XA**)

Pt: I felt … I felt angry. (Deep swallow. The patient's hand comes to her mouth to stifle nausea.)

Th: So … anger. (**XA**)

Pt: Yes … I felt angry that he'd come in and said those things … I'd spent a lot of time preparing the dinner … and he just came in and started … to … criticise and … and … (defence of rationalisation).

Th: (Interrupting) So, when you talk about this … with me … when you talk about how he comes in and starts to criticise the meal you've prepared … the feeling towards him now is anger? (**XA**)

Pt: Yes.

Th: How does that anger feel physically? (**XA**)

Pt: Tension. There's tension in my back and legs and stomach. My stomach is … is churning again … butterflies. I also feel sick … nauseous … not like I'm going to be sick though.

Th: OK, so let's slow down a bit. Because what I see is that you confuse anxiety with anger. You say that you're angry but what you describe is not anger but tension. The symptoms that you describe are not signals of a rising anger, but of anxiety. (**AA**)

Pt: That's not anger?

Th: No. The internal experience for you is anxiety that manifests as physical tension. That's not anger. (The therapist differentiates between the A and X poles of the Triangle of Conflict.)

The ego adaptive capacity of the patient is greatly improved. She is able to provide a specific example without becoming flooded with anxiety. Unfortunately, however, there is an inability to distinguish between anxiety (A) and the impulse/feeling of anger (X). Thus the patient cannot differentiate between the poles of anxiety (A) and impulse/feeling (X) on the Triangle of Conflict. The therapist could have helped the patient with this differentiation by reiterating the parasympathetic manifestations of anxiety (i.e., churning stomach, nausea) and distinguishing these from anger.

In the above assessment, restricted to sixty minutes, there was not time to continue with a psycho-diagnostic investigation. The therapist therefore summarised the findings of the initial interview:

- Uncertainty about attendance
- Poor recognition of physical manifestations of anxiety
- Poor regulation of anxiety
- Difficulty in exploring anger towards husband
- How the exploration of anger led to high levels of anxiety and, subsequently, to autonomic reactions and cognitive-perceptual disruption
- How the ability to regulate anxiety improved, somewhat, over the course of the initial interview
- That the patient was unable to distinguish between anxiety and her experience of anger.

On the basis of the initial interview, the therapist saw the patient as having high Superego pathology. In particular, she had begun to do to herself that which had been done to her. She ignored and neglected her feelings and placed her needs second to others. She tolerated relationships that were destructive. She ignored the pain and tension in her body. She pushed through discomfort without attending to her needs. Last, she had a poor tolerance to impulses and feelings, in particular anger, which provoked high anxiety that was channelled into her musculoskeletal, sympathetic, parasympathetic, and cognitive-perceptual systems. These tendencies (i.e., caregiving, emotional suppression, self-neglect, and perfectionism) have been noted previously in patients who present with polysymptomatic somatic conditions such as chronic fatigue syndrome (Kinsella, 2007).

The next vignettes, taken from the first therapy session, show the gains made after the initial assessment session. It begins with the patient reporting growing insight into the acrimony in her marriage. Mrs D opened the session by describing an incident where Nick had criticised her new haircut.

Session 1 (12.04–13.50 minutes)

Th: So there was a feeling? (**XA**)
Pt: I thought … (defence of intellectualisation).
Th: (Interrupting) But the feeling? (**XA**)
Pt: Irritation (defence of minimisation).
Th: Irritation?
Pt: No … anger. I thought … (defence of intellectualisation).
Th: (Interrupting) Hold on … hold on … let's not go to thought (block to defence). Thought takes you away from how you're feeling (**DA**: clarification of function of the defence). How did you experience that anger physically? (**XA**)
Pt: Heat … and … power … in my hands (patient begins to clench fists and to shake them).
Th: Power in the hands? (**XA**)
Pt: Yes.
Th: So what do the hands want to do? (**XA**)
Pt: Punch him on the nose.
Th: Imagine that … imagine punching him on the nose … imagine that power coming out through those fists. (**XA**)
Pt: (Sits back in the chair and moves her hand to her chest and throat. There is an audible gastrointestinal disturbance.) It's back … I … I got the acid and … and my stomach is churning. (A)
Th: OK … so let's review what just happened. Do you see as soon as you connect with your anger towards Nick (X) … the anxiety comes (A) … it comes straight in and blocks everything. Do you see? (**HP, AA,** building awareness of causality)
Pt: Yes.

Mrs D opens the session with defences of intellectualisation and minimisation at the forefront. However she quickly connects with her anger. There is a cognitive awareness of anger, a physiological response, and a motoric activation (see Coughlin Della Selva, 1996). Unfortunately the patient can only tolerate a small amount of anger before her anxiety increases. To assist in the regulation of anxiety the therapist summarised what had occurred. This summary had two functions: (i) it provided insight into the sequence of events for the patient, helping the patient to understand causality, thereby building ego adaptive capacity (ten Have-de Labije, 1999), and (ii) it allowed the anxiety to reduce to a manageable level before a further round of pressure to impulse and feeling was applied (see Davanloo, 1990).

Session 1 (13.50–15.09 minutes)

Th: So you connect with your anger and then anxiety comes in and blocks the true feelings. Do you see? (**HP, AA,** building awareness of causality)
Pt: Yes.
Th: So what happens to the anger?
Pt: It stops inside.
Th: It stops inside. So you end up with it. (**HP, DA**)
Pt: I guess I do.
Th: I guess you do. (Pause) That sounds unfair to me. (**RE, XA**)
Pt: It does.
Th: Do you want to do that? (**SO**)
Pt: Not at all. I don't want to do it all.
Th: OK. Good ... so let's see what we can do to get it out ... to direct the anger at the correct person. (**XA**)
Pt: OK.
Th: So let's look at how the anger would come out. In fantasy, you say you would punch him on the nose. (**XA**)
Pt: Yes.
Th: Then what?

The patient subsequently described a fantasy of punching her husband on the nose. He falls to the ground and the attack continues. She imagined kicking him repeatedly in the lower back. The attack culminated in his murder. It was followed by a sense of guilt and profound grief. During the portrayal of sadistic murderous rage towards the husband, the patient did not experience any physical tension. Her movements were in fact both fluid and powerful. Interestingly, following this portrayal the patient described a reduction in tension and back pain. Furthermore, the fact that much of the sadistic rage during the portrayal had been focused on the lower back of her husband had not gone unnoticed by either the patient or the therapist. This can be understood in terms of the defence mechanism of projective identification (that the patient does to herself that which she unconsciously wishes to do to the other). Following this portrayal of impulse, the patient associated to her childhood relationship with her father (C-P link on Triangle of Others).

Session 1 (22.45–26.32 minutes)

Th: Tell me … what comes to mind? (**HP**)
Pt: I was thinking of my father … the way he used to treat me … the horrible things he used to do. He was strict … strict to the point of nastiness. You never knew where you were with him … one minute he was kind and loving … and the next … the next he would lose it … shouting, swearing … he would hit us … not just a smack … (Patient becomes tearful).
Th: There's a feeling coming up? (**XA**)
Pt: Just … (patient reaches for tissues).
Th: Let it come … let it come … don't stop the tears. (**XA**)
Pt: (Patient begins to sob)
Th: Let it come. (**XA**)
Pt: He was horrible …
Th: (Interrupting) Don't push them down. (**XA**)
Pt: (Patient sobs heavily)
Th: There's such a deep sadness in you … such a deep sadness … just let the tears come … (**XA**)
Pt: It's not right … it's not right to treat … to treat children in that way (defence of generalisation).
Th: No … it's not right that he treated you in that way (block to the defence of generalisation). (**DA**)
Pt: (Sobbing) No … no … I hated him … hated him. I was the one who got it all … I was the eldest … I was the one who was supposed to look after the others … the one that had to come last … the one that had to care for everybody else … make sure they were OK.
Th: How awful … how awful.
Pt: (Sobbing) It was … it really, really was.

Following a mobilisation of anger in relation to her husband, Mrs D then associates to her father. There is a passage of grief as she begins to remember the demands placed on her in childhood. She then moves on to voice hatred towards her father. Lastly, we see the origins of the caregiving tendency.

Session 1 (26.32–29.45 minutes)

Th: So you became the carer? (**HP**)
Pt: I was always the carer … always … always.
Th: But who gave you that role? (**HP**)
Pt: Both of them … but I hated him more … a lot more (Patient sits back in chair. She looks to be experiencing gastrointestinal discomfort.) I hated him a lot, lot more than her.
Th: (Noticing rise in anxiety) Do you see that the anxiety comes as we look at your anger towards your father? (**HP, AA**)
Pt: It's in my chest … my throat … acid …
Th: How's your stomach? (**AA**)
Pt: Queasy.

Th: Pain in your back? (**AA**)

Pt: Some ... some ... but not as bad as usual.

Th: OK ... so ... when we look at your anger towards your father there is an immediate rise in anxiety. This comes out in acid in the throat, queasy stomach and pain in the lower back. Is that right? (The therapist provides a recapitulation so as to regulate anxiety.) (**HP, AA,** building awareness of causality)

Pt: Right.

Th: Tiredness? (**AA**)

Pt: Yes.

Th: Disturbed vision ... racing thoughts? (**AA**)

Pt: No ... not now.

Th: Right. So just talking of your anger fills you with anxiety ... just the way it did when talking about your anger towards Nick. So we begin to see that anger is a problem for you ... that for some strange reason you see anger as wrong ... so it gets suppressed. (The therapist differentiates between the X and A poles of the Triangle of Conflict.)

Pt: I never get angry.

Th: So we need to understand why.

Pt: Yes.

Th: So let's start first by looking at the anger towards your father. Can we do that together? (**XA, RE**)

Pt: Yes.

The mobilisation of anger towards the father led to an immediate rise in anxiety. This was channelled directly into the smooth muscle of the gut. It was also associated with an increase in lower back pain and the emergence of fatigue. Having seen this immediate rise, the therapist regulated the anxiety (AA) by providing a cognitive recapitulation of the events that had just occurred. This slow process of pressure to affect, regulation of anxiety through recapitulation, and subsequent return to pressure for affect, through a process of restructuring, gradually increases the patient's ego adaptive capacity, including her ability to regulate anxiety. Of particular note, in the above example, is the absence of cognitive-perceptual disruption when exploring anger towards her father—a clear demonstration of the increasing ability of the patient to self-regulate, that is, the gradual development of ego adaptive capacity in this fragile patient. Having helped the patient to regulate her anxiety, the therapist attempted once more to explore her feelings of anger towards her father (XA).

Session 1 (29.45–31.12 minutes)

Th: So your father treated you poorly. (**HP**)

Pt: Yes.

Th: OK. So when you look back on this ... on this unfair childhood ... what's the feeling towards him now? (**XA**)

Pt: Hatred ... absolute hatred ... (defence of intellectualisation).

Th: But the feeling? (**XA**)

Pt: Oh, anger … I could kill him … I really could … the things that he used to make me do … (defence of diversification).

Th: (Interrupting) But if we stay with the feelings. You say that you could kill him. Right? (**XA**)

Pt: Not in reality …

Th: (Interrupting) No … of course. In reality we know that you're a loving, kind and compassionate person … someone who struggles even to talk of anger … but in fantasy … where no harm can come to you … in fantasy there is a strong anger towards him? (**SO, AA, XA**)

Pt: Strong …

Th: So let's look at how this anger would come out? (**XA**)

Pt: I hit him … in the stomach. Hard … right in the stomach.

Th: Then what?

Pt: He's stunned … falls to the ground … he doesn't know what's hit him … and it feels good … really good … liberating … like getting my own back for all those years.

Th: Then what?

Pt: I kick him … right in the stomach … hard … watch him crumple up … watch him crumple up into a little ball … and then bam … bam … in the back … with my foot … right there … hard.

Th: Then what?

Pt: I'd keep kicking … kicking hard … right in the back … hard with the point of my shoe … bang, bang, bang.

This portrayal continued to the murder of her father. There were subsequent feelings of guilt and remorse. Mrs D connected with her grief and talked of her longings for a father who could have acknowledged and attended to her needs and desires as a young child. She moved on to talk about the passivity and compliance of her mother. This in turn led to anger directed towards her and to feelings of guilt, grief, and longings for a loving relationship. From this vignette, the gradual development of ego adaptive capacity is clearly evident. Mrs D entered the assessment session with little access to her affective state. She failed to acknowledge or attend to her feelings. Exploration of feelings led to an instant rise in anxiety that spread throughout the entire musculoskeletal, autonomic, and cognitive-perceptual systems. In contrast, by the mid-point of the first therapy session, we see a marked improvement. She is now able to experience her feelings, including anger, rage, love, grief, guilt, and sadness. She can explore these without recourse to defence or impairment to functioning. More importantly, Mrs D has recognised the effect that her suppression of feelings has had on her physical state.

The course of the treatment was relatively slow (as is quite often the case with poly-symptomatic somatic patients). Mrs D struggled to take in that which was offered and the therapist had to repeatedly challenge the defences of ignoring and neglect. However, despite the slow pace there were significant improvements within a short time-frame. The first clear indication of an improvement was a return to work. Mrs D returned to work following the sixth session and has not experienced significant physical pain or chronic fatigue since. This implies having given up a significant part of her defence of somatisation. The next important shift was in terms of giving up her defence of the professional caregiver. Mrs D began to attend to her own needs and desires and not dedicate her life to the service of others. This led to marked tension in her marriage. However, it also saw her engage with interests and hobbies that she had neglected for many years. She rediscovered the pleasures of painting and reading. She also started to attend pilates and yoga classes. Mrs D also reported a significant improvement in her mood. Despite the strain in her marriage, she did not feel the despair that she had felt prior to attending therapy. On the basis of this, she stopped her antidepressant medication. There was also a reduction in her experience of pain—she had entered treatment with diffuse chronic pain (diagnosed previously as fibromyalgia). Over the course of twelve sessions this reduced in intensity by 80 per cent and she stopped all analgesia. There was a similar improvement in her fatigue symptoms. Once again, she rated her improvement in this area as approximately 80 per cent. The vignette below, taken from the start of the eleventh session, illustrates some of the gains detailed above.

Session 11 (00.00–02.45 minutes)

Th: (Smiles) Hello.
Pt: (Smiles) Hello.
Th: How are you? (**HP**)
Pt: Fine. (Pause) No … it's better than fine. Fine is an … an underestimate of how I'm feeling.
Th: I see.
Pt: Yes … an underestimate.
Th: OK … so tell me what stuck from last session?
Pt: Boundaries … I've been thinking about boundaries this week … how I tend to put others first … how I need to develop better boundaries and stop looking after everyone else and start looking after me. (Pause) Those were the main things. (The patient has reflected on treatment between sessions and does seem to have metabolised some content. This also shows the development of an observing and attentive Ego: the patient slowly coming out from the shadow of the punitive and neglectful Superego.)
Th: So what did you do?
Pt: I don't … how do you mean?
Th: To change this pattern.
Pt: Oh … right … I'll give you an example.
Th: Good … I like examples.
Pt: They wanted me to take a late shift at work … to cover for someone who was sick. But it was short notice … really short notice … plus I'd worked all week. Normally I'd have done it even though I wouldn't have wanted. I'd have been thinking about how I'd be letting them down and the impression … and how I needed to be seen to be helping. But … and this is the change … I thought … "No, I'm not going to do it!" I thought … "I've worked all week and I need a break." So I said that I couldn't.
Th: How did that feel? (**XA**)
Pt: Scary.
Th: It generated anxiety? (**AA**)

Pt: Yes … but not for long. It was scary at first but it soon went. Then I felt good. I felt like I'd done something positive … something, you know, something positive for me.

Th: So changing this pattern generated some anxiety, but rather than defend against this by becoming submissive or compliant (the therapist highlights the poles of the Triangle of Conflict) … you took a different course … and that felt good. It felt positive. (The therapist highlights the positive consequences of relinquishing the defences.) (**HP**)

Pt: Yes … yes … very good.

Th: How did you experience that physically? (**XA**)

Pt: The good feeling?

Th: The good feeling. (**XA**)

Pt: Positive … it felt … well … it felt positive (defence of intellectualisation).

Th: But how did it feel physically? (**XA**)

Pt: I'll tell you how it felt … it felt powerful … like … like I could take on the world. I felt strong.

Th: Now when you say that … when you tell me you felt powerful … you have this great smile on your face. Now tell me how you feel right this minute … if you look carefully at your body? (**MI, XA**)

Pt: I don't …

Th: Tell me how your body feels? (**XA**)

Pt: It feels relaxed … calm … it feels relaxed and happy and light (patient laughs). It's weird.

Th: Is it weird or is it nice? (**DA**)

Pt: Nice.

Th: Nice. Not weird. Not weird at all. (**DA**)

Pt: No.

Th: So where's the tension? (**AA**)

Pt: There is none. I don't feel tense at all.

Th: Back pain? (**AA**)

Pt: No.

Th: Tiredness? (**AA**)

Pt: No.

Th: (Pause) Now, I have a question for you. Do you prefer this state of being or do you prefer the old state? (**SO**)

Pt: This feeling.

Th: Good. OK. This feels better. So when you feel powerful what happens to the tension? (**AA**)

Pt: It goes.

Th: Exactly. So when you start to attend to your needs … when you start to attend to your body … to put up boundaries and look after yourself … this feels good … you feel … empowered … like you can take on the world … and the pain and the tiredness and the tension goes. Now, if it was me I would want this good feeling more and more. I wouldn't want to live a life where I ignored myself and put myself second … where I carried the burden for everyone else … where I carried the pain and tension for everyone else … I would want the feeling that you have now … and I'd work hard to make sure I kept that and I didn't fall back. That's what I'd do. **(SE, SO, HP)**

Pt: (Smiles) Me too … definitely.

Conclusions

Patients who present with poly-symptomatic somatic conditions such as chronic pain, chronic fatigue, fibromyalgia, daily headaches, and IBS pose a challenge to traditional services. Due to this, there has been an increased interest in the role of psychological therapy in the treatment of these conditions. This has led to NICE recommending that psychological therapy be included in packages of care for patients suffering from CFS and chronic pain (low back pain). Despite the evidence for the effectiveness of CBT, there remain an appreciable number of patients who do not benefit from this approach. For these treatment refractory patients, experiential dynamic psychotherapies offer a credible alternative.

Herein, the opening phase of the therapy of a thirty-four-year-old woman with poly-symptomatic somatic complaints was presented. From the above, it appears that EDT can be effective in relieving entrenched and treatment-resistant somatic difficulties. Over the course of twelve sessions there was a marked reduction in the patient's levels of chronic pain and chronic fatigue. The patient stopped all analgesia and returned to part-time employment. There was a significant improvement in her mood and she stopped taking her antidepressant medication. Moreover, the patient began to attend to her own physical and emotional needs, and make adaptive lifestyle choices.

In the author's opinion, the effectiveness of EDT in this case is not due solely to the undoing of projective identification. The patient did describe some relief from somatic symptoms when she became aware that she did to herself that which she unconsciously wished to do to others. However, the majority of gains came from the patient relating to her Self and to others in a different manner. By separating the healthy (but overwhelmed) Ego from the grip of the neglecting and punitive Superego, the patient was able to attend to her Self and make far more adaptive choices. Hence, she began to treat herself with compassion rather than cruelty.

It is interesting to compare the EDT treatment of poly-symptomatic somatic patients to cognitive-behavioural interventions. In CBT the treatment protocol (for both CFS and chronic pain) is based on graded exercise, relaxation, activity scheduling, and cognitive restructuring of pathogenic beliefs. The goal would be to facilitate the management of a chronic condition to assist in the adjustment process. In EDT, the therapist is far less prescriptive—although the goals ultimately remain the same: that is, for the patient to relinquish the maladaptive defences (coping strategies) that they have become reliant on over the course of years. The difference, however, lies in how these goals are achieved. In the case presented the emphasis was on helping to separate the healthy part of the patient (i.e., Ego) from the unhealthy part (i.e., neglectful and punitive Superego). Once this had been accomplished, the patient naturally moved to a position where she was able to make adaptive choices. This shift towards health and well-being is reminiscent of the belief of Horney (1950), who maintained that patients have an innate predisposition towards self-actualisation and that the aim of the therapist should be in helping them to remove the obstacles to health and happiness. Thus, in this case, the therapist did not have to recommend particular healthy pursuits (i.e., graded exercise, relaxation, or activity rescheduling) as the patient moved naturally towards these.

In conclusion, experiential dynamic psychotherapies can produce significant improvements in those patients presenting with treatment-resistant poly-symptomatic somatic conditions. However, experiential dynamic psychotherapies should not be viewed as a panacea and there remain a large number of people who gain little or no benefit from treatment and who continue in pain and distress.

References

Altieri, M., Giambattista, R., Diclemente, L., Fagiolo, D., Tarolla, E., Mercurio, A., Vicenzini, E., Tarsitani, L., Lenzi, G. L., Biondi, M. & Dipiero, V. (2006). Combined pharmacological and short-term psychodynamic psychotherapy for probable medication overuse headache: A pilot study. *Cephalagia, 29*: 293–299.

American Psychiatric Association (2000). *Diagnostic and Statistical Manual of Mental Disorders—Fourth Edition—Text Revision.* Washington, DC: American Psychiatric Association.

Barber, J. (1997). *Hypnosis and Suggestion in the Treatment of Pain: A Clinical Guide.* New York: W. W. Norton.

Bradley, L. A., Young, L. D., Anderson, K. O., Tuner, R. A., Agudelo, C. A., McDaniel, L. K., Pisko, E. J., Semble, E. L. & Morgan, T. M. (1987). The effects of psychological therapy on pain behaviour of rheumatoid arthritis patients. *Arthritis and Rheumatism, 30*: 1105–1114.

Crook, J., Weir, R. & Tunks, E. (1989). An epidemiological follow-up survey of persistent pain sufferers in a group family practice and specialty pain clinic. *Pain, 74*: 1–3.

Davanloo, H. (1990). *Unlocking the Unconscious: Selected Papers of Habib Davanloo, MD.* Chichester, UK: John Wiley & Sons.

Dijkstra, A., Vlaeyen, J. W. S., Rijnen, H. & Nielsen, W. (2001). Readiness to adopt the self-management approach to cope with chronic pain in fibromyalgic patients. *Pain, 90*: 37–45.

Grant, M. & Threlfo, C. (2002). EMDR in the treatment of chronic pain. *Journal of Clinical Psychology, 58*: 1505–1520.

ten Have-de Labije, J. (1999). Maintaining Davanloo's discovery for uncovering the unconscious: Attempt at formulating operational definitions of the dependent variables. Part 1. *Ad Hoc Bulletin of Short-Term Dynamic Psychotherapy: Practice and Theory, 3*: 4–16.

ten Have-de Labije, J. (2001). Red and green traffic lights on Davanloo's road to the unconscious. In: J. ten Have-de Labije (Ed.), *The Working Alliance in ISTDP: Whose Intrapsychic Crisis?* (pp. 41–98). Amsterdam, Netherlands: VKDP—Dutch Association for Short-Term Dynamic Psychotherapy.

ten Have-de Labije, J. (2006). When patients enter with anxiety on the forefront. *Ad Hoc Bulletin of Short-Term Dynamic Psychotherapy: Practice and Theory, 10*: 1–38.

Horney, K. (1950). *Neurosis and Human Growth.* New York: W. W. Norton.

Kennedy, T. M., Chalder, T., McCrone, P., Darnley, S., Knapp, M., Jones, R. H. & Wessely, S. (2006). Cognitive behavioural therapy in addition to antispasmodic therapy for irritable bowel syndrome in primary care: Randomised controlled trial. *Health Technology Assessment, 10*: 19.

Kinsella, P. (2007). *Cognitive Behavioural Therapy for Chronic Fatigue Syndrome: a Guideline for Clinicians.* London: Routledge.

Malan, D. H. (1979). *Individual Psychotherapy and the Science of Psychodynamics.* New York: Plenum.

Morley, S., Ecclestone, C. & Williams, A. (1999). Systematic review and meta-analysis of randomized controlled trials of cognitive behaviour therapy and behaviour therapy for chronic pain in adults, excluding headaches. *Pain, 80*: 1–13.

NICE (2007). *Chronic Fatigue Syndrome/Myalgic Encephalomyelitis (or Encephalopathy): the Diagnosis and Management of CFS/ME in Adults and Children*. Retrieved May 8, 2011 from http://www.nice.org.uk/nicemedia/pdf/CG53FullGuidance.pdf.

NICE (2009). *Low Back Pain: Early Management of Persistent Non-Specific Low Back Pain*. Retrieved May 8, 2011 fromhttp://www.nice.org.uk/nicemedia/live/11887/44334/44334.pdf.

Osimo, F. (2003). *Experiential Short-Term Dynamic Psychotherapy: A Manual*. Bloomington, IL: AuthorHouse.

Turk, D. C. & Rudy, T. E. (1991). Neglected topics in the treatment of chronic pain patients: Relapse, noncompliance, and adherence enhancement. *Pain, 44*: 5–28.

Note

1. Ego adaptive capacity is defined as "the extent to which the ego mediates constructively between the external (the subjectively interpreted and/or objective demands of various persons in different situations) and internal demands (the instinctual demands of the id and the moral, punitive ones of the Superego" (ten Have-de Labije, 1999, pp. 5–6).

CHAPTER NINE

Intensive Experiential-Dynamic Psychotherapy in the treatment of long-standing depression[1]

Ferruccio Osimo

Introduction

This chapter highlights the unique way in which Intensive Experiential-Dynamic Psychotherapy (IE-DP) can undo the triggering and maintenance of depressive mechanisms. Severe depressive symptoms inhibit and disguise the expression of the Self, depriving the individual of their individuality and making them depleted, neutral, and lacking vital energy, similar to a physically ill person. For this reason, depression is often mistaken for a purely medical condition to be treated only with drugs. The aetiology of long-standing depression is more complex than this and three levels need to be considered: (i) brain function and genetics (e.g., Panksepp, 1998; Rosenthal, 1971), socio-cultural milieu (e.g., Stevens & Price, 1996), and psycho-emotional processes (Arieti, 1978; Freud, 1917e). When we practise experiential dynamic therapy we are in a real human relationship *and* use techniques, interacting mostly at the psycho-emotional level (intrapsychic), and with the way individuals interact with their socio-cultural milieu and significant Others (interpersonal). Consistent with a holistic view and with findings of affective neuroscience, in so doing we may, to some extent, also affect brain function in a favourable way. By promoting emotional experience in mind and body, EDT sets in motion a benign circle of being oneself, feeling in touch with emotion, and having a sense of being oneself and capable of feeling. As a patient is starting to access emotion and comes back to feeling alive, they realise what they have been missing and this has a powerful motivating effect, enhancing the conscious and unconscious therapeutic alliance. The therapist will then be in a position to confront the patient as to whether they want to stay open to their emotions and become the owners of their inner life, or shut down again and stay depressed. Without the specific fuel of an adequate emotional experience, the healing engine cannot be started. The case study of long-standing depression presented in this chapter highlights a few salient dynamics, often characterising depressive patients, and their treatment with Intensive Experiential-Dynamic Psychotherapy (Osimo, 2003). Among the therapeutic ingredients, we will especially focus on some aspects of the patient-therapist relationship (RE), handling of the Superego (SE) and character defences with the help of the character hologram (DA), and restructuring the relationship with Self and Other (SO).

Case study

Little Johnny

This man, in his late sixties, had a long history of relapsing depression and previous psychotherapies, and was on antidepressant and neuroleptic medication at the start of his Intensive Experiential-Dynamic Psychotherapy (IE-DP) treatment. He was the son of a depressed father, who was subdued to the patient's mother, a powerful character running the family business. The patient had a younger brother who was also subdued to the family matriarch. "Little Johnny" was the affectionate but diminishing name given to him by his mother. Notwithstanding his passive and compliant character, the patient—already retired at the start of therapy—had had a satisfactory career. Even during symptomatic remissions, however, he never felt himself, and rather felt he was living like an actor playing a character. At consultation he appeared very depressed, reported spending all day lying on a sofa, and could not see any light ahead of him or plan his future. As a consequence of this he was seriously jeopardising the relationship with his wife. They had married over twenty years earlier. Excerpts from the initial part of therapy will highlight the crucial role played by emotional connection with the therapist in enabling the safe in-session experience and regulation of conflicting feelings, impulse, and anxiety.

Real relationship and character hologram

For organisational reasons, this therapy did not start with the usual extended trial relationship interview, but with sessions of about seventy-five minutes' duration. The following dialogue is from the beginning of session 4. During the preceding three sessions there had been a positive response to the relationship with the therapist, and the experiential focus was the patient's physical perception of the "depressive cloud" coming over him, carrying Superego demands and preventing him from feeling himself. The character hologram (Osimo, 2009) was visualised as the "sad and eager puppy" and the "Pierrot" mask.[2] This brought about rapid, though partial, symptomatic relief, and the patient was able to give up medication. The way he opened session 4 clearly implies a distinction between the "work" ahead of therapist and patient, and other, supposedly lighter, aspects of their relationship. The patient is smiling and appears eager to be a "good patient" and please the therapist:

Pt: Which will we do first? Shall we do the work first? Or …

Th: Hmm, you choose … but let me just say that I noticed that, as we were walking in the corridor, here, you almost put a hand on my shoulder … but you actually … **(RE)**

Pt: … stopped myself, yes.

Th: So that's also something meaningful … I don't know whether it refers more to the present or to the past, you choose, but that is certainly meaningful (**RE, TCP**)

Pt: Yes, yes, hmm … why did I hesitate … from putting my hand on your shoulder, which is natural for me to do? I think it was my concern that it might be … misconstrued as being … how can I put it … over-eager … hmm … too needy, too … you know, those things … and I didn't feel that way at all, but as though it's just a sense of, you know, it may be misconstrued. As it was when we met last session that I was just this … little puppy who wanted just like shake your hand and, you know, just so eager, so … so desperate!

The patient is referring to the character hologram. The therapist clarifies his projection:

Th: So, the idea is that I would misunderstand your real desire to be close, to be friendly. (**RE, DA**)

Pt: My, it's me, it's not you, and it's my control of me not wanting to appear anxious (tactical defence of saying what he does not feel, and not what he feels).

Th: Yes, but this doesn't say what you do want to appear, what is it? (**DA**)

Pt: It would have seemed just natural to me to put my hand on your shoulder and ask about your holiday.

Th: So it was genuine interest in me? (**RE**)

Pt: Absolutely, absolutely … nothing … and I stopped myself … whether it was your face, my sense of seeming to be … too anxious. But not, but I'm still going back to … the old way.

Th: Yes, but what is the feeling, because, as you say this, your voice almost breaks, so what is the feeling that you have here? (**XA**)

Pt: Ahm … of being judged, of being judged as being … probably in my own mind, of being too eager, too anxious, too needy, too friendly, too … being judged, and maybe that goes back to …

Th: (Interrupting) I see that but, hang on, "being judged" for what? I mean, what is the feeling that you have for me and that you are afraid it gets misjudged, or misunderstood? (**DA, XA**)

Pt: I feel as though I have a friend, and I've only known you for three or four hours, basically, and yet I have a sense of friendship towards you. And I think it's as simple as that, and yet, you are also my doctor, my therapist, and so there is a … a distance, that I …

Th: So, you almost made it, but you left the distance …! (**DA**)

Pt: That's right, exactly, exactly.

Th: So, you feel friendly towards me … I mean, is it you that perceive this friendship, want me to be your friend … or you feel that I am friendly with you? (**RE**)

Pt: I sense it's both ways. I sense … your friendliness. You asked me once, "You like me?" very openly, "Do you like me?" and I sort of said "Yes". And so, that sort of … was a sign of … not just "doctor-patient", but indeed that I can be very open, that I can talk about stuff within me … without editing! And so yes, I feel as though there is a friendship that's developed, yes (snorts).

Th: Why you go snorting? (**DA**)

Pt: Well, you know, that's why I'm sort of saying … that's how I feel, and I feel that …

Th: (Interrupting) Do you enjoy this? (**XA**, **RE**)
Pt: Yes, sure, absolutely, it makes …
Th: (Interrupting) Will you let yourself enjoy it? (**SE**)
Pt: I'll try …

The above excerpt from session 4 mainly illustrates the role played by the real relationship in overcoming distancing and defences against emotional closeness. The patient starts to become familiar with some aspects of his character that lead him to please instead of seeking longed-for affection. The next vignette, from session 5, again starts from the sense of trust and authenticity with the therapist, fiercely opposed by the patient's sadistic Superego, dictating that he must reject the closeness he desires, a form of sadism towards himself. This type of self-sadism, by way of depriving oneself of what one most desires, is one of the mechanisms that maintains depressive states and may trigger relapses.

Unconscious therapeutic alliance: making friends

The therapist confronts the patient's defence of distancing and rejecting closeness and his anxiety of really trusting the therapist. There is a clear interference of the Superego, speaking with his mother's voice:

Th: … and the other thing is that it is too dangerous to come close to me. (**AA**)
Pt: My mother is saying that, or I am saying that?
Th: You. To rely on me, to pat my shoulder, to really feel close, to really … trust that there can be not only a "nice" and pleasant relationship between us, but a real closeness and a strong basis, that gives you the strength you need. That is dangerous to believe, for you. (**AA**)
Pt: Yes, yes, yes, it is.
Th: It is almost impossible to believe. It is frightening. (**AA**)
Pt: Yes, yes … it is giving it away … it is giving me away, and the prisoner inside, is almost afraid to open the door and … and come out.
Th: What is the fear with me (sighs) regarding letting you do that? (**AA**)
Pt: It's the same fear that I have of taking … a pill, I guess, I'm afraid I will become dependent on you …

The patient is now rather shaken and this last sentence could be perceived as an attempt to rationalise. Having seen various therapists before, he is knowledgeable in psycho-jargon, like "becoming dependent". The therapist needs to point out this defence:

Th: (Interrupting) That is good language. I want more! What is the fear that it would happen then? (**DA**, **AA**)
Pt: What if you couldn't help me! What if I allow myself into your hands, and … it doesn't work … that do I go back again into the depression? So it's like, it's like … my fear inside … there's no question it's my bloody fear, it's like I'm afraid to give it over to you. For sure, for sure … why?

This "why" would introduce a new attempt to rationalise that the therapist wishes to prevent:

Th: (Interrupting) No, no, no! I'm not so interested in "why", I'm interested in the fear, hmm … because you know many "whys" … (**DA**)
Pt: (Snorts)
Th: … but we see this fear and this need to control and to give scores to sessions, and was it good-enough, or wasn't it good-enough … which is very mother-like … (**DA, SE**)
Pt: Yes.
Th: (Role-playing the mother) "Johnny, are you good-enough or are you not good-enough?" … I don't want to put myself in your place with your mother and I don't suspect you want to be there still, remain there … (**SE, RE**)
Pt: No.
Th: Then the other option is to get close to me … and not to me-Good-Johnny, me-your-mother or me-therapist, but to me-me! Now, I don't know if you can get close to me … (**SE, RE**)

In this way the therapist brings a direct challenge to the Superego questioning if the patient can avoid following his habitual inclination and, instead, allow himself to be close with the therapist.

Pt: I don't know either, the question I was going to ask is how do I open the gate, how do I put aside the fear?
Th: Try, for instance, to tell me what you want this relationship with me to be like, you wanted to put an arm on my shoulders last time. Now. What do you want? (**SE, RE**)
Pt: I want to be free of depression; I want to have my kite fly, so I know what I want to do for the rest of my life. I want to be without fear, I want to understand … maybe "understand" isn't the word, I want to feel freedom and joy and elation over things, and to end my reserve, to end my, my control …
Th: OK, so, can you have this joy now, or … is there something preventing you from feeling joy? (**SE**)
Pt: It's difficult for me to even think of joy, I'm dressed in dark and … I don't feel a cloud, but I feel sad, I feel sad, I feel … that I can't … and the wave that comes to me, the feeling that comes is that I want to be able to say to you that I'm full of joy, that I'm free, that I'm open and the sadness is that I don't feel that, I feel so … blocked that way, so blocked.

The patient actually conveys sadness (X) and, at the same time, his being is clearly stifled (A) by his sadistic Superego. The therapist decides to focus on the actual experiencing:

Th: Are you blocked or are you sad? (**HP**)
Pt: Sad, sad … yes.
Th: And what is the sad thought? (**XA**)
Pt: (With effort) The sad thought is that I can't just … feel free, I just can't open up, I can't, I can't … laugh.
Th: You can't laugh if you are sad, but where is the sadness in your body? (**XA**)
Pt: In my body it's here (points to his chest)

Th: What do you feel there? (**XA**)
Pt: Heavy, heavy, yeah, yeah …

Exploring and sharing the physical sensation and emotional experience of the patient evokes in the therapist the image of a coffin with a dead body inside. The therapist decides to share this image with the patient, hence the next intervention. In response, the patient has an image of his brother lying dead. The brother is actually alive, and this fantasy clearly reflects the patient's rage at his brother for also being subdued to mother, and siding with her. Moreover, the image of the dead brother is likely to represent the patient's Self, made to live as an emotionally dead person by his Superego.

Helping the patient to stalemate his Superego

Th: And who is there in the tomb? (**XA, HP**)
Pt: Here inside? My brother …
Th: What is the image of your brother that comes to mind? (**HP, XA**)
Pt: Just lying peacefully … there is no more shaking, there is nothing, just lying peacefully. I've had images of his death this week.

This statement about having already had images of the brother's death shows that the image of the coffin and dead body, crossing the therapist's mind, was not his independent ideation, rather the result of unconscious patient-therapist communication. The term and concept of "countertransference" usually refers to a feeling or state of mind elicited in a therapist while interacting with a patient, and related to the patient's dynamics. When working closely with the patient's physical sensations at an experiential level, even physical sensations can be transferred to the therapist. This phenomenon can be regarded as countertransference in a broader sense and can be traced back to mirror neurons (see Osimo, Chapter 3, pp. 50–51). As we will see, the therapist decides to use this fantasy to engage the patient in the fight against his Superego:

Th: So, in a way, you still don't know where you want to stand! With your brother, who was subdued to your mother but, like her, also tries to manipulate you, OR if you want to say NO, as you recently did to your brother for the first time, but never to your mother … (**SE**)
Pt: Or to my brother before.

Engaging the patient to focus on the here-and-now of the session:

Th: So, the real point is what do you want to do now, since you are standing in between; on the one hand you are like your brother; can't follow your colourful kite, dress like Pierrot … are adrift in your life … on the other hand, you perfectly know who you are and want to do, like buying a new house … so there is a part of you that wants to be the driver of your life and to be happy. Because, of course, you cannot be happy if you are not yourself, do the things you want to do and let them come … no doubt about that. (**SE**)
Pt: No, I agree.

The patient can now see clearly the feeling and desiring part of him—or the Self—and the Superego part—personated by his brother and mother—that stifles his lust for life. To enable him to separate his Self from his Superego, the therapist decides to *accompany* the patient to his mother's funeral. The patient's mother died twelve years earlier, but the patient is still identified with her. A technical procedure introduced by Davanloo (1990) to help patients get in touch with their complex and multi-level feelings for someone they love relies on inducing a guided fantasy of acting out the murderous rage, through to the actual killing, last goodbye, and burial of the loved person. In this case, instead, the therapist decides to help the patient get in touch with his feelings by guiding him to re-experience his mother's death, without having to "kill" her in fantasy. This will make out his sadistic impulse in a natural situation, making it even more *real* than in an imagined one.

The sadistic trap

Th: So you haven't buried your mother ... (**DA**)
Pt: No, probably no (tactical defence).
Th: Surely not. (**DA**)
Pt: Yeah, yes.
Th: So, do you want to bury her? Or not? (**SE**)
Pt: Yes, it's time, it's time to ...
Th: So, let's go to her funeral ... when did she die? Were you there? What was this death like? (**HP**)
Pt: I saw her die ... it was very gruesome ... and I think one of the things that sticks with me is that there were two women serving her lunch and I saw one of them putting some powder in her glass, and asked, "What is that?", and they said, "Oh, it's to lower her blood pressure." And that has haunted me since that time, and I did nothing about it. I didn't consult the nurse, I didn't consult the doctor ... she died that night; she exploded inside and I remember so vividly her sitting upright in bed, her mouth open in anguish, in anguish ... and she was gone ... and I'm haunted by that.
Th: And we don't know what that powder was ... (**HP**)
Pt: No, I don't, and I didn't have the guts to go further and ask. I had a similar situation, about a month ago when I was walking in a field and there was a bird caught in a trap ... and I didn't let the bird out of the trap ...

At this stage of Superego work, the patient's self-sadism starts being redirected from the Self—symbolically the mortally trapped bird—towards its real targets:

Th: So there are feelings that you have for your mother that make you want to inflict something on her ... (**XA**)
Pt: Yes ... yes I felt so angry towards her, for creating the thing within me that stops me from being free ... and yet I've always thought of myself as being free, and that's why I'm so angry ...

The patient gave a nice definition of his depressive Superego as "the thing within me that stops me from being free". The therapist will now help him see the details of this mechanism in order to further motivate him to give it up:

Th: Ah! Tell me about this trap that she made, and how it works … (**SE**)
Pt: The trap started when I was a child; you can't go swimming because you'll drown, you can't go on a boat, you can't go walking in the woods because there are lions … you can't, you can't, you can't … so her fear became my fear.
Th: So what do you want to do or to say to her if she is here now? (**HP, XA**)
Pt: (Becoming emotionally aroused) Just, let me go! LET ME GO, just let me go! Allow me to be free, allow me to just, just … allow me to just fly!

The patient is activated emotionally, but still is showing a dependent position:

Th: So you want to go on staying passive and ask her to do something for you! But what do you want to do or to say if you take the lead? (**HP, DA, SE**)
Pt: And … you are right! If I wanted to be free … (tactical defence)
Th: If you want to be free, what do you tell her? What do you do to her? When she says you can't do this and you can't do that and you can't do that, don't swim and don't … (**HP, XA, SE**)
Pt: (Becoming like paralysed on his chair) What do I say to her …?
Th: If you don't want to stay paralysed forever … trapped! What do you want to do? Because you are immobile! (**HP, DA, AA, SE**)
Pt: Immobile, totally …
Th: So, do you want to remain immobile? (**AA, SE, DA**)
Pt: No! No!
Th: Because if you want to remain immobile, there you are … (**DA, SE**)
Pt: (Suddenly animated) No! I, I, I, I, I, I want to move on!
Th: Let's see how you move on! From that position … how do you move on? (**AA, SE**)
Pt: I move on by stopping the voices of "don't, don't, don't, you can't, you can't".

There is no reason to doubt the patient when he states he wants to "stop the voices" but we know that, crucial as it is to be able to state his intention, only the actual experience of his rage and sadism will give him a sense of really owning his feeling and impulse. The therapist has to bring a further challenge until the patient can experience fighting his sadistic Superego, here still personated by his mother:

Th: How do you stop the voices? How do you stop her voice? (**HP, SE**)
Pt: I don't know!
Th: So you can't, you can't! Your mother is right; you want to remain there! (**DA, SE**)
Pt: (Very animated) No! I don't believe that! I don't believe that! I believe that I can! I believe that I can stop that!
Th: So what do you tell her because she keeps on saying you can't?! (**HP, SE**)
Pt: Fuck off! Leave me alone! Just, just …

The patient's attitude is different now; he is sitting up straight and hits the chair arm with his fist. The therapist wishes to highlight and consolidate the new position:

Th: Are you joking, or are you serious? (**DA**, **SE**)
Pt: No, I'm serious, I'm serious. Just …
Th: So, what is the way you want to tell her seriously, as a man! (**HP**, **DA**, **SE**)
Pt: As a man, I'm able to go on in my life without hearing her voice, without being fearful because she's there watching me. I can't go on the rest of my life being fearful of what she will think or say or … or Joan [wife] will say, or my mother will say, or my father will say, or my brother will say!
Th: So do you want to go on coming here with the cloud? Or spend five days out of seven like Pierrot? (**SE**, **DA**)
Pt: No, no … no, I don't. No, I don't.
Th: So, how do you say goodbye to your mother? (**HP**, **SE**)
Pt: I don't know, how do I say goodbye?

At the prospect of real separation the patient goes back into passivity, probably related to his rage, interfering with letting her go in peace. The therapist invites him to portray the last hours until the decision of letting his mother off the assisted ventilation and letting her die. We rejoin the session about ten minutes later.

Th: So, you want to give her a last goodbye now or keep her alive … artificially? What feeling are you hanging on to? (**DA**, **SE**)
Pt: I'm still trapped with her words. Her don't do, don't do, don't do … my father's don't do, don't do, don't do … and I would love to be free, of all those "don'ts".
Th: But you don't. (**SE**, **DA**)
Pt: I don't know even how to reach in and take that emotion, it's like it's strangling up here (pointing to his throat).
Th: You have a physical something here? (**AA**)
Pt: Yes, yes, yes, exactly. So it's just that it's here and it's here … (pointing to his neck).

The patient is reporting a sensation of getting strangled, and this reminds the therapist of a highly traumatic incident when the patient's father asked the patient to help him hang himself. The Superego is now using his father's voice, and the patient needs to look at the feelings towards his father.

Undoing the identification with father

Th: So you end up strangled! I wonder if your father now is in the way, because he asked you to help him … (**HP**)
Pt: … hang himself …
Th: And you didn't want to help him that way … (**HP**)
Pt: No, no … he put a rope in my hand and said, "pull" … in the basement.
Th: Is there something that you want to tell him, now, about this? (**HP**, **SE**, **XA**)

Pt: How cruel could you have been to do that to me …! How sadly sad your life was … that you couldn't stand up to your wife and so you wanted me to kill you and be burdened with your death. You just wanted to hear me say "Daddy, daddy, don't do it."

Th: So that was even crueller than what your mother did; with your father there was no way whatsoever (sighs) of living … (**XA**)

Pt: No, he was so sad … such a sad man … he was so angry at everyone, at everything … I don't remember him ever laughing, never ever, ever saw him laughing.

Th: So, in a way, all the times that you are not enjoying life you are faithful to that … (**SE, DA**)

Pt: I'm being my father. And I'm being my father in my role with my wife, aren't I? Giving in, being placating, being angry … not showing the emotion, but feeling it.

Transference and real relationship

The patient's experience of powerful emotion in the session cannot but lead to mobilisation of feelings towards the therapist. Some of this is transference, in the redirection to the therapist of feelings from other relationships. However, some of the feelings arose from the real relationship with the therapist as a consequence of having shared very painful experiences and memories with him:

Th: How is it now for you to be here saying this, sharing this with me? (**RE**)

Pt: (Very moved) Feels good, feels good, I feel like crying because it's … there's some relief in sharing it, there's some relief in … in actually feeling that I could … I could actually say goodbye …

Th: To? (**DA**)

Pt: To both of them …

Th: So, you want to say goodbye to both of them? (**XA**)

Pt: (Sobbing) Yeah, yes. With all that I think that I loved them very much, with all that I think that, I think that … I miss them like hell. When my mother died, I think that I felt very alone, that there wasn't anyone to look after or direct me or to… It's mine now, it's not theirs, it's mine, and so it's my life and … as my mother used to say, "It's your package".

Th: So, in a way, your mother, in her own way, gave you what she had and could give … (**XA**)

Pt: Yeah, I believe that.

The last goodbye

Pt: (Moved) I am tired! Wow …

Th: So, you want to say goodbye to her now? (**XA**)

Pt: Yes.

Th: What is the way you say goodbye to your mother? (**XA**)

Pt: (Crying) Goodbye, I loved you very much, yeah …

Th: I believe in your love, but I'm not sure you forgave her … (**DA**)

Pt: No, I really haven't. I can't let go, like really let go.

The patient's words of separation from his mother are genuine and emotionally charged. Something is, however, still in the way of giving her up for good. The therapist guesses that what the patient does not want to renounce is the mother's genuine love for him as a lively, but compliant, Little Johnny. Hence the next passages, aiming to enable the patient to renounce the compliant, self-diminishing position, though retaining the good part.

Let's do hats together!

Th: And what are you afraid of letting go? Little Johnny? (**AA**)
Pt: Yeah, sure, sure …
Th: Keep him with you! (**AA**)
Pt: I don't want to.
Th: Why? (**AA**)
Pt: Because, as long as Little Johnny is with me, then I will never … be free!
Th: Well, you can keep him with you, not be him … I mean, he is in you anyway … you don't want to kill him!? (**SO**)
Pt: NO! I don't, I don't, I don't want to kill him. He is me!
Th: The point is, can you keep Little Johnny with you, but be different? Being just him is not practical for you (**SO**)

The therapist helps to restructure the patient's relationship with the part of himself that is identified with "Little Johnny" so as to achieve a better separation and integration of his parts. In the next line Little Johnny is located "beside" the patient, thus in a different position, and with the separation of parts, intrapsychic communication is possible and integration of parts can proceed:

Pt: It would certainly be easier to have him beside me, than to try and … kill him, to try and eliminate him totally …
Th: Maybe you can talk to him … what can you tell him? (**SO**)
Pt: Let's go back and make hats together! Let's go and do portraits of teachers! Let's go and swim together … all those things that I did well before I was eight years old …
Th: Let's put our strength together! Our creativity, our joy for life … (**SO**)

Close of session

Pt: (Joyous and moved) Yes, yes, I like that a lot! I like that a lot!
Th: You are moved … what is the feeling or the thought? (**XA**)
Pt: (Moved and very excited) Two things have happened, that I … I've trusted, I'm giving over to you … It feels … very nice! Yes … Just the blocks that just came out are just incredible … I'm, I'm at least allowing myself to … share … I'm able to actually express an emotion!
Th: What is your emotion with me? (**XA, RE**)
Pt: Ooh, it's just like I'm, I'm joyous that I can … I can just let it go, can open up, yeah …

Th: So you have a feeling for me! What feeling? I'm interested! (**XA**, **RE**)
Pt: I'm able to trust you! I'm able to sort of just ... cry! I'm able to just ... let it out. It feels ... it feels so good! Wow ... yeah, yeah ... there is more of light in the sky ...
Th: It's so important to make contact with each other! (**RE**) And where do you visualise your mother now? (**HP**)
Pt: Just lying in bed, just peacefully with her eyes closed. She's dead and she's quite peaceful.
Th: And your father? (**HP**)
Pt: I think I can let go of him too ... yeah I think so ...
Th: What would you say to him to ... to say goodbye, to let him go? (**HP**, **SE**)
Pt: I hope you have peace now. I hope you have ... finally put an end to your anger ...

This session created a good therapist-patient relationship (RE), fostering the unconscious therapeutic alliance and acting as a matrix fuelling technical work on defences (DA) and Superego restructuring (SE). The surfacing of deep feeling and impulse mobilised anxiety, and the patient automatically took a paralysed position. The therapist invited the patient to relinquish their position of paralysis and passivity (DA), and regulated the patient's anxiety (AA), uncovering self-sadism and, eventually, intense feelings of rage, guilt, grief, and love. Finally, the patient was able to start separating emotionally from his primary attachment figures, coming to terms with the inner representation of himself as a little, desperate puppy, only eager to please others. All this supplied therapist and patient a clear vision of the main dynamics involved in perpetuating the depressive mechanism. Moreover, the patient experientially realised that getting in touch with deep buried emotion is the opposite of being depressed and, consequently, even at the age of sixty-seven, it would be possible to leave his depression behind. This is not to say that the therapeutic work hitherto was enough to bring about a permanent change in the patient's functioning and approach to life. Rather, it served to fully motivate the patient to take advantage of the therapeutic help being offered to him.

The depressive habit

A crucial aspect of long-standing depression is that, whatever the respective shares of different aetiological factors involved in each single case, the individual's emotional as well as physiological and behavioural regulatory systems are set to the depressive way of life. We might call this a "depressive habit", relying on a generous amount of passivity and passive aggression, having a pessimistic stance—that is, ignoring positive signals and amplifying the negative ones—and indulging in re-enactments of sadomasochistic relational interchanges, whereby the Self gets its daily dose of abuse and punishment. In dynamic terms, this amounts to a sadistic ill-treatment of the Self, perpetrated by the Superego. If we wanted to translate this into CBT language (Beck, 1967; also see Meijers, 2012) we could say that, since the patient's mother (P) and then his wife (C), are perceived as overpowering and devaluing, this represents the Antecedent event. This Antecedent triggers the Belief, "I am worthless and can only be loved if I am subdued and eager to please". This Belief brings about the Consequent state of mind, "The future is hopeless, I cannot stand it, and I am depressed". Even looking at it from different theoretical viewpoints, if we want to prevent relapses, we will need to direct all of the individual's emotional energy to the unbalancing of the depressive homeostasis, establishing a healthier one. In IE-DP, consolidation of a new healthier equilibrium, once the balance is tipped, mostly relies on the ingredient of "Self-restructuring" (SO). Leigh McCullough et al.'s (2003) description seems very suited to depressive patients:

> Many patients who need Self-Restructuring work are unaware of their own inner signals, neglect them or don't feel entitled to respond to them or to voice their own needs. Generally they were taught as children to adapt to situations by denying parts of themselves. Many patients were taught to be receptive to other people's needs, but not receptive to their own needs. When this lack of "receptive capacity" to one's own wants and needs continues in adulthood, it can create a constant state of self-inflicted deprivation. (p. 238)

Hence the need to promote a shift whereby perceived oppression and devaluing become capable of triggering healthy anger, adaptive beliefs about Self, and adaptive assertion. In this way the individual can be assisted in the unlearning of depressive modes until a new homeostasis is established that honours the individual's emotional and interpersonal needs.

Improvement and relapse

At around session 9, the patient's wife went back to their country of origin to spend a few months there and the patient—for the first time in twenty-five years—decided not to go with her. This was a first move towards independence and enabled him to attend sessions regularly, committing himself fully to the therapeutic work, and experimenting with new and better strategies in his everyday life. Over Christmas, however, he decided to give his wife a surprise by joining her in time to celebrate together. When the patient left he was bold and enthusiastic but, after a few days, he fell back into his depressive, powerless, and self-devaluing position. The trigger was the patient's perception of his wife and old friends doubting the results of his efforts to heal, disbelieving his recovery, stigmatising him as a depressed person, and recommending some "really" sound therapeutic intervention. Needless to say, whatever his wife and friends may have said and done got intercepted by the patient's sadistic Superego, which regained power to crush his recently reclaimed sense of personal worth, strength, and initiative.[3] The patient quickly flew back and, in session 18, complained with the therapist about his relapse. The therapist empathised with his suffering, and showed him his projected Superego by using the metaphor of "friendly fire":

Pt: I'm just dragging my ass … just there is no … no joy, I'm rigid … I thought I was starting to spark a little, but it's not, it's not … I'm feeling as though I'm back at the beginning, Ferruccio, back at the beginning, and it's so … disheartening to be there, it's like it comes on (snaps fingers) like that! And the guarantee—we talked about that—the guarantee was that I would never have depression again! I want the guarantee! In defence of myself, I said to everyone that I was with … who were expounding drug therapy, this therapy, that therapy, religion … I said, "No, I will never be depressed again, I am conscious it will never happen to me again" (snorts). I've lost that consciousness. I've lost that and I don't know what's triggered it … I do know, I do know, I mean, yes it is emotional. Joan sort of talking to all of our friends and it was like, again war.

Th: Well, the answer is that you need to defend your little plant from your and others' attacks on it, by finding better and better ways of responding immediately to whatever attack, as you do … but not enough, as it seems … and … I sympathise with you; since you found yourself in an adverse situation, being attacked on many sides at the same time … it is like the friendly fire … hmm …? **(SE)**

Pt: Yeah, you can still die …

Th: It's horrible, because you expect to be fired at by the enemy, not by a friend! So it's more difficult to defend oneself against the friendly fire. Also, it gave you a lot of anxiety, because if you counterattack someone who loves you, you are afraid of losing the friend and destroying the love! **(SE)**

Facing friendly fire

Although exposure to his wife's and old friends' communications about his recovery had led to a sudden, but severe, relapse, subsequent exposure to the relationship with the therapist gave the patient immediate relief. Only by developing an independent ability to face his Superego, however, is the patient able to consolidate his change and make it stable. This was the focus of sessions 19–21, which centred on the intrapsychic dynamics (SE), as well as on the handling of real life situations in relation to the therapist and significant Others (SO, TCP). From session 19:

Pt: Well, it's been a better week, for sure … I spent a couple of days in the garden. It was just joyous, and I had a very pleasant dinner with some people …

Th: Yes: I am sure you can now feel well, but we don't want to be blind and disregard this potentiality you have … to feel a wreck, hmm? Part of this, anyway, was healed last week by feeling that you could stay with people … me … a friend or a neighbour … I mean, in a good way … in a different way, without all this … **(SE, RE, SO)**

Pt: … control …

Th: … control and devaluing, bossing and bullying … so, it is very therapeutic to have a different type of interchange with others; the good one … but … what to do with the other type? There is a part of you that hasn't renounced it completely, for some reason … you call it back, and find it difficult to unthread … to take away the good, and keep it with you leaving the negative part … **(SE)**

Pt: Hmm … yes! I'm trying to think of … was it Joan that triggered that within me? I don't think so necessarily, I'm not sure, or was it simply that I … set myself up for it? Because … I arrived and we all had dinner together, and … and it was absolutely marvellous!

Patient and therapist carefully restructure the inner dynamics of the patient, Little Johnny, his mother's voice, and his father's voice. Was he able to grow independent on all this?

Pt: Yeah, yeah … you see … we had let go of him [Little Johnny], and there was a real … it was very visual for me; the "letting go" of him. We did that for both of them [parents] of letting go … but they are still with me, at least my father is with me, for sure … in the treatment of my mother to my father, of the women that I've been with … she [wife] still has this feeling that chemical therapy is the only answer … and you and I have never ruled that out, but we've never gone there … and, you know, maybe there is some need for her to come and spend … an hour, the three of us, I don't know … and that's something for you to think about and we should talk about I guess … I don't know how you feel …?

Th: No problem on my side, I don't think you need that … but … (**SO**)

Pt: I'm not sure I do either. I suggested that she come here on her own and she seemed reluctant to do that …

This is a delicate moment; the patient senses that if his change becomes steady and permanent, his wife will need to go through a process of adaptation, that is, she will need to change too.[4] He therefore suggested to her that she comes to therapy, but she was totally against this option. The therapist could have seen the wife if she so wished, but knows that the patient needs to change, independent of what the wife will or will not do. He therefore decides to first put all the responsibility on the patient, though leaving a door open to seeing patient and wife together, as including the wife cannot make up for any diminishment of the patient's full and unambiguous commitment to change. So, the patient can start trying his best on his own before involving the wife:

Pt: … so, yes, no I think I need some time to sort of just digest what we've done, and just, you know, go on from there … because I literally played the role, in order for Joan to react in a certain way, and I'm doing it these days … giving her the tools … come on, hit me again! When I don't feel good about me, I give her the ammunition to put in the gun to shoot me! The same as I did with our old friends … and one friend in particular, literally, she and her husband had the guns. I had loaded them for Joan and she gave them to them, and it was like bang, bang, bang, bang!

The following dialogue is an example of Self-Other restructuring and Superego work:

Th: … so, the two things are true, and you should acknowledge with Joan that you are angry with her for what she did, but you recognise that you played a role in that … is she as rigid as you? (**SO**)

Pt: No … (sighs) I hamper her … I hamper her spontaneity …

Th: That is self-destructive! Do you want to go on hampering it? (**SE, SO, DA**)

Pt: I could tell you … say to you, "NO", but my actions don't speak that way, I say "No" intellectually, I don't want that …

Th: So, you mean you don't want to change your action! (**SE, DA**)

Pt: I want to change my actions …

Th: So, what do you do? Because either you do it or not …! (**SE, DA**)

Pt: Well … why do I put my shoes at the front door …?

Th: There is no "why" ... either you change, or you keep on putting the shoes like that ... if your intention is to go on putting your shoes like that, there is nothing anybody can do if it is your choice ... and decision, but ... you cannot blame someone for bullying you, I mean, if you don't want to change anything of your behaviour in the least. (**SE**, **SO**, **DA**)

The next description by the patient is effective in conveying the effort required to totally renounce the depressive habit:

Pt: ... (sighs) ... I have to tell you that I am comfortable in that rigidity ... I'm comfortable in ... in that environment. I've been comfortable in that environment without Joan there, and it's been my space and my organisation, and my tidiness, whatever ... and ... it's been OK! So I'd like to sort of say, "Yes, I want to be free! I want to just throw everything everywhere!", but that's, that's, that's ... not who I've been! I've been this way all my life ... I've never thrown things on the floor, not capped toothpaste, or ... haven't made the bed ... all those things, it's like ... sort of like it's, it's the beginning of the day for me, or the end of the day for me when, you know, it's ... it's like things are put back in place ...
Th: So, no concession! (**SE**, **DA**)
Pt: I hear you, I hear you ... not easy ... not easy for me to sort of ... go that way ... not easy ... not easy ...
Th: (Ironical) I wonder what is the fear that you have, if you ... let go some of this, I mean, it's very useful to have a husband who tidies up! (**AA**, **DA**)
Pt: Yeah ... it's so funny! ... if I'm going to ... be true to me ... (tactical defence) I have to find ...
Th: (Interrupting) If I'm going to ...? (**DA**)
Pt: ... if I'm going to be true to myself, then I must speak with her honestly and candidly and ... we both have to work through this ... I can't ... I can't, I won't go back and go through what I went through of just placating and just being the fake ... I want to feel everything again ... and I had that! I had that! It did come!

The patient is now determined to change and does his best to operationally restructure his couple relationship. The feedback is convincing and the therapist leaves it with him whether or not to invite his wife to come to a session with him.

An unusual last session

The patient's wife was not willing to undertake any therapeutic work. However, she accepted the patient's invitation to attend session 22 together, after making plain that she would only come "for him". She was sceptical about the patient's recovery process, and the prospect of trusting in his change made her very anxious. She enquired about how much of the patient's "illness" was hereditary and, in spite of the encouraging signals, she still leaned towards a "heavy" medical and pharmacological approach for him. She disbelieved his change and, to the direct question posed to her by the patient, "Do you see me as a depressed person or am I not depressed?", she was unable to give a straight answer. During the session, the patient was gentle but very assertive when making plain to the wife that they seemed to see two different things and that, at any rate, he wished to have back a real and satisfactory couple relationship or give it up altogether. In so doing, he gratefully recognised the many good things that happened in the course of their relationship hitherto. The therapist openly contemplated a few couple sessions but the wife confirmed her lack of motivation for any form of individual or couple help. The therapist then did his best to regulate the wife's anxiety at the prospect of accepting the authenticity of the patient's change, and engaging in a new phase of their relationship. Both patient and wife were cheerful when leaving the session. Although it had not been planned that this would be the last session, the patient did not have a sense that he needed or wished to come again. However, he kept in touch with the therapist by mail.

Sixteen-month follow-up

More than one year after the last session, the therapist asked the patient to come for a follow-up session. He did this for an outcome study and, consequently, the session was not charged to the patient. The patient was in an excellent mood and looked younger. After the initial playful remarks and mutual updating, the therapist started enquiring about a recent move to a new house and city. To this the patient answered:

Pt: (Changing subject) First of all, let me say one thing to you that I think is important. I've been depression-free for a lot of time now and it's been wonderful … hmm and … your lessons were very clear for me …

Th: … my lessons?

Pt: (Smiling) Yes … yes, your … words and that "You don't have to have depression ever again in your life".

Th: Did I say that!?

Pt: Yes, you did! … well, maybe there was some qualification that I'm not sure, but actually you did, I think …

Th: … well, we have the tapes, so we can listen again …

Pt: … yes, we can, but … it's been a wonderful … whatever length of time it's been … not without pains and difficulty but … but not with depression … not with feeling down in the abyss, without hope … so, we moved to […] … Joan and I are well … we've come together … not always in agreement, but I'm no longer being bullied, which is very nice and … Sometimes that leads to moments of … "non-communication", but we have a new appreciation for each other …

Th: That's very good to hear …!

Pt: Yes, to me too, to me too … I've come to realise that some of my rigidity, of my "everything must be in order" has also eased, that I'm not as rigid … which is very nice … so that's good and we are laughing a little more and … it's quite a rich life these days … as I say, not always, but each day … we grow … so, that's good …

At this point the therapist enquires about some more specific situations that, in the past, would have triggered a depressive response in the patient. The patient gives two examples of depressive cognitive-emotional states that were triggered in him. One was related to the impact of the world financial crisis on his finances, the second was an incident in which he was run after by two dogs while walking in the countryside, and was fearful. As the reader may remember, his mother used to terrify him with phrases like, "You can't go walking in the woods because there are lions …", which makes this incident particularly (C-P) meaningful. On both occasions, however, the patient was able to quickly interrupt his initial depressive response, feel well, and resolve the situations. This feedback was very rewarding for the therapist. Since it would be unthinkable that things might really improve without any modification in the couple relationship, the therapist then specifically asked about that. The patient answered:

Pt: … Joan had some very difficult times at the beginning …

Th: Yes, I imagine something of that, I mean, when the two of you came together, she was really in difficulty with you …

Pt: Yes, terribly! … and that still comes up from time to time and I think the thing that is changed is that I don't accept it, I don't accept her bullying, don't accept her "my way or the highway" … and so we've come to new ground … it's really good! … not always good, but … good!

Th: Do you still feel that she is blaming you on past things … going back to the past to nail you to something … this was something you felt she did …

Pt: Yes, this is part of what she did … what she is doing now—and even that is lessening a little—is to say "You must find a passion, an interest, a job, so that you have some involvement," and I agree with her, but, you see, Joan is a woman that becomes very entrenched in an idea and doesn't let it go, to the point where it becomes bullying, and that's very difficult for me to accept now … I don't need the pounding. I don't need the reminder that I need to get involved in something.

Th: So, what is the way you respond to that when it happens?

Pt: Oh, we fight! I'm not afraid to raise my voice, nor is she … and then we don't talk for a couple of days and … I think there was one threat and she said, "This isn't working for me!" And I remember sort of saying, "Well, perhaps we sell the house, we should separate!"

Th: Was it this house?

Pt: This house. This was four months ago … and she stopped, stopped!

Th: Good for you!

Pt: And so … we celebrated our twenty-fourth anniversary two days ago … it was a very loving, wonderful day … yeah, terrific!

Concluding remark

A salient characteristic in long-standing depression is a sadistic Superego stifling the Self. Another is what I have called a depressive habit, whereby the individual has become accustomed to a pessimistic view of themselves and life in general, deeply influencing all life strategies. A real and genuine human interchange, coupled with an efficient use of techniques, can bring about the emotional experiencing of hitherto buried feeling and impulse, enabling the patient to reclaim their emotional life. The experiencing of buried emotion is, in itself, the opposite of feeling depressed, which calls to mind the saying, "Nothing succeeds like success". This gives patients enough motivation to commit themselves to a demanding therapeutic process. Subsequent therapeutic work will focus upon the undoing of the depressive habit, in order to stabilise healthy mechanisms and prevent depressive relapse.

Post scriptum, that ... "I'm not sure what"

Over three years after the end of therapy, the therapist sent his former patient the draft of this chapter. What follows is an extract of their email correspondence:

> Dear John,
>
> I enclose a chapter I wrote for a forthcoming book, based on your "case". I hope you find it reflects things in a respectful way. If not, please feel free to point out anything that you would like to change. Also, in case, by any chance, you wished to add your own feelings/comments/considerations on this therapeutic journey, I am certainly interested + might consider adding them to the chapter.
>
> Ferruccio
>
> ....
>
> My dear Ferruccio,
>
> Thank you. I read "my chapter" when your letter arrived, and then again this moment, a few days later. You describe the journey so well. I would add only that there was a moment near the beginning of our therapy that I became committed to the healing, that I decided to not be the actor and say the things that I knew you would want to hear, which I had done so often with previous therapists. I had trust and felt our bond ... It was quite wonderful. One small detail: my brother is older than me.
>
> John

On receiving this answer, the therapist felt he wanted to get a deeper understanding of what exactly enabled the patient to make the most out of this therapy and go through such a deep transformation. Hence the next letter:

> Dear John,
>
> Thanks for pointing out your brother's correct age position. Regarding what you wrote:
>
> "... there was a moment near the beginning of our therapy that I became committed to the healing, that I decided to not be the actor and say the things that I knew you would want to hear ..."

Can you try and make out what factors, in your recollection, came into play inside you, the "moment" when your will/attitude changed?

Ferruccio

....

Good morning Ferruccio,

There were several factors that played into my commitment: the terrible experience that summer with a narcoleptic psychiatrist in [...], who fell asleep during our session, the pressure to go on drug therapy from Joan and friends, the subsequent drug therapy with another psychiatrist recommended by our family doctor, an awful woman, that after 15 minutes, decided that I was bipolar and immediately put me on meds, which did not work, and then my reaching out to P.K. [one of John's former therapists] who I had worked with and liked, who knew you, who made our connection. I remember, on the almost 5 hour trip to Milan, that I decided that I could no longer go on being the actor. That if I felt a link, trust, I would commit to the work. In our first session, you negated drug therapy for the moment. Your wanting to hear my story, your ... I'm not sure what, was insurance enough for me to stop being the actor. As you pointed out I have been a depressive since I was quite young. I have seen many psychiatrists, and, I had for them, always played the role.

Abbracci, John

References

Arieti, S. (1978). Sociocultural Factors, Sociology of Knowledge, and Depression. In S. Arieti & J. Bemporad, *Severe and Mild Depression: The Psychotherapeutic Approach*. New York: Basic.

Beck, A. T. (1967). *Cognitive Therapy and the Emotional Disorders*. New York: International Universities Press.

Davanloo, H. (1990). *Unlocking the Unconscious*. Toronto: John Wiley & Sons.

Freud, S. (1917e). *Mourning and Melancholia. S. E., 14*. London: Hogarth.

McCullough, L., Kuhn, N., Andrews, S., Kaplan, A., Wolf, J. & Lanza Hurley, C. (2003). *Treating Affect Phobia: A Manual for Short-Term Dynamic Psychotherapy*. New York: Guilford.

Meijers, J. (2012). Experiential short-term psychodynamic psychotherapy from the perspective of a cognitive behaviour therapist: a personal account. In: F. Osimo & M. J. Stein (Eds.), *Theory and Practice of Experiential Dynamic Therapy*. London: Karnac.

Osimo, F. (2003). *Experiential Short-Term Dynamic Psychotherapy: A Manual*. Bloomington, IN: AuthorHouse.

Osimo, F. (2009). The character hologram. *Ad Hoc Bulletin of Short-Term Dynamic Psychotherapy: Practice and Theory*, *13*: 25–50.

Osimo, F. (2011). Intensive Experiential-Dynamic Psychotherapy with patients suffering from long-standing depression. *Ad Hoc Bulletin of Short-Term Dynamic Psychotherapy: Practice and Theory*, *15*: 29–45.

Osimo, F. (2012). The essence of experiential dynamic therapies. In: F. Osimo & M. J. Stein (Eds.), *Theory and Practice of Experiential Dynamic Therapy*. London: Karnac.

Panksepp, J. (1998). *Affective Neuroscience: The Foundations of Human and Animal Emotions*. New York: Oxford University Press.

Rosenthal, D. (1971). *Genetics of Psychopathology*. New York: McGraw-Hill.

Stevens, A. & Price, J. (1996). *Evolutionary Psychiatry: a New Beginning*. London: Routledge.

Wikipedia (2011). *Pierrot*. Retrieved May 2, 2011 from http://en.wikipedia.org/wiki/Pierrot.

Notes

1. This chapter is based on a previous article (Osimo, 2011).
2. "Pierrot ... is a stock character of pantomime and Commedia dell'Arte whose origins are in the late seventeenth-century Italian troupe of players performing in Paris and known as the Comédie-Italienne. ... His character in postmodern popular culture—in poetry, fiction, the visual arts, as well as works for the stage, screen, and concert hall—is that of the sad clown" (Wikipedia, 2011).
3. A similar example of depressive relapse, soon before concluding therapy, can be found in another case study (see Osimo, 2003, pp. 262–264).
4. To some extent, it is normal that a partner takes a longer time to adapt to the new situation arising when the other partner has gone through deep change.

CHAPTER TEN

Using Intensive Experiential-Dynamic Psychotherapy to treat an underachieving gifted adolescent

Ronete Cohen

In this chapter, the reader is introduced to the problem of underachievement in gifted adolescents. Issues relevant to psychological therapy with underachieving gifted students will be described and links will be made between the presenting problems and specific therapeutic activities of experiential dynamic therapies (EDT). Transcripts from a psychological therapy with a young gifted adolescent will be presented to illustrate how an Intensive Experiential-Dynamic Psychotherapy (IE-DP) perspective informed the clinical work undertaken, in particular, anxiety work, and separating healthy Ego from harshly critical Superego. Patient- and therapist-reported changes at termination of therapy will be outlined.

Underachievement in gifted adolescents

A significant proportion of my caseload consists of gifted children and adolescents who are seriously underachieving in that their school results fall far short of what would be expected from someone with their ability. Since there is no question of a lack of ability, the causes must lie elsewhere. Extensive and diverse research on the subject has consistently identified both internal and external factors. For example, Baum, Renzulli, and Hébert (1995) identify emotional problems as a major contributor to underachievement. Clemons (2008) finds that social and cognitive factors may also influence a student's level of achievement. For example, she determined that the motivation to achieve is strongly influenced by self-perception that, in turn, is influenced by the child's attributional style, that is, beliefs about whether success or failure is controlled by internal or external factors. This attitude (also known as "locus of control") affects motivation, self-esteem, behaviour, and the level of risk one is prepared to take. The more an individual believes their own actions and behaviours influence events, the more positive their perception of their ability. In contrast, a belief that events are determined by others, or by fate or chance, has a negative influence on self-perception of ability.Neihart, Reis, Robinson, and Moon (2002) found that positive self-concept was associated with challenge-seeking and the willingness to take risks.

Parents also play a very important role. Their levels of involvement and responsiveness are a major influence on the child's motivation (Clemons, 2008). In particular, their expectations and the value they place on achievement are associated with the student's level of achievement (ibid.). Grobman (2006) found that supportive and appropriately involved parents helped to decrease the intensity of social, parental, and educational conflicts. Baum et al. (1995) reported that positive relationship with adults, self-regulation behaviour, and self-understanding were a precursor to achievement.

Issues facing underachieving gifted students

Researchers emphasise that the gifted are as well-adjusted as the rest of the population and that they do not suffer higher levels of dysfunction (Colangelo, 2002; Neihart, 1999). This may indeed be true of many, or even most, gifted students, even those who temporarily find themselves in a situation where they are square pegs being forced into round holes, but not for the ones I tend to see in my practice. They would not come to me if there were nothing wrong. The presenting problem is something that is obvious to their environment (underachievement) which is a symptom of the (largely hidden) underlying problems. They suffer high levels of dysfunction, whether as a result of a lack of fit that has been ignored for too long, or as a result of an equally ignored pre-existing level of dysfunction within their family system. Neihart (1999) suggests that research findings on the subject can be misleading, because comparing the well-being of the gifted and the non-gifted as a dichotomy does not lead to meaningful conclusions. Instead, we should be looking at the psychological well-being of the gifted student in relation to the type of giftedness (verbal or mathematical—mathematical is less socially accepted and therefore leads to more social isolation and other problems), the educational fit (i.e., are the student's educational needs being catered for?), and the student's personal characteristics, such as self-perception, temperament, and life circumstances.

Practitioners who treat gifted adolescents often encounter a familiar process that precedes referral. In my experience, during the first few years of school, a significant proportion of the learning process happens so rapidly and automatically for the highly gifted, that they do not need to give conscious thought to organisation and procedure. As they reach adolescence, however, and learning becomes more complex and demanding, they often find themselves lacking age-appropriate, learning-related, organisational and procedural skills as well as the discipline to spend time and effort on getting work done. The gifted student quickly falls behind—a huge shock to the system for those who previously knew themselves as exceptionally bright. The shame associated with a self-perception of "becoming stupid" is great. They will often create an elaborate deception to disguise what is really happening, and provide what they consider to be a more plausible and less shameful reason for their declining achievements. For example, they will deliberately sabotage their schooling by not doing any work, or disrupting lessons until they get sent out of class, or even expelled; or they will engage in self-destructive behaviours, such as drug taking, eating disorders, or self-harm. It is noteworthy that Colangelo and Assouline (1995) found that the self-concept of gifted students is lower in high school than elementary school. They also found that as gifted students progressed in school, they became more anxious and isolated, that they had relatively positive self-concepts in relation to their academic functioning, but more negative self-perceptions in relation to their interpersonal functioning. Gifted adolescents perceived giftedness as positive when it came to personal understanding and to performance in academic subjects, but negative when it came to relations with peers (Kerr, Colangelo, & Gaeth, 1988, cited in Colangelo & Assouline, 1995).

Based on these frequently observed behaviours, Whitmore (1980) developed a diagnostic checklist to identify gifted individuals who underachieve. Indicators include poor test performance, daily work frequently incomplete or poorly done, superior comprehension and retention of concepts when interested, persistent dissatisfaction with work accomplished, and avoidance of new activities to prevent imperfect performance, linked to perfectionism and self-criticism. Additional signs include showing initiative in pursuing self-selected projects at home, a tendency to withdraw or be aggressive in the classroom, not functioning comfortably or constructively in a group of any size. These individuals are characterised by low self-esteem, and show an acute sensitivity in their perceptions that are related to self, others, and life in general. They have a tendency towards unrealistic self-expectations, for example, setting goals that are too high or too low. They demonstrate an indifferent or negative attitude to school, and resistance to the efforts of teachers to motivate or discipline behaviour in class. Robinson (2002) noted arrogance, depression, and social isolation.

The issues underlying the problems described above are highly relevant to therapy as they interfere with the gifted adolescent's ability to achieve at a level commensurate with their intellectual ability. Strop and Goldman (2002) highlighted anger, fear of failure, a strong need to control, low self-esteem, and fear of success. The underachieving gifted individuals I see in my practice typically experience anxiety when faced with anything that is directly or indirectly linked to school learning, have low self-esteem, and doubt their ability to achieve. In particular, they fear and overestimate the probability of failure, and do everything they can to avoid activities that they deem to be risky, where there is potential to fail. Gifted individuals often display high levels of perfectionism (Grobman, 2006; Schuler, 1999), but underachieving gifted students are effectively crippled by their perfectionism. Schuler's (1999) research supported the theory of perfectionism as a continuum between healthy and dysfunctional perfectionists. She found that healthy perfectionists were ordered and organised, tolerated mistakes, enjoyed high parental expectations, coped positively with their perfectionist tendencies, and viewed personal effort as an important part of their perfectionism. In contrast, dysfunctional perfectionists were terrified of making mistakes, had extremely high standards, perceived excessive expectations and negative criticisms from others, questioned their own judgement, lacked effective coping strategies, and had a constant need for approval. Baum et al.'s (1995) small-scale, qualitative study revealed family and emotional issues including family dysfunction, an extraordinary need for attention, perfectionism, and depression. From their account, it is evident that high levels of anxiety were also an issue. In the context of underachievement and self-destructive behaviour, Grobman (2006) noted perceived strangeness and isolation, a sense of being controlled rather than in control, guilt, fear of envy and retaliation from others, and fear of losing ability.

Recommended treatment approaches

Psychological interventions consist mainly of identifying giftedness through testing, and then advising the parents and the school how best to serve the gifted adolescent's educational and environmental needs, with the assumption that, once this has been done, the student will start achieving at an appropriate level. Rather than provide clear therapeutic guidelines on how to treat underachieving gifted individuals, recommendations (e.g., Schuler, 1999; Clemons, 2008) tend to focus on what areas need to be addressed: for example, self-concept, educational, and family issues. Interventions tend to be delivered by school counsellors.

Baum et al. (1995) identify several precursors to achievement including positive relationships with adults, self-regulatory behaviour, and self-understanding. However, most recommendations focus on adapting the school environment so that it can accommodate gifted students with behavioural problems, assuming that once the environment fits, everything will be OK. It *is* important for the gifted individual to be placed in the right learning environment, but the adolescents who reach therapy tend to have fallen so far behind—academically, behaviourally, and emotionally—that they still have a long way to go before they can even be considered eligible for such an environment. Even if they were allowed on a programme for underachieving gifted students, they would not be able to function successfully enough to benefit from it because too many issues remain in the way. Guidance on how to deal with these issues is hard to find.

Jerald Grobman, a rare example of a psychotherapist who works extensively with underachieving adolescents (though admittedly from functional backgrounds, and stable and supportive social environments), provides dynamic guidelines that can be more easily translated into a treatment plan (see Grobman, 2006). He recommends helping the patient understand the avoidance and denial that serve as defences against the emotional distress they are feeling, and helping them to learn to trust others so that they can gain insight and accept guidance. There is no information about what kind of therapy works and what does not.

In my view, experiential dynamic therapies, including Intensive Experiential-Dynamic Psychotherapy (see Osimo, 2003), are valuable in that they not only give a clear picture of what is going wrong and where (i.e., "what" needs to be addressed), but also provide clear therapeutic guidelines concerning "how" to intervene. In particular, the Triangles of Conflict and Others provide a framework for understanding underachievement as a defence against the anxiety-provoking and/or painful feelings evoked in an individual's significant relationships. In addition, EDT provides clear guidelines for how to work with Superego pathology, and understanding an external attributional style/locus of control in terms of Superego pathology makes therapeutic sense. Furthermore, unlike the adults discussed elsewhere in this book, the children referred to me do not always want to see me, or sometimes they agree to see me after pressure from their parents or school, but are generally unco-operative. Developing and dealing openly and honestly with the real patient-therapist relationship is central to EDT, and is a valid and important part of therapy with underachieving gifted individuals. This genuine and personal approach makes it easier to bring any resistance or awkwardness into the room, and deal with it explicitly and directly. Both patient and therapist can find a comfortable way in which to discuss their feelings about the process. Indeed, an EDT therapist learns not to fear such discussions but rather considers them a natural and integral part of the process of therapy.

Often the initial sessions are spent gaining the patient's trust and helping them relinquish the barriers they have put up, working within the Triangles of Conflict and Others.

When working with adolescents, and, in particular, exceptionally gifted ones, it is important to fully understand how they differ from adults in order to adapt EDT to suit their specific circumstances. A major difference between adults and adolescents is that, for the latter, the past and present in the Triangle of Others overlap to some degree, since they are still living with one or both of their parents. Adolescents, gifted or not, are also still developing, so character and character defences are fluid. The nature of the patient-therapist relationship is also very different. A unique characteristic of the exceptionally gifted is that they can sometimes experience an extreme emotional intensity, something that needs to be taken into consideration when working with the Triangle of Conflict. These aspects of treatment are illustrated in the case study presented herein and are discussed at length in the conclusions at the end of this chapter.

Case study

In my practice, children, adolescents, and families are seen in their own homes. Referrals are via parents and/or schools. Individual sessions normally take place in the child's room, or in another private room in the house. The usual process is to have an intake session with one or both parents, followed by another intake with the child. Intake sessions last between one and two hours. Julia, the fifteen-year-old female patient presented herein, was referred by her mother as she had been doing extremely poorly at school for several years (despite being highly gifted). Her parents were struggling to deal with her, and apparently she no longer cared about learning. Specifically, the mother reported that if her daughter's school performance did not improve significantly she would have to repeat a school year, that she had made subject choices that did not meet with the mother's approval and which she refused to change, and that she wanted her to be happy but she was not. Julia was both verbally and mathematically gifted. Since quite early on in her education there had been a distinct lack of educational fit, in that the schools she attended could not meet her needs or deal with her reaction to that. She insisted that she was doing badly at school simply because she was lazy. She wanted to be left alone so that she could drop out of school and become a world-famous rock star (she could neither sing nor play a musical instrument, but she did not consider mere practicalities to be important).

Very little about Julia's behaviour and general demeanour seemed to genuinely reflect her inner world. She was working very hard to impress the therapist with how unique she was, and yet it was all barely skin-deep. I slowly came to recognise (and, if I failed to do so, she would helpfully point it out to me) that she borrowed large chunks of what she said from movies or TV series. Her clothes were carefully selected to express the mood she wished to convey—they replaced words, like a time-delay response to various ongoing conversations. This was different from the not unusual teenage practice of "trying on images for size". None of her peers believed in these attempts to convey maturity and sophistication via a false self, but her mother was deeply impressed and proud of her daughter's persona. Julia admitted to not being able to feel any real emotions but was afraid that without her false persona no-one would like her.

The patient was seen weekly in her school's counselling office, as she did not want her sister to know she was seeing a therapist. The therapist was in her first year of Core Training in IE-DP. Transcripts will be presented from the twenty-sixth and twenty-eighth sessions of a fifty-seven-session therapy that was terminated prematurely when the family moved away.

Overview of therapy with Julia up to the twenty-sixth session

In the Triangle of Others, it was not just Julia's past (P) and current relationships (C) that were problematic, but also her relationship with me (T). Her false Self was so unbelievable and phoney that I would experience a deep irritation with her that would distract me and sometimes make it difficult for me to empathise with her. I used this transference and countertransference to help me identify the feelings she brought to the surface in the people around her, so that I could better understand her current relationships (C). Julia's family system was also dysfunctional. I came to realise that she only received mothering by demonstrating her false Self. As therapy progressed, she increasingly experienced me (T) accepting her true Self. Perhaps because of the rage and/or grief about the lack of acceptance in her family of origin, acceptance by me was associated with Julia experiencing extreme anxiety (A). She had never before experienced someone being loving and kind to her as her true self, since her mother (P and C) always reacted with the threat of abandonment in similar situations.

Julia's mother collaborated with Julia's hypochondria, taking her to increasingly obscure alternative practitioners up and down the country whenever her behaviour got out of hand. She continued to do so during her daughter's psychological therapy, often sabotaging any progress that had been made. This was especially noticeable whenever the treatment led to Julia asserting a degree of autonomy and control over her life. An example of such an occasion was when, as a result of successful anxiety regulation (AA), Julia started being aware of rising anxiety (A) and became able to reduce it by practising mindfulness. When she told her mother about it, she immediately gave Julia a homeopathic remedy for anxiety, thereby not only medicalising a reaction to real emotions (regardless of whether it was done with the use of a placebo or not) and encouraging her hypochondria (D), but also acting to remove her growing sense of control over her own life, and re-instilling a sense of helplessness and dependence (on mother) (D).

Extract from the twenty-sixth session of therapy with Julia

Julia had deep feelings (X) that she could not allow herself to experience. Whenever they threatened to rise to the surface, she experienced huge anxiety (A) and her defences (D) were immediately mobilised. For example, an immediate defensive reaction to acute anxiety was a sudden and overwhelming sleepiness (D), which happened both in sessions and in real life. In the following extract from our twenty-sixth session, Julia begins by stating that she is nervous (A):

Pt: I'm a little nervous.
Th: About what? **(HP, AA)**

The therapist could have helped the patient to label her anxiety (AA) but instead responds with an enquiry that has the potential to regulate anxiety (HP, AA).

Pt: What if I don't pass this year (**D**)? That was in the back of my head (**D**) and I'd like it to stay in the back of my head (sighs). I totally agree that it was necessary for [the teacher] to talk about it, but … (her body tenses up)

The therapist then enquires about the physical experience of anxiety but in a vague way (AA) before drawing the patient's attention to the muscle tension in her body (MI). At this point, she could have pointed out that anxiety (AA) is linked to feelings (XA), and that attributing it to not passing her exams is a defence (DA).

Th: How does it make you feel? (**XA**)
Pt: Panicky …? (**D**)
Th: I can see your body tensing up. (**AA, MI**)
Pt: I didn't do this year so well and it feels like shit (**D**) (eyes tear up, starts to fidget, avoids eye contact). (**D**)

The patient is ignoring the therapist and dismissing what she has said (D).

Th: You're looking sad now (**XA, MI**)
Pt: You don't say … (**D**)
Th: What's the worst thing about doing badly at school? (**AA**)
Pt: I must be stupid or something (**D**) (starts tapping on the chair). (**A**)

The patient expresses self-criticism and the therapist sees that the patient is becoming anxious. The self-criticism could be addressed (SE) and/or the therapist could point out to the patient what she is seeing that tells her that the patient is anxious (MI, AA) as well as link the anxiety to process, that is, what is happening in the therapeutic relationship and in the session at that moment (AA). She proceeds to acknowledge the anxiety that is at the forefront but, instead of exploring it further, or helping the patient to understand what underlies the anxiety, she moves to enquiry about feelings (XA) as, with adolescents, the therapist's repeated attempts to confront defences or explore anxiety can be experienced by the patient as "badgering", which can lead to the therapeutic relationship being damaged.

Th: I can see that this is making you feel anxious. (**AA**) How else is this making you feel?
Pt: Nothing. (**D**)
Th: Do you think that your explanation of stupidity is a good one? (**DA**)
Pt: Well, it's the only one I can think of. (**D**)
Th: Well, I think that, when you take everything that's going on into consideration, you've actually done pretty well. I think you have made great progress. (**AA, RE, SO**)
Pt: (Makes eye contact but says nothing)
Th: If I think of what you were like a few months ago, I think you've done really well to get as far as this. You've made a big switch in your brain: you've dropped a lot of your defences … (**HP, RE, SO**)
Pt: (Nods)

Th: … you know, all that stuff on the outside that you would spend so much energy on. And that was a complete barrier. You weren't really experiencing anything because everything was happening to that barrier. (**DA, SO, XA**)

The therapist is referring to something already familiar to the patient: her former ever-present defence of false "selves" and hypochondria that prevented her from having access to her real emotions and constituted a barrier to emotional closeness with others. The patient would resort to a large repertoire of defences to get her through her day-to-day life, and ensure a "life on the surface" that never came near to her true emotions. Her normal existence was in the form of an all-encompassing defence: the creation of an ever-present false Self (D). There were alternative selves on hand to suit each occasion, including a very angry and destructive one who caused havoc and punished those around her. These selves were unsophisticated and stereotypical to the point of having a two-dimensional comic-book quality to them. Whenever she found herself in a situation that would normally call on her (inaccessible) emotions, she experienced great anxiety (A) and rationalised (D) what she considered to be a suitable reaction in the form of a false emotion (D) that she then displayed with exaggerated facial expressions and body language, or even with clothing or hairstyle. She would wear black to convey depression (her term). When her "mood" (D) changed, the colour and style of what she wore changed in line with it. There was no experience of the feeling in her body; it was a pure display for the benefit of her environment and it replaced age-appropriate dialogue.

The patient also resorted to hypochondria (D) to disguise the anxiety (A) she experienced in situations when feelings (X) threatened to rise to the surface. It gave her an acceptable form of expression for her distress (X), and distracted from the powerful emotions (X) that were associated with everything that was so troubling in her life. She had a long list of non-existent ailments (D), which without exception had neither visible nor measurable symptoms. The therapist witnessed "panic attacks" and "hyperventilation" that she would not have been aware of if it were not for the patient's self-report. Other "life-long ailments" were unknown to medical science or would by now have led to hospitalisation or death if the patient really did suffer from them.

The therapist tries to show her that her harsh self-criticism is not validated by the facts and is therefore unjustified (SE). The patient responds by assuming a more relaxed posture and the therapist continues to provide positive feedback (SO).

Pt: (Moves in her chair to a more relaxed position)

Th: You've also started rediscovering your passion for different things. You're slowly beginning to understand what you want and who you are. You've still got some big issues, but you're dealing with them. (**SO**)

Pt: (Makes a cartoonish series of facial expressions, followed by hand gestures for me to fast-forward what I'm saying)

Th: I'm guessing that means you've got something to say? (**HP**)

Pt: (Nodding and smiling)

Th: Do you realise that I am saying something positive about you and the progress you have made and you are kind of ignoring it? (**RE, DA**) How does it feel to hear what I was saying? (**XA, RE**)

Pt: I don't know ... I guess it's true.
Th: How does it feel? (**XA**)
Pt: Normal. (**D**)
Th: What does that mean? I think it means that you are avoiding what you feel. (**RE, DA**)
Pt: (Laughs) (**D**)
Th: I notice you're having trouble telling me about how you feel about something: that means you are getting nearer to your real emotions. (**DA**) Does it make you feel nervous or uncomfortable? (**AA**)
Pt: Maybe. (**D**)
Th: Does the progress you've made make you feel a bit anxious? (**AA**)
Pt: Sometimes, maybe. (**D**)
Th: It must be scary not having the shield you had, but you're doing OK. (**AA, SO**)

Relinquishing her shield and getting in touch with her true feelings was a double-edged sword for the patient. The reality of the patient's life was that most of her peers found her behaviour ridiculous and childish. She was largely alienated because they found it impossible to communicate with her, so being more genuine had its benefits. But her mother—her primary attachment figure—approved of her false selves and encouraged her hypochondria. As with all other things that she either approved or disapproved of, the threat of abandonment by her mother was always there should Julia dare to act in any other way.

At this point, the therapist intends to start working on the Triangle of Others by asking the patient if this feels like any other situation she has experienced, but the patient changes the subject and starts to talk about her relationship with her mother (P). An opportunity to make an explicit connection between what the patient had been telling the therapist about teachers (C) and her experience with her mother (P) has been missed.

Pt: When my mum went away for a week, me and my dad didn't have a single argument. When she isn't there, everything's OK.
Th: How did that feel? (**XA**)
Pt: Weird. I don't know. (**D**) That my mother's the problem? (Remains calm) Well, my mother is always the problem. She's always been the problem.
Th: So you're saying that the relationship with your mother is the most problematic thing in your life? (**HP**)

The therapist is touching on a very challenging aspect of working with adolescents; their parents are not a distant influence but are very much present, in both senses of the word: they are not yet in the past (P), and they are a constant presence in the adolescent's life.

Pt: (Biting her nails) (**A**) I totally agree. And she's finding ways to totally seep into my life and attack my personal space as much as possible.
Th: Can you give me an example? (**HP**)
Pt: We had an argument last week. I didn't agree with what they were saying and they said I was breaking the rules. That's when I snapped. (**D**)

Th: It feels to me like I'm missing chunks of conversation here. (**HP**)
Pt: But that's the thing. I don't even know what I did wrong.
Th: What did you do? What did you say? (**HP**)
Pt: I don't remember the entire conversation. (**D**) There was yelling, but I seriously don't remember. Things became very dark, I just exploded. (**D**) I've barely slept at home the last week. It's been insane.

Not sleeping at home can be seen as a way of avoiding confrontation, which is technically a defence (D). I think that since a teenager like Julia is not an independent person, there is a limit to the degree of assertion that she can safely exercise. I therefore see not sleeping at home at that age as an indirect expression of anger and a form of self-assertion (X).

Th: What is this darkness you talk about? (**XA**)
Pt: I noticed myself falling into it and I didn't know why.
Th: I notice that you use the word dark or darkness when you talk about rebelling or standing up for yourself. (**XA**)
Pt: It wasn't rebelling and standing up for myself anymore, it was just pointless rage. (**D**) It wasn't just rebelling, it was rebelling aimlessly. (Becomes animated in a theatrical way) (**A**) Rebel without a cause! (**D**)
Th: Do you realise that you were quite natural and non-Hollywood when you were telling me about how you felt about your mother? And then when you started to tell me about the argument, you slipped back into using dramatic words, even movie titles. (**DA**) You tend to do this when you are anxious, a kind of way to distance yourself from what has happened. (**DA**) Does that feel right?
Pt: Maybe. OK. I don't know. (**D**)
Th: What is it about rebellion that is making you anxious?
Pt: It's not rebellion. It's aimless! (**D**)
Th: What can you feel when this rebellion happens? (**XA**)
Pt: Mad as hell!
Th: When someone has not rebelled when it comes to things that really really disturb her, then anger grows inside her, a deep anger that makes you rebel against everything to do with the person who is doing this to you. (**XA**) Do you recognise that?
Pt: Well that's what happened.
Th: Why is that dark? (**HP**)
Pt: I just burst. I felt myself becoming horribly mean. (**D**)

Julia is feeling guilty (A) about expressing anger (X).

Th: I think that what you're describing as "horribly mean and dark" could be your guilt about standing up for what you want and not putting up with things anymore.
Pt: (Looks away) (**D**)
Th: I think that's the reason it's so hard for you to stand up to … (**AA, XA**)
Pt: (Her hand twitches suddenly and violently) (**D**)
Th: Is that just a random movement (**AA**) or did you have one of your "spasms"? (**DA**)

The therapist is referring to something familiar to both therapist and patient—one of the patient's quite common defences, a faked physical "reaction", which she uses to convey a defensive "feeling". One was an exaggerated shaking/twitching of her hand (D) that appeared on cue whenever she needed to get herself out of a situation that she was trying to avoid (A) (while avoiding having to face up to her true emotions and the real reasons for this), or—in session—whenever her anxiety rose (A) and she was attempting to make me believe in a fake two-dimensional feeling (D). Another was trying to avoid (D) the exploration of the physical side of emotions because of the anxiety that this caused, by adding fantasy or a supernatural element to physical sensations (D). It is important to note that these defences were purely within the patient's control and that they were carefully calculated. The supposedly uncontrollable physical twitches were well-choreographed and their manifestation was always an overly familiar expression of an emotion or state of mind depicted in popular culture. When the therapist would focus on these defences in an attempt to help her relinquish them (DA), she would reluctantly admit that she could control them (which she would then go on to demonstrate without visible effort). The same was true of highly exaggerated and clichéd "masks" of primary emotions (D) that she used to manipulate her environment and avoid direct confrontation and assertiveness.

At this point in the session, the patient is undoubtedly experiencing anxiety, but her reaction to that is the usual (and mostly effective) defence that normally gets people to leave her alone and helps her avoid any further exploration of her true emotions. It is not an involuntary movement, but a carefully choreographed one that she can start and stop at will. She is trying this with the therapist as a last resort attempt to avoid having to explore her feelings (D).

Pt: (Smiling) (**D**) It was one of my spasms. (Looks away) (**D**)

Th: Isn't it interesting that whenever we talk about this kind of situation then this kind of thing happens? (**DA**)

The therapist refers to this defence in rather vague terms, since both patient and therapist know exactly what is being referred to due to this being a common occurrence.

Pt: (Without making eye contact) (**D**) It's actually more interesting how I think I've had this spasm less than five times in the last three weeks that I haven't seen you (**D**). (She starts to fidget) (**A**)

Th: Could it be that it's because you've been able to avoid facing up to things while I've been away? (**DA**) I'm thinking that there is a very strong feeling of guilt, which is an anxiety related thing—it's an anxiety causing thing—about you wanting to assert yourself and to rebel against the people who are hurting you. There's nothing wrong with rebelling. Whenever you do explode—what you call "rebel without a cause" … (**HP**)

Pt: (Laughs exaggeratedly and then becomes serious) Well, I was rebelling without a reason! (**D**)

Th: But you mostly don't rebel when you do have a reason. (**DA**) The frustration and the anger build up and then you explode, and then you rebel against everything. (**DA**) And then you feel like you're bad. (**SE**) Basically, you see rebellion as a bad thing whereas rebellion is a healthy thing. (**SE**) It makes you feel guilty. (**AA**)

Pt: (Aloof and exaggeratedly knowingly) Well, there's a difference between the normal rebellion that I do when there is a cause and just nonsense rebellion like what happened then. (**D**)

Th: Can I challenge you on something? (**DA**)

Pt: Go right ahead.

Th: You mentioned that you do rebel when there is cause … (**DA**)

Pt: Yeah. (Looks away, tense; exhibits pronounced and distracted fidgeting) (**D, A**)

Th: … but, I want to challenge you on that, because I think you don't. Mostly when you do have a cause you end up hurting yourself. You don't stand up for yourself. (**DA, SE**)

Pt: (Smiles a tight-faced smile, her eyes glaring at me, (**D**) and says quietly and hesitantly) I have been rebelling for what I believe in recently.

Th: Tell me about it. (**HP**)

Pt: That time when I stood up against my mother and walked out of the house despite her trying to pull me back.

Th: Yes, you are beginning to do that, which is great, but much of the time you still tend to … (**DA**)

Pt: (Looks down and whispers) … hurt myself. Yeah.

Th: Yes, you take your anger and frustration and redirect it at yourself. (**DA**)

The patient tells the therapist about a specific incident, the details of which are omitted in order to protect her identity.

Pt: … and then I was thinking: I can imagine what Ronete's going to tell me about this.

Th: And what was that? (**RE**)

Pt: (Challenging me with a smile) You're hurting yourself to hurt your mother again. (Laughs) (**D**)

Th: Do you notice how you're laughing when you're telling me something so terrible? It's your defence from the emotions that you feel in such a situation. (**DA**) Can you tell me how you feel? (**XA**)

Pt: Angry.

The therapist sees this anger as defensive anger (D) rather than an emerging emotion (X) because it is not directed at those who are hurting the patient but at the patient herself. It is self-destructive and not self-assertive as healthy anger should be.

Th: It's sad that you're already hurting (**XA**), but you would rather hurt yourself more than do something that you think will hurt your parents. (**SE**) When it comes to you standing up against your parents, it's scarier for you to actually directly confront them than to do this kind of thing. (**AA**)

Pt: I'd like to know how to confront them, but the thing is I don't have anything to confront them with. I've got nothing. They own me. I'm not even allowed to have secrets, because that's breaking the rules.

Th: How does that make you feel? (**XA**)

Pt: I want to hurt her. (**X**)

When the therapist tried to help the patient to get to the anger and talk about how she wanted to hurt her mother, Julia changed the subject (D). There was just enough time to deal with her anxiety before the session ended.

Extract from the twenty-eighth session of therapy with Julia

The following extract from our twenty-eighth session returns to the issue of Julia's relationship with her mother. There is no clear separation between mother and daughter; the mother does not recognise Julia as a separate and autonomous individual, and Julia believes she has no choice but to accept this as reality (D). This contributes to her general sense of helplessness and hopelessness, to her ineffective way of dealing with what life throws her way in general, and—to go back to the social cognitive model of gifted underachievement—it is a major factor that affects her attributional style and her self-perception. Julia has been invited to stay with her young and Bohemian aunt in London for a week. It will be the first time she has spent any length of time away from her mother. Although she puts on a facade (D) of really looking forward to the freedom this will afford her, it is obvious that she is also very scared (A), but does not know how to acknowledge her hidden feelings (X) and deal with them. When we discuss the trip, she immediately starts to construct a list of reasons why it will be impossible for her to take advantage of her newly acquired freedom (D). The therapist starts by summarising what Julia has told her, but blocks the defences that the patient had put into operation. The therapist tries to expose the patient's defences (DA) and show the blunt reality of what she is saying. Similarly to the previous extract, from a social cognitive point of view, known factors that are significant to underachievement are being addressed: in particular, self-perception and the parental role (Clemons, 2008).

Th: You are going to stay with your aunt. Your mother isn't going to be there and you can do what you like—something you've been really looking forward to … (**HP**)

Pt: (Laughing and fidgeting) (**A**) The world is my oyster. (**D**)

Th: … yet you are planning to behave as though your mother will be there by doing what she would be telling you to. (**DA**) How does that feel? (**XA**)

Pt: (Sighs) It is a scary thought. (**A**)

The therapist could have immediately pointed out the defensive function of the patient's interruption (DA), but, at the time, decided to ignore it, because she wanted the truth to be out in the open before addressing the patient's defence. The therapist implicitly acknowledges the patient's anxiety (A) and the defence of interrupting the therapist (D):

Th: Is that why you tried to draw attention away from this by interrupting me? (**DA**)

Pt: (Nods)

The therapist continues with anxiety regulation (AA):

Th: What is scary? (**AA**)

Pt: The scary part is that I agree. I am doing exactly what my mother would expect me to.

Th: I also noticed that when I asked you about the best thing about going away, you mentioned several things. The last one was that your mother wasn't going to be there … (**DA**)

Pt: (Laughs and says loudly in an exaggerated voice and manner) (**D**) Save the best for last! (**D**)

Th: But you whispered it. (**DA**)

Pt: (Laughs and hides her face) (**D**) You're going to search for hidden meanings in everything, aren't you? (**D**)

Th: I just want you to notice what I see so that you can't go on ignoring it. (**DA**) It seems very hard for you to hear this. You keep trying to draw the attention away from what you're doing. (**DA**) When I try to draw your attention to these things, you interrupt me; you have tried to deny it by saying "Save the best for last", or have tried to make what I'm saying sound ridiculous by saying that I'm searching for hidden meaning that doesn't exist. (**DA**)

Pt: (Slumps in her chair and looks sad)

Th: And now you're getting very uncomfortable. (**AA**)

Pt: (Laughs and says loudly and in an exaggerated voice and manner) You don't say! (Laughs and hides her face) (**D**)

Th: How are you feeling right now listening to all this? (**XA**)

Pt: Pathetic. (**D**)

Th: You're being really hard on yourself. You're attacking yourself. The way you react to situations connected to your mother is the way you learnt very early on. It's what helped you survive until now. Learning to see this is what's making it possible for you to change. (**SE**)

Pt: She's got this creepy power over me. It's insanity.

Th: How do you feel about this? (**XA**)

Pt: I'm mad. (**X**)

Th: What are you mad about? (**XA**)

Pt: At my mother. I hate that woman for what's she's done to me. I hate her for what she's doing to me. I hate her! And you know what?

At this point, the therapist could have challenged the patient's passivity and helplessness (D) by showing her that she allows her mother to have power over her and that she is neglectful, dismissive, and harshly critical towards herself.

Th: What? (**XA**)

Pt: I don't even feel guilty about that anymore. She deserves it. It's her fault, not mine.

Th: Remember how you used to almost fall asleep each time I tried to talk about things connected to your mother? Well, you've learnt to deal with this anxiety and it stopped happening. Then we could finally talk about her and you were able to deal with the anger you feel towards her, but it still made you feel guilty. And now you've dealt with the guilt and can look at what you really feel towards your mother. Can't you see how much progress you've made? (**HP, SO**)

Pt: Yes, I guess so … But I'm still stuck here.

Subsequent progress noted by patient, schoolteacher, and therapist

These are just two extracts from a long and very intensive journey. There were ups and downs along the way, but despite all this, things slowly improved. Julia's level of achievement at school slowly improved, roughly in line with her ability to gradually shed her defences and face up to her true feelings. The change in her was noticeable to everyone who knew her, including her teachers. She became involved with her learning and other school activities and, for the first time, she started making serious plans for her future. Her relationship with her mother remained problematic, but now it was due to her growing assertiveness. Unfortunately, I am unable to go into any further detail on this aspect of the case in the context of this chapter. Finally, just as things were looking extremely hopeful for Julia, her family moved away, and treatment was terminated prematurely.

Conclusions

The work I have done with Julia and with others like her has shown EDT to be very useful and effective in addressing the known contributors to underachievement in gifted adolescents. It is, however, important not to lose sight of how different working with adolescents is from working with adults. There are both advantages and disadvantages, often requiring the therapist to adapt techniques to suit their unique circumstances.

As has already been pointed out, the Past and Current poles of the Triangle of Others have a significant overlap for the adolescents I see, who still live at home with their parents. When they use projection and externalisation as a defence, they have readily available real-life examples of their parents' actions to "prove" their case. Trying to help them see how their Superego is a unique entity that is distinct from their actual and live relationship with their parents is a long and frustrating process. Learning to practise control over their Superego and letting go of defences is an uphill struggle for them. They are exposed to daily reinforcement of the belief that the parents control their lives, their feelings, their actions, and there is little either therapist or patient can realistically do to stop, or even limit, this exposure. There is a never-ending supply of fresh interactions, many more than any antidote the therapist can provide during therapy. The idea of a Superego and the adolescents' role in placing these restrictions on themselves is constantly eclipsed by their repeated daily experiences of the external reality that they have also internalised. It is incredibly difficult to be able to hold on to this distinction when one finds oneself under a continuing onslaught. Adolescents have never had the chance to distance themselves from their parents for long enough to develop better insight. They have never had the chance to mature enough emotionally to enable themselves to better understand such complex mechanisms. Working on Superego issues brings up a lot of anxiety and resistance in them. The therapist has to be gentle and firm and, especially, extremely patient, repeating the process again and again, and providing positive reinforcement to counteract the control by the parent that the patient is exposed to outside therapy.

That the Current and Past poles of the Triangle of Others are, to some extent, merged when the patient lives at home with parents makes therapy with adolescents slower than one would expect it to be with an adult who has experienced a similarly dysfunctional childhood but who is now at least physically removed from his or her parents. In therapy, there are several ways to make things easier for the adolescents. However, whichever way you choose, the core of the whole process is helping the patient work through the Triangles of Conflict and Others. The more the patient relinquishes defences and experiences feelings, the more of a sense of self and autonomy he or she develops. In my experience, the defences such adolescents tend to have are ones that maintain or increase their dependence on the parent (e.g., Julia's hypochondria makes her helpless and allows her mother to take control and "care" for her), so relinquishing them is a big step in the right direction. Experiencing their own unique feelings is experiencing their own unique identity as an entity that is entirely separate from their parents. As for the Triangle of Others, since the P and the C poles are partially merged, I tend to accentuate the distinction between the (early) past (P)—when patterns were set—and illustrate how these patterns influence what is now current (C). I do this by helping the patient see how she was formed by the earlier influence of her parents (P) to deal with her parents in this particular way now (C). Although the early past is not so distinct and distant in the case of an adolescent, it is still effective to keep highlighting this process during therapy.

When working with adolescents, the therapist needs to be mindful that, at any time, the patient can get up and leave the room and not come back. In order to prevent the therapeutic relationship from being damaged, the therapist may choose to work on engagement and undoing projection, rather than on defence restructuring. As soon as the therapist tries to exercise any degree of pressure on the patient to experience feelings and/or gain insight into their defensive patterns, the painful and/or anxiety provoking feelings begin to surface and the patient becomes anxious and starts to project. The therapist stops being the person who is trying to help them heal and gain autonomy, and becomes "just like my parents", "attacking", "badgering", and making them as powerless as their parents have done. In particular, patients will start to see the therapist as an extension of their parents in a way that differs from what you would find with an adult, who tend to be individuated and living separately from their parents. Adolescent patients, who project their parents on to the therapist, perceive the therapist/parent in a much more vivid and threatening way. This is linked to the Past (P) and Current (C) poles in the Triangle of Person overlapping. When their parents are a more vivid presence, the transference is overwhelming. It is not an undercurrent that may take some exploration to uncover—it provokes an immediate and dramatic reaction in the patient. These adolescents are likely not to have had close and trusting relationships before now. Their primary attachments are unsafe, damaging their capacity for trust and for experiencing closeness with others. In order to ensure a good therapeutic relationship, it is necessary to pay attention to Other-restructuring by helping the adolescent patients identify what the therapist is really doing and feeling, and enabling them to make a distinction between their parents and the therapist. This takes both time and patience. Every time the patients go home, the Past (P) once again becomes Current (C), so it is usually a matter of two steps forward, one step back, and sometimes, even one step forward, two steps back. Avoiding too much pressure and confrontation is a step in the right direction.

Sometimes, helping the patient develop autonomy is not an option in an extremely dysfunctional family, because it could lead to an unsafe and unliveable environment for the patient. In such cases, it could help to make the patient aware of why he or she is behaving in a particular way, and how it is a coping mechanism or a survival technique that cannot yet be relinquished because the consequences (while still living at home) will be too serious. It helps the patient to understand that this is simply a character defence that can be relinquished when the time comes, and not who he or she really is. It also helps to show how, as the patient gets older, even the "past" (P) that is now current (C) will in the not too distant future truly become past (P). This helps give the patient hope and motivation to carry on. This is far from ideal, but the therapist and the adolescent patient are not free to make the best choices for the patient—the parents have the ultimate control. The therapist can make it possible for the patient to grow and develop to a certain extent outside the restrictive environment of the home, in preparation for the time when the patient can leave home and leave the past behind.

The fact that adolescents still live at home does have one positive aspect; the Self- and Other-restructuring takes place with their parents. This can have huge benefits for the rest of their lives. But there are also disadvantages, even dangers. Experiential work has to be handled with extreme care. Bringing some emotions to the surface can have serious consequences and one needs to consider the implications. Due to the merging of the P and C poles, it makes sense that adolescents experience difficulties distinguishing between their Superego, which is internal, and genuine parental control, which is external. As previously stated, they may have reduced awareness of the mechanisms of the Superego and their ability (and responsibility) to control their own behaviour. This not only complicates Superego work, it also means that what is experienced in the room with the therapist can sometimes overflow into real life. I have more than once had to either abandon or tone down anger work because it became apparent that it would be re-enacted in real life. The objects of their anger (almost always the parents) are within easy reach and the actions that cause them such anger continue to happen on a daily basis (because they are unable to effectively remove themselves from their environment). It is easy to explode under such circumstances and do something that will have grave consequences. In Julia's case, it was necessary to limit experiential work in order to prevent it from "leaving the room". She had poor impulse control (she would suppress her emotions until she "exploded"), and lacked the ability to fully distance herself from her mother. If she were an adult who was not living with her parents, it would have been possible (and advisable) to do a lot more anger exposure work. It is vital to assess the adolescent patient for suitability for anger exposure. If in doubt, it is best to stick mainly to non-experiential talk and psycho-education. It is the therapist's duty to protect adolescents from doing what they will later regret and which could lead to a significant worsening of their situation.

At the same time as working with the patient, working with the parents can be hugely beneficial, but also very challenging. It all depends on how open the parents are to the idea that this is not just about their child, but that everyone needs to change. Ideally, in such cases, the parents too would be undergoing EDT, but often, parents in the more dysfunctional families who could benefit most from that, are resistant to the idea. Some parents, for a variety of reasons (usually their own problems), are unable to parent adequately (i.e., be a stable and reliable presence in their child's life and accommodate his/her emotional needs), and they find it too difficult to face up to this. When their child's problem serves the purpose of deflecting attention from what is going on with them, it plays a special role in the family dynamics. In such cases, most parents are reluctant to change anything that could uncover their own issues. When the therapist encounters such parents, it can become almost impossible to help the patient.

The biggest disadvantage of working with adolescents is that they are not in control of the therapy; they do not pay for it and, therefore, remain at the mercy of their parents, who may also be largely responsible for their predicament. Parents can withdraw treatment at any time and, when their child's improvement threatens the parental position as the healthy family members who just happen to have a dysfunctional child, they often do. Some parents do not directly withdraw treatment, but instead sabotage it in a variety of more subtle ways. Some try to destroy the patient-therapist relationship by criticising and attacking the therapist and their work in the presence of the patient. This can be very distressing for an adolescent who has developed a close and positive attachment to the therapist. Some will do their best to reverse any progress made in therapy that makes them feel like they are losing control over their child (e.g., Julia's mother providing homeopathic remedies for anxiety). Other parents stop paying for their child's treatment, and place the therapist in the impossible situation of not wanting to withdraw vital treatment from the child, but having to change the rules of engagement with the parent in order to recover the debt. In private practice, it puts the therapist in the awkward position of having to be both debt-collector and therapist, two very different roles that require the nature of the interaction between therapist and parent to jump backwards and forwards from firm and uncompromising to flexible and empathic. This is an impossible juggling act that rarely fails to have an indirectly negative effect on the patient—when parents are already sabotaging treatment, they are likely to make the child aware of what is going on in order to show him/her that the therapist "isn't really the ally he/she pretends to be".

Whatever the situation, it is important not to forget that the therapist's most important alliance is with the patient. It will often become necessary to develop an additional alliance with the parents in order to stop therapy from failing. As long as this alliance remains within the boundaries of understanding and taking into consideration the parents' own difficulties in dealing with the situation, it can be done. When the alliance with the parents starts to threaten the alliance with the patient (e.g., when the patient perceives it as a conflict of loyalties and starts to lose trust in the therapist), or when the alliance with the patient threatens the alliance with the parents (e.g., when the therapist frequently witnesses the damage done to the patient by a narcissistic parent, it becomes impossible to be objective and sympathetic to the parent), it is advisable to refer the parents to another therapist, preferably one who (with the consent of both the parents and the patient) has no objections to working as a team with the child's therapist, and, possibly, agrees to having family sessions (attended by the parents and the patient and both therapists) from time to time, as the need arises. This, again, can only be done if the parents agree to it. The reality is that some parents will accept nothing beyond the therapist "fixing their child". One such parent explained to me that, when she takes her car to the garage, they return it fixed. She expected me to do the same with her son and could not see why she had to be dragged into "this whole situation"—she saw this as my failure as a therapist. If the parent does not stop therapy prematurely (which is likely), then it is possible to continue helping the patient make the best of a bad situation. However, the scope of what can be achieved may be very limited as the patient returns to his or her dysfunctional environment after each session where parental behaviours and attitudes threaten or actively undermine progress. In such cases, I am not entirely sure that helping the patient to make the best of a bad situation is always the best approach. On the one hand, the therapist perceives that the patient—a defenceless and dependent minor—is being abandoned to his or her fate, which is a very difficult thing for a therapist to have to deal with. On the other hand, the lack of any real change eventually leads to frustration on the patient's side and a growing hopelessness about the possibility of anything ever changing or, even worse, a growing conviction that he or she will never amount to anything. In very extreme (and rare) cases where the psychological damage done to the adolescent is very severe, it may become necessary to work with the school and social services and find her alternative living arrangements that will allow sabotage-free treatment to take place and provide the patient with better prospects for the future.

Adolescents are still very much "growing into themselves", which means that their characters are relatively fluid and character defences are not as ingrained as they are in adults. On the one hand, this makes them easier to address. However, one must bear in mind how fragile this emerging adult is and how easy it is to go too far and "impose a character" in the absence of significant resistance. It is easy to overlook an adolescent who is eager to please the therapist by giving the impression of shedding a defence, when in reality she is replacing it with a seemingly adaptive behaviour that is a more carefully disguised defence. Adolescents are so used to trying on images/characters for size, that they can give the impression of real change when what is actually happening is purely cosmetic. Noticing when character defences have been truly relinquished, or when they have just been replaced by others, is a delicate balancing act that requires the therapist to always be sensitive and alert. With character defences out of the way, there will still be fluidity of character—experimentation that does not cause the patient any damage. With adolescents it is necessary to just sit back and watch this happen without intervention. What the therapist needs to do is remove the maladaptive aspects, but then not to (help) create a new character, but let the adolescent do that gradually, only interfering if new character defences start to emerge. Working with the Triangles of Conflict and Others is guidance enough to point the adolescent in the right way to developing her own character.

Experiential work helps underachieving gifted adolescents to get in touch with feelings that, for some, are only just entering their emotional vocabulary and, for others, would not have done so otherwise. It helps them make sense of their internal world and become emotionally literate in a speeded-up, yet fully supported, way. They mature more quickly than their peers as a result. Where, normally, the dysfunction in their lives would have held them back emotionally, they now have a clear advantage (as far as emotional maturity is concerned) over their peers that comes with the experiential work they have done. In comparison with adults, adolescents generally tend to have significantly fewer barriers standing in the way of experiential work. Working on the patient-therapist relationship is of vital importance here. With adolescents, through transference, the therapist often takes on the role of a healthier version of the dysfunctional parent. Once this relationship has been formed, they are more likely than adults to trust the therapist and feel comfortable experiencing very deep feelings in their presence. Gaining that trust is not easy. Adolescents who have trust issues because of their dysfunctional family situation require this trust to be reciprocal. This often means the therapist allowing more self-disclosure than when working with an adult patient, for example, letting the adolescent patient turn the table and take the role of interviewer for a while. It can also mean spending time just building the relationship by talking about what they are interested in—it helps to have some exposure to teenage culture (being able to quote from episodes of *South Park* or *Doctor Who* has been an invaluable tool in my practice). Some adolescents who have only negative experiences of closeness will keep their distance at first and the therapist needs to respect that and give them time without trying to push their boundaries. Unfortunately, those who have been too deeply damaged may never be able to allow anyone to come too close. For those who are able to build a strong and positive relationship with their therapist, the experience of a secure and caring attachment is so positively overwhelming for them that it has dramatic effects; it reduces their anxiety and use of defences, making feelings more readily accessible.

In comparison with adults, adolescents are more emotionally unstable (Fischer & Lamborn, 1989; Hare et al., 2008; Larson, Moneta, Richards & Wilson, 2002). This emotional instability, when coupled with the social and biological changes typical for that age, produces the "*Sturm und Drang*" (storm and stress) of adolescence, leaving them generally more susceptible to anxiety (Fischer & Lamborn, 1989). Effective anxiety regulation is therefore very important when working with adolescent patients. The therapist can (and should) teach the patient to identify anxiety and to use self-regulation techniques in order to reduce it. However, an adolescent is still not totally independent. There will be times outside sessions when anxiety levels rise and the adolescent needs help and support in dealing with it. This is a natural part of parenting, but these adolescents live in dysfunctional homes where parenting is inadequate; they do not get the care they need and, subsequently, are also not very good at self-care. With adolescents, the patient-therapist relationship often takes on the nature of a child-parent relationship. The patient will develop a dependence on the therapist and will seek help and support from the therapist in such moments. There will be text messages, emails, phone calls, and instant messages. The therapist can place boundaries on such intrusions, such as helping the patient understand that the therapist is not always available but will get back when he or she has the time, or creating an MSN or Skype account that is for patients only and which the therapist can choose when to log into so as not to be constantly interrupted when online. Adolescents do need more support than adult patients. If they do not receive this at home, they will need to receive it from somewhere in order to develop in a healthy way and eventually learn to care for themselves. Like any healthy parenting relationship, the aim is to teach the adolescent how to cope and then help him or her gradually to take responsibility and control so that the therapist can then let go. The parents of many of the adolescents I see cannot do this; they either do not provide the care and support when their child needs it, or are unable to let the child go when the time comes for him or her to start developing into an adult. The therapist-adolescent patient relationship helps the patient to make up for this by letting the patient experience a healthy attachment from start to finish.

The experiential side of therapy needs to be handled with extra care in the case of exceptionally gifted individuals. More often than not, this small group, at the top end of the giftedness scale, experiences emotion at an intensity that can be overwhelming to the individual. This is part of what is also known as over-excitabilities (Dabrowski, 1972), an intensity that is psychomotor, physical, intellectual, imaginational, and emotional. The implications of emotional over-excitability include heightened, intense feelings, extremes of complex emotions, a very strong sense of empathy, and what, to the uninitiated, can seem like highly exaggerated affective expression (Piechowski, 1991). This is very different from what we see in the case study presented in this chapter, where *false* emotions are melodramatically *displayed*. Over-excitability is a very intense *actual experience* of emotions. Exceptionally gifted children and adolescents will often have at least one sense (e.g., hearing, smell) that is acute to a level that any sensation in that area invades their whole consciousness and cannot be ignored. Emotions for someone with over-excitability can be extremely overwhelming and can only be accommodated, not controlled. For example, when they occur at school and cause great embarrassment to the child/adolescent, it is possible to make teachers aware of it and agree on a way that the child can signal to the teacher that this is happening, so that he/she is allowed to leave the class and go somewhere private without having to enter into conversation or draw the attention of his/her peers to what is going on. Being present when a child or an adolescent is experiencing such overwhelming emotions can be very upsetting for anyone: a parent, a teacher, or a therapist. In terms of the Triangle of Conflict, you could say that the D corner is almost bare, while the X and the A happen simultaneously—they are defenceless in the face of emotion and the resulting anxiety. They cannot modify these intense emotions/sensations in order to suit their environment. The emotions are very real and strongly reflected in corresponding physical sensations. Anyone doing experiential work with the exceptionally gifted needs to understand this and, on a case by case basis, assess the advisability of such an approach. It is possible to attenuate anxiety by moderating the exposure to feelings, and working gently. It is also advisable to teach the patient to identify early warning signs and take action before the feelings spin completely out of control and become distressing. In sessions, exposure work needs to be moderated; the patient must be carefully observed for signs that he or she is becoming overwhelmed by emotion.

In relation to the case presented herein, on re-examination of the session tapes, there are some things I think I would have done differently. Now that I am more experienced, I can look back and see that, while still an EDT novice, sitting in a room with a patient and trying to notice everything that is going on and then addressing it, is a huge challenge. If Julia were referred to me today, I would like to believe that she would find a more effective EDT therapist. I have no way of telling, though, whether this would have made a huge difference to the outcome of treatment. It is possible that more rapid progress from Julia would have led to an even more premature termination of treatment by her parents. I would have worked more closely with the Triangles of Conflict and Others, paying more attention to redefining what the patient is telling me in terms of the different poles of both triangles. Ideally, I would work on the P and C poles while paying special attention to reducing conflict within the family. I was already placing strict limits on anger exposure, so, in addition to that, I would try to reduce conflict by helping her gain more maturity through specifically relinquishing the defences that make her more dependent on her parents, in particular her mother. During therapy, these defences were Julia's "last frontier" and she would fight tooth and nail to avoid even discussing them. I fear that this was not without good reason. Considering the reality of what her mother was really like, any degree of independence would have been impossible for her to achieve while still living at home. All things considered, I am not entirely sure whether I can stand on the sidelines and say how much I would really change. I would have to be put in the room with Julia once again and keep assessing and reassessing the situation as it develops.

To conclude, based on what is known about underachieving gifted adolescents, and my experience of working with them, if one is careful to always bear in mind special considerations, and to incorporate any necessary adjustments to accommodate the differences between adults and adolescents and the unique characteristics of the exceptionally gifted, EDT becomes an effective way of helping them.

Summary

In this chapter, it was demonstrated that experiential dynamic therapies are a suitable form of therapy to address some of the problems of underachieving gifted adolescents. The factors contributing to underachievement in gifted adolescents were identified, and presenting problems were linked with specific therapeutic activities of EDT. Parts of a therapeutic process were illustrated with transcripts from a psychological therapy with a young gifted adolescent, demonstrating how an IE-DP perspective informed the clinical work undertaken, in particular, anxiety work, and separating healthy Ego from harshly critical Superego. At (premature) termination of therapy, significant and measurable improvements in aspects of the presenting problem were observed.

References

Baum, S. M., Renzulli, J. S. & Hébert, T. (1995). *The Prism Metaphor: A New Paradigm for Reversing Underachievement* (CRS95310). Storrs, CT: The National Research Center on the Gifted and Talented, University of Connecticut, University of Virginia, Yale University.

Clemons, T. L. (2008). *Underachieving Gifted Students: A Social Cognitive Model* (RM08234). Storrs, CT: The National Research Center on the Gifted and Talented, University of Connecticut, University of Virginia, Yale University.

Colangelo, N. (2002). *Counseling Gifted and Talented Students.* Storrs, CT: The National Research Center on the Gifted and Talented, University of Connecticut, University of Virginia, Yale University.

Colangelo, N. & Assouline, S. G. (1995). Self-concept of gifted students: Patterns by self-concept, domain grade level, and gender. In: F. J. Mönks (Ed.), *Proceedings from the 1994 European Council on High Ability Conference.* New York: John Wiley & Sons.

Dabrowski, K. (1972). *Psychoneurosis is Not an Illness.* London: Gryf.

Fischer, K. W. & Lamborn, S. D. (1989). Mechanisms of variation in developmental levels: cognitive and emotional transitions during adolescence. In: A. de Ribaupierre (Ed.), *Transition Mechanisms in Child Development: the Longitudinal Perspective.* Cambridge: Cambridge University Press.

Grobman, J. (2006). Underachievement in exceptionally gifted adolescents and young adults: A psychiatrist's view. *Journal of Secondary Gifted Education, 17*: 199–210.

Hare, T. H., Tottenham, N., Galvan, A., Voss, H. U., Glover, G. H. & Casey, B. J. (2008). Biological substrates of emotional reactivity and regulation in adolescence during an emotional go-nogo task. *Biological Psychiatry, 63*: 927–934.

Larson, R. M., Moneta, G., Richards, M. H. & Wilson, S. (2002). Continuity, stability, and change in daily emotional experience across adolescence. *Child Development, 73*: 1151–1165.

Neihart, M. (1999). The impact of giftedness on psychological well-being: What does the empirical literature say? *Roeper Review: A Journal on Gifted Education, 22*: 10–17.

Neihart, M., Reis, S. M., Robinson, N. M. & Moon, S. M. (2002). *The Social and Emotional Development of Gifted Children: What Do We Know?* Washington, DC: National Association for Gifted Children.

Osimo, F. (2003). *Experiential Short-Term Dynamic Psychotherapy: A Manual.* Bloomington, IN: AuthorHouse.

Piechowski, M. M. (1991). Emotional development and emotional giftedness. In: N. Colangelo & G. A. Davis (Eds.), *Handbook of Gifted Education*. Needham Heights, MA: Allyn & Bacon.

Robinson, N. M. (2002). *Assessing and Advocating for Gifted Students: Perspectives for School and Clinical Psychologists* Storrs, CT: The National Research Center on the Gifted and Talented, University of Connecticut, University of Virginia, Yale University.

Schuler, P. A. (1999). *Voices of Perfectionism: Perfectionistic Gifted Adolescents in a Rural Middle School.* Storrs, CT: The National Research Center on the Gifted and Talented, University of Connecticut, University of Virginia, Yale University.

Strop, J. & Goldman, D. (2002). The affective side: Emotional issues of twice exceptional students. *Understanding Our Gifted, 14*: 28–29.

Whitmore, J. (1980). *Giftedness, Conflict and Underachievement*. Needham Heights, MA: Allyn & Bacon.

CHAPTER ELEVEN

Experiential dynamic therapy in a university counselling service

Amanda Baker

In this chapter the context of university counselling will be described and the needs of students as counselling clients will be outlined. A rationale will be given for the inclusion of experiential dynamic therapy-informed work among the range of therapeutic responses offered by a university counselling service. Links will be made between the issues facing university students, developmental issues relevant to therapy with university students, and specific therapeutic activities of experiential dynamic therapy. Transcripts of excerpts from a therapy with a student presenting to a university counselling service in a post-1992 English university will be presented to illustrate how some experiential and dynamic interventions were applied within the counselling work undertaken. There is an emphasis on taking care of the real relationship (Osimo, 2012), restructuring the client's sense of self and others, and facilitating use of fantasy, to explore hidden impulses and desensitise the client to the experience and expression of anxiety-provoking and painful feelings, especially anger. Short-term follow-up will be presented.

The context of university counselling

As elsewhere in the world, alongside their core business of teaching and research, universities and colleges in the United Kingdom usually provide a range of support structures, with the task of facilitating students' capacity to be fruitfully engaged in learning (May 1999). These services address the need for support and advice relating to financial, housing, disability, and academic skills issues, among others. In addition, counselling has maintained a strong place in UK universities, and the process of enabling therapeutic change has held its validity as central to the educational support remit (Rickinson & Rutherford, 1995). This context, in which the residue of radicalism still resonates perhaps more freely than within the NHS, continues to be one in which a psychodynamic ethos thrives. Ellen Noonan, a psychologist who worked in the 1960s under David Malan in the brief psychotherapy workshop at the Tavistock Clinic, became a pioneering student counsellor and developed the specialist psychodynamic student counselling training at Birkbeck College. This programme influenced a generation of counsellors who have been involved in the development and expansion of university counselling across the UK in subsequent decades (Maitland, 2007). However, as this expansion has continued in recent years, there has been a move towards more multidisciplinary specialist provision. A university counselling service often now employs a range of therapists representing cognitive behavioural, psychodynamic, humanistic, cognitive analytic, and other modalities, as well as a mental health advisor and/or consultant psychiatrist. This reflects a shift towards a diagnostically oriented focus on counselling as treatment.

Most counselling within a university or college counselling service is very short term (even two decades ago, in a comparable American context, it was often between just three and seven sessions—see May, 1988) which, as May points out, has a lot to do with students' developmental stage (as well as with university calendars). For example, the autonomy-building transitional life stage of most students (the majority being aged between eighteen and their mid-twenties) means that they are often dependence-averse, and, for most, long-term therapy would be incongruent with their developmental circumstances. Rather, a brief dose of university counselling is often a crucial catalytic part of a transformative process unfolding within an overarching encounter with the bigger organisation, the university system, which is both facilitator and authority structure (O'Carroll, 1997). Therapeutic interventions which can rapidly and focally engage students are well suited to this context.

Students can have difficulties on several fronts. Firstly, of course, they can encounter the same loss, trauma, illness, or other misfortune as the wider population. Secondly, university life itself entails particular situation-specific pressures including rapid change, and new financial, academic, and social demands. Thirdly, the majority of students, who are in late adolescence or early adulthood, are going through developmental change. In particular, attachment and separation challenges arise as they attempt to master more radical differentiation from their parental worlds, extend their attachment needs into other relationships, and, at the same time, prepare themselves for adult roles. At university, the way an individual is used to being in the world can be experienced very differently, with different benefits and, sometimes, new costs. These maturational moves can precipitate a natural crisis, as students are newly encountering and re-forging their sense of identity (Casey, 2004; Coren, 1997). Fortunately, the majority of students manage most of these challenges with remarkable resilience, and without a need for counselling. In those cases where the crisis at university becomes disabling, it is often the result of long-standing emotional problems interacting with the new circumstances associated with attending university. The residual emotional conflicts associated with a history of abuse or neglect, for example, may come to a head as a student encounters the emotional and relational pressures of this new environment. These emotional troubles can often be manifest in eating difficulties, self-harm, social isolation, depression, and anxiety, all of which are common presentations to university counselling services.

In relation to the therapeutic work, in comparison with traditional psychodynamic therapy, features of the university context outlined above shape therapeutic relationships in student counselling in such a way that the work tends to be more short-term, focal, active, and less transference-based (O'Carroll, 1997). Transferences within the institutionalised authority structure can be complex, and students can be highly anxious about the necessity of interacting with teachers, counsellors, and others. A classic transference-oriented analytic stance can leave students feeling alienated and produce misalliances. Interpretation of high anxiety, or ignoring it by leaving long silences, is often experienced as persecutory, nonsensical, and unfriendly, which can simply compound earlier attachment problems. With students, transference interpretations of endings and breaks can be shed like water off a duck's back since, in their adolescent omnipotence, they often cannot conceive of endings except in the moment of experiencing them.

Experiential dynamic therapy and counselling with university students

Some of the ways in which experiential dynamic therapy (EDT) handles the problems outlined above are attractive for working with students. For example, the EDT therapist is overtly collaborative, and, rather than foster transference neurosis, works with both the real relationship (Osimo, 2012) and the transference in a here-and-now mirroring fashion. This approach enables the essential links and insights on the Triangle of Person to be made, while attending to the real relationship gives students a comfortable and usable bond with their counsellor, who can also model the alternative parent, by formulating dynamic interpretations in a psycho-educational tone and manner. The softer short-term psychodynamic psychotherapy approaches to anxiety-regulation and defence-validation (see Fosha, 2000; McCullough Vaillant, 1997), and the "graded format" (Abbass & Bechard, 2007) are particularly appropriate. EDT is a brief therapy, and its brevity suits the rhythms of the academic cycle and the phases of students' lives. Its collaborative therapeutic stance gives these (usually) young adults an appropriate stake in their counselling process, which enhances engagement and has the potential to increase therapeutic gain. The trial therapy initial session, combining dynamic assessment with intervention, offers a way of working which can be engaging and effective from the first encounter. In addition, using a dynamic formulation offers students a comprehensible, but not too medicalised "diagnosis", along with a framework for understanding and addressing their difficulties. The EDT therapist's active attention to regulating moment-to-moment anxiety is particularly helpful therapeutically and psycho-diagnostically (Frederickson, 2008), since anxiety is a ubiquitous experience among students who ask for help from a university counselling service.

Case study[1]

Katie, a twenty-one-year-old student in the third and final year of a photography degree, approached the university counselling service feeling troubled by anxiety and low mood. She was worried that her jealous compulsive checking of her boyfriend's computer for traces of "cheating" (infidelity) was beginning to undermine their relationship. Her mother had been newly diagnosed with cancer just at the time when Katie first left home to attend university. When she presented for counselling, she was fearful of a recurrence of her mother's cancer, but was expressing more generalised anxiety that her boyfriend or parents would come to harm when she wasn't with them, especially following partings.

In terms of the character hologram (Osimo, 2009), Katie came across as someone with her own strong perspective on life, and a core of self-reliance, creativity, and resourcefulness which had clearly helped her to thrive in many ways. She expressed herself in an obliging manner, seeming eager to please. She kept herself composed, conveying herself as someone who would always be courteous and not cause disturbance or make unwanted demands. The flip-side of this was a fearfulness about taking an independent lead or expressing the full individuality of her views or feelings if these might entail conflict or risk disagreement. As she and the counsellor worked together, what emerged was an underlying fear that her real self, if unleashed in all its shapes and colours, would somehow cause damage or loss, and this fear drove the generalised suppression of self which was associated with her low mood and anxiety.

Katie had twenty-one sessions of counselling incorporating aspects of EDT, plus a follow-up session at three months. While this is a longer therapy than the usual handful of sessions in university counselling, the work exemplifies an approach of which aspects can be used in much briefer frameworks too. The counsellor was in the first two years of a Core Training in Intensive Experiential-Dynamic Psychotherapy.

We join the counselling in the fifth session. During the preceding sessions, the work focused on understanding and normalising Katie's separation anxiety and guilt in relation to her parents, given she had left home at the time her mother developed cancer (HP, AA, SE), the anxiety she felt in her relationship with her boyfriend, and self-other restructuring (SO) to enable freer expression of her own needs. Katie responded with great relief to the normalising effect of her early sessions and began to accept and express her feelings without taking a dismissing and punitive position towards her Self:

Pt: … it seems to put into perspective, more, what I'm feeling … why I was annoyed … and then you explained and said it's understandable that you're annoyed, it puts it into perspective, making me realise that other people would have felt that had happened … and that it's a normal thing to get annoyed about.

Session 5

It can be argued that lasting therapeutic change within EDT arises via the combination of affective arousal and cognitive reframing (Meijers, 2012), and a major shift for Katie came after allowing, experiencing, expressing, and processing a moment of anger towards the counsellor for a comment she made about Katie's boyfriend (XA). Katie had been telling the counsellor about an incident when her boyfriend had angrily threatened to leave her.

Pt: Once the shock had worn off, I was upset. I took it the wrong way (**SE, D**) and thought that he meant he needed to move out.

Th: Well, maybe he did in that moment, and it was a sort of ambiguous message with a hurtful twist to it. (**HP**)

Pt: Mm. Yeah.

Th: But again, I think you cover up for him, a bit. When you say you took it the wrong way. (**DA**)

Pt: (Nodding, silent, then timidly) Yep, maybe I took it the way he meant it at the time.

The counsellor notices a rise in the client's anxiety and shifts to exploring the client's experience in the relationship with the counsellor (AA, XA, SO, RE):

Th: Mm. Mm. It's possible, isn't it? But what's it like to think that here, or to hear me say something like that here?
Pt: Um—I'm not sure. I don't know if it makes me feel a little bit annoyed.

The counsellor could have addressed the client's defences of helplessness, uncertainty, and minimisation (DA), but instead continues to explore the client's feelings towards her for blocking the client's self-denigrating position and drawing attention to the hurtful behaviour of the boyfriend (XA):

Th: Just here?
Pt: Yeah.
Th: Anger towards me, maybe?
Pt: (Laughs) Maybe, yeah (nodding).
Th: Yeah. And if you stay with that feeling, what's it like to just be with, now?
Pt: Initially, it makes me feel annoyed, and then it makes me want to defend him.

Katie recognises for herself that the moment the counsellor draws her attention to the hurtful behaviour of the boyfriend she experiences anger and wants to take the position of defending her boyfriend, signalling the emergence of a more attentive ego. The defence against anger towards the counsellor serves both to keep the client's anger towards her boyfriend out of the client's awareness and to maintain a barrier between the client and the counsellor. The defence has been put into operation by the client in obedience to a dismissive superego leading her to avoid the counsellor's validation and facilitation of her experience of anger towards the boyfriend, maintaining a position of minimising feelings. The counsellor continues to focus on Katie's feelings towards her (XA):

Th: Right, to sort of fix things.
Pt: Yeah.
Th: But if you stay with the annoyed bit, what's it like, just to be annoyed with me?
Pt: I don't know (looking uncomfortable, fidgeting in chair and smiling).

As Katie becomes more anxious and takes a helpless, unknowing position, the counsellor could have drawn Katie's attention to the anxiety (AA) or defence (DA). She continues with her focus on Katie's feelings towards her (XA):

Th: But you know you're feeling it. You recognise it, something inside you.
Pt: Not annoyed to start with. I sort of wanted to defend him straight away, and … make an excuse.

Katie notices her defence of wanting to make excuses and also notices that awareness of her defensive reaction had led her to recognition of her anger towards the counsellor.

Th: OK, but you also said you were annoyed.
Pt: Yes.
Th: Is it difficult to get at it?
Pt: Yeah. I can't explain other than saying annoyed.

As Katie's anxiety is blocking her experience of anger, the counsellor begins to explore Katie's experience of talking with the counsellor (RE, SO) and her anxiety (AA):

Th: And what's it like to just talk about it a bit and let me know?
Pt: It makes me feel nervous.
Th: Right, and how's that in you at the moment?
Pt: ... in case of your reaction.
Th: OK. What do you imagine I'm going to do, with my reaction?
Pt: Don't know (pause) I don't know. I don't know whether it's just the fact that I've said straight away that it annoyed me.

Self-other restructuring reveals that Katie's anxiety relates to a belief that acknowledging her anger in the real relationship would lead to retaliation, which, in turn, would lead to escalation of her own anger.

Th: Yeah. But that would be you being scared of your reaction. But I think you said you were scared of getting annoyed with me, because you were scared of what might happen, what I might do, is that ... (**SO, AA, RE**)
Pt: Yeah.
Th: What is it you feel I would do, what do you expect, in that moment? (**SO, AA, RE**)
Pt: I don't know. Maybe if you say something else, and come back with something else, that would make me more annoyed.

The counsellor is beginning to wonder about links to what Katie experiences with her parents (TP), but continues to explore her here-and-now experience of talking with the counsellor (RE, SO), and regulates her anxiety (AA) via further self-other restructuring (SO):

Th: But those fears you have about being challenged or pushed, or me coming back and doing something which would make you even more angry, is that what you experience from me at the moment? Is that what I am doing, or what it feels like at the moment?
Pt: No. No.
Th: What does it feel like?
Pt: Like you're trying to help the anxiety.

Following an increase in the therapeutic alliance the therapist continued to explore Katie's anxiety about expressing her feelings. After this session, Katie began to relinquish her defences against expression of her anger, and reported a deepening of her relationship with her boyfriend as she became more assertive towards him. She continued to experiment with self-expression, and as she connected with her emotion, especially sadness and anger, her anxiety symptoms decreased, her checking behaviour reduced, while she described feeling more often sad and less panicky in response.

As Katie found more space for what she previously perceived as unacceptable aspects of herself, her difficulties began to surface in a way which newly disturbed her; Katie told the counsellor that she had been home to visit her parents, and, since then, had been having nightmares and daytime waking fantasies about her parents being killed in accidents or car crashes. She said these were "graphic and horrible, with blood". In one dream she lay down next to her father's body, longing to stop anyone from taking him away. Katie also had a dream of graphic self-harm—holding up bloody wrists which she had cut.

The recent past and events around the time of her mother's cancer began linking back to patterns from the more distant past and her childhood relationship with her mother. In particular, Katie described how emotional expressiveness in her childhood had often resulted in misinterpretation, intolerance, reprimand, punishment, separation (being banished to her bedroom), and being held to blame for her mother's distress. Katie described a perpetual feeling of insecurity, precariousness in her attachments, and danger, with a sense that she might at any minute lose her boyfriend or her parents. Her mother's cancer had of course amplified this, as perhaps originally had her father's job—working abroad in dangerous places for weeks at a time—throughout her childhood. The counsellor hypothesised that her deepest anxiety about her parents coming to harm was that such harm would be a result of her own retaliatory sadistic impulse originating from the early experience of being neglected and punished herself. An unconscious defence against the guilt which accompanied this seemed to be to disown any agency, as though she herself must simultaneously be at the heart of things going wrong, but without there being anything she could do about it; an Alice-in-Wonderlandish predicament. Katie described a sense of being helpless to avert inevitable disaster. She was becoming obsessionally vigilant lest her parents come to harm or her boyfriend desert her. Hence the checking and separation anxiety.

A task of therapy was to uncover and normalise the punitive rage, to help Katie to forgive herself, and understand how natural and normal it was that she might at times want her parents to feel hurt. In so doing, she could re-own these impulses and also feel and discover that the actual misfortunes, including her mother's cancer, were in no way linked to her own natural rage, which could be received in a way which was not damaging to either, and in a way which might even be attentive. This way she could discover her real loving bond with her parents surviving, maturing, and hopefully also being strengthened.

The counsellor developed a dynamic formulation whereby any form of demonstrative self-expression (X) gave rise to fear (A) of (originally parental) dismissiveness or reprimand. A major defence (D) was what she described as "going quiet" in interaction with others (the counsellor, or her parents or boyfriend), but combined with this was a pre-emptive turning her rage back onto herself. Katie's Superego thus kept on deflecting the rage from its natural—external—target and turning it against her. If Katie could be helped to safely experience her own angry impulse towards her parents or her boyfriend when she felt let down by them, such new awareness would have unearthed the root cause of her anxiety about losing them, de-escalating her anxiety.

We rejoin the therapy in the seventh session.

Session 7

The counsellor re-contracted with Katie to continue their work on a more open-ended basis, and suggested they start working in a more emotion-focused way. As part of the collaborative re-contracting, the counsellor asked Katie what she wanted to work on (RE, HP):

Pt: I think I'd want to explore more the sort of holding back my feelings.
Th: Cos it strikes me that you've done some of what you wanted to do, and that's been really good, and in the process of doing that it's almost as though things shift so we become more aware of underlying difficulties around expression of deep feeling.
Pt: Yeah. I think the main reason I first came here was because of the anxiety and the what I thought was paranoia and stuff. And that's gone now.
Th: Yes.
Pt: Yeah—as we've got more into it, it's my parents.
Th: It's tracked back to them.
Pt: Yes.

The counsellor explores with Katie her sense of what is wrong between herself and her parents, and she describes frustration about the superficiality of their interactions, and a perception of emotional distance. The counsellor wants to clarify whom Katie perceives the distance to be created by, herself or her parents. We rejoin the session about a minute later:

Th: Do you feel pushed away by them?
Pt: Not—really, I mean, it feels a little bit as though I'm pushing myself away by not saying to them, like they're being narrow-minded and stuff at the photography show.
Th: So you're aware that part of you responds to some things by creating distance rather than showing your feelings.

They go on to explore what the painful experience is which this distancing defends her from feeling or expressing to her parents (HP, DA, XA):

Pt: ... it seems as though they've really moved on from things, from when my mum was ill, and are therefore now different from me ... I dunno, it feels as though they almost like don't—I know they care, but it feels as though they don't care that much, because they don't talk to me about it, they've never talked to me about it.
Th: About ...
Pt: About all emotional stuff since mum was ill.
Th: Mm, mm.
Pt: And like they ask, how am I, and then I say yeah fine, and then it goes to what I've done in the day.

Noticing a rise in emotion, the counsellor brings the focus into the here-and-now (XA):

Th: What do you feel just now as you talk about this?
Pt: Um, kind of sad.

Th: Yeah—like there's some emotion there.
Pt: Yeah (biting lip).
Th: Can you describe what that's like?

Katie's attention moved to her defence, to which the counsellor responds by asking a mirroring question (MI, DA) and brings it into the relationship (RE):

Pt: Um, makes me feel like I just want to be quiet.
Th: Do you think you hold it back, the sadness?
Pt: Um, sometimes, yeah.
Th: Are you doing that now?
Pt: No, not now, but sort of sometimes I think if I get upset, I say I want to be quiet, I sit there and like with nothing in my head to stop it.

Katie deflects the highlighting of her here-and-now experience (D), and the counsellor recapitulates with a validating comment linking feeling, anxiety, and defence (MI, XA, AA, DA):

Th: So how painful this sadness is, it kind of disturbs you so that you want to shut it down, keep it out.
Pt: I think I either go so I cry and cry loads, and get really worked up and emotional, or instead of doing that I'd just sit down and blank and stuff.

In order to facilitate Katie's fuller experience of her emotion, and to regulate the anxiety it arouses, the counsellor again focuses gently with Katie on what is happening in the moment as they are talking (XA, AA, RE):

Th: Where is it now, as we talk about it?
Pt: Um—sort of in there (gesturing to throat).
Th: You feel that lump?
Pt: It's not a lump as if I'm going to cry, 'cos I'm not stopping myself crying, it's just an uncomfortable feeling in there.
Th: What's it like?
Pt: Um—it's not like a lump, but it's getting tighter, it feels like. And I feel like I need to swallow to make it not so tight, the way my voice is and stuff.

The counsellor explores Katie's experience of anxiety a bit further, and we return to the session a few moments later as the counsellor again links Katie's anxiety to her feeling of sadness (MI, XA, AA), thereby helping Katie to develop her understanding of causality and building ego adaptive capacity (see ten Have-de Labije, 1999):

Th: One of the things you've said is that when you feel sad, you tend to go a bit panicky when you feel sad.
Pt: Yeah.

Th: As though the sad feeling is very closely related in you to the experience of anxiety that it triggers off. You get anxious about yourself in an emotional state.

The counsellor is also helping Katie to differentiate her experience of anxiety from her deep feeling of sadness which triggers her anxiety (AA, XA). The counsellor asks Katie what would happen if she became more openly emotional in the session, and Katie describes how her emotion leads her into (Superego) responses she finds intolerable:

Pt: I dunno, just what normally happens. I would just cry and it feels worse and worse, and then more things seem to come up and make me upset … Like there's always the initial thing that makes me upset, but then that goes away after a couple of minutes and I start crying and it gets into deeper things like that I haven't got friends here and it just sort of escalates into more stuff.

Th: It sounds like what happens is you start to criticise yourself. That first you feel this gut feeling of sadness, sometimes it's been about being alone, sometimes it's been about something to do with your relationship with Dave, or about your parents … When you start to experience that, when you start to let your feelings flow, to cry, part of you comes along and starts to really lay into you and say, and start to criticise you, is that right?

Pt: Yeah. It always like every time I notice it gets worse and worse, and then it gets really bad, so … like in my head I kind of like shout at myself … And then afterwards, I sort of feel sorry for myself and feel really low for, sometimes it's like a couple of hours and sometimes it's like the following day I feel really low and lonely and sorry for myself.

Th: So you kind of beat yourself up and it gets into a frenzy really, and then you go down. You feel very low.

Pt: Yeah.

Th: And feel sorry for yourself in what way—in a compassionate gentle way, or in a critical way?

Pt: In a critical way … I just sort of think, "Oh, pull yourself together". I think to myself, "Go into uni and sort of talk to people and make sure you make friends", and sort of tell myself to do it.

Th: Mm.

Pt: In my head. But then inside, I feel really low. So I never actually do go out and talk to people.

Recapitulating (MI, DA, SE, XA):

Th: Mm. OK, so it sounds as though the original sadness gets thoroughly shut down by all these self-critical thoughts, and commands that you give yourself, that try to push you back into coping.

Pt: Yeah.

The counsellor first validates Katie's past use of her defence that is put into operation in obedience to a harshly critical Superego, then goes on to point out its cost (DA):

Th: And that's in some ways worked for you over the years. You have coped extremely well. But on the other hand, there's a sacrifice or there's a cost that is attached to that about your emotional world really, and the space to feel sad, and the space to seek real comfort from other people.

This work continues to deepen the alliance, and the client confides more about her inner reactions, including the impulse to self-harm, which is something she has not previously revealed:

Pt: Yeah. I haven't mentioned this to anyone, but like sometimes, not recently, before I came here for the first time, for a few times I've been really bad, like real almost panicky state. And I've thought about like harming myself … And then—it sort of gets into that I tell myself stuff rather than actually physically do stuff.

Th: … so almost like this berating of yourself is almost a substitute for harming yourself.

Pt: I've never harmed myself but there's been a few times when I've been standing in the kitchen and thought, oh well, sort of cut this, and do stuff. I've thought about it, and then I think "Don't be stupid", and then it stops when I think "Pull yourself together, don't be stupid".

Th: And at one level that does—it is protective. It does keep you safe in a way. But at another level it shuts down any thinking, or forgiveness, or understanding or anything really to do with what was this feeling about, that made you feel so desperate that you wanted to hurt yourself.

Pt: I don't know. That is sort of in the middle of everything, after I've been upset and then that's when I'm thinking I, first I think I want to go home. Then I think I haven't got friends here, and I'm lonely here.

In a recapitulating and mirroring comment, the counsellor links Katie's emotion-regulatory impulse (X) to the prohibitions of a harsh Superego, and Katie's anxiety and defences (A and D), before normalising her impulse (X).

Th: So initially you feel sad, then you want to go home. Which seems like a really natural urge, to go back to your parents for safety, to get some love and TLC [tender loving care]. But somehow that's got out of bounds. And maybe we need to give ourselves more time to understand this. So then you've learnt to connect that up with a kind of prohibition: "Not allowed to go home". "Not allowed to need anything from them, I've got to get it here instead from friends, although I don't have any friends" … So almost like the healthy thought of longing to seek something from one's parents, triggers off a whole lot of things which feel quite, um, harsh on yourself.

Pt: Yeah. Yeah. They seem quite extreme.

Th: Mmm. There hasn't been much space for the original feeling, the longing, the sadness, the emotion.

Pt: No.

Th: Somewhere along the way, you've learnt—that's a sort of association, you've learnt. Not consciously, not rationally, but it's an experiential, emotional experience kind of learning.

> It may go way way back. But somehow you've learnt that the longing for comfort and the longing to have space for feelings, especially with your parents, has to be prohibited because somewhere along the line ... you've associated that with some kind of other bad experience, something not working out how you expected ... And coming here to talk to me I think is the part of you that does have a healthy urge to share your feelings with somebody ... in a place where it feels safe and it's possible to do that. And that as you've done that more and more, developed a kind of appetite to do that.

Subsequent work focused on linking this self-punishing and self-depriving superego reaction with Katie's avoidance of feeling and avoidance of acknowledging sadistic impulses towards others, which were deflected but indirectly acted out in fantasised and dreamed gestures of self-harm. Unsurprisingly, crucial shifts followed Katie's recognition of the censored sadistic part of her angry impulses towards her parents, and working through the anxiety and Superego self-punishment which she had been carrying, which she had believed to be "extreme". As the dreams ceased, what they had raised for her—punitive impulses towards her mother—was now clearly on her agenda and needed to be consciously faced.

Session 11

Katie was upset about a recent phone conversation with her mother which had again brought up anger, this time about the superficiality of her mother's questions to her about how she was and how university was going. The counsellor asked what this meant to her:

Pt: Thinking that she doesn't, not that she doesn't care, but she's not worried about whether I'm sad or even ill or anything.
Th: What does that do to you just now, as you think about it?
Pt: It makes me feel angry to start with, with her, and then deflated again.

The counsellor focuses on emotional maieutics (XA), trying to help Katie to take a different position from the deflated one, through the use of a fantasised conversation with mother:

Th: If you were to tell your mum about the anger, now, just in fantasy, what would it be that you would want to tell her, about how she didn't notice and she wouldn't even care if you were ill?
Pt: Just that I think, that it feels that I'm completely separate from them and not part of the family.
Th: How would you say it, just in fantasy, at the moment?
Pt: Probably in an upset way.
Th: How would that sound?
Pt: Almost like when parents are talking to a child, that they're disappointed in them.

Katie was becoming more aware of her impulse to act on her disappointment in them. As this awareness grew, so did her guilt and superego activity, expressed in worries that she was being "extreme".

Session 14

After a Christmas break, Katie referred back to her frightening dreams and her fear that they meant there was something wrong with her. Wanting to do further superego restructuring (SE), the counsellor responds to her implicit request for reassurance, not by directly reassuring her, but opening up Katie's own concerns (AA):

Th: It's ... one of the anxieties you've ... brought here right from the start, "Am I normal or not?" ... Each thing that happens, or each thing you go through, or each thing that you tell me about, part of what you are doing is checking to see if it's normal or not. Is that right?

Pt: Yeah. With some things. Not so much now, but the paranoia side, the disturbing dreams seem so extreme.

Th: Mm. Tell me what's extreme, for you, what it is that, because it's almost like you're so—part of you is fixed on whether I'm going to think it's normal or not, whether, in a sense, it's acceptable or not. But I think you're also telling me that, for you, it's unacceptable, or part of you feels frightened or extreme, or ...

Pt: Yeah.

Th: ... like this isn't normal.

Pt: I think frightened because they're so disturbing.

Th: So can we go there and have a look, and see what's disturbing for you?

Pt: I think, partly, because of the fact that I've never physically hurt anyone, or never hurt myself, or anything, and yet there's still thoughts of badly hurting people, in dreams.

Th: Mm. What are the ones that come to mind just now, when you say that, badly hurting people? Who at the moment?

Pt: It's the dream when I sort of cut myself and then was bleeding everywhere (gesturing slitting wrists and holding them up).

Th: Mm. Badly hurting yourself. And is that also hurting anyone else?

Pt: Not physically.

Th: But ...

Pt: Well, if I did it, it would emotionally hurt other people.

Th: Does anyone come to mind?

Pt: My parents and stuff.

Th: OK, so that might be part of that as well. What do you feel about it, do you think? What's the feeling that comes with you ...

Pt: Almost a scared feeling (high, thoughtful, soft but unrestrained voice).

Th: Can you describe it?

Pt: Yeah. I mean, the way the dream was, that scared me, was almost like watching a scary movie.

Th: Mm.

Pt: And the scene was like a film.

Th: What's it like now to remember it?

Pt: It makes me not want to think about it, because it's so horrible.

Th: You're shutting it off.

Pt: Yeah.

The counsellor recognises and identifies Katie's defence of avoiding exploring the meaning of her violent dream (DA) and continues to draw her attention to the defence (DA):

Th: So seeing it in like a film, like a movie, almost makes it unreal, or makes …
Pt: Yeah.
Th: … it distances it, maybe.
Pt: Yeah.
Th: Are you feeling any of it just now, or just thinking about it?
Pt: More just thinking about the dream, yeah …

After more work on Katie's defence (DA), and her anxiety that was being discharged through hand movements, the counsellor refocused on her fear (AA):

Pt: When I think about the scariness of them, inside, when I think about that dream, it's almost like terror, inside.
Th: Right—is that what you feel now?
Pt: Yeah.
Th: Yeah, so can we stay with that bit, and describe it? Where do you feel the terror?
Pt: In there (pointing into chest), but it's not a physical feeling, it's like, just like a screaming feeling, makes the image more disturbing at the same time.

Sensing that Katie is now able to tolerate more contact with her feelings, the counsellor encourages her to use fantasy to explore her feelings (XA), sometimes referred to as a portrayal (Coughlin Della Selva, 1996; Fosha, 2000; Malan & Coughlin Della Selva, 2006; McCullough Vaillant, 1997; Osimo, 2012). This involves guiding a client through a fantasised scene in which she experiences and expresses the underlying impulse, with the aim of desensitising the impulse and freeing her from associated anxiety. It is framed "as if" the client were there, while client and counsellor remain aware of being safely in-session together.

Th: What would you be screaming?
Pt: I don't know if it is me. Well, it's inside my head, not screaming anything, just noise.
Th: Mm. And yet you talk about it so calmly here, at the moment, and you sit here very calmly—so it's like one part of you is screaming, and maybe screaming to be able to get at that feeling here, but another part of you is being very polite and conversational almost. You keep everything damped down.

In this mirroring comment which highlights her conflict (MI), the counsellor continues to identify Katie's defences as they emerge (DA).

Pt: Yeah I think so.
Th: Is that something you recognise?
Pt: Now, I do, now that you said that.
Th: Right, what's that like?

Pt: I suppose I do it quite a lot probably.
Th: What's that like to notice that?
Pt: It makes me think that I'd like to actually not like embrace the feelings—it's not a nice feeling, but to not shut it down.
Th: Right. Maybe embracing things, or un-trapping things a bit?
Pt: Mmm.

There is a rise in Katie's motivation to relinquish her defence of shutting down, which the counsellor continues to clarify with her and scaffold. This continues to deepen rapport and enable a safe enough alliance for Katie to talk increasingly openly about feared parts of her inner experience:

Pt: I think the only way I imagine myself expressing the feelings of being scared and the terror from the dream is to like, very, extremely, like screaming and …
Th: Can you stay with that thought, that fantasy, that expressing them would be extreme screaming?
Pt: Yeah, almost like having to be restrained and …
Th: … what would happen if you weren't restrained?
Pt: I don't know. But sort of a feeling of expressing it would be to sort of loudly shout and maybe sort of run and burst out of doors and …
Th: Where would you be, bursting out of the doors?
Pt: I don't know, but I can picture pushing double doors, and then (laughs) …
Th: And you laugh again then.

The laugh indicates a surge of anxiety, and the counsellor highlights this (MI) to help contain and regulate it (AA), and to help Katie stay connected with her emotional experience (XA).

Pt: Yeah. I don't know where the image is. Not like the double doors down there or that door, or anything … they're almost like hospital doors, in the corridor …
Th: Are you going into a hospital?
Pt: Running out, I think.
Th: What are you screaming?
Pt: Not sure. Not words. There's not words in my head.
Th: Mm, what does it sound like?
Pt: Like, a painful screaming.
Th: Somebody in pain.
Pt: Yep.
Th: What's the pain?
Pt: I've never heard, almost like someone in labour … or like, agony, screaming.
Th: Agony.
Pt: Yeah …
Th: And what's the pain in you, what's the agony?
Pt: I'm not sure. When I said almost like hospital doors, the image of my mum in hospital, visiting her when she was ill, came to mind.

Th: What comes with that?
Pt: A scared feeling.
Th: Scared.
Pt: I'm not sure, not scared about losing mum. Just scared about revisiting the actual image where I saw her really ill in bed.

This confirmed that the fear was not about the imagined loss itself, terrible though this was for her, but that there was something anxiety-provoking arising as she revisited this image.

Th: Mm. What was it like, to see her?
Pt: It wasn't very nice, because she had one of those bags of blood next to her … all attached to her when I was in the room. Then she hid it when my brother went in the room.
Th: Mmm. What did that mean to you? You were very upset.
Pt: I think, I know she wanted to protect Tim [brother] and not make him feel disturbed by it.
Th: Mm, but she treated you differently.
Pt: Yeah.
Th: How did you feel about that?
Pt: Quite upset. But I think she thought, I don't know, maybe I was older and would be able to handle it … It always feels like they expect me to be the strongest one.

Katie's feelings about her own true needs being overlooked was part of her core conflict. Those feeling still provoked anxiety (A), and she was still partially diluting them and explaining them away, averting the full force of her experience (D). The counsellor offers scaffolding guidance, reiterating, normalising, and accompanying Katie through the scene, hoping to continue restructuring the Superego (SE).

Th: So what would you feel towards your mum, in that moment?
Pt: I'm not sure, possibly a bit of anger.
Th: Does that seem real now?
Pt: Yeah … I was on holiday when she was in hospital, when I got back. So I don't know whether Tim had been to visit her before me, but …
Th: But if you stay with the anger part, what would you want to say to your mum in fantasy?
Pt: I don't know what I would say, but I would want to ask her why she let me see the bag.
Th: How would you say that, what would be the sentence, in fantasy?
Pt: Probably like, "Why would you let me see that when you must know how scared I was?"
Th: Why would you let me see that when you must know how scared I was?
Pt: Yes. She must have known how scared she and dad was, and therefore, because she's my mum, it was probably worse, the thought of losing my mum.
Th: So part of you is screaming, "She must have known how scared I was!"
Pt: Because she must have been scared herself.
Th: That's the detective part of you … you didn't see the evidence that she knew [how scared you were].
Pt: Yeah, she didn't show that she knew.

Th: Mm, and that leaves you feeling?
Pt: Angry with her, yeah.
Th: That's the part that's screaming, "Mum, why?"
Pt: Yeah. It was as if she either didn't notice, or noticed but didn't do anything about it herself. And left it up to the family support person, who didn't really do much.
Th: So, for whatever reason, something really important about your needs got completely neglected, a feeling that your mum wasn't there helping you with this horrendous experience.
Pt: I don't quite understand why she wouldn't think to cover it up to me.

The counsellor noticed a hesitation in Katie's voice, although she remained highly engaged and unusually emotionally open throughout this part of the session.

Th: What did you feel just then?
Pt: Anger again, but confused at the same time ... it's as if she knew that Tim was scared, but didn't think I would be.
Th: What do you feel about that?
Pt: Upset, and a bit confused. As far as I'm aware, I didn't do anything differently from Tim.

The confusion seemed to be a defensive deflection away from her awareness of anger towards her mother, and the counsellor offers further normalising mirroring recapitulation (HP), to support the self-other restructuring (SO) which is enabling Katie to let go of her guilt and begin to experience more fully her disappointment and anger towards her mother.

Th: It's like there's part of you that's casting around to see what you did to make it like that ...
Pt: Yeah.
Th: ... but what you're actually saying is, mum did this, she treated us differently and it felt awful ...
Pt: Yeah.
Th: ... she expected something different from you, you said, felt very difficult. So it's as though that's rubbed something into the wound.

It seemed important to explore the anxiety that was still inhibiting Katie's anger and bringing guilt with it. Katie had a fantasy that if her mother had recognised her distress, it would ignite her mother's own distress, leading to an escalation of distress, and ultimately to hysterical panic, with Katie being "torn away" from her mother who she so desperately needed, and being restrained, and banished to a psychiatric hospital. She then made the link back to her childhood experiences of being banished to solitary confinement in her bedroom whenever she became emotionally expressive of anger, fear, or excitement, or expressed an emotional need to her parents. Katie learned from her parents' reactions that her core emotional experiences were "something wrong"—they were effectively pathologised—and became actively associated with real experiences of being left frightened and alone in her bedroom. She did not experience her mother as attending to, recognising, containing, or regulating her emotional states—her mother seeing how the wound was affecting her, and attending to her pain. Rather, her mother became very distressed, anxious, or helplessly frustrated, for which Katie was held responsible, and which led to escalating consequences—isolation just when she most needed comfort.

Following this phase of work, there was a significant breakthrough in Katie's current relationship with her mother after a visit home. Katie described how she had been explaining her university work to her mother who was "grilling her" with questions, leaving Katie with a sense of being dismissed and feeling annoyed. Katie, uncharacteristically, stopped her mother and said, "Why are you asking me all these questions?" For Katie, this was a moment of defiance she had previously avoided, and which she experienced as direct expression of her own anger towards her mother. It was the first time she had experienced herself standing up to her mother in this way, and her mother then told her about her own feelings of inadequacy over supporting Katie, which shifted Katie into feelings of connection and compassion, with a new awareness "that she cares about me". Letting go of her defence by interrupting her mother thus had rewarding consequences, as well as dissolving the associated anxiety. In the session she then recognised a moment when she'd been taking the lead, followed by an anxious reaction, and a defensive nervous laugh. Her new awareness was consolidated by linking the Triangle of Conflict with links on the Triangle of Person, in this case T-C-P (mother in the present and in the past). Subsequently, Katie reported a consistent absence of her old anxiety symptoms, as well as elevated mood.

Session 18

Katie introduced the question of ending "soon", and immediately experienced high anxiety. This turned out to be a transferential fear that the counsellor would become angry with her for voicing her wishes in this way, and immediately cut off the sessions, requiring an assertive or angry response from her.

Th: What would it mean? Because it's quite a powerful fantasy, that you come here and tell me you're feeling ready to move towards an end, and then I say, "Well, OK, then, we won't meet again!"

Pt: Mm.

Th: What is that, do you think?

Pt: When you were saying that, I sort of thought about mum, all of a sudden, saying that, "You're being noisy—go up to your room." I don't know if it's a reaction to that.

Th: You'd be banished.

The client makes the dynamic transference-past (TP) link for herself.

Pt: Yeah. That's what came to mind. So it would be a sudden stop, like mum used to, when we didn't know we were doing anything wrong … I don't know why, I imagine you saying it the way mum did, which was sort of, no warning, all of a sudden, like, yeah, "You're being noisy, go upstairs. You're not allowed to play with that any more." Almost like, "Yeah, bye, don't come back next week." Straight away.

The counsellor and Katie processed this again in the real relationship, weaving in links with past and current relationships. This enabled Katie to be more vividly and thoughtfully in touch with her punitive anger, and to restructure, with the counsellor, the guilt which had been inhibiting it.

Pt: … imagine sort of blurting it out and you being taken aback. And then, sort of, shrinking and really upset.
Th: Me shrinking and really upset.
Pt: Yeah, because it hurt you.
Th: Mm.
Pt: Yeah, almost like I can physically see that it hurt you, even though it's in your mind, if that makes sense.
Th: So it's hit home, and I kind of crumple.
Pt: Yeah.
Th: And then what would happen?
Pt: I think then it would actually hit home to me that I'd hurt someone that much.
Th: And what would happen then?
Pt: I suppose I would feel guilty and upset (in a smaller voice).
Th: What would happen then, what would you do with the upset, what would you say?
Pt: I don't know. I don't think I would apologise. If it was that situation that happened, then I would obviously want to hurt.
Th: OK, so you would be holding onto something in you.
Pt: Yeah. I don't think I would apologise and say I didn't mean it. Because in that situation if I'd said it then I would have meant it.
Th: Yeah, so you did mean it … so, what would you be saying, when you saw me crumpled and hurt, because of what I've done and then what you've done? What would you want to say, if you didn't want to say …
Pt: I think I'd want to sort of be stubborn, and then say, "Oh well, there you go, that's hurt you, tough!"
Th: Right.
Pt: Rather than, I'd like to carry on being strong.
Th: Right, so holding your ground somehow.
Pt: Yeah.
Th: And saying, "There you go, tough!"
Pt: Yeah, almost as if I was saying, "Oh well, there you go, you shouldn't have said something to me in the first place."
Th: Right.
Pt: Yeah, that kind of feeling.
Th: And that sounds quite angry as well.
Pt: Yeah.
Th: You want to really let me know how angry you felt, because I shouldn't have done that in the first place.
Pt: Yeah.

Th: Mm. And how would you be feeling then?
Pt: Probably quite strong and confident then.
Th: Mm. Strong and confident. And what would happen then?
Pt: Probably, in my head, at the moment, I'm thinking as if it was Jan [ex-flatmate], I think then I would sort of feel, not proud that I'd hurt her, but almost pleased that I finally did something.
Th: OK. So some pleasure, you'd feel some pleasure that you'd been able to hurt her, been able to do something strong.
Pt: Yeah. Rather than just thinking that I would say that.
Th: Right. And then what happens?
Pt: I'm not sure.
Th: And how does it feel now?
Pt: It makes me feel bad just now.
Th: What's the feeling that's coming?
Pt: I think guilt, maybe. That I've admitted that I would get pleasure out of hurting her.
Th: Guilt towards who? Just then, or guilt here to say that?
Pt: Just to admit it, that I would like to hurt someone.
Th: So it's hard for you to let there be space for the part of you that has those impulses, the wish for revenge.
Pt: It makes me want to justify it again.
Th: Right.
Pt: Yeah, and …
Th: Mm. So the guilt is the part that's been inhibiting the part of you that actually wants to stand up for yourself.

The counsellor makes a link between Katie's tendency to suppress her expression of anger—self-inhibition—and the guilt she is experiencing in session following expression of her impulse to hurt both the counsellor and her ex-flatmate.

Pt: Yeah I think so. But, I. Yeah, maybe the guilt of, someone thinking that I want to hurt her.
Th: But this is real. Those feelings are really there. And, they are there. What's bad about them, for you?
Pt: I don't know. I think I feel bad admitting that I would feel happy that I hurt her, because I think someone would think that I'm a horrible person.

Katie expresses her fear that she would be perceived as a horrible person and the counsellor responds by inviting her to investigate her feelings and experience of the counsellor's response in the real relationship (RE), potentially leading to a restructuring of Katie's sense of others (SO):

Th: Is that how you feel here, that telling me you would take pleasure in punishing her makes you worry that I would think you're horrible?
Pt: Yeah, maybe.
Th: And is that how it feels?

Pt: Yeah, like …
Th: Are you feeling at the moment that I'm thinking you are horrible?
Pt: No, I'm not feeling that. But while I was saying it, I felt bad in case you did think I was horrible. Which makes me want to explain it more. So you know there's a reason I want to be nasty.

Katie acknowledges that she does not sense criticism or judgement from the counsellor but again refers to the critical and dismissing Superego part that provokes guilt when she accepts its perspective on her anger, and her defence of rationalising and justifying her anger. The counsellor links this to a defence Katie uses which together they had early on noticed and described as "packaging", whereby she minimises her description of something to seem more palatable to the other person in order to try to control the other's reaction. Katie had found this observation revelatory early in the work. The counsellor refers to the effect of this defence within the real relationship now, pointing out its self-defeating nature (DA):

Th: Well, that's the packaging part that wants to control my reactions.
Pt: Yeah.
Th: That part cheats you of the opportunity to discover, actually, how people do react, and how I am reacting.

The counsellor invites Katie to explore her thoughts and feelings (XA) in the real relationship (RE), continuing to work towards restructuring Katie's sense of others (SO):

Th: But what do you think, what do you feel now?
Pt: Now I feel normal, like calm, and not anxious.

The invitation to notice the real relationship and the counsellor's real reaction (SO) served to regulate Katie's anxiety (AA), in part, through normalising and making space for her to understand that her sadism did not make her a "horrible" or flawed person (XA, HP).

Th: OK.
Pt: I don't feel bad or guilty any more.
Th: The guilt's gone?
Pt: Yes.

The counsellor moved to cognitive recapitulation and meta-therapeutic processing.

Th: So that seemed to go through checking out something with me, about whether I thought you were horrible. Is that right?
Pt: Yeah. Yeah, because I know that you don't think I'm horrible. Or I know that you know it's a normal thing to actually want to hurt someone.

The counsellor then invites Katie to explore her feelings towards herself, working towards restructuring Katie's sense of herself (SO):

Th: OK, so what does that do to your feeling about yourself?
Pt: It makes me think that it is OK to want to stand up for myself.
Th: So it makes a bit more space for those feelings maybe?
Pt: Yeah.

The counsellor recapitulates, making links between Katie standing up to her in session and her recent assertive breakthrough with her mother (TC), both of which had led to freer communication, emotional closeness, and a more adaptive sense of self and others. The counsellor continues to work on restructuring Katie's sense of herself and others (SO):

Th: You did actually stand up for yourself by saying, "Mum, why are you asking all these questions?" I don't know exactly how you worded it but …
Pt: Yes.
Th: … or what the tone was, but …
Pt: Yeah, I asked her why she was asking so many questions.
Th: Mm. So that had that quality of sticking up for yourself, and at that moment being able to let her know.
Pt: Yep.
Th: And at that moment, you weren't afraid of damaging either her or you.
Pt: Yeah.
Th: And in the fantasy, just now, you weren't afraid of damaging me … So those feelings were survivable. In that fantasy of them, you found that actually …
Pt: Yes.
Th: … they weren't that awful.
Pt: Yes.

Deciding to end counselling was a formative step for Katie. Standing up to the counsellor by expressing her wish to end the sessions coincided with standing up to her mother. The counsellor explored transference with her from a position of supporting and not over-interpreting her need to end. They worked through her transference fantasy that the counsellor would respond to her wish to end by immediately punishing her and cutting off any remaining sessions, linking the transference to her past (TP). Katie then began to experience the counsellor as affirming her excitement about being able to take this step for herself. This provided a new opportunity to understand her "well-behaved" compliance—how she had been depriving herself of the fullness of the connection she craved by blocking the contagious potency of her own emotion. She had often told the counsellor about excitement while remaining inexpressive, disconnected from her feeling, and displaying no animation. She now saw that she had been disabling the infectiousness of her excitement because of the remembered fear both of directly angering her mother, and also of inciting her brother to the boisterousness which then got both of them into trouble (TP). The real relationship allowed Katie and the counsellor to talk about this as it was happening in the session.

Session 19

Following the self-other restructuring work (SO) which released Katie from her fear of the counsellor's punitive reaction to her wish to end her counselling, there was a moment when Katie, unusually, held onto her excitement within the session, and found it feeling "bigger". This followed a recapitulative comment from the counsellor that announcing her wish to end the counselling had not resulted in the anticipated punishment. They had been discussing Katie's excitement and sense of achievement about the work they had done together, and the possibility of ending.

Pt: When I said I feel excited about the sense of achievement, you seemed to feel excited and animated.
Th: OK, so when you pick up a resonance in me …
Pt: Yeah. It seems to, like, almost like, back up what I'm saying and push me more.

Noticing this shift in the experience between them (SO) opened the possibility of understanding what had previously been inhibiting connection in the real relationship (RE). In particular, Katie's expectation of rejection, that had historically followed her self-expression, was again challenged, and it became possible for Katie and the counsellor to look more closely at the mechanism Katie had been putting into operation to obstruct authentic connection (DA, SE):

Th: And there's another part of you that's fearing and expecting a very different response from that [acceptance of your feelings and emotional expression], like you had from your mother: "If you get over-excited, I'm going to get cross. And banish you" … And the part that expects to be banished almost does it for, pre-empts it, and banishes yourself by going sheepish …
Pt: Yeah. Yes, that always comes, that's, yeah (sounding very definite).
Th: Right. So that part you hide, the effect of that part is that, you hide your excitement, so that the other person can't maybe feel it. Does that make any sense?
Pt: Yep (nodding decisively; pause). So you wouldn't be able to react to it, like, either way.

In this moment, Katie clearly digested the counsellor's mirroring feedback which then enabled them together to realise the part she was playing in blocking the counsellor's attunement in the real relationship, even though she longed for it. Subsequently, through further exchanges with her mother Katie gained a new appreciation of her mother's circumstances, and the impact of these on her mother's parenting. At the same time, Katie's new independent-mindedness seemed to elicit a change in her mother's communications. For example, Katie was moved by her mother's acknowledgement of her "strictness" towards her children, and some explanation of her own anxiety with her husband often away and unable to be the disciplinarian, leaving her feeling stuck in a role which she had not been comfortable with. This too was a revelation and relief for Katie, who heard from this that her mother had always cared about her. The thought of her mother's cancer by now had ceased to be laden with resentment, neglect, terror, and foreboding, and, having resolved her conflict around her anger sufficiently there was a rise in feelings of love, compassion, and connection with her mother.

It became clear that Katie's rumination and fear about her mother's cancer returning was in fact linked to guilt and Superego activity in response to her angry impulses towards her mother. Her initial reaction to her mother's cancer, in the context of these angry impulses towards her mother, who, for example did not hide the bag of blood from Katie when she visited her mother in hospital, gave rise to a punitive attack on herself, "beating myself up because it happened to my mum". By the end of her counselling, following a stage in which she was able to tolerate recognising that sometimes her angry and vengeful impulses were towards her mother, rumination and fear about her mother's cancer returning had been replaced by a mature realism.

Session 20

Pt: Now I don't really think: "What if it comes back?" … I think it's 'cos I've almost moved on from that thought. And maybe would cope with it better if it did come back … It doesn't scare me that much any more.

This also coincided with resolution of separation anxiety with her boyfriend:

Pt: Even like when Dave goes to work, and stuff like that, it doesn't bother me any more.

Perhaps most significantly, as it signalled a restructuring of Katie's sense of self, she reported the discovery of a much more solid sense of self:

Pt: It seems like I'm more noticeable, if that's the word, like, for, just me.

This made her feel:

Pt: Quite excited. I think it's made me feel more independent.

Session 21

At termination of counselling, Katie talked about giving support to other carers of cancer sufferers:

Pt: I'm just really excited to be able to say to people [carers of people with cancer] I've been through what you're going through now.
Th: What does that mean to you?
Pt: It means quite a lot. It makes me feel quite emotional, but in a happy way (becoming openly tearful for the first time in counselling).
Th: Mm. Happy, and what else?
Pt: Proud of my mum. I'll be able to say to people my mum's gone through it and survived. Before I didn't feel any of that pride, or anything, and I'm excited to feel it.

Follow-up

At three-month follow-up, Katie described additional gains including being more outgoing and open with others, maintaining a more positive attitude towards herself, being more self-aware, improvements in her self-confidence, and a reduction in her anxiety:

Pt: I think now I'm more open about things ... Now it feels like I'm the centre of my life ... I feel a lot more confident in myself. Last week I went to London on my own for the day, and I noticed that I was marching around really confidently, walking different. I bought some white jeans the other day and I never would have bought white jeans. I don't think I was confident enough to wear them with heels and stuff. I'm more confident and outgoing ... I think now I am strong-minded and confident about myself, rather than just kicking my heels in and being stubborn against someone. So I know my own mind, rather than deliberately opposing someone ... a couple of times I've felt a bit down, but not anxious or nervous about things.

At the outset of counselling it was hypothesised that, if Katie could unearth and resolve the conflict around her punitive anger towards her parents, and could recognise that the harm she most feared was the harm she imagined her own sadism must cause, then her anxiety symptoms and rumination worries would subside. At follow-up, Katie clearly articulated her own understanding of the change, in terms of her anger (X), the anxieties it had caused her (A), the relinquishing of defences (D) as she had started to free herself to express her anger, and the positive change which came in place of the anxiety and defences—realness and normality, calm and security. Describing how things were with her boyfriend, she talked of trust, being happy together, and a sense of equality:

Pt: I think now, by making that anger more ... normal ... I can be angry with Dave ... We can argue together and we can be happy together. So I think the not trusting has gone from that maybe ... It (anger) doesn't feel scary. I think before it was more than scary to express it. I couldn't conceive of expressing it ... Like everything was going to go drastically wrong if I did. But now it's normal, and I can cope with expressing it ... It seems more equal ... Everything seems more realistic, now, like the anger doesn't seem really really scary, and the anxiousness has gone.

In reflecting on the counselling process, Katie attributed therapeutic gains to the willingness of the counsellor to support Katie in expressing her emotions, in particular, grief, and learning how to be, and reconnecting, with herself:

Pt: I think I needed someone like you to make me say my emotions. Not like force me to. But someone to talk to about my emotions. Then I think they wouldn't have got so bad ... I think the grief and anger. I think the grief was what I completely blocked. And then, because of that, the anger got worse, and was then blocked again. So it all built up and up, and I never came here until it was quite a panic, rather than sad ... I think the really bad times, when I used to cry in my room—I didn't have any friends and stuff. It got so bad it turned into something else ... Because when I came here I was really anxious, and depressed and stuff, and I almost wonder how you got me out of it. I think, towards the end, I was sort of making steps on my own, so I had confidence to make steps on my own, and realise stuff during the week before I came to see you ... I think I thought almost sort of in wonder, how the process of just talking has made everything change. It seems like, almost like ... magic.

Th: ... part of it is that, part of the way we actually develop, including our emotional self, develops in relationship. The way you are gets profoundly shaped by the relationships you are in, especially with your mum and your dad (HP). Part of your emotional self felt inhibited, like you'd been squashed and suppressed. We take it on board and suppress ourselves. We talked about it, but it's not just knowing about it. You experienced yourself again in a relationship. You were here with me, and also with Dave. I think one of the times when things started to move for you was when you were able to discover that it was alright to feel a bit angry with me. Anger was one of the suppressed emotions. You then immediately started to find it was OK to be angry with Dave. Then your emotional world started to unlock.

Pt: Almost like learning stuff again.

Th: Unlocking, yeah, learning.

Pt: I think that's maybe where some of the bad dreams came from. Because I didn't have dreams about hurting myself or people dying when I first came. It was in the middle of the process.

Th: What do you think caused those?

Pt: I think, maybe, unlocking different stuff. Because I don't have them any more. So I think it was in the process of unlocking stuff that ... Yes. Almost like it sort of unlocked my unconscious thoughts and then made me realise them.

Conclusions

Separation from parents, which is a major preoccupation even from within a secure attachment pattern, and more so in avoidant, clingy, or disorganised attachment patterns, involves prising oneself loose from one's loyalty to the defensive constellation which arose at one's parents' (usually unconscious) bidding. Especially if there is insecurity, relinquishing this loyalty, while being more necessary, often feels like a betrayal. Students can feel protective of themselves and their parents while they are in these early stages of finding any alternative foothold in their newly expanded world. Dynamic formulation—using the Malan (1979) link between the Triangles of Conflict and Person—is a helpful way to de-stigmatise the questions students may need to explore about the impact of their own and their parents' behaviour. It is helpful for them to understand that their "problems" are internalised continuations of patterns learned in encounters outside themselves and beyond their own control in the past, and that their current emotional suffering (often depression, anxiety, identity, and self-esteem problems) has arisen because their automatic, chronic perpetuation of these patterns resulted in the exclusion of part of the range of their authentic self-experience and self-expression. Dynamic formulation helps a student to recognise how present pain arises from the pain this gave them in the past, as self-expressive options became associated with consequences (parental reactions) which upset or frightened them as children, and an "affect phobia" developed (see McCullough et al., 2003). Suppression of expression of anger is typical, but suppression of joy, closeness-seeking, or fear is equally important. Children from emotionally undemonstrative, affect-averse, or destructively affect-expressive families struggle when they need to use assertion and self-expression to build new relationships, especially intimate ones, and it is this struggle which students are often newly encountering.

In this case study I have highlighted an aspect of the clinical work which addressed anger towards parents which had been diverted and turned against the client's Self. Conflicts around anger usually constitute the heart of the troubles psychotherapy aims to unravel, since, of all emotions, anger is often the most heavily censored, and tends to be perceived as destructive, and unacceptable. For people who have grown up in affect-shy family milieux, there is a discovery to be made which is that healthy anger is a natural and, in any case, unavoidable response to the inevitable aspects of being let down which every childhood entails; that this anger in itself need not threaten the love between a child and parent; and in fact that if it can be openly known about along with the full palette of other emotions, this love can be said to be more richly and nourishingly manifest, to the greater satisfaction of all. However, parents who themselves avoid anger are often protected from their child's anger as the child automatically and obediently learns to deflect this inwards. Unfortunately, this deflection results in the child being frustrated and doubting their Self, rather than casting appropriate doubt on their parents.

For students in late adolescence, anger towards parents can be especially heavily censored while they still remain partially dependent on their parents. The experience is of being unconsciously held to ransom, not wanting to risk an imagined catastrophic breakdown of relations by differently or newly rocking the boat. Yet, in another part of themselves, they know they need to rock the boat, at least inside themselves, to stop the suppressive depressive self-undermining which is the perpetual price being paid internally for outward emotional silence. As in the present case, counselling can help a student un-depress themselves by liberating the full range of their natural feelings towards parents (and others)—including anger—and discovering that this need not destroy any of them. However, student clients are often initially highly resistant to the casting of any doubt that threatens to disillusion them about their parents before they can afford to lose the idealisation. The counselling work described above involved gradual de-escalation of the anxiety the client felt, as she increasingly made contact with her anger towards her parents, and through feeling it, managing it, and beginning to express it, learned that this did not threaten to undermine the real love and attachment which existed between them. At the end of this work she was describing a fuller and more open relationship, especially with her mother, as well as with her boyfriend, experiencing the love and connection in both these relationships blossoming.

It was extremely useful to incorporate EDT into Katie's counselling, since the presenting problem could be conceptualised as an "affect phobia". Her presenting complaint of anxiety and rumination was linked to the problem of blocking her adaptive feeling of anger. It was hypothesised that Katie's presenting symptomatic anxiety sprang from unconscious emotional reactions in her relationships that she had learned to suppress because, in her family of origin, emotional demonstrativeness was associated with painful consequences. Katie had been left with little conscious awareness of her underlying emotions, but intense awareness of insecurity, especially fearing that those close to her might come to harm, a fear which was exacerbated in reality by her mother's recent cancer. She was becoming helplessly hypervigilant lest they either desert her or come to harm, hence her jealous checking and separation anxiety. However, Katie was not conscious that her own emotional impulses might be the potential threat she most feared; that the harm she imagined might be a result of her own wish to punish them. The dynamic core of her difficulties was her suppression of her feelings by taking a position of "being strong"—so as to comply with parental pressure to go ahead with university—rather than give in to her own intense urge to change her plans in order to be near her mother. The immediate cost of this decision was that she became very lonely, isolated, and low in mood as soon as she got to university. Another consequence of "being strong" was that it took nearly two years before she presented for counselling, her help-seeking being precipitated by the onset of anxiety symptoms and behaviour which were threatening her relationship with her boyfriend.

The initial short-term counselling outlined above focused on normalising Katie's feelings, and building assertiveness in her interactions with her boyfriend, and in relation to the need to grieve and process the complicated separation experience when her mother was diagnosed with cancer just as Katie was coming away to university. As the counselling progressed, Katie became disturbed by a new experience of violent and vivid dreams, accompanied by a powerful Superego reaction manifest in urges to self-harm, and a harsh, internal critic. The counsellor re-contracted with Katie to extend the work to formulate and address her core conflict psychodynamically.

In her experiential dynamic approach, the counsellor worked via a collaborative stance within a steady and comfortable alliance with the client, restructuring the client's sense of herself and others, normalising, and using fantasy to help undo the client's tendency to turn anger against her Self. At heart this work required the uncovering of sadistic anger towards her parents, and desensitisation to it. Anger towards parents may be especially heavily censored while there is still a degree of instrumental and/or emotional dependence, and it was important that the counsellor helped Katie to know that her feelings towards her parents would not destroy either her or her parents.

The traditional psychodynamic phenomenon of anger experienced towards the counsellor (which, as in the central dynamic sequence—see Baker, 2012; Malan & Coughlin Della Selva, 2006—can be a powerful route to uncovering the core experience in early relationships) did emerge early on. Although this was only mildly expressed, it appears to have been a crucial experience in restructuring Katie's Superego. The counsellor's sense was that direct defence-challenging work, which might have crystallised resistance in the transference, and allowed for a more intense breakthrough of anger towards the counsellor with subsequent unlocking of the core neurotic structure, would have been experienced by the client as persecutory, colluding with the client's own active Superego. In contrast, an open real relationship was thought to have the potential to, and, in fact, did, provide the scaffolding needed by the client while she mustered the courage to question her assumptions about the relationship she had with her parents. Hence, rather than directly challenging or highlighting defences and Superego activity, the counsellor modelled a position in which she did not see things the same way, and this allowed Katie to arrive for herself at a motivation for taking a different position towards herself, and to begin to believe in the possibility of that more self-accepting and self-expressing stance.

That Katie attributed therapeutic gains to the willingness of the counsellor to support Katie in expressing her emotions, in particular, grief, is interesting given that most of the uncovering work had focused on anger which had perhaps been in turn protecting her from underlying grief. She had clearly got to this grief in any case. Much of the experiential work with Katie was framed in a hypothetical way, and moments of direct emotional experiencing were understated but, nevertheless, were very significant. She used these experiences to uncover and normalise the existence of censored reactions while keeping a level of composure in session, and then tended to use the emotional learning in her outside relationships with boyfriend and parents.

When students seek counselling, they often derive from the counsellor's responses a transitional "auxiliary" frame of reference to scaffold them while they are building their own. Transference to the counsellor often has an element of idealisation and compliance, allowing the young adult to feel safe enough to dissolve their idealisation of parents and others before they have enough autonomy to dissolve idealisation more fully. A universal psychodynamic goal is restoring someone's access to a wider range of their authentic emotional reactions in their major relationships, especially those with their parents, but this can only help if it does not feel to the student as though it robs them of their basis for respecting and loving the parents or parent-figures they often still very much need.

This therapy was atypical in being longer than usual within the university context, but nevertheless illustrates aspects of EDT which are applicable in shorter-term work too. The move away from a traditionally transference-focused psychodynamic relationship, while allowing the interaction to be rooted in the real relationship, helps with many aspects of counselling including anxiety regulation, collaboration, attunement to here-and-now reactions and needs, and cognitive processing. By focusing on the relationship itself as a laboratory with the client, and using dynamic formulation as a way of understanding how this relates to the student's core difficulty, EDT maintains the psychodynamic potency to offer "corrective emotional experience" (Alexander & French, 1946). At the same time, it provides a space wherein the student can feel sufficiently supported to de-repress, experience, and understand unresolved painful feelings from the past, and do their grief work in relation to the things that have been wrong, or missing, in their lives. It may also be that the actuality of this work bears resemblances to what many university counsellors are doing under different banners—EDT therefore represents a useful conceptual framework for formulating a constellation of therapeutic phenomena which is not unique to EDT, but rather an "assimilative integration" (see McCullough & Andrews, 2001). Returning to the present case, counselling within an EDT framework helped Katie to stay at university and complete her degree successfully with optimism, excitement, confidence, and energy. These attitudes and feelings also supported Katie into the beginning of her post-university, adult life.

Summary

The history and nature of university counselling was outlined as a context for the case presented. Developmental issues relevant to counselling with university students were identified, in particular, the significance of attachment and the importance of recognising the instrumental and emotional dependence of some young people on their parents. The range of counselling interventions offered in counselling services within higher education settings was outlined. Links were made between the issues facing university students, developmental issues relevant to therapy with university students, and specific therapeutic activities of experiential dynamic therapies. Transcript of excerpts from a therapy with a student presenting to a university counselling service was presented to illustrate how some experiential and dynamic interventions were applied within the counselling work undertaken. There was an emphasis on taking care of the real relationship, restructuring the client's sense of self and others, and facilitating use of fantasy, to explore hidden impulses and desensitise the client to experience and expression of anxiety-provoking and painful feelings. Three-month follow-up was presented.

Acknowledgements

I am deeply indebted to Katie for her willingness to allow me to write about my work with her, and very grateful for this opportunity to describe a counselling process which was so fruitful.

References

Abbass, A. & Bechard, D. (2007). Bringing character changes with Davanloo's intensive short-term dynamic psychotherapy. *Ad Hoc Bulletin of Short-Term Dynamic Psychotherapy: Practice and Theory, 11*: 26–40.

Alexander, F. & French, T. M. (1946). *Psychoanalytic Therapy, Principles and Application.* New York: Ronald Press.

Baker, A. (2012). David Malan and the genesis of experiential dynamic psychotherapy in the UK. In: F. Osimo & M. J. Stein (Eds.), *Theory and Practice of Experiential Dynamic Therapy.* London: Karnac.

Casey, M. (2004). What's so special about students? *Oxford Psychotherapy Society Bulletin, 39*: 24–27.

Coren, A. (1997). *A Psychodynamic Approach to Education.* London: Sheldon Press.

Coren, A. (2001). *Short-term Psychotherapy: A Psychodynamic Approach.* Basingstoke, UK: Palgrave.

Fosha, D. (2000). *The Transforming Power of Affect: A Model for Accelerated Change.* New York: Basic.

Frederickson, J. (2008, May). *Assessment of ego strength in depression.* Paper presented at the Second Oxford Conference on Experiential Dynamic Therapy, Oxford.

ten Have-de Labije, J. (1999). Maintaining Davanloo's discovery for uncovering the unconscious: An attempt at formulating operational definitions of the dependent variables, Part I. *Ad Hoc Bulletin of Short-Term Dynamic Psychotherapy: Practice and Theory, 3*: 4–16.

ten Have-de Labije, J. (2006). When patients enter with anxiety on the forefront. *Ad Hoc Bulletin of Short-Term Dynamic Psychotherapy: Practice and Theory, 10*: 35–69.

Maitland, J. (2007). Ellen Noonan. Retrieved April 14, 2011 from http://www.guardian.co.uk/news/2007/dec/06/guardianobituaries.mentalhealth.

Malan, D. H. (1979). *Individual Psychotherapy and the Science of Psychodynamics.* Oxford: Butterworth-Heinemann.

Malan, D. H. & Coughlin Della Selva, P. (2006). *Lives Transformed: A Revolutionary Method of Dynamic Psychotherapy.* London: Karnac.

May, R. (1988). Brief psychotherapy with college students. *Journal of College Student Psychotherapy, 3*: 17–38.

May, R. (1999). Doing clinical work in a college or university: How does the context matter? In: J. Lees & A. Vaspe (Eds.), *Clinical Counselling in Further and Higher Education.* London: Routledge.

McCullough, L. & Andrews, S. (2001). Assimilative integration: Short-term dynamic psychotherapy for treating affect phobias. *Clinical Psychology: Science and Practice, 8*: 82–97.

McCullough, L., Kuhn, N., Andrews, S., Kaplan, A., Wolf, J. & Lanza Hurley, C. (2003). *Treating Affect Phobia: A Manual for Short-Term Dynamic Psychotherapy.* New York: Guilford Press.

McCullough Vaillant, L. (1997). *Changing Character: Short-Term Anxiety-Regulating Psychotherapy for Restructuring Defenses, Affects, and Attachment*. New York: Basic.

O'Carroll, L. (1997). Psychodynamic counselling in an education setting: Containing, transference and clientele. *Psychodynamic Counselling, 3*: 303–320.

Osimo, F. (2009). The character hologram. *Ad Hoc Bulletin of Short-Term Dynamic Psychotherapy: Practice and Theory, 13*: 24–49.

Osimo, F. (2012). The essence of experiential dynamic therapies. In: F. Osimo & M. J. Stein (Eds.), *Theory and Practice of Experiential Dynamic Psychotherapy*. London: Karnac.

Rickinson, B. & Rutherford, D. (1995). Increasing undergraduate student retention rates. *British Journal of Guidance and Counselling, 23*: 161–172.

Note

1. The case study presented herein is written with the agreement of the client, Katie, and in order to protect her confidentiality, identifying details have been modified.

CHAPTER TWELVE

A client's perspective[1]

Derek

(Endnote by James Macdonald)

I always felt that I experienced depression in a cyclical fashion and that I could feel my mood slipping over a long period of time before it "bottomed out" and started coming back up again. Sometimes, the transition was very fast, but on reflection I think that this is just the final stage of the mood drop and that the background change was still probably over a longish period—a bit like the funnel shape of going into a black hole—the last bit is the steepest. I also used to have what were probably manic episodes, especially when I was younger—I used to quite enjoy these periods of intense energy and drive, apart from the fact that you knew there would be the negative payback at some point. I'm sure I was probably hard to live with at those times too!

The most recent depressive episode was brought to a head when I was subject to fairly relentless bullying from my line manager and I felt that I had nowhere to go for support and that the backlash from taking formal proceedings would have made the process pointless. While this period was the trigger point, it was, I am sure, not the whole reason for the episode—I had been aware of feelings of despair or hopelessness for some time, the difficulty being that I was so familiar with this that I tended not to do anything about it and treated it as just the general default position of my life. Being depressed was a state of being and I managed it through sheer determination. I never took time off work, even when I felt utterly dreadful and continued to hold a responsible job. The main effects were a sort of nihilist attitude to life, devoid of colour, interest, and excitement and a deep, deep tiredness that permeated everything I did. I read a lot, as I always have, mainly as an alternative to living and getting out there and doing. It became a safe way of opting out. I didn't make plans, think about going on holiday, or making friends. My main focus was to maintain my job and to be organised and in control.

After meeting with the psychiatrist at my local hospital as part of my regular routine appointments we discussed about my going for an assessment for a talking therapy. I was very happy to do this. I had decided that enough was enough and that I was tired of being on the depressive merry-go-round and that really tackling some of the issues would be a useful thing to do. I was also tired of taking medication with all the side effects that they have—such as putting on weight, which made me feel bad, etc., etc. After the first assessment there was a long time gap and eventually I went for another assessment before starting therapy in the summer of 2009. My thoughts and feelings about going were mixed. I was excited at the thought of facing some of the demons that I knew I had been suppressing for many years, but there was also some anxiety about being in a situation where I would do just that! I remember being frightened that I would not be able to control the emotions that I might tap into and I would end up in a heap on the floor. I was especially afraid of unleashing feelings of anger that I had repressed for decades. Additionally, I had concerns about being taken seriously, or that the things that I felt were important would seem insignificant to the therapist and that I would be made to feel weak or a bit useless. As a child I had always been told that there were always people worse off than myself—which of course, there are—but the effect of this was to be trained to believe that whatever I felt or thought was worthless and irrelevant. From this perspective, it was a frightening idea that I would be put in a position where I would be asked to talk about issues which affected me in the full expectation that whatever I said would be diminished. However, my initial fears were groundless as I found that the first session went well, I was listened to and taken seriously. I had tremendous feelings of relief that I was going to be supported on this journey and that I didn't have to carry everything any more—writing this I feel quite emotional at the recollection of the burden being shared at last.

I recall [the most distressing] part of the therapy [sessions four and five, when Derek's symptoms increased] very clearly and I remember feeling dreadful for a period. The work we were doing was becoming challenging and was bringing up a lot of very old memories, impressions, and behavioural responses that were geared up to maximise the survival of a very lonely and frightened little boy. To revisit all of this, even in the very safe and supportive environment that was created during the sessions was extremely difficult. I think the hardest part was trying to approach the anger that I felt about events in my early years which still resonated in the adult me and the grief that I felt about the loss of "what might (or should) have been". I remember James saying that for some people therapy was not the right path to take and I felt very anxious and was afraid that he was going to give up on me, which immediately translated into my being unworthy of continuing with and so on. I think I expressed this and he saw my concern and stated very clearly that he would make sure that he didn't say things like that in the future—this certainly helped me to continue as I felt he was being supportive and interested in me. I remember crying a lot during this period, both in and outside the sessions and it seemed for a while that going to therapy was becoming driving off for my weekly howl. I do remember wondering if it would ever stop—for me it was very exhausting to be at this stage, and I used to leave after the hour ready to go for a rest rather than drive straight to a whole day's work. I do recall a turning point when the tears became real grieving- there is a different quality to them and the emotions seem to come from a very different part of you. It was very clear that I was reaching back into some very deeply buried feelings and that I felt much better afterwards—exhausted, but somehow lighter. I don't remember ever being ambivalent about the work we were doing—I knew that it was going to be tough at points and that to some extent it would get worse before it got better. I went into the therapy with the very clear aim of making it work and that I was going to use the opportunity I had been given as fully as possible. I do think that I continued to "hold back" during our sessions, especially in the first eight to ten. I was still learning to trust James and myself—I also think I was afraid to let go, not knowing what would happen—being a bit of a control freak, I suppose.

I remember finding the role play sessions difficult to start with, not because I am uncomfortable with role play, but it was difficult to visualise my parents and to keep them focused while I was talking to them. However, it was a very powerful tool which enabled me to confront all kinds of issues and be able to express how I felt about things that had happened to me when I was young. I most remember being almost goaded by James to get angry and really express it—which I found really difficult—and when I felt at the point of letting it all out it suddenly dissipated into nothing. I thought I would feel angry at not being able to express anger, but on reflection I think I was expressing the anger—but in a way I didn't expect. I had no residual feelings of anger or anxiety afterwards and I was particularly surprised and moved to realise that I had sympathy for my parents and some understanding of what their angers and griefs may have been about. I felt that I understood them more and could forgive them for many of the things that they had caused—I didn't condone it but I felt able to understand it and let it go. The release of pressure was huge and I think it was then that I felt I had turned a corner and was beginning to embrace the "me in the middle of me", to allow myself to be an OK person—which up to then I had never thought I was. It was a very lovely awakening to see that I was—and am—a good person. At this point I was able to start being less hard on myself for every little error and fault and started to enjoy being me. I even drove all the way to [name of city] to buy an electronic keyboard and started to play the piano again, which I had not done for years—it will take time, but I will play that Beethoven sonata!

It was around this time that James and I started to talk about self compassion and mindfulness. I bought a couple of books and CDs and started to follow the meditations with very rapid and satisfying results—it was all so simple but effective and I continue to do the meditation (though not as often as I ought to) and recite the "may I be ..." mantra very often—I find it helps to centre myself when I get a bit stressed, or even do it when I am feeling fine as I can then enjoy the feeling of well-being that it brings. For me it was the combination of working through the sessions with James and being able to be proactive by doing things for myself outside them. Essentially, I was being given permission to be me, and for someone who had always lived for others and been moulded by their demands this was a wonderful revelation.

As I have mentioned above, I started to follow the guided meditations in mindfulness and to actively learn self compassion, catching myself when I erred and started to have negative thoughts about myself. I also spent a lot of time reflecting on the work we had focused on in the sessions by going through some of the role plays that I had done, and explored my feelings about these and thinking and feeling through the dialogue with James. The technique of feeling where an emotion was in my body and identifying what it felt like was useful in staying in the moment and really exploring the feelings that I was experiencing. I learned a lot about accepting my emotions as valid and human instead of being ashamed of them.

I have to say that I believe I was very fortunate to have James as my therapist. He made me feel comfortable immediately and was both very supportive and challenging as required—it would have been easy for me to hide away but his experience saw all of those little strategies and made it easier for me just to be open and honest. I found the sharing of information reasonably easy as I don't feel that I am closed off or ultra-private in that respect. But of course the level of sharing is very high and there were times when I felt exposed and open to judgement or ridicule, especially in the earlier phase of the therapy. As trust developed it was easier to disclose information and to be comfortable about exploring it. Although I was very open to James and he was extremely supportive and warm towards me I always felt and knew that it was a therapeutic relationship. This didn't stop me from experiencing the warmth and genuine interest that James directed to me as an acceptance and permission to say what needed to be said, feel what needed to be felt, and still be held in positive regard. He did remove most of the elements of fear from the process.

The most useful part of the whole process was the regularity of the sessions, and that they were (most of the time) in the same room. The familiarity of both the person and the space was important in helping me to feel valued—it's odd, but if the room had changed a lot I would have felt that I wasn't being taken seriously and was just being fitted in here or there with little regard for how I felt about it. We were able to maintain the continuity of the sessions by planning any breaks well in advance and by my determination to attend, regardless of how difficult the previous session might have been. I didn't feel negative towards it at all and I think this mindset really helped me focus on the work that I was doing. The really interesting thing is seeing at the end of it all that the "solutions" are actually very simple, but as you are your own problem there is no way you can deal with them on your own—with James as facilitator and therapist I was slowly drawn towards the end of what had been a very long tunnel.

I still have days when I feel very down and maybe even depressed. However, I now accept these as part of the human condition as I do my realisation that I too am human. Learning to be kind to myself was a major achievement for me and I hold on to that whenever I get difficult times. I have always been kind and compassionate to others—I am now experiencing that myself, and it feels good. My relationships at work have improved enormously, especially with regard to one person, and I think my going to therapy has done him a wonder of good! I feel more confident and less likely to feel anxiety when things go wrong or if I have to deal with a difficult situation. I suppose I am more centred and although I always appear calm I actually am calm (or at least calmer). My piano playing continues to develop and I am trying to learn a lot of new pieces—Beethoven and Mozart are favourites at the moment. I haven't really got back into composing, though I did start a string quartet last summer—I may pick it up again this summer. My personal relationships are better and I continue to work at being both more assertive and more compassionate with my partner—as in any close relationship there will always be issues—I hope now that I am able to confront them before they get twisted out of all proportion and erupt in an uncreative and messy way. This is not always the case, but the percentage is getting better. I actually feel as though I have finally grown up. I am now able to fully acknowledge my responsibility for myself and those around me, and find that I don't blame other people or resent them for something that they should (or should not) have done. The role plays with my parents were highly influential in this in that I finally forgave and understood my parents more than I ever had before, and that I could now be free of the repression and unkindness that they had directed my way. I had learned to understand them as people from the perspective of being an adult, not carrying the childhood memories and impressions, with all their faults and imperfections being accepted. During the progress of the therapy I felt as though I was growing into myself and becoming more aware of my ability and viability. It's a bit difficult to describe, but it felt as though I was finally, properly, inhabiting my body and mind in a real way and that I could be proud of that, of who I am and the things that I have done and continue to do. The main achievement is the lessening of fear and anxiety—about anything and everything. I can approach life and its challenges in a more level-headed, calm, and confident way, knowing that there will always be "stuff", but that it is nothing to be afraid of—I actually laugh at it much of the time now and find that any anxieties usually fade away pretty quickly. I have a much better sense of the future and although it is likely to be difficult in some ways over the next few years due to elements out of my control I find that I can imagine a number of alternative scenarios that are comfortable and will bring along with them a whole new world of challenges and surprises. Therapy is an ongoing adventure and although the sessions came to an end some time ago, I find that I use the strategies that I learned all the time and that I enjoy being a work in progress.

Endnote (by James Macdonald)

Derek is in his mid-fifties. He has had a successful career and currently holds a senior job in his employing organisation. Derek reported a twenty-year history of recurrent depression, and one brief hospital admission following an overdose twenty years ago. Derek had been assessed by another clinician and had been waiting for treatment for one year before starting therapy. I work as a clinical psychologist specialising in psychotherapy. I trained in EDT between 2006 and 2008 and have a long-standing interest in experiential approaches to therapy, having spent six years training in Gestalt therapy in the late 1980s and early 1990s. My use of EDT with Derek involved working collaboratively to identify emotional conflicts through, for example, mirroring defences, underlying feelings, and anxiety, helping Derek to regulate guilt, shame, and anxiety about his feelings, helping him identify and experientially confront Superego/ self-attacking processes, supporting an attitude of self-compassion, and supporting him in emotion-focused restructuring of his internalised relationship with his parents. The work was done within the UK National Health Service and was limited to twenty sessions.

Several months after his therapy had ended, and with his agreement, Derek responded to the questions presented in Table 1, to provide his perspective on his therapy.

Table 1.

Questions put to Derek by James several months after the termination of his therapy with James
Derek, could you say something about the nature of the depression you suffered, what it felt like, and how it affected you?
Could you say something about what it was like to come to therapy for the first time, what you expected, what you noticed, and what your initial impressions were about what would be involved, and so on? How did you feel after the first session(s)?

(Continued)

Table 1. *(Continued).*

Questions put to Derek by James several months after the termination of his therapy with James
The session-by-session symptom scores during the therapy show that you actually were feeling considerably worse—more anxious and depressed—around sessions four and five. I guess at this point we were working on feelings and memories that were very painful. I wonder if you could describe how you felt in the therapy at that time and how you experienced the work we did? What did you find hardest? Were you able to fully let me know how you felt at that time? Were you at all ambivalent about our work then? Were there any other times which were particularly hard?
Also, I'm wondering if there was a tipping point for you, when it began to feel as though you were going in the right direction and you started feeling better? Was there anything we did together that sticks in your mind as being particularly helpful? Did your motivation fluctuate during the therapy, and if so, were there any elements of our work together that influenced that?
Could you comment on what you did outside the sessions to support the work we were doing? Generally, I was thinking of the things you did to make the therapy work between the sessions.
It would be great if you could reflect on the therapeutic relationship, for example, what it felt like to share so much of yourself with a therapist? What different impressions about the relationship crossed your mind? How you experienced my interest in how you were feeling? Any moments that were especially difficult or especially helpful, and so on.
What other aspects of therapy did you find more helpful?
Finally, how are you now? For example, any persistence of difficulties, your well-being, relationships, work, creativity, and so on. It would be great if you could say something about the impact of the therapy on your life now. How things have changed in your life? Any differences you are aware of in relationships, how you handle conflicts or stressful situations, how you feel in yourself, your sense of the future, etc.? Also perhaps any limitations to what we were able to do in the time we had.

Note

1. The present chapter evolved from collaboration between the first author, Derek, and his therapist, Dr James Macdonald, who emailed several questions to Derek about his experience of a therapy that had terminated some months earlier. The questions and background information are presented in an endnote for the interested reader.

CHAPTER THIRTEEN

Receiving the invitation to open up

Arno L. Goudsmit

In this contribution, theoretical insights from object relations theory that underlie my therapeutic approach will be introduced. These can be seen to fit in well with an experiential dynamic therapy approach. In particular, I will discuss and illustrate the development of an interpersonal transitional space (cf. Winnicott, 1971) in which corrective emotional experiences can take place, that is, the therapist becoming an object to the patient thereby offering the patient a relationship working model that was missing or lost in childhood. In particular, the therapy can offer a new interpersonal space, from which the patient can develop a new or an enhanced Ego position. That is to say, the deep affects cannot be conceived just to "exist" somewhere inside the patient, if the subject who is to experience them has not yet arrived, or has sought shelter elsewhere. (The "subject" is the epistemic carrier of the affects, where the "individual" is the physical person.)

Object relations and relatedness

The core of object relations theory, as I understand it, entails quite a revolutionary shift, or inversion, of emphasis from the primacy of the individual to the primacy of the relation. If we take relatedness as primary, and prior to individuality, then this inversion has some implications for the idea of a subject, for then relatedness is conceived to be the substrate of individual subjectivity, rather than the subject being conceived as the primordial carrier of relationships. The latter view is the more traditional way of conceiving, but it may be useful not to stick to it in all circumstances.

One reason to consider the primacy of relations, at least in some situations, has to do with the simple fact that subjectivity, the quality of a person to make up his own mind and to have access to his own experiences, desires, and thoughts, is a capacity that has to be developed while growing up. Though the raw experiences may be present, the person will have to learn how to deal with them, to recognise and process them. Individual subjectivity, therefore, can be understood as the outcome, rather than as the point of departure, of relations with other persons, especially parents. Psychodynamic therapies, those of the experiential dynamic therapies (EDT) family included, are usually assuming a suffering subject inside the patient. This, of course, is not flatly wrong, but it may also be helpful for the psychotherapeutic practice to do the inversion of concepts as described in object relations theory.

In particular, when very early traumas are being dealt with in a therapy, it is not so evident that the infant did have the subjectivity to experience the variety of affects that an adult person would have available. Generally, parents contain their infant's deep affect in an act of protection (usually without too much reflection) before the infant becomes capable of tolerating a particular frustration and of "digesting" the facts that gave rise to it (cf. Bion, e.g., 1962). This protecting containment is missing when aggression, also mental abuse, comes from the parents themselves. It is here that trauma can be inflicted easily, as the infant does not have the capacities, cognitive and bodily, to act as a subject and to contain its own affects and digest them, let alone to defend itself adequately.

Although it is clearly important to offer patients a relationship wherein these therapeutic ingredients can be delivered, accepted, and made use of, a therapy that departs from individual subjectivity might overlook the aforementioned infantile incapacity.

Bowlby's (e.g., 1969) work extensively demonstrated the importance of attachment bonds between parents and infants. He focused not so much on the child's functional needs, on a set of metapsychological assumptions about unconscious destructive and other phantasies in the child, as did Klein (e.g., 1975), but rather on the empirical observation of attachment patterns. This was a basic issue in infant psychology and attachment theory: should parent-infant interactions be understood in terms of the existing social context or in terms of the child's functional needs? Neborsky (2010, p. 121) makes an interesting point in suggesting that Davanloo (1990) made a kind of "re-union" between Klein's and Bowlby's divergent stances, in that he considered guilt and Superego problems in a person to stem from a *continuum* between both positions, that is, between the relationships and the functional needs of the infant.

This is of major interest to the practice of Davanloo's original technique and of those therapeutic techniques derived from or inspired by it, such as the EDT family. For it entails that within the therapeutic interaction a pattern of transference resistances or other transferential behaviours and affects can occur, in which not only early relational issues between infant and parent are being re-enacted, but in which the therapist also has a major opportunity to encounter and counter these issues. This is to say that a major part of the therapeutic process takes place on the continuum between metapsychological constructs, such as unconscious phantasies, and real interactions, and that, through the latter, the psychotherapist can address the former and deal with them. Thus, deep affects can not only be observed within the actual therapeutic interaction, but through these observations they can also be encountered within the originating phantasies that gave rise to them or that were meant to handle them. Especially when this handling is immature the patient cannot "digest" the facts experienced, and as a result relies on very early defence mechanisms, such as projective identification and splitting. It is here that the subjectivity of the patient cannot be assumed to exist as a container of the various deep affects. Rather, this subjectivity is to be understood in terms of relatedness towards others, both in the past (parents) and in the present (therapist). It is here that, as ten Have–de Labije (2010, p. 247) puts it, a conscious or unconscious working alliance with the patient is often mistakenly assumed by the therapist to have been established, where in fact the patient is so much dominated by destructive Superego forces, to the extent of not being able to act from the position of an adaptive Ego and accordingly to accept the working alliance.

Anger and indignation towards maltreating parents cannot be supposed to exist in a child, if the parents are defining (and confining) the child's identity and if the child does not have the opportunity to escape easily to other persons who do offer the containment and the opportunity for the child to develop its own subjectivity into an adaptive and adequately functioning Ego. Accordingly, I am suggesting that object relations theory offers some valuable insights which can be integrated into our EDT concepts, without devaluing any of the available techniques. The present contribution aims to illustrate some aspects of this, in that it presents some episodes of an approach to early trauma in a woman who did not manage to contain or digest the concomitant affects.

A note on video recording therapy sessions

At EDT Maastricht, we record therapy sessions, as mpg files, onto a memory stick that the patient can take home with them immediately after the session. If the patient gives their permission, the therapist will make a copy of the file. At home, the patient can review the session recording, enabling them to retain a better memory of the session, so that the next session can profit from that. Furthermore, study of the session recording offers new opportunities for the patient to understand what has been said in the session, as well as for recognising their own (non-verbal) behaviours and emotional expressions. Finally, watching the video often activates the patient's regular Superego responses, and thus helps us *within the session* to unravel Ego and Superego positions; the Superego and its criticisms can often be situated at the "other" side of the camera—the unfriendly spectator that is going to watch and judge the patient. The patient's anticipatory fears concerning these judgements can be explored, which also helps to make the Superego's disapprovals less ego-syntonic. It is then particularly useful to join the patient in finding a stance towards this anticipated "evil eye".

Case study

The patient, a woman in her fifties, had been suffering from long-term depressions and compulsive disorders. In particular, she had a particularly strong disapproval of herself, which can be understood as a hostile introject, stemming from her parents' long-term disapproving attitude towards her. As a child, she had felt utterly unwelcome with her parents, with no escape from their harsh and derogatory regime. She can remember often having been sent to her room and left to her own fantasies. As a result, she found ways to attain her parents' approval, and identified with their opinions about her. It is with the same harshness that she imposed upon herself a variety of demands, most of them in the domain of behaviours considered by her to be "decent" and "appropriate". Depressed mood, sadness, stress, and other unpleasant feelings were deemed undesirable behaviours and were criticised relentlessly, leading to vicious cycles in which her subsequent fears of disapproval were sufficient to heighten stress, lower her moods, etc. During the preceding fifteen years, several therapies had failed to bring much relief, or had even contributed to her conviction that, due to their failures, she was not a "good patient".

After the ninth session the patient gave permission to video record her subsequent sessions. The transcript presented below includes the major part of the eleventh session. The patient had mentioned her fear of watching the video recording of the previous session. She suggested that she might first practise and watch some old holiday videos, in order to get accustomed to how she looks on video. She mentioned that she was usually not bothered when other people had critical opinions of her, but rather, was afraid of her own self-criticism. We join the session at 6 minutes 58 seconds, and the therapist is enquiring about the patient's self-criticism:

Session 11 0:06:58

Th: So it happens especially when you are doing it [the criticism] yourself? (**HP**)
Pt: (Nods)
Th: And what is it, when you are doing that; how does it get into you? What is so offending, so grim?
Pt: Well, then I get stuck internally.
Th: Yes, is that what happens?
Pt: Yes, I get stuck. I withdraw entirely into myself (moves her head between her shoulders).
Th: And you move with your shoulders. Do you withdraw like that? (**MI**)
Pt: Yes.
Th: As if you are being beaten up …
Pt: Yes.

The therapist tries to focus upon the underlying feelings of helplessness and despair. The idea is that, before any anger can be felt by this patient towards her parents and other caregivers, this despair is the only affect that she is capable of experiencing as owned by herself and situated in herself as an individual, separate from the parents. This despair is the outcome of the various kinds of violence and punishment suffered by the patient, augmented by her own self-disqualifying and self-annulling gestures and acts. As soon as the latter (coded DA in the transcript) can be made recognisable to her, a more authentic Ego position can be helped to come into existence and express itself.

Th: … and no way for you to defend yourself any more at such a moment? (**XA**)
Pt: No.
Th: You cannot avoid the beating.
Pt: Yes … I cannot disconnect from that.
Th: What would be a way for you to defend, when being beaten up? Is there something you might need, a thing you could use?
Pt: I don't know …
Th: You're defenceless. (**MI**)
Pt: Yes … yes … it happens to me in many respects, this kind of cramp.

Here the therapist makes an implicit connection to the childhood experiences:

Th: Yes, defenceless, huh, without anything to defend you with. There is no tablecloth that you could get, no protecting blanket, no protecting wooden shield, nothing to find shelter, nothing.
Pt: No.

Again the therapist addresses the despair:

Th: Nothing, there's nothing you can crawl under? So unprotected? (**XA**)
Pt: Yes.
Th: Like a child that is being beaten up, without a chance to withdraw, that's how I imagine this.
Pt: Hm hm.
Th: You are watching yourself on the video recording, and you punish yourself, you cower, with no options to reciprocate. (**SE**)
Pt: Hm hm (nods).
Th: I would wish you to learn to reciprocate. It is very hard, you didn't learn it ... And it is there that you could learn to do more than you do now. You do not have it readily available, you should discover how to do it. (**RE, DA, SO**)
Pt: Hm hm.
Th: At least you might say something in return: keep your hands off me, don't mess with me, look at someone else, get lost, I don't need your judgement, I don't need your criticisms, I don't want your shit, I can do without you ... I'm just trying something ... (**SO**)
Pt: Well, yes, I do try even those things at times ... or rather, quite often, but they don't work.
Th: So you do try them.
Pt: Yes, I try.
Th: OK, so they don't work, but at least you do try them. That's very important. These things are not sufficient ...
Pt: No.
Th: ... but you do perform them. (**SO**)
Pt: Yes.
Th: What kind of things are they? What is it you are doing then? (**HP**)
Pt: Well, inside, I try ... to get out of something ... telling myself, "What are you involved in?" or "So what!"
Th: "So what"? How do you mean?
Pt: Something inside myself ...
Th: How do you mean?
Pt: When something happens to me, "So what?"
Th: That's what you're telling yourself, "So what? What does it matter?" (**DA**)
Pt: Yes! But it doesn't work!
Th: Aha, so you're saying "What does it matter", but in fact things do matter very badly ... (**MI**)

Pt: Yes.
Th: ... and you start reproaching yourself. (**SE**)
Pt: Yes.
Th: But fortunately there's at least something you are doing; you're not entirely quiet. (**SO**)
Pt: No, I'm not fully passive, I don't think so. No, I'm sure of it.

The therapist continues to reinforce the adaptive Ego functions rather than focusing on their self-punishing effects (**SO**):

Th: So there is a real kind of resistance, even though it is not good enough.
Pt: Yes, and that resistance just should stop! I oppress it! (patient demonstrates, with fists, her own self-oppression).

The therapist takes the patient's anger about her self-oppression as a signal that the self-oppression has become more ego-dystonic, and continues to support and reinforce the patient's adaptive expressions (**SO**):

Th: Yes, that's what it looks like.
Pt: I always oppress it, put it away.
Th: Yes.
Pt: And that's why I trivialise them .... I can often hear myself say, "Let it go, it's not that bad, it's not that bad!" But I've been telling this myself for all my life! (yelling) "It's not that bad! It's not that bad!"
Th: But about what are we talking? What is not that bad? (**DA**)
Pt: Eh, eh ... I don't know ... anything.

Notice that what is being called "resistance" here is considered by the therapist as a very authentic, though failing, attempt by the patient to protect herself.

Th: You're saying, "I trivialise the resistance, telling myself, 'It isn't that bad'". You are resisting something, and then ...
Pt: And then I nevertheless put it off ...
Th: So you're telling me that you oppress the resistance?
Pt: Yes ... and then I put it off ... and ... eh ...
Th: Then what are you opposing?
Pt: First I start with resisting, and then I tell myself, "Oh, leave it, oh, it isn't that bad, it doesn't matter."
Th: "Don't resist," that's what you're telling yourself. (**DA**)
Pt: Yes, actually I'm saying, "Don't resist."
Th: And "It doesn't matter" is about what? Being beaten? (**DA**)
Pt: Anything! Nothing matters any more!
Th: OK, so you just have to give up your resistance.
Pt: Yes! I just used to give it up!

Th: So the resistance is being attacked from behind, so to say, and then you drop it …
Pt: Yes, then I drop it.
Th: OK, so this is a very healthy resistance, but you do not keep it up. (**SO**, **XA**)
Pt: Indeed. And whenever it is there, it is there only for a moment!
Th: So it is already there. (**XA**)
Pt: Yes, but it does not go on.

The therapist perceives the patient as attempting to continue her anger towards herself for failing to maintain her resistance, and continues to support the adaptive Ego (**SO**):

Th: It does not go on, and it is not sufficient, not strong enough, not convincing enough.
Pt: Indeed.
Th: But it does exist, in fact, fortunately! (**XA**, **SO**)
Pt: Yes, but I cannot display it …
Th: … utilise it.
Pt: … go on with it, give it more expression … pfew!
Th: Yes … you cannot really unfold it. (**MI**)
Pt: No.
Th: Elaborate it, so that it can serve you. (**MI**)
Pt: Yes.
Th: And then again you are left behind, defenceless against all criticisms.
Pt: Yes, and then I get angry again, at myself, and so it goes and goes …
Th: Angry for having done what?
Pt: … then I get angry again, thinking things like, "Why didn't I resist, why didn't I do this or that?"
Th: So then you also get angry at yourself for not opposing? (**HP**)
Pt: Yes.

The therapist introduces the notion of a choice for her to defend or not defend herself. The anger at herself is restructured as intended by her for the activation of her own self-defence.

Th: Aha, so then in fact you have let yourself down, which you can become angry about, and so you can go on … (**DA**)
Pt: Yes, it goes on and on, I always keep going on in this circle.
Th: So … quickly … your anger is always your first response to yourself. (**HP**)

Here the patient has accepted and acquired the idea of self-defence as a desirable option. Hence, anger towards others can now become a topic of exploration, whereas it used to be only possible as a punishing anger towards herself, introjected from the parents. First this latter anger is kept in focus, and only after the independent Ego position has become more solid, can the former be explored more fully.

Pt: Yes, and that's so strange … when I'm angry and want to express it … I just put it aside …
Th: Hm.

Pt: … and then nothing has happened.
Th: Yes, you're good at that, huh, putting it aside … and then afterwards you get angry again for having done that. (**DA**)
Pt: Yes.
Th: So it is one boiling mass. (**MI**)
Pt: Yes.
Th: And what is missing is good protection, protection against your anger, protection against all nasty criticisms, of yourself against yourself, like criticisms that you do not hold your teacup as you should, or that you do not protect yourself well enough, or that you give up your resistance, or that there's something else that you're doing not well enough … Each time there's a new attack. (**SE**)
Pt: Hm hm.
Th: And you don't protect yourself well enough against all those attacks, huh? And from there new anger comes … And so you keep reproaching yourself for not defending yourself well enough against the reproaches …
Pt: Yes.
Th: And so the circle is closed. Right?
Pt: Yes, right. Yes.

00:17:25

Th: And what you need is a much better protection against all this anger. (**DA**)
Pt: (Nods)
Th: For it is not a pleasure to always be immersed in all that anger. (**XA**)
Pt: (Silent and non-responsive)

This may be correct, but nevertheless it may have been hard for the patient to deal with at this moment. The therapist therefore tries to re-establish contact with her, after he notices her withdrawal:

Th: I feel I have spoken too much and that I lost contact with you. (**RE**)
Pt: No, it's correct.
Th: And where are you … (**RE**)
Pt: I'm here.
Th: … and what are you feeling right now? (**XA**)
Pt: Restlessness! (sighs).
Th: Please describe it to me.
Pt: Restlessness, emptiness …

The therapist does not believe this:

Th: Emptiness?
Pt: Also sadness, I presume … a feeling of myself as … as just nothing.

Th: Aha, this is what you also said last time; I am just nothing at all!
Pt: Yes, and I'm feeling it again.
Th: And "nothing" is another word for "hopeless". (**XA**)
Pt: Hopeless, yes, you took the right word … hopeless.
Th: So very sad indeed.
Pt: Yes (angry voice), nasty, that's how I just feel, dismal, nasty.

The patient takes a position that is ambiguous, between active and passive. The therapist emphasises the suffering and passive position (**MI, DA**):

Th: So very much unprotected.
Pt: Y-yes.
Th: I think that is what it amounts to, that you are very vulnerable, and very much hurt …
Pt: Yes.
Th: … without being capable to do something against it, without having been able to withstand it …
Pt: Yes (whispering).

Again the therapist emphasises the passive experiences, hoping to trigger a more active Ego position:

Th: And nobody notices the sadness, because you are hiding yourself completely. (**MI**)
Pt: Yes, correct (whispering).
Th: Can you feel this hopelessness?
Pt: Yes (whispering) … yes (sighing).

The therapist does not want the patient to withdraw:

Th: Yes. Please describe it to me. (**RE**)
Pt: The shame also.
Th: Also that …
Pt: It flashed through my mind (swings her left hand horizontally, from left to right, along her face, as if to apologise and to illustrate the strength of the impulse).

00:21:04

Th: Yes.
Pt: You looked at me …
Th: I look at you?
Pt: Yes, and then … (repeats the hand movement several times) … I just feel ashamed.
Th: You also feel ashamed … because I am looking at you. (**RE**)
Pt: Yes.
Th: Because of everything that is being shown to my eyes.

Pt: Yes.
Th: And what are those things that are being shown? What is it that makes you feel ashamed so much?
Pt: Well, perhaps it is because I am vulnerable.
Th: Yes, might be … yes, that is what is shown to my eyes, that you are vulnerable …
Pt: (Nods)
Th: … and in fact this should not become visible to me.
Pt: (Nods) Indeed.

The therapist probes for projections (**DA**):

Th: And then you feel my mockery, my contempt?
Pt: It does flash through my mind, yes.
Th: Does it? And do you also notice it on me, do you see it on me? (**RE**)
Pt: No, I don't think so.
Th: But that's what you think.
Pt: But your gaze is so penetrating.
Th: Do you notice any mockery or contempt in my attitude or manners?
Pt: No, but just this penetrating thing already makes me nervous.
Th: Makes you already afraid that I may feel this, feel the contempt, so that you will feel compelled to be ashamed for me looking at you …
Pt: Yes.
Th: … for then I can see something that I am not entitled to see, huh? That cannot be good, or so …
Pt: Well, another flash goes … "stupid", "stupidness".
Th: That I find you stupid? (**DA**)
Pt: Yes.
Th: Aha. … Is that also what you can see on me, that I find you stupid? Or just a thought? (**RE**)
Pt: It just flashed through my mind.
Th: Aha. It must be very unrealistic to you that I come to see so much of you, whereas actually I do not behave in the way that you're so afraid of. You're afraid that I feel contempt, that I find you stupid, ridiculous … that you will have to be ashamed towards me. All this flashes through your mind, but actually in my behaviour there is not so much that would indicate any such thought in me. (**RE**)
Pt: Yes, but it is because of that penetrating way of looking at me …
Th: Yes, but this very look of me is not yet the same as any opinion of mine that you are stupid, or is it?
Pt: No, it isn't.
Th: I look at you, yes, I have been looking at you, yes, indeed, that's what I have been doing, that's right, but it is a way for me to stay concentrated.
Pt: Yes, I know, but I can't help it, but actually I then feel like hiding there in the corner of the room.

The therapist senses that the patient is feeling guilty, following the therapist's explanation for his penetrating gaze that sounded like an apology. The therapist offers a mirroring intervention (**MI**), in order to continue ego-enhancement and in order to offer an alternative to her own explanation of the gaze.

Th: But actually that's also what I stay looking at … while looking at you, I have been imagining a child hiding itself in a corner, perhaps that's why my looks are like that … I have been watching that child, imagining you hiding yourself somewhere … And apparently this feels very unpleasant to you, when I look at you that way.
Pt: (Nods)
Th: As if I find you stupid … Imagine that I do not find you stupid, imagine that I do not feel contempt for what you have been telling me and for what you have been showing me. Can you imagine that, or is it too far-fetched, too hard? (**SO**)
Pt: (Sighs) Yes, but only rationally so.
Th: Only rationally, for your feelings are telling you the opposite.
Pt: (Nods)
Th: So now you are projecting upon me all mean judgements about you; I have become the angry eye, watching you like you might watch yourself when seeing today's video recording … It is with such a meanness that I am looking at you right now. (**DA, RE**)
Pt: (Nods)
Th: So now it is between us, huh? (**RE**)
Pt: Yes.

The therapist aims at inducing a further rise of transference:

Th: And can you still find a way to protect yourself against me, against my looks, my mean looks, my mean judgements about you? (**DA**)
Pt: (Makes the "flashing" hand movement) At times by rationalising.

The therapist senses a deepening of the patient's affect, in particular, of her sadness.

Th: That's what you're capable of; to realise that it is not like that.
Pt: And in the meantime, there was a dreary … (makes the hand movement) and I felt. You're looking at me in such a way, I will be beaten.
Th: Beaten by me?
Pt: Yes!
Th: Is that how I am looking at you? (**RE**)
Pt: Yes!
Th: To that extent! So you are not only seeing how angry I am looking at you, but also that I am abusing you. (**DA**)
Pt: I do know that that's not the case, but it does flash through me! (flashing hand movements, now with both hands, desperate voice).

Th: It's good that you are aware that that is not how it is, but it also shows how very vulnerable you are feeling. When you feel so vulnerable, someone may promptly start to beat you, abuse you … Very grim, painful. And you can protect yourself by thinking "Oh no, that is not what he is doing; oh no, that is what I am myself making out of it; this is not what is really happening here." (**SO, MI, DA**)

Pt: (Nods)

Th: But you do feel as if I can start doing so right now. I would not even dare to think of doing so, of course.

Pt: Indeed (whispering).

Th: But you nevertheless do have the fantasy that I would be willing to do so … It reveals how vulnerable you are feeling, undefended … that if you are feeling so undefended, someone just might beat you … without any chance for you to strike back. I would be happy if you would learn in fact to strike back, to do more, though I don't want you to beat me, but to defend yourself better. (**DA, MI, XA, RE, SO**)

Pt: (Sigh, whispering) Yes, so would I.

Th: And what you have learned is that it never works and that it is never good enough, so that you'd better not try it. (**XA**)

Pt: (Nods)

Th: "Resistance is futile" is the expression, huh?

Pt: Yes.

Th: Utterly fruitless.

Pt: That's the point … ehm … ehm … I don't have control of myself … I would like to … but I do not manage … Like what happened right now … I feel that myself becoming hard and stiff …

Th: And then you become very anxious … you responded with a lot of fear. (**AA**)

Pt: And then … I am no longer capable of responding.

Th: Yes.

Pt: And …

Th: Then you are so much afraid, that you tense up entirely. (**AA, MI**)

Pt: Yes.

Th: Yes, and you need to discover that I will not do you any harm; that I do not feel the contempt that you are projecting; that I do not find you stupid, as you are projecting; that I am not going to abuse you, as you are projecting. All these things seem to be impending at the moment, and it is so hard to relax and get out of the cramp. (**RE, DA**)

Pt: Hm hm.

The therapist notices that the patient is less tense and mirrors to the patient that she is more relaxed (**MI**):

Th: There seems to be some relaxation right now, as if you discover that things are not that bad.

Pt: (Nods)

Th: Do you see me right now as a person involved in treating you aggressively? (**RE**)
Pt: No.
Th: With contempt in my eyes, mockery, and the like ... (**RE**)
Pt: No.
Th: Not.
Pt: Not now, but just a while ago it all came to the surface and flashed around.

The therapist tries to make the unconscious alliance more explicit and to reinforce the patient's openness towards him, both by recognising the patient's emotional qualities and by pointing out that the communicative acts performed by the patient are steps in which her Ego acted less inadequately than before:

00:32:16

Th: Yes, yes I can believe that ... And at least you can tell me all these things. (**RE**, **SO**)
Pt: Yes, yes (smiles).
Th: So to that extent there is still some confidence [in me, as a therapist], huh? **(RE)**
Pt: Yes, that is a true word.
Th: Actually it's a beautiful thing, this also being the case.
Pt: Yes.
Th: We've been together into a horrible abyss, where tremendous fear and hopelessness exist, hopeless, helpless ..., where only evil is to be expected ... but you managed to show it to me. It was a kind of guided trip for tourists; not so nice a one ... but perhaps it is a tasteless metaphor ... I came as a kind of outsider and I was introduced by you, in order to explore this area. **(RE)**
Pt: Yes.
Th: If I were to do this every day on my vacation, I would not have nice holidays, so I would not recommend this for tourists. It is hard work, and it has been hard work for you to show me, but very important for you to do so.
Pt: (Nods) Yes.

The therapist recognises, more explicitly, the isolation in which the burden has been carried:

Th: For I think you have been lonely here for a very long time. (**XA**)
Pt: Funny, isn't it.
Th: What?

Patient happily receives the recognition about her own communicative steps:

Pt: As you put it, "You have shown it to me", it relieves me, actually.
Th: I am happy to hear so. At least it decreases your isolation, huh, when you can show it, even though it is ghastly what you show ... It comes from very far ... It has been there for a long time. It is not over, but it is less hidden now. (**XA**)

00:35:55

The patient recognises her own communicative steps and her enhanced Ego position:

Pt: Yes ... I think, the way you put it, is very beautiful (voice breaking with sadness).
Th: What is it you heard me saying?
Pt: This idea that you're a tourist and I am guiding you.

The therapist begins to conclude the session. We rejoin the session three minutes later:

00:38:22

Pt: Strange! ... there is kind of gladness in me now, due to all this.
Th: Great!
Pt: Glad and sad.
Th: Yeah, how different from angry. (**XA**)
Pt: Therefore I think it I should watch the video!
Th: Be careful, small fragments may be sufficient.
Pt: Yes but I feel it as "today's video, I want to watch it!"
Th: Yes.

Subsequent developments

The therapy unfolded as follows. There was an ongoing growth of self-respect and awareness of her capacities to protect herself against her family and others, and, more basically, against her own self-criticisms. Depressive and compulsive phenomena diminished and openness towards the therapist increased. The patient shared and elaborated with the therapist a variety of additional traumatic experiences. Although the therapy was not yet finished at the time of writing, the developments described herein turned out to have been crucial for the course of her recovery during the half year that was to come.

Conclusions

In the therapy described above, the patient accepted the therapist's invitation to introduce him into her fantasies of being dismissed, and her subsequent mixed sense of joy and gladness can be understood as a confirmation that she did receive the therapist's presence as an *amendment* to her fantasy of being dismissed, thereby experiencing an interaction that opposed and countered the long-term traumatic neglect perpetrated by her parents. What mattered was that the patient introduced the therapist into her realm of isolation, where an adequate differentiation between self and other had been missing and where the patient's sense of identity was predominantly defined by hostile introjections. Though this can be understood in terms of therapeutic maieutics, that is, helping the deep affects be excavated towards their full expression (Osimo, 2003), it is, I think, not only the expression of the deep affect that was of importance here, but also the origination of a kind of relationship that was new to the patient—one in which she was allowed to export her intolerable feelings and project them onto and into the therapist, who was willing to contain them. As a result, she opened up and made her hostile issues accessible as topics of conversation. The therapist's job was to create a safe environment in which the patient was enabled to distinguish her own Ego position as the locus of her own identity, as distinct from her self-dismissing Superego. It is the creation of this space and the patient's experience of it that, I think, comes before the deep affects can be worked through. Interpersonal transitional space was created as transference rose.

The patient's self-disapproving, self-demanding, self-dismissing, self-devaluing, self-rejecting, self-neglecting, and self-ignoring attitudes were manifestations of her Superego pathology, but the patient could not recognise them as alien to her as she had a strong identification with her parents who had disapproved of her so strongly. The therapist therefore offered special support to the part of the patient that suffered from all these criticisms, approaching it as the abandoned child, or the unsupported Ego, that had sought refuge in her room all those years ago. First, the therapist drew the patient's attention to the abandoned child part of her that deserved their attention. Second, it was highlighted as a position in serious need of a better defence against the Superego reproaches and criticisms. Third, new ways for it to defend itself were identified, and previous authentic (though failing) attempts at its own defence that had already been ventured were recognised, affirmed, and validated. This task was dominant throughout the entire session. Connections between the patient's current self-criticism, and the past criticisms of the parents, were pointed out to the patient, to render the self-criticisms less ego-syntonic. Therapeutic interventions were primarily concerned with clarifying these links to the patient and helping her to turn against the self-dismissing part of her Superego, thereby helping her move towards relinquishing the self-harming defences and demands, and to better make use of her new experience and knowledge of her emotional life in order to develop more self-valuing and self-compassionate internal representations. More specifically, the therapeutic job was to deal with the punishing Superego, and to undo the patient's identification with it. Hence, many interventions are coded as SE. However, the therapist's attempts to approach and support the hidden child brought the patient into a state of alarm, as if they constituted for her a new type of attack. Nevertheless, an unconscious alliance was established between us, becoming manifest in her various explicit reports of hostile projections towards the therapist that "flash" through her mind, that she was willing, and even eager, to mention. When, by the end, the therapist mentions this alliance (in terms of her confidence in him, due to which she could take him on the "guided tour") she could recognise it and feel both joy and sadness. This can be taken as a more open position, in which her ego-adaptive capacities had become enhanced so that self-criticisms were less dominant, and less damaging. The invitation to open up had been accepted.

In helping the patient to shift into a more open position, the therapist worked on their real relationship. First, as previously stated, the patient's Ego was vulnerable and in need of support, and the therapist directed the patient's attention to that vulnerability, and the necessity for her to regain powers in order to defend herself. Then he created the opportunity for the patient to experience and express her paranoid fears. This permissive role not only confirmed the existence of those feelings, but also situated them within an ongoing conversation with the therapist, thus contributing to the definition of their real relationship as one in which feelings can be expressed and investigated safely—without undermining the relationship. At the same time, the therapist repeatedly brought the patient to relate her fears to his actual behaviours. Thus the real relationship was confirmed simultaneously to the exploration of the fears. As a result, a safe space was built in which the patient could both explore her feelings, and experience the stability of the contact with the therapist.

A final remark: naïve objects

It is clear in the above vignette that the patient's self-reproaches had a self-referential character. They pertain to her lack of ego-power and her subsequent self-negation. Accordingly, she reproaches herself for being too submissive towards her own reproaches. It is of interest, both practically and theoretically, that this vicious circle breaks down as soon as the identification of her Ego with a harshly judgemental Super-ego position starts to weaken.

The practical interest, of course, is that it helps a patient escape from self-directed impairments. Theoretically, however, the issue is of interest as it illustrates the absence of a critical distance for this patient, whereby she does not distinguish (the positions of) her two parts—her Ego and Superego—that she sees as identical. It is the impossibility for the patient to make this distinction that is most difficult to imagine for the critical observer, the therapist. I have called this type of non-distinction a naïve way of perceiving, and the objects thus perceived "naïve objects" (Goudsmit, 1998, 2009). Naïve objects are experiential entities, defined in terms of an absence of differentiation between what is perceived and how it is being perceived. Hence, a naïve object is experienced as an immediate given, and by definition its way of being experienced is not reflected upon. This is a more general formulation of the idea, as presented in object relations theory, that individual subjectivity has to develop within social relationships. In the case presented here, the patient does not differentiate between her angry self-reproaches and the incapacitated Ego. Her upcoming distinction between these two is not an abstract intellectual accomplishment. Instead, it happens through the creation, within (and due to!) the shared space, of a new naïve object. In the case presented here this new naïve object pertains to the patient herself, as suffering from her own vulnerability. This is what she comes to experience as a really existing identity of herself. Thus, the new naïve object comes to replace the old one. Experiential dynamic psychotherapy explicitly deals with such new naïve objects, and the interpersonal therapeutic space can be made available as their locus of origination.

References

Bion, W. R. (1962). *Learning from Experience.* London: Heinemann.

Bowlby, J. (1969). *Attachment. Attachment and Loss, Vol. 1.* London: Routledge.

Davanloo, H. (1990). *Unlocking the Unconscious: Selected Papers of Habib Davanloo, MD.* New York: John Wiley & Sons.

Goudsmit, A. L. (1998). *Towards a Negative Understanding of Psychotherapy.* (Doctoral dissertation, University of Groningen, the Netherlands, 1998.) http://irs.ub.rug.nl/ppn/174290861.

Goudsmit, A. L. (2009). Sense and self-referentiality in living beings. *Biosemiotics*, *2*: 39–46.
ten Have-de Labije, J. (2010). *The Collected Writings of Josette ten Have-de Labije, PsyD*. Minneapolis, MN: Tasora.
Klein, M. (1975). *Envy and Gratitude, and Other Works, 1946–1963*. New York: Free Press.
Neborsky, R. J. (2010). *The Collected Writings of Robert J. Neborsky, MD*. Minneapolis, MN: Tasora.
Osimo, F. (2003). *Experiential Short-Term Dynamic Psychotherapy: A Manual*. Bloomington, IN: AuthorHouse.
Winnicott, D. W. (1971). *Playing and Reality*. London: Penguin.

PART III

TRAINING AND RESEARCH

CHAPTER FOURTEEN

Group Intensive Experiential-Dynamic Psychotherapy in a public mental health service

Silvia Landra

This chapter describes how EDT, specifically Intensive Experiential-Dynamic Psychotherapy (IE-DP), was applied in a group setting within the Servizio Sanitario Nazionale (Italian national health service), specifically the School of Psychiatry of Milan University, by two co-therapists, Silvia Landra and Ferruccio Osimo. The origins and some relevant aspects of group analysis will be introduced. The rationale for the group approach and several relevant aspects of the group IE-DP treatment, including selection of patients, information about their presenting problems, and outcomes at one-month follow-up will be described. Nine learning points that emerged from review of video recordings of the group therapy sessions will be summarised and illustrated with transcript from the group psychotherapy. It will be noted that, in comparison with individual therapy, the sense of the co-therapists was that, within the group setting, there was an acceleration of the process in which patients learn to recognise anxiety manifestations and defences, and focus on emotional experience. The importance of a trial relationship prior to group treatment will be highlighted, and indications and contraindications for a group treatment approach will be outlined. The author concludes that the group IE-DP approach yielded encouraging results for resistant patients with Superego pathology, and that the group setting lends itself to Self- and Other-restructuring.

Group analysis and IE-DP

Group analysis is almost one century old. The term itself was introduced by Burrow (1927) and taken up by Foulkes (1964), who systematised the theoretical concepts of group psychotherapy. With Bion, Foulkes formed various therapy groups in 1948, at the Tavistock Clinic, elaborating on the clinical experience gained with soldiers during World War II. This enabled him to better articulate innovative concepts such as "matrix", a term also first introduced by Burrow in the first decades of the twentieth century.[1]

The theories on group dynamics already investigated in social psychology (e.g., Levy Moreno, 1932; Lewin, 1936) cross-fertilised productively with the foundations of psychoanalysis, to the point that Foulkes (1975) defined group-analytic psychotherapy as "a method of treatment by the group of the group, including its conductor … The therapist-analyst helps in this process and puts his or her knowledge and education at the service of the group" (pp. 97–99). Paraphrasing Neri (1995), in groups we deal with a "network" because the individual is seen as a nodal point of a number of relationships, symbolically represented in the group. Moreover, we are in a "field", the special space formed when various individuals place their mental contents, unconscious fantasies and images in the same container, so as for these to be processed by the group itself, with the therapist's guidance, producing emotional transformations and thought operations.

Various authors regarded the group as having the potential of enhancing and deepening the therapeutic work of each individual, thanks to the materialising of a group psychic apparatus, described by Kaes (1993) as a "system involving a high number of disparate elements, in multiple relations, generator of sub-systems" (pp. 123–124, translated by the author from the French original). According to Bion (1961), the activation of an individual's Self in the group enables the individual to get in touch with primitive aspects of the mind, and a space is created in which different time frames overlap and many relationships among group members in the here-and-now are made possible.

More recently, Yalom (1995) discussed the potential of group therapy to instil hope through group members witnessing improvements in others, and how patients who tended to be socially isolated and lacking emotionally intimate relationships could feel more in touch with the world through learning that others have similar problems. Yalom also highlighted how, through helping fellow group members, a patient can develop a more positive sense of Self, and how helpful it could be to receive responsive, honest, and direct feedback from fellow group members on interpersonal behaviour and defences. In the Netherlands, residents at De Viersprong (The Crossroads) in Halsteren participate in an intensive treatment programme that combines individual and group psychotherapy. Of interest to the present chapter, as part of their treatment, a group of nine patients each undertake an individual Intensive Short-Term Dynamic Psychotherapy (ISTDP) within a group setting, that is, with the other group members as an audience (Cornelissen & Verheul, 2002). This provides an opportunity for the patients to learn from others and about themselves through their own experience of therapy as well as through witnessing the work of fellow patients. In particular, they can "see each other in the same position they themselves are, over and over again. As such, they might for instance focus on witnessing the development of the working alliance with the psychotherapist or choose to resist it, depending on whether this reflects their own problems with this aspect of the treatment" (Cornelissen, 2001, p. 152). Cornelissen further suggests that "witnessing each others' sessions indirectly enhances the level of the working alliance and also helps to acquaint oneself with the basics of ISTDP … [which] will prove to multiply the effect and outcome of the therapy for each individual member" (p. 152). We had good reason to believe that offering a group IE-DP would harness the same therapeutic factors.

The context and rationale for group IE-DP

The IE-DP approach and related methodologies offer us therapists the opportunity to engage in a real and lively relationship with our patients, in which we combine depth of analytical understanding with every effort to foster the acceleration in the therapeutic process by means of the three main dynamic activities: (i) defence restructuring, (ii) anxiety regulation, and (iii) emotional maieutics (Osimo, 2003). In 2007, Ferruccio suggested to his team the idea of testing IE-DP in a group context within the School of Psychiatry of Milan University. At first, I wondered to what extent the speed and power of the model would retain their effectiveness in a group setting, and whether the therapeutic ingredients of IE-DP might successfully combine with the energy and power of group analysis in catalysing an effective therapeutic process. On thinking this through, however, the challenge felt more and more appealing. First, in public health services any choice that allows us to respond to the greatest number of requests, working in the shortest possible time, is welcome. Group treatment certainly allows these two objectives to be achieved, particularly in a context (such as the Italian one) in which public psychotherapy is not yet resourced sufficiently to meet the actual and growing demand of the public for treatment. Second, in the field of psychotherapy it is important that practitioners have the courage to try out and evaluate new ways of working, as this will lead to innovation and development of more effective approaches. Third, merging two consolidated approaches into something new may give a chance of understanding their strong and weak points even more deeply. Fourth, if "only the presence of a good technique, accompanied by a relationship characterised by genuineness, spontaneity and authenticity can make the therapeutic work really effective" (Palvarini, 2009, p. 144), the group presents a significant number of real relationships whose energy can be therapeutically oriented.

Forming the group

We endeavoured to recruit patients who were similar in terms of life conditions and age in order to foster mutual identification, and reduce the risk of in-session emotional isolation. The usual contraindications for group therapy were considered. In particular, we excluded patients with psychotic illness, paranoid personality, severe episode of major depression and high suicidal risk, manic and agitation states, as well as those who relied heavily on projection.

In March 2007, eight patients were selected—four men and four women—between twenty-three and forty-one years of age, who sought help from the Servizio Sanitario Nazionale in Milan, mostly complaining of symptoms of anxiety and depression. In one case, obsessive-compulsive symptoms were present. Three patients had recently completed an individual psychotherapy. In each case, diagnostic assessment revealed a personality disorder that indicated dynamic-experiential therapy. About half were taking SSRI and/or benzodiazepine medication at the start of the group therapy.

As part of the selection procedure, each group member first participated in an individual, extended trial relationship session (see p. ?) in which their prevailing defensive styles, and the painful areas behind their initial complaints were identified. This helped the future group members to become familiar with the experiential-dynamic approach, producing some shift from the

Table 1.

NAME	*AGE*	*AXIS I AXIS II dagnosis*	*Personality profile, character defences, notes of personal history*	*GAF*
PETER	28	Dysthymia Narcissistic	*Highly self-sabotaging / flees one step away from the goal.* Reports many incidents in which he failed to attain meaningful goals even though they were consistent with his lively intelligence and many practical skills, for example, shortly before undertaking therapy, refused a job in director's office. Poor sense of Self and future planning. Past history of humwiliating and sadistic treatment from mother, the only parent who lived with him. Lives with his girlfriend. Frequent misunderstandings and fights give him a chance to take the blame on himself "because [he] behaves weird and wrong".	42
MADELEINE	23	Anxiety disorder Borderline	*Puts herself across as an exuberant and slightly rebellious adolescent, jaunty and outgoing, a horse-lover, this being her life passion.* This conceals very painful experience as a child brought up by her grandparents after her parents' stormy separation, and who often ended up in the emergency unit for "certain stomach aches that got better with Valium". As an adolescent, suffered from bulimia. Now asks for therapy due to anxiety and depressive inner feelings that in the past she always obstinately dealt with, "without asking anyone for help". Family were very blaming and abusing, for example, she recalls father told her, "If you do badly at school, I will kill myself," and her grandmother often telling her, "If you misbehave, remember that this is not your home and that I am not obliged to put you up." She is unable to find a steady job or to graduate (fine arts), but has a seemingly good-enough relationship with her boy friend. Is on SSRI at the start of therapy.	40
ROBERT	35	Depressive episode Avoidant	*Isolates himself and puts a distance with others.* At consultation reported a not-wholly-resolved depressive episode, much more pervasive than previous ones, following yet another separation from his girlfriend after moving in with her. Wonders in amazement "what makes it always go wrong!?". Comes from a family of musicians, is a musician himself, and teaches singing to musical performers. His working performance is excellent, as is his social presentation, but, "In my intimate relations my handbrake is on." Father irascible, puts him down, mother absent-minded and "childish". Experienced his relationship with both parents as "vague and superficial". Is on SSRI at the start of therapy.	46

(Continued)

Table 1. *(Continued)*.

NAME	*AGE*	*AXIS I AXIS II dagnosis*	*Personality profile, character defences, notes of personal history*	*GAF*
ANNIE	39	Dysthymia Dependent	*Falls into silence and fades away*. Holds back a lot of painful feelings in an ongoing effort not to be a burden for anyone. Learnt this from very early" in her life when her mother, a serious heart disease sufferer and often bedridden, unconsciously designated her, her youngest child, as her nurse and carer. She would do her homework at mother's bedstead, could not raise her voice nor touch her mum too much, and often her gestures of affection were not returned, "because mum is very tired". After mother's death, when Annie turned ten, she went on successfully with her school and social activities. Currently, she works for the disabled, holding a management role. Nonetheless keeps on concealing her Self and is afraid of encroaching upon others, to the extent of being unable to speak out vis-à-vis her colleagues, and, in spite of her personal sensitivity, cannot get deeply involved with anybody. At the start of therapy she is on SSRI, and has a boyfriend who lives 400 miles away, but seems unconcerned with the distance problem.	48
GEORGE	41	Panic Attacks Obsessive-Compulsive	*Jokes about everything*. For some years, gripped by frequent and severe panic attacks, for no apparent cause, involving admission at the emergency unit, followed by discharge with prescription of anti-anxiety medication. Married to a Peruvian woman, and is the father of a two-year-old girl, whom he described proudly, but with whom he had fits of rage. A physics graduate, he is unhappy with his current job, tormented by his role and by regarding his personal skills as inadequate. States that "paternal authority" was always difficult for him to deal with and reports difficulty in handling his anger, which is often disproportionate to the stimulus. Is on SSRI and benzodiazepine at the start of therapy.	46
HELEN	34	Agoraphobia Dependent	*Uses phobic symptoms in passive-aggressive way, often resorts to the mechanism of splitting*. For about two years she has been afraid to move about alone—even only performs simple everyday chores if accompanied by friends/acquaintances. She defines as "frank" the way she sees her symptom. However, it rather sounds like a remarkably split perception of reality, separating the good from the bad and opposing the "befores" and the "afters", for instance, she would not speak with her mother-in-law "because she is a snake"; she shares nothing with her husband "because he is a saint". Frequently attacks without appeal those who desert/do not value her, just as in the past her parents allegedly often did. Mother of two young girls, is married to a man "who does not give her any emotion". She works in the administration of a small family-run business. At the start of therapy, displayed various certainties that were beyond discussion, but perceived her phobic symptom as weird and utterly incomprehensible.	46

(Continued)

Table 1. *(Continued).*

NAME	*AGE*	*AXIS I*	*AXIS II dagnosis*	*Personality profile, character defences, notes of personal history*	*GAF*
JOHN	40	OCD	Obsessive-Compulsive	*Calm, patronizing attitude, tends to hide his own needs from others.* Often involves his wife and two young children (one is a few months old) in his frequent and wearying rituals, centred around tidiness, cleaning, the care and perfect order of household objects. He is a train maintenance worker, where precision and time-keeping are his assets, but at home a practical operation can cause lengthy delays, his wife loses her temper, and children cry. Harbours great rage inside that he finds hard to feel and express. Often feels crushed by comparing himself with his authoritarian father. Painfully critical of his symptoms, but feels at a total loss with them. Is on SSRI medication, with poor effect, at the start of therapy.	46
SUSANA	32	Anxiety disorder	Avoidant	*Avoidant / tends to please.* Though being in a phase of her life in which many difficult issues seem to have settled, is often overcome by anxiety symptoms, depressive crying, and lack of self-confidence in making even small everyday choices in life. Knows how to put others at their ease, but is constantly worried lest she does not appear adequate, nor does she share her deeper emotions, especially anger. She is Peruvian and moved to Italy four years ago. Works in a haute couture fashion store and is an outgoing and refined shop assistant. Married for a year, she describes her emotional relationship in positive terms. However, makes frequent comparisons with the relationship between her parents, described as "dependent". Perceived her mother as a strong and authoritarian character "who would carry her husband like a rucksack", and would often ill-treat her children, the patient above all.	48

request to free them from their anxious, depressive, or compulsive symptoms, to a motivation to improve their own unsatisfactory relational patterns. Each of the two therapists conducted a trial relationship with four patients, and the selection was based on (i) detecting at least one Axis II disturbance on top of Axis I symptomatology; (ii) good-enough level of emotional activation, and (iii) lack of clear contraindications.

Patients who were suitable for group treatment were offered weekly group therapy sessions of one and a half hours' duration. A summary of their presenting problems is presented in table 1. It was decided to offer a one-year therapy (from April 2007 to April 2008) consisting of thirty-eight sessions which were scheduled in advance of the group starting. All sessions were video recorded. Outcome evaluation (see table 2) was based on the administration of the Symptom Checklist-90-R (Derogatis, 1994) and clinical interviews consistent with the approach described by Malan (1976a, b). Both the clinical interview and the SCL-90 were administered on three occasions: (i) at assessment, (ii) at mid-therapy, and (iii) one month after termination. At termination of therapy, five patients achieved satisfactory results and did not require or request further therapy. Two patients were improved, and asked to continue with individual sessions. One patient dropped out after session 8.

Table 2.

NAME	*GAF AFTER (BEFORE)*	*MEDICATION AFTER (BEFORE)*	*Life situation, one month after the end of group IE-DP. Life changes and psychodynamic considerations. Medication, AXIS I, AXIS II, and GAF modifications.*
PETER	52 (42)	No medication (no medication)	Peter's emotional involvement in the group alternated between phases of utter pessimism and remoteness, and those of apparent excitement and optimism. The way he portrayed his life—from past to current—was always depicted in inescapably sadistic and utterly hopeless colours. This split and conflict-laden perception of life did not fail to imbue the therapeutic pathway as well. In session thirty-seven, Peter actually threw to the group a defeatist and radical description of what he called his own therapeutic failure. The therapists, with the help of a by now expert group, were able to recognise this massively regressive acting out, triggered by the threat of breaking the group bond, in view of the imminent end of the therapy, turning it to the benefit of the whole group. An extract of this session is reported herein. In the individual post-therapy session, Peter was able to acknowledge what he accomplished, that is, a partial, but meaningful, crack in his ruthlessly sadistic Superego, which denied him praise or reward over his accomplishments. He was actually able to express his joy over the news that his girlfriend at last managed to get pregnant. *Overall:* GAF moderately increased; some sense of worthiness and personal value. Partial, but crucial, modification of his all-pervading sadistic Superego. Negligible personality modifications.
MADELEINE	40 (40)	SSRI (SSRI)	Her presence in the group was erratic and, after her second consecutive absence, she welcomed the therapist's telephone proposal to interrupt the therapy. In an individual session she was helped to express her own malaise in dealing with the others whom she perceived as "further ahead and more capable". She had a sense of being like a sponge, absorbing others' suffering. The unit met her request to undertake individual psychotherapy. *Overall:* no change. Her ego-fragility was wrongly assessed at consultation—she was bright and insightful with others, which made us underestimate the extent to which she would passively resonate with others' anxiety, feeling unable to elaborate on her own feelings. The group had a chance to elaborate Madeleine's abandonment, by sharing inner feelings of fear and failure in the subsequent sessions. What springs to mind is Madeleine's statement, "I am someone who leaves the scene before showing her faults." As therapists, we were left wondering whether it could have been possible to grant her even more support in the group setting.

(Continued)

Table 2 *(Continued)*

NAME	*GAF AFTER (BEFORE)*	*MEDICATION AFTER (BEFORE)*	*Life situation, one month after the end of group IE-DP. Life changes and psychodynamic considerations. Medication, AXIS I, AXIS II, and GAF modifications.*
ROBERT	60 (46)	No medication (SSRI)	Robert is the patient who most of all expressed effort to "learn the method" on the others, so as to later apply it upon himself. In the early sessions, the therapists let him take the position of the interested spectator, who "does not know what to say of himself", but "listens willingly", consoling himself at hearing that others too have problems in their close relationships. In this way, Robert gains meaningful understandings of the whole group and, unlike Madeleine, manages to "give them back" for everyone to work on it. In session 7 he is "put into a corner" by the others, who invite him to focus on his inability to "be with women"—which he by now calls his *leitmotif*—a hitherto un-modifiable, ego-syntonic character defence. At that point, the therapists contribute a close challenge, allowing Robert to experience intense sadness over his deep loneliness that has old roots. He is able to elaborate on his childhood memory in which "he never well knew whom to talk to". In the course of therapy Robert got engaged to a girl younger than him, feeling rather amazed at this bond, since he had always had relationships with women older than him. At first he tended to minimise and devalue that relationship, but then began to deal with his fear of being accepted and his terror of being left alone again. At the end of the therapy interview he declares that his symptoms have gone, which is confirmed by the SCL-90. *Overall*: GAF substantially increased; depressive and anxiety symptoms resolved; resolved the fear of loneliness, breaking free from self-depriving Superego and renunciation of avoidant position.
ANNIE	65 (48)	No medication (SSRI)	In the early sessions Annie seldom spoke, and only if stimulated by others. However, her capacity to slip into the dialogue gradually and steadily increased, revealing that she was actually working a lot within herself, sometimes by means of the steps accomplished by others. Around halfway through the therapy, with the therapist's active help, Annie managed to fully re-experience her grief, mourning the loss of her mother. She came to the awareness that she needed to break free from the role of "carer", "who has to bear the mourning" and thus cannot feel any joy. In the subsequent weeks she made the decision to move to another city to live with her boyfriend, after having searched carefully for a new job, suiting her professional skills. At the end of the therapy Annie reported the disappearance of her anxiety and of the depressive states that had often gripped her. *Overall*: GAF much increased; symptom resolution; broke free from imprisoning Superego and renunciation of dependent position.

(Continued)

Table 2 *(Continued)*

NAME	*GAF AFTER (BEFORE)*	*MEDICATION AFTER (BEFORE)*	*Life situation, one month after the end of group IE-DP. Life changes and psychodynamic considerations. Medication, AXIS I, AXIS II, and GAF modifications.*
GEORGE	58 (46)	No medication (SSRI + Benzodiazepines)	From the start, George expressed himself a lot in the group, having fair communicational skills, and often resorted to the tactical defence of trivialisation. This was repeatedly pointed out by the therapists and, later, in an advanced phase of therapy, also by his fellow group members, who helped George to focus on his fits of rage over which he felt unpleasantly helpless. In session 3, he experienced an important breakthrough of anger at his overpowering and emotionally distant father. Idealisation of father reduced, and he gained a new awareness of the connection between the rage inside him and his panic attacks. However, after a phase of symptomatic and subjective improvement, during which he almost stopped resorting to benzodiazepines to prevent panic attacks, George declared he was having a relapse of this symptom. Elaborating on this, transference feelings of anger and abandonment emerged in relation to the therapists and the end of the therapy. During therapy, he managed to change his job, finding one that suited his skills and interests. The relationship with his daughter was much improved. At the post-therapy individual session, one of the therapists (SL) met the patient's request for a few individual sessions. After eight individual sessions, centred on rage about separation, he seemed more stabilised. *Overall*: GAF moderately increased; panic attacks and rage symptoms much improved; evolution of Superego from punitive, sadistic, and devaluing/idealising, to more accepting, compassionate, and relaxed.
HELEN	56 (46)	No medication (no medication)	Helen participated actively from the very start, appearing resolute and self-confident, but staying locked behind her splitting mechanism, showing only one side of her. The group was often provided with opportunities to elaborate on her splitting defence, thanks to Helen's very special capacity to give many examples, share theories, and ask questions. The whole group often gave her their attention, co-operating with the therapists striving to get in touch with her emotional experiences, pausing on the contradictions in her reasoning. Helen was the first to disclose an important aspect of her life, her extramarital affair, giving herself a chance to elaborate on it with the help of the group. During the last few sessions, she managed to speak with her husband, asking to divorce him. This eventually made it possible to address various aspects of her relationship with others, along with her frequent splitting and denial. By the end of therapy her symptoms were significantly improved, but had not disappeared. *Overall*: GAF moderately increased; symptom much improved; partial freeing from depriving Superego, and reduction of dependence.

(Continued)

Table 2 *(Continued)*

NAME	*GAF AFTER (BEFORE)*	*MEDICATION AFTER (BEFORE)*	*Life situation, one month after the end of group IE-DP. Life changes and psychodynamic considerations. Medication, AXIS I, AXIS II, and GAF modifications.*
JOHN	53 (46)	SSRI (SSRI)	As with Annie, in the early sessions John seldom spoke, and only if stimulated by others. John, however, seemed more fearful. Although sporadically, and only if stimulated, he shared his own shy attempts at becoming more assertive with his wife and became more keen to focus on his own emotional experience, especially his fits of rage in interacting with his children. He slightly improved his ability to refrain from putting unfair prohibitions on his children and showing angry reactions if they failed to comply. While he was able to come to see the connection between his emotional aspects, anxiety, and exacerbation of his obsessive symptoms, at the end of the therapeutic path John reported substantial persistence of his OCD symptoms. He, however, made some subjective gain, since he asked to be put on a waiting list in order to take part in a future EDT group therapy. *Overall*: GAF slightly increased; symptoms virtually unchanged; some slight reduction of harshness of Superego and character rigidity.
SUSANA	62 (48)	No medication (no medication)	As early as the tenth session we observed, through frequent recognition by the group members themselves, a significant change. Renounced her anxious crying and continuous mulling over small daily decisions. Much more self-confident, she was able to resonate with the intense suffering of the child Susana who always had a sense that she had done wrong and was bound to match her harshly critical mother's expectations, without finding any support in her emotionally absent father. Much improved relations with work colleagues, whom she saw as less judgemental. Much more assertive. Emotional activation in the fourth session, when she wondered in a heartfelt manner, "What mother shall I become!", seemed pivotal to deep change. In session 6, revealed to the group she was pregnant, and her relief, alongside the trepidation, that she would have a chance to be a good mother to the child to be born. At the end of the therapy reported that her anxiety symptoms for which she sought help had disappeared. Did not need or request any further therapy. *Overall*: GAF much increased; symptom resolution; remarkable reduction of self-devaluing Superego and reduction of avoidant position.

Based on an analysis of the video recorded sessions, nine learning points arising from the fusion of two approaches, group analysis and IE-DP, stand out as being crucial in bringing about meaningful therapeutic effects. Although the relevance of these factors to outcome was not measured using specific scales, there is good evidence of their significance for the implementation of the experiential-dynamic activities (Osimo, 2003) and the EDT therapeutic ingredients in a group setting. In the pages that follow, these learning points, and the application of the therapeutic ingredients will be highlighted and discussed alongside transcript of the therapy.

Learning points and vignettes

When we think of IE-DP as a group treatment, from a dynamic and experiential perspective, the following nine points turn out as being especially relevant to a successful healing process.

1. PATIENTS AS CO-THERAPISTS

Patients tended to learn how to apply IE-DP techniques first in interactions with others, becoming "co-therapists", drawing fellow patients' attention to what was important therapeutically. The action of several observing and attentive Egos facilitated the therapeutic process, and tended to precede the individual patient focusing on their own internal dynamics and behaviour in relation to Self and Other.

2. DEFENCE RESTRUCTURING

From early group sessions, tactical defences become increasingly easy for patients to recognise, comment on to others, and undo. Even character defences could be addressed by fellow group members.

3. GROUP ANXIETY-REGULATION

The group setting brought about and facilitated a natural interaction in which anxiety was regulated through the tendency of group members to step in and take the floor. This natural phenomenon can be used by therapists to regulate anxiety.

4. OPPOSING SUPERFICIALITY

Therapists working within an IE-DP framework in a group setting may need to focus particularly on helping patients to recognise and relinquish defences of intellectualisation, rationalisation, trivialisation, and covering up with humour.

5. ALTERNATING GROUP AND INDIVIDUAL INTERVENTIONS

The overall IE-DP group process—based on this first experience—was characterised by a harmonious alternation between phases of emotional resonance in the whole group, in which group dynamics were at the forefront, and phases in which the focus was on one of the group members. Especially in "history taking, perspective, and portrayal" (HP) interventions (see Osimo, Chapter 3, pp. 54–60), when focusing on a specific incident in a group member's life, it was crucial to harness all the available attention, enhance the emotional sharing, and prevent diversions. In order to attain this, therapists' interventions were necessary in the early sessions. After the first breakthroughs had taken place, however, the other group members acted maieutically and, in so doing, these many "midwives" provided an exceptionally powerful holding environment to the experiencing person.

6. VIBRATING BY SYMPATHY

Characteristically, during phases of individual work on emotional experiencing, at which times the therapist (usually one at a time) was more active, there was attentive silence from other group members, who themselves tended to be experiencing mobilisation of feeling that was subsequently expressed to the group.

7. EMOTIONAL ACTIVATION

As in other group treatment approaches, members of an IE-DP group who were more guarded about or afraid of expressing themselves were desensitised to emotional experience and expression—or experienced a reduction in their affect phobia (McCullough et al., 2003)—and were encouraged by witnessing the efforts of their peers in expressing their feelings. Moreover, the IE-DP group therapist actively attended to the real relationship, enabling them to regulate their anxiety, and express their emotion.

8. TRANSFERENCE AND REAL RELATIONSHIP

Similar to other group treatment approaches, as an effect of the group interaction, transference phenomena involved not only the therapist(s) but other group members as well. This partitioning of transference facilitated the work of the IE-DP therapists, who were willing to enhance and value the most personal—and real—aspects of the relationships. Group members often "draw the therapists into the fray" thereby giving them an excellent chance to work on the here-and-now of the relationship, the same as in an IE-DP individual approach, disclosing personal aspects and feelings, and, in turn, inviting group members to recognise the emotions they experience towards the therapists. The possibility of exploring the emotions that emerged, while immersed in a social context, was an added value offered by the group setting. Moreover, the group itself represented a subject with which to interact. Indeed, we can consider the group "as totality, a set, an object representation" (Rouchy, 1998, p. 220, translated by the author from the French original), we must expect that there are "shifts of affect upon the group as an entity" (ibid., p. 221), and work fruitfully on these.

9. EMOTIONAL FOCUS

Patients experienced the process of recognising and naming emotions as a collective, stimulating and gratifying endeavour. They often had a sense of being like hounds, striving to detect something inside them, that they are not used to focusing upon and identifying in everyday life. It sometimes happened that a group member defensively demanded of a fellow group member that they are able to identify and name their emotion, as a deserved recompense to the patient-as-co-therapist's effort. This is indeed reminiscent of the initial phases of EDT training, in which trainees demand of a patient to deliver their emotion, again, as a deserved recompense to their therapeutic effort!

These points will be further highlighted in the clinical vignettes. The main therapeutic activities will also be highlighted, using the codes applied within the transcripts of the individual EDT treatments presented in other chapters of the book. A new code, "**GI**", is introduced here for therapist interventions addressing the group as a whole. Within the abundance of our videotaped material, amounting to fifty-seven hours of group sessions, I chose to focus on a few vignettes that illustrate the above learning points. Rendering the complexity of group interaction in writing was not dissimilar to the task of Sisyphus. In the transcript that follows, the therapists and patients are identified by their surnames and given names respectively.

Inhibitory forces and anxiety regulation

"When that hatch opens, you will be scared"

In the first session we observed that the patients, at least in the initial half hour, resorted to tactical defences (Davanloo, 2000), raising general issues with few specific examples from their own experience, and demonstrated paucity of contact with their emotions. They tended to direct their gaze downwards, sitting with arms crossed or hands placed beneath their legs. We could "breathe" a great deal of anxiety; some voices were trembling, others inexpressive. Some ironic comments by George aroused some nervous laughter. Most of the group members expressed in a veiled way the symptoms that led them to undertake psychotherapy. Robert favoured dialogue in an often pertinent and witty way, without ever mentioning the problem afflicting him. Susana and Helen tended to express concepts with many words, which most of the time distanced them from emotional experience. In contrast, John and Annie expressed themselves with few words, almost as if witnessing the ongoing dialogue "from afar". Madeleine seemed concerned about providing accurate answers and often asked for confirmation from others in regard to the validity of what she had said.

As each patient had already participated in an individual trial relationship extended interview, the *natural* task of the first group session was to measure up to the anxiety of sharing painful feelings with strangers. Therefore, in comparison with their behaviour in the trial relationships, the therapists limited their interventions to a focus on emotional state in the here-and-now (How is it for you being here? What does this arouse in you?), seeking to facilitate "making friends" and therapeutic alliance. After each therapist intervention there was an increase in the level of anxiety, and tactical defences were more frequently put into operation. It was immediately apparent that the group had the power to disperse anxiety through avoidance and diversion of attention away from emotional topics. The first observation I wish to make, therefore, is that, especially in the initial phase, the therapist was constantly faced with the choice of whether to let the group get rid of anxiety or, instead, keep the group's attention focused on the same subject, while regulating the anxiety, thereby enabling one or more participants to approach deep emotion.

As in an individual EDT, anxiety regulation can be attained by means of the therapist's direct intervention, as they detect anxiety signals and mirror them to the patient (vignette A-1, first part). However, from review of the group therapy video recordings we noted that direct anxiety regulation by the therapist was used less and less as therapy progressed. Rather, we observed a greater tolerance to anxiety by the group as a whole, and a growing disposition of the participants to reciprocally share episodes or images in which they recognise themselves, in this way regulating anxiety via collective work on the incident or metaphor described (vignettes A-2 and A-3). In addition, as the therapy progressed, the group members demonstrated an increased capacity to regulate each other's anxiety (vignette A-1, second part).

Vignette A-1—from session 1

Susana's tears are a manifestation of her anxiety, together with her fast speech and logorrhoea. The therapist realises that, by adequately regulating her anxiety, he can improve Susana's contact with her "small", insecure, and fearful part, which is seeking encouragement. In the previous half hour the group has been talking about fear of undertaking something new.

Susana: In the session [trial relationship] with Dr Osimo something emerged that got me thinking a lot; there is an adult Susana who deals with the situations when she has to—I must go to work, I must pay the bills, I must do the shopping … then, however, there is a completely different Susana who has to solve the simplest things that are a mountain for me. I am not able to climb up it! I am in anguish. I say to myself, I won't be able to make it, I won't make it, I won't make it and then at times I manage and at others I can't do it. The concept is a little ambiguous and I don't know exactly what it is that scares me. I find myself in a fruit salad or a stew and I can't solve it. At times I feel more at ease when I am on my own, because I have done many things in my life, I used to travel often and I get along fine with myself. When with others instead it feels like hard work to always be nice! In the three hour session I discovered that there is a child Susana inside me who drags some things along (tears well in her eyes): it is a Susana who has perhaps suffered for some things and for that reason at times I say, I can't make it, I don't believe in myself, it is a hard situation to manage (crying). Then I get very angry with myself and say that I had lived up to the age of eighteen years with my family, with mother who made me feel oppressed. Then I went to study in [name of city] and for ten years I lived on my own, and I took this chance to do things that I couldn't do in the small village. I travelled a lot, had various boyfriends. Before, nothing would happen, I would read a lot and say, I would like to have a life like that, more active. Then the time started when I was unable to have confidence in myself, until five years ago when I met my husband and he was a great help to me, above all in the moments when I felt the anguish and felt I would never make it (galloping and agitated speech). When I drove the car—I drive very badly and I could kill someone—he helped me say, who cares, these are just fears, but I have to do things! It makes me angry that I believe I have the capacity, and don't know why I find it hard to do things. So the anguish rises, my throat closes and I cry because I cannot control it. (Addressing the other group members) I see myself in everything you are saying and then I have some big problems with my small Susana. The problem that grips me is, one day, if I become a mother, how will I manage to do everything that a supermom does today?

The last question is almost disconnected from the previous discourse and confirms the patient's growing anxiety. The therapist reads many signs of anxiety but also grasps the sadness that is surfacing and tries to foster its expression.

Osimo: (Interrupting) How does the small Susana feel in telling these things to all of us? (**AA**, **XA**, **RE**)

Susana: At first, while I was talking, the anguish rose; now that I have said it, I feel a little better.

The first result obtained is that the patient "feels a little better"—that is, she is less anxious, slows down her speech, and lets herself get in touch with a part of her sadness. So the therapist invites her to stay with the small Susana, imagining a dialogue.

Osimo: What would this small Susana like to hear us say to her, to make her feel less sad? (**XA, RE**)

Susana: I don't know ... (sad facial expression and crying), maybe that I will be able to do some things, in any case, that I can make it, that I could be liked.

Her speech is slow now, but her breathing is in short breaths. Her facial expression conveys intense sadness.

Osimo: (Empathically) That we are very keen on her managing to do it! (**XA, SE**)

Robert: (Interrupting) Not making it does not mean losing. It is not a knockout race. It doesn't matter if you are not able to do something!

Madeleine: If you don't think too much about it, you might make it!

Susana: (Smiling) ... at times I relax, and then I manage to do things. At times I do the crazy thing of interacting with people I do not know to try and have a go and have the courage to say my own thing. There are times that I grant myself what I want and not what I must do.

Two patients stepped in to regulate Susana's anxiety "who relaxes and then manages", alluding unwittingly to a chance of victory over her own harshly judgemental Superego, which opposes "what I want" with "what I must". This shows the group's learning ability from the first session, as the two patients co-operate with the therapist as he intervenes to regulate Susana's anxiety (learning point 1). While Susana shares a part of her sadness vis-à-vis a "small Susana" who very rarely was able to speak out, for the benefit of all the participants she deals with the main group theme, that is, the fear of plunging into a new experience (the group therapy) paralysed by the fear of both the inner (Superego) and external (group) judgement. It is remarkable that Susana actually refers to interacting with people who she does not know as a "crazy thing" and, although she is referring to her past experiences, the link to the group session setting is very clear.

The patients' fear of emotional-affective involvement, and thus also their fear of letting themselves go to the group's welcoming relational experience, is one of the earliest group-related themes that emerged in this context. Wherever the group analyst would pick up the group's theme and elaborate on it, the IE-DP therapist would rather deepen the emotion involved by focusing on the group member who is more capable of feeling it.

Vignette A-2—from session 1

In this second fragment, Robert provides an effective metaphor that allows several people to deal with "the terror of leaping", that we may regard as anxiety about the breaking out of deep emotion within the group. This is also clearly linked to the level and quality of the conscious and unconscious therapeutic alliance with the therapists as well as with the group. Helen has just explained her fear of going out of her house alone as a result of which, for two years, in her day-to-day life she has only been to places when accompanied by someone.

Annie: At times the worst bit is the fear of being afraid.

Robert: (Arms folded, monotonous tone of voice) Once I used to feel the need to do something to get over things, so I had this parachutist friend of mine who told me, jump out! I went and trusted him. I must say that I suffer from dizziness, and I'm the kind of person that at the funfair wouldn't even go for a ride on the caterpillar, so you can get some idea; I am always afraid of falling. And he got me to do a whole minute's free falling!

Susana: But at that moment, didn't you think to yourself, "Oh my goodness, what on earth am I doing here?" Didn't you regret it?

Madeleine: I think he didn't think of anything at that very moment.

The interest of other group members modifies Robert's emotional participation, and he now seems less detached. He utters the following remarks leaning forwards, with a heartfelt tone of voice, searching for the gazes of those present. From this moment, the group are experiencing intense collective anxiety, with a sudden change in the group atmosphere. Before the therapist intervention that linked the terror of leaping with fear of throwing oneself into the new therapy experience, various patients performed anxiety-regulating interventions, keeping anxiety within a tolerable range (learning point 3).

Robert: I thought to myself. I trust him! I trust the airplane, I trust the parachute, I trust him, I trust myself, I trust the fact that 400 jumps are done like that every day and nothing happens. At first I didn't want to, but then I jumped out.

Helen: Let's say that it is one of the things you would never have done in your life and then instead you did it.

Robert: This made me think that it was a limit I had set by myself. Helen, perhaps the day will come that you can think you might make it, that nothing will happen … well, I would not like to be in their [therapists'] shoes (laughs).

Helen: I think that if one day I will overcome this thing I will say, "What a stupid thing!"

Robert: There is nothing stupid about it. For my friend, something "stupid" was that I did not want to jump. For me it can be "stupid" that someone is afraid to sing a song in front of people. Everyone knows what he or she can do. Trust is the element that has led me to do this thing. I trust, it can be done!

Osimo: (Empathic) Trust is like accepting the unknown factors in the relationship. Because this instructor put himself forward and, at first, you would say, "I am a fool!" But then you faced this new, unknown factor. (**AA**)

The therapist intervened to support Robert in the effort he was making to pluck up courage and summon up trust. In individual IE-DP, the therapist does not leave a patient alone, rather they support emotional experience by being present and conveying their emotional participation with words and non-verbal communication. In a group setting, however, mirroring phenomena are different and more complex than in a dyadic setting. Besides using words and an understanding tone of voice to facilitate emotional experience, a firm, active reinforcement of expression may be necessary to prevent other group members from interrupting the expression of the one who is conveying emotionally rich content.

Robert: Yes, trusting his words. Trust me, it is not like going on the helter-skelter. Trust me that you won't have your heart in your throat. Remember that when the hatch opens you will be afraid! Trust me that when the hatch opens you will be afraid ... he repeated that to me so often that I was practically unafraid when the hatch really did open.

Madeleine: Oh, come off it, it's not true!

Robert: No, it is true.

Landra: Robert, earlier on you said you wouldn't like to be in us therapists' shoes. (**AA**, RE)

Robert: Yes, but I was saying it meaning that I did not want to take over your role!

Landra: OK, so that's my association; you jump but it is the instructor's task to say be careful, that when the hatch opens you will be afraid but ... (**AA**, **RE**)

Robert: ... but you can make it!

Landra: We are not doing an obvious thing, something that is leaving us neutral while we are starting this group. (**GI**, **HP**, **AA**)

In the last part of the vignette the therapist brings attention back to the transference relationship which the patient unwittingly referred to earlier. This reminds us of Stone's (1999) advice that, "The task of the group therapist is to understand the metaphor of transference and to then find a way of working within the shift, carefully heeding the way in which the members 'metabolise' the intervention" (pp. 220–221). The therapist mirrors the idea of the parachute jump as a representation of what the participants are experiencing—an important and risky action of trust towards the therapists and the group. The overall climate of the group changes visibly after Robert has told of his parachute jump adventure. In the subsequent part of the session, anxiety signals diminish, voices tend to overlap, and almost everyone tries to tell of a similar experience in sport or on some exciting funfair attraction. The group as a whole appeared to be less detached and, at times, were even excited. There was the sense of a great desire to trust and leap into a new experience.

Vignette A-3

The next vignette, from a little later in session 1, particularly illustrates the role patients gave to the therapists, and the emotional ambivalence that was generated in this regard. It is noteworthy that the therapists do not actually intervene but are indirectly very much present in the group members' communications.

Peter: Excuse me, to me this is important because, for me, what he [Robert] just said about one of the problems that I must solve. I was struck by something you said—"I trusted the instructor and everything else but I also trusted myself." For me this is an important thing. Actually, I do not trust myself. I have castrated my working career and a part of my life because I do not trust myself. It is one of the things that I need to solve, sorry, but I needed to underline this.

Helen: Instead one thing that struck me a lot is when the hatch opened and you were no longer afraid.

Susana: So your greatest nightmare might not come about.

Peter: But are you prepared to do a course in which you come to use your hands to open the parachute?

Robert: Yes.

Peter: Fuck off (laughs).

Robert: The first year you do the course, they told me, you jump with two instructors holding you, otherwise you can't make it.

What is striking is the analogy between the two instructors and the two group therapists. Robert is elaborating the fear and, interestingly, is the only member of the group who has not already made explicit the reason for his own suffering.

Peter: But do I deal with the risk of my life only banking on my own capacity? I should reiterate, until now I have not done it because every time someone has believed in me at work—I wanted to be a director, I went to film school—when I understood that two weeks later they would give me some shows, I handed in my resignation and restarted the job from the start somewhere else.

Madeleine: But there are also skills that are not just technical at stake, but also a certain sensibility.

Peter: No, it is just technique.

Madeleine: Ah, it is just technique, and you felt sure about the technique?

Peter: If you don't put your snout right into the trough you can't know. I never felt prepared for what I was doing. That was not the only company I ran away from. I always come to a stage when I avoid the exam. I do not know if it is the fear of succeeding instead of the fear of not succeeding. Also, in my family I was always handled and considered to be stupid for my school performance. I have never been accepted. My teachers never dealt with my refusal to study. I had teachers who would throw my notebook out of the window. But it was because of my problems, not because I wanted to spite them with my failure. Then at work I found I was good, putting a lot of effort into it, and for me it was a surprise. However, when the going gets tough, Peter legs it! Because you are there you do all you can to show you are there, that you're good, able to satisfy the expectations of whoever gave you the job and trained you, but the fear of making a bad show …

Madeleine: But with other people or with yourself?

Peter: No, with other people. I am used to myself by now!

Madeleine: But if you have never even tried!

Peter: Well, I can deal with it, but with other people I would be afraid, because for me other people's opinions are very important. For example, now I would not be able to go out to go to the toilet because maybe while I am outside you might say something about me, as is quite normal.

It is not necessary to interpret the link between the fear of other people's opinions expressed by Peter and Madeleine in their dialogue, and the fear of trusting the group, because Peter himself expresses it by going from one narrative concerning his own work to the specific situation in which he would not even leave the room for fear that the others might start speaking about him in his absence. Also interesting is Madeleine's mention of technique and sensibility as though they were two alternative dimensions; the group wonders how much humanity, how much "real relationship", and how much professional skill the therapists are able to put into the path that is starting. The real relationship with therapists and among group members will often be facilitated and made explicit in the course of therapy as a necessary ingredient for a successful IE-DP treatment (learning point 7). The group proceeded by putting forward some thoughts and reactions.

Peter: … in order not to undergo the judgement of others I prefer to stay alone in my little orchard and not see anyone.

Madeleine: Instead I am not afraid to cut a poor figure with other people. When I say that I end up winning a horse race, it is simply with me. My biggest fear is to discover my limit. I cannot go any further than that. I would like to be very good and if I realise that I am mediocre, it is me, it is my fault. The worse opinion about me is my own. Like it is for beauty; I never find someone is ugly; the flaws, the flab, I say looks all right, but it is all right. But if I see it on myself, I say it is ugly, how can anyone go round looking like that! I am very nasty to myself and nice to everyone else.

Peter: There is definitely also the fear of revealing myself to myself, of course.

Madeleine: (Addressing Peter) In other words … we do the first part of the process in the same way, then maybe we run away from things for this fear, but for different fears; you from the opinion of others, and me from my own.

Peter: This makes me think to my inner self more than I ever imagined.

In these last two excerpts from the session there were no verbal interventions by the therapists, but we can notice how important processes of comparison and identification were starting up among the group members, which fostered an initial partial acknowledgment of defensive positions and Superego incursions.

Restructuring character and tactical defences

"Maybe it's something that is not exactly yours … rather something that you can leave behind!"

In a group setting the therapist, even if he or she wanted, could not possibly mirror each patient's tactical defences. In this regard, we have observed an interesting capacity on the part of the group to intuitively identify many verbal or postural signals indicating defence, inhibitory feelings, or anxiety. For example, in a subsequent vignette, George points out that Helen is playing with her cell phone so as not to express the emotion that she is experiencing vis-à-vis the group. In contrast, the therapist appeared to play a crucial role in identifying and describing character defences, and addressing individual members or the whole group to enhance awareness of the defence and make it ego-dystonic.

We identified four main ways of working on character defences within the group, according to the patient's degree of awareness of the defence, its ego-syntonicity, and the motivation of the patient to renounce it:

1. The therapist explains to the whole group what a character defence is and how it can be self-sabotaging (vignette B-1).
2. A patient shows a clear intention to put his or her character defence into operation and this mobilises the group therapeutic alliance towards working deeply on the defence brought to their attention (vignette B-2).
3. The therapist specifically asks a group member who has hinted at their defence in a vague and general way to focus on a specific incident (vignette B-3).
4. The therapist portrays the character defence for a patient who is still very far from seeing it, so as to help them begin focusing their attention on a dysfunctional character trait (vignette B-4).

Vignette B-1—from session 2

The following extract is presented to highlight a therapist intervention that introduces the group to the concept of character defence. Similar interventions are made frequently during the therapy, and aim to provide the group with an understanding that facilitates discussion and exploration by the group members within the group process. The therapist escorts the group members in a gradual and increasingly incisive way to acknowledge that it is necessary to work on "attitudes that we do not like", but which "we can grow fond of".

John: I often happen to be uncaring and impolite, above all when I am tense or tired, it happens with my one-year-old kid or with my brothers ... not always though, but when I am tense, a small trigger suffices ...

Osimo: Always been like that? (**HP, DA**)

John: Well I believe it was a bit less, then with the passing of time it has got worse.

Answering the therapist's question, John begins to realise that he is not talking of one of his usual obsessive-compulsive symptoms, but of his overall attitude towards change, and he tries to describe it:

John: I am realising that whenever there is a change in my life I struggle to ... whether it's a small or a big thing—even my wife points it out to me—and then habits have to change and, if there are problems and complications, I start wondering how to go about it. I start getting nervous, and maybe it is something unimportant. Now, with my family I realise it more, maybe with my brothers I didn't pay attention to this. Now even the slightest change feels hard to me.

Osimo: This is a very interesting aspect, because here we are dealing with change. As Helen was saying, at times we risk taking an attitude we do not like and may see that in people around us, and you described your father as being in different ways, depending on one's point of view. At times, it is true that we get fond of certain attitudes, even when they are no longer useful. (**DA, GI**)

George: I like the way you have put it. We get fond of certain attitudes. It's true, it's true!

By calling attention to defence as a pattern that is used and that one can stop using when we perceive it is no longer needed, the therapist introduced a theme that is highly relevant to dealing with patients' character defences. In particular, casting doubt on a defence does not mean mortifying a part of the person, but identifying a way of being that one can and may wish to change. In order for a strong therapeutic alliance to develop in the group, all the group members need to realise that the attack is on their defences and not on the Self.

The therapist's intervention in response to John triggered George's excited comment. George had not yet "come out into the open", often hiding his feelings by way of witty remarks, but he now begins to sense that, in the group, there is room for him to disclose his pervasive and self-sabotaging enraged attitude with his wife and daughter. This will be given attention in the two subsequent sessions.

Vignette B-2—from session 5

In the vignette that follows, the therapists, supported by most of the group, seek to welcome Peter who is disclosing his anxiety and guilt linked to his sense of being "selfish and arrogant" for not feeling an interest in other people. The self-sabotaging aspect of this narcissistic defence is that it prevents him from satisfying his deep need to be cared for and loved without being criticised. The group focuses on Peter and "works" on an important character defence. The group is learning that attention will be focused on a single individual whenever an especially tough resistance requires a direct and systematic intervention by one of the therapists.

Having sensed an emotional activation in Peter, and not wishing to allow a group member to step outside the group's boundaries by speaking to the therapists before the others have arrived—that is taking his own space outside the setting, the therapist starts the session:

Osimo: Today Peter arrived a moment before you and, when he was alone with us, he told us that last Sunday he was furious … (**HP**)

Peter: (Sarcastic) It was my daily pleasant state of constant anger … the nervous state I am in every day …

Osimo: I understood that it was more accentuated than usual. (**MI, HP**)

Peter: Yes, because I was at home with my girlfriend, I did not feel like talking, listening to her, I was restless, lately I have been more like that, so I was mad, it is practically a relentless state of mind. This comes from states of impatience, not feeling at all well.

Helen: I too have the feeling all the time. Even if you try to get out of it—at times I realise that I really am unbearable—the fact is that I don't feel well with myself.

Peter: That's what I said, "I didn't feel well with myself." It is not as if someone has done anything to me.

Helen: No, actually, others have nothing to do with it!

Peter: Of course not, poor fellows … well, however, it's not as if we live in a greenhouse.

Helen: At times I realise that I think things that make me sick of myself. At times I think when my husband is speaking, "What a bore!" In other words, I do not want to listen.

Peter: And he's a man! Think if you had a woman on the other side who talks three times as much (laughs).

Helen: It's not the right thing … it is a nasty thing … compared with how I was before when I would listen to absolutely everyone. Now I listen a lot less. On the daily and futile things I do not listen any more, only if it is something important.

Peter: I am unable to listen. With Osimo in the three-hour interview I said that I cannot listen and that I refuse to listen.

George: You don't know or you refuse? That's a different thing.

Peter: I don't know, I am here to understand this as well …

George: Are you annoyed by listening to someone or do you get distracted a lot? For instance, I get very distracted listening, but I do not get annoyed.

Peter: But do you know where the distraction comes from? It might be … the child who gets distracted at school due to a pathological deficit …

Helen: They used to tell me that. I was branded a dunce.

Peter: … I … definitely there is a lot of arrogance, I am trying to be so less and less, because I come from an arrogant family, there were three of us and no one ever listened to anyone. The fish in the bowl would listen! (laughs). I had to be with a person who very much needs to be listened to and was not listened to in her family, and for this she suffered a lot.

Osimo: Do you think Peter seems like someone who cannot listen? (**GI, DA, MI, SO**)

Here, we notice that the therapist seemingly takes attention away from Peter to bring it upon the group.[2] The aim of this intervention is not to take attention away from the issue but rather to highlight that there is much interest in the personal issues brought to the session, while, at the same time, enabling Peter and the whole group to discern the incongruence of his defensive attitude (learning point 4).

Peter: But here I make a big effort, though, for example, I do not know a single name in here! (Pointing one by one to the members of the group.) The physicist, the railwayman, the entrepreneur, the Peruvian, the clerk, the painter, and the musician.
(The group laughs)

Osimo: Ah! You don't need the name! (**RE, HP**)

Peter: It would take too much effort, too much concentration.

George: The first name I learned was hers! (points to Susana). Maybe because she is Peruvian …

Susana: That happens to me at times as well … it is not that I do not listen, it's that I do not pay attention, which is something different. For many years I have had to travel, eat with a lot of people. I happened to be at dinner with people I was not interested in, but I had to eat anyway. Perhaps I was at dinner in a city with fourteen people because a new sales point was going to be opened and I would have rather stayed on my own, I wasn't interested in those people so I didn't remember their names. It was like making a selection.

Peter: Excuse me … I have already gone over my forty to fifty seconds of attention, so I have already got lost (slightly sarcastic).

Here Peter brings attention back to him, being particularly keen to say how he is so little interested in what the others have to say. In the last lines of this vignette, we observe a rapid shift from an individual focus to a group focus and back to the individual (learning point 5). In this way, the capacity to listen, that of being attentive and observing, became a group theme, lending itself to elaboration by the individuals within the group. This appears to have been useful for deepening the work on character defences.

George: (Ironically stressing the syllables, addressing himself to Peter) Me Geor-ge!
Peter: Yes, the physicist, I know.
George: Eh, so then yours is a refusal!
Peter: Well, we are at the fourth, fifth, or sixth session?

Peter notices that the linearity of his argument is undermined; the others do not believe he is careless because in actual fact they see him as careful and interested. From this point onward he almost exclusively addresses the therapists.

Osimo: Fifth. (**HP**)
Peter: I have had two strong impressions: (i) and this is definitely your technique, the two of you (addressing the therapists) knew all the names from the first session.
George: Oh come on, psychiatrists and psychologists must learn the names!
Peter: Be quiet for a moment, damn it! (said in local dialect) (laughs). Sorry, I was joking. No, it's not true, but it was significant, eight people, eight unknown faces … definitely a technique. And then I was struck by the fact that from the second meeting, everyone, especially the musician—I noticed—knows why the others are here. I don't! I took absolutely no notice of anyone. I swear. And yet I like to come here a lot. And at the fourth session, last time, I started to make out something—the panic attacks, your problem (addressing Helen). I had a lot of trouble memorising it, as well as that of our musician friend. Not even you (he turns to Annie) …
Annie: I have not yet said what it is!
Peter: You haven't yet said it and you missed the second session! But this is not out of a real form of nastiness or indifference. I come here and make the biggest effort possible. But I really have difficulty having the right sort of respect and consideration for others …
Osimo: You really make a big effort! (**MI, RE**)
Peter: I am here to make a big effort.
Osimo: This pleases me greatly but … you are describing yourself as someone who does not listen and, instead, look at how many things you have in your mind about us! (**MI, RE**)
Peter: About me!
Osimo: About us! (**MI, DA**)
Peter: About me!

Annie: Also about us! I remember that, after two or three sessions, you remembered one thing that I said at the first session.

As if in a relay race, Annie intervenes and continues the challenge started by the therapist.

Peter: About the fiancé you have in [name of city]?
Annie: Yes.
Helen: You were sitting here when you said it!
Peter: That's because it was something I was very interested in.
Annie: (Laughs) Fancy that! … you were interested in the fact that my boyfriend is in [name of city]!?

As if she got the message that it is an important operation, Annie continues to challenge Peter's defence:

Peter: (Blushing for embarrassment, and tense in his speech for increased anxiety) For me, [name of city] is the rest of the world … I am someone who would pack his suitcase and run away. Well, I have picked something about each one who is here, it's not as if I don't take an interest, for heaven's sake, but I have a very low threshold of tolerance. I have a problem in relationships with people. In friendly relations, working relations. I do not know if it's because my mother would shout and beat me like hell …
Susana: Perhaps that's one thing … I do not know how to say it in Italian, we say "desapevo" in Spanish, which means not getting attached to people. I find her nice (points to Annie) because we take the train together, so I remember her and I put her into my life …
Peter: No, no, no, no (with a disapproving tone).
Susana: … and you keep them all far distant.

At this point the baton had been taken up by Susana who described the narcissistic defence in clear terms—"keep everyone distant".

Peter: No, it's not a matter of affection. I think it is merely a form of arrogance.
Landra: (To Peter) I was immediately struck by your way of looking after us a lot. I remember, for example, when you helped Helen to say what she was feeling, in the second session. (**HP, DA, SO**)

Again the therapist steps in so the attention to the topic does not "cool off", highlighting the discrepancy between what Peter is portraying about himself (i.e., aspects of his ego-syntonic character), how he behaves, and how he is perceived by others.
Helen: Actually, I feel he is always very present mentally.

Peter: Only because I was greatly interested in what she was saying! I felt involved.
Landra: I find you made some very specific points and in a tough way too. Was it a way of talking about your own things?

Peter: (To Landra) Well, you talk about me helping others. I don't know if I was helping others or myself. It was just a momentary performance.

Now various elements have been assembled and Peter is showing more intense signals of anxiety (voice is tense and sharp, gesticulation increased) in response to the feelings stirred up by the collective interventions on his character defence. The therapist continues with an individual focus, offering a clear representation of what, to Peter, had been previously an unseen aspect of his character in the context of the dynamics of his family of origin:

Osimo: Perhaps, to begin from your family context where, as you pointed out, there were three of you but no one ever listened to anyone, you were left with the inner feeling that what is good for one can't be good for others, and no action can possibly go to everyone's advantage. It feels like you keep on seeing yourself as selfish, and others stick out as great people, exceptionally skilled … you even stated we [therapists] are so clever because we can remember everyone's name. (**TCP**, **SO**, **HP**)

Helen: (Referring to the therapists who remember all names) They've just been more attentive!

Annie: (Jokingly) And they must have reviewed the three-hour interview that we all recorded. I want to believe that they have done their homework about us! (laughs).

Peter: She is just amazing! (referring to Annie). She says a couple of words in a calm and serene manner and then you feel like an idiot! Her capacity to analyse is outstanding.

Peter's inclination to idealise is even clearer.

George: When, at work, we took a class on communication, there was a psychologist who remembered everyone's name …

Peter: In any case, there is also a technique for this, the same as for remembering the numbers in a table, like he (turns to John) has to remember a series of operations to manoeuvre a [type of vehicle]. Oh come on (turning to the therapists), you have this technique, guys!

Peter resorts to the defence of trivialising the issue and devaluing the therapists.

Helen: It happens to everyone—to treat people you don't like with arrogance. For example, there is my uncle, who loves me deeply—this is what he says—but I despise him. I am sorry for my mother who is his sister-in-law.

Helen goes on to describe her uncle as a liar, always opposing others, and taking advantage of grandmother's money. She states that she did not open the door to him when he came to see her. In this phase, Helen is identifying with Peter, comparing his alleged spite for others with her dislike of her uncle. In so doing, she supports the idea that certain people are the way they are "because of their character", and there is no other option. As Helen often tries to bring attention back to herself, especially when she sees the therapists are busy challenging someone else's defences, the therapists have to choose whether to address Helen's defence or keep the focus on Peter. Of course, two birds with one stone would be a great option!

Helen: Listening to everyone is also a gift, like talking. Some talk a lot and some say barely two words torn from their mouths. We can't all be the same and all perfect.

Peter: It is true, it is a point of character, even if for me the key is how interested you are in getting to know the other person. Here, for example, I am trying to be polite and at my best. But I can be the sort of person always interrupting others and wanting to be right.

Osimo: (Turning to Peter) So it's a matter of character, you say. (**DA**)

Here we notice that Peter had taken advantage of Helen's story about her unpleasant uncle in order to strengthen his theory on the immutability of human character. The therapist decided to stay with Peter's defence since Peter had been generally reluctant to focus on himself, and more often elaborated on what other group members said.

Peter: Character means a way of being. We carry with us some virtues and some non-virtues.

Osimo: What you described is an aspect that can change. (**DA**)

Peter: Sorry?

Osimo: It is a changeable aspect, I say. (**DA**)

Peter: Er, I don't know, you tell me, since you are the doctor!

Landra: It is a question we can put to everyone. You experience this part of yourself as a negativity. And yet this way of relating to others must have some use. If you had not explained so well this part that does not listen, it would not be clear to us, since we see you as someone who listens a lot. But you keep on saying you only listen to what you are interested in. Let's look together at what the meaning of this position taken by Peter might be. (**DA, MI, GI, SO**)

Once again Peter is offered a validation of his character defence, underlining that it is a part of him and not him as a whole. This time the therapist addressed Peter directly but then straight afterwards opened the work up to the rest of the group, so that the process of understanding the defensive position can be to everyone's benefit.

Helen: To understand it well, we should see the way he is in his everyday life. Here he is making an effort.

Peter: Here I do not look nuts! (laughs).

Helen: Wait. Let me finish. It is important for him to have come to see this negative side that he wants to overcome.

Annie: Perhaps, more than character, this thing of yours is tied to your family past, that is, to your own way of asserting yourself—that you could not help but be a little aggressive. Let alone the fact that you are taking a chance in a situation in which you can't do it … here you cannot assert yourself aggressively.

Peter: That's right.

Annie: But inside it still arouses some things in you ... Maybe it's something that is not exactly yours ... rather something that you can leave behind!

Peter: Um yes, well I do hope so! I should make a small premise—I did not come to this point with my own deductions, but it was explained to me. By whom? By my partner who can't stand it any more.

Annie has exactly grasped the nature of the defence and the situation. At last, Peter does not reject this possibility (i.e., that there is a useless and self-sabotaging part that can change). He even said he hopes for a change. Although he cannot yet take full responsibility for this, since he calls in his girlfriend, Peter's overall attitude has changed; he is no longer anxious, detached, and sarcastic, but instead looks eager to talk and more in touch with his emotions.

Susana: Can you talk about this? Because I am very interested!

Peter starts elaborating on his ambivalent relationship with his girlfriend and describes himself as being imbued with love for a unique and enchanting creature, and hatred for an unbearable part of her. It is worth remembering that all this defence work—predominantly centred on Peter—started from the rage he had experienced with his girlfriend the previous Sunday. It was after the therapist asked Peter to talk about it, that he raised the issue of his lack of interest in other people. In the subsequent phase of the session, not reported here, Peter talks about his girlfriend in a realistic way and admits to the rage he felt towards her.

To the therapists, what stands out in the above long and intense extract from the fifth session is probably one of the most stimulating aspects of the application of IE-DP to group therapy—the patients in the group showed a surprising learning capacity, especially in grasping the practical value of the three experiential-dynamic activities. Another observation is that they tended to apply the activities on others first, and only later focused their attention on their own inner worlds and behaviour. For example, we can recall that, in the second session, Peter was strongly allied to the therapist when trying to perform emotional maieutics with Helen. By the fifth session, the group therapeutic alliance made it possible for the therapists to challenge character defences, and other group members (i.e., Annie, Susana, and Helen) worked on Peter's anxiety and his character armour. These are examples of learning points 1, 2, 4, and 5.

Vignette B-3—from session 2

The following short passages illustrate HP interventions that aimed to help the group members to focus on specific incidents, and recognise dysfunctional and self-sabotaging character traits. Some participants focused on the emotional experience of rage, making it the current group theme.

George: The last time I felt such strong rage was when I went to the DIY store and I did not find the screws I was looking for. There were all types except the ones I needed. I asked, and the shop assistant said, "They are due to come." I did not shout, but felt an amazing, disproportionate build-up of rage inside. Since I planned to get the right screws to do that job, my rage was sky-high. I even feel silly in telling it, but I believe it's the right place. There it wasn't my wife's fault, so we did not fight, but had she been involved …

Osimo: Those screws must really mean a lot to you if they arouse such a strong feeling! (**MI, HP**)

The group immediately perceives the importance that the therapist gives to the incident described by George. From then, "George's screws" became a favourite metaphor used by the group for the bottled up feelings they did not allow themselves to experience and displaced elsewhere.

George: Because I could not do the job. I take years to do a job in the house. Then when I do it I am happy. If I have twenty screwdrivers, I need the twenty-first that I have not bought … then I get really angry. My wife pushes me and says, "That job needs to be done, when are you going to do it?" Then I go and do the shopping and a particular screw is missing and then I want to destroy the world. One thing that I said to Dr Landra [trial relationship interview] is that I feel really bad when we fight in front of our daughter, who is unable to defend herself. I would like to have the will power … it is silly of me to get angry over some petty matters.

Susana: Aren't you angry over making a huge effort to do the thing you don't want to do?

George: No, no, I also get angry when it's something I like to do.

Susana: I get angry like that when I am at the limit of my energies and I know I must do something and I force myself to do it and I get angry at myself if in some case someone prevents me from doing it.

George: I am a guide at the [name of place] and I am very happy to do it, but if they keep on changing my schedule this does annoy me. I become angry even though I say nothing to my colleague.

Helen: I get angry like hell when I am determined to do something, and then I am unable to because of someone's fault.

The therapist notices Helen's generalisation and invites her to be more specific.

Osimo: Will you tell us one? (**HP**)

Vignette B-4—from session 2

In the following extract, the therapist puts pressure on Robert (who still seems very reticent in talking about himself) by drawing attention to a metaphor that he had used a few comments earlier when talking about a long-lasting relationship. Of course, there will also be reference to the famous "screw" (wall plug) that encompasses George's failed anger.

Osimo: (Turning to Robert) I was struck when you spoke of spending your life in prison, referring to a relationship that has lasted a long time. Perhaps we should understand what is at stake here, which "plug" is actually missing. (**HP, SE**)

Robert: Then, after the first session I realised that I did like with my students at school, and wrote down everybody's name, because I do not remember names, and going home I reread your names and tried to reconstruct what everybody's main problem was. But then I further realised that I had not expressed my own difficulty. Do you remember my difficulty (turning to Susana)?

Susana: No, I remember that you told us about your jump.

Landra: With the jump you got us going and then you yourself did not speak. (**DA**)

Robert: Earlier on, when you (addressing Osimo) spoke of the person I am close to, I realised that I live with a moat all around me. If the relationship is fairly detached, then I am important, I am a good friend, I am an adviser. When someone comes close to me, they will fall into the water in my moat and, automatically, I am unable to build a bond—that person never crosses to my side.

Osimo: What happens? (**DA**)

Robert: What happens is that many relationships ended up this way. I see you married with children, lucky you! I do not know what is happening to me, everything that is close it's as if I could not see it, I do not see it, I can't value it, can never foster a relationship. Kind of the initial inertia by which the relationship got started suddenly drops, and I throw in the towel and do something else.

George: There is a moat that swallows everything up. You are a castle!

Robert: Yes, a ruin! (laughs). I do not actually feel like a castle. I see a moat and realise that the closer people get, the more I throw them down. Actually, a friend of mine says to me, "For you the neighbour's garden is always greener" … when I have a girlfriend, then I live like that [looks far afield], what is here I no longer see. Not that I am looking for other relationships. Just that I can only see and understand what is far afield, for instance, I am a lucid planner in my working decisions.

Landra: Here are we having the same effect on you as with your students at school or are we closer as compared with the last session? (**DA**, **RE**)

"The patients must be given the chance to enhance their own capacity to manage their feeling conveyed by means of metaphors, but the therapist must also respect their reactions, which can mark a feeling of danger" (Stone, 1999, pp. 220–221). In this case, Robert, by means of images (the prison, the plug, the moat)—all metaphors of emotional states that he struggles to communicate—appeared more in touch with a deep emotion. The therapist therefore interrupted him to focus his attention on something that he was experiencing in the here-and-now of the session. Such an intervention is typical of the transference/real relationship work of IE-DP.

Robert: Here I am able to say that I stand on this side of the moat and it is for me to make the effort to come closer. But here we owe each other nothing. You cannot criticise me for not taking something into account.

Susana: But in every relationship there is a certain commitment. With us, instead, you have no commitments.

Robert: (With a very sad face) As I said to the doctor [alluding to the trial relationship], I never had second thoughts, went backwards and made a blunder. I just realised that I was always repeating a certain pattern in relationships. You (turning to George) used to say, "What I do not like about myself" … well, what I do not like about myself is living through relationships, drying them up, and then leaving them to do something else …

In the above vignette, the therapists and group members helped Robert to get in touch with deep sadness about his self-defeating pattern in relationships. This occurred in the relationships with his fellow group members who, differently from his students at school, are on the same level with him, which makes it difficult for Robert to allow closeness. Both the therapist and Susana put to Robert the here-and-now of his real and transference relationship with the group (learning point 8).

Emotional activation and emotional maieutics

"… that is, it must give you some emotion, it's chemistry!"

In one of the first group IE-DP sessions we explored how to apply emotional maieutics in the group setting. As we know, by means of the dynamic activity of emotional maieutics, we focus on deep emotion as it is rising, and accompany it with the patience and the determination with which a midwife accompanies childbirth. As in an individual therapy, it is crucial to regulate the anxiety associated with the surfacing of emotion as soon as feeling begins to be experienced. In the group, however, the anxiety mobilised in many by the surfacing of a deep feeling in one of the group members can cause turmoil—an intense buzz, the overlapping of voices, the excitement of several people at the same time, massive resort to rationalisation, and discussion.

In the following sequence, as Helen reveals that, for some years, she has had an extramarital affair, the therapists notice that the other group members are anxious.

Helen: What I cannot understand is which my real needs are, because I have even betrayed him.
George: Does he know?
Helen: Oh no, he doesn't!
Susana: Are you sure you know what your needs are? Because you say that you want to understand what yours are …
Helen: Well, before my husband I never had any sentimental experiences and this is a mistake. What you miss if you don't try before, you catch up on afterwards.
John: It's true, you miss something later.

Even John, who mostly listens in silence, makes his comment, showing some emotional activation.

Helen: I live well like that; my husband and my family on the one hand and then my world outside. These two lives live in parallel.

Helen expresses with unconscious clarity the defence of splitting, which she often resorts to in her life.

Helen: What my husband gives me is not enough and so I go and look for it in another person. Not that my husband gives me little ... this is my mental masturbation. What do I lack?

Osimo: That's what we can look at in here! (**DA**)

Helen: I am here for this.

The therapist starts to focus attention on Helen who is keeping to her usual tone of voice, conveying self-assurance and emotional detachment.

Robert: Would you not think that the pedestal (he refers to a metaphor previously used by Helen to describe her relationship with her husband) where you husband puts you not only puts you up high but also holds you still?

George: Can I ask you a nasty question? If you found out that your husband betrays you, would you accept that?

Helen: I would rather not find out and if I should find out, I would ask for the reason and then, with a small self-analysis, I might forgive him.

Both Robert and George were anxious and intervened as if they had not heard what the therapist had said to Helen, and as if they were not even listening to each other. Helen, who was probably feeling more emotion inside than she revealed, does not miss the chance to answer her two fellow group members instead of the therapist, choosing the best road to avoid the issue and disperse the anxiety that she was feeling. On the whole, however, the group climate is heating up.

Peter: I'd like to understand. You believe that betraying your husband does you good and can do good to you both.

Helen: I don't believe that, it's just like that.

Peter: You don't think that, you know it.

Robert: You'd be a worse wife without the betrayal.

George: If I had another relationship I'd be afraid, I'd be scared of the risks involved. Aren't you scared?

Helen: On the contrary, this is the most adventurous thing. I like it. It makes me feel good.

Peter joined in with those who interacted as though Helen was the only interlocutor. Their voices are louder, and overlapping. The therapist has to make a drastic intervention.

Osimo: I am sorry to interrupt you. (**DA**) (Turns openly to Helen) How does it make you feel to be talking of this with us? I think you made an important opening ... (**XA**, **RE**)

Helen: Because I am here and I can say whatever I want to, since we get to know each other here and things stay here. I am here right to say this thing that is important to me.

Helen shows many signals of anxiety in her upper body. The therapist insists on the emotional level.

Osimo: What's it like to say it? (**XA**)

Helen: Indifferent. Makes no difference to me one way or the other. For me it's a normal thing.

Helen has already reverted to her usual resolute tone and her anxiety is less visible. The therapist continues.

Osimo: I see, but saying it here … (**XA**)

Helen: Yes, it causes a pinch of embarrassment, but not even that much.

Robert: Because you do not experience it like something sinful …

Helen: I don't experience it as something so sinful. For me this is a good thing.

John: It is good because it improves your relationship …

Robert interfered with the therapist's intervention by introducing a new rationalisation, offering Helen a defence on a silver plate. John was about to foster a debate, thereby amplifying the rationalising defence. The therapist tries to get in the way of the defences and shift attention back to an emotional aspect by exploring Helen's phrase "a good thing":

Osimo: What is the "good thing"? (**XA**)

Helen: It's good to be able to talk about it.

Robert: If it's a good thing, where's the problem?

Helen: Many people might think that it's something not so right.

Robert: But you said you were here for that very reason. You are here for what?

Helen: To understand why … then, my problem is staying alone (referring to her agoraphobic symptom). If this emotional thing has a link with my own problem, expressing it can help me.

Involuntarily, Robert goes along with what the therapist too is trying to do (i.e., help Helen to focus on her emotional experience), the moment she focuses on the problems that motivated her to undertake therapy in the first place.

Peter: But what for? To keep on doing it or not to do it any more? I do not think that declaring you betray your husband will help you to learn staying alone. It can relieve your guilt and even give you greater gratification. According to me, Helen did not say this difficult thing of hers by pure chance …

Robert: I will try to answer for her. She put it on the table and it is not like saying, "I like hot chilli peppers", it is an important moment that can help to understand exactly why she is unable to stay alone.

Peter: I think that … I was interested in Dr Osimo's question that he asked you, I think, what emotion does it give you to say it and I am interested in the answer!

Just as the group was moving towards more and more rationalisation and away from Helen's emotion, here Peter surprisingly interrupted Robert's explanation (which, however, brought the attention back to the symptom), and posed the therapist's question once again.

Helen: … because I think that in order to say it …

Peter: No, I am not interested in your reasons, he [Osimo] is asking you (says slowly) what you feel in saying it out loud. I am satisfied, I feel ashamed, I excuse myself … that is, it must give you some emotion, it's chemistry (raises his voice)!

Helen: Ah, it must give me that? (smiles). It is honest to say so …

Peter: So it gives you a feeling of relief?

Helen: More than relief … I'd say it is knowing oneself deeply, it is right to say so! I can think it. I too have a fault, I have many faults!

The group again expresses anxiety by means of a loud buzz. The therapist chooses to intervene in the group as a whole, drawing attention to the emotional experience of other group members.

Landra: However, it looks like hearing this has given others too a chance of feeling an emotion … (**GI, XA**)

Peter: Of course, it is not like the story of the transfers! (referring to George's telling the group about an incident in childhood when he had suffered because his mother had taken the liberty to remove "transfers" from the wall of his room).

The therapeutic intervention was de-powered by Peter's trivialising defence. The group laughs. The therapist keeps on with her intervention, focusing on Peter who, having earned success through laughter, tries to extend the trivialisation. We repeatedly noticed that, when the group uses its power of amplifying individual defences, intense emotion is not far away.

Landra: Peter, would you like to start telling us your emotion, since you have helped Helen to try to do it? (**XA**)

Peter: Well, let's say that Helen's communication has been the strongest part of the session, the most provocative thing. I am really keen on transfers (laughs).

At this point Helen takes out her mobile phone. The therapist notices and decides to intervene directly with her.

Osimo: And what about Helen? (**DA**)

John: (Whispers) If something like that had happened to me …

Helen: Because it's not something I tell everyone, but with you I wanted to be honest.

Osimo: (Empathic) There is this strong desire for reconciliation … so what does it arouse in you telling us now? (**XA**)

There are a few seconds of silence. Helen continues to look at her mobile phone.

Peter: I am very curious about the answer.

Peter has reinforced the therapist's intervention.

Robert: I have admired her for her courage. Perhaps what I cannot admire is her being so quiet now …

Robert has attacked Helen's defence of remaining silent.

Helen: I am not feeling worthy right now …

The therapist can easily go back to the request for an emotion without interrupting the group's communication flow.

Osimo: Well, you could tell us the way you do feel, instead. (**DA, XA**)
George: Yes, because, apart from your weak spots, you are able to take quite a strong position. You are not so shy!
Helen: The moment I thought of saying it, I felt it was something honest vis-à-vis what is being done here.
George: I want to tell you about two emotions that I have experienced. One—so I will try to be brave as well—a little envy, because I told myself, at bottom, I too have thought several times of betraying my wife; when I start to chat with a good-looking girl on the train, perhaps I even betray my wife with my thoughts. Second thing, and we know that we all judge, a judgement occurred to me about coherence. I told myself that if I am to accept that I can go to bed with another woman, I must also allow my partner to do the same, regardless of whether I do so or not. Otherwise it means that I give more value to her than to me.

George is concentrating and does not trivialise as he often does. Rather, he is emotionally resonating in response to the therapists who often brought the group's attention back to the group members' emotions that were hidden beneath anxiety signals. In this case, George answered "in Helen's place" as if he was showing her that it is possible to look at what she feels.

Susana: But you have to discuss this with your wife.
George: Well, to a greater or lesser extent we all make judgements, and in a situation like this … even if Helen conquers her embarrassment by reading her mobile phone (laughs) … since we cannot look at the floor as we are not in a lift (laughs) … anyway I thought it was right to say what I felt. As soon as Helen told us I thought, "Oh, what a bitch, she can get away with betraying her husband without telling him and he can't!"

Here we notice George's timely intervention of pointing out Helen's tactical defence (learning point 2)—attending to her mobile phone. As often, George gives more thoughts than feelings. However, when saying, "… what a bitch …" etc. he conveys a kind of envious, angry excitement. Helen, "brought to order", puts away her phone and appears much more attentive.

Peter: Mind you, she said she might accept her husband's betrayal.

George: No, she said, she might forgive him, and so there is the imbalance. If she looks for forgiveness, this means her husband would be doing something negative, but when she refers to herself, she says that betrayal is a good thing.

Osimo: Well there is no perfect solution, and Helen has suggested one (defence validation: **DA, GI**)

Peter: She actually put it to us that her affair is being therapeutic, so she feels better and everyone is better.

Peter attempted to stop the group elaboration of Helen's betrayal, whereas Robert and George handled their anxiety in a different way. That is, by continuing to speak about her in a slightly excited way. So much so that Helen must interrupt them to be able to speak again:

Robert: But she doesn't feel well! Then you (turning to Helen) say that if he leaves you alone even for a quarter of an hour, you get angry.

George: All right, but that is another problem.

Helen: Wait, I have to answer! My affair is not sexual. I would have ended the affair with this person if he had been someone who comes for sex and nothing else. The truth is that he makes me feel like a princess.

Helen uttered this last remark with a hushed tone of voice which is unusual for her as, in the group communication, she usually talks over others and holds the stage.

George: How I envy you!

Robert: So it is for this reason that you are afraid of staying alone. If you are alone who will make you feel like a princess?

Robert is offering an interesting reading of Helen's phobic symptom, by insightfully picking up on the connection between the desire to feel unique and loved "like a princess" and Helen's total inhibition to move around on her own.

Helen: So, why do I feel like that?

As Helen articulates her words we perceive her emotion—a rare occurrence in interactions with Helen.

Robert: You cannot stay alone because there would be no one making you feel like a princess. You are unable to see yourself a princess and can't value yourself unless others put you up on this pedestal.

We can see that George and Robert perform an important co-therapeutic function in these sequences. In particular, they point out, in their own way, Helen's character defence of needing a pedestal, the position of a princess and, consequently, the constant physical presence of someone to support her as she cannot recognise her value nor think of herself as being lovable.

These continuous and fast-flowing interventions keep Helen more and more in touch with a deep feeling that eventually surfaces thanks to the therapist's maieutic action. All the while, the therapist kept his attention focused on Helen, conveying to her, in a non-verbal way, that he was observing with keen attention the emotion that was gradually surfacing within her. He offers her the chance to express her emotional state:

Osimo: It is really a big desire, your desire to feel … (**XA**)
Helen: … loved! (her voice is broken by emotion and she starts sobbing).
Osimo: (Empathic) Loved. It goes through that form … it is an interesting way! (**XA, DA**)

Now the group is silent. At last, Helen is more in touch with her deep feeling of sadness and intense desire to feel loved. This emotional experience gives rise to an intense and very involved silence in the group which, in turn, facilitates the emotional experiencing (learning point 6).

The final phases of the group therapy

"For the first time I felt like changing"

Vignette D-1—from session 37

Peter starts out by stating he has never felt authentic in the course of the whole group therapy, that he only expressed a marginal part of himself, and totally lacks personality. The concepts are absolutes, the tone is peremptory, the process of splitting evident. He then announces that his wife is pregnant.

Peter: … perhaps this child is the only thing of my life that I am doing with conviction and joy. Yesterday we did the, the ultrasound.
Osimo: What emotion did that give you? (**XA**)
Peter: An extraordinary emotion. The only problem is that it's been ages since I last felt emotionally in touch with what happens to me. It's my partner who has led me here, because in life I am always waiting for the others before doing anything myself.
Osimo: Ah, you don't want the baby? (**DA**)
Peter: Of course I want it. But I want to say that in my life I was never ever able to initiate a choice based on my needs.
Osimo: What you are saying is very meaningful. I will underline two things. The first is that you clearly feel you are telling us about aspects of yourself that you had never had the courage to speak about before. The second is your statement that you never did things of your own choice. Allow me to cast doubt over the latter remark, as, for example, this baby is coming because you let yourself be led along but also because, you said, you wanted it. You too want the child, but it is still hard to say this out loud!
Peter: No, doctor (disconsolate), the thing is longer and more rotten than that.

A long discussion begins between the therapists and Peter, in which the group is silently involved. Peter becomes more and more emotionally aroused although for about twenty minutes he stubbornly goes on juxtaposing the part of himself that is happy for the child, and a sadistically self-denigrating Superego part. At some point, a grim image comes—he sees himself walking along a path of which the end cannot be seen. The ground is made of large stones and, as he walks, he cuts his abdomen, tearing away pieces of red flesh and throwing them into the wind.

Osimo: Does this image scare you a lot? (**AA**)
Peter: (Visibly excited, anxious, and sort of alarmed) Yes, because I see myself as a lunatic.
Osimo: It is the visual form of … (**XA**)
Peter: … madness!
Osimo: … of something mixed up … (**XA**)
Peter: … yes, a desire to open up, damn it! (raises his voice).
Osimo: What do you feel like doing? (**XA**)
Peter: Like getting up.
Osimo: Get up! (**XA**)
Peter: No! I am ashamed …
Osimo: Then we'll get up ourselves! (**DA, XA**)

The therapists stand up while Peter shakes his head and shields himself, appearing really scared by this chance of doing what he likes, without letting himself be held back by his self-sabotaging inner part. One at a time, all the group members rise to their feet. George then holds out his hand to Peter and vigorously invites him to stand up.

When applying IE-DP techniques in the group, we repeatedly observed that seeing a fellow group member striving to express their emotion was immensely helpful in that it facilitated others in the group to make contact with their feelings. When the group members stood up it symbolically affirmed that they were not ashamed of the emotion they were feeling, and were brave enough to do so inasmuch as they saw Peter's labour as a reflection of their own labour (learning point 9). In this final excerpt, it is apparent that, by now, when intense feeling is being faced, the group as a whole is tuning in.

Peter: (Is getting up, dragged up by George) No, but I don't need tenderness! What you are asking me for is pure violence!
Osimo: So, let's see this violence you are feeling. (**XA**)

Everyone sits back down.

Peter: It's wanting to smash stuff, digging out strength and power, punching the concrete, hurting myself!
Osimo: Why punish yourself so harshly? (**SE**)
Peter: No, I don't want to punish myself, it's just that after thirty-seven years I know that I am stronger than concrete, that I can punch and don't hurt myself.

Peter's last remark highlights the weak rationale behind his thinking, being prey to a defence of total denial. The therapist again has to stop him and provide an explanation that highlights the contradiction.

Osimo: Peter, I would like you to see how many emotions have emerged for having spoken about such a deep part of yourself and how much guilt you feel in expressing it, so much so that you have to punish yourself. (**XA, SE**)

Peter: I feel ashamed about all of this (with a barely audible voice)... Actually, no! (loud voice). I do not want to feel shame for what is happening in the group. It's my damned free-trade area, where I can say whatever I like, and at last I have found it! (raises his head and smiles while looking at everyone).

Besides working on the self-sabotaging part, in this penultimate session, for the most part focused on Peter, the group measures up to their fear of the end of the therapy through the many contradictory references that Peter addressed to the group—defining it, on the one hand, as a place of non-authenticity and, on the other, a free-trade area in which one can be oneself. When all the group members rise to their feet, they spontaneously represent the group internal cohesion and, at the same time, the strong dependence fostered by the group which Peter rebels against, feeling the violence inside himself, and representing on behalf of everyone the need to separate himself and to be "reborn". Peter's baby is about to be born and this, besides being a beautiful fact, represents the part of each group member who might see the light of day and become independent.

Conclusions

This chapter presented some initial thoughts in regard to IE-DP in a group setting. Attention was particularly focused on the interactions that developed in the early group sessions when the patients learned from the therapists the use of three main dynamic activities: (i) defence restructuring, (ii) anxiety regulation, and (iii) emotional maieutics.

For the two therapists, the early sessions were also a stimulating discovery about how the therapeutic process can benefit from the group's learning capacity of the therapeutic method. Also in individual EDTs, the patient is progressively trained in recognising the signals of anxiety, their defences and dysfunctional character patterns implemented in their relations with others, and in focusing on emotional experience. We noticed that, in comparison with an individual EDT, this type of learning is faster and more efficient in the group setting. The reason may be that, in the individual setting all the teaching, explaining, and stimulating relies on the therapist, whereas these activities are boosted through being performed by the therapist and other members of the group in the group setting. The therapeutic process that unfolded over the course of the thirty-eight sessions involved tremendous learning on the part of the group members in the use of the experiential-dynamic activities, generating a greater awareness of their own inner obstacles, the full expression of their emotions, and the possibility to freely manifest a more authentic Self. This finding is consistent with Cornelissen's (2001) views on the advantages of offering individual ISTDP in a group setting. In particular, Cornelissen suggested that the group setting provides opportunities for group members to learn from each other through witnessing each others' therapeutic work. Furthermore, he suggested that a shared knowledge or understanding of dynamic concepts and their uses develops within the group, and which group members can use to help themselves and each other.

> They will see someone struggle for emotional closeness, or in the painful process of trying to establish a meaningful relationship, and they may reflect on how each group member behaves at such moments. In this way the patients gather information they can use to help each other ... most important though, when we discuss the advantages of this format, is the impact on the patient when he observes the defensive patterns of his fellow patients in the ISTDP session. Of course, witnessing helps him to reflect consciously on his own behaviour, but contributes at the same time to the unconscious rise of the transference. Witnessing other group members grubbing their defences and experiencing feelings, or seeing the growing potential in others to resolve their problems, must also give rise to positive transference feelings. Maybe one could even say that this doubles or triples the effect of their own individual work ... Becoming aware of the positive forces of therapy can help to direct the patient against the undermining forces of the superego and stimulates the awakening of the ego and its consequent restructuring process, and thus assists in the recovering of its adaptive capacities. In other words, we expect this simultaneous therapy to contribute to the restructuring process of the ego. Not only the working alliance is enhanced, also the ego strength is improved. One could argue that this format functions as a therapy accelerator. (Cornelissen, 2001, pp. 152–153)

Some final considerations

The first application of IE-DP to a group described in this chapter was rewarding for both therapists, who decided to further this experience with a view to refine group EDT techniques. Some final considerations, based on experience gained from further IE-DP group therapies are described here.

The first observation is that it seems crucial to have offered an individual trial relationship extended interview *before* starting the group sessions. This gave each prospective group member a clear idea of what lay ahead, that is, along which lines the therapeutic work would unfold. The therapists' impression was that this facilitated the group process a great deal. As frequently is the case when investigating a new field, new issues emerge that require further investigation. One of these concerns patients with low ego-adaptive capacity, like Madeleine, Peter and, to some degree, Helen. Madeleine dropped out after session 8. Peter and Helen made a modest improvement. Madeleine, in particular, presented with an inability to stay within herself. When exposed to the group she let others' thoughts and feelings invade her inner space. This may represent an absolute contraindication to an experiential, emotion-focused group therapy. In contrast, regarding resistant patients with major Superego problems, group IE-DP gave mostly encouraging indications, in that their character and Superego underwent at least some positive modifications. However, John's improvement in this respect was minor.

Another clinical observation was that the group setting especially lends itself to Self- and Other-restructuring interventions (SO). This may have been further enhanced by the IE-DP inclination to privilege the real, personal aspects of the therapeutic relationship (RE). All in all, SO and RE interventions were administered even more generously than in the individual setting.

A final happy annotation is that the group was blessed with three pregnancies. Susana's pregnancy went virtually in parallel with the group therapy, and her baby was introduced to the group in the penultimate session. After trying for a baby for a long time, Peter's girlfriend got pregnant before the end of the group therapy and, at a later follow-up, Peter reported that a healthy baby girl had been born and welcomed by her parents. Finally, as a result of the therapy Annie moved to another city, and started a new phase of her life with her new boyfriend. At a later follow-up she too had become a happy mother.

References

Bion, W. R. (1961). *Experiences in Groups.* London: Tavistock.

Burrow, T. (1927). The group method of analysis. *The Psychoanalytic Review, 14*: 268–280.

Cornelissen, K. L. M. (2001). With Davanloo under your pillow: The ISTDP of Dr H. Davanloo in a residential setting. In: J. ten Have-de Labije (Ed.), *The Working Alliance in ISTDP: Whose Intrapsychic Crisis?* Amsterdam: VKDP—Dutch Association for Short-Term Dynamic Psychotherapy & the Netherlands Foundation for Intensive Short-Term Dynamic Psychotherapy.

Cornelissen, K. L. M. & Verheul, R. (2002). Treatment outcome of residential treatment with ISTDP. *Ad Hoc Bulletin of Short-Term Dynamic Psychotherapy: Practice and Theory, 6*: 14–23.

Davanloo, H. (2000). *Intensive Short-Term Dynamic Psychotherapy: Selected Papers of Habib Davanloo, MD.* Chichester, UK: John Wiley & Sons.

Derogatis, L. R. (1994). *Symptom Checklist-90-Revised: Administration, Scoring and Procedures Manual.* Minneapolis, MN: National Computer Systems.

Foulkes, S. H. (1964). *Therapeutic Group-analysis.* London: Allen & Unwin.

Foulkes, S. H. (1975). *Group-analytic Psychotherapy.* London: Gordon & Breach.

Kaes, R. (1993). *Le groupe et le sujet du groupe (Group and the Group's Subject).* Paris: Dunod.

Levy Moreno, J. (1932). *Psychothérapie de groupe et psychodrame. Introduction théorique et clinique à la socioanalysis (Group Psychotherapy and Psychodrama. Theoretical and Clinical Introduction to Socioanalysis).* Paris: Poche.

Lewin, K. (1936). *Principles of Topological Psychology.* New York: McGraw-Hill.

Malan, D. H. (1976a). *The Frontier of Brief Psychotherapy.* New York: Plenum.

Malan, D. H. (1976b). *Toward the Validation of Dynamic Psychotherapy.* New York: Plenum.

McCullough, L., Kuhn, N., Andrews, S., Kaplan, A., Wolf, J. & Lanza Hurley, C. (2003). *Treating Affect Phobia: a Manual for Short-Term Dynamic Psychotherapy.* London: Guilford Press.

Neri, C. (1995). *Il Gruppo (The Group).* Rome: Borla.

Osimo, F. (2003). *Experiential Short-Term Dynamic Psychotherapy: A Manual.* Bloomington, IN: AuthorHouse:

Palvarini, P. (2009). La relazione reale come fattore terapeutico in psicoterapia (The real relationship as a therapeutic factor in psychotherapy). *Psicobiettivo, 19*: 131–147.

Rouchy, J. C. (1998). *Le group espace analytique: clinique e theorie.* Ramonville Saint-Agne, France: Edition Erès.

Stone, W. N. (1999). *Group Psychotherapy for People with Chronic Mental Illness.* New York: Guilford Press.

Yalom, I. D. (1995). *The Theory and Practice of Group Psychotherapy.* New York: Basic.

Notes

1. By "matrix" is meant the group's function of fostering the interplay between relationship patterns and the therapeutic process.
2. In the individual trial relationship interview—which, by the way, Peter often mentions—the therapist would have already engaged in a tit-for-tat with the patient to allow the contradictions to emerge, underlining, in real time, two sniggers, showing the character defence and probing for Peter's willingness to give it up.

CHAPTER FIFTEEN

Privileging relationships within our places of work: what can the principles of experiential dynamic therapy bring to public services?

Naomi Wilson

The aim of this chapter, using the metaphor of maieutics, is to give birth to a new dialogue about how the experiential and relational expertise of professionals needs to be privileged, rather than ignored, within the NHS. There is accumulating evidence of the centrality of the therapeutic relationship, attunement, and a highly affective focus as prerequisites to psychological healing (Schore, 2009). Moreover, this aspect of the work can be motivating for caregivers, and emotional connection is personally and professionally sustaining—what works for patients works for us too, which can only be good for service provision. In this way, the emotionally intimate relationship between therapist and patient in experiential dynamic therapy (EDT) constitutes the core of humane and effective interventions. Although humane and effective treatment is a goal of public services, the culture of our care systems in Western Europe in the twenty-first century is one where quality indicators of care are objective and almost exclusively derived from scientific or economic epistemologies. I will argue that these are divorced from people who provide care and render the relational dimension of professional knowledge invisible (Reinders, 2010). This puts professionals at risk of not being able to work as empathically as is needed, which is not just an ethical concern but one that threatens our most effective tool of change, the real relationship. Recent work within neuroscience about the unhelpful predominance of "left hemisphere" understandings of the world also illuminates this over-reliance on reductive and potentially dehumanising processes of accountability within public services (McGilchrist, 2009). Theoretical frameworks from EDT can help us formulate how the political and professional contexts of our workplaces often act as barriers to emotionally effective care, and may become solidified into emotionally defensive practices. Finally, I will discuss how the relationship and relational techniques privileged by EDT can be applied to systemic problems by those working in mental health services.

Therapeutic relationships promote effective change in EDT and sustain professionals in their work

Osimo (2003) and McCullough (1997) propose that in EDT the real relationship, rather than the transferential one, is arguably more important to personality change. The therapist who is collaborative and committed to a growing emotional connectedness with the patient (as long as not to the personal gratification of the therapist) offers a real and "enlightened involvement" (McCullough, 1997, p. 199). This enables the therapist to "(a) assist in the desensitization of conflicted affects and attachments, (b) offer a new or 'good enough' model for attachment, and (c) help validate, clarify, and label inner experience, when necessary" (ibid., p. 433).

EDT continues to diverge from other psychodynamic and psychoanalytical practices in being more explicit about the use of active relational strategies. For example, Fosha (2000) identifies how patient-therapist relational experiences can be noticed and recruited to positive therapeutic end. For instance, therapists may show support and affirmation for their patient by appreciating the person and their experiences, express care, compassion, and concern, offer encouragement, and validate and amplify healthy responses (such as self-empathy or self-compassion). In addition, the therapist will ask for permission to share authentic emotional responses to the patient's Self and life experiences (with appropriate boundaries that are made explicit), and will also explore the patient's response to these communications. Very important is how the patient reacts to the therapist's empathy, as many, particularly those who lack receptive capacity (see McCullough et al., 2003), will block, discount, or minimise this.

In her writings, Fosha (e.g., 2000a, b) discusses how the therapist's expression of real affective experience might occur within EDT. This could include the acknowledgement of errors or limitations, being receptive to the patient's impact on them, self-disclosure to counteract therapeutic omnipotence and, again, *exploring the patient's reaction* to this communication. Small incremental steps in attunement and enquiry about the patient's response to this are recruited in the pursuit of increasing intimacy and closeness. This is by no means an exhaustive list of the use of the therapeutic relationship within EDT, but what these aspects have in common is that they all include not just the therapist's intervention and patient's response, but a "metaprocessing" (Fosha, 2000b) of affective-relational experience. This explicit interchange occurs regardless of where the therapeutic activity is taking place on the Triangle of Others and offers a continuous feedback that iteratively informs the therapist's *and* the patient's understanding of their inner and relational worlds. This "bringing to life" of interpersonal space is a paradigmatic shift from previous dynamic therapies, where much of the patient responses would be noted, but not clearly pointed out to him or her. Significant therapeutic factors are, therefore, the therapist's ability to work within the real relationship, and willingness to explore affective-relational experience.

Trauma (either in early life or in adulthood) can result in overwhelming, unprocessed, and unintegrated emotional states (van de Hart, Nijenhuis & Steel, 2006; van der Kolk, 1994). In order to cope, individuals withdraw from their emotional world or employ defensive strategies that limit further emotional experiencing. Aloneness is the inevitable outcome of such ways of being. Within trauma work, it is of utmost importance to facilitate a secure enough attachment in the therapeutic dyad, as this is a necessary, but not sufficient, condition of change that provides the foundation from which experiential, emotionally focused therapeutic work can begin. Restructuring strategies (see McCullough, 1997; McCullough et al., 2003) are also needed, but my focus here is to emphasise the role of the relationship in EDT in facilitating healing. Given that the first stage is to establish a secure relational base from which to proceed, what follows is a clinical example of the active use of the therapeutic relationship, specifically the therapist's empathic response and disclosure of affective impact of the patient on her, towards this end. It should be evident that the tentative beginnings of relational work around positive affect within the therapist-patient relationship builds resilience, reduces "aloneness", and enhances a sense of togetherness and trust. Such safety in the relationship means that, later in the therapeutic process, as other emotions and pro-attachment experiences such as intimacy, closeness, and togetherness surface, the patient will experience less anxiety, and defences are less likely to be put into operation. This deep level of interaction is in stark contrast to the histories of traumatised patients who have experienced much interpersonal abuse and abandonment.

So, to the clinical example. Previously in the session the patient has talked about an overwhelming sadness (X) that she carries within her. She often cries at home alone for hours, but with relatively little relief. In session, she allows herself some tears but tends to start to analyse (D) why she is feeling like this with the therapist rather than allowing herself to stay with the feeling, for fear that "it will never stop" (A) as "it feels as if there is an ocean of tears" (X). The therapist has been exploring with the patient, with increasing specificity, what it is like to cry alone, with the intention, initially, of bringing to light the maladaptive character defence of coping alone, and hiding her inner world from others, which keeps her imprisoned from the vitality of close, intimate and warm relationships (DA). During this, the therapist discloses to the patient how sad it makes her feel when she hears that the patient is grieving but that she does this alone (affective self-disclosure—RE, SO, XA).

Th: You have these tears, this sadness, this longing to cry (**XA**), a feeling that it could go on forever. (**AA**)

Pt: Yeah (weeping, but blowing nose and trying to wipe tears away).

Th: That it might never stop. (**AA**) So, there are different parts. Part that wants to be able to share this feeling (**XA**) but part that feels safer not to share what you really need, (**AA**) and another part that is defiantly saying "We are not going to do this together". (**DA**)

Pt: I don't think it is that, I think there is something in there, in the defiance but it is also the fact that there is something in there that is going to make you [the therapist] sad.

The therapist takes this open and revealing correction of the therapist's formulation by the patient as an indication that an atmosphere of collaboration and sharing views has been established. The therapist conveys to the patient that she is OK with her sadness and will not be overwhelmed or damaged but rather is OK with emotional closeness and connection (RE, SO):

Th: Oh, OK, OK. Well perhaps I should let you know that it is OK for you to make me feel sad. It is OK for me. I am a human being and being touched by you is fine. I am not overwhelmed by it, it is not damaging to me.

Pt: Yeah. And I suppose another way of wanting to look at it in a more constructive way is that if I don't [think you will be] sad then I could allow myself to cry more. Which would help me, you would be less sad or not sad at all (D against intimacy).

The therapist persists with affective disclosure and makes it clear to the patient that she expects to continue experiencing feelings in relation to the patient throughout the therapy (RE, SO):

Th: Hm, hm. For me, it is OK. Sometimes you might make me sad, you might make me happy, or I may have other feelings, but that is OK. They are just feelings, information, and whatever comes up here is OK. (**XA**) For you one of the things that seems to happen in relation to your feelings, particularly with others, is that lots of activity starts to happen up here (pointing towards her head). (**DA**) Is that right?

Pt: Yes.

The therapist continues to point out the patient's defensive position of ruminating about whether or not she should cry and the patient notices this makes her "freeze" (A). What follows is therapist activity focused on anxiety regulation and an invitation to work together to not respond defensively to the anxiety. It should be noted that the therapist validates the defence but invites the patient to think about a more adaptive strategy (DA):

Th: What if you were not to freeze? (**AA, DA**) Because on the one hand it is important that you work out a way of holding on to your thoughts so you can go back and get them, but …

Pt: … if I didn't do that …

Th: If you were not to freeze? (**DA**)

The pace of therapy is slower here, with the intention of being anxiety regulating. It is also intended to allow the patient to explore her internal dynamics in a paced way that is not overwhelming.

Pt: Is that I would probably go deeper into it. I am not really sure. I guess it is because it is not something that I ever really do!

Th: It's new territory!

Pt: Yes it is new territory, something that I need to explore (laughs).

Th: (Laughs).

The therapist and the patient are perhaps experiencing a little trepidation at the start of a new journey and the prospect of emotional closeness, but there is also shared pleasure in their collaboration and emotional contact.

Th: Yeah? Can we do that here together?

Pt: Yeaaah.

Th: If you just notice anything you might feel in relation to me saying that what you say makes me sad, touches me, what do you notice comes up? (**RE, SO, XA**)

Pt: It's a really good feeling to hear.

The patient says this quietly, indicating some anxiety and some defensive diminishing of her voice. The therapist gently encourages the patient to continue (AA, XA):

Th: Hm, hm, OK.
Pt: Yeah. It almost gives, it is kind of like a green light to go. I guess it does feel like a safe, like it would be safe, yes it is safe.
Th: It feels safe, it feels like a green light to go, yeah? What's that like? Having "a green light to go"?
Pt: It's like, again it's unexplored.
Th: New?
Pt: Yeah.

The therapist mirrors the patient's stance and pace.

Th: Tentative?
Pt: It's definitely tentative, it is new, but then of course it brings all this fear.

The patient beautifully articulates the link between feeling and anxiety, and the therapist acknowledges the patient's anxiety (AA):

Th: Yes it brings up fear.

A few moments later.

Th: So your openness allows you to explore, which is a real gift I think you have, this real deep enquiry you have about yourself and desire to understand and be more open to your feelings. But it also makes you say, at some point, "OK that is enough." The anxiety comes in and you say, "I am going to go away for a bit." (**AA**)
Pt: Yes I think I do that a lot.

A few minutes later in the session the patient recognises one of her problematic patterns of relating with others, acknowledges an adaptive alternative, and refers to her automatic tendency to put a wall between herself and others:

Pt: I think that happens a lot in relationships. I have been told in the past that there is only so much I give then nothing comes after. I suppose in a relationship it takes people to one level and you can explore and develop it more. I guess there is no end to it really, yeah, but I put a wall.
Th: So what we just noticed together here is that there is real capacity in you, a desire to feel more connected and freer with your feelings but then actually when I say "OK let's take another step," you say, "No, what I was thinking was" …
Pt: (Laughs)
Th: (Laughs) … but you have a very beautiful picture of what is happening. So how would it be to stay a little quietly with what is bubbling up? (**XA**)

Exploration of the patient's tendency to cry alone, outside therapy continues. At some risk of over-attending to the use of this defensive strategy, the therapist returns to the use of the therapeutic relationship to try to foster core emotional work.

Th: What is your experience of crying alone compared to crying here with me?
Pt: There is no exchange (referring to being alone).
Th: What is your experience of [this] exchange?
Pt: It's two of us, but, from you I get the guidance, there isn't the personal ...

The patient denies (D) the personal aspect of her relationship with the therapist, simultaneously denying the reality of the therapist as a person who can be personally affected, but then relinquishes her defence, referring to the therapist's earlier affective self-disclosure. The therapist explores the patient's experience of their personal connection (RE, XA, SO):

Pt: ... well, there is the personal side when you say that you are sad that I don't allow myself to do something, or are touched by something I say.
Th: What is that personal connection like for you?
Pt: It's good (voice lifting, looking directly at therapist), it's helpful (looks away and clears throat then looks back up at therapist and with arms expressive) it's like cotton wool.

The therapist has a warm tone of voice and is receptive to the patient expressing something about her experience of receiving empathy from the therapist (XA, SO).

Th: (Smiling) Uh, huh.
Pt: But I guess it does feel very new, but it feels good, yeah.
Th: Mmm, yeah, where do you notice it feels good?
Pt: In my head.

It is noteworthy that the patient gives a very rapid, clear, and direct response that is in stark contrast to the relative hesitancy of her previous utterances, indicating a growing connection to her authentic feelings. As the therapist is aware that the patient has a habit of spending a great deal of time ruminating on why she struggles so much in life, fantasising about alternative life scenarios, and dissociated, that is, losing time or "spacing out" during interpersonal exchanges, the therapist is interested to know what is happening when the patient says that she feels good in her head (HP):

Th: In your head? Yeah? It has an impact on your head. What happens to your head?
Pt: It clears my head.
Th: It clears your head.

There is a pause as the therapist takes in the significance of the patient's communication.

Th: Wow.

The patient goes on to describe that there are a couple of friends who she tries to be more open with, and who she thinks know "about her" but realises that her exchange with the therapist is different. The patient is smiling towards the therapist who begins to help the patient deepen their affective-relational experience (XA, RE):

Th: There's a difference. I notice that this brings a smile to your face. It gives you a warm feeling?
Pt: (Smiles and nods) Yeah.
Th: There's a difference, it seems, for you that here your tears are responded to.

The therapist then goes on to provide psycho-education about the adaptive function of tears of grief, that is, that they alert others around them to the person's distress and need for comfort. She describes the experience of *receiving* comfort in the patient's words of feeling like she is "surrounded by cotton wool" when the therapist responds with concern to her tears. The patient says that this understanding of the role of tears is new information. However, she then connects this to her own feeling of wanting to help people if she sees them crying. The therapist points out to her how sensitive she is to others and how warm she can be. The patient's face lights up, indicating that her receptive capacity is developing and recounts an anecdote of her close friend explaining to her that others come to her because of *her receptiveness* to others' difficulties. The session is coming to an end and the therapist alerts the patient to this, and prompts for meta-therapeutic processing.

Th: How has it been for you today?
Pt: Um, OK. Um, good. Well I feel, I suppose I feel, perhaps you don't think this.

The patient laughs nervously indicating anxiety about sharing her true feelings, but there is also concerted effort on the patient's part to stay connected to her experience after the earlier benefits of doing this with the therapist.

Pt: It's somehow easier, it's becoming easier to … I guess to relate to you and think of the work together.

Throughout the therapist is saying, "Yeah", "Umm", and offering non-verbal communications of her receptivity to the patient's brave attempts to relate more openly.

Th: So we have something to celebrate!
Pt: (Smiling and laughing) Yes.
Th: Yeah.

The therapist does not deepen the feeling experience further as the session is drawing to a close and instead continues with meta-therapeutic work to build a cognitive understanding of what has happened within the session.

Th: So this is a new way of learning about yourself, exploring. And every relationship is unique and takes time to evolve.

Pt: Yes, it has been helpful.

As is evident from the extract above, this type of work can be immensely motivating for the therapist; emotional connection that facilitates the transformation of our patients is personally and professionally sustaining. In my experience as a therapist, these moments are deeply moving and sustaining. The preceding example demonstrated that the first step involves therapist and patient constructing a relational frame that is safe for the client to begin exploration of their inner world in relationship with the therapist. The emphasis within EDT of checking and rechecking of the patient's response to therapist interventions, regardless of where on the Triangle of Conflict we are working, is another illustration of how the therapeutic relationship is used to foster security and safety within the relationship. The patient's responses are the most important aspect of any interchange—whether defensive, or indicative of anxiety or core feeling. All require attention to further understanding of the patient's dynamics, and to continue the processing of what has just been experienced, leading to a further round of experiencing. What is also powerful about this intervention is that new relational experiences with the therapist can be named and the therapist and patient have an opportunity to differentiate these from past experiences and appreciate their adaptive potential.

Fosha (2006) demonstrates that this degree of therapist emotional engagement, enquiry about patient response, and an attachment orientation facilitates a rapid relinquishing of defences, regulation of anxiety, and fosters connection with adaptive, core affect that results in "quantum leaps" of change in a positive direction. That is, it is not only trauma that can have a sudden and enduring emotional impact on individuals. This challenges some of the psychodynamic zeitgeists of slow, therapeutic change in the context of a more emotionally distanced and interpretive (primarily cognitive) relationship with the patient.

The meta-therapeutic processing of the *affective-relational experience* processes the patient's experience of transformation with the therapist and can minimise disavowal. Of interest is that in this model the relational experience is attended to at either end of the therapeutic process; the conditions (secure enough attachment) for therapy are clearly set up via relational mechanisms at the outset and then we return to the same at the end; "How was it to have those experiences here with me?" I believe that this processing of affective experiences within such a well-developed relational frame is unique to EDT.

What is important here is an authentic interaction that gives the patient a different attachment experience. One caveat in my presenting here the processing of "positive affect" and intimacy, is that the therapist clearly also needs to be able to deal equally directly, albeit sometimes in a graded way, with all the other feelings and material that the patient brings to therapy. Idealisation is evidently not going to help the patient (Malan & Coughlin Della Selva, 2006), but the purpose here is to illustrate the explicit attention made to the fear of feelings, closeness with others, and to the emergence of transformative healing affects of accomplishment, pride, joy, wonder, and of simply being well and accepting of oneself. This meta-processing of transformational experiences within a secure attachment relationship with the therapist enables patients to "engage a wider range of life enriching behaviours and affects" (Ogden, 2009) and to activate "new resources and capacities", which become constitutive of the Self (Fosha, 2009, p. 201) and herald new relational opportunities.

What we have seen thus far is that the relationship between therapist and patient in EDT, especially with people who have experienced multiple interpersonal trauma, is not only at the core of the work but is made explicitly so. What is unique about working with other human beings, especially, but not exclusively, in psychotherapy, is that changes are largely possible via close and intimate relationships (Meininger, 2005). Patients' goals may be to become less depressed, to return to work, to have happier relationships, to stop hurting themselves. However, the route by which transformation is possible requires a dialectic process of the therapist putting a premium on the closeness of the relationship with the client, as well as self-understanding of the caregiver in order to do this.

Professionals need to be relationally sophisticated

Many of our patients have histories of developmental trauma, often with interpersonal abuse on the part of primary caregivers. We know from neuropsychological understandings (e.g., Shapiro, 2001) that when entering a similar situation now (i.e., an attachment relationship with the therapist), earlier complex stored perceptual information is elicited, and the child's perspective comes to the fore. Specifically, the same emotions, somatic experiences, perspectives, and beliefs *of the child* at that time are experienced by the patient; to a degree it is who they are in that moment. In this way the dependency of the patient on the therapist is clear and knowing and healing is an intimate, affect filled, relational and, on the part of the therapist, highly attuned and technically sophisticated dance between the two of them.

In this way, regardless of our patient group, "tacit knowledge" (Reinders, 2010), that is, a real relationship that attends to personal, affective, and relational interactions are important in the provision of care. More than this it is an epistemological claim; high quality relationships and pro-attachment behaviours are the means by which we garner professional knowledge and orientate ourselves to how we can help others. Moral sensitivity in health care requires a capacity for relatedness rather than an ability to make "objective" assessments (e.g., Jaeger, 2001). Nienaber's (2011) study of nurses' experiences of suicide policy in psychiatric inpatient settings revealed that none of the policy documents discussed relationships. Yet repeatedly it was the relationship with others that nurses and patients attested to as "saving lives". Specifically a "bridging" between death and life was offered as the nurses reflected an image of humanity, guided the patient back to life, and helped them learn to live again.

In the same way, organisational learning that sustains improvement over time is enhanced by collaboration between managers and clinicians (Rushmer, Kelly, Lough, Wilkinson & Davis, 2004). In Nienaber's (2011) study there were times *in extremis*, when referral to policy documents and increased documenting or systematising of care provided nurses with adaptive defences, as such practices offered emotional and legal protection that enabled them to continue in their work, particularly at times of acute anxiety following suicide attempts. However, when such defensive practices were not relied upon, the relationship with the patient, positive risk taking (involving shared team responsibility), a no blame culture and an emphasis on engagement rather than control, were all privileged as the most effective mechanisms of care.

Clearly in contexts such as these, if we are to work with any emotional care or openness, let alone sophistication with our patients, there cannot be an emotional vacuum. Therefore, we need to turn our attention to the context in which psychologists and psychotherapists work, as this impacts on how effectively we carry out our therapeutic task of helping other human beings to heal and live well. Practitioners too need their capacity for relatedness to be fostered. When in close and secure relation to others (at work this is our colleagues, referrers, trainers, managers, policy makers) who are, among other things, attuned to our emotional needs, capacity for relatedness is likely to be enhanced. This becomes even more important when professionals are, rightly, under pressure to provide sensitive, humane, and effective services within the NHS. But what is the current context of the workplace?

Current context of work in public systems

In the last twenty years, choice and competition have been consistently offered as the panacea by which patient care can be improved in the NHS. This is despite a paucity of evidence that there exists any such positive relationship between what is, on the one hand, a political and economic ideology about allocation of resources and, on the other, a philosophical, moral, or altruistic ideal to which society aspires. In short, that we take care of each other when in ill health. As the architecture of our healthcare system is premised on economic models, this means measurement is foremost focused on the quantity or amount of time spent in transaction between provider (normally a professional person or team of professionals) and patient, or "episodes of care" rather than the quality or nature of care given.

Quality of care is an increasing focus of attention but, interestingly, measures most congruent with economic models, for example, quantitative outcome measures of symptom reduction (already a less than individualistic tool of evaluation), are most easily and readily employed. These inadvertently support the premise that the evaluation of service provision, including psychological care, is primarily quantitative and *can* be divorced from the professional (or their relationship with the patient) which enables change (Wilson, Meininger & Charnnock, 2009). There is often an assumption inherent in these models that a technique can be applied to a particular end (without even the most basic acknowledgement that the "technique" is a human interchange). This means quality assessments are presumed to be independent of the person(s) providing a service and encourages the tendency across all public sector practices to reduce variability in provision so that the full leverage of competition and choice can be realised. We thus offer the "same" (application of technique) for "less" (financial cost), normally only possible by "cheaper" (less well trained and less well supported) professionals, or mechanisation of services.

All of this has been dependent on another economic premise, which is the artificial split between purchaser and provider in the NHS. This again, has been the focus of attention in the White Paper, *Equity and Excellence: Liberating the NHS* (Department of Health, 2010). The most radical aspect of this particular NHS reform is the collapse of Strategic Health Authorities and removal of Primary Care Trusts (historically commissioners of services as well as the education of health professionals). These are to be replaced by a greater number of smaller GP commissioning groups. The rhetoric has been that this enables the government to put patients first and sets an agenda of continuous improvement in healthcare.

What has been interesting about the re-evocation of market mechanisms to "improve quality of care" has been the virtually unanimous response from health care professionals and patient and carer groups. They have not condoned the purchaser–provider split; rather, the consensus is that patient care will only be enhanced through multidisciplinary co-operation, service integration, the sharing of professional and patient expertise within commissioning groups, extending these beyond GPs, as well as the removal of any explicit intention to "promote competition" (Mental Health Foundation, 2011; NHS Future Forum, 2011; Rethink, 2011). However, even prior to 2011 there seems to have been little appetite for reform. For example, when the public is offered choice, almost all opt to stay with local NHS services and resist the equality of opportunity of service provision that has been opened up to the private and voluntary sector.

The NHS is in the position of having to provide services for all. There are no exceptions to provision of care, even when the work is difficult, distressing, and complex. There are also times when each of us reaches the limit of our expertise in helping particular patients (Wilson, Clegg & Hardy, 2008). One of the advantages of commissioning organisations that serve larger populations (rather than the proposed smaller GP commissioning groups) is that financial risk management is at a tolerable level. This is because there are both "high" and "low" cost individuals, meaning there is inevitable overspend that is offset by surplus capital. Unspoken in this is the nature of the relationship between all members of society that implicitly is one of allocation of resources based on need and collaboration, not competition.

The *Equity and Excellence: Liberating the NHS* White Paper (Department of Health, 2010) advocates that improving outcomes of patient care will be possible by liberating clinicians to innovate. On the surface, it would appear that this is closely allied to what clinicians are aiming for in their work. However, differences start to become apparent when we examine the mechanisms of change at a political rather than clinical level. Whereas psychological knowledge—specifically here, EDT—promotes better relational skills as the tool of change, the mechanisms of implementation within all health-related policy documents (certainly those from the UK in recent years) are based on the principle of market forces.

Reinders (2010) argues that the impact of this type of bureaucracy is changing the practice of care in detrimental ways, specifically, having an adverse effect on the personal dimension. Care standards are not irrelevant but care is not entirely reducible to "quality standards". If the context of professionals' work is one of increased scrutiny and accountability of care, but in a relatively mechanical way, it can also leave clinicians, who do not rely exclusively on these types of knowledge, unsure about the validity of their work. Practitioners may become reluctant to offer creative caring interventions to their patients, as, in addition, such measurement at a societal level has a paradoxical effect of creating a culture of public suspicion rather than trust (O'Neill, 2002).

So, what about the humane dimensions of care within our work if the political discourses are largely devoid of this in content or tone? We are not faced with an anonymous individual to whom a finite amount of financial resources are allocated, but particular others with whom we have unique personal relationships (Clegg, Murphy, Almack & Harvey, 2008). A functional rather than relational concept of the other is not only dehumanising to patients, but also to professionals, who may be left to navigate the tragedies and joys of their patients' lives within bureaucracies that distance themselves from this, in order to implement political rationalities that are sometimes at odds with the real human endeavours within our work. In this way, some of the unhelpful behaviour of our organisations parallels that of the past caregivers of our patients; there is a neglect of relational-affective experience and a valuing of achievement of targets over systemic well-being. In this context, it is easy for professionals to believe that their endeavours are not valued and that any regard is conditional on reductionist measures of success.

I wonder, why, when we are skilled to work so closely in therapeutic relationships with our patients that we do not always bring this level of experiential knowledge to our work within the systems of which we are part? There seems to be some urgency to find (or re-find) ways of theorising and measuring the relational nature of our work with other human beings if we are to avoid further inescapable shifts in the meaning of the professional self.

Formulation and remedies

Having made clear some of the political, institutional, and systemic barriers to undertaking high quality work that clinicians face in the NHS, this section will explore how EDT and recent neuropsychological insights deepen our understanding of how "emotionally detached" organisational cultures in public services are sustained. Secondly, some of the EDT techniques that promote better relational skills and restore healthy functioning will be offered as possible remedies to the organisational pathology described.

Osimo (2012) describes character defences as well established patterns of being that have become crystallised into the personality. Their aim is to repel intimacy and they are put into operation automatically in an attachment relationship due to anxiety about sharing feeling or due to an alliance with a pathological Superego that would respond as disparaging, dismissive, or neglectful of any such feelings. Arguably, the systems in which professionals are operating in the twenty-first century have many of the features of a personality that exhibits maladaptive character defences. For example, at best, their philosophies are benignly neglectful of relational processes, and, at worst, are similar to those of a pathological Superego that scorns such ways of knowing and positions them as illegitimate. In her early work, Menzies-Lyth (1988) argued that professionals in organisations inevitably experience anxiety during the course of their work, and unhelpful social defence mechanisms can evolve that become embedded within their structures, functioning, and culture: for example, taking a position of detachment, denial of feelings, avoidance of close relationships with patients, and renunciation of unique personal characteristics (through uniforms or "uniformed" procedures). If they become concrete, a defensive, self-defeating position towards caring work is sustained as they foster depersonalisation of others, categorisation, and denial of the significance of the individual, again all of which we know are counter-therapeutic. Since Menzies-Lyth's observations, the relentless redefinition of our public services in the last twenty years as ever more abstract, technical, and (ideally) goal seeking (Mowles, 2011), means that professionals are even more increasingly pushed into taking paranoid positions. If coupled with a manic response to the demands of "hyper-accountability" it is indeed hard to stay close to the vitality and vulnerability associated with the bringing to life, or losses and deaths of our patients, the services in which we work, and, indeed, the NHS itself. Such a terrorised state of affairs cannot be helpful, not least, as there is a risk of trying to limit exposure to emotional connections that are at the heart of our work. This means that professionals and services tend not to be encouraged to develop the emotional sophistication to deal effectively with relational and emotional issues.

McGilchrist's (2009) exceptional thesis on the primacy of left-brain thinking within the Western world, and the dangers of this, has much to offer us when we examine the types of knowledge that underpin our bureaucracies. He argues that we are operating within structures that both implicitly and explicitly endorse a "left-brain" epistemology of healthcare. The value of the left hemisphere (LH) is that it "yields narrow, focussed attention" (p. 27) that is relatively detached, mechanistic, and affectually disengaged (lacking empathy). It enables us to isolate objects from their context for close analysis and is highly useful in making linear and logical deductions. Representation of the world (in our case the NHS) solely from this perspective yields a view that is "relatively mechanical, an assemblage of more or less disconnected 'parts'; it would be relatively abstract and disembodied; relatively distanced from fellow-feeling; given to explicitness utilitarian in ethic; over-confident of its own take on reality, and lacking insight into its problems" (p. 209). The right hemisphere (RH), in contrast, "yields a broad, vigilant attention, the purpose of which appears to be awareness of signals from the surroundings [...] and is involved in bonding" (p. 27). This prioritises a knowing through experience, including the noticing of anomalies. The RH perceives the whole and is involved in emotional connection with others. Moreover, the RH "grounds" the LH; it has ontological supremacy.

Reinders (2010) disentangles theories of knowledge that are empiricist and assumed valid within evidence-based care, and those that do not presume you can disentangle knowledge from the person who holds that knowledge; "The connection between knower and what is known cannot be severed without loss" (p. 32). He proposes that the difference in epistemologies is the difference between knowledge and insight. This echoes McGilchrist's (2009) position that a retreat from reality (according to the RH gestalt) increases the rigidity and focus of LH thinking to which we become increasingly enslaved but at enormous cost to understanding. Science here attempts to eliminate the "contamination" of the unique interpersonal current, whereas for Reinders (2010) "The quality of professional judgment depends upon among other things, the intentionality of being attached and attuned to the particularities of the client" (p. 32). This "necessary embodiment" of knowledge or insight means the personal dimension needs to be cultivated for professionals, which is in contrast at times with standardisation. This is not to deny any need for scientific enquiry or instruments of measurement, but is a reminder that these are not adequate premises for guaranteeing good professional judgement.

How might EDT principles be applied within services to promote organisational health?

EDT makes explicit the Triangle of (intrapsychic) Conflict, the Triangle of Others, and the technical interventions employed by the therapist that are intellectually and emotionally informed by the real relationship. This requires an approach from the therapist that is not just verbal and rational but also encompasses other ways of attending. We are asked to continually "notice" the patient's way of being and relating in a myriad of ways, some of which involve verbal communication while others include the attitude of the patient, bodily postures, actions, and affect expression. We make sense of these using both our conceptual capacity and technical knowledge but also our own emotional responses. This at best then helps us to convey a knowing that integrates all aspects of the relationship and that we can relate back to the whole person, something encapsulated in Osimo's (2009) conceptualisation of the "character hologram".

If we want to foster healthy systems, a key question is how can we enable similar *organisational* knowing or insight in a sustainable way? It would seem that the success and vitality of institutions are likely to be related to their capacity to value systemic attention to the emotional and relational needs and wisdom of their workforce, having effective mechanisms to contain anxiety (Menzies-Lyth, 1988) around the deeply affectual aspects of our work (whether they be around clinical or organisational work), and being able to identify those defence mechanisms, including those embedded and characterological, which threaten the healthy functioning of staff and, therefore, service provision. Before expounding this further, it is important to say that these cannot operate in isolation but a gestalt perspective is required in order for more actively engaged relationships between professionals and professional groups to be sustainable. Rather than a linear process, this relies on a circular moving back and forth between or round these positions (at each level and between levels) within services. Instead of risking becoming detached from the life of their organisations, professionals and teams can become more attached to each other, and develop confidence in addressing problems in mature, resilient, and sustainable ways.

This is a challenge, but in practice a start might be to recognise that we are caught in powerful systems and processes that are technical and rational in epistemology. In contrast to this we need to assume that, at core, and like our fellow human patients, professionals are motivated by the desire for attachment and, at least in part, by altruism and compassion for the other in distress. A second assumption would be that for professionals this connectedness or real and "enlightened involvement" (McCullough, 1997, p. 199) extends to their colleagues and systems of which they are part. At an organisational level, explicitly "bringing to life" the interpersonal space within the system (and the services within these) would be the equivalent of acknowledging the primacy of real relationships in EDT. Envisioning a valuing of relationships and networks and actively incentivising reciprocity in relationships between services (counter to the commissioner-provider split in the NHS) would extend and consolidate this position further.

If we continue to formulate individual professionals or professional groups using the Triangles of Conflict and Others, then anxiety or healthy caution around relating to others (whether patients, colleagues, managers, or policy makers) should rightly be acknowledged and feature in our thinking. This process is partly informed by frameworks of ethical practice that foster an awareness and adherence to professional practices that also set safe boundaries and encourage integrity. It is beyond the scope of this discussion to unpack this further, but what is not being advocated is a relinquishing of ethical thinking, other than to make the caveat that these also have their own epistemologies that may or may not be congruent with relational understandings of human behaviour.

Within services, such valuing of relationships would lay the foundation for the setting up of supervisory and reflective practices that encourage attention to the relational and emotional aspects of our work and the knowledge this affords us. For example, an interesting exercise to this end would be to set out to openly discuss or ask the questions of teams, "What helps us help people to repair their lives, and what touches and sustains us?", "To whom and what do we feel connected and where do people trust each other?", "Where do good relationships exist?", and "When does the team work well?" It would also be important to articulate where frustrations and challenges lie but it is, within the current context of public services, even more valuable at this juncture to recognise where we experience achievement and joy. Genuine relational involvement is life-giving and sustaining within our systems and enables survival. Neurological evidence is such that adaptive affects move outwards and mobilise positive activity whereas anxiety has a dynamic motion of moving inwards to restrict, constrict, and disable adaptive action (ten Have-de Labije, 2010; Neborsky, 2010). Systemic relational work might also be enabled via the explicit mapping of and investment in the professional networks of which we are part, and the support of ongoing collaboration across organisations in the public sector (and beyond) to foster positive alliances.

It would seem feasible to bring Fosha's (2006) concepts of meta-therapeutic processing in here. Wherever, or perhaps we should now be saying *whoever* in the system we turn our attention to, affective-relational processing offers ways of affirming transforming affects within the work which are sustaining; as we have seen, they bring a focus to the positive affects such as curiosity, creativity, and positive risk-taking that mobilise and energise. Whether we reflect on the process of facilitating change with patients, how teams are working, or relationships with other services, this should have the effect of reducing professional isolation and enhancing togetherness. You will recall that in EDT, explicit attentjon to creating a sense of safety in the relationship means that adaptive emotions can surface and pro-attachment experiences such as intimacy, closeness, and trust become possible as defences are relinquished. In this way the effect of rapidly enhancing mastery within the workplace and across the systems and localities in which we work becomes more achievable. One further way of protecting such reflective processes is to understand that, inevitably when under pressure of deadlines, targets, and financial strictures to which we are held to account, these life-giving aspects of our work are easily de-prioritised.

In summary, we need our service and senior managers in public services to empower staff to invest time and energy in meeting with each other to support each other, express care, and compassion to each other, affirm their good work and validate and amplify healthy collaborative functioning. Overall we need them to envision and allow professional practices that value emotional knowing. What we know from our clinical work is that those in leadership positions will only do this when they fully understand the importance of building personal relationships and secure attachments to foster change, and that this is not only with respect to our patients but vitally important to professional well-being. If enabled to invest in transformative processes that enhance emotional and relational health within and between services, only then will we truly foster cultures of psychological wisdom rather than compliance to reductionist economic epistemologies of care.

References

Clegg, J., Murphy, E., Almack, K. & Harvey, A. (2008). Tensions around inclusion: reframing the moral horizon. *Journal of Applied Research in Intellectual Disabilities, 21*: 81–94.

Department of Health (2010). *Equity and Excellence: Liberating the NHS*. London: The Stationary Office.

Fosha, D. (2000a). *The Transforming Power of Affect: A Model for Accelerated Change*. New York: Basic.

Fosha, D. (2000b). Meta-therapeutic processes and the affects of transformation: Affirmation and the healing affects. *Journal of Psychotherapy Integration, 10*: 71–97.

Fosha, D. (2006). Quantum transformation in trauma and treatment: Traversing the crisis of healing change. *Journal of Clinical Psychology, 62*: 569–583.

Fosha, D. (2009). Emotion and recognition at work: energy, vitality, pleasure, truth, desire, and the emergent phenomenology of transformational experience. In: D. Fosha, D. J. Seigel & M. F. Solomon (Eds.), *The Healing Power of Emotion: Affective Neuroscience, Development & Clinical Practice*. New York: W. W. Norton.

ten Have-de Labije, J. (2010). *The Collected Writings of Josette ten Have-de Labije*. Del Mar, CA: Unlocking Press.

Jaeger, S. M. (2001). Teaching health care ethics: the importance of moral sensitivity for moral reasoning. *Nursing Philosophy, 2*: 131–142.

Malan, D. & Coughlin Della Selva, P. (2006). *Lives Transformed: A Revolutionary Method of Dynamic Psychotherapy*. London: Karnac.

McCullough, L. (1997). *Changing Character: Short-Term Anxiety Regulating Psychotherapy for Restructuring Defenses, Affects and Attachment*. New York: Basic.

McCullough, L., Kuhn, N., Andrews, S., Kaplan, A., Wolf, J. & Hurley, C. L. (2003). *Treating Affect Phobia: A Manual for Short-Term Dynamic Psychotherapy*. New York: Guilford Press.

McGilchrist, I. (2009). *The Master and his Emissary: The Divided Brain and the Making of the Western World*. New Haven, CT: Yale University Press.

Meininger, H. P. (2005). Narrative ethics in nursing for persons with intellectual disabilities. *Nursing Philosophy, 6*: 106–118.

Mental Health Foundation (2011). *Response to the NHS Future Forum's Recommendations on the Health and Social Care Bill. London: Mental Health Foundation*. Retrieved September 21, 2011 from http://www.mentalhealth.org.uk/our-news/news-archive/2011/11-06-14/?view Standard.

Menzies-Lyth, I. (1988). *Containing Anxiety in Institutions: Selected Essays, Volume 1*. London: Free Association.

Mowles, C. (2011). Planning to innovate. Designing change or caught up in a game? *Perspectives in Public Health, 131*: 119–123.

Neborsky, R. (2010). *The Collected Writings of Robert J. Neborsky, MD*, Del Mar, CA: Unlocking Press.

NHS Future Forum (2011). *Summary Report on Proposed Changes to the NHS*. London: The Stationary Office.

Nienaber, G. (2011). Searching for a balance: a grounded theory approach to exploring nurses' experiences of suicide prevention policy in a psychiatric inpatient setting. (Unpublished thesis, submitted for the degree of doctor of psychology, University of Surrey.)

O'Neill, O. (2002). Called to account. *Reith Lectures 2002—A Question of Trust*. Retrieved September 21, 2011 from http://www.bbc.co.uk/print/radio4/reith2002/lecture3.shtml.

Ogden, P. (2009). Emotion, mindfulness, and movement. Expanding the regulatory boundaries of the window of affect tolerance. In: D. Fosha, D. J. Seigel & M. F. Solomon (Eds.), *The Healing Power of Emotion: Affective Neuroscience, Development & Clinical Practice*. New York: W. W. Norton.

Osimo, F. (2003). *Experiential Short-Term Dynamic Psychotherapy: A Manual*. Bloomington, IN: AuthorHouse.

Osimo, F. (2009). The character hologram. *Ad Hoc Bulletin of Short-Term Dynamic Psychotherapy: Practice and Theory, 13*: 25–50.

Osimo, F. (2012). The essence of experiential dynamic therapies. In: F. Osimo & M. J. Stein (Eds.), *Theory and Practice of Experiential Dynamic Psychotherapy*. London: Karnac.

Reinders, H. S. (2010). The importance of tacit knowledge in practices of care. *Journal of Intellectual Disability Research, 54*: 28–37.

Rethink (2011). The Listening is Over, Now it's Time to Act. Retrieved September 21, 2011 from http://www.rethink.org/how_we_can_help/news_and_media/press_releases/the_listening_is_ove.html.

Rushmer, R., Kelly, D., Lough, M., Wilkinson, J. E. & Davis, H. T. O. (2004). Introducing the learning practice—III. Leadership, empowerment, protected time and reflective practice as core contextual conditions. *Journal of Evaluation in Clinical Practice, 10*: 399–405.

Schore, A. (2009). Right brain affect regulation: an essential mechanism of development, trauma, dissociation, and psychotherapy. In: D. Fosha, D. J. Seigel & M. F. Solomon (Eds.), *The Healing Power of Emotion: Affective Neuroscience, Development & Clinical Practice*. New York: W. W. Norton.

Shapiro, F. (2001). *Eye Movement Desensitization and Reprocessing: Basic Principles, Protocols and Procedures*. New York: Guilford Press.

van der Hart, O., Nijenhuis, E. R. S. & Steele, K. (2006). *The Haunted Self: Structural Dissociation and the Treatment of Chronic Tramatization*. New York: W. W. Norton.

van der Kolk, B. A. (1994). The body keeps the score: Memory and the evolving psychobiology of posttraumatic stress. *Harvard Review of Psychiatry*, 1: 253–265.

Wilson, N., Clegg, J. & Hardy, G. (2008). What informs and shapes ethical practice in intellectual disability services? *Journal of Intellectual Disability Research*, 52: 608–617.

Wilson, N., Meininger, H. P. & Charnnock, D. (2009). The agony and the inspiration: professionals' accounts of working with people with learning disabilities. *Mental Health Review Journal, 14*: 4–13.

CHAPTER SIXTEEN

Experiential short-term psychodynamic therapy from the perspective of a cognitive-behaviour therapist: a personal account

Joop Meijers

In the mind of many, psychodynamic and cognitive-behaviour therapies are two worlds apart. A huge gulf separates them. In this chapter, I hope to show that the gulf need not be seen as a separating barrier but may, instead, be seen as a connecting stream. In the first part of this chapter I will focus on differences and similarities between the two therapeutic approaches, arguing for the possibility and desirability of a more integrative approach. I will then illustrate some of the ideas presented in the first part of the chapter with a transcript from my work with one patient whom I treated with experiential dynamic therapy.

Introduction

In a world where labels and boxes count, I "am" or at least "am known as" a cognitive behaviour therapist. Since my clinical internship during, and after, my MA studies in the Netherlands in the Seventies (of the last century) I have learned, trained in, and practised Cognitive Behaviour Therapy (CBT). I was lucky in having as my clinical teachers and supervisors the founders of CBT, like Aaron Beck, Albert Ellis, and Donald Meichenbaum. In Holland, I was supervised by the late Ron Ramsay, the pioneer of CBT-based Grief Therapy (Ramsay & Happee, 1977). For my post-doctoral studies I went to Canada where Donald Meichenbaum taught me the basics of Cognitive-Behaviour Modification with children. In the Eighties and Nineties, I trained in New York at the Rational Emotive Behavior Therapy (REBT) Institute with the late Albert Ellis and his staff. Later, I visited Philadelphia, where I trained with Judy Beck who taught me Cognitive Therapy as developed by her father, Aaron Beck. Over the years, as teacher and therapist, I have integrated the different approaches and applied my own "blend" of CBT in my work with my patients (adults and children).

I was formed as a therapist in a Dutch mental health climate which, already in the Seventies, had surpassed the "old-fashioned and non-scientific 'psychodynamic model'", but after immigrating to Israel, suddenly I was confronted by the dominance of the psychodynamic models. I tried to keep my distance from anything smacking of psychoanalytic thinking.

The psychodynamic therapists were the "others": treasurers of what I considered to be a fossilised, psychoanalytic nature reserve, where the natives protected the old and crumbling civilisations as a museum for future generations. CBT was the future, Freud, the past.

A few years ago my opinion changed. Through my contacts with a Dutch colleague,[1] who like myself, shared the Dutch CBT background, I heard for the first time about a therapy orientation that—so she said—could be a bridge between CBT and traditional psychodynamic therapy. Through personal circumstances, she had been in contact with one of the founders of Dutch CBT, who over the years had become interested in a therapy orientation called Intensive Short-Term Dynamic Psychotherapy (ISTDP), pioneered by a Canadian surgeon turned psychotherapist by the name of Habib Davanloo. After watching hundreds of hours of his videotaped therapies, Davanloo developed an extremely effective and efficient short-term psychodynamic therapy for people, even, and especially, those with severe personality disorders. He showed how it was possible to cure them within a relatively short time (sometimes twenty to thirty sessions). Davanloo apparently knew about Behaviour Therapy (BT) and he integrated BT principles and techniques in his ISTDP, although he does not explicitly credit BT or CBT.

My Dutch colleague decided to join one of the first Dutch ISTDP training groups, supervised by Josette ten Have-de Labije, co-founder of the Dutch CBT foundation, and pupil of Davanloo. My colleague radiated her enthusiasm for this method to me. I was curious, and began to read about Davanloo's approach and became enthusiastic as well. Here and there, unsupervised, I even began to apply some of his ideas in my own clinical work. To my surprise, and maybe even to my shock, it sometimes worked! In the summer of 2009 I decided the time had come to immerse myself in the method; I took part in a week-long, intensive, immersion course in Italy, delivered by a "star team" of EDT practitioners. The course (it was called a "summer school") was based on lectures, and hours and hours of watching videotaped therapy sessions by the EDT therapist-supervisors who had no difficulty in openly and honestly sharing with us their work with their clients. I became even more interested and decided to take part in an intensive training course that takes place every few months in London (UK) together with an international group of trainees like me.

So here I am, a CBT therapist, learning to apply and integrate principles of psychodynamic therapy into his work with clients. At this juncture of my career, I feel the need and necessity to clarify, to my clients, my colleagues, and myself, how I see the relationship between CBT and the experiential psychodynamic therapies; why it is important or even necessary to relate and integrate. What I hope to accomplish is to present an account or narrative that, in itself, forms a "bridge over troubled waters", to connect two worlds that—at least in my personal history—always were so apart.

CBT and EDT—two pillars of a bridge

Since there are many excellent introductions to CBT and the various experiential dynamic therapies, my aim at this point is to summarise the main principles of both approaches, the way

I understand them. For an extended review of the basics of CBT, the reader is referred to Aaron Beck (1967, 1990, 1979), Judith Beck (1995), and Albert Ellis (1962, 1996). For an introduction to the experiential dynamic therapies the interested reader is referred to Coughlin Della Selva (1996), Davanloo (1990, 2000), Fosha (2000), Frederick (2009), ten Have-de Labije (2010), Malan and Coughlin Della Selva (2006), McCullough Vaillant (1997), McCullough et al. (2003), Neborsky (2010), and Osimo (2003).

Cognitive Behaviour Therapy (CBT)

The original point of departure of CBT was that problematic feelings and behaviours, the focus of psychotherapy, were first and foremost a function of (caused by) illogical, distorted, irrational thinking and perceiving. One could summarise this approach as follows: If you do not feel well, it is because you do not think well. For example, if after having been ditched, the rejected lover thinks, "This proves that I am a worthless human being, no one will ever love me again, I will remain unhappy the rest of my life, how horrible, I cannot stand this," that person would no doubt feel and become depressed. But if they thought and believed, "This is a very unfortunate experience, that proves our relationship did not work out, but it does not change who I am and there will be other opportunities in the future, I do not like this but it is not the end of the world," they will feel appropriately sad and frustrated but not depressed. Of course, this is a stereotypical example but it exemplifies the original scheme of CBT. Over the years, Beck and other CBT theoreticians could not deny that sometimes emotions precede cognitions so they had to change their model into a more circular one in which pre-existing emotions cause cognitions that in turn may exacerbate, escalate, and/or add to the pre-existing emotions (Clark, Beck & Alford, 1999). But even within the revised model, which looks at problems through the lens of interconnected chains of emotions and cognitions, cognitions are still considered to be the primary focus for therapy. The main assumption, supported by a wealth of excellent quality theoretical and empirical research, is still that it is possible and desirable to change cognitions and that, by changing cognitions (information processing in the widest sense of the word), it is possible to change emotions and behaviour. So, in the preceding example, the therapist's task is to help the patient first, through Socratic questioning, to challenge the distorted beliefs and assumptions, and/or the "core irrational schemas", then change his way of thinking about himself, others, and the future so that where pathological depression was, appropriate sadness shall be. The rich literature of CBT shows that this is indeed a feasible and effective way of therapy for some patients, some of the time, with some problems.[2] To schematically summarise their model, many CBT theorists and clinicians will use the following equation:

$$A \rightarrow B \rightarrow C$$

where

A = the (attended, perceived) Antecedent event (trigger)
B = the Belief (evaluative interpretation, cognition) about A
C = the Consequent emotion or behaviour or both

In our preceding simplified example
A = being left or rejected by lover
B = the Belief: I am worthless, the future is hopeless, I cannot stand it
C = the Consequent emotion: extremely sad

According to Ellis's "Rational-Emotive Behavior Therapy" (REBT) (Walen, DiGiuseppe & Dryden, 1992), and for the comparison with the EDTs, a crucial addition is the "C" in the equation. That is, the consequent affect, feeling, emotion, and/or behaviour that can in turn become a new antecedent event, called A_2, that will then be followed by a B_2 (evaluative belief about A_2), that will then lead to a C_2, a new, secondary emotional and/or behavioural consequence.

Ellis originally conceived of the ABC model as a unidirectional model, but the model has evolved into a circular one, in which pre-existing emotions can change the perception of an event which then will lead to new and different or more intense emotions (Ellis, 1996).

In our example, let us suppose that the rejected lover reacted to the original A with appropriate sadness and/or anger, but then the sadness or anger (C_1) became a new, secondary Antecedent event, trigger (A_2) for B, the belief, "I should and must not be sad, to be sad is unworthy of me" (B_2). As a consequence, the individual would then develop "a secondary emotional disturbance" (Walen, DiGiuseppe & Dryden, 1992, p. 85), namely being angry at (or afraid of) their sadness. This would set in motion a negative emotional chain that could lead to a variety of emotional problems. According to the theory of REBT (ibid.), many problems in psychotherapy are secondary emotional problems. that is, a negative emotion about another negative emotion, leading to avoidance and escape of the emotion and the emotion arousing situation.[3] In those cases, the therapeutic priority is to treat the secondary emotional problem before the primary one (ibid.). It is important to re-emphasise that for Ellis, and Rational Emotive Behaviour Therapy, in particular, the Bs, the Beliefs about the emotions and the triggering situations are of central importance. It is possible, and often enough, to change the B in order to bring about change at the level of C (emotion and behaviour). In a way, analysing the A, B, and C, with the client, is still part of the diagnosis (diagnosis with a therapeutic value). After having established, with the full co-operation and agreement of the client, the A, B, and C, the core work of therapy can begin. Ellis (1996) added two letters to the original three-term equation:

D = Disputing (challenging, Socratic questioning) the "irrational" (problematic) B

So that as a result the client will change his iB (irrational Belief) into a more rational, healthy Belief (rB) with, as a result:

E = creating an alternative, more healthy Emotional and behavioural consequence.

So, for Ellis, but also for Beck, the pioneers of CBT, the problem may very well be that the patient has an emotion (e.g., anxiety) about an emotion (e.g., anger). Yet, according to the ABC model, the problem to focus on is not the emotion per se but the Belief about the Emotions. The emotional problem is to be treated by changing the cognitions about the emotions.

Experiential dynamic therapies

What follows is my personal understanding of an EDT approach, at this stage of my experiential work with and in this school of therapy, being aware of CBT filters operating in my understanding. The core of the orientation can be summarised as follows: many of the emotional problems of our clients are a function of, caused by, the different ways in which they, over the years, have come to defend themselves against the "anxiety" that is aroused by strong, authentic, adaptive impulses and feelings. Those authentic, biologically determined, evolutionary-based feelings were or are still being aroused in or in anticipation of interpersonal situations. For a variety of reasons, the client, if and when not able to cope with or accept those strong feelings and impulses, consciously or unconsciously, has "learned" to escape from and/or avoid those feelings and/or situations that arouse or are associated with those impulses and feelings. But since the body "does not forget" the authentic impulses and feelings, what remains is the anxiety or tension, as a reminder of the authentic emotions and impulses. Often the defence, avoidance, escape from the aversive anxiety, is what forms the problem or causes the problem for which the patient comes into therapy in the first place.

An example—a person comes in with assertiveness problems. In situations in which they are treated in an unjust way, they remain silent, bottle up their anger, and let the abuser get away with the abuse. The individual who has suffered abuse then becomes depressed. It turns out that as a child they were severely criticised and/or ignored or neglected by one of their parents. As a child, they felt very angry but knew from experience that, if they or one of their siblings would express anger towards the parent, that parent would become aggressive, or reject the child. What started as an appropriate protective fear of expressing anger, in a child, still heavily dependent on their parents, gradually became a generalised, internalised fear of *experiencing anger* and then led to a repression of the anger, and later of other strong emotions in general—a process that can be explained easily by modern learning theories as well as by Freud's second signal anxiety theory (Freud, 1926d). Over the years, the child, who in all probability also had a timid temperament, became more and more depressed, and suffered from extreme lack of assertiveness in many situations where they were and are confronted by authority figures.

Many texts of EDT (e.g., Osimo, 2003) present the aforementioned model in schematic form, referred to as the Triangle of Conflict (first developed by Ezriel, 1952, cited in McCullough, 1997), and popularised by Malan (1979), and the Triangle of Others (first developed by Menninger, 1958, cited in McCullough, 1997). Since the triangles are extensively described elsewhere in this book (see Osimo, 2012a), I will only present them in their graphic form (see Figure 1), so they can be of use in the comparison of the ABCDE model of Albert Ellis (1996) and the EDT approach to the understanding and treatment of emotional problems.

It seems to me that, in the EDT model, the root trigger in the historical development of the problem is the so-called attachment trauma, that is the (perceived) rejecting, neglecting, punitive, abusive responses of attachment figures or later important others to the child's authentic feelings, wishes, and longings (see for example, Fosha, 2001). Contrary to the ABC model of Ellis, within the Triangle of Conflict, in EDT, there is no symbol for the original or present trigger, but it is assumed that a stimulus (in the context of a meaningful relationship) triggers "X" (authentic feeling/impulse) that, because of the rejecting and abusive reactions of the other, leads to anxiety and defences, for example, repression of the feeling. A situation stirs up feeling (X), that is painful or provokes Anxiety (perceived as something unpleasant and dysfunctional). To defend against, avoid, and escape from Anxiety (and indirectly from X), a Defensive response is developed or learned. Often the Defensive response is an appropriate response in the original

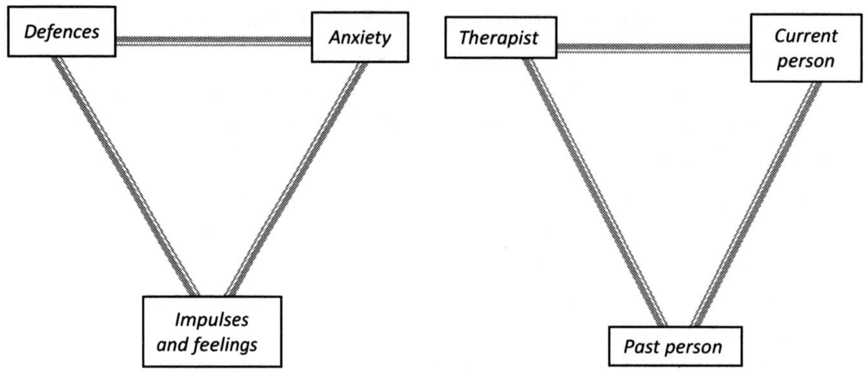

Figure 1. Triangle of Conflict and Triangle of Others.

learning situation (e.g., to avoid being hit and/or rejected, the child, being dependent on their parents, has no choice but to repress their anger). However, what originally might have been a good defence becomes problematic when maintained for too long, for example, becoming automatic and habitual, and/or when it is put into operation in situations where other behaviours are possible and desirable, and the cost of relying on the defence is ignored. In an excellent paper, Kalpin (2001) stated that, within the EDT approaches cognitions are the secondary outcome of repressed emotions. The adult who has learned to repress their anger due to the anxiety it arouses, now "believes" that they absolutely need the appreciation of the other and that if they become angry at the other, the other will reject them, which would be unbearable since, as Ellis (1962) would say, "I absolutely *must* have their love and attention, otherwise I am doomed and lost."

As previously stated, to the Triangle of Conflict a second triangle has been added; the Triangle of Others. This triangle clarifies the interpersonal context of the Triangle of Conflict. The Triangle of Others emphasises how the learning process of repression cannot be isolated from the interpersonal situations in which emotions are aroused and repressed. In the tradition of other psychodynamic models, there is an underlying assumption that the process often starts in childhood with a parental or other attachment figure, and is then repeated in interactions in the here and now with significant others including, as the third leg of the triangle, the therapist. The interpersonal context is inseparably bound up with the process of repression and therefore the therapeutic relationship too plays a crucial role in the process of de-repression (Coughlin Della Selva, 1996). We still see how the role of the therapeutic relationship is heavily underrepresented in CBT, especially in the original CBT models, but less so in newer CBT approaches, like Young's Schema Therapy (Young, Klosko & Weishaar, 2003). So, if for a CBT therapist, at least in the pioneer years, distorted and irrational cognitions are the "cause" of the emotion, it seems that for an EDT therapist the cognitions, like automatic thoughts, come in the wake of and between the authentic feelings and impulses and the emergence of anxiety. When the patient identifies with the "automatic thoughts" the result is defences, the secondary result of, or a defence against, the anxiety that is being triggered by the apparently not completely repressed experiencing of the authentic emotion.

To sum up so far, the framework within EDT is that due to an abusive learning history, the anxiety/fear of authentic feeling leads to defences (avoidance/escape) that in turn cause (or maintain) the pathology to be treated. So the therapeutic implication is to help the client give up the defences, relate the anxiety to the authentic feelings, and help the person feel, fully, experience, and then express the authentic emotions in interpersonal situations that are relevant to them, beginning in the authentic interactions between therapist and client. Ferruccio Osimo, who like Albert Ellis, had studied the Greek classics in his youth, coined the beautiful term "maieutics" (Osimo, 2003, p. 49), which in old Greek means "characteristic of a midwife" and was used by Plato to describe the Socratic dialogue in which Socrates, as a midwife, helped his partner in dialogue to give birth to the truth. Osimo uses the term for one of the central activities of the therapist: to help—as a midwife—bring the client to the point where they can feel and express the authentic emotion in a meaningful interpersonal relationship. When the anxiety is too intense, the therapist will help the patient regulate the anxiety to a level that is tolerable, before the so-called "defence restructuring" can begin.

Socrates as midwife of Osimo (EDT) and Ellis (REBT)

Although not immediately relevant to the focus of this chapter, I cannot refrain from commenting on an interesting parallel between one of the leading therapists in EDT, Ferruccio Osimo and a pioneer of CBT, Albert Ellis.[4]

Both of them mention the Greek philosopher Socrates as an important "maia" (Osimo's term) or symbolic midwife of their thinking about therapy. Socrates's mother, apparently, was a midwife. She also, no doubt, must have been an important, and probably healthy, attachment figure for the young Socrates. Socrates himself emphasised the cognitive aspect of human functioning, the freedom and potential of human beings to give meaning, to use their critical faculties to get to the "truth" as Socrates conceived it; the good and the beautiful, that which is ethically and aesthetically right. The correct understanding of what happens to us will ultimately bring us happiness. So what Ellis learned from Socrates was that, "If you do not feel right, it is because you do not think right." But to learn that skill you need a teacher you trust, you feel attached to. The same Socrates, who taught us how to think well, also is the father or mother of the dialogue. The dialogue is a necessary condition for learning. Socrates, with his mother-midwife as attachment figure, no doubt knew how to create the emotional conditions that would enable his partners in dialogue to be open to internalise what he wanted to teach them. So Osimo's maieutics are a necessary (but not always sufficient) condition for the dialogue that ultimately leads to better understanding and more happiness. From this point of view—and I am aware of my own filters—the midwife gave birth to twins that may need each other for the necessary dialogue that will help the two of them to be happily feeling and good thinking human beings.

A first comparison between CBT and EDT

In my view there are some striking similarities but also differences between the two therapeutic approaches described above.

One striking similarity is that both CBT and EDT assign a prominent role to avoidance/escape/defence as a factor that is responsible for escalating a difficulty into a problem. Let me explain. From an evolutionary point of view, anxiety is a normal, natural, and necessary emotional response that alerts the organism to real, existential danger. It forces the organism to pay attention to a life-threatening situation. Anxiety is a built-in danger signal to which the organism will respond with an evolutionary survival reaction of escaping or avoiding the danger, if at all possible. If successful, the avoidance/escape/defence will be followed by a reduction of anxiety which is experienced as gratifying (reinforcing). Thanks to an evolutionary conditioning mechanism, in the future, similar dangerous situations will be reacted to in the same or similar way. But what happens when the danger is not a real danger but a false alarm? In that case, the successful escape or avoidance response will prevent the organism from learning, and experiencing that the feared situation is not really as dangerous as thought/feared. For example, it is a nice and warm summer day. A person who enjoys swimming jumps in the water but, when confronted by the "cold water", immediately gets out of the water because it feels too cold. By immediately leaving the "cold water" they get immediate relief of the coldness of the water. However, they never will learn and experience that if they had stayed a bit longer in the water, their body would have adjusted its temperature to the real temperature of the water, and they would have enjoyed the relatively warm water. Jumping out is a solution that solves a temporary difficulty but at the cost of creating a bigger problem that is maintained by the solution i.e., that the person will stop swimming. Theory and research in CBT (Allen, McHugh & Barlow, 2008; Foa, 2006) shows that so-called "exposure" to the feared stimulus, that is, techniques that enable the patient to stop escaping and avoiding in order to learn that the alarm or danger is a false alarm (or that the water is warm enough to enjoy swimming in it), is an effective way of reducing anxiety and other unpleasant feelings. So a common therapeutic task in both CBT and EDT is to create conditions under which the client is willing and able to risk stopping/interrupting the escape and avoidance responses, or defences, in order to learn (cognitively), and experience (emotionally), that the feared situation/emotion is not really as dangerous as thought or feared.[5] However, an important difference between CBT and EDT seems to be the focus of the exposure-procedure in practice, with CBT exposing the client to the external situation (and indirectly and implicitly to the beliefs associated with that situation) in which the anxiety occurs, while EDT exposes the client to his authentic feelings and impulses that are being triggered in an authentic interpersonal situation.

Another striking similarity, closely related to what has been stated above, has to do with the stimulus that supposedly triggers the anxiety. From a classic learning theory perspective, in many emotional problems, an unconditioned stimulus (UCS) automatically and reflexively triggers an unconditioned response (UCR). This can best be explained by the paradigm of Pavlonian conditioning (Davey, 1989). For example, a traumatic event, like being hit by a parent (UCS) triggers pain, anger, fear, and anxiety (UCR). It is easy to see how, over time, especially if the episode is repeated, the child will try to escape or, if possible, avoid any situation that is associated with the likelihood of being hit again. Over time not only the traumatic situation itself (UCS) will be escaped from or avoided but also feelings associated with the situation. If, for example, the child was hit after having been angry and expressing anger towards a parent, the feeling of anger (a UCR), in response to the parent's aggression (the UCS) can become a CS (conditioned stimulus) in itself that will trigger an internal CR (conditioned response) that will terminate the CS—the experience and expression of anger. So both CBT and EDT look for the UCS. The UCS can be an external situation (parent hits child) or an internally experienced emotion (like anger). So, often, CBT will focus on the link between the external (perceived) situation and the following thought or belief that then causes anxiety, while EDT will focus on the link between the internal UCS and the anxiety. The choice of focus is, or should be, guided more by practical, and pragmatic, rather than ideological considerations. But more about this, later.[6]

As stated above, a striking difference—at least in my view—is the role of the interpersonal therapeutic situation in the theory of CBT and EDT. Although, as stated above, within CBT more attention nowadays is paid to the importance of the interpersonal relationship in therapy (e.g., Leahy, 2008; Safran, 1998), CBT is still lacking a coherent theory that explains the interface between working on the Triangle of Conflict (or in CBT terms, the ABCDE model) and the Triangle of Person, that in CBT has no equivalent. Since many or most emotional problems are closely related to and associated with interpersonal situations, the emotional and cognitive relearning also should take place in an interpersonal meaningful context. It seems that EDT, more so than CBT, is eminently suited to the treatment of emotional problems where the main problem has to do with anxiety that is aroused (and the defences that are put into operation) in relation to the experience and expression of authentic impulses and feelings in interpersonal situations.

So far I have been guided by theoretical considerations in attempting to build a tentative, preliminary, bridge between CBT and EDT. In the following section I will present a case example to clinically illustrate some of the understandings and insights mentioned so far. The case is a recent one from my clinical practice. For obvious reasons, I have changed some of the identifying characteristics of the case to guarantee the privacy of my client. I hope that I have succeeded in retaining the core of the problem he wished to learn to deal with in therapy.

The case of Ronen

Ronen is a twenty-three-year-old, first-year student in the humanities. He was referred to me because of severe obsessive-compulsive disorder (OCD). His main symptoms had their onset during childhood but had become worse over time. They included compulsive hand washing, fear of contaminating objects, fear of contaminating people or being contaminated by them, and avoidance of public places and public transport. Related to this, he had become more and more isolated as he began to avoid most social contacts. He left school and studied at home, although he attended lectures when there was no choice. Because of his problems he was exempted from army service. Ronen has an older brother and younger sister. His father died quite suddenly when he was still a toddler. His mother is an academic professional, well known in her field. His mother, brother, and sister are outgoing, assertive people who easily make contacts. When I spoke with Ronen over the phone to make a first appointment, it turned out that he was already seeing a CBT therapist who had begun treating his OCD. The CBT therapy focused exclusively on the severe symptoms of his OCD, in accordance with the state of the art in evidence-based psychotherapy, where research shows the efficacy and efficiency of CBT as treatment of choice for OCD (Franklin & Foa, 2008).

Since I usually do not accept a client who is already being treated by another therapist, I asked him why he wanted to see me, while he was already in therapy. His short answer was that he was convinced the OCD had to do with traumas experienced in late childhood and early adolescence:

Pt: My therapist helps me a lot with the symptoms, but I am convinced that I have to work on my trauma as well and that is something my therapist does not think is necessary.

I asked Ronen to provide written permission to contact the other therapist, which he did. The other therapist, an excellent CBT expert, confirmed what Ronen had told me over the phone:

CBT Th: I focus on the OCD. It is my experience that there is no need to go into more personal and emotional issues. But if Ronen wants to work on those issues, that is fine with me and I do not see that as a threat or competition. So if he wants to see you and you him, go ahead but let's stay in touch.

In the first session, which was conducted along the lines of a trial therapy (Osimo, 2003), Ronen touched upon the tip of the trauma iceberg; several times during his late childhood and early adolescence he had been the victim of severe bullying and, in some instances, sexual abuse by his peers. Being a very shy and sensitive person, in all these cases, Ronen had not defended himself. He had experienced extreme feelings of humiliation, powerlessness, anger, and later sadness. In the beginning he told his mother and teachers what had happened to him. When they referred to the incidents as "children's play", told him, "Do not pay attention to it", and failed to take any active steps to stop the abuse and punish those who had bullied and abused him, Ronen's anger, humiliation, shame, and feelings of helplessness only increased. He felt alone, and lost, and had to cope on his own without any help or empathy from those closest to him. Around this time the first symptoms of OCD appeared.

The symptoms became severe after an incident which, though not an explicit form of sexual or physical abuse, apparently reactivated in Ronen all the feelings and impulses that had been aroused in the past but had to be repressed in order to survive, mentally and emotionally. To protect Ronen's anonymity, I can only give a rough outline of what happened. Ronen, age fifteen, had to undergo a medical procedure. While waiting for the anaesthesia, a "friend of the family" happened to be around. Although this person was a "friend of the family", Ronen despised and hated him for a variety of reasons. While Ronen was already somewhat drowsy and in the beginning of the anaesthesia, the "friend" approached Ronen, who was lying in his bed, and stroked his hair, no doubt meant as a friendly gesture just before the surgery. Eight years later, Ronen remembers how he felt at that moment; furious for what he experienced as an invasion of his privacy, and helpless—"I was almost under anaesthesia and could not do a thing"—feeling extreme disgust towards the man, and humiliation. A few days after the operation, severe symptoms of OCD erupted. In particular, an obsessive fear of his hair touching and contaminating any nearby object or person. Since, by necessity, his hair came into contact, directly or indirectly, with a variety of objects (e.g., pillow, comb, blanket, sweater, floor of the shower, towels, soap etc.), all the "contaminated" objects had to be removed. Washing them was not enough. They had to be thrown away, burned, or destroyed. Without going into further details, it is clear how Ronen's life became a hell. He devoted a great deal of time and energy to avoiding or neutralising contamination by getting rid of contaminated objects or avoiding situations where he risked his hair touching objects or people. His room became one big mess since no one was allowed to clean the room, which caused huge fights with his mother, who demanded the room be clean and orderly "as long as you live in *my* house".

CBT or EDT?

Let us assume that Ronen had been referred to me in the first place. What could have helped me in deciding what course to steer? As I mentioned in the preceding section, from an evidence-based perspective, based on a *Diagnostic and Statistical Manual of Mental Disorders—Fourth Edition* (DSM-IV), diagnosis of OCD (APA, 2002), the treatment of choice is CBT, since so far, in addition to pharmacological treatment, CBT is the only therapy proven to be effective for this condition. However, the evidence (Stewart, Geller & Jenike, 2004) also shows that 30–40 per cent of all cases do not or hardly profit from CBT.

It may very well be that in cases of severe OCD (e.g., OCD with co-morbidity, patients with pathological family conditions), either many more CBT sessions or different approaches altogether are needed. Conceded, there is no evidence base right now for EDT as a treatment of choice in such cases. However, I want to argue that, in cases where OCD develops in reaction to traumatic life circumstances, EDT alone or combined with CBT may well be a treatment of choice. What brings me to this assumption? It may sound paradoxical but a case conceptualisation derived from classic and cognitive learning theories points the way to the application of an EDT model of treatment.

Two conceptualisations compared

Based on the clinical research literature (e.g., de Silva & Marks, 1999), and stress-diathesis models (e.g., Rosenthal, 1971), we assume that OCD has a high probability in people who are born with a biological predisposition to anxiety disorders, in general, and OCD, in particular, especially after they are exposed to severe stress. In the case of Ronen, the severe symptoms, fear of contamination and the urge to neutralise contaminants, erupted after an event he experienced as particularly stressful (i.e., the hair-stroking incident) which came after a series of incidents in which he had been the victim of abuse. From a learning theory point of view, the original incidents were UCS (unconditioned aversive stimuli) that triggered UCR (unconditioned emotional responses, like anger, sadness, and sense of helplessness, humiliation). The original OCD (e.g., the hand washing), in all probability developed as a Conditioned Avoidance Response (CAR) whose function was to reduce (repress!), or escape from and avoid, the intensity of the overwhelming emotions (UCR). From animal research, we know that compulsive behaviours (like licking or washing the skin) in experimentally stressed animals serve as an anxiety- and stress-reducing response, reinforced by the reduction of tension which is then experienced as relief, and thus has reinforcing properties (Szechtman, Sulis & Eilam, 1998). So even before the critical incident, Ronen was already sensitised to events that were perceived as an invasion of his privacy under circumstances in which Ronen felt he had no or little control or help from outside. The incident of the hair-stroking by the "friend of the family", towards whom Ronen felt disgust and hate in the first place, was a stimulus that easily triggered the response of anger, helplessness, and humiliation.

I hypothesise that what happened next was that all these feelings and perceptions (CR) now came to be associated with, and generalised to, the hair that had been touched by the disgusting and hated "friend", with the hair becoming a further CS for a plethora of feelings experienced by Ronen. Through a process of verbal conditioning, the hair served as a trigger for the intense feelings that, instead of being experienced in full, were being neutralised (repressed) immediately through either avoidance or removal of anything that had been touched by the hair.[7]

The first session with Ronen coincided with my becoming familiar with Malan's (1979) Triangle of Conflict, so when I listened to Ronen's account I could not refrain from formulating with the Triangle of Conflict in my mind's eye (see Figure 2).

From an EDT perspective I assumed that Ronen, when he experienced the original abuse, had authentic and normal feelings of anger and indignation when he was attacked. Due to his inherent shyness, introverted personality, and realistic fear of the bullies who had threatened him in the past with knives, he perceived no way of expressing these feelings. So helplessness, humiliation, sadness, and passivity replaced constructive anger. In a way, those feelings protected Ronen against the anger and aggressive impulses that he had learned were too dangerous to experience, let alone express. A few years later, when he was confronted by the "family friend" (a man he experienced as disgusting and hateful) stroking his hair, the anger and aggression were immediately and automatically repressed. What remained was a vague and uncomfortable experience of anxious feelings that were directed at a controllable object (i.e., the hair and what touched it), instead of towards the "family friend", who was uncontrollable and unpredictable.

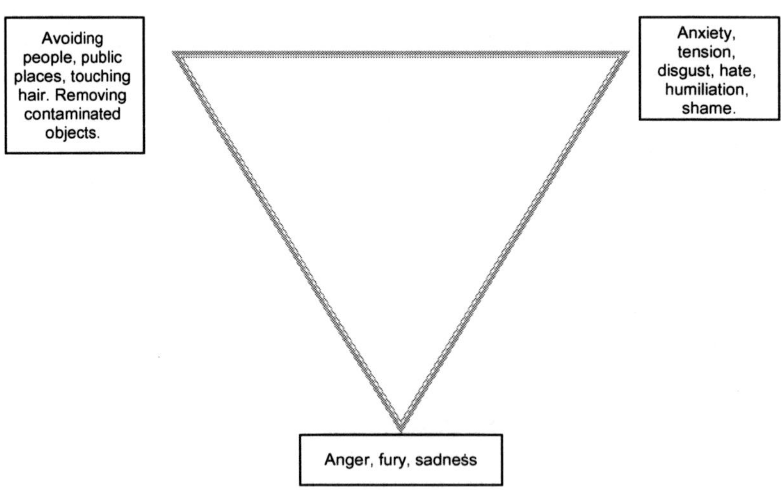

Figure 2. Preliminary formulation using the Triangle of Conflict.

So it seems that two "narratives" or "conceptualisations" are equally possible. I am well aware of the danger of throwing everything on one heap and saying that it is all the same, there is no real difference. CBT therapists might claim that what the psychodynamic therapists do is "what we are doing all the time", and vice versa. But if there is a difference, what is the difference that makes a difference?

What follows is an account of my thinking during the earlier stages of Ronen's therapy. By treating his symptoms, so I believed and still believe, through the evidence-based method of exposure and response prevention, my colleague was helping Ronen to give up his defences, or in CBT terminology, avoidance behaviours and his perceived need to neutralise by compulsions. However, I also believe that, by exclusively focusing on the debilitating symptoms, and disregarding the learned repression of healthy, constructive, evolutionary adaptive feelings, both their full experience and expression, Ronen would sooner or later again be helpless, traumatised by new incidents in which he—realistically or not—would perceive that his privacy and core self was violated. To be helped, it would also be necessary for him to be able to fully experience the repressed or avoided feelings, first, in the relative safety of the therapist's presence, and later, in his relationships with others.

Here I want to add a comment that is related to the second triangle, the Triangle of Others, that Malan, Osimo and others place alongside the Triangle of Conflict. In the second session with Ronen, he told me how, when he first had been exposed to the sexual abuse, he had told his mother in the hope that she would deal with it on the level of the school and the authorities. Neither of the two happened. Mother thought he exaggerated, that the kids had meant it as a game, and that he was making a fuss about nothing. She did not validate his feelings, was not empathic, and did not support him. After his father had died at an early age, Ronen had become extremely dependent on his mother who took care of the household, children, and income, and did an incredible job of keeping the family together. When mother did not give him the backing he expected, and did not validate his feelings, he also felt very angry with her. Here too, given his dependent position, his shyness, his developing or developed fear of feeling and expressing anger, he easily and understandably repressed his fury at his mother. Later, when he was again exposed to abuse, he would not tell his mother any more, and bottled up his feelings, preferring isolation and helplessness over the pain and anger associated with mother's disappointing reaction.

From the point of transference it is interesting to speculate that the defensive silence and passivity towards his mother (also later in relation to the bullies) was transferred to the CBT therapist. Ronen had decided not to tell his CBT therapist about the traumas. He gave two reasons:

Pt: First, from the beginning my therapist said he was not interested in the causes of the OCD, that we did not need to deal with it and second, I believe that my OCD is different than the OCD that is normally being treated by CBT.

Since the symptoms of the OCD were treated by my CBT colleague, I allowed myself to focus on the experiential part of the therapy, and after providing "psycho-education" about the approach, was able to focus on Ronen's inner experience.

To conclude, a transcript from the third session with Ronen will be presented to illustrate his connection with his feelings of anger and how, in fantasy, for the first time, he began to experience his aggressive impulses towards the hair-stroking "friend of the family". He had chosen the hair-stroking incident as the stimulus to explore with me, even though it was very high on his stress-scale (an imaginary scale from 1–10, used in CBT by the client to denote the level of stress he feels in relation to anxiety-arousing situations).

Th: Can you try to imagine the situation where you are already on the bed, on the verge of the anaesthesia, Mr J (the friend of the family) coming in, seeing you, getting near, touching your hair. If it helps you, close your eyes and picture the situation as you remember it; the place, how he looks, how he is dressed, where you are. (**HP, XA**)

Pt: Yes, I so often think about it, I can still see it. I am in a small room, white walls, a nurse at my side, I am on the bed, with all kinds of tubes connected to my hands. I cannot move my hands. Suddenly I see J. I wonder what he is doing here. Then I remember that he is married to the nurse who is a friend of my mother. I hate his guts. He is a nasty, vulgar, disgusting man. He approaches me, stretches out his right hand, touches my hair and says something like, "It will be OK." I feel angry, powerlessness, cannot do anything, do not want to make a scene. He smiles at me, then turns around and leaves the room. I shake, my whole body trembles. Then the nurse tells me she will now give the anaesthesia through the vein. Then I do not remember anything any more, till I wake up after the surgery.

Th: You felt very angry then, and powerlessness. Now in fantasy, if you could have given free rein to what you felt, just in fantasy, what would you have liked to do? (**XA**)

Pt: I do not know. I never thought about that. I just kept it inside. It happened so long ago.

Th: I know. And of course we are not talking about what you would do in reality. But as we discussed before, every feeling has an impulse part of it, which is a normal part of the feeling. So again, only in fantasy, when you felt the anger, or even now when you feel the anger again, what is it you would have liked to do. (**AA, XA, SO**)

Pt: It scares me to think about it, but yes, I would have wanted to punch him in the face, in his bulgy stomach, to hit him on the head. To smash his face. To pull out his hair … Wow, I never thought I could have these ideas, this is so unlike me.

Th: Again I want to emphasise that we are dealing with your feelings and what—in your fantasy—you had wanted to do to him. Now, you have hit him, smashed his face, pulled out his hair. Then what? (**AA, XA**)

Pt: I could have killed him but I would not. He is lying on the floor. Blood is flowing. He is screaming, crying for help. He is in pain. I do not help him. Let him suffer. Now I feel that my anger is diminishing. He got what he deserved. Then I feel sad. I cannot undo what he did to me. He touched me without my consent.

Th: Let's stop here for a moment. How do you feel right now, with me in the room, imagining what happened then? (**XA, RE**)

Pt: Wow, I cannot believe it. This is the first time ever, I dared to defend myself, to do something to someone who hurt me. I know, it is only fantasy, imagination, but so far even in fantasy I never dared to go there.

Th: What do you mean, to go there? (**HP**)
Pt: To even think about expressing my anger in a concrete way.
Th: So, how do you feel right now? (**XA**)
Pt: As if a burden has lifted. I cannot believe it. Lighter.
Th: You know, you are very courageous. This is only the third session. You dared to permit yourself to feel and in fantasy express the feeling, something you have not done ever. I feel happy for you. (**SO, RE, XA**)
Pt: But I could and can never do this in reality. Often I am very angry with my mom, but there is no way I can express it. Not in words and not in deeds.
Th: You must probably ask yourself, what good it does to experience this in fantasy, if I cannot do these things in reality. (**HP**)
Pt: Yes. What happened, happened, I cannot turn back the clock.
Th: For the time being, the more important thing is that you will learn not to be afraid of your feelings and impulses. For that it is already a huge accomplishment if you dare to feel the feelings and impulses, here with me in the here and now and imagining yourself in abusive situations of the past. Once you are not afraid any more to feel what there is to feel, of course we are going to work on how to express the feelings depending on the person, the situation. We will work on that as well. (**SO, AA, RE**)

Follow-up

Soon after this session, Ronen decided to end the CBT therapy. He felt that it was not very helpful any more and he also disliked the exclusive focus on his symptoms and what he perceived as a lack of empathy on the part of the therapist. In the same way that he was not able to express anger towards his mother, he was also not able to let the CBT therapist know that he was not satisfied; he told the therapist that "for the time being" he wanted to take a break and maybe come back to therapy at a later stage.

In our therapy we focused on two issues: (i) supporting and reinforcing the experiencing and—in fantasy—expressing of feelings of anger and rage towards those who had bullied and harassed him, and (ii) accepting the authentic sadness that what had happened could not be reversed. Another issue was his difficulty in confronting his mother in the here and now and expressing both his feelings of anger but also of love whenever he felt them. To bolster his self-confidence I encouraged him to return to the gym and take lessons in self-defence, two activities I thought would be helpful both to strengthen his inner resources as well as preparing him for his army duty which was to take place in the near future. Gradually his depression lifted and the symptoms of OCD decreased in intensity and frequency even though they did not go away completely, which is consistent with most of the research (Abramowitz, 2006) that finds OCD to be a chronic disease, where the symptoms wax and wane over a lifetime.

Personal conclusions

What can I conclude after having been a CBT therapist for almost forty years and—in addition—an EDT therapist for two to three years?

To be(come) a therapist is a lifelong learning process. Every encounter with a new patient, a new approach, a new research finding, a new theory, a new thought, impacts and transforms me and becomes part of who I am, like a kaleidoscope in which every additional piece and new movement leads to a completely new pattern, comprised of pieces of glass in ever-changing formations that offer endless new perspectives. Among the pieces of coloured glass two stand out: (i) *thoughts*, and (ii) *feelings*. As a CBT therapist I have come to appreciate both the dysfunctional and the very functional aspects of rational and logical thinking and problem solving. Research and practice have taught me how therapeutic it can be to identify, analyse, and then change dysfunctional and irrational thinking into more logical, reality-based thoughts. So-called dysfunctional thoughts are not necessarily defences in the psychodynamic sense. Sometimes/often the psychopathological cycle starts with dysfunctional thoughts and illogical or irrational conclusions and changing those thoughts can be a royal road to change. The other conspicuous set of pieces in the kaleidoscope is the feelings and emotions. From EDT I have learned how much psychological misery is related to the fear of the patient to fully experience and express their feelings in intimate relationships, or any relationship deemed important enough to share their emotion with the significant other. To help the patient to connect to what were previously repressed feelings, and have the courage to express their feelings, is sometimes/often the expressway to change and well-being.

How can I know what is needed with whom?

I believe that process and outcome research will be helpful in teaching us what works best for whom, how, and in which circumstances. However, I also believe that, in the end, it is the very real personal relationship between therapist and client that is going to determine how we will be working together and to what degree we will focus on thoughts or feelings (or both). That decision will no doubt also be influenced by unconscious forces. With hindsight, we always can find good reasons to justify why we did what we did, but let us be honest, the reason is *not* the cause. So even though I am a CBT therapist, I accept that not everything I do can be scientifically or rationally justified. After having loyally followed my thoughts for over forty years, it is time to also loyally trust my feelings and intuitions. Paraphrasing Albert Ellis, not only is it true that if we think well, we will feel well. It is also true that if we feel well we will think well!

Summary

The aim of this chapter was to compare and, hopefully, build a bridge between two streams of therapy—Cognitive Behaviour Therapy (CBT) and Experiential Dynamic Therapy (EDT)—that, on the surface, seem very apart from, if not contradictory to each other. Mainstream CBT focuses on the role of cognitions as a determinant of emotions and, therefore, in its interventions stresses the importance of changing beliefs, interpretations, and perceptions, in order to bring about change in emotion and emotion-driven behaviour. EDT assumes that cognitions linked to early learning experiences in attachment relationships mediate between feelings and inhibitory anxiety and/or, in the case of rumination, are a (defensive) outcome of a process in which authentic feelings and impulses, because of early learning experiences, are repressed and avoided due to the anxiety engendered by experiencing and/or expressing those emotions. To bring about change it is necessary to help the client overcome his anxiety and again fully experience and express his true feelings. Cognitions will either change as a natural consequence of giving up the repression or will be dealt with after the repression has been lifted and feelings are again being experienced and expressed. In this chapter, I have tried to show how understandings of CBT and EDT (and techniques deriving from those understandings) can complete each other and be integrated. My thesis was illustrated by presenting and reflecting upon the case of a patient with obsessive-compulsive disorder. In this particular case, the OCD was first treated with traditional CBT (exposure therapy). Then, after the patient thought that the CBT was not helpful enough, he approached another therapist, the author, who, being trained in both CBT and EDT, decided to change the approach and apply principles of EDT. In the EDT part of therapy the therapist helped the patient overcome some of the fear of his authentic feelings of anger, which was associated with a significant decrease in OCD symptoms and improvement in the patient's well-being and functioning. This was accomplished without using the typical CBT techniques of exposure and response prevention. The hope is that this chapter will contribute to the dialogue between two schools of therapy that can only gain by learning each other's language, and—eventually—create a new, richer, language that merges and integrates the existing ones.

References

Abramowitz, J. S. (2006). *Understanding and Treating Obsessive-Compulsive Disorder: A Cognitive-Behavioral Approach*. Mahwah, NJ: Lawrence Erlbaum.

Allen, L. B., McHugh, R. K. & Barlow, D. H. (2008). Emotional disorders. In: D. H. Barlow (Ed.), *Clinical Handbook of Psychological Disorders*. New York: Guilford Press.

American Psychiatric Association (2002). *Diagnostic and Statistical Manual of Mental Disorders (4th ed., text rev.)*. Washington, DC: American Psychiatric Association.

Beck, A. T. (1967). *Cognitive Therapy and the Emotional Disorders*. New York: International Universities Press.

Beck, A. T., Freeman, A., Pretzer, J., Davis, D. D., Fleming, B. & Beck, J. S. (1990). *Cognitive Therapy of Personality Disorders*. New York: Guilford Press.

Beck, A. T., Rush, A. J., Shaw, B. F. & Emery, G. (1979). *Cognitive Therapy of Depression*. New York: Guilford Press.

Beck, J. S. (1995). *Cognitive Therapy: Basics and Beyond*. London: Guilford Press.

Butler, A.C., Chapman, J.E., Forman, E.M. & Beck, A.T. (2006). The empirical status of cognitive-behavioral therapy: A review of meta-analyses. *Clinical Psychology Review*, 26, 1: 17–31.

Clark, D. A, Beck, A. T. & Alford, B. A. (1999). *Scientific Foundations of Cognitive Theory and Therapy of Depression*. New York: John Wiley & Sons.

Coughlin Della Selva, P. (1996). *Intensive Short Term Dynamic Psychotherapy: Theory and Technique*. New York: John Wiley & Sons.

Davanloo, H. (1990). *Unlocking the Unconscious*. New York: John Wiley & Sons.

Davanloo, H. (2000). *Intensive Short-Term Dynamic Psychotherapy: Selected Papers of Habib Davanloo*. Chichester, UK: John Wiley & Sons.

Davey, G. C. L. (1989). UCS revaluation and conditioning models of acquired fears. *Behaviour Research and Therapy, 27*: 521–528.

de Silva, P. & Marks, M. (1999). The role of traumatic experiences in the genesis of obsessive-compulsive disorder. *Behaviour Research and Therapy, 41*: 129–137.

Ellis, A. (1962). *Reason and Emotion in Psychotherapy*. Secausus, NJ: Citadel Press.

Ellis, A. (1996). *Better, Deeper, and More Enduring Therapy: The Rational Emotive Behavior Therapy Approach*. New York: Brunner/Mazel.

Foa, E. B., Huppert, J. D. & Cahill, S. P. (2006). Emotional processing theory: An update. In: B. O. Rothbaum (Ed.), *The Nature and Treatment of Pathological Anxiety*. New York: Guilford Press.

Fosha, D. (2000). *The Transforming Power of Affect: A Model for Accelerated Change*. New York: Basic.

Franklin, M. E. & Foa, E. (2008). Obsessive-compulsive disorder. In: D. H. Barlow (Ed.), *Clinical Handbook of Psychological Disorders*. London: Guilford Press.

Frederick, R. J. (2009). *Living Like You Mean It: Use the Wisdom and Power of Your Emotions to Get the Life You Really Want*. San Francisco, CA: Jossey Bass.

Freud, S. (1926d). *Inhibitions, Symptoms and Anxiety. S. E., 20*. London: Hogarth, pp. 87–156.

ten Have-de Labije, J. (2010). *The Collected Writings of Josette ten Have-de Labije*. London: Karnac.

Kalpin, A. (2001). The integration of cognitive and dynamic approaches in the short-term treatment of depression. In: J. ten Have-de Labije (Ed.), *The Working Alliance in ISTDP: Whose Intrapsychic Crisis*. Amsterdam: VKDP.

Leahy, R. (2008). The therapeutic relationship in cognitive-behavioral psychotherapy. *Behavioural and Cognitive Psychotherapy, 36*: 769–777.

Malan, D. H. (1979). *Individual Psychotherapy and the Science of Psychodynamics*. London: Butterworth.

Malan, D. H. & Coughlin Della Selva, P. (2006). *Lives Transformed: a Revolutionary Method of Dynamic Psychotherapy*. London: Karnac.

McCullough Vaillant, L. (1997). *Changing Character: Short-Term Anxiety-Regulating Psychotherapy for Restructuring Defenses, Affects and Attachment*. New York: Basic.

McCullough Vaillant, L., Kuhn, N., Andrews, S., Kaplan, A., Wolf, J. & Hurley, C. L. (2003). *Treating Affect Phobia: a Manual for Short-Term Dynamic Psychotherapy*. London: Guilford.

Neborsky, R. J. (2010). *The Collected Writings of Robert Neborsky*. London: Karnac.

Osimo, F. (2003). *Experiential Short-Term Dynamic Psychotherapy: A Manual*. Bloomington, IN: AuthorHouse.

Ramsay, R. W. & Happee, J. A. (1977). The stress of bereavement: components and treatment. In: C. Spielberger & I. Sarason (Eds.), *Stress and Anxiety* (Vol. 4). London: John Wiley & Sons.

Rosenthal, D. (1971). A program of research on heredity in schizophrenia. *Science, 16, 3*: 191–201.

Safran, J. D. (1998). *Widening the Scope of Cognitive Therapy: the Therapeutic Relationship, Emotion, and the Process of Change*. London: Jason Aronson.

Stewart, S. E., Geller, D. A. & Jenike, M. (2004). Long-term outcome of pediatric obsessive-compulsive disorder: A meta-analysis and qualitative review of the literature. *Acta Psychiatrica Scandinavica, 110*: 4–13.

Szechtman, H., Sulis, W. & Eilam, D. (1998). Quinpirole induces compulsive checking behavior in rats: a potential animal model of obsessive-compulsive disorder (OCD). *Behavioral Neuroscience, 112*: 1475–1485.

Walen, S. R., DiGiuseppe, R. & Dryden, W. (1992). *A Practitioner's Guide to Rational-Emotive Therapy* (2nd ed.). New York: Oxford University Press.

Young, J. E., Klosko, J. S. & Weishaar, M. E. (2003). *Schema Therapy: A Practitioner's Guide*. New York: Guilford Press.

Notes

1. Hilda van der Steen, to whom I am very thankful for having introduced me to a whole new world of therapy.
2. For an excellent summary of the research evidence in support of CBT the interested reader is referred to Butler, Chapman, Forman, and Beck (2006).
3. It is important to emphasise that when Ellis speaks about a "negative emotion" he means an emotion that is experienced as aversive.
4. I want to thank Ferruccio Osimo for the inspiration that led to these comments.
5. For an excellent EDT treatise on "affect phobia" the reader is referred to the major contribution by McCullough Vaillant (1997).
6. This is the basis of McCullough's model of affect phobia (see McCullough et al., 2003).
7. From a classic psychoanalytic perspective it is intriguing to speculate about the meaning of hair in a young adolescent, but at this stage I do not want to antagonise some of my "relational" colleagues more than is absolutely necessary.

CHAPTER SEVENTEEN

EDT in the context of psychotherapy research and mental health policy in the UK

James Macdonald

Introduction

Anyone versed in psychotherapy research will wonder why we need another brand of therapy? Over thirty years of meta-analysis and comparative trials have pointed to equivalent outcomes for different models of therapy (Lambert & Ogles, 2004; Wampold, 2001). The Dodo bird's verdict from the Caucus race in *Alice in Wonderland* (Carroll, 1865)—that "Everyone has won and all must have prizes"—has long been declared in the context of the equivalent effectiveness of different therapy models (Luborsky, Singer & Luborsky, 1975; Rosenzweig, 1936; Wampold, 2001). True to the Dodo bird's pronouncement, the only comparative trial comparing an experiential dynamic therapy (EDT) with another non-psychodynamic model of therapy found equivalent outcomes between EDT and cognitive therapy (Svartberg, Stiles & Seltzer, 2004). In spite of recurrent evidence of the equivalent effectiveness of different psychotherapy models, there has been a prolific expansion of different brands of therapy, with in excess of 400 models of therapy in existence (Garfield & Bergin, 1994). This trend towards proliferation can be seen within the field of experiential dynamic therapies, where currently it is possible to distinguish derivatives of Davanloo's (1990) and Malan's (2001; Malan & Coughlin Della Selva, 2006) work, including Intensive Short-Term Dynamic Psychotherapy (ISTDP) (e.g., Coughlin Della Selva, 1996), Accelerated Experiential-Dynamic Psychotherapy (AEDP) (Fosha, 2000), Intensive Experiential-Dynamic Psychotherapy (IE-DP) (Osimo, 2009), and Short-Term Affect-Regulating Therapy (START) (McCullough Vaillant, 1997; McCullough et al., 2003).

Is this process of fragmentation necessary to the development of psychotherapy? Certainly in the United Kingdom, the development of evidence-based practice in the National Health Service (NHS) has largely confined itself to the validation of particular models of psychotherapy, found to be effective for treatment of particular diagnoses. This is enshrined in the Department of Health's National Institute for Health and Clinical Excellence (NICE) guidelines. Further development along these lines would logically lead to the proliferation of new therapies each tailored to a specific diagnosis, a venture which is both practically and scientifically questionable (Westen, Novotny & Thompson-Brenner, 2004). However, in the broader field of psychotherapy research, another approach to the dissemination of evidence has begun to emerge. This latter approach consists of systematic attempts to summarise the current state of our knowledge of "principles of therapeutic change"—in other words, what psychotherapy research tells us, so far, about the therapeutic processes which contribute to positive outcomes in psychotherapy. These principles, derived from studies relating therapy "process" to therapeutic "outcome", may be operational to a greater or lesser extent in a range of therapeutic models (Castonguay & Beutler, 2006a), and for this reason have sometimes been referred to as "common factors". In this chapter, an attempt will be made to justify the entry of a further acronym into the psychotherapy world by arguing that EDT represents a promising integration of a number of therapeutic principles of this kind. Following this, there will be a review of empirical studies of the efficacy of EDT. The chapter will conclude with a brief outline of EDT within current mental health policy in the National Health Service in the UK.

For the purposes of this chapter, EDT will be defined broadly as short-term psychodynamic psychotherapy that draws mainly on Malan's (2001) theoretical framework and Davanloo's (1990) clinical methodology. It prioritises active engagement by therapist and client on manifestations of defence, anxiety, and underlying feeling as these occur in the here and now of the therapeutic relationship. The objective is to clear away the barriers to a "corrective emotional experience" (Alexander & French, 1946) in which both the client and the therapist are attuned to the client's previously avoided affective experience. This corrective emotional experience is assumed to enable the client to become more energised as a result of being in touch with underlying emotional experience or needs, more able to connect in an emotionally alive way (evoking appropriate responses from others and greater capacity for emotional intimacy), and to give up handicapping emotional defences.

Principles of therapeutic change in EDT and the evidence

The first decade of the twenty-first century yielded several systematic reviews of evidence-based "principles of therapeutic change" in psychotherapy (Castonguay & Beutler, 2006a; Norcross, 2002; Orlinsky, Rønnestad & Willutzki, 2004). Castonguay and Beutler assembled a working party of psychotherapy research experts, drawn from across the spectrum of theoretical models, to conduct what, to date, has been the most comprehensive review of the process-outcome research. Their goal was to cut across the different models of therapy in order to pinpoint evidence-based principles of therapeutic change. In their review, the working party distinguished between principles associated with the *technique*, the *therapeutic relationship* and the *participants* in therapy. Evidence will be presented relating to each of these three domains as it pertains to the practice of EDT.

Technique

EDT is of course characterised by a primary focus on affect as it manifests in the here and now of the therapy situation. Therapeutic strategies are directed at raising awareness of barriers to adaptive affective experience (the Defence pole in Malan's Triangle of Conflict), evoking underlying adaptive affective experience (the Feeling pole in Malan's Triangle of Conflict), and regulating affective experience (by acting to reduce inhibitory emotions such as shame, guilt, or anxiety, associated with the Anxiety pole in Malan's Triangle of Conflict. In addition, therapeutic interventions aim to promote insight into the nature of emotional conflicts (the relationship between the three poles in the Triangle of Conflict), their relational origin, and current interpersonal contexts (Malan's Triangle of Person) (see Malan, 2001; Malan & Coughlin Della Selva, 2006).

While the theoretical basis of EDT remains rooted in Malan's (2001) psychodynamic framework, therapeutic strategies aimed at achieving these objectives can be drawn from or are congruent with the strategies of a variety of schools of psychotherapy (McCullough et al., 2003). In addition to traditional psychodynamic techniques (such as clarification, confrontation, and interpretation), recent versions of EDT (particularly as conceptualised by McCullough and colleagues) can encompass techniques shared with Gestalt therapy (interventions aimed at deepening emotional experiencing), behaviour therapy (graded exposure to feared affect), CBT (Socratic exploration of anxiety), mindfulness (awareness and acceptance of thoughts and feelings, developing self-compassion), and motivational enhancement therapy (motivational work on giving up maladaptive defensive strategies) (see table 1).

A distinctive aspect of EDT is the rigorous work on defences, and the focusing on emotional experiencing in body-and-mind, particularly as it manifests in the context of the therapeutic relationship. While psychodynamic and humanistic approaches have always emphasised the centrality of emotional experience, recent theoretical and clinical innovations in both cognitive and behavioural therapy have also begun to see emotional avoidance as central in maintaining psychopathology, and the achievement of new emotional experiences in therapy as key to recovery (see Ehrenreich, Buzzella & Barlow, 2007, for an example). In this review of the

Table 1. Examples of strategies drawn from various therapeutic models that contribute to achieving the psychodynamic aims of EDT.

Edt strategy	*Model*	*Examples of congruent principles of change*
Raising awareness of barriers to adaptive affective experience	CBT: motivational enhancement therapy Psychodynamic therapy	Motivational work on giving up maladaptive defensive behaviours Clarification, interpretation
Evoking underlying adaptive affective experience	Gestalt therapy CBT: mindfulness	Deepening emotional experience Awareness and acceptance of here and now experience
Regulating inhibitory affective experience	Behaviour therapy CBT CBT: mindfulness	Graded exposure to feared stimuli Socratic exploration of anxiety Developing self-compassion
Gaining insight into the interpersonal roots of emotional conflicts	Psychodynamic therapy	Interpretation

evidence on therapeutic technique, I shall highlight the evidence as it relates to focusing on affect as a key to therapeutic change.

Although there is little published research on process-outcome relationships in EDT, the approach appears congruent with evidence that techniques relating to the client's affective experience may be important mediators of therapeutic outcome (see Malan & Coughlin Della Selva, 2006). Orlinsky et al.'s (2004) review of process-outcome research highlighted the potency of "experiential confrontation" (affectively evocative techniques generally studied in the context of humanistic "process-experiential" therapy), as well as the strong evidence relating client openness (versus defensiveness) to therapy outcome. In the context of psychodynamic therapy, Diener, Hilsenroth, and Weinberger (2007) have conducted a meta-analysis of well-conducted studies examining psychodynamic therapists' focus on affect and concluded that "the more therapists facilitate the affective experience/expression of patients in psychodynamic therapy, the more patients exhibit positive changes" (p. 939).

One problem with research on affect in psychotherapy is that distinctions among different affective experiences (e.g., between activating and inhibitory emotions, McCullough et al., 2003) are often omitted, resulting in some confusion in this area (as noted by McCullough & Magill, 2009, and illustrated in some mixed findings in this area reviewed by Orlinsky et al., 2004). A small but intriguing body of process-outcome research in EDT, linked to two randomised controlled trials involving EDT (the Beth Israel Medical Center study, by Winston et al., 1991, and the Trondheim study, Svartberg et al., 2004), has used the "achievement of therapeutic objectives scale" (ATOS) (McCullough et al., 2008) to distinguish the relative proportions of "activating" (related to Malan's Feeling pole in the Triangle of Conflict), and "inhibitory" (relating to Malan's Anxiety pole in the Triangle of Conflict) emotions in psychotherapy sessions. This enables researchers to differentiate between the impact of work on regulating inhibitory affect and on activating underlying adaptive emotions. Findings to date are outlined in a recent chapter by McCullough and Magill (2009). In summary, process-outcome research by McCullough's group suggests that, while outcomes were equivalent between EDT and cognitive behavioural therapy (CBT) in Svartberg et al.'s study, this may have been achieved by different processes, with EDT appearing more successful in increasing the experience of adaptive activating affects, and CBT appearing more successful in helping clients decrease problematic inhibitory affects such as anxiety.

Returning to the broader research field, Castonguay and Beutler (2006b), summarising the main principles identified by their psychotherapy researcher panels, concluded that, with regard to emotion, existing research evidence supports the effectiveness of two principles of therapeutic change: (i) "Therapeutic change is likely if therapists help clients accept, tolerate, and at times, fully experience their emotions" (p. 364) while at the same time, (ii) "Interventions aimed at controlling emotions can [also] be helpful" (p. 365). EDT, with its fine distinctions between varieties of affective emotional experience, and its well-specified techniques aimed either at deepening adaptive affective experiences, regulating inhibitory emotional experiences, or addressing defences and blocks to emotional awareness and experience, provides a comprehensive theoretical and clinical resource for accomplishing the complex engagement with client emotional experience hinted at in Castonguay and Beutler's two principles. It may be that further process-outcome research will result in enhanced effectiveness of EDT techniques and possible integration of strategies that work in both CBT and EDT. If so, it is likely that modifications to technique will not require reworking of the theoretical model in EDT, which, as noted above, suggests that "many roads can lead to Rome" or at least to the "achievement of therapeutic objectives" as described by Malan (2001).

The therapeutic relationship

Early formulations of EDT, for example, the work of Davanloo (1990), emphasised innovations in the technique of working with defences and emotion rather than the therapeutic relationship. However, it was assumed that challenge to defences could only be successful when there was an "unconscious therapeutic alliance" in which the client tacitly recognises that the therapist values the client and is on the side of liberation from destructive defences. Davanloo's "graded approach" (Abbass & Bechard, 2007; Davanloo, 1990) emphasises a variety of means of regulating the client's experience of anxiety, shame, and guilt in order to prevent negative therapeutic effects and, by implication, to maintain a positive therapeutic relationship. Some recent developments in EDT have highlighted the role of the therapeutic relationship in providing a corrective emotional experience that can resolve the emotional conflicts associated with problematic attachment relationships in the past. This has been most fully elaborated by McCullough Vaillant (1997) and Fosha (2000). These clinicians have emphasised techniques designed to increase the client's capacity to receive the corrective emotional experience of the therapist's positive feelings and, in so doing, challenge the client's defences against emotional closeness and intimacy.

In a review of 2354 findings in process-outcome studies, Orlinsky, Grawe, and Parks (1994) concluded that "the strongest evidence linking process to outcome concerns the *therapeutic bond* or alliance, reflecting more than 1000 process-outcome findings" (p. 360; see also Orlinsky, Rønnestad & Willutzki, 2004). However, the actual size of the effect is relatively modest, suggesting, perhaps not surprisingly, that the therapeutic relationship accounts for a moderate amount of the effectiveness of psychotherapy, but other ingredients are important too (Horvath & Bedi, 2002). Following the series of expert reviews in Castonguay and Beutler (2006a), the authors concluded that there is evidence that a strong therapeutic alliance, a high level of collaboration, therapist empathy, caring, warmth, acceptance, and congruence are all likely to contribute towards positive outcomes in therapy (Castonguay & Beutler, 2006b).

Within the field of EDT there have been different views on the manner of confronting clients with their self-damaging defences and underlying feelings (McCullough & Kuhn, 2009). It is probably fair to say that Davanloo's work may have failed to take root at an earlier date in the UK due to the perception that his approach lacked empathy towards the client, that is, this approach may have been perceived as lacking the relational qualities that have subsequently been demonstrated to lead to positive therapeutic outcome. Malan has since argued that Davanloo's own personal style is not a necessary ingredient of the effectiveness of his approach, and has recently highlighted the degree to which EDT therapists after Davanloo have been able to achieve the same therapeutic objectives while adopting a more validating and empathic stance (see Malan & Coughlin Della Selva, 2006). However, there continue to be different shades of opinion within the EDT community as to the degree to which pressure towards underlying feeling should ever be, as Davanloo (1990) put it, "unremitting". Advocates of more "unremitting" pressure towards feeling have increasingly stressed the importance of very careful ongoing assessment of signs that the client may be overwhelmed, so that the focus can, when necessary, be redirected to regulating the client's anxiety (Abbass & Bechard, 2007; ten Have de Labije, 2001, 2006). Others (e.g., Fosha, 2001; Lamagna, in press; Lamagna & Gleiser, 2007; McCullough Vaillant, 1997) have emphasised means of accessing underlying feeling which do not require the same level of interpersonal challenge and potential for ruptures in the therapeutic relationship. In particular, these latter writers have elaborated on ways of maximising the therapeutic impact of therapist empathy (Fosha, 2001; McCullough Vaillant, 1997), exploration of the emotional stances involved in client ambivalence (e.g., Lamagna, in press; Lamagna & Gleiser, 2007), and consideration of the strengths as well as the weaknesses of the client's defensive strategies (McCullough Vaillant, 1997). Osimo (2003a) has likened these two broad approaches to the stances adopted by the Sun and the Wind in Aesop's Fable of the *The Sun and the Wind*, although, in contrast to the spirit of the fable, he sees both approaches as valid and believes many styles are possible, with each therapist's approach reflecting their own unique personality.

There is little evidence to assess the relative merits of the more "challenging" versus the more "validating" styles within EDT. One of the few randomised controlled trials involving an EDT compared Davanloo's "anxiety-provoking" model of EDT with a more supportive psychodynamic approach (Winston et al., 1991; Winston et al., 1994). This study found no significant differences in outcome between the two different approaches. This would suggest that a more confrontational style neither adds to nor subtracts from the therapeutic effect. However, follow-up process research on this data, summarised recently by McCullough and Magill (2009) suggests that, contrary to the expectations of the researchers, "*supportive, empathic*, and *clarifying* methods generated more affect than did *confrontive* interventions" (p. 258, italics in the original). They describe previously unpublished work that examined "confrontations sustained over 1–9 minutes, hypothesising that it was the *continued confrontation* that would 'break through' the defences to underlying feeling" (p. 258). This work, they report, found that, in fact, "confrontation did not predict improvement", while further research appeared to show that confrontation in general elicited more defensive behaviour, but confrontation "given along with a supportive or empathic statement by the therapist ... resulted in greater likelihood of expression of affect" (p. 259). McCullough and Magill do not advocate abandoning confrontation on the basis of these findings but rather stress ways of modulating confrontation (for example by working on increasing self-compassion) so that "when confrontations are given, they are not experienced as attacking" (p. 259). While further research in this area would clearly be desirable (see McCullough & Kuhn, 2009), the findings described by McCullough and Magill are in keeping with the broader conclusions of Castonguay and Beutler (2006b) regarding the importance of therapist empathy, caring, warmth, and acceptance.

Participants

It has been estimated that approximately 40 per cent of the variance in outcome in therapy is attributable to "client factors", and events which happen outside therapy (Asay & Lambert,

1999). In this category, client level of psychological functioning is a very significant predictor of outcome. Castonguay and Beutler's (2006b) first participant "principle" is that "clients with a high level of impairment are less likely to benefit from therapy than those with a better level of functioning at pretreatment" (p. 355). Further related principles include the fact that clients diagnosed with personality disorders, clients with financial and occupational difficulties, and clients who have experienced significant interpersonal problems during their early development are all less likely to be able to benefit from psychotherapy (Castonguay & Beutler, 2006b).

Current UK mental health policy, manifest in NICE guidelines, takes a diagnosis-led view of what treatment is appropriate for an individual client. However, diagnostic categories are not reliable indicators of client level of functioning or prognosis (see Duncan, Miller & Sparks, 2004, for a review of this literature). In the current author's experience within the NHS, diagnosis-led NICE guidelines can result in confused and inappropriate expectations on the part of both clients and referrers when no account is taken of client level of psychological impairment. In routine clinical practice a more pragmatic approach is to tailor treatments to suit the client's level of functioning.

In EDT, Davanloo (1990) described a "spectrum of psychopathology". Based on patients' responses to invitations to explore here-and-now emotion within a "trial" clinical interview, an assessment of "character structure" is possible through consideration of the type of defences used, the level of dystonicity/syntonicity of defences and how unconscious anxiety is channelled and manifests within the body. This has informed ten Have-de Labije's (2001) "traffic light" framework for "taking the road to the unconscious". In other words, observable aspects of the patient's experience are used to inform the nature of the work so that an appropriate balance can be maintained between more supportive/cognitive and more challenging interventions. McCullough Vaillant (1997) has linked this aspect of EDT to the Axis V 'Level of Functioning' Scale of the Diagnostic and Statistical Manual (4th Edition) (American Psychiatric Association, 1994), and described a variety of means of "self and other restructuring" that may be required before clients who suffer with more severe psychological impairments can tolerate greater awareness of their affective experience. In this way, EDT has evolved mechanisms for adapting in significant ways to the needs of clients with varying degrees of psychological impairment.

In addition to the client's level of functioning, EDT also contains a focus on the client's motivation to change. This typically occurs when the client has recognised the self-destructive defences associated with their psychological problems, and the therapist either highlights the fact that it is only the client who can decide whether they will go on living with these defences, or explores with the client the consequences of maintaining and/or relinquishing them. To my knowledge, neither the motivational aspect of EDT nor the adaptations tailoring EDT for different levels of client functioning have been subjected to systematic research, although numerous individual case studies testify to their helpfulness for many clients (e.g., Davanloo, 1990; Malan & Coughlin Della Selva, 2006).

In summary, the EDT literature provides a clear description of different levels of functioning, and Davanloo and his followers have provided a useful blueprint for how to modify therapeutic techniques in order to tailor therapy to clients with various degrees of impairment.

Summary of evidence-based principles of change and EDT

In the preceding section it was suggested that the psychodynamic objectives associated with Malan's theoretical model provide a robust framework within which it is possible to integrate a variety of principles of therapeutic change drawn from other models of therapy, including emerging "evidence-based" principles of change. In this way the core theory of EDT provides a "meta-perspective" which can encompass a plurality of strategies for achieving the objectives of therapy. It was noted that the research literature suggests the helpfulness both of accessing and of regulating emotional experiences. It was suggested that EDT provides the clinician with a particularly rich and helpful set of distinctions between the varieties of different emotional experience and thus orients clinicians to respond flexibly to emotion, depending, for example, on where the affect is located on the Triangle of Conflict. With regard to the therapeutic relationship, while this stratum of the therapy has received hardly any attention in the small research literature on EDT (in contrast to the voluminous empirical literature on the therapeutic relationship in the broader field of psychotherapy research), the relationship has been given prominence by some EDT theorists, who have emphasised the capacity of the real relationship with the client to provide a corrective emotional and relational experience within therapy. Further empirical work in this area might enable EDT clinicians to gain greater consensus on handling risks to the therapeutic relationship posed by more affectively challenging interventions. Finally, I have outlined how EDT theorists have addressed the issue of the client's level of functioning, which research indicates is a robust predictor of therapeutic outcome. I have highlighted how different strands of EDT recommend important adaptations to the therapeutic approach in response to the client's characteristic defensive style and capacity to tolerate emotional exploration.

Research on the effectiveness of EDT

A brief note on the orientation to evidence and transparency

EDT was initially developed by Davanloo from study of videotapes of his own work, which enabled him to notice what appeared to be most effective. Further refinements to theory and practice have also taken place after the detailed examination of videotaped therapies (e.g., McCullough Vaillant, 1997), and training and dissemination of EDT has emphasised video-based supervision and video demonstrations of effective therapies by expert therapists. In addition to the focus on what actually happens in therapy via observation, Malan (e.g., Malan & Coughlin Della Selva, 2006; Malan & Osimo, 1992) pioneered the use of idiographically oriented follow-up interviews demonstrating the long-lasting effects of EDT.

More recently, a number of leading EDT therapists have worked hard on developing the evidence base for this form of therapy in more formal ways, most notably Allan Abbass and Leigh McCullough. In comparison to more traditional forms of psychodynamic therapy, the theoretical clarity and emphasis on observation in EDT lends itself relatively easily to research and, as we shall see below, it appears to have punched above its weight (in the sense of the number of practitioners of EDT in the UK) in a recent UK attempt to map the evidence-based "competencies" of psychodynamic therapy.

Current evidence base in EDT

I have reviewed how EDT encompasses therapeutic processes that have been shown to contribute to positive outcomes in the wider psychotherapy research literature. In this section, I aim to do a quick round-up of the major relevant studies of EDT, and place them in the context of the evidence for psychodynamic therapy more generally. An overview of the relevant studies is presented in table 2.

The first randomised controlled trial (RCT) of EDT is the Beth Israel Medical Center study of Winston et al. (1991). Study participants were thirty-two clients diagnosed with DSM-III (American Psychiatric Association, 1980) personality disorders (including compulsive, avoidant, dependent, passive-aggressive, histrionic, and mixed personality disorders, but excluding paranoid, schizoid, schizotypal, narcissistic, and borderline diagnoses). They were assigned either to short-term dynamic psychotherapy based on the work of Davanloo (the EDT condition) or to a less confrontational and more cognitive type of psychodynamic therapy known as brief adaptational therapy. The outcomes of each therapy following approximately forty sessions were compared with each other and with a waiting list control. The results demonstrated the effectiveness of both treatments relative to the control, however, (as we might expect from the "Dodo bird verdict" described above) the two treatment groups had similar outcomes. Winston et al. (1994) reported from the same study, with a larger sample of eighty-one clients, and arrived at the same conclusions. Hellerstein and colleagues reported on an entirely new data set collected as an extension of the same research project, this time comparing the Davanloo-based short-term dynamic psychotherapy with another psychodynamic model, brief supportive psychotherapy (Hellerstein et al., 1998). Once again, they found equivalence in the outcomes of the two types of treatment.

A second major psychotherapy research project, the Trondheim study of Svartberg et al. (2004), randomly allocated fifty patients to short-term dynamic psychotherapy or CBT. The short-term dynamic psychotherapy model used in the study was the "anxiety regulating" adaptation of Davanloo's model developed by McCullough (1997). Therapists in the EDT condition received training from McCullough, and therapists in the CBT condition received training from well-known American schema-focused therapists, such as Jeffrey Young. As noted at the beginning of the chapter, this is the only RCT to compare an EDT with a non-psychodynamic model of therapy, and the study was carefully conducted with monitoring of adherence to each model. As noted above, the (perhaps by now) unsurprising conclusion of this RCT was that both models of therapy were effective, and that there were no significant differences between the two models.

More recently, Abbass, Sheldon, Gyra, and Kalpin (2008) conducted a study comparing Intensive Short-Term Dynamic Psychotherapy (ISTDP) with a pre-treatment control group. The clients were twenty-seven clients with personality disorders. The five therapists in the study were all experienced practitioners who had been trained by Davanloo. Abbass and colleagues reported significant improvement relative to the control condition, an 83 per cent reduction of personality disorder diagnoses, and 74 per cent of treated clients coming off psychotropic medication. In addition to this, the authors estimated cost effectiveness benefits in the form of reduced disability benefits and reduced costs of medicines that were noted to exceed three times

Table 2. Characteristics of four randomised controlled trials (RCTs) featuring an EDT.

Study	*Client sample*	*No. clients*	*Dropout*	*No. sessions*	*Therapists*
Winston et al. (1994)	DSM-III PD (excluding paranoid, schizoid, schizotypal, narcissistic, and BPD)	81	6 STDP 2 BAT (not included in n of 81) ns	40	13 STDP 11 BAT (STDP av 10 yrs experience)
Hellerstein et al. (1998)	DSM-III PD (predominantly cluster C or Not Otherwise Specified)	49	10/25 STDP (40%) 7/24 BSP (29%) ns	30–40	23 STDP 11 BSP (STDP av 6.5 yrs experience)
Svartberg et al. (2004)	DSM-III-R Cluster C PD (other PD excluded)	50	1 dropout (was not included in n of 50)	40	Experienced full-time clinicians trained in each model for the study 8 STDP (av 6 yrs experience with this model) 6 CBT (av 4 yrs experience with this model)
Abbass et al. (2008)	DSM-IV PD	27		Av 28 (range 2–64)	5 therapists with a minimum of 5 yrs supervision with Davanloo

Abbreviations: STDP: short term dynamic psychotherapy; BAT: brief adaptational therapy; BSP: brief supportive psychotherapy; DSM: Diagnostic and Statistical Manual; PD: personality disorder; BPD: borderline personality disorder; SCL-90 GSI: Symptom Checklist (90 item) General Symptom

Model of EDT	*Comparison group*	*Measures*	*Follow-up*	*Outcome*
Davanloo STDP	Brief adaptational therapy (BAT) Waiting list control	SCL-90-R GSI Social Adjustment Scale Target complaint ratings	6 months—4.5 years (av 1.5 yrs)	Equivalent outcomes between treatments Both effective Effectiveness maintained at follow-up
Davanloo STDP	Brief supportive psychotherapy (BSP)	SCL-90-R GSI IIP Target complaint ratings	Termination scores used in analysis. Follow-up means reported but no indication of length of follow-up	Equivalent outcomes between treatments Both effective (though STDP did not reach significance on IIP)
McCullough STDP	Schema focused CBT	SCL-90-R GSI IIP Millon Clinical Multiaxial Inventory	2 year follow-up	Equivalent outcomes between treatments Both effective Effectiveness maintained at follow-up (About 50% of STDP clients returned to general population functioning) Effect size for STDP in this study noted to be 3x higher than in Winston et al. 1994 study
Davanloo ISTDP ("graded technique")	W/L control	BSI-GSI IIP GAF SCID-II PQ Medication Employment Disability costs	2 year follow-up	Major benefits of treatment on all outcomes (e.g., 83% reduction PD, 74% stopping meds) Effectiveness maintained at follow-up

Index; IIP: Inventory of Interpersonal Problems; GAF: Global Assessment of Functioning; SCID-PQ: Structured clinical interview for DSM disorders personality disorders questionnaire.

the cost of treatment by two year follow-up. Abbass and colleagues noted that the outcomes in this study were superior to those reported in the Beth Israel Medical Center study, and they speculate that this may be due to innovations in technique since Winston et al.'s (1991, 1994) work (specifically the development of Davanloo's "graded technique" for treatment of fragile patients), and the participation of more experienced therapists. In addition to randomised control trials, Abbass (2002) conducted a "naturalistic" study of eighty-nine consecutive patients treated by himself in private practice, demonstrating considerable effectiveness of his approach. Another naturalistic study by Abbass, Joffres, and Ogrodniczuk (2008) involving a consecutive sample of thirty patients showed significant improvement in client symptoms following trial therapies consisting of one long session and a single five week follow-up.

In summary, randomised controlled trials of EDT are comparatively few in number, and have all focused on personality disorders. Although both the Beth Israel Medical Center and Trondheim studies focused on DSM Cluster C personality disorders, the Abbass et al. (2008) study encompassed a broader range of personality disorders. Where studies have compared EDT with another therapy, in all cases, to date, the results have conformed to the "Dodo bird verdict" of equivalent effectiveness. These findings are consistent with findings from research into psychodynamic therapy in general. For example, Leichsenring, Rabung, and Leibing (2004) conducted a meta-analysis of psychodynamic therapy, focusing only on well-conducted RCTs of short-term psychodynamic therapy.[1] They found seventeen such studies, including the EDT studies of Winston et al. (1994), Hellerstein et al. (1998), and Svartberg et al. (2004)—the RCT by Abbass et al. (2008) had yet to be published. Leichsenring et al. concluded that psychodynamic therapy "yielded significant and large pretreatment-posttreatment effect sizes" (p. 1208), although no differences were found between short-term psychodynamic therapy and other forms of therapy. More recently short-term psychodynamic therapy has also been subjected to a systematic Cochrane review by Abbass, Hancock, Henderson, and Kisely (2006). Their review included twenty-three studies, including two EDT studies. They concluded that there was evidence that short-term psychodynamic therapy was a promising treatment with modest to moderate benefits, which were often sustained over time.

EDT and mental health policy in the UK

As we have seen, the evidence suggests that EDT is neither more nor less effective than any other bona fide therapy. However, neither EDT nor psychodynamic therapy in general has found itself well-positioned in the current implementation of evidence-based practice' in the NHS. In part, this is because comparatively few RCTs of psychodynamic therapy have been conducted—only seventeen methodologically sound studies in the Leichsenring et al. (2004) meta-analysis, for example. Thus, while those seventeen studies point to the general utility of psychodynamic approaches, they are spread thinly across the range of psychological disorders: for example, four RCTs of psychodynamic therapy for depression, and only one for anxiety disorders, compared with large numbers of RCTs examining the effectiveness of CBT for specific disorders.

The National Institute of Health and Clinical Excellence (NICE) guidelines, which are intended as a guide to the commissioning of evidence-based treatments, are diagnosis-based, meaning that they review the evidence of the effectiveness of treatments tailored to specific disorders, based on RCTs of treatments of that specific disorder—an approach to the evidence on psychotherapy that has been questioned by a number of commentators, for example, Westen et al. (2004). The paucity of RCTs examining the effectiveness of psychodynamic therapy means that NICE guidelines make bleak reading for psychodynamic therapists working in the NHS. For example, the NICE (2005a) guideline for OCD states that "there is doubt as to whether it [psycho-analysis] has a place in mental health services" (p. 104). The guideline for PTSD states that "the review did not find support for any clinically important benefits of [psychodynamic] treatments" (NICE, 2005b, p. 70). The guideline for depression states that there is "C class evidence" (a low level of evidence) for psychodynamic therapy for depression, but only when it is co-morbid depression (NICE, 2004a). Although the NICE (2009) guideline for borderline personality disorder is more open to the potential usefulness of psychodynamic therapy, it states that the evidence is at an early level of development. In fact the only NICE guideline that seems to contain a positive endorsement for psychodynamic therapy is that for eating disorders (NICE, 2004b) which recommends "focal psychodynamic therapy" for anorexia.

In 2007 the UK government committed £173 million towards its "Improving Access to Psychological Therapies" (IAPT) programme, designed to enhance access to evidence-based psychological therapies in primary care. While the main emphasis has been on increasing access to CBT (for example, twenty-three centres have been commissioned to provide CBT training), there has been some acknowledgement that other therapies can be of value. The former health secretary, Alan Johnson, stated in 2008 that, although CBT "will remain at the core of the psychological therapies programme … it will not do so at the exclusion of other equally valid [i.e., NICE approved] forms of therapy" (Johnson, 2008). Although there does not appear to have been parallel investment in non-CBT approaches to therapy, in 2008, a document (Lemma, Roth & Pilling, 2008) on "psychodynamic competencies" was published as part of IAPT based on an expert reference group's review of psychodynamic approaches that have proved efficacious in RCTs,

Lemma et al. (2008) derived their competencies from the "manuals" of therapy used in RCTs. Because research trials monitor therapists' adherence to the manuals, as they put it, "[T]his makes it possible to be reasonably confident that if the procedures set out in the manual are followed there should be better outcomes for clients" (p. 7). Although the RCTs used to derive the competencies are not listed in this document, the authors state that McCullough et al.'s (2003) book is one of a small number of "widely-cited texts" that were used in developing the guidelines "which explicate psychodynamic terminology and provide clear descriptions of how these concepts translate into clinical practice" (p. 8). Appendix B of the document lists thirteen manuals used in the compilation of the competencies (four of which are unpublished), including Osimo's (2003b) published description of EDT. It therefore appears that, despite its relatively undeveloped potential within the UK, the efforts of those who have conducted research into EDT, and the clarity with which EDT has been explicated, have resulted in recognition that the EDT approach embodies important aspects of evidence-based "psychodynamic competencies". It remains to be seen whether this translates into increased acceptance of EDT within the psychoanalytic community in the UK, particularly as, to date, EDT has adopted a very different model of training from more traditional psychodynamic therapies, emphasising video demonstrations, and micro-process video supervision, as compared to the more traditional emphasis in psychodynamic training on the trainees' own psychotherapy, and supervision that does not emphasise direct observation and the learning of skills.

Conclusions

In this chapter an attempt has been made to spell out the key elements of EDT, linking them with evidence-based "principles of change" derived from process-outcome research, and examining the evidence base for EDT relative to other therapies and to psychodynamic therapy. A question posed at the beginning of the chapter concerned what value, if any, is added by introducing yet another brand of psychotherapy into the already teeming pot of branded therapies. The review of EDT's place relative to both the empirically derived principles of change, and evidence to date of its efficacy, suggest a number of strengths. Firstly, the theoretical basis of the model, as outlined originally by Malan (2001), is both clear and parsimonious. As a result it is relatively easy to define the objectives of therapy while being open to a variety of means of achieving those objectives. EDT is therefore an approach in which it is possible to be theoretically coherent while being technically creative or eclectic (e.g., responding to the preferences and needs of different clients), thereby maximising the therapeutic potential of different therapist-client dyads. An attempt was made early in the chapter to link a variety of evidence-based principles of change to the therapeutic objectives from an EDT point of view. Secondly, the specific techniques of EDT, deriving from the study of videotaped psychotherapy, are clear and specific. The variables of relevance to EDT are generally directly observable, as are the outcomes of specific techniques, and this lends itself to effective demonstration, training, and supervision of therapy skills. Thirdly, EDT's focus on affect is congruent with the evidence that successful outcome in therapy involves varieties of both emotional experience and emotional regulation. As we have seen, EDT provides us with a rich set of differentiations between different manifestations of affect (for example as underlying Feeling, inhibitory Anxiety, or affect used as Defence). Finally, as a result of its emphasis on observation and the clear specification of techniques, EDT lends itself to empirical scrutiny. In this respect, EDT has earned a place in the vanguard of psychodynamic therapy models that have embraced the challenge of research, and is comparatively well represented in the small canon of RCTs in psychodynamic therapy. The work summarised illustrates one recent trajectory through which psychodynamic theory has continued to develop and evolve vigorously from its origins in the nineteenth century, through the latter part of the twentieth and now into the twenty-first century.

Acknowledgements

Leigh McCullough's work originally inspired my interest in EDT and her ideas about psychotherapy integration were a starting point for this chapter. I was fortunate to meet Leigh when she was in the UK in March 2010 and I remain very grateful to her for the clarity and insight of her writing and for her personal warmth, support, and encouragement. Leigh read an earlier draft of this chapter and was encouraging about its aims. In fact, to my delight, she offered to collaborate, although sadly illness prevented her from making any further contribution. This chapter is dedicated to Leigh and to the clarity, breadth, and wisdom of Leigh's contribution to the field of psychotherapy. I would also like to thank Joel Town for his helpful comments on an earlier draft of this chapter and for our discussions of ISTDP.

References

Abbass, A. (2002). Intensive short-term dynamic psychotherapy in a private psychiatric office: clinical and cost effectiveness. *American Journal of Psychotherapy, 56*: 225–232.

Abbass, A. & Bechard, D. (2007). Bringing character changes with Davanloo's intensive short-term dynamic psychotherapy. *Ad Hoc Bulletin of Short-Term Dynamic Psychotherapy—Practice and Theory, 11*: 26–39.

Abbass, A., Hancock, J. T., Henderson, J. & Kisely, S. (2006). Short-term psychodynamic psychotherapies for common mental disorders. *Cochrane Database of Systematic Reviews*, Oct. 18 (4).

Abbass, A., Joffres, M. & Ogrodniczuk, J. (2008). A naturalistic study of intensive short-term dynamic psychotherapy trial therapy. *Brief Treatment and Crisis Intervention, 8*: 164–170.

Abbass, A., Sheldon, A., Gyra, J. & Kalpin, A. (2008). Intensive short-term dynamic psychotherapy for DSM-IV personality disorders: a randomised controlled trial. *Journal of Nervous and Mental Disease, 196*: 211–216.

Alexander, F. & French, T. (1946). *Psychoanalytic Therapy*. New York: Ronald Press.

American Psychiatric Association (1994). *Diagnostic and Statistical Manual of Mental Disorders (4th edition)*. Washington, DC: American Psychiatric Association.

Asay, T. P. & Lambert, M. L. (1999). The empirical case for the common factors in therapy: quantitative findings. In: M. Hubble, B. Duncan & S. Miller (Eds.), *The Heart and Soul of Change: What Works in Therapy*. Washington, DC: American Psychological Association.

Carroll, L. (1865). *Alice's Adventures in Wonderland and Through the Looking-Glass and What Alice Saw There*. London: Penguin, 1998.

Castonguay, L. & Beutler, L. (Eds.) (2006a). *Principles of Therapeutic Change that Work*. New York: Oxford University Press.

Castonguay, L. & Beutler, L. (2006b). Common and unique principles of therapeutic change: What do we know and what do we need to know? In: L. Castonguay & L. Beutler (Eds.), *Principles of Therapeutic Change that Work*. New York: Oxford University Press.

Coughlin Della Selva, P. (1996). *Intensive Short-Term Dynamic Psychotherapy*. London: Karnac.

Davanloo, H. (1990). *Unlocking the Unconscious: Selected Papers of Habib Davanloo*. Chichester, UK: John Wiley & Sons.

Diener, M. J., Hilsenroth, M. J. & Weinberger, J. (2007). Therapist affect focus and patient outcomes in psychodynamic psychotherapy: A meta-analysis. *American Journal of Psychiatry, 164*: 936–941.

Duncan, B., Miller, S. & Sparks, J. (2004). *The Heroic Client: A Revolutionary Way to Improve Effectiveness Through Client-Directed, Outcome-Informed Therapy*. San Francisco, CA: Jossey-Bass.

Ehrenreich, J., Buzzella, B. & Barlow, D. (2007). General principles for the treatment of emotional disorders across the lifespan. In: S. Hofman & J. Weinberger (Eds.), *The Art and Science of Psychotherapy*. New York: Routledge.

Fosha, D. (2000). *The Transforming Power of Affect: A Model for Accelerated Change*. New York: Basic.

Garfield, S. & Bergin, A. (1994). Introduction and historical overview. In: A. Bergin & S. Garfield (Eds.), *Handbook of Psychotherapy and Behaviour Change*. New York: John Wiley & Sons.

ten Have-de Labije, J. (2001). Red and green traffic lights on Davanloo's road to the unconscious. In: J. ten Have-de Labije (Ed.), *The Working Alliance in ISTDP: Whose Intrapsychic Crisis?* Amsterdam: VKDP—Dutch Association for Short-Term Dynamic Psychotherapy.

ten Have-de Labije, J. (2006). When patients enter with anxiety on the forefront. *Ad Hoc Bulletin of Short-Term Dynamic Psychotherapy, 10*: 35–69.

Hellerstein, D., Rosenthal, R., Pinsker, H., Samstag, L., Muran, J. & Winston, A. (1998). A randomised prospective study comparing supportive and dynamic therapies. *Journal of Psychotherapy Practice and Research, 7*: 261–271.

Horvath, A. & Bedi, R. (2002). The alliance. In: J. Norcross (Ed.), *Psychotherapy Relationships That Work*. New York: Oxford University Press.

Johnson, A. (2008). Psychological therapies in the NHS: science, practice and policy. (Speech by the Rt Hon Alan Johnson MP, Secretary of State for Health, 27 November 2008 at the New Savoy Partnership Annual Conference.) Retrieved April 11, 2011 from http://webarchive.nationalarchives.gov.uk/+/www.dh.gov.uk/en/MediaCentre/Speeches/DH_091251.

Lamagna, J. (in press). Of the self by the self: Internal attachment, attunement and psychological change. *Journal of Psychotherapy Integration*.

Lamagna, J. & Gleiser, K. (2007). Building a secure internal attachment: An intra-relational approach to ego-strengthening and emotional processing with chronically traumatised clients. *Journal of Trauma and Dissociation*, *8*: 25–52.

Lambert, M. & Ogles, B. (2004). The efficacy and effectiveness of psychotherapy. In: M. J. Lambert (Ed.), *Bergin and Garfield's Handbook of Psychotherapy and Behaviour Change*. New York: John Wiley & Sons.

Leichsenring, F., Rabung, S. & Leibing, E. (2004). The efficacy of short-term psychodynamic therapy in specific psychiatric disorders: A meta-analysis. *Archives of General Psychiatry*, *6*: 1208–1216.

Lemma, A., Roth, A. & Pilling, S. (2008). *The Competencies Required to Deliver Effective Psychoanalytic/Psychodynamic Therapy*. London: Research Department of Clinical, Educational and Health Psychology, University College London. Retrieved April 11, 2011 from http://www.ucl.ac.uk/clinical-psychology/CORE/Psychodynamic_Competences/Background_Paper.pdf.

Luborsky, L., Singer, B. & Luborsky, L. (1975). Comparative studies of psychotherapies: Is it true that "everyone has won and all must have prizes?" *Archives of General Psychiatry*, *32*: 995–1008.

Malan, D. (2001). *Individual Psychotherapy and the Science of Psychodynamics*. London: Arnold.

Malan, D. & Coughlin Della Selva, P. (2006). *Lives Transformed: a Revolutionary Method of Dynamic Psychotherapy*. London: Karnac.

Malan, D. & Osimo, F. (1992). *Psychodynamics, Training, and Outcome in Brief Psychotherapy*. Oxford: Butterworth-Heinemann.

McCullough, L. & Kuhn, N. (2009). The varieties of STDP experience: Taking our theories lightly. *Ad Hoc Bulletin of Short-Term Dynamic Psychotherapy—Practice and Theory*, *13*: 5–15.

McCullough, L. & Magill, M. (2009). Affect-focused short-term dynamic therapy. In: R. Levy & J. S. Ablon (Eds.), *Handbook of Evidence-based Psychodynamic Psychotherapy: Bridging the Gap Between Science and Practice*. New York: Humana.

McCullough, L., Kuhn, N., Andrews, S., Kaplan, A., Wolf, J. & Lanza Hurley, C. (2003). *Treating Affect Phobia: A Manual for Short-Term Dynamic Psychotherapy*. New York: Guilford Press.

McCullough, L., Larsen, A., Schanche, E., Andrews, S., Kuhn, N., Lanza Hurley, C., Carley, M., Francis-Ranier, E., jia Cui, X., Meyer, S., Schlager, E., Ewalt, S. & Wolf, J. (2008). *Achievement of Therapeutic Objectives Scale: ATOS Scale (Representing Well-Established Common Factors in Psychotherapy)*. Retrieved April 11, 2011 from http://www.affectphobia.org/docs/VideoATOS/ATOSManual.pdf.

McCullough Vaillant, L. (1997). *Changing Character: Short-term Anxiety-regulating Psychotherapy for Restructuring Defences, Affects, and Attachment*. New York: Basic.

National Institute of Health and Clinical Excellence (NICE) (2004a). *Depression: Management of Depression in Primary and Secondary Care—NICE Guidance*. Retrieved April 11, 2011 from http://www.nice.org.uk/CG023.

National Institute of Health and Clinical Excellence (NICE) (2004b). *Eating Disorders: Core Interventions in the Treatment and Management of Anorexia Nervosa, Bulimia Nervosa and Related Eating Disorders*. Retrieved April 11, 2011 from http://www.nice.org.uk/CG009.

National Institute of Health and Clinical Excellence (NICE) (2005a). *Core Interventions in the Treatment of Obsessive-Compulsive Disorder and Body Dysmorphic Disorder*. Retrieved April 11, 2011 from http://www.nice.org.uk/CG031.

National Institute of Health and Clinical Excellence (NICE) (2005b). *Post-traumatic Stress Disorder (PTSD): the Management of PTSD in Adults and Children in Primary and Secondary Care*. Retrieved April 11, 2011 from http://www.nice.org.uk/CG26.

National Institute of Health and Clinical Excellence (NICE) (2009). *Borderline Personality Disorder: Treatment and Management*. Retrieved April 11, 2011 from http://guidance.nice.org.uk/CG78.

Norcross, J. (Ed.) (2002). *Psychotherapy Relationships that Work: Therapist Contributions and Responsiveness to Patient Needs*. New York: Oxford University Press.

Orlinsky, D., Grawe, K. & Parks, B. (1994). Process and outcome in psychotherapy—noch einmal. In: A. Bergin & S. Garfield (Eds.), *Handbook of Psychotherapy and Behaviour Change*. New York: John Wiley & Sons.

Orlinsky, D., Rønnestad, M. & Willutzki, U. (2004). Fifty years of psychotherapy process-outcome research: Continuity and change. In: M. Lambert (Ed.), *Bergin and Garfield's Handbook of Psychotherapy and Behaviour Change*. New York: John Wiley & Sons.

Osimo, F. (2003a). Annotations for "The Sun and the Wind". *Ad Hoc Bulletin of Short-Term Dynamic Psychotherapy, 7*: 23–46.

Osimo, F. (2003b). *Experiential Short-Term Dynamic Psychotherapy: A Manual*. Bloomington, IN: AuthorHouse.

Osimo, F. (2009). The character hologram. *Ad Hoc Bulletin of Short-Term Dynamic Psychotherapy—Practice and Theory, 13*: 25–49.

Rosenzweig, S. (1936). Some implicit common factors in diverse methods of psychotherapy. *American Journal of Orthopsychiatry, 6*: 412–415.

Svartberg, M., Stiles, T. & Seltzer, M. (2004). Randomised, controlled trial of the effectiveness of short-term dynamic psychotherapy and cognitive therapy for cluster C personality disorders. *American Journal of Psychiatry, 161*: 810–817.

Wampold, B. (2001). *The Great Psychotherapy Debate: Models, Methods and Findings*. Mahwah, NJ: Lawrence Erlbaum.

Westen, D., Novotny, C. & Thompson-Brenner, H. (2004). The empirical status of empirically supported psychotherapies: assumptions, findings, and reporting in controlled clinical trials. *Psychological Bulletin, 130*: 631–663.

Winston, A., Laikin, M., Pollack, M., Samstag, L., McCullough, L. & Muran, J. (1994). Short-term psychotherapy of personality disorders. *American Journal of Psychiatry, 151*: 190–194.

Winston, A., Pollack, J., McCullough, L., Flegenheimer, W., Kestenbaum, R. & Trujillo, M. (1991). Brief psychotherapy of personality disorders. *Journal of Nervous and Mental Disease, 179*: 188–193.

Note

1. Meta-analysis is a way of statistically combining the findings of a number of studies.

INDEX